PETER OF SPAIN
(PETRUS HISPANUS PORTUGALENSIS)

SYNCATEGOREUMATA

STUDIEN UND TEXTE
ZUR GEISTESGESCHICHTE
DES MITTELALTERS

HERAUSGEGEBEN VON

Dr. ALBERT ZIMMERMANN

PROFESSOR AN DER UNIVERSITÄT KÖLN

BAND XXX

PETER OF SPAIN
(PETRUS HISPANUS PORTUGALENSIS)

SYNCATEGOREUMATA

PETER OF SPAIN
(PETRUS HISPANUS PORTUGALENSIS)
SYNCATEGOREUMATA

First Critical Edition
with an Introduction and Indexes by
L. M. DE RIJK, PH.D.
with an English Translation by
JOKE SPRUYT, PH.D.

E.J. BRILL
LEIDEN • NEW YORK • KÖLN
1992

The paper in this book meets the guidelines for permanence and durability of the Committee on Production Guidelines for Book Longevity of the Council on Library Resources.

Library of Congress Cataloging-in-Publication Data

John XXI, Pope, d. 1277.
  [Syncategoreumata. English & Latin]
  Syncategoreumata / Peter of Spain (Petrus Hispanus Portugalensis); first critical edition with an introduction and indexes by L.M. de Rijk; with an English translation by Joke Spruyt.
      p.   cm.—(Studien und Texte zur Geistesgeschichte des Mittelalters, ISSN 0169-8125; Bd. 30)
  English translation and original Latin text of: Syncategoreumata.
  Includes bibliographical references and indexes.
  ISBN 9004094342
  1. Logic—Early works to 1800. I. Rijk, Lambertus Marie de. II. Title. III. Series.
  BC60.J56313   1991
  160—dc20   91-39214
                                                                                          CIP

ISSN   0169-8125
ISBN   90 04 09434 2

PRINTED IN THE NETHERLANDS

to Jettie
to Frank

CONTENTS

PREFACE

Some twenty years after the publication of Peter of Spain's *Tractatus*, we can present a critical edition of his *Syncategoreumata*. The need for such an edition has been felt for a long time, not only considering the author's renown, but also because research has shown the enormous importance of Mediaeval treatises on syncategorematic words in general. Translations are always welcome, to make their contents accessible to present-day readers. An English translation of Peter of Spain's *Syncategoreumata* by J. P. Mullally has been available since 1964. However, it was based on two Cologne editions which, as a result of a large number of omissions and interpolations, are not a very reliable source for Peter's original work.

10

The present edition is a first critical edition of Peter of Spain's *Syncategoreumata*. Indexes have been added to facilitate the reader's orientation in the book. In the translation an attempt has been made to stick to the Latin as closely as possible. In a number of cases the Latin words Peter discusses have not been translated, especially where he deals with problems that only occur in the Latin language and in those cases where the words he discusses allow for more than one translation.

We would like to thank all the people who have contributed to the completion of this book. We are very grateful to Professor Braakhuis for letting us use his first draft of this work based on the manuscripts from Milan and Cordoba, and to Professor Moreira da Sa for lending us his film of the manuscript from Tarragona. We are highly indebted to the Conservators of the manuscript collections of many libraries, especially the ones of Cordoba, Ivrea, Milan, Naples, Prague, and Vatican City. Dr. C.H. Kneepkens has helped us greatly by casting light on some difficult grammatical expressions. Finally we would like to express our deepest gratitude to Ms Jettie de Wal and Ms A.A.C. Spruyt-de Geus for devoting so much of their time, energy and care to typing out the Latin and English texts.

L. M. de Rijk
J. Spruyt

INTRODUCTION

Peter of Spain (ca 1205-77) who, in 1276, became Pope under the name of John XXI, was the author of an impressive number of scholarly works, *inter alia* the *Tractatus* (a textbook of logic, widely known afterwards under the title *Summule logicales*) and the *Syncategoreumata*.[1] The latter work, which deals with syncategorematic terms, is here critically edited for the first time, together with an English translation.[2]

Peter's authorship of the *Syncategoreumata* is beyond all doubt: it is confirmed again and again by nearly all our manuscripts. As to the date and place of origin of the *Syncategoreumata* : they were surely written after the *Tractatus* (which were written not later than the 1230's, see my *Introduction* to the edition of this work, p. LV-LVII). There is no reason at all to assume a connection between the *Syncategoreumata* and Peter's stay at the University of Paris, which he left in 1229, before the composition of the *Tractatus*. Clearly, Paris does not play any role in the early diffusion of the *Syncategoreumata*. It seems highly probable, therefore, that the *Syncategoreumata* were written by Peter in the same region where he wrote the *Tractatus*, i.e. Northern Spain or Southern France. The work's most likely date is between 1235-1245 (cf. my *Introduction* to the *Tractatus* , pp. XXXIV-LXI). From Peter's use of *lectio* (see X, cap.8) it may be concluded that the *Syncategoreumata* were meant as a piece of schoolteaching.

---

[1] For Peter's life, career and other works, see L.M. de Rijk, *Peter of Spain*, Tractatus *called afterwards* Summule logicales. First Critical Edition from the Manuscripts with an Introduction (Philosophical Texts and Studies, 22), Assen 1972, *Introduction*, pp. XXIV-XLIII and the works mentioned there. Professor J.M. da Cruz Pontes rightly pleas for an up to date biography of Peter in 'A propos d'un centenaire. Une nouvelle monographie sur Petrus Hispanus Portugalensis, le pape Jean XXI, est-elle nécessaire?' in *Recherches de théologie ancienne et médiévale*, tome XLIV (1977), 220-30.

[2] For a study of the first two chapters of this work, see Joke Spruyt, *Peter of Spain on Composition and Negation*. Text. Translation. Commentary (diss. Leiden 1989), Ingenium Publishers, Nijmegen 1989. See especially 97-102 and the works mentioned there (esp. Gabriel Nuchelmans, *Theories of the Proposition. Ancient and Mediaeval Conceptions of the Bearers of Truth and Falsity*, Amsterdam-London 1973; H.A.G. Braakhuis, *De 13e eeuwse Tractaten over syncategorematische termen* (2 vols.): Inleidende studie; II Uitgave van Nicolaas van Parijs' *Syncategoreumata* (diss. Leiden 1979), Meppel 1979).

1. *The Manuscripts Used*

Peter's *Syncategoreumata* have come down to us in quite a lot of manuscripts, most of them dating from the 13th up to the 15th centuries,
and also in several old editions,[3] which are, however, marred by a
great number of interpolations, pseudo-corrections and arbitrary
interventions due to later commentators and editors who proudly
announced their editions as *emendatae.*

Not all the manuscripts are equally valuable. Some of them, especially the later manuscripts dating from about 1350, are downright
unreliable as a source for Peter's text as their scribes obviously made
use of exemplars written by authors who considered it their task to
produce easily accessible schoolbooks rather than to hand down
Peter's work and who lavishly interpreted, elucidated or even 'corrected' Peter's text. Most printed editions are also adaptations, inten-
tional adaptations even, compiled by people who were themselves
well-known masters of logic and famous heads of schools.

Other manuscript copies suffer from the negligence or incom-
petence of their scribes who, without batting an eyelid, committed
the most unbelievable errors. However, every editor of medieval
texts is well aware that manuscript copies from the hands of slow-
witted, but dedicated and faithful, scribes may be quite valuable
intermediaries of the texts involved: a naive scribe is very much
inclined to conscientiously copy the *exemplar* at his elbow, however
meagre his understanding of the content of what he is copying. The
scribe of our Ivrea manuscript (*E*) obviously belongs to this category
of copyists.

In all the 13th century manuscripts the *Syncategoreumata* come right
after the *Tractatus.* Since, in each manuscript, the *Syncategoreumata*
and the *Tractatus* are in the same hand we may assume that features
that are characteristic of the *Tractatus* copies are also characteristic of
the copies of the *Syncategoreumata.* Our appraisal of the *Syncategoreumata* manuscripts, therefore, can be based on our evaluation of the
Tractatus manuscripts. My studies have shown that the following
manuscripts deserve the special attention of the editor:[4]

---

[3] See Carl Prantl, *Geschichte der Logik im Abendlande III*, Leipzig 1867 (repr. Graz
1955), 35-40.

[4] See the five papers I wrote 'On the Genuine Text of Peter of Spain's *Summule
logicales* ', in VIVARIUM, *A Journal for Medieval Philosophy and the Intellectual Life
of the Middle Ages*, 6 (1968), 1-34; 69-101; 7 (1969), 8-61; 120-62; 8 (1970), 10-55 in
which I have made an attempt to reconstruct the original text of Peter's *Tractatus inter alia* by an examination of the oldest commentaries on Peter's textbook

Tarragona (Spain), Library of the Palacio Arzobispal, cod.2. The   **T**
handwritten catalogue tells us that this manuscript originates from
the Convent of Preveres de Valls. Later it came into the possession of
the Arxiu Històric Arxidiocesà de Tarragona. It has been described
by S. Capdevila[5] as containing the *Dialectica de "Petrus Hispanus"*
segle XIII, consisting (still according to Capdevila) of 50 parchment
folios of two columns and measuring 205 x 140 mm. When visiting
Spain in 1968 I consulted the catalogue that gives us the following
information:

> Armari No 15, Estant 3 er: Petri Hispani—Philosophia—Dialectica. Llibre
> de pergami; manuscrit del segle XIII. Procedent de la Comunitat de Pre-
> veres de Valls.

Unfortunately, the manuscript had disappeared. I was told by the
librarian that it was probably removed during the Civil War (1936-
39). Cordiolani, however, claims that the catalogue of the Library of
the Palacio mentions (under no 85) a work entitled *Tractatus philo-*
sophicus et de dialectica by Peter of Spain.[6] In 1972 (see the *Introduction*
to my edition of the *Tractatus*, p. CX) I concluded from several pecu-
liarities of this manuscript, as given by Capdevila, that the Tarragona manuscript must have contained a really valuable copy of Peter's
works. This much is certain, the provenance of the Tarragona
manuscript should be seen in connection with the fact that Southern
France and Northern Spain were the scene where Peter's *Tractatus*
found their first renown: the earliest commentaries on this work (by
Robertus Anglicus and Guillelmus Arnaldi) originated there.[7]

---

that have come down to us. See also the *Introduction* to my edition of the
Tractatus, pp. CII-CX. It should be noted that the Avignon MS (Musée Calvet,
cod.311) only contains the opening lines of the *Syncategoreumata* (ff.62ra-63vb).
The inferior manuscript *Reg. Lat.* 1205 of the Vatican Library (used by Bochen-
ski for his edition) which belongs to the *codices minus adhibiti* of my edition of
the *Tractatus* (the SIGLA en face p.1 of the edition should be corrected to that
effect) does not contain the *Syncategoreumata*.
[5] S. Capdevila, Prev., 'Notes d'Arxius I: De l'Arxiu arxidiocesà de Tarragona',
in *Analecta sacra Tarraconensia*. Anuari de la Biblioteca Balmes 6(1930), 295-6.
[6] A. Cordiolani, 'Hispania Sacra', in *Rivista de Historia Ecclesiastica* 5 (1959),
132. I do not know whether Cordiolani did actually see the manuscript or only
compiled some bibliographical data. This much is certain, the manuscript
meant by Cordiolani must be identified with *T* since there is no trace of
another manuscript of this kind in the Chapter Library.
[7] For these commentaries, see my studies in VIVARIUM 7 (1969), 8-61 and
120-62.

In June 1981 Professor Artur Moreira de Sá from Lisbon University kindly lent me a microfilm (the only one in existence, it seems) of the Tarragona manuscript, a photostat of which now is in the Library of the Instituut voor Middeleeuwse Wijsbegeerte (Filosofisch Instituut, University of Nijmegen). The following observations are based on this photostat.

On the cover the indication 'No 2' is found. On its backside the title must have been mentioned. However, on the photostat only the last words of each line are visible. No doubt, it runs as follows (cf. the entry of the old handwritten catalogue):

<No 15 [or 85?], Estant 3 er> Petri
<Hispani Philosophia Dialectica, Procedent>
de la <Comunitat de Preveres de> Valls

The codex, which was, according to Capdevila, well conserved, consists of 52 folios (two more than Capdevila says). The *Tractatus*, beginning on f.1 ra and ending on f. 25 rb, are written in two columns of 44 lines each (the written surface of each page is 92 x 125 mm, as the photographer informs us on folio 1). The first folio is slightly damaged by damp stains, as are the next three, but to a lesser degree. The first folios contain quite a lot of marginal notes and some diagrams, most of them in a contemporaneous hand. The first folio contains a beautifully illuminated *D* (of *Dialetica*) representing, as Capdevila tells us, a sitting master who is teaching (the photostat is rather blurred); on the blank spot to the right of the upper part of the *D* a later hand wrote *Incipiunt tractatus magistri petri yspani*.

The text of the *Tractatus* is found on ff. 1 ra-25 rb, line 40 (where it ends without any colophon). It is marred by many omissions that cannot all be ascribed to the loss of folios or quaternios. There is a rather extensive omission beween folio 1 *recto* and *verso*, which cannot, of course, be the result of a loss of folios. The gap corresponds to about sixteen chapters of our edition (I, 9, p. 5,5 up to 24, p. 15, 9). There is another omission after fol. 1 v corresponding to chapters II 9 (p.19, 20) up to II 21 and IV 1-3 (p. 44, 21) of my edition. The latter omission, however, may be due to a loss of folios (the foliation was added afterwards).

The twelve tracts of the *Tractatus* are found in the following order:

I   *De introductionibus* : 1 ra-rb; [...] 1 va
II   *De predicabilibus* : 1 va-vb [...]
IV   *De sillogismis* : [...] 2 ra-vb
V   *De locis* : 2 vb-5 rb
III *De predicamentis* : 5 rb-7 ra

So the order is the same as that found in Napels, *Univ.* F VIII.29 (our *N*), Prague, *Metropol.* 1380 (our *P*), *Vat Reg. lat.* 1731 (our *R*), Cordoba *Capit.* 158 (our *C*) and Milan *Ambros.* H. Inf. 64 (our *H*). *T* has the *Caliditas* interpolation in *De predicamentis* (f.6 vb) as well as the *ycos* interpolation in *De locis* (3 ra-b). However, *T*, together with *P, N, C* and *R*, has the *Exemplum* (in V 3, p. 58, 6-7) in what may be taken to be the original reading: *Legionenses—Astoricenses—Zamorenses*. The usual interpolation in the opening lines of the *Tractatus* found in most MSS (*sola enim dialetica probabiliter disputat de principiis omnium artium*, which words seem to have been taken from the *Summula* of Lambert of Auxerre or from Lambert's source) is missing in *T* (as well as in *P* and *E*).

The *Syncategoreumata* which are found on ff. 25 rb-51 ra are almost complete. The treatise opens at the bottom of 25 rb (where the *Tractatus* end without any colophon) and is introduced merely by *Sequitur de sinchat* (!), written by the same hand that added the title of the *Tractatus* on f.1 r. There is a small rubrica ('Ab') and a marginal note was added: *Nota quod est hoc verbum aliquando est purum verbum ut homo est aliquando pura copula ut homo currit idest homo est currens et tunc est sincategoreumatica dictio aliquando partim verbum partim copula ut homo est albus.*

The text is nicely written, in two columns of 44 lines each, in a neat 13th century gothic minuscle. It contains several corrections, some of them by the same hand that wrote the tract, the others by a contemporaneous hand. There are a few glosses also, dating from about the same period. After ff. 35 v and 36 ra two folios, which must have contained a text corresponding to IV 40 up to V 29 of the present edition, are missing. The work ends on f. 51 r, line 25, without colophon. The last words are: *Si autem aliquis in istis voluerit esse peritus oportet eum frequenter exercitari in huiusmodi* (Capdevila wrongly has *huiusmodis*) *sillogismis*. Rubricas are found at the beginning of each chapter. Folio 51 ra has only 25 lines. The bottom of this folio has been torn away rather carelessly; its verso side contains some random notes, as is the case with f. 52 r. Fol. 52 v was presumably left

blank. The photostat of the back cover of our manuscript makes me think that the codex was closed by means of a simple leather clasp.

I have made a complete transcription of the *Syncategoreumata* version in *T*.

P   Prague (Praha, Czechoslovakia), Metropolitan Chapter, codex 1380 (=M27) dating from about 1300.[8] This codex consists of 91 parchment folios and two paper folios (10 and 11) and measures 188 x 142 mm. The fly-leaf at the beginning was taken from a 12th century missal, it seems. On the verso side of this fly-leaf, the first folio, we find the words *Alexii baccalarii*. On f.4 r there is a multi-coloured diagram. The codex consists of nine unequal quaternios. Between ff. 7 and 8 (the foliation was added later) a folio has been torn out. There is also a folio missing between ff. 17 and 18 and three folios between ff. 76 an 77.

The *Tractatus* are found on ff.1 ra-45 ra in the order I-II-IV-III-V-VI-VII-VIII-IX-X-XII-XI. They are followed by a part of John le Page's *Appellationes* (ff. 45 ra-50 vb) that have been edited by professor Alain de Libera from the only two copies hitherto known (Paris, *B.N. lat.* 11.412 and 15.170).[9] The title *Appellationes* is found immediately after the explicit of Peter's *De relativis*. After some blank lines the text begins. In this manuscript the *Appellationes* are incomplete and anonymous. They end abruptly at f. 50 vb (II, cap. 53 in de Libera's edition).[10] Next follow Peter's *Syncategoreumata*: ff. 51 ra-90 vb.

In the *Tractatus* the interpolation in the opening lines is missing, but the *Caliditas* and *ycos* interpolations are there. The *Exemplum* passage has the names *Arimenses* (!), *Saxones*, *Boemos*, *Morawos*, the last three of which are apparently due to a patriotic scribe. At *Syncateg.* VIII, 15 the usual *Yspania* is replaced by *Polonia*.

Following the final words of the *Syncategoreumata* we find an explicit and a colophon in the same hand: *Expliciunt sincategoreumata* [this word *in rasura*] *magistri petri hispani qua* [*sic* !] *scripsit Willelmus. Explicit iste liber, qui scripsit sit modo liber et ipsum deus custodiat.* The

---

[8] See A. Podlaha, *Catalogus codicum manu scriptorum qui in Archivio Capituli Metropolitani Pragensis asservantur*, Prague 1923, p.285. Podlaha failed to recognise the *Syncategoreumata*. He was probably misled by the cover title of the codex: *Textus sumularum Petri Hispani*.

[9] 'Les *Appellationes* de Jean le Page' in *Archives d' histoire doctrinale et littéraire du moyen-âge* 51 (1985), 193-255.

[10] The *Appellationes* in *P* end as follows: '...non autem quantum ad suam formam. Item. Dicimus quod terminus accidentalis apponens verbo de preterito et de futuro debet'.

remaining part of the column is taken up by short descriptions of
the proper subjects of the seven liberal arts. Folio 91 is left blank.

I have made a complete transcription of the *Syncategoreumata* text
as given in *P*.

Naples, Biblioteca Universitaria, codex F VIII 29, olim Capestianen-   N
sis. This is a parchment codex, consisting of 88 folios, written in
Italy in a gothic minuscle in two columns of 37 lines each and
dating from the beginning of the 14th century, it seems.[11] The
codex, which has a number of multi-coloured capitals, consists of
nine quaternios numbered *A* to *L* (on f. 86 v we read: 'A...L quinterni
sunt 9 et fol. 88'). It stems from San Bernardino de L'Aquila. In
addition to Peter's works it contains several other tracts. No corrections are found.

N contains the *Tractatus* on ff. 1 ra-41 vb in the same order as *T* : I:
1 ra-3 va; II: 3 vb-5 rb; IV: 5 rb-6 vb; V: 6 vb-9 vb; III: 9 vb-12 vb; VI: 12
vb-14 va; VII: 14 va-33 vb; VIII: 33 vb-35 rb; IX: 35 rb-vb; X: 35 vb-36 ra;
XI: 36 ra-37 va; XII: 37 va-41 vb.

Although *N* in *De predicamentis*, cap. 29, line 18-9 reads *ut albedo in
cigno et nigredo in corvo et carbone aut in ebano* instead of the usual *ut
albedo nivi et caliditas igni*, it does have the *Caliditas* interpolation (f. 12
rb). The *ycos* interpolation in *De locis* is also found in *N* (f. 7 ra). Unfortunately, the *Exemplum* passage is corrupt due to haplography (*ut
legionenses contra aristoricenses* (!) *pugnare malum est utrumque enim est
pugnare affines contra affines*). Nevertheless, where the bulk of the
later MSS have quite arbitrary, 'local' readings, the Naples MS does
have the correct version. As far as the opening lines of the *Tractatus*
are concerned, *N* has (with *R*, *C* and *H* and nearly all later MSS)
the interpolations *scientia scientiarum* and *sola enim dialetica probabiliter
disputat de principiis omnium artium* (taken from Lambert of Auxerre's
Logica).

The *Syncategoreumata* are found on ff. 41 vb-84 vb, right after the
explicit of the *Tractatus*. The former are introduced by the title:
Incipiunt sincategoreuma ta ma gistri petri hys pani. Our treatise opens
with a nice multi-coloured rubrica and, like the *Tractatus*, is written
in two columns of 37 lines each by the same hand that wrote the

---

[11] For a codicological description, see Cesare Censi O.F.M., *Manoscritti frances-
cani della Biblioteca Nazionale di Napoli* II, Grottaferrata 1971 (Spicilegium
Bonaventurianum VIII), pp 856-7. His description of the contents of the manuscript is not correct.

Tractatus . Some corrections are added by a contemporaneous hand, but the greater part of the omissions are not remedied. At first glance this copy makes a favourable impression, it is written in a nice hand. In fact, however, the scribe was quite careless and hasty, as may appear from the many omissions (most of which are due to haplography).

At the end of the *Syncategoreumata* no explicit[12] or colophon is found, but our treatise is followed by the title *De fallacia accidentis* introducing a short tract written by the same hand. Its opening lines run as follows:

> Nota ad cognoscendum fallaciam accidentis consideranda sunt quatuor. Unum est utrum aliqua duo sunt in se eadem secundum substantiam et respectu tertii alicuius. Secundum si diversa secundum substantiam et respectu tertii. Tertium si eadem secundum substantiam in se, respectu autem tertii diversa. Quartum utrum diversa secundum substantiam in se, respectu autem tertii eadem.

We find this small tract on ff. 84 vb-85 ra. It is followed by a set of logical rules, the first of which runs: *Quandocumque hoc signum 'omnis' coniungitur termino generali, multiplex est locutio.* Similar rules are given concerning other syncategorematic terms, the last of which runs: *Quandocumque additur negatio ad verbum consequentis, multiplex est locutio eoquod potest determinare ipsum in comparatione ad antecedens vel consequens simpliciter.*

On f. 85 vb-86 ra we find an introduction to the art of logic. I give here the complete text:

Quoddam prohemium

> In principio cuiuslibet tractatus debent quinque principaliter precognosci. Primum est quid sit introductio. Et quia introductio dicitur ab introducendo: quia in aliquid introducat, debet secundo precognosci in quid [quod *N*] introducit. Illud autem est ars. Et ideo secundo videndum est quid est ars. Sed quia ars non introducit in qua<m>libet artem in medietate sed in artem specialem et particularem, tertio est cognoscendum quid est illa ars specialem. Hec quoad [quod ad*N*] presens est logica. Et ideo videndum est quid logica. Sed quoniam sermo imitatur naturam et hoc non operatur nisi per debitum instrumentum, sic nec logica, cum sit scientia sermocinalis, operatur nisi instrumento aliquo mediante. Hoc autem est argumentum. Et ideo quarto videndum est quid [quidem*N*] est argumentum. Preterea, sicut <dicit> Aristotiles in principio *Posteriorum,* de subiecto scientie oportet supponere quod est et quid est. Et ideo ad introitum scientie necessaria est aliqua

---

[12] The explicit does not occur until f.86 ra; see below, p. 18. Censi wrongly regards the various tracts found before f.86r as belonging to the *Syncategoreumata.*

precognitio ipsius subiecti. Propter hoc quinto videndum quid sit subiectum in logica tota. Quod est [quoniam in *N*] sillogismus.

Introductio sic solet distingui (sic!): introductio est facilis et compendiosa traditio necessaria ad notitiam totius operis subsequentis. In prima parte huius descriptionis tanguntur tria, scilicet facilitas, brevitas et utilitas. Facilitas per hoc quod dicit 'facilis'; brevitas et utilitas per hoc quod dicit 'compendiosa', quia compendium et dispendium sunt opposita. Unde quemadmodum dispendium <est> longum et inutile, sic compendium breve et utile. Et consignanter ponuntur ista tria ibi, quia sicut istorum trium opposita, scilicet difficultas, prolixitas et <in>utilitas, retrahunt hominem ab incepto opere et retardant, sic tria [sic tria *bis in N*] superius predicta, facilitas, brevitas, utilitas, ad cognoscendum opus excitant [exitant *N*] et invitant. Unde facilitas reddit [*86 ra*] docilem auditorem, brevitas benivolum, utilitas sollicitum et attentum.

Ars autem inquantum introducit, in generali est secundum Marchum (!) Tullium collectio preceptorum ad eundem finem tendentium. Secundum autem Aristotilem ars est notitia unius ad alium per experimenta singularium.

Ars autem specialis que est logica, est scientia discernens verum a falso. Aliter autem sic, secundum quod patet in littera: dialetica est ars artium ad omnium methodorum principia viam habens. 'Methodus' autem grece 'semita' latine; unde sunt methaforice. Methodus enim proprie est semita compendiosa per quam dispendium strate publice devitatur, per quam vadunt garciferi [grooms] cum militibus incedentes.

Argumentum secundum Boetium est ratio rei dubie faciens fidem. Unde dicit 'argumentum quasi [quam *N*] 'voces [vos*N*] arguentes mentem'.

Sillogismus autem, sicut dictum est, est subiectum totius logices, aut secundum se aut per suas partes. Sed confectus est <ex> propositionibus, propositiones autem ex terminis. Et notitia totius dependet a partibus; ideo non possumus sillogismum aliter declarare nisi per litteram precedentem.

Et sic terminatur introitus huius totius artis et debet in fine reponi.

On f.86 rb there is a marginal note referring to an omission made in Tract IV (*De syllogismis*) of the *Tractatus*:

⁜ istud debet esse in fine sillogismorum.

As a matter of fact, the same sign ⁜ is found on f.6 vb after the words "... ideo utilis est coniunctio (sic!) talium terminorum" ⁜ followed by the instruction: *require in tali signo in fine libri quod deficit*. The text to be supplied in *De syllogismis* is the text given by the Tarragona and Ivrea manuscripts (our *T* and *F*), whereas the Milan MS (our *H*) has this passage with some additions and both the Vatican MS (our *R*) and the Cordoba MS (our *C*) give a far more extensive redaction.

After some blank lines under the first column of f. 86 r the same hand that wrote the preceding texts added a colophon

> Explicit iste liber sit scriptor crimine liber

followed by the postponed explicit of both the *Tractatus* and the *Syncategoreumata* in a different, contemporaneous handwriting:

> Expliciunt tractatus Magister petri
> hyspani et sincategoremata eius.

On f. 86 va thirteen lines are found in a contemporaneous hand which contain a logical text about *opposita*. The remaining part of f. 86 va and the entire second column of this page (86 vb) give a somewhat later text which is almost illegible due to damp stains. Its incipit runs:

> Incipit tractatus magistri Johanini de inventione medii. Quoniam principium sillogizandi unamquamque propositionem est medius terminus....

This small work has sometimes been ascribed to Thomas Aquinas. On f. 86 vb we find the explicit:

> Et hec de inventione medii termini dicta sufficiant. Amen.

Follows the first half of the alphabet (*a* to *l*). Folio 87 r contains a diagram of the different kinds of supposition. The pages 87 v, 88 r and 88 v show some *tentamina plumae* in a later hand (*inter alia*: 'ergo putinus (?) iacobi est asinus', on f. 87 v).

I have made a complete transcription of the *Syncategoreumata* text of *N*.

E   Ivrea (in Piemont, Italy), Biblioteca Capitolare, codex 79.[13] This parchment codex, originally consisting of 194 folios, seems to date from the end of the 13th century. It measures 256 x 175 mm and is written in one column of 28 lines on the middle of the page, which is rather unusual for a manuscript of this period, but can be explained if we assume that the scribe intended to add marginal glosses. The codex is not foliated, with the exception of the fourth page which is numbered f. 1. The four preceding pages are numbered *a*, *b*, *c* and *d* . A contemporaneous gloss commentary[14] on *Tractatus* I-V is written on the folios *c* and *d* and in the margins of

---

[13] The catalogue by Alfonso Professione (*Inventario dei manoscritti della Biblioteca Capitolare de Ivrea*. Edizione riveduta a cura di Ilo Vignono, Alba 1967) gives (p.64) only scanty information about this manuscript.
[14] For this commentary, see my study in VIVARIUM 8 (1970), (10-55), 19-28.

ff. 1 r-33 v (on f.33 v in the left margin only). Several folios have
been torn out on account of the beautiful initials at the opening lines
of each new section. Some illuminations, however, are still there
(ff.1 r, 31 r, 54 v, 99 r, 113 v, 127 v, 135 r, 147 v, 156 r, 161 v, 167 r, 179
r, 188 r, 189 r, 192 v). The folios 98, 174, 181 and 191-2 are missing
(see below). The codex is somewhat damaged in several places; the
first pages are partly illegible as a result of damp stains, especially
the glosses. The pages that are numbered *a* and *b* seem to contain
fragments of Prosper of Aquitania. At the bottom of page *b* we come
across the following note in a 15th century hand: *Iste prosper est antor
fili <...> de filo <...> de jucomolio de arusio. quem deus benedicat* AMEN.
Since page *c* is much more damaged by damp stains than *b* we
may conclude that *b* served as a fly-leaf in a later binding. At the
top of page *c* we find a note reading *Qaln XIV.*

  E contains a complete copy of the *Tractatus* and nearly the complete text of the *Syncategoreumata*. The *Tractatus* occur in the following
order: I (1 r-7 r); II (7 r-11 r); III (11 r-17 v); IV (18 r 22v); V (22 v-30
v); VI (31 r-35 r); VIII (35 r-39 r); IX (39 r-40 r); X (40 r-v); XXI (40 v-44
v); XII (44 v-54 vv) and VII (54 v-97v). The position of tract VII is quite
unusual. It has the explicit: *Et hec de fallaciis et earum reductione dicta
sufficiant.* DEO GRATIAS AMEN. The *Tractatus* themselves have
neither colophon nor explicit. Surprisingly, *E* lacks both the *Caliditas*
and the *ycos* interpolation. In the *Exemplum* passage our MS gives the
remarkable combination *Mediolanenses-Londenses-Papienses*, thus un-
derlining its Italian origin. The familiar interpolations in the opening lines of the *Tractatus* (see above, p.13f.) are happily missing in
E. The gloss commentary is remarkable in that has retained some
of the *couleur locale* of Peter's text: it instances (f.15 ra) *homo Tolosanus*
(as opposed to *homo Anglicus*).

  The text of the *Syncategoreumata* begins acephalously (due to the
loss of the first folio) on f.99 r: *par vel impar de numero, habere tres
angulos equales duobus rectis de triangulo* (*Introduction*, cap. 4 of the present edition). The text is written carefully and it is quite legible, but
it contains a great number of dreadful errors which betray a serious
lack of understanding on the part of the scribe (or of the scribe's
exemplar). For a short anthology of these errors, see below, p. 25.

  The text is illuminated with some multi-coloured rubricas in the
opening lines of several tracts: 99r, 113v (at the beginning of *De
dictionibus exclusivis*), 127v (beginning of *De dictionibus exceptivis*), 135r
(*De dictionibus consecutivis*), 147v (*Incipit, desinit*), 156r (*Necessario, contingenter*), 161v (*De coniunctionibus*), 167r (*vel*), 179r (*De reduplicativis*),
188r (*Quanto*), 189r (*Quam*), 192v (*De ostensione syllogismorum*). The

folios 174, 181, 191 and 192 were torn out, by the same villain, no doubt, who also laid violent hands on the first folio (f. 98) of the *Syncategoreumata* text on account of its rubrica.

The *Syncategoreumata* tracts are found in the following order (that turns out to be the usual one):

> *Introductio* : [...]-99 r
> I *De compositione* : 99 r-106 r
> II *De negatione* : 106 r-113 v
> III *De dictionibus exclusivis* : 113 v-127 v
> IV *De dictionibus exceptivis* : 127 v-135 r
> V *De dictionibus consecutivis* : 135 r-147 v
> VI *De 'incipit' et 'desinit'*: 147 v-156   r
> VII *De 'necessario' et 'contingenter'*: 156 r-161 v
> VIII *De coniunctionibus* : 161 v...173 v [...] 175 r-180 v [...]-188 r
> IX *De 'quanto', 'quam' et 'quidquid'*: 188 r-190 v [...] 193 r
> X *De responsione* : 193 r-[...]-194 r.

I have made a complete transcription of the *E* MS copy of the Syncategoreumata and have consulted it continuously.

R Vatican Library (Città del Vaticano, Rome) codex 1731 of the *codices Reginenses* , of Italian origin as is apparent from the handwriting and from several notes and *tentamina plumae* on the fly leaves. It is a parchment codex consisting of 80 folios and dating from the first decades of the 14th century. It measures 195 x 144 mm (written surface 117 x 94 mm) and is written in two columns of 42 lines each (except for ff. 1 and 2 which have 44 lines). There are a few marginal notes and some occasional corrections throughout the entire manuscript, most of which are written in a somewhat later hand. Peter's works are followed by the *Tractatus de sphera* of John of Sacrobosco (ff. 57 r-end). Peter's *Tractatus* are found on ff. 1 ra-29 va (in the same order as in *T*). The explicit runs: *Et de distributionibus dicta sufficiant. R* has both the *Caliditas* and the *ycos* interpolations but, in spite of its Italian origin, it does give the topographically correct version of the *Exemplum* passage: *Legionenses-Astoricenses-Zamorenses.* Unfortunately, it has the usual interpolations in the opening lines of the *Tractatus* (see above, p.13f.).

The opening lines of the *Syncategoreumata* immediately follow the *Tractatus* : *Ab eo quod res est...*etc. (29 va, line 17). The *Syncategoreumata* end on f. 55 vb. The order in which they occur is the usual one:

Introductio (29 va-30 ra); I (30 ra-31 vb); II (31 vb-34 ra); III (34 ra-38 ra); IV (38 ra-40 ra); V (40 ra-43 rb); VI (43 rb-45 vb); VII (45 vb-47 rb); VIII (47 rb-53 vb); IX (53 vb-55 ra); X (55 ra- vb)

On f. 55 rb the explicit runs: *Expliciunt sinchategoreumata* (!) *magistri petri hispani,* followed (ff. 55 rb-56 va) by a few stray logical notes (most of them logical rules) quite similar to those occurring in the Naples MS (see above, p. 16), the last two of which concern the *ars obligatoria.* The remainder of f. 56 contains some (practically illegible) notes in a different handwriting (probably identical with the hand that corrected the *Syncategoreumata* in this MS and added some captions in the margin as well as some logical diagrams.

The text of the *Syncategoreumata* is nicely written in a gothic minuscle and dates from the second half of the 13th century. The corrections and diagrams ((e.g. one demonstrating the different kinds of *compositio* (at the bottom of f. 30 r) and another elucidating *negatio* (on f. 31 v)) are in a somewhat later hand.

I have used a complete transcription of this copy of the *Syncategoreumata.*

Cordoba (Spain), *Biblioteca del Excellentissimo Cabildo,* codex 158 (formerly 318).[15] It is a parchment codex of Spanish origin measuring 190 x 135 mm (irregularly) and consisting of 126 folios in two columns. The first part is written in a 12th century gothic minuscle, the remainder in a hand dating from the beginning of the 14th century, which shows a remarkable similarity to the *manus corrigens* of the Vatican MS. (our *R*). Part of f. 36 r and the entire 36 v are written in yet another, somewhat later, hand. The quaternios consist of 10 or 12 folios and the number of lines in the first part varies, whereas the second part has 29 lines in each column. The codex has a few illuminations.[16]

The manuscript contains the following items:[17]

— 1 r-19 v: Boethius, *De differentiis topicis* (incomplete; the text ends abruptly in the last section of Book III, col. 1205 A 10-2, ed. Migne: Ab

C

---

[15] The old number 318 was mentioned by Heinrich Denifle, who discovered this manuscript in Cordoba (see his *Chartularium Universitatis parisiensis* I, 542). When visiting this library in 1968 I found the manuscript under no. 158.

[16] For a detailed codicological description, see Antonio Garcia y Garcia, Francisco Cantelar Rodriguez and Manuel Nièto Cumplido, *Catalogo de los manuscritos e incunables de la Catedral de Cordoba,* Biblioteca Salmanticensis VI Estudios 5, Salamanca 1976, 297-9.

[17] See the printed catalogue, *loc. cit.*

antecedentibus et consequentibus, mixti cum pluribus. A repugnantibus
ciceronis, idem a temistio).
— 20 r-29 v: The same, *De syllogismis categoricis* (incomplete; the text ends
abruptly in Book II, col. 826 A 17-8, ed. Migne: Et resolvitur primus sic
conversa enim prima universali).
— 30 ra-72 vb: Peter of Spain, *Tractatus* (the tracts of which are in the same
order as in *T* and *R*) without any explicit.

C has the *Caliditas* interpolation in the same form as our Milan MS
(see below, p. 23) and, unlike the other MSS, it has the *ycos* interpolation at the end of V4 (in my edition) after the *Exemplum* passage
and not in the *entimema* section. The version of the *Exemplum* passage in *C* is correct, but the opening lines of the *Tractatus* contain the
usual interpolation (see above, p. 13).

The *Syncategoreumata*, immediately following the *Tractatus* and
introduced only by INCIPIUNT SINCHATHAGA[73 r]REUMATA
(*sic* !) were written (ff. 72 vb-110 rb) by the same scribe who copied
the *Tractatus*. There are some marginal notes in this same hand. At
the beginning of the tract we find some glosses in a different hand.
The *Syncategoreumata* tracts occur in the usual order: *Introductio* (73 ra-
va); I (73 va-76 rb); II (76 rb-79 va); III (79 va-85 rb); IV (85 rb-88 ra); V
(88 ra-93 ra); VI (93 ra-96 rb); VII (96 rb-98 va); VIII (98 va-108 ra); IX
(108 ra-109 vb); X (109 vb-110 vb). Strangely enough, the marginal
caption added to tract V contains the same error as is found in *R* :
Sequitur de dictionibus consequentivis (!). For that matter, *C* has some
readings which also occur in the margin of *R*. On f. 110 vb the
explicit is found:

> Expliciunt sinca^{ta} magistri petri hispani. Laus tibi sit Christe quoniam
> liber explicit iste.
> Hic liber est scriptus. Qui scripsit sit benedictus.

Before the same hand makes a fresh start with an incomplete gloss
commentary (f. 111 ra-126 vb) on the *Tractatus* there are some stray
notes (on f. 110), written by a somewhat later hand, on the four
causae huius operis (e.g. *causa efficiens in isto libro est ipse magister
petrus*). The commentary opens as follows:

> **Dialetica est ars** etc. Quia instrumentum proprium et completum dyaletice
> disputationis est sillogismus di<aleticus>, ideo accedentibus ad dyaleticam
> necessarium est habere notitiam de sillogismo.[18]

Professor Braakhuis kindly lent me his complete transcription of
this MS.

---

[18] For the rest of the opening lines and some other quotations from this commentary, see my study in VIVARIUM 8 (1970), 38-40.

Milan (Italy), *Biblioteca Ambrosiana* H. 64 Inf., a parchment codex   H
consisting of 100 folios, measuring 200 x 147 mm (written surface
121 x 97 mm) each. This codex was apparently written in Northern
Italy and came into the possession of the Biblioteca Ambrosiana *ex
legato Bernardini Ferrarii mediolanensis machinatoris anno 1830*, as we are
told on the first fly leaf. Two different hands can be distinguished
(ff. 1 r-96 va and 96 va-99rb) dating from the end of the 13th and the
first quarter of the 14th century, respectively. Part of the stray notes
found on ff. 99 v and 100 r are by the second hand. Up to f. 99 r the
codex is written in two columns of 37 lines each. On the first fly-
leaf a later hand wrote: *Petri Hispani—qui et Joannes PP XXI ab aliquibus dictus est—Dialectica. L. An. Seneca—De remediis fortuitorum.* Folio
1r is badly damaged by damp stains. A third hand, which seems
somewhat later than the one that wrote the *Tractatus*, added a number of marginal notes, especially on the first folios.

The *Tractatus* are found on ff. 1 ra-49 vb in the same order as in *T,
R* and *C*. The Milan codex has the *Caliditas* interpolation in the
same redaction as in *C* and the *ycos* interpolation as in *T* and *R*. In
the *Exemplum* passage the Italian scribe did not adapt the *couleur
locale*. On the other hand, *H* (which, on the whole, is rather sus-
ceptive of interpolations), has the usual interpolation in the opening
lines of the *Tractatus* (see above, p. 13). The text of the *Tractatus* ends
on f. 49 vb: *Et hec de distributionibus dicta sufficiant.* DEO GRATIAS:
AMEN:
On f. 50 r the *Syncategoreumata* begin without any title: *Ab eo quod
res est.....etc.* The complete text of this treatise takes up ff. 50 ra-96 va.
The explicit runs (96 va):

EXPLICIUNT SICATHEGOREUMATA (!)
MAGISTRI PETRI YSPANI. DEO
GRACIAS: AMEN: AMEN: AMEN.

After the *Syncategoreumata* we find Seneca's work in the 14th century hand.[19] Folio 99 r contains a number of stray notes on logical
matters, written in various hands (s. XIV), among which a rather
extensive note on *consequentia* .

---

[19] For further information, see the *Introduction* of my *Tractatus* edition, p. CVI
f. The Milan MS is also mentioned in A. Amelli, 'Indice dei codici manoscritti della Biblioteca Ambrosiana' in *Rivista delle Biblioteche e degli Archivi* 21
(1910), 152.

Nota quod ad hoc quod aliqua consequentia sit bona exigitur quod non possit
ita esse a parte rei sicut importatur per antecedens nisi sit ita a parte rei
sicut importatur per consequens. Ideo hec consequentia non bona de forma:
'ego sum Troie; ergo hec est vera "ego sum Troie"'. Quod non sit bona patet,
quia possum esse Troie absque hoc quod hec propositio sit 'ego sum Troie'.
Ergo absque hoc quod ipsa sit vera. Igitur consequentia non bona. Et sic de
paribus et similibus. Et non requiritur quod antecedens non possit esse
verum sine consequente, ut aliqui dicunt, quia sequeretur quod nulla consequentia esset bona; quod ipsi negarent. Probo. Et premitto primo quod
antecedens et consequens non sunt nisi due propositiones; secundo quod
'verum' et 'falsum' et similes dictiones attribuantur propositioni. Tu<n>c sic:
Omnium duarum propositionum una potest esse sine alia. Ergo potest esse
vera absque quod alia sit. Et sic cuiuslibet consequentie antecedens potest esse
verum absque consequente. Ultima consequentia patet. Sed probo antecedens
prime consequentie quia nulla propositio dependet ab alia. Et consequentia
prima tenet, quia quando prima non est, non <est> vera. Declaro secundum
quia: Verum et falsum si convenirent rei, tunc propositio de musca volante
formica ipsa quiescente alterarentur [*sic!*]. Item. Verum est adequatio rei ad
intellectum. Sed talis adequatio est ens rationis. Et sic tali enti convenit. Sed
tale ens est. Propositio igitur sibi attribuitur. Et hoc est quod dicit Philo-
sophus in libro *Predicamentorum* : "ab eo enim quod res <est> vel non est,
oratio vera vel falsa dicitur.

Folio 100 r contains an *Ex<tractum>* *de sponsalibus* in seven lines,
written in a handwriting from about 1400.

I have used the complete transcription of *H* made by Professor
Braakhuis after a first draft copied by myself in 1955.

2 *The ratio edendi*

I started the present edition by preparing a provisional text based on
the transcription of *H*. When collating some other earlier MSS I
realised that this version of the text was unsatisfactory in several
respects. *H* is marred by serious omissions and major errors and
corrupted by some arbitrary interpolations and 'corrections' that are
rather isolated variants, as will be clear from our *apparatus criticus*.
Nevertheless, though, *H* has some merits too: together with *T* and
N, for instance, it omits the interpolation at V, 54, which, in various
forms, occurs in *PERC* (and which, for that matter, is also added by
the *manus corrigens* of *H*). At *Introd.* cap. 2 *H* has, together with *T*
and *N*, the correct reading *predicativum* where others read *predicamentum* (*P*), *predicatum* (*R*), or *predicabilis* (C). For other instances of
H 's reliability, see our *apparatus criticus*. All things considered, I
decided to relegate *H* to the *codices minus allati* .

In assessing the value of the earlier manuscripts, I started with the

results of the critical examination I conducted when preparing the *Tractatus* edition. First of all, I examined the Ivrea manuscript which, together with the Avignon manuscript (Musée Calvet, 301, unfortunately containing only the opening section of the *Syncategoreumata*), is unaffected by the three major interpolations that occur (at least part of them) in all other MSS of the *Tractatus*. For that matter, *E* nearly always has quite plausible readings, where many other MSS have less satisfactory or downright unacceptable ones. To mention only one example: at II, 33 *E* has (with *T* and *P*) the correct *nullus homo* instead of *nullum animal* (which is an impossible reading from the viewpoint of logic). All other instances are mentioned in our *apparatus criticus*. *E* (or *E* 's exemplar), however, commits many omissions by homoeoteleuton (by an error of the eye the scribe returns to what seems the last word he copied, but which, in reality, is the same or a similar word occurring a bit further along in the exemplar). Sometimes these omissions are incredibly long. On top of that, *E* contains a great many errors where the copyist was unable to decipher his exemplar and gave free rein to his phantasy. The resultant text often makes no sense whatsoever. Some examples (out of a staggering quantity): *Introd* . 5: in the discussion on 'est' and 'non' *E* has 'illud' and 'non'. At I, 5 *E* has *triaregulim* instead of *ut figura triangularis*. At I, 6 *generandi* instead of *significandi* (confusing logic and biology, it seems); II, 23, *deperit* for *reperit* . The usual confusion of *esse* and *omne* is, of course, not wanting in *E* (e.g. I, 8) neither is that between *materia* and *modo* , between *subiecto* and *substantia* (e.g. I, 9) and between *eam* and *causam* (*ibid.*). At I, 15 *E* has *ut vita* instead of *perfectio unitur*. At III, 26 the scribe even ventures to propose a theological opinion: instead of *nichil est dictu 'tantum ens'* *E* reads *nichil est 'deum timetis'*. The scribe's geographical knowledge is not quite up to the mark: at VIII, 15 he writes *Yspanania* instead of *Yspania* . At VIII, 32 our good man has *communitas platonis* instead of *communitas predicationis* .

These errors, however, are so obvious that they cannot throw us off the right track. What is more, we are indebted to the *E* scribe for many a correct reading where more intelligent scribes forsake us. At VIII, 29 *E* has, with *T*, the correct *encleticum* where the other MSS wrongly have *encleticus, enclelica* or *elenticum* (!); similarly *E* has, with *R* , the correct reading *inclinativum*. At VIII, 42 *E* has, together with *T* and *N* , the correct *per insertionem* and it is the only MS that correctly reads *collatione,* where *P* has *collectione* (!) and *T* and *H* the strange reading *collu, idest collatione* and *N* and *R* the correct reading accompanied by an explanation: *collatione, idest colligatione.* At IX, 3 *E*

gives what must be the correct reading *subversionis* whereas all other MSS read *eversionis*. At II, 2 *E* has the most probable reading *exercitio* (supported by *R* 's *exercito* (!)) where *T* has the possible reading *exercitium* and all the other MSS the akward reading *exercitus*. Thus *E*, together with *T* and *N*, often has the correct reading (see the *apparatus criticus*). In spite of its unquestionable merits I could not help categorising *E* as one of the *codices minus allati* because of its grave errors and frequent omissions.

The manuscripts *R* and *C*, the *Tractatus* copies of which proved to be related[20], are also related as far as the *Syncategoreumata* are concerned (as may appear from the *apparatus criticus* throughout). As I have mentioned before (above, p. 22), *R* and *C* have the same strange marginal caption at the beginning of tract V of the *Syncategoreumata* : *Sequitur de dictionibus consequentivis* (!). For that matter, the *manus corrigens* in *R* (which wrote most of the marginal notes, including the captions) much resembles the hand that wrote *C* . The two may even be identical. Sometimes *R* and *C* have the most credible reading, e.g. at *Introd* . cap. 6 *etiam* , which is omitted by all other MSS. However, *C* sometimes has unwarranted additions which are (correctly) missing in *R* , for instance, at *Introd*. cap. 2 *et alia est dispositio* or at I, 4, where *C* , with *H* , has the addition *nomen significat substantiam cum qualitate*. Agreement between *C* and *H* , by the way, is no exception. *CH* often take isolated positions in the *apparatus criticus*. Compared to the Tarragona MS, which has its origin in the region where Peter in all probability wrote his logical works, *R* and *C* are not very helpful. I have deemed it less useful to record all their minor variant readings and I have classed them with the *codices minus allati* .

Because of its origin the Tarragona manuscript deserves our special attention, the more so, as *T* is one of the very few manuscripts that do not have the interpolation in the opening lines of the *Tractatus* (see above, p. 13), which is also missing in the earliest extant commentaries on this treatise (see above, p. 10, n.4). Frequently, *T* is the only manuscript to have the correct reading. E.g. *Introd* ., cap. 5, where only *T* reads *negatione* (wrongly) omitted by all other MSS. At I, 15 *T* correctly has *quare*, where others read *quia* and at III, 48 only *T* has the correct *in hiis duobus modis*, whereas all other MSS have the corrupted *hiis duobus modis* . At VIII, 77 *T* has *ordinationem* , which is to be preferred to *ordinem*. *T* 's *manus corrigens* (*T^c*) is mostly a felicitous one: e.g. at I, 24 *T^c* alone has the correct reading *propter*

---

[20] See the *Introduction* to my edition of the *Tractatus* , pp. CVIII and CX and the *apparatus criticus*.

predicta male intellecta , rightly cancelling the explanatory addition which, in various forms, occurs in the other MSS and in *T* itself. A similar situation can be found at VIII, 41 in the passage *unum genere .... diffinitione* (see *ad locum*).[21]

However, *T* is surely not perfect. It has its omissions and corrupted readings. E.g. at *Introd.*, cap. 6 *T* reads *res* instead of *dispositio*, or I, 2 where *T* has *metaphisicam* instead of *mathematicum*. At II, 1 *T* has *ex* instead of *et* ; at II, 26 *T* has *cogitando* instead of the correct *cognoscendo*. In spite of its flaws, however, *T* is a comparatively sound manuscript and I have used it as a basis for establishing the text.

There remain two other manuscripts, the Naples MS (our *N*) and the Prague MS (our *P*).[22] *P* sometimes is the only manuscript that has the correct reading. E.g. *Introductio*, cap. 5: *aliis* , wrongly omitted by all other MSS. At II, 15 *P* has the correct *rem* instead of *rationem* (all other MSS). At III, 33 *P* correctly reads *per modum eius quod est quid* , where *E* has *que est quid* and all the others, apparently not aware of the meaning of the phrase 'id quod est quid' read *qui est quid*. At VI, 31 *P* is the only MS that always gives the correct *indesinens* instead of *indeficiens*. At I, 25 *P* has, together with *N*, the correct *quam* , where the other MSS have *quia* and at I, 27 *P* does not omit the indispensable *suam* , which all others lack except *N* . On the other hand, *P* sometimes has a pedantic streak, as it were. It shows a marked tendency to correct the master: several times Peter's (unusual) '*abire* in infinitum' is changed into (the usual) '*ire* in infinitum'. At II, 28 *P* changes *negatio enim negat unum de altero* into *ab altero*, which seems to be a hypercorrection. At VIII, 45-46 *P*^c errroneously changes *de pari* into *disparate*. In VIII, 41 *P* contains a rather extensive interpolation which is found in none of the other MSS. At VIII, 88, 3 *P* has *hostis*, where all others have the usual (but incorrect) *ostis*, but *P*, too, analyses it into *os* and *tis*. On the whole, *P* seems to be one of the better manuscripts. The *apparatus criticus* mentions all its significant alternative readings.

The Naples MS (*N*) is not of a constant quality. On the one hand, it shows an abundance of omissions (often due to haplography) and it contains some rather nonsensical readings. E.g. *Introd.*, 4: *equum* for *enim, lune subiectu* for *lune obiectu* and *pars par* for *par,* II, 23: *differre* for *destruere*. The words *ita, ista* and *prima* are frequently confused (which is easy to explain from a paleographical point of view). On

---

[21] For other instances, see our *apparatus criticus* .

[22] When I prepared the *Tractatus* edition these MSS were not yet at my disposal.

the other hand, *N* is the only MS not to leave out the indispensable *termino* at II,3; similarly, at VIII, 4 only *N* has the correct reading *cum legit quare legit*, where other MSS give a variety of (wrong) readings. Also, *N* (with *T*) correctly omits a rather extensive interpolation at V, 54. Many times *N*, together with *T* and *P*, has good readings.

All things considered, none of the extant MSS is perfect. There are several passages, therefore, where the editor has had to correct all of them, or attempt a conjecture. E.g. I, 6 (*antiquum*); II,33 (*fallacia* instead of *locus*); III,39 (*tentum* instead of *tantum*); VI, 6 (*consequenter* for *consequitur*); VI, 9 and 17 (*alterativo* and *generativo*); VIII, 64 (*negativo*, twice). At VIII, 83 *ad medium ordinatur utraque extremitas* seems to present itself as an inevitable correction of the (apparently) corrupt (different) readings of the MSS. Likewise, at IX, 1 my conjecture *cum notatione* (or something to that effect) imposes itself. At VIII, 76, where all MSS have *Ar.* (=Aristotle), one should read *ars* since the opinion mentioned there cannot be traced back to Aristotle, but is an element of logical doctrine from the 13th century onwards.

Summing up, the MSS *ETPN* seem to be our most reliable sources (leaving aside the transparent and harmless omissions and flaws in *E* and *N*) and have served as the basis for our edition. All the readings of *TPN* are mentioned in the *apparatus criticus* (except for insignificant deviations in spelling and word-order as well as some recurrent variables such as *ergo-igitur* ; *iste-ille* ; *autem-vero* ; *sive-vel* etc. and the omission of *est* in set phrases (e.g. *subiectum inquantum subiectum <est>*)). However, as it would have been rather tiresome to list all the errors and omissions of *E* in the *apparatus*, I had to relegate this MS to the *codices minus allati. R, C* and *H*, as they seldom have a plausible reading where our basic MSS fail, have also been classed as *codices minus allati*. The classification *minus allati*, therefore, does not refer to the actual use of the MSS involved but to their presence in the *apparatus criticus*.

Finally, in spite of some undeniable family relations between the MSS (clearly shown by the *apparatus*), it seems to be rather useless to set up a stemma, since, in order to account for the intricate relationships between our MSS, it would have to contain too many postulated intermediary codices.[23]

---

[23] There is, for instance, an unmistakable relationship between *R* and *C*, as well as between *T, P* and *N* , but sometimes the former two show similarities with *N* where *N* deviates from *TP*.

ARGUMENTUM

TRACTATUS IV: DE DICTIONIBUS EXCEPTIVIS

TRACTATUS V: DE DICTIONIBUS CONSECUTIVIS

TRACTATUS VI: DE HIIS VERBIS 'INCIPIT' ET 'DESINIT'

SIGLA

T = *Tarraconensis*, Bibl. Capit. 2 (s. XIII *ad fin.*)
P = *Pragensis*, Bibl. Capit. 1380 (c.1300)
N = *Napolitanus*, Bibl. Nat. F. VIII 29 (s. XIV *init*.)

codices minus allati

E = *Eporedianus* 79 (s. XIII *ad fin*.)
R = *Vaticanus Reginensis* 1731 (s. XIV *init*.)
C = *Cordubensis*, Bibl. Capit. 158 (s. XIV *init*.)
H = *Ambrosianus* H 64 Inf. (s. XIII *ad fin*.)

T^c (P^c) etc. = manus quae correxit *T (P) etc.*
T^m (P^m) etc. = manus in margine *T (P) etc.*

]	=	scripsi (scripsit, scripserunt)
......	=	usque ad
coni.	=	conieci
<......>	=	supplevi
[......]	=	seclusi
?	=	fortasse
!	=	sic
add.	=	addit, addunt
om.	=	omittit, omittunt
coll.	=	collato, collatis
codd.	=	plerique omnesve codices
cett.	=	ceteri codices

LATIN TEXT
AND
TRANSLATION

INTRODUCTIO

De significatione dictionum sincategorematicarum in genere

1   [*T25rb, P51ra, N41vb*] Ab eo quod res est vel non est oratio vera vel falsa dicitur. Sed a dictionibus sincategorematicis (ut 'tantum', 'solus',[1] 'nisi', 'preter', et consimilibus[2]) causatur veritas vel falsitas in oratione. Ergo dictiones sincategorematice [*T25va*] significant res aliquas. Sed non significant res subicibiles vel predicabiles. Ergo significant res que sunt dispositiones subicibilium vel predicabilium,[3] quia nichil est in oratione vera vel falsa nisi subiectum et predicatum et eorum dispositiones.

2   'Res' enim dupliciter dicitur. Quia quedam est res subicibilis vel predicabilis (ut[1] 'homo' vel 'equus', 'ambulat'[2] vel 'currit') et alio modo est[3] res que est dispositio subicibilis[4] vel predicabilis. Sed dispositio item,[5] sive res que est dispositio,[6] est duplex, quia est quedam dispositio eius quod est subiectum vel eius quod est predicatum (ut 'albus', 'niger', 'bene', 'male' et consimilia). Et talis dispositio subicitur cum subiecto et predicatur cum predicato (ut 'homo albus currit bene'). Subiectum enim et id[7] quod est subiectum differunt sicut pater et id quod est pater, quia sicut pater dicitur ad filium et econverso, ita[8] subiectum[9] ad predicatum et econverso; sunt enim *ad aliquid*, sive relationes, ut[10] pater et filius. Alia[11] est dispositio subiecti inquantum est subiectum vel[12] predicati inquantum est predicatum (ut 'tantum', 'solus', 'necessario',[13] 'contingenter' et sic de aliis) et ille non subiciuntur neque predicantur, quia sunt ipsius[14] subiecti in[15] comparatione ad predicatum et econverso. Et tales dispositiones significantur per dictiones sincategorematicas; [*N42ra*] dicunt[16] enim comparationes[17] sive habitudines subiecti[18] inquantum subicibile et predicati[19] inquantum predicabile. Et dicitur[20]

INTRODUCTION

On the signification of syncategorematic words in general

1   It is because a thing <involved> is or is not that a proposition is said to be true or false.[1] Now the truth or falsity in a proposition is caused by syncategorematic words (such as 'only', 'alone', 'unless', 'but', and the like). Therefore syncategorematic words signify something or other. Now they do not signify things that are capable of functioning as subjects or as predicates. Therefore they signify things that are dispositions of things capable of functioning as subjects or as predicates, for there is nothing in a true or false proposition except the subject, the predicate and their dispositions.

2   'Thing' is in fact said in two ways. [1] In one way a thing is something that is capable of functioning as a subject or as a predicate (*e.g.* 'man' or 'horse', 'walks' or 'runs') and [2] in another way a thing is a disposition of something that is capable of functioning as a subject or as a predicate. Now a disposition, furthermore, or the thing that is a disposition, is twofold. [1] In one way there is the disposition that belongs to that which is a subject or that which is a predicate (*e.g.* 'white', 'black', 'well', 'badly', and the like), and a disposition of this kind is made subject together with the subject and is made predicate together with the predicate (as in 'A white man runs well'). For the subject and that which is the subject differ from each other as father and that which is the father. For just as father is said in relation to a son and the other way round, likewise subject is said in relation to a predicate and the other way round, for they are relatives (*ad aliquid*), or relations, like father and son. [2] The other is the disposition that belongs to a subject insofar as it is the subject or to a predicate insofar as it is the predicate (*e.g.* 'only', 'alone', 'necessarily', 'contingently', and so on). And these are not made subjects or predicates, since they are part of the subject as such in comparison with the predicate and the other way round. And the dispositions of this kind are the ones signified by syncategorematic words; for these words indicate relations or conditions that accompany a subject insofar as it can function as a subject and accompany a predicate insofar as it can function as a predicate. And 'syncategorema'

---

1   Cf. Aristotle, *Categ.* 5, 4b8-10; 12, 14b21-3.

sincategoreuma a 'sin', quod est 'con', et 'categoreuma', quod est
'predicativum'[21] vel 'significativum', quasi: 'consignificativum'.

3   Habito quod dictiones sincategorematice significent dispositiones subiecti inquantum subiectum et predicati inquantum predicatum, et[1] sic cognita significatione earum in genere, nunc[2] dicendum est de significatione uniuscuiusque earum[3] in specie; et prius
de prioribus, quia, ut vult[4] Aristotiles: de prioribus prior est speculatio.
Cum ergo in dictionibus[5] sincategorematicis per se intelligantur 'est'
et 'non' et non econverso, ideo 'est' et 'non'[6] sunt priora illis. Et ideo
de hiis prius est dicendum.

De 'est' et 'non'

4   Sed ad[1] videndum quomodo 'est' et 'non' per[2] se intelliguntur
in istis, sciendum[3] quod 'per se' dicitur quatuor modis. Primo autem
modo per se insunt quecumque cadunt in diffinitione[4] rei, sive
predicentur sive non de[5] diffinito. Quedam enim[6] diffinientia predicantur de diffinito (ut 'animal[7] rationale et mortale' de homine).
Quedam autem non predicantur de[8] diffinito, ut 'punctum'[9] non
predicatur de linea et cadit in diffinitione eius; linea enim est
longitudo sine latitudine cuius extremitates sunt duo puncta. Neque
linea predicatur de triangulo et cadit in diffinitione eius; est enim
triangulus figura plana tribus rectis[10] lineis contenta. Secundo autem
modo[11] per se insunt quecumque recipiunt sua subiecta in suis diffinitionibus. Et hoc est quando propria passio sive per[12] se accidens
predicatur de sua[13] diffinitione, ut 'omne[14] privatum lumine a terre
obiectu[15] deficit sive eclipsatur'; hic enim *deficere* sive *eclipsari* est
per[16] se accidens sive propria passio et predicatur de sua diffinitione.
Similiter si propria passio predicetur de parte sue diffinitionis, ut
'numerus est par[17] vel impar', 'linea est recta[18] vel curva', quia 'par'
diffinitur per numerum et[19] 'rectum' per lineam. Est enim par:
numerus divisibilis[20] in duo equalia; rectum[21] vero est[22]: linea cuius
medium non exit ab extremis. [*T25vb*] Tertius autem [*N42rb*] modus
est quando propria passio predicatur de proprio subiecto, ut rectum
vel curvum de linea et par[23] vel impar de numero et habere tres

with

derives from '*syn*', that is 'with', and '*categorema*', that is 'predicative' or 'significative'; thus it amounts to 'consignificative'.

3   Now that we have said that syncategorematic words signify dispositions that belong to a subject insofar as it is the subject and dispositions that belong a predicate insofar as it is the predicate, and thus have knowledge of their signification in general, we must now discuss the signification of each kind of them specifically. First of all, we must discuss the primary ones, because, according to Aristotle,[2] the exploration of primary things comes first. Therefore, since 'is' (*est*) and 'not' (*non*) are understood 'per se' in syncategorematic words and not the other way round, 'is' and 'not' are prior to them. And so they must be discussed first.

On 'is'(est) and 'not'(non)

4   Now in order to see in which way 'is' and 'not' are understood per se in these words, note that 'per se' is said in four ways. [1] In the first way all those things which fall within the definition of something, whether or not they are said of the definitum, inhere in it per se. For some definientia are said of the definitum (*e.g.* 'rational animal and mortal' of man). Other definientia, however, are not said of the definitum, *e.g.* 'point' is not said of line, and yet it falls within its definition; for a line is a longitude without latitude whose extremes are two points. Similarly, 'line' is not said of triangle and yet it falls within its definition; for a triangle is a plane figure enclosed by three lines. [2] In the second way all those things which receive their subjects in their definitions inhere per se in them. And this happens when a proper quality or a *per se* accident is said of its definition, *e.g.* in 'Everything deprived of light by the earth's screening wanes or is eclipsed'; for in this case 'to wane' or 'to be eclipsed' is a *per se* accident or proper quality and is said of its own definition. The same thing would happen if a proper quality were said of a part of its definition, *e.g.* in 'A number is an even one or an odd one' or 'A line is a straight one or a curved one'; for 'even' is defined by 'number' and 'straight' is defined by 'line'. 'An even <thing>' is in fact a *number* divisible into two equal parts and 'a straight <thing>' is a *line* of which the middle does not depart from the extremes. [3] The third way is when a proper quality is said of its proper subject, *e.g.* when 'straight' or 'curved' is said of a line, and 'even' or 'odd' is said of a number and 'to have three angles equal to

---

2   Where?

angulos equales duobus rectis de triangulo. Subiectum enim et propria passio dupliciter comparantur, quia[24] uno modo secundum quod subiectum est causa passionis et diffiniens passionem, et sic pertinet ad secundum modum; alio autem modo sumitur subiectum inquantum subiectum et propria passio inquantum est accidens eius; et sic pertinet ad tertium modum. Quartus autem modus est quando effectus qui est propria[25] passio, concluditur de subiecto per suam causam. Et iste quartus modus est semper in habitudine premissarum[26] ad conclusionem demonstrativam, ut

'omne privatum lumine a terre obiectu deficit
sed luna est privatum lumine a terre obiectu
ergo luna deficit'.

5   Sciendum ergo quod 'est' et 'non' intelliguntur in dictionibus[1] sincategorematicis secundum primum modum eius quod est 'per se', quia intelliguntur in diffinitionibus sive[2] descriptionibus earum. 'Solus'[3] enim sive 'tantum' est 'non cum alio' et 'desinit': 'quod est et de cetero non erit' vel 'nunc[4] ultimo est', et sic de aliis. Et ideo 'est'[5] et 'non' sunt priora aliis[6] dictionibus sincategorematicis. Et[7] 'est' prius est[8] quam 'non', quia affirmatio prior[9] est negatione sicut habitus privatione. Et etiam <quia> negatio non habet esse[10] nisi per affirmationem; unde affirmatio dat ei esse; ergo prior est negatione;[11] intelligitur[12] enim affirmatio in negatione et non econverso. Et etiam quia negatio non cognoscitur nisi per affirmationem. Ergo prius dicendum est de affirmatione quam de negatione. Et sic prius dicendum est de 'est' quam de 'non'.

6   Nota ergo[1] quod hoc [*P51va*] verbum 'est'[2] consignificat compositionem,[3] et etiam alia verba. Sed hoc verbum 'est' per prius consignificat[4] eam, cum natura prius sit aliis verbis et in eis intelligatur. Sed compositio non solum repperitur in verbo sed etiam[5] in rebus aliis. Et ideo prius est dicendum de compositione in communi et postea de specialibus compositionibus.

two right ones' is said of a triangle. For a subject and the proper quality are related in two ways: [a] in one way according as the subject is the cause of the quality and its definiens, and then we are dealing with the second way; [b] in another way the subject is considered insofar as it is the subject and the proper quality insofar as it is its accident, and then we are dealing with the third way. [4] The fourth way is when an effect which is a proper quality is concluded of the subject via its own cause. And this fourth way <of saying 'per se'> is always present in the relation the premisses have to a demonstrative conclusion, as in:

> *'Everything which is deprived of light by the earth's screening is eclipsed;*
> *the moon is deprived of light by the earth's screening;*
> *therefore the moon is eclipsed.'*

5   Note therefore that 'is' and 'not' are understood in syncategorematic words in accordance with the first use of 'per se',[3] because they are understood in the definitions or descriptions of syncategorematic words. For 'alone' or 'only' is 'not with something else' and 'ceases' is 'that which is and afterwards will not be' or 'that which is now for the last time', and so on. And so 'is' and 'not' are prior to other syncategorematic words. Now 'is' comes before 'not', because an affirmation precedes a negation in the same way as a possession its privation. And also because a negation only has being via an affirmation; that is why an affirmation grants being to a negation, and therefore precedes it. For an affirmation is understood in a negation and not the other way round. Moreover, because a negation can only be known by means of an affirmation. Therefore we must discuss affirmation before negation. And so we must discuss 'is' before 'not'.

6   Note therefore that the verb 'is' consignifies a composition and that other verbs do so as well. But the verb 'is' consignifies it primarily because it naturally precedes other verbs as it is understood in them. However, a composition is not only found in a verb but also in other things. And so we must first discuss composition in general and the different kinds of composition later.

---

[3]   Cf. above, cap. 4.

TRACTATUS PRIMUS

DE COMPOSITIONE

De compositione in communi

1   Sciendum est[1] quod compositio *ad aliquid* est, quia compositio est compositorum compositio et composita sunt compositione composita; quare[2] compositio in predicamento [*N42va*] *Relationis*[3] est. Dividitur[4] autem compositio primo[5] per duas partes. Compositionis[6] autem alia est rerum, alia modorum significandi. Compositio[7] vero modorum significandi pertinet ad gramaticum[8] secundum quod in nomine[9] est compositio qualitatis cum substantia et in participio et[10] in verbo compositio[11] actus cum substantia.

De specialibus compositionibus

2   Compositio autem rerum fit quinque modis. Quia quedam est forme cum materia, ut anime cum corpore; alia accidentis[1] cum subiecto[2], ut coloris cum corpore; alia est potentiarum sive virtutum cum eo cuius sunt, ut intellectus et aliarum virtutum anime[3] cum anima[4]; alia est partium integralium ad se invicem in suo toto, ut partium linee in linea ad punctum et superficiei in superficie ad lineam; alia est differentiarum cum[5] genere ad constitutionem speciei.[6] Harum autem compositionum que sunt rerum, quedam pertinent ad naturalem, quedam vero ad mathematicum[7], alie vero ad logicum.[8] Item. Compositionis que est modorum significandi alia est[9] qualitatis cum substantia, et hec significatur per nomen, sicut in hoc nomine[10] 'homo' et in quolibet alio nomine; alia est actus cum substantia, de qua postea dicetur. Sed prius dicemus[11] de qualitate nominis.

CHAPTER I

ON COMPOSITION

On composition in general

1   Note that composition is a relative: a composition is of things that are composed and the things that are composed are composed by composition. Therefore composition belongs in the category of 'relation'. Composition is first of all divided into two parts: one type of composition concerns things and the other concerns modes of signifying. Now the composition of modes of signifying is the domain of the grammarian in that in a noun there is a composition of a quality with a substance and in a participle and in a verb there is a composition of an act with a substance.

On the different kinds of composition

2   A composition of things occurs in five ways. [1] One is <a composition> of form with matter, as that of a soul with a body, [2] another is <a composition> of an accident with a subject, as that of a colour with a body, [3] another one is <a composition> of powers or faculties with what they belong to, as that of the intellect or other faculties of the soul with the soul, [4] another one is the mutual <composition> of integral parts in their whole, as that of parts of a line in a line in relation to a point and that of the parts of a surface in a surface in relation to a line, [5] another one is <a composition> of differences with their own genus as to the constitution of the species. Of these compositions of things some concern the philosopher of nature, some concern the mathematician and some the logician. Again. Of the composition of modes of signifying one type is of a quality with a substance; and such a composition is signified by a noun, e.g. in the noun 'man' and in any other one. The other type is the composition of an act with a substance, which will be discussed later. Now first we must discuss the quality of a noun.

De compositione substantie cum qualitate

3 Omne ergo[1] nomen significat substantiam cum qualitate. Verbi gratia: homo[2], ut ita dicam, est *res habens humanitatem*; et res est substantia eius, humanitas [*T26ra*] autem, secundum quod significatur per hoc nomen[3] 'homo', est qualitas eius, et non secundum quod significatur per hoc nomen 'humanitas', quia hoc nomen 'humanitas' est nomen aliud et diversum ab hoc nomine 'homo', et unum non est qualitas alterius neque econverso. Sed qualitas uniuscuiusque nominis per ipsum nomen significatur; 'homo'[4] enim significat suam substantiam et suam qualitatem et hec duo sunt unita in eo[5], ita quod unum significatur in altero sive per alterum.

4 Sed obicitur circa[1] qualitatem nominis, quia: Cum qualitas et substantia sint diversa et[2] omne nomen significet[3] substantiam cum qualitate[4], ergo omne[5] nomen significat diversa; et est sillogismus[6] in primo prime. Sed omnis dictio significans diversa est equivoca. Ergo omne nomen est equivocum. Et[7] hoc est inconveniens. Non ergo in nomine est compositio qualitatis cum substantia.

5 Solutio. [*N42vb*] Quatuor modis[1] contingit[2] significare diversa per dictionem eandem[3]. [*P51vb*] Primo[4] quando diversa[5] equaliter significantur per eandem[6] dictionem, ut in hoc nomine[7] 'canis'. Secundo quando diversa significantur secundum prius et posterius, ut in hoc nomine 'sanum', quod[8] proprie non significat diversa sed rem unam secundum[9] modos diversos; et[10] similiter 'ens'. Tertio[11] modo significantur plura per dictionem unam quando unum significatur[12] ex impositione et reliquum ex[13] transsumptione, ut in hoc verbo 'ridet', quod ex impositione significat[14] ridere et florere significat transsumptive[15]. Et isti tres modi faciunt equivocationem. Quarto modo significantur diversa[16] per dictionem unam quando unum est ratio intelligendi alterum (sive[17] quando unum est principium intelligendi[18] alterum, quod idem est), ut forma est ratio sive principium intelligendi[19] illud[20] cuius est, et cognoscendi ipsum. Ut[21] figura triangularis oblonga sic disposita est ratio sive principium intelligendi cultellum[22] et cognoscendi ipsum.

6 Et hoc modo[1] nomen significat substantiam cum qualitate. Qualitas enim nominis est ratio sive principium intelligendi ipsum

On the composition of a substance with a quality

3   Every noun then signifies a substance with a quality. For instance, a man is, so to speak, *a thing which has humanity*; and the thing is its substance, and humanity, insofar as it is signified by the noun 'man', is its quality. However, humanity is not its quality insofar as it is signified by the noun 'humanity'; for the latter is another noun and different from the noun 'man', and the one is not a quality of the other nor the other way round. On the contrary, the quality of each individual noun is signified by <the noun> itself: 'man' signifies its own substance and its own quality and these two are united in the noun in such a way that one is signified *in* the other or *via* the other.

4   However, as to the quality of the noun it is argued to the contrary: a quality and a substance are different things and every noun signifies a substance with a quality; therefore every noun signifies different things (and this is a syllogism in the first mood of the first figure). Now every word that signifies different things is equivocal. Therefore every noun is equivocal. And this is absurd. Therefore in a noun there is not a composition of a quality with a substance.

5   Solution. One and the same word can signify different things in four ways. [1] In the first way when a word signifies different things equally, like the noun 'dog' (*canis*). [2] In the second way when a word signifies different things, one primarily and the other secondarily, like the noun 'healthy', which does not really signify different things but one thing in different modes of signifying; and the same goes for 'being' (*ens*). [3] In the third way one word signifies more than one thing when it signifies one thing on account of its imposition and the other metaphorically, like the verb 'laughs', which means 'to laugh' by imposition and 'to flower' metaphorically. And these three ways produce equivocation. [4] In a fourth way, however, different things are signified by the same word when one thing is the rationale of understanding the other thing (or when one thing is the principle of understanding the other thing, which amounts to the same); for example, a form is the rationale or principle of understanding and knowing the thing it belongs to, like a triangular and oblong figure as arranged in this particular way is the rationale or principle of understanding and knowing a lance-head.

6   Now in this last way a noun signifies a substance with a quality. For the quality of a noun is the rationale or principle of under

nomen et[2] suam substantiam. Et sic qualitas[3] significatur per nomen ut principium intelligendi. Substantia vero[4] significatur per ipsum nomen ut quod intelligitur per ipsam qualitatem. Et quia[5] unum intelligitur per alterum, ideo non sunt ibi[6] diverse significationes sed una. Et propter hoc iste modus significandi[7] plura non facit equivocationem, sicut cum[8] video coloratum et suam magnitudinem[9] non sunt due visiones sed una, quia[10] color est ratio et principium videndi[11] magnitudinem[12] in qua est . Et ideo[13] dictum antiquum[14]: "ubi unum propter alterum[15], tantum unum est"[16].

7   Item. Queritur utrum compositio qualitatis cum substantia sit[1] aliquid vel non. Si non est aliquid[2], ergo in nomine non est compositio qualitatis cum substantia[3]. Si est aliquid sed[4] non est substantia neque qualitas, ergo est tertium ab istis. Ergo per nomen significantur tria. Ergo debet[5] dici quod nomen significat substantiam cum qualitate et[6] compositionem earum. Quod non est verum.

8   Solutio. Compositio qualitatis cum substantia est aliquid. Et in nomine non sunt nisi duo secundum rem[1], scilicet substantia et qualitas, tria[2] vero secundum rationem, scilicet [N43ra] substantia et qualitas et compositio earum, quia qualitas seipsa[3] componitur cum substantia propter inclinationem quam habet ad substantiam. Omnis enim forma et omnis qualitas, et etiam[4] omne accidens, naturalem habet inclinationem ad id[5] in quo est, quia non habent esse actuale (sive esse in actu) nisi[6] in eo in quo sunt. Unde de accidentibus dicit Boetius quod[7] accidentis esse est inesse, hocest: accidentis esse [T26rb] est esse in alio.[8] Similiter esse[9] actuale ipsius forme est esse in materia[10]. Unde qualitas nominis per inclinationem quam habet ad substantiam nominis, stat in ratione[11] compositionis; ipsa autem[12] qualitas[P52ra] nominis secundum se est unum compositorum. Et ideo dicendum quod cum[13] qualitas secundum se et qualitas inclinata ad substantiam sint[14] idem secundum rem[15] et[16] substantia nominis sit alterum extremorum[17,] propter hoc in nomine non sunt nisi duo secundum rem et tria secundum rationem, quia alterius[18] rationis est qualitas secundum se et qualitas inclinata, et substantia est tertium. Et ideo dixi[19] quod in nomine erant[20] duo secundum rem et tria secundum rationem. Unde quia gramaticus loquitur[21] de

standing the noun itself and its substance. And so the quality is signified by the noun as a principle of understanding. The substance, then, is signified by the noun as that which is understood via its quality. And because the one is understood via the other, therefore there are not different significations in this case, but just one. Hence this mode of signifying more than one thing does not produce equivocation, just as when I see something coloured and its magnitude, there are not two acts of seeing but just one, for colour is the rationale and principle of seeing the magnitude in which the colour resides. That is why there is an ancient saying: "Where there is one because of the other, there is only one".

7   Furthermore, there is a problem whether the composition of a quality with a substance is something or not. If it is not something, then in a noun there is no composition of a quality with a substance. If it is something but it is neither a substance nor a quality, then it is a third thing apart from those. Hence a noun signifies three things. Therefore one ought to say that a noun signifies a substance with a quality and their composition. And this is not true.

8   Solution. The composition of a quality with a substance is something. And in a noun there are only two things in reality, viz. a substance and a quality, but there are three things formally, viz. a substance, a quality and their composition. For a quality unites itself with a substance on account of the inclination it has towards a substance. For every form and every quality, and even every accident, has a natural inclination towards the thing it resides in, because they only have actual being (or being in actuality) in the thing they reside in. That is why Boethius says[1] the following about accidents: the being of an accident is to inhere, which means that the being of an accident is to reside in something else. Similarly, the actual being of the form is to inhere in matter. Hence the quality of a noun, through the inclination it has towards the substance of the noun, is a formal element of the composition; the quality of a noun in itself is one of the things that are united. And so the answer should be that since a quality in itself and a quality as inclined towards a substance are the same thing in reality and the substance of the noun is the other extreme, therefore there are only two things in reality but three things formally. For the quality in itself and the quality as having an inclination are formally different, and substance is the third <element>. And that is why I have said that in a noun there were two things in reality and three things formally.

---

[1]   Cf. In Categ. Arist., 170D-171A.

rebus[22] significatis per partes orationis, ideo dicitur[23] quod nomen
significat substantiam cum qualitate et non[24] debet dici quod
nomen[25] significat substantiam cum qualitate et compositionem
earum.

9   Si autem aliquis querat quid sit[1] illa compositio, dicendum quod
iam patet ex predictis, quia est inclinatio qualitatis ad substantiam. Et
quia inclinatio unius ad alterum nichil est nisi per illud cuius est et
per illud ad quod est, ideo ista compositio quamvis sit aliquid, tamen
non[2] est aliquid nisi per sua extrema. Non enim potest esse res
aliqua media inter qualitatem et substantiam que componat unum
cum altero, quia sic contingeret abire[3] in infinitum. Oporteret[4] enim
quod illa res media aut[5] esset substantia vel[6] qualitas. Et sic[7], si esset
substantia, oporteret ponere compositionem ipsius cum qualitate. Et
sic[8] esset ulterius questio[9] de illa[10] compositione utrum res esset
aliqua; et similiter si esset qualitas.

10   Item. Queritur de compositione qualitatis cum substantia[1] in
nomine, quare non est duplex, scilicet[2] unita et ut distans, sicut
[*N43vb*] est quedam compositio actus uniti cum[3] substantia (ut in
participio) et alia ut distantis[4] (sicut in verbo). Quia[5] videtur quod
aliquando sit[6] qualitas ut[7] unita substantie (ut 'homo albus'), aliquando[8] ut distans (ut 'homo est albus', quando[9] 'homo' ponitur in
subiecto[10] et 'albus' in[11] predicato). Ergo debet[12] esse duplex compositio qualitatis[13] cum substantia.

11   Et dicendum quod compositio actus cum substantia dicitur[1]
dupliciter (et non compositio qualitatis cum substantia), quia 'actus'
sumitur[2] duobus modis. Uno modo sumitur secundum quod habet
inclinationem ad[3] substantiam, secundum quam inclinationem
dicitur de altero. Verbum enim, ut vult Aristotiles, est nota eorum
que[4] de altero predicantur. Alio autem modo sumitur 'actus' privatus
illa[5] inclinatione; et sic est in participio. Et quia 'actus' hiis duobus
modis sumitur, ideo duplex est compositio actus cum substantia, et
una est in participio, alia in verbo, que est compositio actus ut[6]

And so it is because a grammarian speaks of things that are signified by parts of speech, that therefore it is said that a noun signifies a substance with a quality and one must not say that a noun signifies a substance with a quality *and* their composition.

9   However, if someone were to raise a problem about the nature of this composition,[2] the answer should be that this is already clear from what has been said: it is the inclination of a quality towards a substance. And since the inclination of the one towards the other exists only on account of the thing it belongs to and the thing it is <inclined> towards, therefore this composition, much as it may be something, nevertheless is only something on account of its extremes. For there cannot be an intermediate thing between the quality and the substance which is to unite the one with the other, because in that case there would be an infinite regress. For then it would be necessary that this intermediate thing be either a substance or a quality. Hence if it were a substance one would have to assume its composition with a quality. And thus one would further have to raise the problem about this composition, whether it would be something or other, and likewise if it were a quality.

10   There is also another problem concerning the composition of a quality with a substance in a noun, namely why it is not twofold, *viz.* 'united' and 'as <taken> apart', just as there is one type of composition of an act <taken> as united with a substance (*viz.* in the participle) and another of an act as <taken> apart (*viz.* in the verb). For it may be argued that sometimes a quality is <taken> as united with a substance (*e.g.* in 'white man') and sometimes it is <taken> as apart (*e.g.* in 'A man is white', when 'man' is in subject-position and 'white' in predicate-position). Hence the composition of a quality with a substance should be twofold.

11   The answer should be that the composition of an act with a substance is said in a twofold way (and not the composition of a quality with a substance). For an act is taken in two ways: [1] In one way it is taken according as it has an inclination towards a substance, after which inclination it is said of something else. For, according to Aristotle,[3] a verb is the sign of things which are said of something else. [2] In another way the act is taken as deprived of this inclination, *viz.* in the participle. Now since 'act' is taken in these two ways, therefore the composition of an act with a substance is twofold. One composition is in a participle and the other in a verb; the latter is a composition of an act as <taken> apart from a substance,

---

2   Cf. above, cap. 8.
3   *De interpr.* 3, 16b7.

distantis a[7] substantia, eoquod verbum per eam[8] est de altero ut predicatum[9] de subiecto. Sed quia predicta inclinatio non potest esse in qualitate sed tantum in actu, eoquod anima non potest inclinari ad res ut enuntiet unum de altero nisi mediante actu et non mediante qualitate, ideo qualitas non potest significari ut distans sed semper significatur ut unita. Et ideo non potest esse duplex compositio qualitatis cum substantia sed[10] tantum una. Que est in quolibet nomine.

12   [*P52rb*] Ad illud autem quod obicitur de hac oratione imperfecta 'homo albus' et de hac perfecta 'homo est albus' quod[1] in una est qualitas unita et in alia distans, dico[2] quod nulla est obiectio, quia[3] loquimur de qualitate unita que est essentialis[4] et que est ratio intelligendi illud [*T26va*] cuius est, scilicet substantiam. Et sic 'homo' habet in se suam substantiam et[5] suam qualitatem et 'albus' similiter suam substantiam et suam qualitatem. Et non loquimur[6] de qualitate accidentali, de qua ipse obicit; 'albus' enim non[7] dicit qualitatem essentialem homini[8] neque[9] est principium intelligendi hominem[10] simpliciter sed hominem talem. Et ideo de qualitate accidentali unita suo subiecto nichil est ad propositum[11]. In hac[12] vero[13] oratione perfecta que est[14] 'homo est albus': quamvis sit qualitas distans: quia tamen[15] hoc non est per inclinationem [N*43va*] qualitatis ut sit de altero sed per inclinationem verbi ibi positi, similiter de illa nichil est ad propositum.[16]

13   Dicto[1] de compositione in communi, cuius alia[2] erat compositio rerum et alia compositio modorum, et item[3] compositio modorum subdividebatur[4], quoniam[5] alia erat compositio qualitatis cum substantia, alia vero compositio actus cum substantia: cum habitum sit de compositione qualitatis cum substantia, consequenter dicendum est de compositione actus cum substantia.

because through that composition the verb is <said of> something else as a predicate of a subject. However, since the above-mentioned inclination cannot be in a quality but only in an act, for the soul can only have an inclination towards things so as to say the one of the other by means of an act and not by means of a quality, therefore a quality cannot be signified as <taken> apart, but it is always signified as united. And therefore the composition of a quality with a substance cannot be twofold but only single. And this composition is found in every noun.

12 Now as to the argument to the contrary that has to do with the incomplete expression 'white man' and the complete expression 'A man is white',[4] to the extent that in the one the quality is united and in the other it is taken as apart, I say that this is no argument to the contrary, because we are speaking here of a united quality that is essential and is the rationale of understanding what it belongs to, *viz.* the substance. So 'man' contains in itself its own substance and its own quality (and similarly 'white' contains its own substance and its own quality). And we are not speaking of an accidental quality, what the opponent was on about; for 'white' does not indicate an essential quality of a man nor is it a principle of understanding a man *simpliciter* but rather such-and-such a man. And therefore speaking about an accidental quality united with its subject, that has no bearing on what has been brought forward. As for the complete expression, 'A man is white', although there is a quality as <taken> apart, it nevertheless has no bearing on what has been brought forward either, for that it be said of something else is not on account of the inclination of the quality, but rather on account of the inclination of the verb used in this case.

13 We have already spoken of the composition in general of which one was the composition of things[5] and the other of modes.[6] Furthermore, the composition of modes was subdivided into compositions of a quality with a substance and compositions of an act with a substance. And now that we have discussed the composition of a quality with a substance, we must next discuss the composition of an act with a substance.

---

4 Cf. above, cap. 10.
5 Cf. above, cap. 2.
6 Cf. above, cap. 2ff.

De compositione actus cum substantia

14 Compositionis ergo[1] actus cum[2] substantia alia est actus uniti[3] (ut in participio), alia[4] est actus[5] distantis[6] (ut in verbo). Quod autem in participio sit compositio actus uniti[7] patet primo per significationem participii, quia: Participium significat actionem vel passionem in substantia[8] vel substantiam sub actione vel passione et non significat tantum substantiam neque tantum actionem[9] vel passionem; quare[10] significat actum unitum substantie[11]. Ergo in participio est compositio actus uniti cum substantia. Patet hoc[12] etiam inductive[13], quia: Hoc participium 'legens' actionem significat cum substantia infinita; 'legens' enim est 'qui legit'. Sed 'qui'[14] dicit substantiam infinitam. Quare[15] in eo intelligitur substantia infinita et actus determinatus. Et hec duo unita sunt[16]. Ergo 'legens' habet in se compositionem actus uniti cum substantia[17]; et sic de aliis participiis specialibus. Ergo participium simpliciter[18] habet in se predictam compositionem. Quod autem in verbo sit compositio actus ut[19] distantis patet per hoc quod actus significatus per verbum semper[20] significatur ut de altero. Cum enim dico 'currit', oportet intelligere subiectum determinatum vel indeterminatum de quo dicam[21] 'currit' ut[22] predicatum[23] determinatum de suo subiecto.

15 Sed queritur, cum sit inclinatio qualitatis ad substantiam et sit inclinatio actus ad substantiam tam uniti quam distantis, qualiter differunt a[1] se invicem ille inclinationes. Et dicendum quod inclinatio qualitatis nominis ad suam[2] substantiam est inclinatio perfectivi (sive perfectionis[3]) ad perfectibile quod per ipsam [*N43vb*] perfectionem perficitur. Quare[4] substantialis qualitas[5] complet[6] et perficit substantiam nominis. Unde inclinatio qualitatis ad substantiam est inclinatio per quam perfectio[7] unitur perfectibili[8] ut sit[9] ex eis unum, quod est nomen. Inclinatio vero actus[10] ipsius participii ad substantiam est inclinatio per quam actus unitur substantie infinite ut sit in illa sicut[11] in subiecto[12] infinito. Inclinatio vero actus distantis sive verbi est inclinatio per quam actus sive verbum est[13] de altero ut predicatum[14] de subiecto. Et[15] sic sunt ille tres inclinationes specie differentes.

On the composition of an act with a substance

14 Now of the composition of an act with a substance one type is of a united act (*viz.* in the participle) and another is of an act as <taken> apart (*viz.* in the verb). That in a participle there is a composition of an act united with a substance appears first from the signification of the participle. For a participle signifies acting or being acted upon in a substance, or a substance as involved in acting or being acted upon, and it does not signify a substance on its own nor acting or being acted upon on its own, which is why it signifies an act united with a substance. Therefore in a participle there is a composition of an act united with a substance. Now the above is also clear by induction. The participle 'reading' (*legens*) signifies an act with an indefinite substance; for 'reading' equals 'he who reads' (*qui legit*). Now 'he who' (*qui*) indicates an indefinite substance. Hence in it an indefinite substance and a definite act are understood. And these two are united. Therefore 'reading' contains in itself a composition of an act united with a substance, and the same goes for other specific participles. Thus the participle *simpliciter* contains in it the above-mentioned composition. However, that in a verb there is a composition of an act as <taken> apart from the substance appears from the fact that the act signified by a verb is always signified as <said> of something else. For when I say 'runs' one must comprehend a subject, whether definite or indefinite, of whom I can say 'runs' as a definite predicate of its subject.

15 However, there is a problem, in what way these inclinations differ from one another, as there is the inclination of the quality both united and as <taken> apart towards the substance. The answer should be that the inclination of the quality of a noun towards its substance is the inclination of something perfective (or of a perfection) towards its perfectible which is made perfect by this perfection. Therefore the substantial quality <of a noun> completes and perfects the substance of a noun. Hence the inclination the quality has towards the substance is an inclination which unites the perfection with the perfectible, so that out of the two one thing arises, *i.e.* the noun. On the other hand, the inclination of the act of the participle towards the substance is the inclination which unites an act with an indefinite substance, so that the former be in the latter as <its> indefinite subject. Finally, the inclination of an act as <taken> apart or the inclination of the verb is the inclination by which an act (or a verb) is <said> of something else, as a predicate of a subject. So these three inclinations are different in kind.

16   Si autem[1] aliquis querat qualiter differat compositio verbi a compositione nominis et a compositione que est in participio, dicendum quod differunt iste tres compositiones sicut [*T26vb*] inclinationes differunt supradicte. Et per se loquendo non[2] differunt iste tres compositiones[3] per hoc quod compositio[4] verbi est subiectum veritatis et falsitatis, alie vero non, quia illa differentia sumpta est a posteriori; preterea compositio verbi non est simpliciter[5] subiectum veritatis et falsitatis, quia hoc est tantum in indicativo modo et non in aliis modis in quibus est compositio.

17   Item. Queritur de compositione[1] verbi, cum habeat componere subiectum cum predicato quantum[2] ad indicativum modum sive suppositum cum apposito quantum[3] ad alios tres[4] modos, quare potius importatur[5] compositio per alterum extremorum quam per utrumque, quia cum[6] compositio equaliter se habeat[7] ad extrema, ergo compositio debet significari cum utroque extremorum. Item. Idem[8] videtur a simili, quia[9]: Compositio qualitatis cum substantia significatur cum utroque extremorum in nomine. Et in participio compositio actus uniti cum substantia similiter[10] fit cum utroque extremorum. Ergo in verbo debet esse similiter. Item. Habito quod ista compositio significetur[11] cum altero extremorum queritur[12] quare potius significatur per[13] verbum (sive cum verbo) quam per nomen, cum equaliter se habeat ad utrumque[14].

18   Et dicendum ad[1] primum quod compositio duplicem habet comparationem. Unam enim habet ad subiectum[2] et aliam ad obiectum[3], sive ad obiecta, sicut visio[4] comparatur ad subiectum in quo est, [*N44ra*] scilicet[5] ad ipsum videns, et comparatur ad obiectum suum[6], quod est res visa (scilicet[7] coloratum). Similiter compositio[8] comparatur ad subiectum suum[9], quod est ipsum[10] componens, et comparatur ad obiectum suum[11] (sive ad obiecta), quod est compositum (vel que sunt ipsa composita), quia composita[12] recipiunt[13] supra se compositionem, sicut visibile visionem. Dico ergo quod compositio secundum comparationem[14] quam habet ad obiectum (sive ad[15] obiecta), equaliter se habet ad utrumque extremorum. Sed[16] secundum comparationem quam habet ad subiectum, quod est ipsum componens, magis se habet ad unum quam ad alterum, quia cum[17] ipsum[18] componens sit anima et anima non possit componere nisi [*P52vb*] mediante actu, ideo magis se habet compositio ad

16   If someone were to raise the problem in what way the composition of a verb, the composition of a noun and the composition of a participle differ from each other, the answer should be that they differ in the same way as the inclinations mentioned above.[7] And speaking '*per se*' these three compositions do not differ from each other in that the composition of a verb is the subject of truth and falsity while the others are not. For this difference is conceived of *a posteriori*. Furthermore, the composition of the verb is not *simpliciter* the subject of truth and falsity, because this is only the case in the indicative mood and not in the other moods in which there is a composition.

17   Now there is a problem about the composition of a verb, for this composition must unite a subject with a predicate as regards the indicative mood and it must unite a *suppositum* with an *appositum* as regards the three other moods: why does one extreme convey the composition rather than both? For a composition relates equally to the extremes and so it should be signified together with both extremes. Furthermore the same would appear from an argument from analogy: in the noun the composition of a quality with a substance is signified with both extremes. And in the participle the composition of an act united with a substance is likewise signified with both extremes. Therefore it should be the same in the verb. Finally, there is a problem why this composition, granted that it be signified by one of the two extremes, is signified rather by the verb (or with it) than by the noun; for the composition relates equally to both extremes.

18   The answer should be that a composition has a twofold relation. For it has one relation to the subject and another to the object (or objects), just as sight is related to the subject it resides in, *viz.* the subject that sees, and is also related to its object, *viz.* the thing it sees (that is, the coloured thing). Similarly the composition is related to its subject, *viz.* the thing that unites, and it is also related to its object (or objects), *viz.* the united thing (or the united things); for the things united receive the composition as something additional, in the same way as a visible thing receives sight as something additional. I therefore say that insofar as it is related to the object (or objects), a composition relates equally to both extremes. However, insofar as it is related to the subject, which is the uniting thing itself, the composition relates to the one rather than to the other, for since the uniting thing itself is the soul and the soul can only unite things

---

[7]   Cf. above, cap. 15.

actum quam ad reliquum extremorum. Et cum actus significetur per
verbum et non per nomen, ideo magis debet significari compositio
per verbum quam per nomen. Et sic patet solutio prime et tertie
questionis. Ad secundum dicendum quod non est simile de nomine
et participio ad verbum, quia in verbo est compositio distantium, ut
dictum est prius; et ideo compositio verbi non potuit significari cum
utroque extremorum. Sed in participio et in[19] nomine est compositio
unitorum; et ideo in illis significatur compositio cum utroque extremorum. In verbo autem non potuit compositio[20] significari cum utroque extremorum, quia compositio actus distantis est compositio per
quam actus est[21] de altero ut predicatum de subiecto[22].

19   Item. Queritur, cum in verbo sit compositio[1] et inclinatio[2] ad
substantiam, utrum compositio precedat natura inclinationem vel
econverso inclinatio[3] compositionem. Et[4] videtur quod inclinatio
precedat compositionem, quia: Cum actus non habeat esse nisi in
subiecto, vel[5] a subiecto, eoquod est proprium[6] accidentis substantie
inesse, ergo actus naturalem habet inclinationem ad substantiam,
etsi[7] non uniatur ei.[8] Sed compositio actus cum substantia non est
nisi cum[9] unitur actus substantie. Ergo[10] inclinatio actus ad substantiam natura[11] precedit compositionem actus cum substantia.

20   Et dicendum quod actus habet duplicem inclinationem ad
substantiam. Et una earum natura prior est[1] compositione, alia vero
natura[2] posterior, quia cum omnis actus [*T27ra*] sit accidens[3] et non
econverso, ipsi[4] actui debetur quedam inclinatio inquantum est
[*N44rb*] accidens, cum omne accidens naturaliter inclinetur ad
suum subiectum; et hec inclinatio natura precedit[5] compositionem.
Alia autem inclinatio debetur actui inquantum accidens[6] est, non[7] ut
in subiecto sed de subiecto, prout[8] anima inclinat[9] se ad enuntiandum[10] unum de altero; et hec inclinatio natura posterior est compositione. Et sic patet quod una inclinatio antecedit compositionem[11]
et[12] altera[13] sequitur illam per naturam[14].

by means of an act, therefore the composition relates to the act rather than to the other extreme; and since the act is signified by the verb and not by the noun, therefore the verb signifies a composition rather than a noun does. And in this way the solution to the first and third problem[8] is evident. The answer to the second problem[9] should be that the relation between a noun and a verb and the one between a participle and a verb do not admit of an argument from analogy. For in the verb there is a composition of things as <taken> apart, as has been said before, and so the composition of a verb could not be signified with both extremes. In a participle and in a noun, however, there is a composition of united things; so in those two the composition is signified with both extremes. In a verb, however, the composition could not be signified with both extremes, for the composition of an act <as taken> apart is a composition by which an act is <said> of something else as a predicate of a subject.

19   Furthermore, since in the verb there is a composition and an inclination towards a substance, there is a problem whether the composition naturally precedes the inclination or, conversely, the inclination the composition. And it may be argued that the inclination precedes the composition. For since the act does not have being except in a subject, or viewed from[10] a subject, because it is characteristic of an accident to inhere in a substance, therefore the act has a natural inclination towards a substance, even though it may not be united with that substance. On the other hand, there is only a composition of an act with a substance when an act is united with a substance. Therefore the inclination of an act towards a substance naturally precedes the composition of an act with a substance.

20   The answer should be that an act has a twofold inclination towards a substance. One of these is naturally prior to the composition while the other naturally comes later, for since every act is an accident and not the other way round, some inclination pertains to the act insofar as it is an accident, for every accident has a natural inclination towards its subject. Well, this inclination naturally precedes the composition. The other inclination, however, pertains to an act insofar as it is an accident, not taken as in the subject but as concerning the subject, insofar as the soul is inclined to assert one thing of another. And this inclination is naturally subsequent to the composition. Thus it is evident that one inclination precedes the composition and that the other naturally follows it.

---

[8]   Cf. above, cap. 17.
[9]   Cf. above, *ibid.*.
[10]   *viz.* when the composition does not actually take place; cf. below.

21 Patet etiam hoc per operationes[1] anime, quia: Cum anima apprehendit rerum similitudines[2], prius[3] cognoscit[4] res sibi invicem convenire et postea consentit et deinde componit eas apud se et postea enuntiat unum de altero. Cum ergo anima[5] prius consentiat[6] quam componat et prius convenientiam videat quam consentiat et convenientia unius rei ad aliam[7] causetur per naturalem inclinationem unius rei[8] ad aliam, ideo oportet quod naturalis inclinatio actus[9] inquantum est accidens[10], precedat compositionem actus cum substantia. Et item cum anima[11] apud se prius natura componat quam inclinet se ad enuntiandum unum de altero mediante actu, ideo compositio actus cum substantia natura precedit inclinationem actus[12] per quam anima inclinatur ut actus sit de substantia. Et per istam secundam inclinationem modus repperitur in verbo.

22 Et ut hoc[1] planius pateat, nota quod cum verbum[2] debebat[3] imponi ad significandum, tunc anima prius apprehenderat[4] [*P53ra*] actum de substantia et postea afficiebatur[5] ad enuntiandum actum eundem de substantia. Et per istum[6] affectum inclinabatur[7] ad enuntiandum ipsum[8] de substantia et per hanc inclinationem enuntiabat[9] iam ipsum actum de substantia. Unde post apprehensionem actus de substantia prius natura est[10] affectus anime[11] respectu ipsius actus ut sit de substantia, quam inclinatio. Et per istum[12] affectum[13] causatur inclinatio ipsius anime ad enuntiandum.[14] Et per istam[15] inclinationem indicat anima vel imperat et sic de aliis. Ipsa autem indicatio[16] vel imperatio vel optatio est modus. Unde quamvis ista tria, scilicet affectus et inclinatio et indicatio[17,] causaliter ordinentur[18]: quia tamen[19] actu posteriora sunt et[20] accidunt ipsi actui qui est, vel esse debet, de substantia (et causa huius est quia tam affectus quam inclinatio quam indicatio non possunt esse nisi in respectu ad actum et ipse actus bene potest esse sine ipsis), — ideo signum quod[21] imponebatur ad significandum ipsum actum, principaliter dat intelligere ipsum actum et predicta tria dat[22] intelligere[23] quasi[24] accidentia eidem actui. Et ideo dicimus quod verbum significat agere vel pati et consignificat affectus[25] et inclinationes et modos. Et sic patet quod modus causatur ab inclinatione sicut a causa proxima[26] efficiente et inclinatio ab affectu[27.] Et omnia ista tria causantur a

21   This is also evident from the operations of the soul. For when the soul apprehends the similarities of things, it first of all knows that these things are in agreement with each other, then it assents to this argeement, whereupon it unites these things for itself, and finally asserts one thing of the other. Now the soul assents before it unites and it sees the agreement before it assents, and the agreement of one thing with another is caused by the natural inclination of the one thing towards the other. Therefore it is necessary that the natural inclination of an act, insofar as it is an accident, precedes the composition of the act with a substance. Furthermore, the soul naturally unites for itself before it has the inclination to assert one thing of another by means of an act; hence the composition of an act with a substance naturally precedes the inclination of the act (by which the soul is inclined) with the result that the act is of a substance. Now it is on account of this second inclination that the mood is found in a verb.

22   And in order that this may be more evident, note that when a verb is to be imposed to signify, then long before <that>, the soul had grasped the act in relation to the substance and was later moved to assert this act of the substance. And it is on account of this affect that the soul was inclined to assert the act of the substance, and by this inclination it finally asserted the act of the substance. Therefore, after the apprehension of the act concerning the substance, the affect of the soul in respect of this very act, such that it is <said of> the substance, is naturally prior to the inclination. And it is by this affect that the soul's inclination to assert the act of the substance is caused. And it is by this inclination that the soul asserts, or orders and so on. Now it is this very asserting, ordering or wishing that constitutes the mood <of the verb>. Therefore, although these three, *viz.* the affect, the inclination and the assertion, are ordered in a causal manner, they are nevertheless subsequent to the act and belong as an accident to the act which concerns or should concern the substance (and this is caused by the fact that an affect, an inclination and an assertion as well can only be in respect of an act, whereas the act can well be without them). Hence the sign which is imposed to signify this act primarily gives to understand the act itself and it gives to understand the afore-mentioned three as accidents of the same act. And therefore we say that a verb signifies to act or to be acted upon and it consignifies affects, inclinations and moods. And thus it is evident that the mood is caused by the inclination as the proximate efficient cause as it is the case with the inclination as caused by the affect. And all these three are caused

compositione actus cum substantia sicut a causa remota finali. Et causantur etiam eadem tria ab anima sicut ab efficiente remota[28] vel[29] initiali.

23 Nota etiam quod hec diffinitio modorum, scilicet 'modi sunt[1] inclinationes animi varios affectus demonstrantes' est causalis, sicut patet ex predictis. Unde inclinatio non predicatur[2] de modis sicut genus sed causaliter. Unde inclinatio significat affectum sicut[3] effectus suam causam et modus inclinationem et[4] affectum tamquam[5] effectus[6] causam. Nota etiam quod generalis [*T27rb*] compositio in verbo debetur ipsi agere vel pati generaliter sumpto[7]. Specialis autem compositio debetur ipsi agere vel pati specialiter sumpto et[8] contracto.

24 Si quis obiciat quod cum anima afficiatur et inclinetur respectu significati[1] cuiuslibet partis, ut[2] ipsum significet et representet per suum signum, ergo quelibet pars orationis erit alicuius modi, cum propter hoc modus accidat verbo, — dicendum[3] quod hec[4] obiectio fit propter predicta male[5] intellecta, quia non dixi quod predictus affectus et inclinatio et modus essent[6] in anima respectu ipsius actus tantum sed respectu ipsius actus ut[7] est de substantia[8] (sive respectu ipsius actus inquantum componitur cum substantia). Nulla autem[9] pars orationis est de substantia nisi verbum, quia in[10] nulla intelligitur compositio ipsius actus[11] cum substantia exteriori nisi in verbo. Et ideo modus solummodo accidit verbo et nulli alii parti orationis[12].

25 Item. Queritur qualiter intelligatur illa[1] compositio quam[2] dicit Aristotiles quod istam compositionem sine[3] compositis non est intelligere. Et dicendum quod compositio actus cum substantia intelligitur per extrema, quia actus seipso inheret suo subiecto, sicut quodlibet aliud accidens seipso inheret subiecto in quo est[4]. Et non aliquo alio[5] [*N44vb*] mediante, quia sic [*P53rb*] contingeret abire[6] in infinitum, ut prius dictum est de qualitate nominis. Unde compositio actus cum substantia fit per inclinationem ipsius actus ad ipsam[7] substantiam ut ad subiectum suum. Et quia inclinatio unius[8] ad

by the composition of the act with the substance as the remote final cause. And these three are also caused by the soul as the efficient remote or initial cause.

23 Note also that this definition of moods, *viz.* 'Moods are inclinations of the soul indicating its various affects', is a causal one, as is evident from what has been said above. Therefore an inclination is not said of moods as their genus, but in terms of causality. Hence the inclination signifies an affect as an effect signifies its cause, and the mood signifies the inclination and the affect as an effect signifies its cause. Note again that a general composition in a verb pertains to the acting or being acted upon taken in general. A specific composition, however, pertains to an acting or being acted upon taken specifically and confined ('contracted').

24 Now someone may argue to the contrary that since the soul is affected and has an inclination in respect of the significate of every part <of speech> to signify and represent it by means of the appropriate sign, hence every part of speech will convey some mood, because for this reason the mood is an accident of the verb. The answer should be that this argument to the contrary arises from a bad understanding of the things mentioned above. For I have not said that the above-mentioned affect, inclination and mood were in the soul with respect to the act by itself, but that they are in the soul with respect to the act insofar as it is <said> of a substance (or with respect to the act insofar as it is combined with a substance). Now the verb is the only part of speech which is <said> of a substance, for only in the verb one understands the composition of an act with an exterior substance. And thus the mood is only an accident of the verb and of no other part of speech.

25 There is also a problem in which way that composition should be understood of which Aristotle says[11] it cannot be understood without the things that are combined. And the answer should be that the composition of the act with the substance is understood through the extremes. For the act by itself inheres in its subject just as any other accident by itself inheres in the subject it resides in. And it is not though some other intermediate, for in that case we would have an infinite regress, as has been said before regarding the quality of the noun. Therefore the composition of an act with a substance occurs by means of the inclination of this act towards the substance itself as towards its subject. And since the inclination of

---

[11] *De interpr.* 3, 16b24-5.

alterum non potest intelligi nisi per illud quod inclinatur et per[9] illud ad quod inclinatur, ideo compositio actus ad subiectum[10] suum, que[11] consignificatur[12] per verbum, non potest intelligi sine extremis. Ideo dicit Aristotiles quod 'est' consignificat[13] quandam compositionem quam sine compositis non est[14] intelligere, cum solum habeat intelligi per illud quod inclinatur et per illud cui inclinatur, quia inclinatio verbi[15], que est ipsius actus ad substantiam, remotis quod inclinatur et cui inclinatur, nichil est[16]. Et ideo compositio sine extremis nichil est. Et quia unumquodque intelligitur per illud quod dat ei esse: cum extrema dent esse compositioni, ideo compositio habet intelligi per extrema, ut dictum est.

26 Nota etiam[1] quod illa compositio secundum suam[2] veritatem est in re[3] et est quoddam indivisibile, in verbo autem est illa compositio ut in signo. Sicut[4] sanitas secundum suam veritatem[5] est in animali ut[6] in subiecto, in urina autem ut in signo. Nota etiam quod ista compositio[7] est per inclinationem actus ad substantiam, inquantum actus est accidens substantie[8]; et[9] precedit alteram inclinationem per quam actus est de aliquo[10], ut dictum est prius[11].

27 Item. Queritur utrum[1] compositio verbalis sit ens[2] simpliciter vel non. Et videtur quod non, quia: Repperitur in rebus existentibus, ut 'homo est animal', et in rebus non existentibus, ut 'chimera est non-ens'[3]. Ergo repperitur in eis per aliquod commune repertum[4] in ipsis, quia, ut vult Aristotiles in fine *Priorum*[5]: si aliqua passio consequitur[6] aliqua[7] diversa[8], oportet quod consequatur[9] ea per aliquod commune repertum in ipsis. Sed nichil est commune enti et non-enti nisi ens quodammodo. Ergo[10] compositio primo[11] sequitur ens quodammodo. Ergo et ipsa est ens quodammodo. Ergo non est[12] ens simpliciter. Et dicendum quod compositio importata per verbum communiter se habet ad[13] compositionem entium et ad compositionem non-entium. Unde primo[14] sequitur ens quodammodo, ut obiectum est. Et ipsa in communi est ens quodammodo et non simpliciter.

the one towards the other can only be understood via that which is inclined and via that towards which it is inclined, hence the composition of an act towards its substance, which is consignified by the verb, cannot be understood without the extremes. Therefore Aristotle says[12] that 'is' (*est*) consignifies a certain composition that cannot be understood without the things combined, since it can only be understood through that which is inclined and through that towards which it is inclined. Indeed, when that which is inclined and that towards which it is inclined has been taken away, the inclination of a verb, which is in fact that of its act towards the substance, is nothing. And so a composition without its extremes is nothing. And since everything is understood in virtue of that which grants being to it, therefore because the extremes grant being to the composition, the composition should be understood through the extremes, as has been said.

26 Note also that this composition as regards its true being is in a thing and cannot be separated from it, whereas in a verb, this composition is as in a sign, just as health as regards its true being is in an animal as its subject, but in urine as its sign. Note again that the composition exists through the inclination the act has towards a substance, insofar as the act is an accident of the substance, and it precedes the other inclination through which the act is <said> of something else, as has been said before.

27 Furthermore, there is a problem whether a verbal composition is a being *simpliciter* or not. And it may be argued that it is not. For it is found in existing things, *e.g.* in the sentence 'A man is an animal', and in non-existing things, *e.g.* in the sentence 'A chimaera is a non-being'. It is thus found in those things in virtue of something they have in common. For, as Aristotle says at the end of the *Prior Analytics*,[13] if some quality is subsequent to things that are mutually diverse, it is necessary that it is subsequent to them in virtue of something they have in common. Now being and non-being only have being-in-a-certain-sense in common. Therefore the composition is primarily subsequent to being-in-a-certain-sense. Therefore it is itself a being-in-a-certain-sense. Therefore it is not a being *simpliciter*. The answer should be that the composition conveyed by a verb is commonly related to the composition of beings and to that of non-beings. Therefore it is primarily subsequent to being-in-a-certain-sense, as was argued to the contrary. And it is in general a being-in-a-certain-sense and not a being *simpliciter*.

---

[12] *Ibid.*.

[13] Cf. *Anal. Priora* II 27, 70b6-32.

28 Item. Queritur utrum compositio verbalis in communi equaliter [*T27va*] se habeat ad compositionem entium (ut 'homo est animal') et ad compositionem [*N45ra*] non-entium (ut 'chimera est non-ens') vel ipsa per prius dicatur de una et per posterius de alia. Et dicendum quod compositio in communi per prius convenit compositioni entium et per posterius[1] non-entium.

29 Item. Videtur[1] quod compositio[2] in communi sit ens simpliciter et non quodammodo et sic non conveniat[3] compositioni non-entium, quia videtur quod extrema ponantur[4] secundum exigentiam compositionis, ut si compositio est ens simpliciter, et extrema. Unde videtur sequi: 'homo est animal; ergo homo est et animal est'. Et si compositio est ens quodammodo, et[5] extrema. Unde non sequitur[6]: 'chimera est non-ens[7]; ergo[8] chimera est' vel 'non-ens est'. Ergo si compositio in communi est ens quodammodo, oportet quod extrema sua sint[9] entia quodammodo[10.] Ergo hec erit[11] vera 'Antichristus [*P53va*] est homo', cum[12] ibi ponatur 'homo' quodammodo et hec sit[13] vera: 'Antichristus est homo quodammodo'. Et[14] ita iste due convertuntur: 'Antichristus est homo' et 'Antichristus est homo quodammodo'. Quod falsum est. Ergo illud ex quo sequitur, est falsum, scilicet quod compositio in communi sit ens quodammodo et non simpliciter.

30 Et dicendum quod compositio in communi est ens quodammodo, ut prius dictum est, et extrema eius[1] similiter[2] sunt entia[3] quodammodo. Sed compositio contracta ad illam partem eius[4] que est compositio entium[5], est[6] ens simpliciter. Unde in hac: 'Antichristus est homo' contracta est ad compositionem entium. Unde non ponitur ibi 'homo' quodammodo sed[7] simpliciter. Et ideo hec[8] non equipollet huic: 'Antichristus est homo quodammodo'.

31 Ad illud[1] autem quod obicit quod extrema ponantur secundum exigentiam compositionis, dicimus[2] quod falsum est, quia cum extrema sint, non propter hoc sequitur quod compositio sit. Ut[3] cum dico 'homo est asinus', extrema sunt[4], non tamen compositio est. Et si compositio est, non propter[5] hoc sequitur quod extrema sint[6]; ut

28 Furthermore, there is a problem whether a verbal composition in general is equally related to a composition of beings (*e.g.* in 'A man is an animal') as it is to a composition of non-beings (*e.g.* in 'A chimaera is a non-being'); or is it said primarily of the former and secondarily of the latter? The answer should be that a composition in general primarily belongs to a composition of beings and secondarily to a composition of non-beings.

29 Furthermore, it may be argued that a composition in general is a being *simpliciter* and not a being-in-a-certain-sense, and thus does not belong to the composition of non-beings. For it may be argued that the extremes should be posited as is required for a composition, to the extent that if a composition is a being *simpliciter*, the extremes would be so as well. And so it may be argued that it follows 'A man is an animal; therefore a man is and an animal is'. Again, if a composition is a being-in-a-certain-sense, the extremes would be so as well. Therefore it does not follow 'A chimaera is a non-being; therefore a chimaera is', or 'A non-being is'. Hence if a composition in general is a being-in-a-certain-sense, it is necessary that its extremes be beings-in-a-certain-sense. Hence the following will be true, 'The Antichrist is a man', because in this case 'man' is used in a certain sense, and the following would be true, 'The Antichrist is a man-in-a-certain-sense'. And so the following two are convertible, 'The Antichrist is a man' and 'The Antichrist is a man-in-a-certain-sense'. And this is false. Therefore what it follows from is also false, namely that a composition in general is a being-in-a-certain-sense and not a being *simpliciter*.

30 The answer should be that a composition in general is a being-in-a-certain-sense, as was said before,[14] and its extremes in general are likewise beings-in-a-certain-sense. The composition confined to that part of it which is the composition of beings, however, is a being *simpliciter*. Thus in 'The Antichrist is a man', the composition is confined to one of beings. Therefore 'man' in this case is not used in a certain sense but *simpliciter*. And so 'The Antichrist is a man' is not equivalent to 'The Antichrist is a man-in-a-certain-sense'.

31 As to the argument to the contrary that the extremes are posited as is required for a composition,[15] my answer is that this is false. For although the extremes *are* it does not therefore follow that there *be* a composition. For example, when I say 'A man is an ass', the extremes *are* and yet the composition *is not*. Also, if the composition *is*, it does not follow therefore that the extremes *be*. For example, <when

---

14 Cf. above, cap. 27.
15 Cf. above, cap. 29.

'chimera est non-ens': illa compositio est, non[7] tamen extrema sunt. Sed hoc sequitur: 'ista[8] extrema sunt sibi invicem convenientia; ergo compositio eorum est'; et est locus a causa; et[9] econverso sequitur: 'compositio est; ergo extrema sunt sibi invicem convenientia'; et est locus ab effectu, quia convenientia extremorum[10] est causa compositionis et compositio est effectus convenientie extremorum.

32 Item. Videtur quod compositio in communi equaliter se[1] habeat ad compositionem entium et ad compositionem non-entium, quia: Ille due sunt simpliciter vere: 'homo est animal' et[2] 'chimera est[3] non-ens'. Ergo[4] veritas earum simpliciter est ens. Ergo subiectum veritatis in utraque est[5] ens simpliciter. [*N45rb*] Sed subiectum veritatis est compositio. Ergo compositio in[6] utraque simpliciter est ens. Sed in una est compositio entium, in altera[7] vero non-entium. Ergo compositio non-entium[8] simpliciter est ens. Ergo compositio in communi non magis se habet ad unam[9] quam ad alteram. Et dicendum quod compositio in communi dicitur secundum prius et posterius de utraque illarum compositionum, ut prius dictum est, quia per prius dicitur de compositione entium et per posterius de compositione non-entium.

33 Ad illud[1] autem quod obicit quod[2] utraque earum est[3] simpliciter vera, ergo veritas earum[4] simpliter est ens, dicendum quod non sequitur, quia veritas entium est ens simpliciter, veritas autem non-entium non [*T27vb*] est[5] ens simpliciter sed quodammodo. Quod patet, quia veritas entium est per[6] convenientiam extremorum, que est causa compositionis in affirmativa <vera> (ut <hic>: 'homo est animal'), vel per repugnantiam extremorum, que est causa divisionis in negativa vera[7] (ut hic[8]: 'homo non est asinus'). Unde veritas entium erit[9] per convenientiam extremorum[10] ad compositionem vel[11] divisionem; et etiam propter[12] hoc quod extrema sunt simpliciter entia. Sed veritas non-entium non habet nisi alteram[13] istarum causarum, scilicet convenientiam extremorum ad compositionem vel divisionem. Et non habet entitatem eorundem, quia

I say> 'A chimaera is a non-being', the composition involved *is* and yet the extremes *are not*. The following, however, does follow: 'These extremes mutually agree with each other; therefore their composition *is*'; and this is a case of the topic 'from a cause'. The converse follows as well: 'The composition *is*; therefore the extremes mutually agree with each other'; and this is a case of the topic 'from an effect'. For the agreement of the extremes is the cause of the composition and the composition is the effect of the agreement of extremes.

32   Furthermore, it may be argued that composition in general is equally related to composition of beings and to composition of non-beings. For the following two are true *simpliciter*, 'A man is an animal' and 'A chimaera is a non-being'. Therefore the truth in both of them is *simpliciter* a being. Hence the subject of the truth in both of them is a being *simpliciter*. Now the subject of truth is the composition. Therefore the composition of both of them is *simpliciter* a being. Now in the one <proposition> there is a composition of beings and in the other one a composition of non-beings. Therefore the composition of non-beings is *simpliciter* a being. Therefore composition in general does not have a relation with the one <type> rather than it has with the other. The answer should be that composition in general is said of the two kinds of composition, primarily and secondarily respectively, as was said before.[16] For it is said primarily of the composition of beings and secondarily of the composition of non-beings.

33   As to the argument to the contrary that since each one of them is true *simpliciter*, therefore their truth is also a being *simpliciter*,[17] the answer should be that this does not follow. For the truth of beings is indeed a being *simpliciter*, whereas the truth of non-beings is not a being *simpliciter* but a being-in-a-certain-sense. And this is evident because the truth of beings *is* in virtue of the agreement of the extremes, which is the cause of the composition in a <true> affirmative proposition (*e.g.* 'A man is an animal') or in virtue of the incompatibility of the extremes, which is the cause of the separation in a true negative proposition (*e.g.* 'A man is not an ass'). Therefore the truth of beings will *be* in virtue of the agreement of the extremes leading to a composition or separation, and also in virtue of the fact that the extremes are *simpliciter* beings. The truth of non-beings, however, only has one part of these causes, *viz.* the agreement of the extremes leading to the composition or separation, and it does not

---

[16]   Cf. above, cap. 28.

[17]   Cf. above, cap. 32.

extrema non sunt entia, immo[14] sunt non entia. Et ideo veritas non-
entium est ens [*P53vb*] quodammodo, veritas autem entium est ens
simpliciter. Et ita[15] compositio entium est ens simpliciter, compositio
autem non-entium est ens quodammodo.[16]

have the same being as they have, because the extremes are not beings, rather they are non-beings. And so the truth of non-beings is a being-in-a-certain-sense, whereas the truth of beings, is a being *simpliciter*. And so a composition of beings is a being *simpliciter*, whereas the composition of non-beings is a being-in-a-certain-sense.

TRACTATUS SECUNDUS

DE NEGATIONE

De negatione in genere

1   Cum[1] secundum diversitatem compositionum diversificetur negatio, ideo post compositionem dicendum est de negatione. Primo autem sciendum est[2], quod 'negatio' dicitur equivoce. Quia uno modo[3] dicitur oratio negativa. Et est species enuntiationis[4]: enuntiationum autem[5] alia est oratio[6] affirmativa, alia[7] negativa[8] (ut 'homo[9] currit', 'homo non currit'); et diffinitur sic: 'negatio est oratio negativa ab[10] aliquo'. Alio autem modo dicitur negatio[11] signum vel instrumentum negandi. Et hoc modo dicitur tripliciter[12]. Quia negatio ut est instrumentum negandi, sumitur uno modo ut substantia (ut in hoc nomine 'negatio')[13], alio autem modo sumitur negatio[14] ut actus, ut[15] in verbo vel in participio (ut 'nego, -as', vel 'negans' et 'negatus'). Et hiis[16] duobus modis[17] sumitur negatio ut concepta [*N45va*] sive per modum conceptus. Alio autem modo sumitur negatio que est instrumentum negandi ut exercita; et sic significatur per hanc particulam 'non'.

2   Et nota quod conceptus et affectus[1] differunt in hoc quod conceptus[2] dicitur esse illud quod est in anima per similitudinem aliquam[3]: cum enim cogito[4] de coloribus et de hominibus[5], similitudines eorum recipio in anima, et non res ipsas. Affectus autem[6] sive exercitio[7] dicitur[8] esse illud quod secundum veritatem est in anima vel in corpore. Ut cum laboro in egritudine, dolor est in anima mea secundum veritatem afficiens[9] eam, et quando curro, cursus[10] est in corpore secundum veritatem exercitus[11] et[12] afficiens ipsum corpus.

3   Item. Negatio isto[1] ultimo modo sumpta est duplex. Quia est quedam negatio que est termini[2], ut in nomine infinito vel[3] in verbo infinito; et est alia que est orationis. Et prima additur termino[4] per compositionem, secunda per appositionem. Item. Negatio termini

CHAPTER II

ON NEGATION

On negation in general

1 Now since negation is diversified in accordance with the diversity of compositions, we must therefore discuss negation after composition. Note first of all that 'negation' is said equivocally. [1] In one way a negation is called a negative proposition. And this is a species of 'enunciation'; for of enunciations, some are affirmative propositions (*e.g.* 'A man is running') and others are negative (*e.g.* 'A man is not running'); and <the latter> is defined thus: 'A negation [*i.e.* a denial] is a proposition denying something of something else'. [2] In another way a negation is a sign or an instrument for denying. And as such it is said in three ways. [2.1] In one way the negation as an instrument for denying is taken as a substance (in the noun 'negation' (*negatio*)); and [2.2] in another way the negation is taken as an act, *viz.* in a verb and in a participle (*e.g.* in 'to deny' or 'denying' and 'denied'). And in these two ways [*i.e.* 2.1 and 2.2] the negation is taken as conceived of (*ut concepta*) or in the manner of a concept (*per modum conceptus*). [2.3] In yet another way the negation that is an instrument for denying is taken as carried out (*ut exercita*) and as such it is signified by the particle 'not' (*non*).

2 Note that a concept and an affect are different in that a concept is that which is in the soul in the form of some kind of exterior resemblance; for when I think of colours and of men, I receive their resemblances in the soul and not the things themselves. An affect or 'carrying out' (*exercitio*), however, is called that which is really in the soul or in the body. For example, when I suffer from a disease, the pain is in my soul really affecting it, and when I am running, the running is in my body really carried out and affecting the body itself.

3 Again, negation taken in this last way is twofold: one type of negation is the negation of a single word, as in an indefinite noun or an indefinite verb, and the other is the negation of a complex expression. And the first is added to a word through composition whereas the other <is added to the word> through apposition. The

est duplex. Quia est quedam que facit nomen[5] infinitum sive
privativum[6] (ut 'non-homo', 'non-lapis') et est alia que facit verbum
infinitum sive[7] privativum (ut 'non-currit', 'non-laborat').

4   Sed videtur quod neque qualitas accidentalis[1] neque actus
possint[2] predicari de substantia, quia[3] sunt diversa et diversa inquantum diversa[4] sunt[5] repugnantia. Ergo unum non vere predicatur de
altero. Ergo sicut hec est[6] falsa: 'Sortes est albedo', similiter sunt[7] hec:
'Sortes est albus' et[8] hec: 'Sortes currit' sicut et hec: 'Sortes est cursus'.
Et dicendum quod dupliciter contingit significari[9] diversa. Quia uno
modo inquantum unum[10] est oppositum alteri vel[11] diversum ab eo
(ut 'Sortes'[12], 'albedo', 'cursus'); et sic unum non potest[13] vere predicari[14] de altero. Alio[15] autem modo contingit significari[16] [*T28ra*]
diversa prout unum est de altero (ut 'albus', 'niger', 'currit', 'legit') et
universaliter quecumque significantur in concretione ad substantiam, sive dicantur denominative[17] (ut 'albus'[18], 'currit') [*P54ra*] sive
non[19] (ut 'studiosus'[20], 'cursor' et 'pugillator' et consimilia, prout
dicuntur[21] 'cursor'[22] et 'pugillator' a naturalibus potentiis). Et hoc
modo unum diversum predicatur de altero.

5   Item. Cum triplex sit compositio, scilicet qualitatis ad[1] substantiam [*N45vb*] et actus distantis a substantia cum substantia et actus
uniti substantie[2] cum[3] substantia, et cuilibet harum trium[4] compositionum sua opponatur[5] negatio, et[6] sic erit triplex negatio. Quare[7]
male ponuntur due tantum. Et dicendum quod[8], sicut prius est
dictum, negatio[9] ut est exercita sive ut[10] afficiens, est duplex in[11]
genere, sicut compositio duplex est in genere, quia est quedam termini, alia[12] vero orationis, ut dictum est. Sed quia[13] negatio illa[14] est
in specie quadruplex[15], eoquod negatio termini[16] subdividitur: quedam[17] enim est que removet qualitatem a substantia, faciens nomen
infinitum (ut 'non-homo', 'non-asinus')[18] et est alia que actum unitum[19] substantie removet a substantia, faciens participium infinitum
(ut 'non-currens', 'non-legens'), tertia vero actum distantem a substantia exteriori removet sive privat a substantia intra[20], faciens
verbum infinitum (ut 'non-currit', 'non-laborat')[21] —quarta vero est
orationis, ut dictum est, faciens orationem negativam —, sic negatio
termini dividitur per partes[22] tres.

negation of a single word is twofold: there is one which makes a noun indefinite or privative (*e.g.* 'non-man' and 'non-stone'); and there is another which makes a verb indefinite or privative (*e.g.* 'does-not-run' and 'does-not-suffer').

4   Now it may be argued that neither an accidental quality nor an act can be said of a substance because they are diverse and diverse things as such are incompatible. Hence the one is not truly said of the other. Therefore, just as 'Socrates is whiteness' is false, so is 'Socrates is white'; and in the same way 'Socrates is running' <is false> no less than 'Socrates is the act of running'. The answer should be that different things can be signified in two ways. One way is insofar as the one is opposite to the other or is different from it (*e.g.* 'Socrates', 'whiteness', 'the running'); and in this way the one cannot be truly said of the other. In the other way, however, different things can be signified insofar as the one is <said> of the other, like 'white', 'black', 'runs', and 'reads', and, in general, whatever is signified in concreteness with a substance, whether they be said denominatively (such as 'white', 'runs') or not (such as 'scholar', 'runner', 'fighter', and the like, insofar as 'runner' and 'fighter' are named after natural faculties). And in this way one different thing is said of another.

5   As composition is threefold, *viz.* of a quality with a substance, of an act as <taken> apart from a substance with the substance and of an act united with a substance with the substance, and to each of these three compositions its appropriate negation is opposed, therefore in that way negation will be threefold as well. Therefore one can hardly propose only two. The answer should be that, as has been said before, negation, as it is carried out or affecting, is of two kinds, just as composition is of two kinds, in that one type is the one of a word and the other type is the one of a complex expression, as has been said. However, negation has four species, for the negation of a word is subdivided <as follows>: [1] one type is the negation of a word which removes a quality from a substance, thus producing an indefinite noun (*e.g.* 'non-man', 'non-horse'); [2] another type is the one that removes an act united with a substance from a substance, thus producing an indefinite participle (*e.g.* 'not-running', 'not-reading'); [3] the third type removes (or takes away) the act <as taken> apart from an external substance from an internal substance, thus producing an indefinite verb (*e.g.* 'does-not-run', 'does-not-read'); [4] the fourth type of negation, however, is of a complex expression, thus producing an indefinite complex expression. And thus the negation of a word is divided into three types.

6 Ad illud autem quod obicit[1] quod triplex est compositio, actus[2] scilicet cum substantia, ergo ex opposito erit triplex negatio, — dicendum[3] quod insufficienter dividit[4], quia relinquit compositionem actus distantis a substantia exteriori cum substantia intra[5]. Et sic sunt quatuor compositiones. Unde ex opposito erunt quatuor negationes. Quod autem sint[6] quatuor compositiones patet. Quia quedam[7] est qualitatis[8] cum substantia, ut in quolibet nomine; et negatio ei opposita facit nomen infinitum[9] (ut 'non-homo'). Et alia est actus uniti substantie cum substantia, ut in participio; et negatio ei opposita facit participium infinitum (ut 'non-legens'). Tertia vero[10] est actus distantis a[11] substantia exteriori cum eadem[12] substantia exteriori (ut 'Sortes currit'); et[13] negatio ei opposita facit orationem negativam (ut 'Sortes non currit'). Quarta vero est actus distantis a substantia exteriori cum substantia intra[14]; et negatio ei opposita facit verbum infinitum (ut 'non- currit', 'non-laborat'). Et sic[15] insufficienter[16] dividebat compositiones istas in specie et negationes eis oppositas.

7 Et nota quod verbum comparatur duplici substantie, scilicet[1] exteriori, que reddit ei [*N46ra*] suppositum[2] (ut 'Sortes currit') et substantie interiori, que infinite[3] intelligitur in ipso, quia 'currit' idem est quod 'res currens' et[4] 'currens'[5] est ipse[6] actus, res vero[7] est substantia interius[8] intellecta.

De negatione in specie

8 [*P54rb*] Dicto de negatione in genere consequenter dicendum est de unaquaque predictarum negationum et[1] in specie. Et primo de negatione nominis infiniti, cum hec sit prior aliis.

De negatione infinitante nomen

9 Circa quam primo queritur utrum nomen infinitum predicetur de quolibet quod est et quod non est. Et videtur quod non, quia: Sicut[1]

6 As to the argument to the contrary that the composition, of an act with a substance, that is, is threefold and therefore, contrariwise, the negation will be threefold,[1]—the answer should be that <the opponent> is making an insufficient division, for he is leaving out the composition of an act as <taken> apart from an external substance with an internal substance. And in this way there are four compositions. Hence contrariwise there will be four negations. Now the fact that there are four types of composition is evident. For one type of composition is of a quality with a substance, as <is found> in every noun; and the nagation opposed to it produces an indefinite noun (*e.g.* 'non-man'). Another type is the one of an act united with a substance with the substance, as in a participle; and the negation opposed to it makes a participle indefinite (*e.g.* 'not-reading'). The third type is the one of an act as <taken> apart from an external substance with the same external substance (*e.g.* in 'Socrates is running'); and the negation opposed to it produces a negative complex expression (*viz.* 'Socrates is not running'). The fourth type is the one of an act as <taken> apart from an external substance with an internal substance; and the negation opposed to it produces an indefinite verb (*e.g.* 'does-not-run' and 'does-not-suffer'). And so <the opponent> has insufficiently specified these compositions and the negations opposed to them.

7 Note also that a verb is related to a twofold substance. It is related to an external substance which renders it its *suppositum* (*e.g.* 'Socrates runs'). It is also related to an internal substance which is indefinitely understood in it, for 'runs' is the same as 'a running thing', where 'running' is the act itself, whereas the thing is the substance understood in it.

On the different kinds of negation

8 Now that negation in general has been discussed, we must next also say something about each one of the previously mentioned negations specifically. First the negation of an indefinite noun must be discussed, because this one is prior to the others.

On the negation that makes a noun indefinite

9 In the first place, there is a problem whether an indefinite noun is said of whatever *is* and whatever *is not*. And it may be

---

[1] Cf. above, cap. 5.

dicitur in *Secundo Perihermeneias,* ad affirmationem in qua predicatur[2] nomen infinitum, sequitur negatio in qua predicatur[3] nomen finitum, et non econverso (ut 'omnis homo est non-iustus; ergo nullus homo est iustus', et non econverso). Ergo affirmatio in qua predicatur[4] nomen infinitum, ponit aliquid[5], quia si nichil [*T28rb*] poneret, tunc[6] converteretur cum negatione. Ergo infinitum solum predicatur de ente. Ergo non de quolibet quod est et quod[7] non est. Ad idem. Cum dicitur 'homo est non-iustus', hic ponitur ens, quia affirmatur[8] esse, neque[9] compositio negatur per negationem ipsius termini infiniti sequentem. Ergo nomen infinitum predicatur solum de ente. Ergo non de quolibet quod[10] est et quod non est.

10 Sed contra. 'Homini' opponitur aliquid secundum negationem[1] et aliquid secundum privationem,[2] ut 'mortuum' opponitur 'homini' privative et 'non-homo' negative. Sed privatio plus participat de ente quam negatio. Ergo 'mortuum' plus participat de ente quam[3] 'non-homo'. Sed 'mortuum' predicatur de non-ente. Quare[4] multo fortius 'non-homo'. Ergo nomen[5] infinitum non solum predicatur de ente sed etiam[6] de non-ente. Item ad idem. Boetius docet convertere universalem affirmativam infinitando terminos[7], ut 'omnis homo[8] est ens; ergo omne[9] non-ens est non-homo'. Ergo 'non-homo' predicatur de quolibet non-ente. Ergo non solum de ente. Item. Ut est in *Secundo Topicorum:* si ad 'hominem' sequitur 'animal', ergo per consequentiam econtrario ad 'non-animal' sequitur 'non-homo'. Sed bene[10] sequitur 'si est homo, est ens'. Ergo sequetur[11] per consequentiam econtrario 'si est non-ens, est non-homo'. Ergo nomen infinitum non solum predicatur de ente sed etiam de non-ente.

11 Solutio[1]. Solet dici quod in homine est duplex compositio. Quia quedam[2] est compositio forme cum materia; homo enim et unumquodque [*N46rb*] aliud a Primo constat ex materia et forma, vel vere[3] vel proportionaliter[4]. Et est alia compositio in homine[5] que est differentiarum cum[6] genere vel cum[7] superiori, sive sint differentie

argued that it is not. For as it says in the second book of the *Periher-meneias*,[2] from an affirmation in which an indefinite noun is in predicate-position follows a negation in which a definite noun is in predicate-position, and not the other way round (*e.g.* in 'Every man is non-just; therefore no man is just', and not the other way round). Therefore an affirmation in which an indefinite noun is in predicate-position always posits something, for if it were to posit nothing, then it would be convertible with a denial. Therefore an indefinite noun is only said of being. Hence it is not said of whatever *is* and whatever *is not*. An argument that yields the same <conclusion> is the following. In the expression 'A man is non-just', a being is posited, for *being* is affirmed and the composition is not denied by the subsequent negation found in the indefinite term. Therefore an indefinite noun is only said of being. Hence it is not said of whatever *is* and whatever *is not*.

10   An argument to the contrary is that to 'man' something is opposed by way of a privation and something by way of a negation, *e.g.* 'dead <thing>' is opposed to 'man' privatively and 'non-man' is opposed to it negatively. Now a privation shares more in being than a negation does. Therefore 'dead <thing>' shares more in being than 'non-man'. Now 'dead <thing>' is said of a non-being. So *a fortiori* 'non-man' is said of it. Therefore an indefinite term is not only said of being but of non-being as well. Another argument to the contrary: Boethius teaches[3] <us> to convert a universal affirmative by making its terms indefinite, *e.g.* in 'Every man is a being; therefore every non-being is a non-man'. Therefore 'non-man' is said of every non-being and so not only of being. Moreover, as it says in the second book of the *Topics*,[4] if from 'man' follows 'animal' therefore by contraposition 'non-man' follows from 'non-animal'. Now the following inference is sound: 'If it is a man, it is a being'. Therefore by contraposition it will follow 'If it is a non-being, it is a non-man'. Therefore an indefinite noun is not only said of being, but of non-being as well.

11   Solution. In *man* there is a double composition. [1] One is the composition of form with matter in it, for a man and everything other than the First Being consists of matter and form, either really or by analogy of proportion. [2] The other composition in *man* is the one of differences with their genus or some <other> higher entity,

---

2   Cf. *De interpr.* 10, 20a11ff..
3   *De categ. syll.*, 807B-C, ed. Migne.
4   *Topica* II 8, 113b17-8.

specifice, ut in speciebus omnibus et generibus subalternis[8], sive sint differentie non-specifice, sicut[9] sunt[10] differentie que[11] secundum rationem finis vel cause alterius[12] adiciuntur enti, per quas differentias[13] genera[14] generalissima differunt[15] a se. Cum enim genera generalissima communicent in ente[16], licet secundum prius et posterius, oportet quod per aliquid differant. Ut[17] patet, quia: Substantia est ens per se[18], quantitas vero est ens mensurativum substantie[19], qualitas[20] vero est ens informativum (vel[21] qualificativum[22]) substantie, relatio vero[23] est ens comparativum[24] substantie, actio vero est ens medium per quod, sive secundum quod, unum agit in aliud; et sic de aliis. Unde hec[25] differentia 'per se'[26] est differentia substantie et 'mensurativum substantie' est differentia quantitatis, et sic de aliis. Et sic per istas differentias, que non sunt specifice, differunt genera[27] generalissima inter se.

12   Formetur[1] autem argumentum sic: In homine est duplex compositio, scilicet forme cum materia et differentiarum cum primo predicabili, ut cum ente. Sed cuilibet compositioni opponitur[2] sua negatio. Ergo[3] duplici compositioni existenti[4] in homine duplex opponitur negatio. Ergo negatio in hoc termino 'non-homo' est duplex. Quia vel removebit compositionem que[5] est differentiarum cum ente. Et sic relinquitur ens, quia cum dicitur 'ens per se corporeum animatum sensibile rationale mortale': si aggregatio istarum differentiarum removeatur[6] (non dico quod unaqueque[7] earum removeatur, sed aggregatio earum, que potest removeri pro una vel pro pluribus sive pro omnibus)[8], tunc relinquitur ens (quia si una sola removeatur[9], iam[10] non sunt ibi omnes; vel si plures vel si omnes, [*T28va*] semper aggregatio earum removetur). Et sic 'non-homo' ponit ens et predicatur solum de ente. Et sic 'non-homo' dicitur terminus privativus. Si autem negatio ista removeat compositionem forme cum materia, tunc nichil ponit actu, sed tantum ponit ens in potentia vel in opinione. Et sic 'non-homo' est terminus negativus[11]. Et sic 'non-homo' ponit potentiale vel opinabile vel ymaginabile. Et sic 'non-homo' predicatur de[12] ente et de non-ente. Et[13] sic nomen infinitum est[14] duplex. [*N46va*] Quod concedimus.

13   Dicendum ergo quod nomen dupliciter potest infinitari, ut ostensum est. Quia[1] uno modo secundum privationem; et sic 'non-homo' ponit ens, removendo aggregationem differentiarum a primo

whether they be specific differences, like in all species and sub-altern genera, or non-specific differences, as are the differences which are added to 'being' as a final or other type of cause, through which the highest genera differ from one another. For since the highest genera share in being, albeit in an order of prior and posterior, it is necessary that there is something through which they differ. And this is evident: a substance is a being *per se*, a quantity is a being that measures substance, a quality is a being that informs (or qualifies) a substance, a relation is a being that relates a substance, 'acting' is an intermediary being by means of which, or according to which, one thing acts upon another thing, and so on. And so the difference '*per se*' is the difference of substance, and 'what measures a substance' is the difference of quantity, and so on. And it is through these differences, which are not specific ones, that the highest genera differ from one another.

12 Let us form the following argument: In *man* there is a double composition: one of form with matter and one of differences with the first predicable, *viz.* with being. Now to every composition its own negation is opposite. Therefore to the double composition that exists in *man* a double negation is opposite. Therefore the negation in the term 'non-man' is double. For either it will remove the composition of the differences with *being*. And in this way *being* will remain, for suppose one says 'being *per se*, corporeal, animate, sensible, rational, mortal', then if the collection of these differences be removed (I do not say that each one of them is removed, but rather their collection, which can be removed <by removing> one or more or all of them), in that case a being <still> remains. (For if only one is removed then no longer do all remain, or if more or all <are removed>, their collection is always removed.) And so 'non-man' posits a being and is said only of a being. And thus 'non-man' is called a privative term. However, if this negation removes the composition of form with matter, then it does not posit an actual being, but only a potential being or a being in the mind. And in this way 'non-man' is a negative term. And thus 'non-man' posits something potential, conceivable or imaginable. Thus 'non-man' is said of being and non-being. And in this way an indefinite noun is twofold. Well, we agree with this.

13 One should say therefore that a noun can be made indefinite in two ways, as has been shown.[5] In one way it is by way of a privation; in this way 'non-man' posits a being by removing the

---

[5] Cf. above, cap. 12.

predicabili. Et sic 'homo' et 'non-homo' opponuntur ut privatio et
habitus et predicantur solum de ente. Alio autem modo potest nomen infinitari[2], scilicet secundum negationem. Et sic 'non-homo'
nichil ponit et est terminus negativus[3]. Et sic 'homo' et 'non-homo'
opponuntur ut affirmatio et negatio et[4] predicantur de quolibet quod
est et quod non est, ita quod hoc vel illud, sicut et[5] quelibet contradictio. Et nota quod ille duplex modus infinitandi terminum est
solum in terminis specialibus, quia[6] termini generales (ut 'ens' et[7]
'aliquid') uno solo modo infinitantur, scilicet secundum negationem, quia in eis non est duplex compositio sicut in specialibus.
Unde 'non-ens' et[8] 'non-aliquid' solum predicantur de non-ente[9].
Nullus enim[10] terminus[11] infinitus potest predicari de eo cuius[12]
forma removetur[13] per ipsum. Unde 'non-homo' non potest predicari
de[*P54vb*] homine neque 'non-ens' de ente. Nullum enim oppositorum predicari potest de sibi opposito.

14   Ad illud autem quod obicit, quod ad affirmationem in qua
predicatur nomen infinitum, sequitur negatio[1] in qua predicatur
nomen finitum, et non econverso, et[2] sic nomen infinitum ponit
ens, — dicendum sicut dictum est prius, quod[3] 'nomen[4] infinitum'
duplex est propter hoc quod vel est infinitum secundum negationem
et sic nichil ponit, vel quod[5] est infinitum secundum privationem et
sic ponit ens, sive sit substantiale (ut homo, animal) sive accidentale
(ut album, iustum, rectum[6], curvum, par vel impar). Unde si predicetur terminus accidentalis infinitus secundum privationem, sic
relinquit subiectum accidentis in esse. Et sic ista: 'homo est non-
iustus' et consimiles ponunt ens. Et sic ad ipsas sequitur negativa de
predicato finito, et non econverso (ut[7] 'homo est[8] non-iustus; ergo
homo non est iustus', et non econverso). Et hoc determinat Aristotiles in principio *Secundi Perihermeneias* dicendo[9] quod sic consequuntur sibi[10] invicem sicut[11] dictum est in *Prioribus*. (Hoc[12] etiam dicit[13]

collection of differences from the first predicable, and so 'man' and 'non-man' are mutually opposed as a privation and a state, and they are only said of a being; in another way, then, one can make a noun indefinite by way of a negation; in this way 'non-man' does not posit anything and it is a negative term. And thus 'non-man' is said of every being different from *man* as well as of non-being. And in this way, 'man' and 'non-man' are mutually opposed as an affirmation and a negation and are said of whatever *is* and *is not*, so that it would be either this or that, as is the case with every contradiction. And note that there is this twofold way of making a term indefinite only in the case of specific terms. For general terms (such as 'being' and 'something') are made indefinite in one way only, *viz.* by way of a negation, because there is not a double composition in them like in the specific ones. Therefore 'non-being' and 'non-something' are only said of that which is non-being. For no indefinite general term can be said of that of which the form is removed by that term. Hence 'non-man' cannot be said of a man nor can 'non-being' be said of a being. For no opposite can be said of its opposite.

14 As to the argument to the contrary, that from an affirmation in which an indefinite noun is in predicate-position a negation follows in which a definite noun is in predicate-position, and not the other way round, and so an indefinite noun posits a being,[6]—the answer should be, as we have said before,[7] that 'indefinite noun' is ambiguous in that it is either indefinite by way of negation and thus does not posit anything, or it is indefinite by way of privation and thus it posits a being, whether it be a substantial being (such as *man, animal*) or an accidental being (such as *white, just, straight, curved, even,* or *odd*). Hence if in predicate-position there is an accidental term indefinite by way of privation, then it leaves the subject of the accident in <the domain of> being. Therefore 'A man is non-just' and the like posit a being. And so from these <types of statements> a negative proposition with a definite predicate follows, and not the other way round (*e.g.* 'A man is non-just; therefore a man is not just', and not the other way round. And this is what Aristotle states at the beginning of the second book of *Perihermeneias*,[8] by saying that in this way they follow from each other, in the same way as was indicated in the *Prior Analytics*. (He in fact says at the end of the

---

6 Cf. above, cap. 9.
7 Cf. above, cap. 13.
8 *De interpr.* 10, 19b30-1.

in fine *Primi Priorum* quod ad privativam affirmativam [*N46vb*] sequitur negativa finita, et non econverso; ut 'hoc est inequale; ergo non est equale'[14], et non econverso; vel[15] 'hoc est non-album; ergo non est album', et non econverso). Si autem predicetur[16] terminus accidentalis infinitus secundum negationem, tunc nichil ponit, ut dictum est. Et sic convertitur cum negativa finita (ut 'omnis homo est non-iustus; ergo nullus homo est iustus', et non econverso). Et similiter dicit[17] in principio[18] *Secundi Perihermeneias* paulum post quod[19] ad negativam finitam sequitur affirmativa infinita (ut 'nullus homo est iustus; ergo omnis homo est non-iustus'). Quod non possit esse nisi converterentur[20] isto[21] modo, scilicet [*T28vb*] secundum quod est nomen infinitum secundum negationem. Et similiter intellige de termino infinito substantiali (ut 'non-homo') sicut de[22] accidentali (ut 'non-iustum')[23].

15 Ad illud autem quod postea obicit, quod in ista: 'homo est non-iustus' ponitur[1] ens, cum affirmetur esse et remaneat[2] compositio affirmata et non negetur per negationem sequentem, — dicendum quod hoc[3] argumentum tripliciter peccat. Quia[4] uno modo[5] secundum equivocationem huius nominis 'non-iustus'[6], quod[7] uno modo ponit ens et alio modo non, ut dictum est prius. Et[8] alio modo[9] peccat secundum consequens, sive secundum quid et simpliciter, quia non sequitur 'affirmatur esse aut[10] ipsa compositio; ergo est', quia affirmatio est tam de ente quam de non-ente. Ergo in plus est affirmatio quam esse secundum rem[11]. Ergo est *consequens*. Unde[12] secundum quod 'non-iustus' est nomen infinitum secundum negationem, non sequitur [*P55ra*] 'homo est non-iustus; ergo homo est'. Preterea est ibi fallacia secundum quid et simpliciter, quia quamvis sit[13] ibi compositio affirmata, non tamen[14] ponitur ibi[15] ens simpliciter sed diminutum[16] per determinationem sequentem. Unde sicut non sequitur 'est opinabile; ergo est', quamvis sit ibi[17] compositio affirmata[18], ita non sequitur 'est non-iustus; ergo est', cum[19] diminuatur esse per deter-

Book I of the *Prior Analytics*,[9] that from a privative affirmative proposition follows a negative definite proposition, and not the other way round; *e.g.* 'This is unequal; therefore it is not equal', and not the other way round, or 'This is non-white; therefore it is not white', and not the other way round.) However, if in predicate-position there is an accidental term indefinite by way of negation, then it does not posit anything, as has been said before. And in this way <the proposition> is convertible with a definite negative proposition (*e.g.* 'Every man is non-just; therefore no man is just', and the other way round). Similarly he says in the second book of *Perihermeneias*, a little further along,[10] that from a definite negative proposition follows an indefinite affirmative one (*e.g.* 'No man is just; therefore every man is non-just'). And that could only be the case if they were converted in this way, *viz.* in the sense that it is a noun indefinite by way of negation. And likewise you must consider an indefinite substantial term (such as 'non-man') in the same way as an accidental one (such as 'non-just').

15   As to the argument the opponent presents further down, namely that in this case, 'A man is non-just' a being is posited because *being* is affirmed and the composition remains affirmed and is not denied by the subsequent negation,[11] the answer should be that this argument goes astray in three ways. In one way <it is mistaken> in virtue of the equivocation of the noun 'non-just', which in one way posits a being, and in another does not, as has been said before. In another way it commits the fallacy of the consequent or of reasoning from something taken in a certain sense to the same thing taken *simpliciter*, for it does not follow '*Being* or the composition is affirmed; therefore it *is*.' For an affirmation concerns being and non-being equally. Hence *affirmation* is of a wider range than really *being*. Therefore there is a fallacy of the consequent. Hence insofar as 'non-just' is a noun indefinite by way of negation, it does not follow 'A man is non-just; therefore a man *is*'. Moreover, in this case there is an occurrence of the fallacy of reasoning from something taken in a certain sense to the same thing taken *simpliciter*, for although a composition is affirmed here, nevertheless no being is posited, but a being diminished by the subsequent qualification. Therefore, in the same way as it does not follow 'It is conceivable; therefore it *is*', even though a composition is affirmed here, likewise it does not follow 'He is non-just; therefore he *is*'. For <in these

---

9   *Anal. Priora* I, 46.
10 *De interpr.* 10, 19b33-4.
11 Cf. above, cap. 9.

minationem nichil ponentem, secundum quod 'non-iustus' est[20] terminus negativus.

16 Sciendum autem[1] quod nullus terminus[2] potest infinitari nisi subicibile[3] vel predicabile. Et[4] ideo signa universalia vel particularia non possunt infinitari, quia sunt dispositiones subiecti inquantum subiectum est, et ita respiciunt predicatum. Et ideo dicit Aristotiles quod hec negatio 'non' non est addenda huic signo 'omnis', quia non significat universale sed quoniam universaliter.

De negatione infinitante verbum

17 Dicto de negatione speciali[1] nominis faciente[2] nomen infinitum consequenter dicendum de speciali negatione verbi faciente verbum infinitum, quia sicut nomen natura prius est[3] verbo, ita nomen infinitum natura prius est[4] verbo infinito. Primo ergo queritur de verbo infinito utrum predicetur de omni[5] eo quod est et quod non est. Et videtur quod sic. Quia, ut vult Aristotiles, verbum infinitum similiter[6] est in quolibet quod est et quod non est. Ergo predicatur de omni quod est et quod non est. Sed contra. Negatio que est in verbo infinito, relinquit compositionem affirmatam[7], removendo actum a substantia[8] de qua predicatur actus. Unde sensus huius 'Cesar non currit', secundum[9] quod 'non-currit' est verbum infinitum, est iste: *Cesar est non-currens*. Sed compositio affirmata[10] ponit ens, quia ponit subiectum in esse. Ergo verbum infinitum ponit ens. Ergo solum predicatur de ente.

18 Et dicendum secundum quosdam quod verbum infinitum[1] extra orationem manet infinitum, sed in oratione non[2] manet infinitum, sed fit semper oratio quando ponitur in oratione, quia[3] negatio est una pars et verbum alia. Sed hoc nichil est, quia[4] moventur eoquod nesciunt distinguere in hac oratione 'Cesar non currit' et in consimilibus, secundum quod sunt propositiones negative[5] et secundum quod sunt de verbo infinito. Unde dicendum quod

examples> the being is diminished by the qualification which posits nothing, insofar as 'non just' is a negative term.

16 Note <thirdly> that a term can be made indefinite only if it can function as a subject or predicate. And therefore universal or particular signs cannot be made indefinite; for they are dispositions of a subject insofar as it is the subject, and so they relate to the predicate. And therefore Aristotle says[12] that the negation 'not' should not be added to the sign 'every', because the latter does not signify a *universal* but that <something should be taken> *universally*.

On the negation that makes a verb indefinite

17 Now that we have discussed the specific negation of a noun that makes the noun indefinite, we must next discuss the specific negation of a verb that makes the verb indefinite. For just as the noun naturally precedes the verb, so the indefinite noun naturally precedes the indefinite verb. Now first there is a problem concerning the indefinite verb, <*i.e.*> whether it can be said of everything that *is* and everything that *is not*. And it may be argued that it can. For according to Aristotle,[13] an indefinite verb is equally in whatever *is* and what *is not*. Therefore it is said of everything that *is* and everything that *is not*. There is an argument to the contrary. The negation in an indefinite verb leaves the composition affirmed while removing the act from the substance of which the act is said. Therefore insofar as the verb 'does-not-run' is an indefinite verb', the meaning of 'Caesar does-not-run' is *Caesar is something not-running*. Now an affirmed composition posits a being because it posits the subject <of the composition> in <the domain of> being. Therefore an indefinite verb posits a being. Therefore it is only said of being.

18 According to some people the answer should be that an indefinite verb outside a proposition remains indefinite whereas in a proposition it does not, and that when the indefinite verb is placed in a proposition one always gets a proposition [namely a negative proposition] because one part of it is the negation and the verb the other one. However, this is nonsense, for their reasoning is brought about by the fact that they are not capable of making the proper distinction in the proposition 'Caesar is not running' ['Caesar does-not-run'] and the like insofar as they are negative propositions and <propositions> containing an indefinite verb. Hence it should be said that an

12 *De interpr.* 7, 17b11-2.
13 *Ibid.* 3, 16b14-5.

verbum infinitum predicatur de quolibet quod est et quod non est et manet infinitum extra orationem et in oratione. Et hec propositio 'Cesar non currit' et consimiles, secundum quod sunt orationes negative, nichil ponunt; et compositio negatur in[6] eis nichil relinquendo, per eos[7]. Secundum autem quod in eis ponitur verbum infinitum, compositio remanet affirmata[8]. Unde isto modo secundum quod in eis verbum infinitum, adhuc sunt duplices, quia verbum infinitum potest infinitari [*T29ra*] secundum negationem et sic nichil ponit; vel potest [*P55rb*] infinitari secundum privationem et sic ponit subiectum in esse, et sic ponit ens.

19   Ad illud[1] autem quod obicit quod compositio affirmata[2] ponit ens, quia ponit subiectum in esse, dicendum quod utrumque est falsum, quia compositio equaliter se habet ad[3] compositionem entium et ad compositionem non-entium; unde neque[4] ponit ens ipsa compositio neque ponit subiectum suum in esse. Et ita virtute compositionis affirmate[5] inquantum est[6] affirmata, nichil ponitur[7]. Sed virtute predicati[8] [*N47rb*] aliquando ponitur subiectum in esse, ut quando predicatum est[9] ens simpliciter[10], et aliquando non ponitur[11] subiectum in esse, ut quando predicatum[12] est ens diminutum vel[13] quodammodo. Et ideo[14] sequitur 'lapis est homo; ergo lapis est' et non sequitur 'lapis est opinabile; ergo lapis est'. Unde sensus huius 'Cesar non currit' secundum quod 'non-currit'[15] est verbum infinitum, est iste: *Cesar est non-currens.*

20   Et similiter intellige de participio sicut et de verbo. Unde ille due 'Cesar non currit', 'Cesar est non-currens' nichil ponunt secundum quod verbum et participium sunt termini negativi. Sed secundum quod sunt termini privativi, sic ponunt ens, quia ponunt subiectum in esse. Et hoc virtute predicati et non compositionis, ut dictum est. De negatione infinitante participium satis patet ex predictis; et ideo relinquatur.

indefinite verb is said of whatever *is* and what *is not* and it remains indefinite outside as well as inside a proposition. And insofar as the proposition 'Caesar does not run' and the like are negative propositions they do not posit anything, and the composition is denied in them, whereby they leave nothing, according to them.[14] However, in the sense that these propositions contain an indefinite verb, the composition remains affirmed. Thus in the latter way, <*i.e.*> insofar as these propositions contain an indefinite verb, they are still ambiguous. For a verb can be made indefinite by way of negation, and in that way it does not posit anything, or it can be made indefinite by way of privation, and in that way the subject is posited in <the domain of> being; and thus it [*viz.* the verb] posits a being.

19   As to the argument to the contrary that an affirmed composition posits a being because it posits the subject in <the domain of> being, the answer should be that both <claims> are false. For *composition* is equally related to the composition of beings and the composition of non-beings. Therefore the composition itself neither posits a being nor does it posit its subject in <the domain of> being. And so in virtue of the affirmed composition insofar as it is affirmed it posits nothing. It is in virtue of the predicate, however, that the subject is sometimes posited in <the domain of> being, as when the predicate is a being *simpliciter*, whereas sometimes the subject is not posited in <the domain of> being, as when the predicate is a diminished being or a being-in-a-certain-sense. And thus it follows 'A stone is a man; therefore a stone *is*', and it does not follow 'A stone is conceivable; therefore a stone *is*'. So the meaning of 'Caesar does-not-run' insofar as 'does-not-run' is an indefinite verb is *Caesar is something not-running.*

20   And the same goes for the participle, no less than for the verb. Therefore these two propositions 'Caesar does-not-run' and 'Caesar is not-running' do not posit anything insofar as the verb and the participle are negative terms. However, in the sense of privative terms they do posit a being, because they posit the subject in <the domain of> being. This <positing of being> is in virtue of the predicate, not the composition, as has been said. As to the negation that makes a participle indefinite, enough is clear from what has been said; and so let us leave it.

---

14   *i.e.* the people mentioned above.

De negatione orationis

21 Determinatis negationibus terminorum dicendum est de negatione[1] orationis. Simplex enim natura precedit[2] compositum. Unde[3]
nomen et verbum natura sunt priora oratione. Unde negatio nominis vel[4] verbi natura precedit negationem orationis. Primo ergo
queritur utrum negatio orationis faciat contradictionem[5]. Et videtur
quod non, quia: Ad hoc quod[6] negatio contradicat, oportet quod removeat compositionem. Sed non potest removere compositionem[7],
quia compositio est subiectum negationis et nullum accidens removet suum subiectum. Ergo non potest facere contradictionem. Ergo
non contingit contradicere. Item ad idem. Quicquid est causatum,
aut[8] est substantia aut accidens. Ergo negatio cum sit causata, aut est
substantia aut accidens. Sed non est substantia. Ergo est accidens.
Ergo est in subiecto aliquo. Sed nonnisi[9] in compositione. Ergo non
removet eam[10]. Ergo non contingit contradicere. Item[11]. Cum
contingat contradicere, quia[12] hoc est principium[13] principiorum in
scientiis, ergo negatio removet compositionem. Sed compositio est
causa modi. Ergo removet modum. Ergo nulla oratio[14] negativa est
alicuius modi. Ergo neque[15] indicativi (locus[16] a genere). Ergo nulla
oratio[17] negativa est vera vel falsa; sola enim indicativa est in[18] qua
est verum vel falsum.
22 Solutio. Sicut hoc nomen 'homo' duplicem habet significationem, scilicet generalem[1] et[2] specialem (generalis significatio est
significare substantiam cum qualitate, specialis[3] vero significare
hanc substantiam que est homo), et sicut[4] in verbo duplex est significatio, scilicet generalis [*N47va*] et[5] specialis: (generalis[6] est significare agere vel pati, specialis vero[7] significare istum actum[8] vel
istam passionem, ut legere vel legi, percutere vel percuti), — similiter duplex[9] est compositio, scilicet[10] generalis et specialis. Generalis[11] autem compositio communiter se habet quantum est de se ad
omnia componibilia. Cum enim dicimus quod verbum consignificat[12] [*P55va*] compositionem, non dicimus hanc compositionem[13]

On the negation of a complex expression

21   Now that the negation of terms has been dealt with, we must next discuss the negation of a complex expression. For the simple naturally precedes the complex.[15] Hence the noun and verb naturally precede the complex expression. Therefore the negation of a noun and verb naturally precede the negation of a complex expression. First of all there is a problem whether the negation found in a complex expression produces a contradiction. And it may be argued that it cannot. For in order to produce a contradiction it is necessary that the negation remove the composition. Now it cannot do so, for the composition is the substrate of the negation and no accident removes its own substrate. Therefore it [*i.e.* the negation found in a complex expression] cannot produce a contradiction. Therefore one cannot have a contradiction at all. There is another argument that yields the same conclusion. Whatever is caused is either a substance or an accident. Therefore in virtue of the fact that it is caused, the negation is either a substance or an accident. Now it is not a substance. Therefore it is an accident. Therefore it *is* in some substrate. Now it only *is* in a composition. Therefore it does not remove the composition. Therefore one cannot have a contradiction at all. Again, as it is possible to have a contradiction, since that is the first principle of the sciences, therefore the negation removes the composition. Now the composition is the cause of the mood. Therefore it [*i.e.* the negation] removes the mood. Therefore no negative proposition is of a certain mood. Therefore it is not of the indicative mood either (the topic 'from a genus'). Therefore no negative proposition is true or false; for only in <propositions of the> indicative mood there is something true or false.

22   Solution. Just as the noun 'man' has a double signification namely a general one and a specific one (the general one is to signify a substance with a quality whereas the specific one is to signify *this* substance, which is a man), and just as the verb also has a double signification, namely a general and a specific one (the general one is to signify acting or being acted upon and the specific one is to signify *this* acting or *this* being acted upon, *e.g.* to read or to be read, to hit or to be hit),—in the same way a composition is twofold, namely general and specific. The general composition in itself relates equally to all things that can be combined. For when we say that a verb consignifies a composition, we do not mean *this* or *that*

---

[15]   Cf. Aristotle, *De caelo* II 4, 286b16-7.

vel[14] illam, sed compositionem in genere; et hec compositio est generalis[15]. Specialis autem compositio est per extrema compositionis. Et negatio removet specialem compositionem, et hoc sufficit ad contradictionem. Et relinquit generalem, ratione cuius accidit modus. Unde adhuc[16] contingit[17] contradicere.

23   Item. Solet[1] dici quod due negationes equipollent affirmationi[2]. Et queritur quare due affirmationes econverso [*T29rb*] non equipollent negationi[3]. Et[4] videtur quod, sicut negatio removet affirmationem, sic econverso affirmatio negationem. Et dicendum quod negatio apta nata est destruere[5] quicquid repperit[6], quia negatio est actus[7] destruens suum obiectum. Unde obiectum negationis, quodcumque fuerit, removetur per negationem. Et quia negatio aliquando[8] est obiectum negationis, aliquando negatio negatur (ut 'non: Sortes non currit') et[9] ideo negatio removetur per negationem, ideo[10] ex consequenti ponitur affirmatio, quia[11] remota negatione ponitur affirmatio, eoquod necesse est semper esse affirmationem vel[12] negationem. Et ideo due negationes equipollent affirmationi. Affirmatio[13] autem non est apta nata destruere[14] suum obiectum, sed ponit ipsum[15] potius et conservat. Et ideo cum res affirmata[16], que est obiectum affirmationis[17], non[18] removeatur per affirmationem, ob[19] hoc due affirmationes non possunt equipollere negationi.

24   Ad illud autem quod obicit quod affirmatio removet negationem, sicut et[1] econverso, dicendum quod due comparationes[2] sunt in affirmatione et due in negatione, diversimode[3] comparate. Una enim comparatio affirmationis est ad illud quod affirmat, aliam[4] vero habet ad illud cui opponitur. Et ille due comparationes affirmationis non[5] sunt respectu eiusdem sed respectu diversorum. Verbi gratia, hec affirmatio 'Sortes currit' affirmat Sortem currere et compositio[6] eius opponitur ei[7] que est Sortem non currere. Et ideo ratione compositionis[8] non potest destruere [*N47vb*] suum obiectum. Sed due comparationes negationis sunt semper[9] respectu eiusdem, quia negatio semper negat aliquid, sicut[10] affirmatio affirmat, et semper negatio opponitur alicui. Sed nonnisi ei quod negat. Et ideo

composition, but a composition in general; and this is the general composition. A specific composition, on the other hand, occurs via the <actual> extremes of the composition. Now the negation removes the specific composition, and this suffices for a contradiction. And the general one is left, which accounts for the mood. Hence it is still possible to have a contradiction.

23   Furthermore, one usually says that two negations are equivalent to an affirmation. And there is a problem why, conversely, two affirmations are not equivalent to one negation. This would seem to be the case, because just as a negation removes an affirmation, so, conversely, an affirmation removes a negation. The answer should be that a negation is by nature apt to destroy whatever it has come across, for a negation is an act which destroys its own object. So the object of the negation, whatever it may be, is removed by the negation. And since sometimes a negation is the object of a negation, the former is sometimes denied (*e.g.* in 'Not: Socrates is not running') and so a negation is removed by a negation. And thus consequently an affirmation is asserted, because when a negation is removed an affirmation is asserted, since it is necessary that there always be an affirmation or negation. And therefore two negations are equivalent to one affirmation. An affirmation, however, is not by nature apt to destroy its own object, but rather it asserts and conserves it. And so since the 'thing' (*res*) affirmed, the object of an affirmation, is not removed by an affirmation, for that reason two affirmations cannot be equivalent to one negation.

24   As to the argument to the contrary that an affirmation removes a negation, just like the other way round as well,[16] the answer should be that an affirmation and a negation contain two types of relations which are differently related. For one relation the affirmation has is to what it affirms, whereas the other it has is to what it is opposed to. And these two relations do not concern the same thing but different things. For example, the affirmation 'Socrates runs' affirms that Socrates is running and its composition is opposed to the <composition> that-Socrates-is-not-running. And therefore in virtue of the composition <the affirmation> cannot destroy its object. The two relations found in the negation, however, do concern the same thing, because a negation always denies something, in the same way as an affirmation always affirms something, and a negation is always opposed to something, but only to what it denies. And there-

---

[16] Cf. above, cap. 23.

negatio ratione sue oppositionis semper destruit suum obiectum quod negabat[11]. Sed affirmatio non opponitur [*P55vb*] ei quod affirmat, ut dictum est. Et ideo affirmatio[12] non destruit quod affirmat[13]. Et sic non est simile de affirmatione ad[14] negationem et de negatione ad affirmationem, ut iam patet per[15] hoc quod negatio opponitur affirmationi et negat eam, affirmatio opponitur negationi et non affirmat eam sed aliud, ut dictum est.

25 Item. Dicit[1] Aristotiles in secundo *Topicorum* quod si aliquid non est susceptivum unius contrariorum, neque alterius. Ergo quod non potest affirmari[2], non poterit[3] negari[4]. Sed ista 'Sortes non currit' non potest affirmari, cum sit negativa. Ergo non potest ei addi altera negatio ut per eam negetur. Ergo due negationes non[5] equipollent affirmationi.

26 Ad hoc dicunt quidam quod negatio quodammmodo est affirmatio, quia negatio[1] habet in se aliquid[2] de ente, scilicet[3] de affirmatione, unde participat[4] naturam affirmationis. Et ideo potest negari per negationem. Et ita huic propositioni 'Sortes non currit' potest addi altera negatio sic[5]: 'non: Sortes non currit'. Et ita due negationes equipollent affirmationi. Sed ego credo quod melius dicitur quod quamvis[6] accidentia nature non possint reflecti supra[7] se agendo in se (sicut[8] caliditas[9] non agit in se sed in suum obiectum), tamen accidentia causata[10] a ratione possunt reflecti supra se agendo in[11] se (sicut ratio supra se cognoscendo[12] se et iudicando[13] de se). Unde negatio, que[14] est accidens causatum[15] a ratione, potest reflecti[16] supra negationem sive[17] supra rem negatam[18]. Et ideo negatio potest negari, quamvis non possit affirmari. Et consideratio Aristotilis[19] debet [*T29va*] intelligi de accidentibus nature sive de contrariis nature (ut 'album-nigrum', 'calidum-frigidum' et consimilia). Item. Iste due 'Sortes currit'[20], 'non: Sortes non currit' equipollent sibi invicem et contradicunt huic 'Sortes non currit'. Sed[21] contra: dicit Aristotiles quod unum uni opponitur. Ergo due propositiones non contradicunt uni.

fore in virtue of its being opposed, a negation always destroys the very object it denied <before>. Now an affirmation is not opposed to what it affirms, as has been said. And so an affirmation does not destroy what it affirms. And so there is no analogy as regards <the way in which> an affirmation <is related to> a negation and a negation to an affirmation, as is already evident from the fact that a negation is opposed to an affirmation and denies it, whereas an affirmation is opposed to a negation but does not affirm it [*i.e.* the negation] but something else, as has been said.

25 Again, Aristotle says[17] in Book II of the *Topica* that if something cannot admit of one of the contraries, it cannot admit of the other either. Therefore what cannot be denied cannot be affirmed. Now 'Socrates does not run' cannot be affirmed because it is a negative proposition. Therefore another negation cannot be added to it so as to deny it. Therefore two negations are not equivalent to an affirmation.

26 In reply to this argument some say that a negation is an affirmation in a certain sense, because a negation in itself contains some feature of being, *viz.* an affirmation, on account of which it shares in the nature of an affirmation. And so it can be denied by means of a negation. And so to the proposition 'Socrates is not running' another negation can be added as follows: 'Not: Socrates is not running'. And so two negations are equivalent to an affirmation. However, I think it is better to say that although natural accidents cannot return upon themselves by acting upon themselves (just as warmth does not act upon itself but upon its object), nevertheless accidents that stem from reason can return upon themselves by acting upon themselves (just as the intellect can do so by knowing itself and judging itself). Therefore the negation, which is an accident that stems from reason, can return upon a negation or the denied 'thing' (*res*). And therefore a negation can be denied, although it cannot be affirmed. And Aristotle's consideration must be regarded as concerning natural accidents or natural contraries (such as the white-the black, the warm-the cold and the like). Furthermore, the two <propositions> 'Socrates is running' and 'Not: Socrates is not running' are mutually equivalent and contradictory to 'Socrates is not running'. An argument to contrary, however, is that Aristotle says[18] that to one thing <just> one thing is the opposite. Therefore two propositions are not the contradictory of one.

---

[17] Cf. *Topica* II 7, 113a33-5.
[18] *De interpr.* 7, 17b37.

27   Et dicendum quod dupliciter[1] fit contradictio, scilicet primo et
ex consequenti. Unde in hiis est primo contradictio 'Sortes[2] currit',
'Sortes non currit'. Sed[3] hec 'non: Sortes non currit' [*N48ra*] contradicit[4] ex consequenti huic 'Sortes non currit', quia, inquantum equipollet, et convertitur cum ista[5] 'Sortes currit'. Unde intellige quod in
contradictione primo[6] semper altera[7] est affirmatio et altera est
negatio. Unde dicit Aristotiles[8] quod contradictio est affirmatio et
negatio opposite. Sed in contradictione que est ex consequenti, negatio potest contradicere negationi.

28   Item. Nota quod negatio [*P56ra*] preposita sive postposita[1]
termino singulari idem significat (ut 'Sortes[2] non currit' et 'non:
Sortes currit'). Sed non similiter est in terminis communibus, quia
hec est indefinita[3] 'homo non[4] currit', hec autem est[5] universalis
negativa 'non: homo currit'. Neque[6] est in[7] contrarium quod[8] dicit
Aristotiles: "transposita nomina vel verba idem significant". Et[9]
intelligatur de aliis dictionibus, quia intellexit[10] de dictione[11] que
est[12] subicibilis vel predicabilis[13] vel[14] que est dispositio ipsius subicibilis vel predicabilis absolute. Et non intellexit[15] de dictione que est
dispositio unius ad[16] alterum, ut sunt negationes et signa universalia[17]. Negatio enim negat unum de[18] altero et signum universale
disponit subiectum in respectu ad predicatum.

Sophismata

29   Item. Queritur de hoc sophismate NULLO HOMINE CUR-
RENTE TU ES ASINUS. Probatio. Hec est falsa 'aliquo homine
currente tu es asinus'. Ergo eius contradictoria erit[1] vera, hec scilicet
'non aliquo homine currente tu es asinus'. Sed[2] 'non aliquo' et
'nullo' equipollent, sicut 'non aliquis' et 'nullus'. Ergo hec est vera
'nullo homine currente tu es asinus'. Sed contra. Nullo homine
currente tu es asinus. Ergo dum nullus homo currit[3], vel si nullus
homo currit[4], vel quia nullus homo currit, tu es asinus. Quod falsum
est.

27 The answer should be that a contradiction occurs in two ways, *viz.* primarily and by consequence. So in the following there is a primary contradiction: 'Socrates is running', 'Socrates is not running'. Now 'Not: Socrates is not running' is by consequence the contradictory opposite of 'Socrates is not running', that is, insofar as it is equivalent to <the former> it is also convertible with 'Socrates is running'. So understand that in a primary contradiction the one is always an affirmative proposition and the other a negative one. Therefore Aristotle says[19] that a contradiction is an affirmation and a negation opposed to one another. However, in a contradiction by consequence a negation can contradict another negation.

28 Note that a negation placed before or after a singular term signifies the same (as in 'Socrates is not running' and 'Not: Socrates is running'). However, the same does not hold for common terms, for 'A man is not running' is an indefinite proposition, whereas 'Not: a man is running' is a universal negative one. And this is not contrary to what Aristotle says,[20] that "transposed nouns and verbs signify the same". And one should understand this same <rule> as concerning other words, for he understood it as concerning a word capable of functioning as a subject or predicate or a word that is a disposition of the subject or predicate itself in an absolute sense. And he did not understand it as concerning a word that is a disposition of one in relation to another, as are negations and universal signs. For a negation denies one thing of another and a universal sign modifies a subject in relation to a predicate.

Sophismata

29 There is a problem concerning the sophisma-sentence NO MAN RUNNING YOU ARE AN ASS. Proof: the following is false, 'Some man running you are an ass'. Therefore its contradictory opposite, *viz.* 'Not some man running you are an ass', will be true. Now 'not some' and 'no' are equivalent, just as 'not someone' and 'no one'. Therefore the following is true, 'No man running you are an ass'. However, there is an argument to the contrary. No man running you are an ass. Therefore while no man is running, or if no man is running, or because no man is running, you are an ass. And this is false.

---

[19] *Ibid.* 6, 17a33-4.
[20] *Ibid.* 10, 20b1-2.

30   Solutio. Prima falsa, hec scilicet 'nullo homine currente tu es asinus'. Quia[1] ista[2] per[3] quam probat eam, peccat secundum divisionem, hec scilicet 'non aliquo homine currente tu es asinus'. Et[4] est duplex, eoquod negatio potest negare tantum participium (et sic est divisa et falsa), vel potest negare participium in comparatione ad verbum sequens (et sic est composita et vera). Et primo[5] modo equipollet prime, scilicet huic 'nullo homine currente tu es asinus'. Sed hec est falsa 'nullo homine *etc.*', quia negatio que est in compositione[6] huius signi 'nullo'[7], non potest ferri ultra participium, per hanc regulam

> *quotienscumque negatio et distributio includuntur in termino uno[8], ad nichil potest ferri unum sine reliquo.*

Sed distributio non fertur[9] ultra participium. Ergo neque [*N48rb*] negatio. Et[10] ita hec est falsa 'nullo homine currente tu es asinus'. Quare et[11] sua equipollens illo modo quo ei equipollet. Et utraque est affirmativa, hec scilicet 'non[12] aliquo[13] homine currente *etc.*'[14] et 'nullo homine currente *etc.*', secundum quod equipollent. Et per hoc[15] patet quod neutra earum contradicit huic 'aliquo homine currente *etc.*', quia affirmativa non contradicit affirmative.

31   Item. Queritur de hoc sophismate NICHIL NICHIL EST. Probatio[1]. Eius contradictoria est falsa, hec scilicet 'aliquid nichil est'. Ergo prima[2] vera. Contra. Nichil nichil est. Ergo nichil nulla substantia est. Et videtur esse[3] locus a genere sive a toto in quantitate, ut 'nichil est; ergo[4] nulla substantia est'. Sed conclusio est[5] falsa, hec scilicet 'nichil nulla substantia est', [*T29vb*] quia equipollet huic 'quidlibet est aliqua substantia', quod falsum est. Ergo et[6] prima ex qua sequitur, est falsa.

32   Solutio. Prima vera, hec scilicet 'nichil nichil est', quia [*P56rb*] equipollet huic 'quidlibet est aliquid', per illam regulam[1]:

> *quotienscumque duo signa universalia negativa ponuntur in eadem[2] locutione, ita quod unum in subiecto et[3] alterum in predicato, primum equipollet suo contrario, reliquum suo contradictorio.*

30 Solution. The original sentence, *viz.* 'No man running you are an ass', is false. For the proposition by which the opponent proves it to be true, namely 'Not some man running you are an ass', is erroneous due to the fallacy of division. And this proposition is ambiguous because the negation can deny <either> the participle only (and in this way it is divided and false), or it can deny the participle in relation to the subsequent verb (and in that way it is compounded and true). And in the first way it is equivalent to the original one, *viz.* 'No man running you are an ass'. However, the following is false, 'No man . . . *etc.*', for the negation that is part of the sign 'no' cannot carry farther than the participle, and this is on account of the following rule:

> *Whenever a negation and a distribution are included in the same term, the one can carry no farther than the other.*

Now the distribution cannot carry farther than the participle. Therefore the negation cannot either. Hence 'No man running you are an ass' is false. And therefore its equivalent according as it is equivalent to the former is false as well. And both, *viz.* 'Not some man running . . . etc.' and 'No man running . . . etc' are affirmative insofar as the two are equivalent. And thus it is evident that neither of them is contradictory to 'Some man running *etc.*', because an affirmative proposition does not contradict an affirmative one.

31 There is a problem concerning the sophisma-sentence NOTHING IS NOTHING. Proof: its contradictory, 'Something is nothing', is false. Therefore the original proposition is true. There is an argument to the contrary. Nothing is nothing. Therefore nothing is no substance. And this appears to be a case of the topic 'from a genus' or 'from a quantative whole', as in 'Nothing is; therefore no substance is'. Now the conclusion, 'Nothing is no substance', is false, because it is equivalent to 'Everything is some substance', which is false. Therefore the original proposition from which it follows is false as well.

32 Solution. The original sentence, 'Nothing is nothing', is true, because it is equivalent to 'Everything is something', on account of the following rule:

> *Whenever two universal negative signs are placed in one and the same locution such that one is in the subject and the other in the predicate, the first is equivalent to its contrary and the other to its contradictory.*

Item. Improbatio peccat secundum consequens communiter loquendo, quia sicut hic[4] est *consequens* secundum communiter loquentes 'quidlibet est aliquid; ergo quidlibet est aliqua substantia', similiter hic est *consequens* 'nichil nichil est; ergo nichil nulla substantia est'.

33   Ad illud autem quod obicit quod videtur[1] ibi esse locus a genere sive a toto in quantitate, dicendum[2] quod non est verum, immo est ibi fallacia[3] secundum consequens, sicut hic 'nullus homo est nullum animal; ergo nullus homo est nullum risibile'. Quia in ista 'omnis homo est nullum animal' 'animal' removetur a subiecto. Et cum apponitur[4] alia negatio per hoc signum 'nullus', removetur predicatum negatum[5] a[6] subiecto sic: 'nullus homo est nullum animal'. Sed removere predicatum a subiecto negatum est ponere ex consequenti in[7] eodem affirmatum. Ergo ista 'nullus homo est nullum animal' equipollet huic 'omnis[8] homo est aliquod[9] animal'; et similiter ista 'nullus homo est nullum risibile' equipollet huic 'omnis homo est aliquod risibile'[10]. Hic autem ponunt *consequens*: 'animal est; ergo risibile[11] est', sicut hic: 'animal currit; ergo homo currit'. Ergo et[12] hic: 'omnis homo est animal; ergo omnis homo est risibile'; et similiter in suis equipollentibus ' nullus homo [*N48va*] est nullum animal; ergo nullus[13] homo est nullum risibile'[14]. Et similiter est in proposito: 'nichil nichil est; ergo nichil nulla substantia est'.

34   Et[1] videtur quod conclusio improbationis sit vera, quia hec est vera 'nulla substantia est nichil'. Quod patet dupliciter, scilicet per predictam regulam, quia equipollet huic 'omnis substantia est aliquid; et etiam quia sua contradictoria est falsa, hec scilicet 'aliqua substantia est nichil'. Ergo[2] hec est vera 'nulla substantia est nichil'. Ergo sua conversa erit[3] vera, hec scilicet 'nichil est nulla substantia'.

35   Et dicendum quod non recte convertit hanc 'nulla substantia est nichil', quia debet ponere signum subiecti supra totum predicatum et reducere[1] ad subiectum[2], ut 'nulla substantia est nichil: nullum ens[3] nichil est substantia'. Sed utraque istarum[4] est vera. Et sic non probat

Moreover, the disproof commits the fallacy of the consequent according to common usage. For just as the following is a fallacy of consequence according to people following common usage, 'Everything is something; therefore everything is some substance', in the same way this is a fallacy of the consequent, 'Nothing is nothing; therefore nothing is no substance'.

33   In reply to the argument to the contrary, that there appears to be a case of the topic 'from a genus' or 'from a quantative whole', it should be remarked that this is not true; rather we have here the fallacy of consequent, as in 'No man is no animal; therefore no man is nothing that can laugh'; for in 'Every man is no animal', 'animal' is removed from the subject. And when another negation is added to it by the sign 'no', the denied predicate is removed from the subject as follows, 'No man is no animal'. Now to remove a denied predicate from the subject is consequently to assert the affirmed predicate in the subject. Therefore 'No man is no animal' is equivalent to 'Every man is some animal', and similarly 'No man is nothing that can laugh' is equivalent to 'Every man is something that can laugh'. However, in the following <argument> they commit the fallacy of the consequent, 'An animal *is*; therefore something that can laugh *is*', in the same way as in 'An animal is running; therefore a man is running'. Therefore this also happens in 'Every man is an animal; therefore every man is something that can laugh'. And the same applies to their equivalent propositions: 'No man is no animal; therefore no man is nothing that can laugh'. And it is similar in our case: 'Nothing is nothing; therefore nothing is no substance'.

34   And it seems that the conclusion of the disproof is true, because 'No substance is nothing' is true. This is evident in two ways, *viz.* from the rule mentioned above,[21] for it is equivalent to 'Every substance is something', and also because its contradictory, 'Some substance is nothing', is false. Therefore 'No substance is nothing' is true; therefore its converse, *viz.* 'Nothing is no substance', will be true.

35   The answer should be that <the opponent> does not correctly convert 'No substance is nothing', for he should place the sign of the subject as ranging over the whole predicate and bring it back to the subject, as in 'No substance is nothing; therefore no being-nothing is a substance'. Now both of these are true and so he does not prove the conclusion of the disproof. Again, the fact that the conclusion of the

---

21   Cf. above, cap. 32.

conclusionem improbationis. Item. Quod conclusio improbationis sit
falsa probatur dupliciter. Quia uno modo per predictam regulam, et
alio modo quia eius[5] contradictoria est vera, hec scilicet 'aliquid est
nulla substantia', ut albedo et quodlibet aliud[6] accidens.

disproof is false is proved in two ways. In one way it is proved via the rule mentioned above,[22] and in the other way because its contradictory opposite, 'Something (whiteness, for example, or any other accident) is no substance', is true.

---

[22] Cf. above, *ibid.*.

TRACTATUS TERTIUS

DE DICTIONIBUS EXCLUSIVIS

Introductio

1   Dicto de[1] negatione et affirmatione consequenter dicendum est de dictionibus exclusivis, ut 'tantum', 'solus'. Circa quas[2] primo queritur propter quid dicatur dictio exclusiva et quid significet dictio exclusiva; secundo[3] quot[4] et que sint[5] cause exclusionis[6] que exiguntur [*P56va*] ad esse exclusionis; tertio[7] quot sunt partes[8] sive species exclusionis; quarto[9] queritur, descendendo[10] ad quandam causam exclusionis, scilicet ad illud quod excluditur, que[11] sint[12] ea que debent excludi; quintum et ultimum erit de differentia harum dictionum 'tantum' et 'solus' in suis exclusionibus.

Quare dicatur dictio exclusiva

2   Circa primum ergo[1] queritur quare dicatur dictio exclusiva. Et dicunt quidam quod dictio dicitur exclusiva quia significat exclusionem. Sed contra. Nulla dictio significat actum quem exercet, ut[2] iste terminus 'homo' non significat suppositionem quam exercet supponendo pro hoc et pro illo, et[3] sic de aliis; sed[4] significat hominem et exercet suppositionem; et sic de aliis dictionibus. Ergo nulla dictio[5] significat actum quem exercet; et est inductio et est[6] locus a partibus sufficienter enumeratis[7]. Sed 'tantum' et 'solus' exercent[8] exclusionem. Ergo [*N48vb*] non significant eam.

3   Item. Exclusio intelligitur dupliciter; scilicet ut concepta [*T30ra*] et ut[1] exercita, sicut cursus significatur ut conceptus[2] per hoc nomen 'cursus' et per hoc verbum 'curro, -ris'; aliter[3] autem cursus significatur ut exercitus, ut cum[4] aliquis[5] exercet ipsum in[6] currendo. Similiter exclusio intelligitur ut concepta, sicut[7] per hoc nomen 'exclusio, -nis' et per hoc verbum 'excludo, -dis'; aliter autem intelligitur ut exercita, ut per has dictiones 'solus' et 'tantum'.

CHAPTER III

ON EXCLUSIVE WORDS

Introduction

1   Now that we have discussed affirmation and negation, we must next discuss exclusive words, namely '*tantum*' ('only') <and> '*solus*' ('alone'). Concerning these words there is *[1]* first a problem why one calls a word exclusive and what an exclusive word signifies, *[2]* secondly what and how many are the causes of exclusion that are required for there being an exclusion, *[3]* thirdly how many are the parts, or kinds of exclusion, *[4]* fourthly there is a problem, by descending to a certain cause of exclusion, namely to that which is excluded, what the things are that are to be excluded, and *[5]* fifthly and finally there is a problem about the difference between the words '*tantum*' and '*solus*' as regards their kinds of exclusion.

Why a word is called exclusive

2   *Ad [1]:* As to the first item, there is thus a problem why a word is called exclusive. And some say that a word is called exclusive because it signifies exclusion. However, there is an argument to the contrary. No word signifies the act it carries out, like the word 'man' does not signify the supposition it carries out by suppositing for this and for that, an so on. Now it signifies *man* and it carries out a supposition; and the same goes for other words. Therefore no word signifies the act it carries out, and this is a case of induction and the topic 'from parts sufficiently summed up'. Now 'only' and 'alone' carry out an exclusion. Therefore they do not signify it.

3   Furthermore, 'exclusion' is understood in two ways, *viz.* as conceived of and as carried out, just as running is signified as conceived of by the noun 'the running' and by the verb 'to run'; in another way, however, running is signified as carried out, namely when someone carries it out by running. In the same way exclusion is understood as conceived of, like by the noun 'exclusion' and by the verb 'to exclude'; in another way it is understood as carried out, namely by the word<s> 'alone' and 'only'.

4 Si ergo 'solus' et 'tantum' significant exclusionem, aut significant eam[1] hoc modo vel illo. Sed[2] si significant eam[3] ut conceptam, ergo iste dictiones 'exclusio, -nis' et[4] 'exclusus' et 'excludo, -dis' erunt dictiones exclusive. Quod falsum est. Ergo non significant eam ut conceptam. Neque[5] ut exercitam, quia sicut se habet dictio in communi ad actum suum communem, qui[6] est significare, similiter[7] se habet dictio specialis ad actum suum specialem. Sed dictio in communi non significat actum suum communem; dictio enim non significat significare sed exercet ipsum. Ergo similiter dictio specialis non significat actum suum specialem sive proprium sed exercet ipsum. Ergo hec dictio[8] specialis[9] 'solus' non significat exclusionem [*P56vb*] sed exercet ipsam[10]. Ergo dictiones exclusive non significant exclusionem ut[11] exercitam[12] neque ut conceptam[13], ut probatum est. Ergo nullo modo significant exclusionem.

5 Quod concedimus dicentes quod dictiones exclusive dicuntur exclusive non quia significent[1] exclusionem sed quia exercent eam, ut 'tantum'[2], 'solus' dicuntur dictiones exclusive ab exclusione exercita et non ab exclusione significata. Sicut[3] securis dicitur incisiva ab incisione exercita et non ab incisione significata. 'Securis' enim nullo modo significat incisionem sed significat securim (sicut[4] 'homo'[5] hominem) et exercet incisionem sive ipsum scindere.

Quid significet dictio exclusiva

6 Ad aliud autem[1] quod queritur[2], quid significet dictio exclusiva, dicendum quod significat idem quod hec oratio 'non cum alio', sive[3] privationem associationis totius ad partem, [*N49ra*] ut 'solus Sortes currit', idest[4] *Sortes currit et nichil[5] aliud* vel *Sortes currit et nullus alius homo currit.* Et sic pars ponitur et totum removetur, quia ponitur Sortes et removetur quilibet[6] alius[7] homo, vel quidlibet aliud, a Sorte. Et ita[8] totum non associatur[9] parti sue. Et sic dictio exclusiva privat associationem[10] totius ad partem suam[11] per suam significationem. Et ideo dicitur[12] significare privationem associationis totius ad partem. Sed ad istam privationem sequitur exclusio omnium aliorum, sicut proprius[13] actus sequitur ad illud per quod exercetur. Et ideo exclusio

4   If therefore 'alone' and 'only' signify exclusion, they signify
<it> either in the former or in the latter way. Now if they signify it
as conceived of, then therefore the words 'exclusion', 'excluded' and
'to exclude' will be exclusive words. And this is false. Therefore
they do not signify it [*i.e.* exclusion] as conceived of. Nor do they
signify it as carried out either, because just as a word in general is
related to its general act which is to signify, in the same way a
specific word is related to its specific act. Now a word in general
does not signify its general act; for a word does not signify 'to
signify' but carries it out. Therefore likewise a specific word does
not signify its specific or proper act, but carries it out. Therefore the
specific word 'alone' does not signify an exclusion, but carries it out.
Therefore exclusive words do not signify exclusion as carried out
nor as conceived of, as has been proven. Therefore in no way do
they signify exclusion.
5   We agree with this saying that exclusive words are called exclusive not because they signify exclusion, but because they carry it
out, like 'only' and 'alone' are called exclusive words after an exclusion carried out and not after an exclusion as signified, just as an axe
is called 'incisive' after an incision carried out and not after an
incision as signified. For 'axe' in no way signifies incision, but it
signifies *axe* (just as 'man' signifies *man*) and it carries out the incision or cutting itself.

What an exclusive word signifies

6   As to the other problem,[1] what an exclusive word signifies, the
answer should be that it signifies the same as the expression 'not
with another', or a privation of the connection a whole has with a
part; *e.g.* 'Only Socrates is running', that is, *Socrates is running and
nothing else* or *Socrates is running and no other man is running.* Thus a part
is posited and a whole is removed, because Socrates is posited and
whichever other man or whichever thing other than Socrates is
removed. Thus the whole is not connected with its part. In this way
an exclusive word removes the connection a whole has with its part
on account of its very meaning. Therefore it is said to signify a
privation of the connection a whole has with a part. Now from this
privation follows the exclusion of all others, just as a proper act
follows from that by which it is carried out. Hence an exclusion is

---

[1]   Cf. above, cap. 1.

importatur per dictionem exclusivam, non ut significata sed ut exercita. Et sic patet[14] primum.

Quot et que sint cause exclusionis

7   Circa secundum queritur in hunc modum. Associatio et privatio associationis opponuntur[1] ut privatio et habitus. Sed privatio diffinitur per habitum, quia cecitas est privatio visus in oculo et per hunc[2] habet esse. Ergo privatio associationis erit per ea per que est associatio, et per illam[3] habebit esse. Sed ad[4] associationem exigitur quod associetur[5] et cui associetur[5] et in quo associetur.[5] Ergo ad privationem associationis exiguntur eadem tria. Quod concedimus.

8   Unde dicendum quod ad exclusionem que sequitur ad predictam privationem, quatuor exiguntur, [*P57ra*] scilicet[1] quod excluditur et a[2] quo excluditur[3] et respectu cuius excluditur; et quartum est[4] ipse actus excludendi. Verbi gratia[5] 'solus Sortes currit'; alii a Sorte excluduntur ut[6] a subiecto et respectu cursus; et actus excludendi[7] importatur[8] per hanc dictionem 'solus'. Et hee quatuor cause exiguntur [*T30rb*] ad exclusionem semper[9].

De quibusdam regulis

9   Ex predictis patet quedam regula. Que[1] talis est:

> *ubicumque vere fit exclusio, semper id respectu cuius exclusio fit, ponitur in eo a quo omnia alia excluduntur.*

Ut 'tantum homo est risibile': hic enim 'risibile', respectu cuius fit exclusio, ponitur in 'homine', a quo omnia alia excluduntur. Unde sequitur 'tantum homo est risibile; ergo homo est risibile'; et 'tantum homo currit; ergo homo currit'.

10   Ex predictis[1] patet quedam alia regula. Que talis est:

brought about by an exclusive word not as conceived of, but as carried out. So the solution to the first problem is evident.

How many and what are the causes of exclusion

7   *Ad [2]*: As to the second item, the problem runs as follows. A connection and a privation of a connection are opposite as a privation and a possession. Now a privation is defined in terms of a dispossession, because blindness is a privation of sight in the eye and in virtue of the latter it has being. Therefore a privation of a connection will be in virtue of the things by which there is a connection, and in virtue of that connection it will have being. Now for a connection what is required is that which is connected, that to which the former is connected and that in which there is a connection. Therefore for the privation of a connection the same three things are required. We agree with this.

8   Hence the answer should be that for an exclusion which follows from the above-mentioned privation, four things are required, namely: [1] that which is excluded, [2] that from which the former is excluded, [3] that with respect to which it is excluded, and [4] the fourth is the act of excluding itself. For example, in 'Socrates alone is running' others than Socrates are excluded as from the subject and with respect to the running, and the act of excluding is brought about by the word 'alone' ('*solus*'). And these four causes are always required for an exclusion.

On certain rules

9   From what has been said above a certain rule is evident, *viz.* the following:

> *Whenever there really occurs an exclusion, it is always the case that that in respect of which the exclusion occurs, is asserted in that from which all other things are excluded.*

For example, in 'Only a man is something that can laugh', 'something that can laugh', in respect of which the exclusion occurs, is asserted in 'man', from which all other things are excluded. Thus it follows 'Only man is something that can laugh; therefore man is something that can laugh' and 'Only a man is running; therefore a man is running'.

10   From what has been said another rule is evident, *viz.* the following:

omnis exclusiva vera relinquit suam preiacentem veram.

Ut patet[2] in predictis exemplis, ut 'solus Sortes currit; ergo Sortes currit'. Propositio autem exclusiva est illa[3] in qua ponitur dictio exclusiva (ut[4] 'tantum', 'solus'), ut 'solus Sortes[5] currit' vel 'tantum homo currit'; preiacens autem[6] dicitur ipsa propositio remota dictione [*N49rb*] exclusiva, ut 'Sortes currit' vel 'homo currit'.

Sophisma

11 Secundum[1] predicta queritur de hoc sophismate TANTUM UNUM EST. Probatio. Unum est et nichil est quod non sit unum. Ergo tantum unum est. Contra. Multa sunt. Non[2] ergo tantum unum est. Item probatio prime, quia: Ut dicit[3] Boetius, unumquodque simulac[4] est, unum[5] est. Ergo tantum unum est. Item ad idem. Dicit[6] Boetius: unumquodque ideo est quia[7] unum numero est. Sed unum[8] numero est unum. Ergo unumquodque[9] est[10] unum. Ergo tantum unum est. Idem[11] patet per[12] regulam quandam. Que talis est:

> *quotienscumque unum convertibilium[13] predicatur de altero: si dictio exclusiva vere[14] adiungatur uni, et reliquo.*

Ut 'tantum homo currit; ergo tantum risibile currit'[15], et econverso. Sed 'unum' convertitur cum ente. Ergo si dictio exclusiva vere adiungatur[16] enti[17], et uni. Sed hec est vera 'tantum unum est'[18]. Ergo hec est vera 'tantum unum est'.

12 Solutio. Prima duplex, quia hoc nomen 'unum' est equivocum, eoquod est quedam unitas que est essentialis, ut illa per quam res existit in esse speciali sive in[1] esse specifico. Et hec unitas est per formam completivam dantem esse rei[2] in separando et distinguendo[3] ipsam rem ab omnibus aliis in sua[4] specie, ut Sortes non solum est in specie hominis per suam formam completivam sed

Every true exclusive proposition leaves the truth of the basic proposition intact,

as is evident in the examples mentioned above, *e.g.* 'Only Socrates is running; therefore Socrates is running'. The exclusive proposition is the one in which the exclusive word is used (like 'only', 'alone'), *e.g.* 'Only Socrates is running' or 'Only a man is running'. 'Basic proposition' is the name of the proposition itself as soon as the exclusive word has been removed, *e.g.* 'Socrates is running' or 'A man is running'.

Sophisma

11 As regards what has been said, there is a problem concerning the sophisma-sentence ONLY ONE IS. Proof: one is and there is nothing that is not one. Therefore only one is. There is an argument to the contrary. Many things are. Therefore not only one is. Again, there is a proof of the original sentence. As Boethius says,[2] as soon as everything is, it is one. Therefore only one is. Moreover, there is an argument that yields the same conclusion. Boethius says:[3] everything is therefore because it is numerically one. Now whatever is numerically one is one. Therefore everything is one. Therefore only one is. The same is evident from a certain rule, *viz.* the following:

> *Whenever one of two convertibles is said of the other: if an exclusive word can be truly adjoined to the one, it can also be truly adjoined to the other.*

For example, 'Only a man is running; therefore only something that can laugh is running', and conversely. Now 'one' is convertible with 'being'. Therefore if an exclusive word can be truly adjoined to 'one', it can also be truly adjoined to 'being', and conversely. Now 'Only being is' is true. Therefore the proposition 'Only one is' is true.

12 Solution. The original sentence is ambiguous, because the noun 'one' is equivocal, in that in one sense it concerns a unity which is essential, *viz.* the one in virtue of which a thing exists in special or specific being. And this unity is in virtue of a consummative form that grants being to something in separating and distinguishing that thing from all others that belong to the same species. For example, Socrates not only belongs to the species *man* in virtue of

---

[2]   Cf. *Contra Eutychen* IV, 35.
[3]   Cf. *ibid.* 40.

etiam[5] per ipsam perficitur in suo esse proprio et[6] separatur et distinguitur ab omnibus [*P57rb*] aliis hominibus. Et hec est unitas essentialis. Alia autem est unitas accidentalis, que est principium numeri. Unde sicut numerus accidit rebus que numerantur, similiter et unitas per quam numerantur et que est principium numeri[7], accidit eis. Quicquid enim numeratur,[8] per hanc unitatem numeratur[8], quia numerus nichil aliud est nisi[9] aggregatio unitatum. Numerus enim est multitudo ex unitatibus[10] aggregata.

13   Et utraque istarum unitatum convertitur cum 'ente'. Sed differunt in hoc quod prima est essentialis (ut dictum est) et secunda accidentalis; et etiam[1] in hoc quod secunda est in prima ut[2] accidens in subiecto; unde secunda accidit prime. Et sicut[3] 'unitas' dicitur equivoce, similiter et unum. Dico ergo quod si [*N49va*] accipiatur unitas[4] essentialis[5] sive unum essentiale[6], sic prima est vera. Si autem accipiatur unitas[7] accidentalis sive unum accidentale, sic prima est falsa, quia dictio exclusiva[8] adiuncta parti numerali destruit suum[9] totum, ut 'tantum duo currunt; non ergo tria'; similiter[10] 'tantum unum est[11]; non ergo duo'[12] vel 'non ergo multa'.

14   Alii autem dicunt quod prima est duplex (hec[1] scilicet 'tantum unum est') eoquod potest fieri exclusio ratione suppositi (et[2] sic est vera); [*T30va*] vel potest[3] fieri exclusio ratione accidentis sive forme (et[4] sic est falsa). Et tunc sequitur[5] 'non ergo multa sunt'. Sed primam solutionem credo esse meliorem[6].

15   Ad probationem[1] dicendum quod procedit secundum[2] quod 'unum' dicit unitatem essentialem, quoniam[3] quicquid est, per suum completivum[4] est, quod dat ei esse. Ut[5] Sortes per suam formam completivam, que est anima ipsius, separatur et differt a[6] qualibet alia re; et dat ipsi unitatem essentialem. Et sic est de omnibus aliis. Ad improbationem autem[7] dicendum quod[8] accipit unitatem accidentalem que per sui aggregationem est principium numeri; et hoc modo tenet improbatio. Ad duo argumenta sequentia dicendum quod

his consummative form, but also in virtue of that form he receives his perfection in his own proper being and thus is separated and distinguished from all other men. And this unity is an essential one. The other unity, on the other hand, is an accidental one, and this is the principle of number. Thus just as number is an accident of things that are counted, in the same way also the unity by which they are counted and which is the principle of number is an accident of these things. For whatever is counted, is counted by this unity, because a number is nothing other than the sum of unities. For a number is a multitude collected from unities.[4]

13   Well, both these types of unity are convertible with 'being'. However, they are different in that the first type is essential (as has been said) and the second type is accidental, and also in that the second inheres in the first as an accident in a subject. Thus the second is an accident of the first. And just as 'unity' is said equivocally, in the same way so is 'one'. I therefore say that if the unity is taken as essential or 'one' is taken as essential, in this way the original sentence is true. If, on the other hand, the unity is taken as accidental or 'one' is taken as accidental, in this way the original sentence is false, because an exclusive word adjoined to a numerical part destroys its whole; *e.g.* 'Only two are running; therefore not three' and 'Only one; therefore not two' or 'therefore not many'.

14   However, others say that the original sentence (*viz.* 'Only one is') is ambiguous because the exclusion can occur with regard to the *suppositum* (and thus it is true), or the exclusion can occur with regard to an accident or form (and thus it is false). And then it follows 'Therefore there are not many things'. However, I believe the first solution is the better one.

15   As to the proof,[5] the answer should be that it proceeds according as 'one' names an essential unity, because whatever is is in virtue of what completes it, which grants it being. For example, in virtue of his own consummative form, namely his soul, Socrates is separated and differs from any other thing; and this form grants him an essential unity. And the same goes for all other things. As to the disproof,[6] however, the answer should be that it takes the unity as an accidental one, which, in virtue of its [*viz.* number] aggregative nature, is the principle of number; and in this way the disproof holds. As to the two arguments that follow,[7] the answer should be

---

4   Note that *unum* ('one') is not a number, but rather the principle of number.
5   Cf. above, cap. 11.
6   Cf. above, *ibid.*.
7   Cf. above, *ibid.*.

accipiunt 'unum'[9] <secundum> unitatem[10] essentialem, sicut et[11] probatio.

16 Ad ultimum dicendum quod bene sequitur 'tantum ens est[1]; ergo tantum unum est', accipiendo[2] 'unum'[3] secundum unitatem essentialem. Sed non sequitur 'tantum ens est; ergo tantum unum est', accipiendo <'unum' secundum> unitatem accidentalem (quamvis unitas accidentalis convertatur cum 'ente'), quia 'unum accidentale' dicit discretionem sive rem discretam, cum sit principium numeri; 'ens' vero dicit rem suam per modum substantie. Et ita peccat secundum figuram dictionis. Sicut hic: 'tantum homo currit; ergo tantum unus [*P57va*] homo currit'; hec[4] autem est falsa 'tantum unus homo currit'. Posito enim[5] quod omnes homines currant et nichil aliud currat, hec est vera 'tantum homo currit', hec autem est falsa 'tantum unus homo currit'[6]. Et est figura dictionis ibi[7] (sicut[8] dictum est), quia 'homo' dicit rem suam per modum substantie, sed 'unus' addit discretionem numeri circa[9] ipsum. Preterea est ibi *accidens*[10]. Quia cum esse conveniat uni et multis: quamvis dictio exclusiva vere adiungatur[11] 'enti' respectu esse (ut[12] 'tantum ens est'), non tamen potest vere[13] adiungi 'uni' dicenti discretionem numeralem[14]. Unde de[15] hoc uno non posunt dicere 'tantum unum est'[16], quia tunc [*N49vb*] excluderet duo et tria et sic de aliis, ascendendo[17] ut 'tantum unum[18]; non ergo duo neque tria'[19] et sic de aliis. Unde ens est ibi res subiecta et unum est accidens eius[20] et exclusio respectu[21] esse assignatur communiter[22] inesse utrique sive fieri ab utroque.

17 Ad illud[1] autem quod obicit per[2] regulam convertibilium, dicendum quod regula[3] debet intelligi remoto accidente, sicut et[4] omnes alie regule. Quamvis enim regula sit[5] sive maxima:

quicquid [6] *predicatur de diffinitione, et de diffinito,*

non tamen sequitur 'animal rationale mortale est diffinitio; ergo homo est diffinitio', quod[7] est propter *accidens*, quod impedit.

that they take 'one' as an accidental unity, in the same way the proof does.

16   As to the final argument,[8] the answer should be that 'Only being is; therefore only one is' is a good inference when taking 'one' as an essential unity. However, <in> 'Only a being is; therefore only one thing is', when taking 'one' as an accidental unity it does not follow (although an accidental unity is convertible with 'being'), because 'accidental one' names a discreteness or a discrete thing, because it is the principle of number, whereas 'being' names its thing in the manner of a substance. Thus the agument goes astray as a <fallacy of> figure of speech. It is the same as in 'Only a man is running; therefore only one man is running'; in fact, the proposition 'Only one man is running' is false. For supposing that all men are running and nothing else is running, the proposition 'Only a man is running' is true, whereas the proposition 'Only one man is running' is false. And this is a <fallacy of> figure of speech (as has been said), because 'man' names its thing in the manner of a substance, whereas 'one' adds a discreteness of number to it. Moreover, this argument contains a fallacy of accident. For although being comes to one and many, <it is nevertheless the case that> although an exclusive word is truly adjoined to 'what is' as regards being (*e.g.* in 'Only one is'), it cannot, however, truly be adjoined to 'one' that names a numerical discreteness. Therefore of this type of one we cannot say 'only one is', because in that case it would exclude two and three and so on, by going upwards, as in 'Only one, therefore not two nor three', and so on. Therefore being in this case is the thing that is the subject and one is its accident and the exclusion as regards being is assigned to commonly extend to both or to occur as an exclusion from both.

17   As to the argument to the contrary that employs the rule of convertibles,[9] the answer should be that this rule must be taken into account when the accident has been removed, just like all other rules. For although there is a rule or maxim:

Whatever is said of the definition is also said of the definitum,

nevertheless it does not follow 'Animal, rational, mortal is a definition; therefore man is a definition'; and this is due to the fallacy of accident which prevents <such an inference>.

---

8   Cf. above, *ibid.*.
9   Cf. above, *ibid.*.

Quot sint species exclusionis

18   Circa tertium queritur quot sint partes exclusionis[1]. Et solent
poni due[2], quia[3] ponitur duplex exclusio: una enim[4] generalis[5] et
altera specialis. Generalis[5] exclusio[6] ponitur communiter quando
excluditur diversum genere; specialis[7] vero quando excluditur diversum specie. Sed contra. 'Diversum' dicitur tripliciter: diversum
genere[8], diversum specie, diversum numero. Ergo si exclusio dicitur
generalis quia diversa[9] genere excluduntur[10] et specialis quia diversa specie excluduntur, ergo debet esse tertia[11] exclusio numeralis
eoquod diversa numero excluduntur. Ergo non solum erunt[12] due
species, sive due partes, exclusionis sed etiam erunt tres.
19   Et dicendum quod non sunt nisi due partes[1] exclusionis, scilicet generalis et specialis. Sed non dicitur exclusio generalis eoquod
diversa genere excludantur, sed quia excluduntur a subiecto aliquo
omnia que communicant cum[2] eo in aliquo genere, sive in aliquo
generali [*P57vb*] ad[3] omnia que sunt sicut[4] in ente. Unde[5] hoc modo
sensus huius 'solus Sortes currit' est talis: *Sortes currit et nichil* [*T30vb*]
aliud vel *nullum aliud ens*. Item. Specialis exclusio non dicitur eoquod
excludatur diversum specie sicut dicebatur, sed dicitur exclusio
specialis quando[6] ab aliquo subiecto excluduntur quecumque communicant cum eo in[7] aliqua specie, sive in aliquo speciali. Et hoc
modo sensus huius 'solus Sortes currit' est talis: *Sortes currit et nullus*
alius homo, ut excludantur alii particulares homines qui communicant cum Sorte in homine. Et similiter 'solus homo currit', idest
homo currit et nullum aliud animal, quia alia[8] animalia communicant
cum homine in animali. Et hec est specialis exclusio. Si[9] autem
[*N50ra*] sensus huius 'solus homo currit' fuerit talis: *homo currit et*
nichil aliud, tunc est exclusio generalis.
20   Ex predictis patet quod idem numero non potest excludi, vel ea
que communicant in eodem numero. Quia cum dicitur 'solus homo
currit', ista ponit quod homo currit, per regulam prius[1] datam, que
talis est:

How many are the kinds of exclusion

18 *Ad [3]:* As to the third item, there is a problem how many are the parts of exclusion. Now one usually posits two, because one posits a twofold exclusion: one is general and the other specific. The general exclusion is commonly posited when something generically diverse is excluded; the specific exclusion, on the other hand, is posited when something specifically diverse is excluded. There is an argument to the contrary. 'Diverse' is said in three ways: generically diverse, specifically diverse and numerically diverse. Therefore if an exclusion is called general because generically diverse things are excluded, and specific because specifically diverse things are excluded, thence as a third kind there must be a numerical exclusion because numerically things are excluded. Therefore there will not only be two kinds, or two parts, of exclusion but there will be even three.

19 The answer should be that there are only two parts of exclusion, namely general and specific. However, an exclusion is not called general because generically different things are excluded, but because from some subject all the things are excluded that have some 'genus', or something that is general in relation to all things that are, in common with the subject, namely *being*. Thus in this way the proposition 'Only Socrates is running' means *Socrates is running and nothing else* or *no other being.* Again, an exclusion is not called specific because something specifically diverse should be excluded, as was said, but it is called specific when from some subject whatever things that have some species, or some specific thing, in common with it are excluded. In this way the proposition 'Only Socrates is running' means *Socrates is running and no other man,* so that other particular men who have *man* in common with Socrates are excluded. The same goes for 'Only a man is running', that is, *a man is running and no other animal,* because other animals have *animal* in common with man. And this is a specific exclusion. If, however, the proposition 'Only a man is running' means *only a man is running and nothing else,* then it is a general exclusion.

20 From what has been said it is evident that what is numerically the same, or those things that have the the same number in common, cannot be excluded. For when one says 'A man alone is running', this implies that a man is running, on account of the rule previously presented,[10] which is the following:

---

[10] Cf. above, cap. 10.

omnis exclusiva vera relinquit² suam preiacentem veram³

Et si excluderetur idem numero cum homine, tunc⁴ excluderetur⁵ risibile vel animal rationale mortale. Et⁶ sic esset sensus *solus homo currit et nullum risibile* vel *nullum animal rationale mortale.* Sed⁷ secundum⁸ hoc ponitur contradictio et⁹ ob hoc non potest fieri¹⁰ exclusio numeralis.

21   Ex predictis patet quod¹, cum quecumque sunt diversa genere vel diversa specie vel diversa numero, communicent in aliquo genere², <vel in aliquo> generali³ ad⁴ omnia que⁵ sunt, ut in ente, aut in aliquo speciali sub ente, quod⁶ non possunt esse nisi due partes exclusionis, scilicet⁷ generalis exclusio⁸ et specialis.

De quibusdam regulis

22   De speciali exclusione solet dari talis regula:

quotienscumque fit specialis exclusio, non tenet argumentum ab inferiori ad superius cum dictione exclusiva neque a superiori ad inferius, neque a parte subiecti neque a parte predicati.

Ut 'solus Sortes currit; ergo solus homo currit'. Et similiter si fiat processus a parte predicati, ut¹ 'solus Sortes currit; ergo solus Sortes movetur', semper² est ibi fallacia consequentis. Et sic patet quod non tenet huiusmodi³ argumentatio, quia posito quod solus Sortes currat et quidam equus, tunc hec est vera⁴ 'solus Sortes currit', faciendo specialem exclusionem, quia sensus est *Sortes currit et nullus alius homo*; hec autem⁵ falsa 'solus homo currit'⁶, faciendo specialem exclusionem, quia sensus est *homo currit et nullum aliud animal,* quod falsum est, cum equus currat. Similiter a parte predicati, quia⁷ posito quod solus Sortes⁸ currat et Plato moveatur sed non currat, tunc hec est vera 'solus Sortes currit', hec autem falsa 'solus Sortes [*P58ra*] movetur'. Et sic patet quod nullum est argumentum⁹. Quod¹⁰ vero ibi sit *consequens* patet, quia premissa in¹¹ se claudit unam affirmativam et alteram negativam, ut 'solus Sortes currit', idest *Sortes currit et nullus*

Every true exclusive proposition leaves the truth of the basic proposition intact.

And if what is numerically identical with man were to be excluded, then what can laugh or a rational mortal animal would be excluded. In that case the meaning would be *man alone is running and nothing that can laugh* or *no rational mortal animal.* However, in that case it would entail a contradiction and therefore there can be no numerical exclusion.

21   From what has been said it is evident that since whatever things are generically, specifically or numerically diverse share in some 'genus' or in something general to all things that are, *viz.* in *being,* or in something specific under being,—<I repeat> that there can be only two parts of exclusion, *viz.* a general and a specific one.

On certain rules

22   As regards the specific exclusion, one usually presents a rule of the following kind:

> *Whenever a specific exclusion occurs, an argument from what is less general to what is more general in combination with an exclusive word does not obtain nor does an argument from what is more general to what is less general, neither by proceeding from what is in subject-position nor from what is in predicate-position.*

For example, 'Only Socrates is running; therefore only a man is running'. And likewise if the inference proceeds from what is in predicate-position, *e.g.* 'Only Socrates is running; therefore only Socrates is moving', there is always question of a fallacy of the consequent. Thus it is evident that an argument of this type does not obtain, because supposing that only Socrates is running and some horse is too, then the proposition 'Only Socrates is running' is true, if it carries out a specific exclusion, because it means *only Socrates is running and no other man.* On the other hand, the proposition 'Only a man is running' is false, if it carries out a specific exclusion, because it means *only a man is running and no other animal,* which is false, because a horse is running. The same applies if it proceeds from what is in predicate-position, because supposing that only Socrates is running and Plato is moving but not running, then the the proposition 'Only Socrates is running' is true, whereas the proposition 'Only Socrates is moving' is false. And so it is evident that the argument is not valid. That there is question of a fallacy of the consequent is evident: the premise includes one affirmative and one negative proposition, *viz.* 'Only Socrates is running', that is, *Socrates is running and no other man,* and 'Only a man is running', that is, *a*

alius homo et 'solus homo currit', idest *homo currit et nullum*[12] *aliud animal.* Et propter negativas[13] non tenet ab inferiori ad superius, sed est ibi[14] *consequens* ab inferiori ad superius negando. Et[15] propter affirmativas non tenet a superiori ad inferius.

23 De generali[1] exclusione [*N50rb*] talis datur[2] regula:

> *quotienscumque fit generalis exclusio, bene tenet argumentum ab inferiori ad superius cum dictione exclusiva a parte subiecti et non a parte predicati.*

Ut 'solus Sortes currit; ergo solus homo currit', quia prima claudit intra se istas duas[3] 'Sortes currit' et 'nichil aliud a Sorte currit', et propositio illata claudit intra se istas duas[4] 'homo currit' et 'nichil aliud ab homine currit'. Sed[5] ratione affirmativarum[6] bene sequitur[7] 'Sortes currit; ergo homo currit'. Et ratione negativarum[8] bene [*T31ra*] sequitur 'nichil aliud a Sorte currit; ergo[9] nichil aliud ab homine currit'. Ergo bene sequitur a parte subiecti faciendo generalem exclusionem, ut 'solus Sortes currit; ergo solus homo currit'.

Que sint ea que debent excludi

24 Circa[1] dictiones exclusivas querebatur <quarto>, descendendo[2] ad unam de quatuor causis exclusionis, scilicet ad illud quod excluditur[3]. Et[4] queritur[5] quid sit illud quod excluditur[6]. Et illa[7] questio continet[8] sub se alias septem. Prima[9] est utrum[10] dictio exclusiva addita 'enti'[11] possit excludere aliquid. Ut 'tantum ens est[12]; ergo nichil aliud est'. Et[13] similiter si adiungatur aliis terminis qui convertuntur cum 'ente', ut sunt isti[14] 'aliquid'[15], 'unum', 'res'. Secunda questio est magis descendendo, scilicet utrum[16] dictio exclusiva adiuncta uni[17] generalissimo excludat alia[18] et econverso, ut 'tantum substantia; non ergo quantitas'[19] vel econverso. Tertia questio est specialior omnibus[20] predictis, scilicet utrum dictio exclusiva addita speciei unius predicamenti possit excludere species alterius predicamenti,

man is running and no other animal. Well, on account of the negative propositions an argument from something less general to something more general does not hold good, but we have in this case a fallacy of the consequent from something less general to something more general. Again, on account of the affirmative propositions an argument from something general to something less general does not hold good.

23 As regards the general exclusion, the following rule is presented:

> *Whenever a general exclusion occurs, an argument from what is less general to what is more general in combination with an exclusive word obtains when proceeding from what is in subject-position and not from what is in predicate position.*

For example, 'Only Socrates is running; therefore only a man is running', because the first proposition includes the two propositions 'Socrates is running' and 'Nothing other than Socrates is running', and the inferred proposition includes the two propositions 'A man is running' and 'Nothing other than a man is running'. Now on account of the affirmative propositions it follows 'Socrates is running; therefore a man is running'. And on account of the negative propositions it follows 'Nothing other than Socrates is running; therefore nothing other than a man is running'. Therefore it follows when proceeding from what is in subject-position when one carries out a general exclusion, as in 'Only Socrates is running; therefore only a man is running'.

What the things are that are to be excluded

24 <*Ad [4]*>: Concerning exclusive words there was a fourth problem, by descending to one of the four causes of exclusion, namely to that which is excluded. The problem is what it is that is excluded. This problem contains under it seven other ones. *[4.1]* The first is whether an exclusive word added to 'being' can exclude anything. For example, 'Only being is; therefore nothing else is'. And the same problem comes up if it is adjoined to other words convertible with 'being', such as 'something', 'one' and 'thing'. *[4.2]* The second problem comes up when descending to a lower level, namely whether an exclusive word adjoined to one highest genus excludes another one and the other way round, *e.g.* 'Only a substance; therefore not a quantity', or the other way round. *[4.3]* The third problem is more specific than the ones just mentioned, namely whether an exclusive word added to a species of one category can

ut 'tantum homo; non ergo color vel albedo'[21]. Quarta[22] questio est
utrum dictio exclusiva addita alicui[23] speciei unius predicamenti
possit excludere alias[24] species eiusdem predicamenti, [*P58rb*] ut
'tantum homo; non ergo equus', 'tantum color; non ergo scientia', et
sic in unoquoque predicamento[25]. Et hec specialior est omnibus[26]
predictis. Et istas quatuor questiones intelligo in terminis substantialibus[27] dicentibus *quid*, sive[28] que predicantur *in quid*, sicut species[29] et
genera uniuscuiusque predicamenti[30]. Quinta questio est utrum dictio exclusiva addita termino[31] accidentali excludat alios[32] terminos
accidentales, ut 'tantum coloratum; non ergo sonorum'[33]. Sexta questio est utrum dictio exclusiva addita uni oppositorum excludat alterum[34] in quolibet genere oppositionis, ut[35] 'tantum album; [*N50va*]
non ergo nigrum' et 'tantum videns; non ergo cecum'[36] et sic de
aliis. Septima questio est utrum dictio exclusiva addita parti[37] excludat totum (vel econverso) et[38] utrum addita maiori[39] numero excludat minorem (vel[40] econverso), ut 'tantum paries; non ergo domus'
et[41] 'tantum tria[42]; non ergo duo'.

Utrum dictio exclusiva addita 'enti' possit excludere aliquid

25   Circa primum[1] obicitur quod dictio exclusiva addita 'enti'[2] vel
suis convertibilibus nichil potest excludere, quia quod excluditur,
debet communicare[3] cum eo a[4] quo fit[5] exclusio in aliquo generali
vel in[6] aliquo speciali. Sed nichil potest communicare[7] cum ente in
aliquo[8] generali sive[9] speciali supra ens duplici de causa, scilicet[10]
vel quia nichil est aliud ab ente vel quia nichil aliud est supra ens.
Ergo nichil potest excludi[11] ab ente. Ergo dictio exclusiva adiuncta
'enti' nichil potest excludere. Item[12] ad idem. Dictio exclusiva non[13]
potest excludere nisi quod est extra terminum cui adiungitur, ut
'tantum homo; non ergo asinus', quia asinus extra hominem est. Sed
nichil[14] est extra ens. Ergo dictio exclusiva adiuncta 'enti' nichil
potest excludere.
26   Item ad idem. Nichil potest[1] excludi nisi quod[2] est diversum
quoad[3] naturalem suppositionem (ut 'tantum homo; non ergo asinus') vel diversum quoad quandam suppositionem[4] accidentalem ut

exclude a species of another category, *e.g.* 'Only man; therefore not colour or whiteness'. *[4.4]* The fourth problem is whether an exclusive word added to a species of one category can exclude other species of the same category, *e.g.* 'Only a man; therefore not a horse', 'Only a colour; therefore not knowledge', and so on in every category. This is a more specific problem than all other ones mentioned. And I understand these four problems when substantial terms are involved that name something as an essence or that are predicated *in quid*, as there are species and genera of every category. *[4.5]* The fifth problem is whether an exclusive word added to an accidental term excludes other accidental terms, *e.g.* 'Only coloured; therefore not sonorous'. *[4.6]* The sixth problem is whether an exclusive word added to one opposite excludes the other in any kind of opposition whatsoever, *e.g.* 'Only white; therefore not black', and 'Only seeing; therefore not blind', an so on. *[4.7]* The seventh problem is whether an exclusive word added to a part excludes a whole (or the other way round) and whether when added to a larger number it excludes a smaller one (or the other way round) *e.g.* 'Only the wall; therefore not the house' and 'Only three; therefore not two'.

Whether an exclusive word added to 'being' can exclude anything

25 *Ad [4.1]:* As to the first sub-item, there is an argument to the contrary that an exclusive word added to 'being' or words that are convertible with it cannot exclude anything, because what it excludes must have some general or specific thing in common with that from which it is excluded. Now nothing can have with being in common some general or specific thing more general than being, for two reasons, namely because there is nothing other than being, or because there is nothing else more general than being. Therefore nothing can be excluded from being. Therefore an exclusive word adjoined to 'being' cannot exclude anything. Again, there is an argument that yields the same conclusion. An exclusive word can only exclude that which falls outside the term to which it is adjoined, *e.g.* 'Only a man; therefore not an ass', because *ass* falls outside *man*. Now nothing falls outside *being*. Therefore an exclusive word adjoined to 'being' cannot exclude anything.

26 Furthermore, there is an argument that yields the same conclusion. Nothing can be exluded except what is diverse as regards its natural supposition (*e.g.* 'Only a man; therefore not an ass'), or what is diverse as regards some accidental supposition like the supposition

quoad eam que fit per aliquid restringens terminum ex eadem parte
(ut 'tantum homo[5] albus; non ergo niger'). Ex hoc patet quod ab
aliquo termino non restricto per aliquid[6] ex eadem parte sed simpliciter sumpto[7] nichil[8] potest excludi nisi quoad naturalem suppositionem[9]. Sed ab ente simpliciter sumpto [*T31rb*] nichil est diversum quoad naturalem suppositionem. Ergo ab ente simpliciter sumpto et[10] predicta restrictione non restricto sive non cohartato nichil
potest excludi[11]. Ergo dictio exclusiva addita 'enti' nichil potest excludere. Item[12]. Quicquid est ens, est, et quicquid[13] est, est ens. Ergo
convertibilia [*P58va*] sunt 'ens' et 'esse'. Sed nichil est dictu[14] 'tantum est' nec[15] aliquid excluditur. Ergo nichil est dictu[16] 'tantum ens'
neque aliquid excluditur.

27   Solutio. Dictio exclusiva adiuncta 'enti' excludit aliquid, quia
excludit omnia alia quoad naturalem suppositionem eorum que sunt
diversa ab ente et a naturali suppositione eorum que convertuntur
cum ente, quia naturalis suppositio non solum est de [*N50vb*] ente
sed etiam de non-ente. Naturaliter enim supponuntur per terminum
tam entia quam non-entia. Unde exclusio non solum est de ente sed
etiam de non-ente. Unde sequitur 'tantum ens est; ergo nichil aliud
ab ente est'.

28   Ad illud quod[1] primo obicit dicendum quod convertit consequentiam. Unde peccat secundum consequens, quia quicquid com-
municat in aliquo generali vel in aliquo speciali cum eo a quo fit exclusio, debet excludi, et non econverso. Non enim oportet quod illud
quod excluditur, sive quicquid excluditur, communicet cum eo a quo
fit exclusio in aliquo generali vel in aliquo speciali. Quare[2] convertit
consequentiam. Sicut hic[3]: 'quicquid est homo, est animal'; et non
oportet[4] quod quicquid est[5] animal quod[6] sit homo. Sicut[7] enim
animal[8] in pluribus est[9] quam homo, sic excludi[10] in pluribus est[11]
quam in[12] communicantibus in speciali vel in generali cum eo a
quo fit exclusio, quia est in istis et in[13] non-communicantibus. Unde
non oportet quod si aliquid excludatur ab ente quod communicet

that occurs by means of some restrictive term in the same <syntactic> position (*e.g.* 'Only a white man; therefore not a black one'). From this it is evident that from some term not restricted by something in the same <syntactic> position but rather taken absolutely, only something can be excluded as regards its natural supposition. Now from being taken absolutely nothing is diverse as regards its natural supposition. Therefore from being taken absolutely and not restricted or limited by the restriction just mentioned nothing can be excluded. Therefore an exclusive word added to 'being' cannot exclude anything. Moreover, whatever is a being, is, and whatever is, is a being. Therefore 'being' and 'to be' are convertible. Now it makes no sense to say 'It only is' nor is something excluded. Therefore it makes no sense to say 'Only being' nor is anything excluded.

27 Solution. An exclusive word adjoined to 'being' excludes something, because it excludes all other things as regards the natural supposition of the ones that are diverse from being and from the natural supposition of the things that are convertible with being, because natural supposition not only concerns being, but non-being as well. For a term naturally supposits both for beings and non-beings. Hence exclusion not only concerns being but non-being as well. Hence it follows 'Only being is; therefore nothing other than being is'.

28 As to the first argument to the contrary,[11] the answer should be that it converts the inference. Therefore it commits the fallacy of the consequent, because whatever has something general or specific in common with that from which the exclusion occurs, must be excluded, and not the other way round. For it is not necessary that that which is excluded, or whatever is excluded, have something general or something specific in common with that from which the exclusion occurs. That is why the argument converts the inference, in the same way as in 'Whatever is a man, is an animal'; and it is not necessary that whatever is an animal be a man. For just as *animal* is found in more things than *man*, in the same way the excluding occurs in more things than what has something specific or something general in common with that from which the exclusion occurs, because the exclusion occurs in those things and in the things that do not have something in common <in that way>. Hence it is not necessary that if something is excluded from being, it have with it

---

[11] Cf. above, cap. 25.

cum eo in aliquo generali vel speciali[14]. Quare[15] convertit consequentiam.

29 Ad secundum dicendum[1] quod hec est duplex 'dictio exclusiva non[2] potest excludere nisi quod est extra terminum'[3], quia 'esse extra terminum' multiplex[4] est, quia[5] vel quoad essentiam (sicut alia est essentia equi[6] et alia hominis)[7] vel quoad naturalem suppositionem (sicut equus non continetur[8] in naturali suppositione hominis nec econverso). Unde dico quod quando fit exclusio generalis, excluduntur ea que sunt extra terminum quoad naturalem suppositionem tam entium[9] quam non-entium. Sed quando fit specialis exclusio, excluduntur ea que sunt extra terminum quoad naturalem suppositionem entium communicantium cum illo a quo fit exclusio in aliquo speciali. Unde licet aliquando excludantur ea que sunt extra terminum quoad [*P58vb*] essentias[10] (ut 'tantum homo; non[11] ergo asinus'), tamen non excluduntur inquantum sunt extra terminum quoad[12] naturales[13] essentias sed inquantum sunt extra terminum quoad naturalem suppositionem. Unde dico[14] quod, licet quoad essentias nichil sit extra ens, quia[15] essentia[16] solum est entium, tamen quoad naturalem suppositionem aliquid est[17] extra ens. Et sic dictio exclusiva adiuncta 'enti' aliquid potest excludere.

30 Ad tertium. Solvendum[1] per interemptionem, quia 'aliquid' est [*N51ra*] extra naturalem suppositionem entis, quia (ut dictum est) non solum supponuntur entia sed etiam non-entia per terminum. Ad ultimum autem dicendum quod non potest fieri exclusio ab hoc actu 'esse', quia iste actus 'esse' comprehendit[2] sub se omnem[3] alium actum, sicut consequens comprehendit sub se quodlibet suum antecedens. Et ideo[4] nullus [*T31va*] alius actus potest excludi ab hoc actu 'esse'. Sed quia 'ens' non[5] comprehendit sub se omne aliud suppositum[6] sed solum supposita sua[7] et suarum partium (quia[8] supposita non-entium impossibilium esse non comprehendit sub se, ut vacui et infiniti et aliorum non-entium), ideo[9] possunt[10] excludi ab ente, cum exclusio fiat ab eo quoad naturalem suppositionem. Quod autem iste actus esse comprehendat sub se omnem alium actum non

[*i.e.* being] something general or specific in common. And that is why it [*i.e.* the argument to the contrary] converts the inference.

29 As to the second argument,[12] the answer should be that the following is ambiguous: 'An exclusive word can only exclude that which falls outside the term', because 'to fall outside the term' has more than one meaning: either it concerns the essence (just as the essence of a horse is one thing and the essence of a man another) or it concerns the natural supposition (just as 'horse' is not included in the natural supposition of 'man' nor the other way round). Hence I say that whenever there is a general exclusion, what is excluded are the things that fall outside a term as regards the natural supposition of both beings and non-beings. However, when a specific exclusion occurs, what is excluded are the things that fall outside the term as regards the natural supposition of beings that have something specific in common with that from which the exclusion occurs. Hence although sometimes the things that fall outside a term as regards essences (*e.g.* 'Only a man; therefore not an ass') are excluded, nevertheless they are not excluded insofar as they fall outside the term as regards <their> natural essences but insofar as they fall outside the term as regards <their> natural supposition. Hence I say that, although as regards essences nothing falls outside being, because essence only belongs to beings, nevertheless as regards natural supposition, something does fall outside being. And in this way an exclusive word adjoined to 'being' can exclude something.

30 As to the third argument,[13] this should be solved by getting rid of it altogether: 'something' falls outside the natural supposition of being, because (as has been said)[14] terms not only supposit for beings, but for non-beings as well. As to the final argument, the answer should be that an exclusion cannot occur from the act 'to be', because the act 'to be' contains under it every other act, just as a consequent contains under it any of its antecedents. Therefore no other act can be excluded from the act 'to be'. However, since 'being' does not contain under it every other *suppositum*, but only its own *supposita* and the ones that belong to its parts (because it does not contain under it the *supposita* of non-beings that cannot possibly be, such as a void, an infinite and other non-beings), therefore they [*i.e.* the *supposita*] can be excluded from being, because the exclusion occurs from it as regards <their> natural supposition. That, however, the act of being contains under it every other act not as regards its

---

[12] Cf. above, *ibid.*.
[13] Cf. above, cap. 26.
[14] Cf. above, cap. 27.

quoad[11] suppositionem sive predicationem sed (ut ita[12] dicam) quoad
antecessionem patet, quia omnes alii actus antecedunt ad istum, ut
'si[13] currit, est'[14] et 'si cogitat, est' et 'si dormit, est'[15].

Utrum dictio exclusiva adiuncta uni generalissimo excludat alterum

31   Circa secundum[1] sic[2] obicitur. Cum dictio exclusiva excludat
diversum[3] quoad naturalem suppositionem[4] et unum generalissimum non sit de suppositione alterius nec econverso (et[5] sic sunt
diversa quoad naturalem suppositionem), ergo[6] dictio exclusiva adiuncta uni generalissimo excludit alterum et econverso. Item ad
idem. Dictio exclusiva excludit ea que sunt diversa[7] a subiecto, sive
excludit diversa subiecta, ut 'tantum gramatica; non ergo musica'.
Sed diversa generalissima[8] non possunt esse subiectum unum,
immo sunt semper[9] subiecta diversa. Ergo dictio exclusiva adiuncta
uni generalissimo excludit alterum et econverso.
32   Sed contra. Dictio exclusiva non potest excludere quod[1] intelligitur in[2] subiecto cui adiungitur, ut 'tantum album currit[3]; non
ergo corpus currit'[4] vel 'tantum gramaticus disputat; non ergo homo
disputat', quia 'album' dat intelligere corpus et 'gramaticum'[5] dat
intelligere hominem. Sed [*P59ra*] quantitas dat[6] intelligere substantiam. Ergo dictio exclusiva adiuncta quantitati non excludit[7] substantiam. Ergo[8] adiuncta uni generalissimo non excludit alterum. Item
ad idem. Omnis[9] exclusiva[10] ponit suam preiacentem[11]. Et ideo[12]
sequitur 'si tantum quantitas est, quantitas est'. Et si quantitas est,
substantia est, quia alia[13] a substantia non sunt nisi in substantia.
Ergo posita quantitate, vel quolibet alio generalissimo, necesse est[14]
ponere substantiam. Ergo a primo: si tantum quantitas est, substantia
est; et sic de aliis generalissimis. Ergo dictio exclusiva adiuncta uni[15]
non excludit alterum.
33   Et dicendum quod dictio exclusiva adiuncta uni generalissimo
excludit alterum uno modo et alio modo non, ex eo quod generalissima alia a substantia duas habent comparationes. Unam secundum

supposition or predication, but as regards (so to speak) what comes first, is evident: all other acts are antecedent to it, *e.g.* 'If he is running, he is', 'If he is thinking, he is', 'If he is sleeping, he is'.

Whether an exclusive word adjoined to one highest genus excludes another

31 *Ad [4.2]:* As to the second sub-item, there is the following argument to the contrary. It is because an exclusive word excludes something diverse as regards natural supposition and one highest genus does not belong to the supposition of another nor the other way round (and thus they are diverse as regards their natural supposition), that therefore an exclusive word adjoined to one highest genus excludes another, and the other way round. Again, there is an argument that yields the same conclusion. An exclusive word excludes the things that are diverse from the subject, or it excludes diverse subjects, *e.g.* 'Only grammar; therefore not music'. Now diverse highest genera cannot form one subject, for they are always diverse subjects. Therefore an exclusive word adjoined to one highest genus excludes the other and the other way round.

32 However, there is an argument to the contrary.[15] An exclusive word cannot exclude what is understood in the subject to which it is adjoined, *e.g.* 'Only a white thing is running; therefore not a body is running' or 'Only a grammarian is arguing; therefore not a man is arguing', because 'white <thing>' gives to understand a body and 'grammarian' gives to understand a man. Now quantity gives to understand a substance. Therefore an exclusive word adjoined to a quantity does not exclude a substance. Hence adjoined to one highest genus it does not exclude another. Again, there is an argument that yields the same conclusion. Every true exclusive proposition asserts its basic proposition, and so it follows: 'If only quantity is, quantity is'. And if a quantity is, a substance is, because there are no things other than substance except in a substance. Therefore if quantity, or whatever other highest genus, is posited, it is necessary to posit substance. Therefore, taking it from the beginning, if only quantity is, substance is, and the same goes for the other highest genera. Therefore an exclusive word adjoined to one highest genus does not exclude another.

33 The answer should be that an exclusive word adjoined to one highest genus does exclude another one in one way, and does not in another way, in virtue of the fact that all highest genera other

---

15 That is, contrary to what has been argued in cap. 31 above.

abstractionem prout unumquodque ordinatur secundum lineam predicamentalem in sua ordinatione[1] ad omnes species eius sive ad omnia individua sub ipso existentia. Et hoc modo potest fieri in quolibet[2] predicamento talis figura sicut illa que[3] est in Substantia, que[4] dicitur Arbor Porphirii. Aliam autem habent[5] comparationem[6] secundum concretionem ad subiecta[7] in quibus sunt; et sic sumuntur omnia per modum accidentis. Sed secundum comparationem primam sumuntur per modum essentie[8] sive[9] per modum eius quod[10] est *quid.*

34   Unde secundum primam comparationem dictio exclusiva adiuncta uni generalissimo[1] excludit alia generalissima et econverso; nisi quando faciunt subiectum unum, quod in paucis accidit, ut 'tantum substantia est colorata'; hic non excluditur superficies, quia[2] superficies et substantia faciunt subiectum unum coloris. Unde nisi diversa [*T31vb*] predicamenta faciant[3] subiectum unum, semper dictio exclusiva adiuncta uni excludit alterum secundum hanc comparationem. Sed[4] secundum comparationem quam habent secundum concretionem ad[5] subiectum, sic dictio exclusiva adiuncta uni[6] non excludit alterum[7]. Unde[8] cum dicitur 'tantum agens currit', non sequitur[9] 'gramaticum non currit' vel 'musicum'[10] vel 'bicubitum' vel tricubitum' vel[11] 'homo', quia[12] Sortes et[13] est homo et est bicubitus (vel tricubitus) et[14] gramaticus (vel musicus) et est etiam agens. Unde[15] dicendum breviter quod si sumantur[16] in concretione, dictio exclusiva adiuncta uni[17] non excludit alterum. Sed si sumantur[18] in abstractione, tunc dictio exclusiva adiuncta uni[19] excludit alterum, [*P59rb*] nisi faciant [*N51va*] subiectum unum[20].

35   Ad[1] duo prima argumenta dicendum[2] quod bene tenent, secundum[3] quod generalissima sumantur in abstractione et non faciant subiectum unum. Ad tertium argumentum dicendum quod unum intelligitur in altero multipliciter. Quia uno modo unum intelligitur in altero essentialiter (ut animal in homine) et[4] tale exclusio non excludit. Unde non sequitur 'tantum homo currit; non ergo animal currit'. Alio[5] modo intelligitur unum in altero per dependentiam accidentis ad subiectum. Unde in omni accidente intelligitur subiectum. Et hoc dupliciter. Quia accidens concretum[6]

than substance have two relationships. One relationship they have is a relationship of abstraction, to the extent that each one is ordered to all its species or to all individuals that exist under it in a categorial line. In this way it can happen that in every category there resides the type of figure like the one we find in Substance, a figure called the Porphyrian Tree. On the other hand, they stand in another relation, one of concreteness, to the subjects in which they inhere. In this way they [*i.e.* the highest genera] are all taken in the manner of an accident, whereas according to the first relationship, they are taken in the manner of an essence or in the manner of that which is the 'what'.

34   Hence according to the first relationship an exclusive word adjoined to one highest excludes the other ones and the other way round, unless when they form one subject, something that can happen in few cases, *e.g.* 'Only substance is coloured'. In this case surface is not excluded because surface and substance form one subject-substrate of colour. Thus unless diverse categories form one subject, an exclusive word adjoined to one always excludes another according to this relationship. On the other hand, according to the relationship of concreteness the categories have to a subject, in that way an exclusive word adjoined to one does not exclude another. Thus, when one says 'Only an agent is running', for example, it does not follow 'A grammarian is not running' or 'a musician' or 'something bicubital' or 'something tricubital' or 'a man', because Socrates is both a man and something bicubital (or tricubital) or a grammarian or a musician, and he is also an agent. Hence briefly the answer should be that if the categories are taken *in concreto*, an exclusive word adjoined to one does not exclude another, but if they are taken *in abstracto*, then an exclusive word adjoined to one does exclude another, unless they form one subject.

35   As to the first two arguments,[16] the answer should be that they hold good insofar as the categories are taken *in abstracto* and do not form one subject. As to the third argument,[17] the answer should be that one highest genus is understood in another in a number of ways. [1] In one way one is understood in another essentially (*e.g. animal* in *man*), and something of this kind an exclusion does not exclude. Hence it does not follow 'Only a man is running; therefore not an animal is running'. [2] In another way one is understood in another in the manner of a relationship of dependence an accident has to a subject. Thus in every accident a subject is understood. And

---

[16]   Cf. above, cap. 31.
[17]   Cf. above, cap 32.

dat intelligere subiectum (ut 'album'[7] dat intelligere corpus) et etiam accidens in abstractione dat intelligere subiectum; color enim non potest esse nisi in corpore[8]. Unde sive[9] accipiam[10] colorem in concretione (et sic proprie dicitur 'coloratum') sive in abstractione, semper per ipsum intelligitur corpus. Et similiter[11] est de aliis novem predicamentis, quia, sive intelligantur[12] abstracta (ut 'quantitas', 'qualitas' et[13] sic de aliis) sive[14] concreta[15] (ut 'quantum', 'quale' et sic de aliis) semper dant[16] intelligere substantiam. Dico ergo quod illud quod intelligitur in accidente concreto[17], non excluditur. Unde[18] non sequitur 'tantum album currit; non ergo corpus' et 'tantum homo currit; non ergo animal'. Sed subiectum quod intelligitur in accidente abstracto, bene excluditur per dictionem exclusivam. Unde 'tantum quantitas est[19]; non ergo substantia'. Et hoc dicendo[20]: nisi illa duo abstracta faciant subiectum unum alicuius[21] accidentis (ut dictum est prius), sicut homo et superficies eius faciunt subiectum unum albedinis vel[22] coloris.

36   Ad quartum dicimus[1] quod revera omnis[2] exclusiva[3] ponit suam preiacentem[4]. Sed in hac propositione 'tantum quantitas est' duo sunt, scilicet hec dictio 'tantum', que est dictio exclusiva, et[5] illud cui adiungitur, scilicet 'quantitas'. Dico ergo quod dictio exclusiva excludit substantiam, sed quantitas ponit ipsam[6]. Et ideo hec[7] propositio 'tantum quantitas est'[8] ponit contradictionem, quia ponit substantiam[9] esse et non esse. Ponit enim substantiam ratione quantitatis et removet eam ratione exclusionis que additur 'quantitati'.

Utrum dictio exclusiva addita speciei unius predicamenti possit excludere
species alterius predicamenti

37   Circa tertium sic obicitur. Cum dicitur 'tantum homo est albus', ex hoc non sequitur 'ergo superficies hominis non est alba'. Ergo dictio exclusiva addita[1] speciei [*N52vb*] unius predicamenti gratia[2] huius non excludit species alterius predicamenti. Sed contra. Magis differunt ea que sunt in diversis generibus[3] quam ea que sunt in eodem genere sive quam[4] ea que sunt sub eadem specie, quia pluribus differentiis differunt. [*P59va*] Sed dictio exclusiva adiuncta

this happens in two ways: a concrete accident gives to understand a subject (*e.g.* 'white' gives to understand a body) and also an accident *in abstracto* gives to understand a subject; for colour can only be in a body. Thus whether I take colour *in concreto* (and in that way 'coloured' is properly said) or I take it *in abstracto,* it always gives to understand a body. The same goes for the other nine categories, because, whether they are understood as abstract (like 'quality', 'quantity' and so on) or as concrete (like 'a quantity', 'a quality' and so on) they always give to understand a substance. Hence I say that that which is understood in a concrete accident is not excluded. Hence it does not follow 'Only a white thing is running; therefore not a body' and 'Only a man is running; therefore not an animal'. However, the subject understood in an abstract accident, can well be excluded by an exclusive word. Thus it follows 'Only quantity is; therefore not substance', and this is the case by saying, '. . . unless these two abstracts form one subject-substrate of some accident (as has been said before), just as man and his surface form one subject-substrate of whiteness or colour'.

36 As to the fourth argument,[18] we say that indeed every true exclusive proposition asserts its basic proposition, but in the proposition 'Only quantity is' there are two items, *viz.*: the word 'only', that is the exclusive word, and that to which it is adjoined, *viz.* 'quantity'. Well, I say that the exclusive word excludes substance, whereas the quantity posits it. And so the proposition 'Only a quantity is' entails a contradiction because it entails that substance is and is not. For it posits a substance on account of quantity and removes it on account of the exclusion added to 'quantity'.

Whether an exclusive word added to a species belonging to one category can exclude the species belonging to another category

37 *Ad [4.3]:* As to the third sub-item, there is the following argument to the contrary. When one says 'Only a man is white', from this it does not follow 'Therefore the surface of a man is not white'. Therefore an exclusive word added to a species of one category does not in virtue of that exclude the species of another category. However, there is an argument to the contrary. The things that belong to diverse genera are more diverse than the ones that belong to one genus or the ones that fall under the same species, because they are different on account of more differences. Now an exclusive word

---

[18] Cf. above, *ibid.*

uni individuo excludit alia individua que sunt sub eadem specie, ut
'tantum Sortes; non ergo Plato'. Ergo multo[5] magis ea que sunt
diversorum generum, quia magis differunt. Ergo dictio exclusiva
adiuncta [*T32ra*] speciei unius predicamenti excludit alias species
alterius predicamenti.

38   Ad[1] quod dicendum quod in genere quinque sunt ea[2] que
debent excludi. Unum est[3] subiectum diversum, ut 'tantum 'Sortes
currit'; excluditur Plato et alii particulares homines, quia non possunt facere subiectum unum sed diversa[4]. Secundum est diversum
loco, ut 'tantum hic; non ergo ibi'[5]. Tertium est diversum tempore ut
'tantum in hoc tempore[6]; non ergo in illo'. Quartum est[7] oppositum[8]
a parte predicati, ut[9] 'tantum Sortes est albus; non ergo[10] niger nec
medio colore coloratus'. Quintum est actus diversus, sive accidens
diversum, similiter a parte predicati positum, dum ita[11] sit quod
unum non[12] insit per alterum. Et ideo sequitur 'Sortes[13] est tantum
gramaticus; non ergo est musicus', 'tantum[14] legit[15]; non ergo currit'. Et non sequitur 'tantum Sortes est coloratus; non ergo est quantus', quia[16] coloratum[17] inest Sorti per hoc quod est quantus. Neque[18]
sequitur 'tantum currit; non ergo movetur', eoquod unum inest[19] per
alterum sive intelligitur in[20] altero secundum concretionem. Et[21]
omnibus hiis quinque[22] modis excluditur diversum[23] per dictionem
exclusivam.[24]

39   Ex predictis[1] patet solutio primi argumenti, quia homo et
superficies eius faciunt subiectum unum coloris et non diversa[2].
Unde non excluditur superficies per hanc[3] 'tantum Sortes[4] est albus'.
Et ita[5] dictio exclusiva adiuncta speciei unius predicamenti[6] excludit
alias[7], dum non faciant subiectum unum vel[8] unum non insit per
alterum, ut dictum est. Patet etiam solutio alterius argumenti[9], quia
dictio exclusiva[10] excludit diversum [*N52ra*] sive differens aliquo[11]
predictorum modorum tentum.[12]

Utrum dictio exclusiva addita alicui speciei unius predicamenti excludat alias
species eiusdem

40   Ex predictis patet solutio quarte questionis, que erat utrum dictio
exclusiva adiuncta speciei unius predicamenti excludat[1] alias

adjoined to one individual excludes all individuals that fall under the same species, *e.g.* 'Only Socrates; therefore not Plato'. Therefore it excludes the things that belong to diverse genera all the more, because they are more different. Therefore an exclusive word adjoined to a species of one category excludes other species of another category.

38   To this argument the answer should be that generically speaking, there are five things that are to be excluded. [1] One is a diverse subject, *e.g.* <in> 'Only Socrates is running'; Plato and other particular men are excluded, because they cannot form one subject but diverse ones. [2] The second is something diverse *qua* location, *e.g.* 'Only here; therefore not there'. [3] The third is something diverse *qua* time, *e.g.* 'Only at this time; therefore not at that time'. [4] The fourth is something opposite to what is in predicate-position, *e.g.* 'Only Socrates is white; therefore he is not black or of a mixed colour'. [5] The fifth is a diverse act, or a diverse accident, likewise in predicate-position, providing it is the case that one does not inhere in it in virtue of the other. And so it follows 'Socrates is only a grammarian; therefore he is not a musician', 'He is only reading; therefore he is not running'. And it does not follow 'Only Socrates is coloured; therefore he is not a quantity', because *coloured* inheres in Socrates in virtue of his being a quantity, nor does it follow 'He is only running; therefore he is not moving', because the one inheres in the other or is understood in the other *in concreto*. In all these five ways something diverse is excluded by an exclusive word.

39   From what has been said the solution to the first argument[19] is evident: a man and his surface form one subject-substrate of colour and not diverse ones. Thus surface is not excluded by the the proposition 'Only Socrates is white'. Hence an exclusive word adjoined to a species of one category excludes others providing they do not form one subject or the one does not inhere in virtue of the other, as has been said. The solution to the other argument[20] is also evident: an exclusive word excludes something diverse or different, <the latter term> taken in one of the ways mentioned above.

Whether an exclusive word added to a species of one category excludes other species of the same category

40   From what has been said the solution to the fourth [[4.4]] problem is evident, i.e. whether an exclusive word adjoined to a

---

[19]   Cf. above, cap. 37.
[20]   Cf. above, *ibid.*.

species eiusdem, quia omnes alie species eiusdem generis excluduntur. Nisi una comparetur[2] ad alteram[3], non solum ut species [*P59vb*] disparata[4] sed etiam ut terminus eiusdem; et ideo non sequitur 'tantum superficies est; non[5] ergo linea est', quia linea est terminus superficiei; et similiter[6] <non sequitur 'tantum corpus est; non ergo superficies', quia> superficies <est terminus> corporis. Unde[7] bene sequitur 'tantum homo; non ergo asinus', quia[8] ille[9] species solummodo comparantur sibi invicem ut disparate[10].

Utrum dictio exclusiva adiuncta termino accidentali excludat alios terminos accidentales

41　Ex predictis patet quinta questio, que erat utrum dictio exclusiva adiuncta termino accidentali excludat alios terminos accidentales, quia dictio exclusiva (ut dictum est prius[1]) habet excludere omne accidens diversum sive[2] disparatum, dum ita sit quod unum non insit per alterum vel[3] non faciat[4] subiectum unum. Unde sequitur 'Sortes[5] est tantum gramaticus; non ergo musicus'. Sed non sequitur 'Sortes[6] est tantum coloratus[7]; non ergo quantus'[8], quia coloratum[9] inest Sorti in[10] eo quod est quantus[11]. Neque sequitur 'tantum album[12]; non ergo corpus', quia ista faciunt subiectum unum[13].

Utrum dictio exclusiva addita uni oppositorum excludat alterum in quolibet genere oppositionis

42　Circa sextam questionem obicitur quod dictio exclusiva adiuncta[1] uni[2] oppositorum excludat alterum in quolibet genere oppositionis, quia duo opposita non possunt facere subiectum unum sed diversa[3]. Sed quotienscumque aliqua non faciunt subiectum unum[4] sed diversa, oportet quod unum excludatur ab alio[5] per dictionem exclusivam. Ergo dictio exclusiva adiuncta uni oppositorum excludit[6] alterum. Quod concedimus, sicut patet in contrariis, 'tantum album currit; non ergo nigrum'.

species of one category excludes the other species of the same category, because all other species of the same genus are excluded. This is unless the one is related to the other not only as a disparate species but also as its boundary, and so it does not follow 'Only a surface is; therefore a line is not', because line is the boundary of a surface; and likewise <it does not follow 'Only a body is; therefore a surface is not', because> surface <is the boundary> of a body. Hence the inference 'Only a man; therefore not an ass' is sound, because these species are only mutually related as disparate ones.

Whether an exclusive word adjoined to an accidental term excludes other accidental terms

41   From what has been said <the solution to> the fifth problem [*[4.5]*] (*i.e.* whether an exclusive word adjoined to an accidental term excludes other accidental terms) is evident: an exclusive word (as has been said before) must exclude every diverse or disparate accident, providing it is the case that the one does not inhere in virtue of the other or does not form one subject [*i.e.* with the other]. Thus it follows 'Socrates is only a grammarian; therefore not a musician'. However, it does not follow 'Socrates is only coloured; therefore not a quantity', because his being coloured inheres in Socrates in virtue of the fact that he is a quantity. And it does not follow 'Only a white thing; therefore not a body' either, because these accidents form one subject.

Whether an exclusive word adjoined to one opposite excludes the other in any kind of opposition whatsoever

42   *Ad [4.6]:* As to the sixth sub-item, there is an argument to the contrary that an exclusive word adjoined to one opposite excludes the other in any kind of opposition whatsoever, because two opposites cannot form one subject, but diverse ones. Now whenever certain things do not form one subject but diverse ones, it is necessary that the one be excluded from the other by an exclusive word. Therefore an exclusive word adjoined to one opposite excludes the other. We agree with this as is evident in the contrary pair 'Only a white thing is running; therefore not a black thing'.

Sophisma

43   Secundum predicta queritur de hoc sophismate TANTUM
VERUM OPPONITUR FALSO. Probatio. Verum opponitur falso. Et
nichil aliud quam[1] verum opponitur falso. Ergo tantum verum opponitur falso. Contra. Tantum verum opponitur falso. Ergo tantum verum et falsum opponuntur. Quod falsum est, quia[2] album et nigrum
opponuntur et calidum et frigidum[3].

44   Et dicendum quod prima est simpliciter vera. Et improbatio[1]
peccat secundum consequens ab inferiori ad [*N52rb*] superius cum
dictione exclusiva, quia 'opponi falso' in minus est quam 'opponi[2]
simpliciter', sicut 'oppositio veri et falsi' in[3] minus est quam 'oppositio', cum hec sit species, illa vero genus. Et sic cum dicit 'tantum
verum opponitur falso; ergo tantum verum et falsum opponuntur',
peccat secundum consequens.

De relative oppositis

45   Item. Dubitatur de relative oppositis, quia[1] ex hac 'tantum pater
est' sequitur hec 'ergo filius est'. Unde[2] si tantum pater est, pater est,
quia omnis[3] exclusiva ponit [*P60ra*] suam preiacentem. Et si pater
est, filius est (a relative oppositis). Ergo a primo: 'si tantum pater est,
filius est'. Ergo dictio[4] exclusiva adiuncta uni correlativorum non
excludit alterum.

46   Et dicendum quod dictio exclusiva adiuncta uni correlativorum
excludit alterum. Sed illa[1] 'tantum pater est' ponit contradictionem,
quia cum dictio exclusiva excludat quecumque non faciunt subiectum unum sed diversa: cum pater et filius faciant diversa subiecta
et non unum (quia[2] nichil est dictu 'pater filius est' secundum[3] quod
'pater' et 'filius' referuntur ad se invicem), ideo[4] dictio exclusiva
adiuncta 'patri' excludit 'filium' et econverso. Unde in ista 'tantum
pater est'[5] excluditur filius ratione dictionis exclusive et pater ponitur
ratione preiacentis. Sed[6] pater est[7] per hoc quod est[8] ad filium. Et ita

Sophisma

43   As regards what has been said, there is a problem concerning the sophisma-sentence ONLY THE TRUE IS OPPOSITE TO THE FALSE. Proof: the true is opposite to the false and nothing other than the true is opposite to the false. Therefore only the true is opposite to the false. There is an argument to the contrary. Only the true is opposite to the false, therefore only the true and the false are opposites. And this is false, because white and black and warm and cold are opposites.

44   The answer should be that the original sentence is true *simpliciter*, and the disproof commits the fallacy of the consequent <by proceeding> from what is less general to what is more general in combination with an exclusive word: 'to be opposite to the false' is less extensive than 'to be opposite *simpliciter*', just as 'the opposition between true and false' is less extensive than 'opposition', because the former is a species, whereas the latter is a genus. And so if <the opponent>[21] says 'Only the true is opposite to the false; therefore only the true and the false are opposites', he commits the fallacy of the consequent.

On opposites of a relative nature

45   There is a matter of dispute concerning opposites of a relative nature: from 'Only a father is' follows 'Therefore a son is'. Hence if only a father is, there is a father, for every exclusive proposition asserts its basic proposition. And if a father is, a son is (by the topic 'from opposites of a relative nature'). Therefore, taking it from the beginning, if only a father is, a son is. Therefore an exclusive word adjoined to one correlate does not exclude the other.

46   The answer should be that an exclusive word adjoined to one correlate excludes the other. Now the proposition 'Only a father is' entails a contradiction, for as an exclusive word excludes whatever does not form one subject, but diverse subjects, it is because they produce diverse subjects, and not one (for it is makes no sense to say 'A father-son is' insofar as 'father' and 'son' are mutually related), that therefore an exclusive word adjoined to 'father' excludes 'son' and the other way round. Hence in 'Only a father is' the son is excluded on account of the exclusive word and the father is posited on account of the basic proposition. Now a father *is* in virtue of his

---

[21]   Cf. above, cap. 43.

ratione preiacentis non solum ponitur pater sed etiam filius; et[9] ratione exclusionis[10] non solum removetur filius sed etiam pater, quia[11] filius est per hoc quod est ad patrem. Et sic ista 'tantum pater est' ponit duplicem contradictionem, quia[12] ponit filium esse et[13] non esse et patrem esse et non esse.

Sophismata

47 Circa predicta queritur de hoc sophismate SI TANTUM PATER EST, NON TANTUM PATER EST. Probatio. Si tantum pater est, pater est[1]. Et[2] si pater est, filius est. Et si filius est, aliud a patre est. Et si aliud[3] a patre est, non tantum pater est. Ergo a primo: si tantum pater est, non tantum pater est. Contra. Ibi assignatur[4] sequi oppositum ad oppositum. Ergo locutio est impossibilis.

48 Ad[1] hoc solvunt quidam quod 'pater' sumitur tripliciter[2]. Sicut 'album'. Quia[3] 'album' uno modo nominat[4] id quod est album, ut hic: 'album potest esse nigrum', secundum quod hec est vera; et[5] hoc est dictu: *hoc[6] quod est subiectum albedinis, potest esse nigrum.* Alio autem modo 'album' dicit [*N52va*] compositum ex subiecto et accidente, ut 'album currit', idest *substantia[7] habens albedinem currit.* Alio[8] autem modo 'album' nominat ipsum accidens, ut cum dicitur 'album[9] contingit uni et eidem inesse et non inesse'. Similiter 'pater' uno modo dicit subiectum paternitatis, ut 'pater generat filium', idest *id quod est pater*; alio[10] modo dicit compositum ex materia[11] et forma, ut 'pater currit', idest *homo* vel *animal* [*P60rb*] *habens paternitatem currit.* Et in[12] hiis duobus modis excluditur unum correlativorum[13] per dictionem exclusivam adiunctam alteri. Alio[14] autem modo 'pater' nominat ipsam relationem que est paternitas; ut cum dicitur 'pater est in genere Relationis'. Et hoc modo non excluditur unum correlativorum [*T32va*] ab alio, quia sic unum[15] ponit alterum et econverso.

49 Sed hoc nichil est, quia cum dictio exclusiva excludat[1] quecumque non faciunt subiectum unum sed diversa[2] et[3] pater et filius non faciunt[4] subiectum unum[5], secundum quod sunt[6] in genere Relationis, nec[7] aliquo[8] alio modo, tunc[9] oportet quod[10] dictio exclusiva

relation to a son. And so on account of the basic proposition not only the father is posited but the son as well; and on account of the exclusion not only the son is removed but the father as well, because a son *is* in virtue of his relation to a father. And so the proposition 'Only a father is' asserts a double contradiction because it asserts that the son is and is not and that the father is and is not.

Sophismata

47   As regards what has been said, there is a problem concerning the sophisma-sentence IF ONLY A FATHER IS, NOT ONLY A FATHER IS. Proof: if only a father is, only a father is. And if a father is, a son is. And if a son is, something other than a father is. And if something other than a father is, not only a father is. Therefore, taking it from the beginning, if only a father is, not only a father is. There is an argument to the contrary. In this case it is indicated that an opposite follows from an opposite. Therefore the locution is impossible.

48   To this problem some have the solution that 'father' is taken in three ways. It happens in the same way as in 'white <thing>': [1] in one way 'white <thing>' indicates that which is white, *e.g.* in the proposition 'A white thing can be black', insofar as it is true; and this is to say: *that which is the subject of whiteness can be black.* [2] In another way 'white <thing>' indicates something made up of a sub-ject-substrate and an accident, *e.g.* 'A white thing is running', that is, *a substance that has whiteness is running* [3] In another way 'white' indicates the accident itself, *e.g.* in the expression 'White can inhere or not inhere in one and the same thing'. Likewise in one way 'father' indicates the subject of fatherhood, *e.g.* 'A father begets a son', that is to say, *that which is the father;* in another way it indicates something made up of matter and form, *e.g.* 'A father is running', that is, *a man* or *animal having fatherhood is running.* And in these two ways one correlate is excluded by an exclusive word adjoined to the other. In another way 'father' indicates the relationship of father-hood itself, *e.g.* in the expression 'Father belongs to the category of "relation"'. And in this way one correlate is not excluded by the other, because in this way the one posits the other and the other way round.

49   However, this is nonsense, for it is because an exclusive word excludes whatever things do not form one subject but diverse ones, and since father and son do not form one subject according as they belong to the category of 'relation', nor in any other way, that it is

adiuncta 'patri' excludat filium et econverso. Quod concedimus. Solutio[11] recta est dicendo quod hec 'si tantum pater est, non tantum pater est' simpliciter est[12] vera, sed suum antecedens est impossibile (hec scilicet 'tantum pater est'), quia ponit contradictionem, quia in hac propositione 'tantum pater est' ponitur[13] hec dictio 'tantum', que[14] removet omne[15] aliud subiectum vel accidens a patre et sic[16] removet filium[17], et est ibi hoc[18] relativum 'pater', quod[19] ponit filium. Et ita ex una[20] parte removet filium (scilicet a parte[21] exclusionis) et ex alia parte ponit ipsum[22] (scilicet a parte sui[23] correlativi).

50 Ad improbationem autem solvendum per interemptionem, quia[1] non sequitur ibi[2] oppositum ad oppositum, sed sequitur una pars contradictionis ad antecedens, quod claudit[3] intra se utramque partem contradictionis. Et sic sequitur pars ad[4] totum, sicut hic: 'Sortes currit et non currit; ergo[5] Sortes[6] currit'. Et[7] est locus a toto integrali; contradictio[8] enim integratur ex[9] suis partibus. Unde posita contradictione necesse est ex ea sequi tam affirmationem[10] quam negationem, per locum a toto integrali.

51 [*N52vb*] Item. Queritur de hoc sophismate POSSIBILE EST SORTEM VIDERE TANTUM[1] OMNEM HOMINEM[2] NON VIDENTEM SE. Probatio. Possibile est Sortem videre tantum[3] omnem hominem cecum. Sed omnis homo cecus est homo non videns se. Ergo possibile est Sortem videre tantum[4] omnem hominem[5] non videntem[6] se. Contra. Si possibile est, ponatur: Sortes[7] videt tantum[8] omnem hominem videntem se[9]. [*P60va*] Tunc[10] aut Sortes videt se aut non videt se. [11]Si non videt se, ergo est homo non[12] videns se. Et[13] videt[14] quemlibet[15] talem. Ergo videt se. Si videt se, ergo est homo videns se. Sed[16] nullum talem[17] videbat. Ergo non videt se[18], quoniam[19] tantum videbat non videntem se.

52 Solutio. Prima est impossibilis, hec scilicet 'possibile est Sortem videre tantum omnem hominem non videntem se'. Et ista similiter

therefore necessary that an exclusive word adjoined to 'father' exclude a son and the other way round. Well, we agree with this. The correct solution is presented by saying that the proposition 'If only a father is, not only a father is' is true *simpliciter*; however, the antecedent is impossible (*viz.* 'Only a father is') because it entails a contradiction; for in the proposition 'Only a father is', the word 'only' is posited which removes every other subject or accident from the father and thus removes the son, and <at the same time> there is in this case the relative 'father' which posits the son. And so on the one hand it removes the son (*viz.* on account of the exclusion) and on the other hand it posits him (namely on account of its correlate).

50 As to the disproof,[22] this can be solved by getting rid of it altogether: in this case no opposite follows from an opposite, but one part of a contradiction follows from an antecedent that includes both parts of a contradiction. Hence it follows as a part from a whole, in the same way as in 'Socrates is running and not running; therefore Socrates is running'. This is a case of the topic 'from an integral whole'; for a contradiction makes up an integral whole of its parts. Thus when a contradiction is asserted it is necessary that from it follows both an affirmation and a denial, on account of the topic 'from an integral whole'.

51 There is a problem concerning the sophisma-sentence IT IS POSSIBLE THAT SOCRATES SEES ONLY EVERY MAN WHO DOES NOT SEE HIMSELF. Proof: it is possible that Socrates sees only every blind man. Now every blind man is a man who does not see himself. Therefore it is possible that Socrates sees only every man who does not see himself. There is an argument to the contrary. If that is possible, one can assert: Socrates sees only every man who does not see himself. Then either Socrates sees himself or he does not see himself. If he does not see himself, therefore he is a man who does not see himself. And he sees every such a man. Therefore he sees himself. If he does see himself, then he is a man who sees himself. Now he did not see any such man. Therefore he does not see himself, since he only saw <a man> who does not see himself.

52 Solution. The original sentence, *viz.* 'It is possible that Socrates sees only every man who does not see himself', is an impossible one. The same goes for the proposition 'Socrates sees only every

---

22 Cf. above, cap. 47.

'Sortes videt tantum omnem[1] hominem non videntem se'[2], quia utraque habet in se contradictionem, ut iam patebit. Probatio[3] peccat secundum consequens procedendo[4] ab inferiori ad superius cum distributione[5] et etiam cum dictione exclusiva. Ut 'omnis homo; ergo omne animal' et 'tantum omnis homo; ergo tantum omne[6] animal', quia homo non videns se in plus est[7] quam homo cecus. Unde sequitur non conversim. Ut 'si est homo cecus, est[8] homo non videns se' et non econverso, quia homo dormiens est homo non videns se[9] et etiam vigilans[10] oculos[11] habens clausos[12] est homo non videns se.

53   Quod[1] ista 'Sortes videt tantum[2] omnem hominem non videntem se' habeat[3] contradictionem in se patet, quia equipollet istis duabus, scilicet[4] 'Sortes videt omnem hominem non videntem se' et[5] 'non videt aliquem hominem[6] videntem se', et iste due sunt expositive[7] illius. Sed ex ista 'Sortes non videt aliquem hominem videntem[8] se' sequitur 'ergo Sortes non[9] videt se videntem se'. Et est locus a genere sive a toto in modo, sicut hic 'Sortes non videt aliquem hominem album; ergo[10] [*T32vb*] non videt se album'. Sed si Sortes non videt se videntem se, Sortes[11] non videt se, quia[12] convertuntur, cum earum affirmationes[13] convertantur, ut 'si Sortes videt se videntem se, ergo Sortes videt se' et econverso. Sed quotienscumque affirmationes sibi invicem convertuntur, necesse est earum[14] negationes sibi invicem converti. Ut[15] si 'homo' et 'risibile' convertuntur, [*N53ra*] et[16] 'non-homo' et 'non-risibile' convertuntur. Et ideo necessario[17] sequitur 'si Sortes[18] non videt se videntem se, ergo non videt se', per locum a[19] convertibili. Ergo a primo: 'si Sortes non videt aliquem hominem videntem se, non[20] videt se'. Et[21] hec est [*P60vb*] altera[22] pars contradictionis. Ex qua cum altera[23] expositiva prime sequitur reliqua pars contradictionis. Et[24] hoc modo[25] Sortes videt omnem hominem non videntem se et ipse non[26] videt se. Ergo videt se. Et sic videt se et non videt se. Hic[27] autem est[28] contradictio. Et sequitur ex duabus expositivis prime. Et ille expositive intelliguntur

man who does not see himself', because both contain a contradiction as will become evident right away. The proof commits the
fallacy of the consequent by proceeding from what is less general to
what is more general in combination with a distribution as well as
an exclusive word, as happens in 'Every man; therefore every animal' and 'Only every man; therefore only every animal', because a
man who does not see himself is more extensive than a blind man.
Thus the converse does not follow, as happens in 'If he is a blind
man, he is a man who does not see himself' and not the other way
round, because a man who is asleep is a man who does not see himself and also a man who is awake with his eyes closed is a man
who does not see himself.

53 That, however, 'Socrates sees only every man who does not see
himself' contains a contradiction is evident, because it is equivalent
to the two propositions 'Socrates sees every man who does not see
himself' and '<Socrates> does not see any man who sees himself',
and these two are what the original sentence is analysed into. Now
from 'Socrates does not see a man who sees himself' follows 'Socrates does not see himself who sees himself'. This is a case of the topic
'from a genus' or 'from a whole in mode', in the same way as
'Socrates does not see a white man; therefore he does not see himself
as a white man'. Now if Socrates does not see himself who sees himself, Socrates does not see himself, because these two are convertible,
as their affirmations are convertible, *viz.* 'If Socrates sees himself
who sees himself, therefore Socrates sees himself' and the other
way round. Now whenever affirmations are mutually convertible, it
is necessary that their denials are mutually convertible. For instance, if 'man' is convertible with 'risible' [*i.e.* something that can
laugh], 'non-man' and 'non-risible' are convertible as well. Hence it
necessarily follows 'If Socrates does not see himself who sees himself, therefore he does not see himself', by the topic 'from a convertible'. Thus, taking it from the beginning, if Socrates does not see
a man who sees himself, he does not see himself. And this is the
other part of the contradiction. And from this one in combination
with the other one the original sentence is analysed into follows the
other part of the contradiction. In this way Socrates sees every man
who does not see himself and he does not see himself. Therefore he
sees himself. Therefore he sees himself and does not see himself.
Here we have a contradiction, however. And it follows from the two
propositions the original is analysed into. And these expository
propositions are understood in the original one, and so the contra-

in prima. Et[29] ita contradictio intelligitur in prima. Et sic claudit[30] intra se contradictionem.

54 Item. Illud[1] idem ostenditur alia ratione, quia[2] si Sortes non videt aliquem hominem videntem[3] se, ergo Sortes videt nullum hominem videntem se, quia 'non aliquem' et 'nullum' equipollent, sicut 'non aliquis' et 'nullus'. Ergo nullus homo videns se videtur a Sorte (convertendo activam in passivam). Ergo Sortes non videt se, quia si Sortes videret[4] se, iam[5] aliquis homo videns[6] se videretur[7] a Sorte. Et dicebatur quod nullus[8]. Ergo a primo: si Sortes non videt aliquem hominem[9] videntem se, Sortes non videt se. Et sic[10] habetur alia[11] pars contradictionis. Ex qua cum altera expositiva prime sequitur reliqua pars contradictionis, sicut prius. Quare prima habet in[12] se contradictionem. Quod concedimus.

55 Item. Probo[1] quod prima est vera, hec scilicet 'Sortes videt tantum omnem hominem non videntem se'. Ponatur[2] quod Virgilius et Plato et Cicero sint homines[3] non videntes se tantum et omnes alii videant se[4]; et ponatur cum hoc quod Sortes videat tantum illos tres, quia hec positio possibilis est. Et[5] tunc hec 'omnis homo non[6] videns se non videt se' convertitur cum hiis tribus singularibus[7] 'Virgilius non videt se', 'Plato[8] non videt se', 'Cicero[9] non videt se'. Et iste tres[10] insimul sumpte convertuntur cum illa, quia sequitur[11] 'omnis homo non videns se legit; ergo et iste et hic et ille legit' et econverso. Sed[12] Sortes videt[13] tantum[14] illos tres. Ergo Sortes videt tantum omnem hominem non videntem se[15]. Et[16] est locus a convertibili, quia ab uno convertibili ad alterum bene sequitur cum dictione exclusiva, ut 'tantum risibile; ergo tantum homo'. Ergo hec est vera 'Sortes[17] videt tantum omnem[18] [*N53rb*] hominem non videntem se'. Item ad idem. Posito quod sint tantum tres homines ceci et omnes alii videant se[19], tunc iste due convertuntur 'omnis[20] homo cecus' et 'omnis homo non videns se'[21]. [*P61ra*] Sed possibile est Sortem videre tantum[22] omnem hominem cecum. Ergo possibile est[23] Sortem videre tantum[24] omnem hominem non videntem se. Ergo prima possibilis est.

diction is understood in the original. And so the original sentence contains a contradiction.

54 Moreover, the very same is shown by way of a different argument: if Socrates does not see a man who sees himself, therefore Socrates sees no man who sees himself, because 'not a' and 'no' are equivalent, in the same way as 'not someone' and 'no one'. Therefore no man who sees himself is seen by Socrates (by changing the active into a passive form). Therefore Socrates does not see himself, because if Socrates were to see himself, then in fact a man who sees himself would be seen by Socrates. And it was said that he saw no such one. Therefore, taking it from the beginning, if Socrates does not see a man who sees himself, Socrates does not see himself. Thus we have one part of a contradiction, from which in combination with the other proposition the original one is analysed into follows the other part of the contradiction, in the same way as before. And therefore the original sentence contains a contradiction. We agree with this.

55 Again, I shall prove that the original sentence, *viz.* 'Socrates sees only every man who does not see himself', is true. Let us suppose that Virgil, Plato and Cicero are the only men who do not see themselves and that all other men see themselves; and let us suppose, in addition, that Socrates only sees those three, because this is a possible position. And in that case the proposition 'Every man who does not see himself does not see himself' is convertible with the three singular ones 'Virgil does not see himself', 'Plato does not see himself' and 'Cicero does not see himself'. And all these three taken simultaneously are convertible with the former, because it follows 'Every man who does not see himself is reading; therefore this man, that man and that man are reading' and the other way round. Now Socrates sees only these three. Therefore Socrates sees only every man who does not see himself. And this is a case of the topic 'from a convertible', because an inference from one convertible to the other in combination with an exclusive word is valid, *e.g.* 'Only something that can laugh; therefore only a man'. Therefore the following is true: 'Socrates sees only every man who does not see himself'. There is another argument that yields the same conclusion. Supposing that there are only three blind men and that all other men see themselves, then the two expressions 'every blind man' and 'every man who does not see himself' are convertible. Now it is possible that Socrates sees only every blind man. Therefore it is possible that Socrates sees only every man who does not see himself. Therefore the original sentence is possible.

56   Solutio[1]. Dico quod prima est falsa et impossibilis, sicut[2] prius dictum est, quia ponit contradictionem, sicut prius patuit duplici ratione. Ad primam[3] autem positionem dicendum quod ponit duo incompossibilia[4]. Et concedo quod[5] utrumque eorum est possibile secundum se sed[6] ambo insimul[7] sunt incompossibilia[8]. Quia hoc est possibile secundum[9] se, scilicet quod tantum sint illi[10] tres homines[11] non videntes se, et aliud similiter est possibile secundum se, scilicet quod Sortes videat tantum illos tres. [*T33ra*] Sed ambo insimul sunt incompossibilia.[12] Quod sic patet, quia: Quando ponit quod isti[13] tres tantum sint[14] non videntes se[15], in hoc ponit quod Sortes videat se[16], cum non sit de numero illorum. Et quando ponit quod Sortes videat[17] tantum illos tres, in hoc ponit quod Sortes non videat se, cum non[18] sit de illis. Et ita ponit[19] quod Sortes videat se et non videat se[20]. Et ita illa duo[21] insimul posita[22] ponunt contradictionem. Et ita[23] sunt incompossibilia[24].

57   Ad aliud[1] dicendum[2] quod similiter[3] hec est vera secundum se, scilicet[4] 'possibile[5] est Sortem videre tantum[6] omnem hominem cecum'[7]. Sed non est possibile posito quod 'homo cecus' convertatur cum 'homine[8] non vidente[9] se', quia si Sortes videt tantum omnem hominem cecum, tunc non videt se. Et si 'homo cecus' convertatur cum 'homine non vidente se', tunc Sortes videt se, cum Sortes[10] non sit cecus. Et[11] a quocumque removetur[12] unum convertibilium, et reliquum. Et sic[13] ponit iterum[14] in hac ratione secunda quod Sortes videat se[15] et non videat se[16]. Et sic non est mirum, si[17] premissa est impossibilis, cum ipsa sequatur ex positione[18] impossibili.

Utrum dictio exclusiva addita toti excludat partem vel econverso

58   Septima questio fuit utrum dictio exclusiva adiuncta parti integrali excludat totum (vel[1] econverso) et adiuncta minori numero excludat maiorem (vel[2] econverso). Et videtur quod adiuncta toti

56 Solution. I say that the original sentence is false and impossible, as has been said before,[23] because it entails a contradiction, as has been made evident before[24] for two reasons. As to the first argument,[25] the answer should be that it entails two incompossible states of affairs. And I grant that each one is possible in itself but both simultaneously are incompossible, because the one is possible in itself, *viz.* that only these three do not see themselves, and the other one likewise is possible in itself, *viz.* that Socrates sees only those three. However, both simultaneously are impossible. And this is evident as follows: when one asserts that these three are the only ones who do not see themselves, one implicitly asserts that Socrates sees himself, because he does not belong to that number of men. And if one asserts that Socrates sees only those three, one implicitly asserts that Socrates does not see himself because he is not one of them. And so one asserts that Socrates sees himself and he does not see himself. And so the two asserted simultaneously entail a contradiction. And in this way they are incompossible.

57 As to the other argument,[26] the answer should be that likewise the proposition 'It is possible that Socrates sees only every blind man' is true in itself. However, it is not possible supposing that 'blind man' is convertible with 'a man who does not see himself', because if Socrates sees only every blind man, then he does not see himself. And if 'blind man' is convertible with 'a man who does not see himself', then Socrates sees himself, because he is not blind. And from whatever one of the convertibles is removed, the other is removed as well. Thus once again one asserts in this second argument that Socrates sees himself and does not see himself. And so it is not surprising, if the premise is impossible, because it follows from an impossible position.

Whether an exclusive word added to a whole excludes a part or the other way round

58 The seventh problem [[4.7]] was whether an exclusive word adjoined to an integral part excludes the whole or the other way round, and adjoined to a smaller number excludes a larger one or the other way round. It may be argued that adjoined to an integral

---

23 Cf. above, cap. 52.
24 Cf. above, capp. 53-54.
25 Cf. above, cap. 55.
26 Cf. above, *ibid.*.

integrali excludat[3] partem, [*P61rb*] quia sequitur 'domus valet tantum[4] centum libras[5]; non ergo [*N53va*] paries'. Ergo addita toti excludit partem (et econverso, ut[6] 'tantum paries est albus[7]; non ergo domus'). Sed contra. Propositio exclusiva[8] ponit suam preiacentem. Ut 'tantum domus est colorata; ergo domus est colorata'. Sed[9] si domus est colorata, paries[10] est coloratus, quia[11] posito toto integrali ponitur quelibet pars eius. Ergo a primo: si tantum domus est colorata, paries[12] est coloratus[13]. Ergo dictio exclusiva adiuncta toti[14] non excludit partem[15].

59 Et dicendum quod tria genera accidentium reperiuntur in toto integrali et in parte sua. Quia quedam accidentia sunt que tantum[1] conveniunt toti integrali, ut componi ex[2] partibus integralibus et[3] habere partes omnes[4] secundum quantitatem; et propter hoc anima non est pars integralis[5] ipsius[6] hominis[7] sed[8] essentialis, et valere centum[9] libras[10] convenit ita[11] toti quod non parti. Alia autem[12] sunt accidentia que conveniunt tantum[13] parti, ut esse minus[14] vel sequi ex toto integrali (videlicet[15] partialitas)[16] vel coniungi alii[17] quanto ad[18] faciendum maius secundum quantitatem. Tertio autem modo[19] sunt quedam accidentia que indifferenter conveniunt toti[20] et parti, ut album, nigrum, calidum[21], frigidum, humidum, siccum et consimilia. Et in primo genere accidentis[22] dictio exclusiva adiuncta toti integrali excludit partem, ut 'domus valet tantum centum libras[23]; non ergo paries'. In[24] aliis duobus generibus accidentium dictio exclusiva adiuncta parti semper[25] excludit totum, et non econverso.

Sophisma

60 Circa[1] predicta queritur de hoc sophismate A SOLO SORTE DIFFERT QUICQUID NON EST SORTES VEL PARS SORTIS. Probatio[2]. A Sorte differt quicquid non est Sortes vel pars Sortis. Et[3] non ab alio[4] a Sorte differt quicquid non est Sortes vel pars Sortis. Ergo a[5] solo Sorte differt quicquid non est Sortes vel pars Sortis. Ergo prima vera. Contra[6]. A solo Sorte differt quicquid non est Sortes vel pars Sortis. Sed Plato non est Sortes nec[7] pars Sortis. Ergo Plato differt a solo Sorte.

whole it excludes a part, because it follows 'Only the house is worth one hundred pounds; therefore not the wall'. Therefore added to a whole it excludes a part (and the other way round, *e.g.* 'Only the wall is white; therefore not the house'). However, there is an argument to the contrary. An exclusive proposition asserts its basic proposition. For instance, 'Only the house is coloured; therefore the house is coloured'. Now if the house is coloured, the wall is coloured, because by positing an integral whole any of its parts is posited. Therefore, taking it from the beginning, if only the house is coloured, the wall is coloured. Therefore an exclusive word adjoined to a whole does not exclude a part.

59   The answer should be that one finds three kinds of accidents in an integral whole and its part. [1] There are some accidents that only belong to an integral whole, *e.g.* to be made up of integral parts and to have all parts in terms of a quantity; and therefore the soul is not an integral part of a man, but an essential part, and to be worth one hundred pounds is an accident of the whole such that it is not of the part. [2] There are other accidents that belong to a part only, *e.g.* to be less than or to follow from an integral whole (*viz.* partiality), or to be combined with something else so as to form something greater in terms of quantity. [3] In the third way there are some accidents that indifferently belong to both a whole and a part, *e.g.* white, black, warm, cold, humid, dry, and the like. And in the first kind of accident an exclusive word adjoined to an integral whole excludes a part, *e.g.* 'Only the house is worth one hundred pounds; therefore not the wall'. In the other two kinds of accidents an exclusive word adjoined to a part always excludes the whole, and not the other way round.

Sophisma

60   There is a problem concerning the sophisma-sentence FROM SOCRATES ALONE DIFFERS WHATEVER IS NOT SOCRATES OR A PART OF SOCRATES. Proof: from Socrates differs whatever is not Socrates or a part of Socrates. And not from something other than Socrates differs whatever is not Socrates or a part of Socrates. Therefore from Socrates alone differs whatever is not Socrates or a part of Socrates. Therefore the original sentence is true. There is an argument to the contrary. From Socrates alone differs whatever is not Socrates or a part of Socrates. Now Plato is not Socrates nor a part of Socrates. Therefore Plato differs from Socrates alone.

61   Solutio. Prima falsa et altera [*P61va*] probativa[1] est falsa, hec
scilicet 'non ab alio[2] a Sorte differt quicquid non est Sortes vel pars
Sortis', quia sua contradictoria est vera, hec scilicet 'ab[3] alio a Sorte
differt quicquid non est Sortes vel pars Sortis'. Et si querat aliquis[4] 'a
quo alio?', dicendum quod nulla est questio, quia iste terminus 'alio'
non tenetur determinate pro uno sed communiter pro pluribus.
Sicut[5] hic: posito quod omnis homo videat proprium equum tantum,
tunc hec est vera 'equum[6] videt omnis homo' nec tamen[7] est querere
'quem equum?', quia iste[8] terminus 'equum' non tenetur determinate pro uno sed communiter pro pluribus.

Utrum dictio exclusiva addita maiori numero excludat minorem
vel econverso

62   Item. Videtur quod dictio exclusiva addita toti [*T33rb*] numerali
possit excludere partem eius sive addita maiori[1] numero possit excludere minorem[2], quia omnes numeri[3] sunt specie differentes (ut
binarius, ternarius[4], quaternarius et sic de aliis), quia[5] sunt diverse
species ex opposito condividentes[6] Numerum, qui est genus omnium specialium numerorum. Ergo dictio exclusiva addita uni[7]
excludit omnes alias[8]. Ergo si dictio exclusiva addatur maiori[9]
numero, excludet[10] quamlibet[11] unitatem <et ita> quemlibet[12] minorem, quia[13] addita quinario[14] excludit quamlibet[15] aliam speciem,
ergo quamlibet minorem speciem. Sed contra. Quilibet numerus
maior semper ponit suum preiacentem[16]. Et ideo dicit Aristotiles si[17]
duo sunt, unum esse; ergo[18] minor numerus semper intelligitur in
maiori. Sed dictio exclusiva non removet quod intelligitur in suo
preiacente. Ergo dictio exclusiva adiuncta maiori numero non excludit minorem.
63   Solutio. 'Numerus' duobus modis sumitur, sicut[1] quodlibet aliud
totum. Quia uno modo sumitur 'numerus' ratione sue totalitatis (sive
ratione totius aggregationis sue, quod[2] idem est). Et sic dictio
exclusiva adiuncta maiori numero[3] excludit quemlibet[4] minorem, ut
'tantum decem[5] sunt paria; non ergo octo[6] neque sex neque quatuor';
et etiam[7] excludit omnes superiores[8], ut, sic[9]: 'tantum decem sunt
paria, non ergo undecim[10] neque duodecim sunt paria' et sic de aliis

61   Solution. The original sentence is false and so is one of the sentences that aim prove it, *viz.* 'Not from something other than Socrates differs whatever is not Socrates or a part of Socrates', because its contradictory is true, *viz.* 'From something other than Socrates differs whatever is not Socrates or a part of Socrates'. And if someone were to ask 'From what other?', the answer should be that this is an absurd question, because the term 'other' does not determinately apply to one but in general to many things. The same goes for the following: supposing that every man sees only his own horse, then 'Every man sees a horse' is true, and nevertheless it would not do to ask 'What horse?', because the term 'horse' does not determinately apply to one, but in general to many.

Whether an exclusive word added to a larger number excludes a smaller one or the other way round

62   It may be argued that an exclusive word added to a numerical whole can exclude a part of it, or added to some larger number can exclude a smaller one, because all smaller numbers are specifically different (*e.g.* binary, ternary, quaternary, and so on), because they are diverse species which as opposites condivide Number, which is the genus of all specific numbers. Therefore an exclusive word added to one <species of number> excludes all others. Therefore if an exclusive word is added to a larger number, it excludes any unity <and thus> any smaller one, because added to a quinary it excludes any other species, therefore any smaller species. However, there is an argument to the contrary. Any larger number always posits the one that comes before it. And so Aristotle says[27] that if there are two, there is one; therefore a smaller number is always understood in a larger one. Now an exclusive word does not remove what is understood in that which is a basic part of it. Therefore an exclusive word adjoined to a larger number does not exclude a smaller one.
63   Solution. 'Number' is taken in two ways, in the same way as any other whole. [1] In one way 'number' is taken in terms of its totality (or in terms of its whole collection, which is the same). In this way an exclusive word adjoined to a larger number excludes any smaller one, *e.g.* 'Only ten are even; therefore not eight, nor six, nor four', and it also excludes all larger numbers, *e.g.* 'Only ten are even; therefore not eleven, nor twelve, are even' and so on in the

---

[27]   Where?

ascendendo[11]. Alio autem modo sumitur non[12] ratione sue totalitatis (sive totius aggregationis), sed ratione [*P61vb*] eorum ex quibus est[13] (vel ex[14] quibus fit). Et sic dictio exclusiva addita maiori numero non excludit minorem, immo[15] potius ponet[16]. Unde non sequitur 'tantum decem currunt; non[17] ergo novem currunt vel septem'[18], immo potius oppositum[19] sequitur, quia[20] si[21] currant tantum decem, sequitur[22] quod novem currant et[23] etiam quod octo [*N54ra*] currant. Et sic patet quod dictio exclusiva adiuncta maiori numero uno modo excludet minorem et alio modo non. Sed addita minori[24] numero semper excludit maiorem.

De quadam regula

64 Unde[1] de parte in quantitate et de parte integrali et de parte in loco et de parte in tempore et de parte[2] numerali talis datur regula:

> *quotienscumque dictio exclusiva adiungitur parti, semper excludit suum totum, excepto toto universali et toto in modo.*

65 Ad duo[1] prima argumenta facilis[2] est solutio[3]. Quia primum argumentum accepit species numeri ratione suarum[4] totalitatum (sive aggregationum)[5]; et sic dictio exclusiva adiuncta uni[6] excludet omnes alias. Secundum autem[7] accepit[8] species numeri ratione eorum ex quibus sunt[9].

Sophisma

66 Circa predicta queritur de hoc sophismate SOLIS TRIBUS SOLA DUO SUNT PAUCIORA. Probatio. Tribus sola duo sunt pauciora. Et[1] non aliis a[2] tribus sola duo[3] sunt pauciora. Ergo solis tribus sola duo sunt pauciora[4]. Contra[5]. Solis tribus sola duo sunt pauciora. Ergo solis tribus duo sunt pauciora.

67 Solutio. Prima duplex, quia potest exponi[1] per dictionem[2] exclusivam existentem in obliquo[3]; et sic probatur[4] et[5] sic est vera; et[6] est sensus 'solis tribus *etc.*' idest *sola duo sunt pauciora tribus et sola duo non sunt pauciora*[7] *aliis a tribus.* Vel potest exponi per exclusionem existentem in rectitudine[8]; et sic improbatur et[9] sic est falsa; et[10] est sensus

upward direction. [2] In another way it is not taken in terms of its totality (or its whole collection), but in terms of the ones [*i.e.* the numbers] of which it consists (or of which it is made up of). In this way an exclusive word added to a larger number does not exclude a smaller one, but rather the former will posit the latter. Thus it does not follow 'Only ten are running; therefore not nine or seven are running', for rather the opposite follows, because if only ten are running, it follows that nine are running and also that eight are running. Thus it is evident that an exclusive word adjoined to a larger number in one way will exclude a smaller one and in another way will not. However, added to a smaller number it always excludes a larger one.

On certain rules

64 Thus as regards the quantitative part, the integral part, the local part, the temporal part, and the numerical part, the following rule is presented:

> *Whenever an exclusive word is adjoined to a part, it always excludes its whole, with the exception of a universal whole and a whole in mode.*

65 To the two first arguments[28] the solution is easy. The first argument took the species of number in terms of their totalities (or collections); and thus an exclusive word adjoined to one will exclude all others. The second argument, on the other hand, took the species of number in terms of the ones it consists of.

Sophisma

66 As regards what has been said, there is a problem concerning the sophisma-sentence THAN THREE ALONE TWO ALONE ARE FEWER. Proof: than three alone two are fewer. And not than others than three alone two are fewer. Therefore than three alone two are fewer. There is an argument to the contrary. Than three alone two alone are fewer. Therefore than three alone two are fewer.

67 Solution. The original sentence is ambiguous, because it can be analysed by the exclusive word used in the oblique case; and in this way it is proved and thus is true; and the meaning of 'Than three alone *etc.*' is *two alone are fewer than three and two alone are not fewer than other ones than three.* Or it can be analysed by the exclusion in

---

28 Cf. above, cap. 62.

'solis tribus *etc.*' idest *solis tribus duo sunt pauciora et non alia quam duo solis tribus sunt pauciora.* Et ideo[11] altera de exponentibus[12] est falsa[13], hec[14] scilicet 'solis tribus duo sunt pauciora', cum[15] duo sint pauciora omnibus aliis numeris ascendendo. Et ita non solis tribus duo sunt pauciora.

De quadam regula

68   Unde solet dari talis regula:

> *quotienscumque duo sincategoreumata ponuntur [T33va] in eadem locutione seipsa[1] attingentia, duplex est locutio, quia[2] unum potest esse determinatio alterius vel econverso.*

[P62ra] Et hoc est quod solebant dicere antiqui quod unum poterat[3] includere reliquum[4] vel econverso includi ab eo aut[5] excludere alterum vel excludi ab eo.

69   Et nota quod in numeris est duplex ascensus[1], quia unus est causarum et alius quantitatis sive augmenti[2] in[3] quantitate. Unde loquendo[4] de ascensu[5] causarum omnes minores numeri sunt superiores maioribus, quia minores[6] sunt causa[7] maiorum. Unde quanto minor est[8] numerus, tanto superior est[9], quia intantum[10] est prior causa; et[11] omnis causa prior superior est. Et ideo supremum principium in numeris est unitas. Et a[12] maioribus numeris (loquendo [N54rb] de ascensu cause) semper est ascendere ad quemlibet[13] minorem et ultimo ad unitatem; econverso est[14] descendere. Sed loquendo[15] de ascensu quantitatis[16] sive de ascensu augmenti quantitatis, tunc[17] maiores[18] numeri superiores sunt et minores inferiores, eoquod[19] maius est augmentum, vel maior quantitas, in maioribus[20] quam in minoribus. Et hoc modo fit[21] ascensus a minori numero ad maiorem; econverso descensus[22]. Et sic ascensus et descensus fiunt[23] dupliciter in ordine numeri[24].

De differentia harum dictionum 'tantum' et 'solus'

70   Hiis habitis habentur septem questiones que fiebant circa quartam[1] questionem, que erat descendendo ad unam causam exclusionis, scilicet que erant ea que debent excludi. Consequenter queritur

the nominative case; and in that way it is disproved and thus is false; and the meaning of 'Than three alone *etc.*' is *than three alone two are fewer and not other ones than two are fewer than three alone*. And so one of the propositions it it is analysed into is false, *viz.* 'Than three alone two are fewer', because two are fewer than all other numbers in the upward direction. And so not than three alone two are fewer.

On a certain rule

68 Hence one usually presents the following rule:

> *Whenever two syncategorematic words are used side by side in the same locution, the expression is ambiguous because the one can be a modification of the other or the other way round.*

And this amounts to what the *Antiqui* used to say, that one could include or, conversely, be included by the other, or that one could exclude or be excluded by the other.

69 Note that in numbers there are two kinds of ascent: one is an ascent of causes and the other an ascent of quantity or an increase in quantity. Thus when speaking of the ascent of causes, all smaller numbers are superior to larger ones, because all smaller ones are the cause of larger ones. Thus the smaller the number the more superior it is, because in that respect it is a prior cause; and every prior cause is superior. Hence the supreme principle in number is unity. And <to proceed> from larger numbers (when speaking of the ascent of cause) is always to ascend to any smaller number, and ultimately to unity; <to proceed> conversely, however, is to descend. On the other hand, when speaking of an ascent of quantity or an ascent of an increase in quantity, in that case larger numbers are superior and smaller ones inferior, because the increase is greater, or the quantity larger, in larger than it is in smaller ones. In this way there is an ascent from a smaller number to a larger one, conversely there is a descent. Thus an ascent and descent occur in two ways in the order of number.

On the difference between the words 'tantum' and 'solus'

70 Now that these items have been discussed, we have dealt with the seven problems that came up concerning the fourth one, which was, when descending to one cause of exclusion, what the things are that are to be excluded. Next we shall deal with the fifth problem

de quinta questione que fiebat in principio[2] huius tractatus, scilicet[3]
qualiter 'tantum' et 'solus' differant in suis exclusionibus. Et dicendum quod hec dictio 'solus' excludit semper ab aliquo casuali[4], sive
ponatur in subiecto sive in predicato, ut 'solus Sortes currit' idest
Sortes[5] *et nullus alius*; in predicato autem, ut 'do[6] tibi solum denarium'
idest *denarium et nullam aliam rem*. Sed hec dictio 'tantum' aliquando
excludit ab aliquo casuali, ut 'tantum Sortes currit' vel[7] 'tantum
album currit' vel 'tantum legens currit' idest *Sortes currit et nullus
alius*[8], et sic de aliis; aliquando excludit ab aliquo actu reliquos actus,
ut cum dicitur [*P62rb*] 'Sortes tantum legit' idest[9] *legit et nichil aliud
facit*. Sed contra. Hec dictio 'tantum' est adverbium. Ergo semper
excludit ab actu, quia adverbium natum[10] est determinare verbum et
ferri ad ipsum.

71   Et dicendum quod sicut dispositio substantie est duplex, quia
una est dispositio substantie secundum se et absolute (ut album,
nigrum et consimilia) et alia est dispositio substantie[1] mediante actu
(ut cum dicitur 'iste incedit superbus', hec dictio 'superbus' in hac
oratione dicit superbiam que inest substantie per actum), — similiter[2] duplex est dispositio actus, quia quedam est actus secundum se
et[3] absolute (ut 'bene', 'male', 'velociter') et talis dispositio actus
semper determinat actum[4] absolute et non mediante substantia, ut
'bene legit', 'velociter currit'; alia est dispositio[5] [*N54va*] actus mediante substantia ut 'tantum', 'tantummodo', 'solum'[6], solummodo'; et
tales dispositiones actus aliquando determinant actum absolute, aliquando[7] vero[8] mediante substantia. Et ideo quando hec dictio 'tantum' determinat actum absolute, tunc excludit ab aliquo actu[9] omnes
alios actus; quando vero determinat actum mediante substantia vel[10]
aliquo casuali, tunc [*T33vb*] excludit ab ipso[11] casuali, ut[12] patuit in
predictis[13] exemplis.

[*[5]*], which was stated at the beginning of this chapter, namely in what way the words '*tantum*' and '*solus*' are different as regards their kinds of exclusions. The answer should be that '*solus*' always excludes from something expressed in a grammatical case, whether it occurs in subject-position or in predicate-position, *e.g.* '*solus Sortes currit*' ('Socrates alone is running'), that is, *Sortes et nullus alius* (*Socrates and no one else*); in predicate-position *e.g.* '*do tibi solum denarium*' ('I give you a *denarius* alone'), that is, *denarium et nullum alium* (*a denarius and nothing else*). The word '*tantum*', on the other hand, sometimes excludes from something expressed in a grammatical case, *e.g.* '*tantum Sortes currit*' ('Only Socrates is running') or '*tantum album currit*' ('Only a white thing is running') or '*tantum legens currit*' ('Only a reader is running'), that is, *Sortes currit et nullus alius* (*Socrates is running and no one else*), and so on; sometimes from a certain act it excludes other acts, *e.g.* in the expression '*Sortes tantum legit*' ('Socrates is only reading'), that is, *legit et nichil aliud facit* (*he is reading and doing nothing else*). However, there is an argument to the contrary. The word '*tantum*' is an adverb. Therefore it always excludes from an act, because the function of an adverb is to modify an act and to refer to the act.

71 The answer should be that, just as the disposition of a substance is of two kinds: one is a disposition in itself and absolutely (*e.g.* a white <thing>, a black <thing> and the like) and the other is a disposition of a substance with an act mediating (*e.g.* in the expression '*iste incedit superbus*' ('He struts proud'),[29] the word '*superbus*' in this sentence indicates pride which inheres in the substance in virtue of the act),— likewise the disposition of an act is of two kinds: one is a disposition in itself and absolutely (*e.g.* 'well', 'badly', 'fast') and this type of disposition of an act always modifies an act absolutely and not with a substance mediating, *e.g.* 'He reads well', 'He runs fast'; the other is a disposition of an act with a substance mediating, *e.g.* '*tantum*', '*tantummodo*' ('only'), '*solum*', '*solummodo*' ('alone'), and these types of dispositions of an act sometimes modify an act absolutely and sometimes with a substance mediating. Hence when the word '*tantum*' modifies an act absolutely, then it excludes from some acts all other acts; when, on the other hand, it modifies an act with a substance mediating or something expressed in a grammatical case, then it conveys an exclusion from the latter, as has become evident in the examples mentioned above.

---

[29] Cf. Iuvenalis, *Satyra* XII, 125-6.

Sophisma

72 Item[1]. Queritur de hoc sophismate SOLUS SORTES EXCLUDI-
TUR, posito quod solus Sortes excludatur ab aliquo subiecto respectu
alicuius predicati et nullus alius[2]. Probatio prime. Sortes excluditur.
Et nullus alius a Sorte excluditur. Ergo solus Sortes excluditur. Contra. Hec est quedam[3] propositio exclusiva in qua excluduntur omnes
alii a Sorte. Non ergo solus Sortes excluditur.

73 Solutio. Prima simpliciter vera. Et improbatio peccat secundum
quid et simpliciter, quia quamvis sit propositio simpliciter exclusiva,
tamen sua exclusio fit respectu huius actus 'excludi'[1]. Sed quod excluditur ab exclusione, non excluditur, sicut quod privatur a[2] privatione, non privatur quia privare a privatione non est privare sed potius
dare habitum, ut[3] privare cecitatem[4] non est privare sed[5] dare visum.
Et sic privare[6] privationem non est privare et privari privatione non
est privari. Et ideo excludi ab exclusione non [*P62va*] est excludi.

74 Item. Videtur quod debeat 'solus'[1] restringere terminum cui
adiungitur, per quandam regulam prius datam:

> *omne adiectivum non diminuens nec habens vim[2] ampliandi adiunctum ex eadem parte*
> *termino communi restringit terminum cui adiungitur.*

Sed[3] hec dictio 'solus' est talis. Ergo debet[4] restringere terminum[5]
cui[6] adiungitur. Et dicendum quod regula[7] debet intelligi de adiec-
tivis[8] specialibus (ut[9] 'albus', 'niger' et consimilia) et non de adiecti-
vis[10] generalibus, quia generalia non restringunt, eoquod restringens debet esse minus[11] commune. Sed 'solus' est adiungibile rebus
omnium generum. Et ideo non potest restringere. Vel dicendum
quod quedam sunt adiectiva que imponuntur ab aliqua qualitate (ut
'albus' ab[12] 'albedine' et 'niger' a 'nigredine') et talia restringunt
quando qualitates [*N54vb*] a quibus sumuntur, sunt speciales. Alia
autem sunt adiectiva que imponuntur a substantia oblique sumpta, ut
'solus'; 'solus' enim est 'non cum alio'. Unde in[13] eo intelligitur iste
ablativus 'alio' significans substantiam diversam[14] in obliquitate. Et
talia non restringunt.

Sophisma

72   There is a problem concerning the sophisma-sentence SO-
CRATES ALONE IS EXCLUDED, supposing that Socrates is excluded
from some subject with respect to some predicate and no one else is
excluded. Proof of the original sentence: Socrates is excluded and no
one other than Socrates is excluded. Therefore Socrates alone is
excluded. There is an argument to the contrary. This is an exclusive
proposition in which all others than Socrates are excluded. Therefore Socrates alone is not excluded.

73   Solution. The original sentence is true *simpliciter* and the disproof commits the fallacy of reasoning from something taken in a
certain sense to the same thing taken *simpliciter*, because although it
is a proposition exclusive *simpliciter*, nevertheless the exclusion occurs with respect to the act 'to be excluded'. Now what is excluded
from an exclusion is not excluded, just as what is deprived of a
privation is not deprived, because to deprive of a privation is not to
deprive but rather to grant a possession, just as to deprive of blindness
is not to deprive but rather to grant sight. And so to deprive of a
privation is not to deprive and to be deprived of a privation is not to be
deprived. Hence to be excluded from an exclusion is not to be
excluded.

74   Again, it may be argued that 'alone' should restrict the term to
which it is adjoined, on account of the rule presented earlier:[30]

*Every adjective which is neither diminutional nor ampliative juxtaposed to a common
term restricts the term it is adjoined to.*

Now 'alone' is such a word. Therefore it should restrict the term it is
adjoined to. The answer should be that the rule is to be taken as
dealing with specific adjectives (*e.g.* 'white', 'black' and the like)
and not as dealing with general adjectives, because general ones do
not restrict, as the restringent must be less common. Now 'alone'
can be adjoined to things of all kinds. Therefore it cannot restrict. Or
the answer should be that there are some adjectives imposed after
some quality (*e.g.* 'white' after whiteness and 'black' after blackness)
and these types restrict when the qualities after which they are
taken are specific ones. There are other adjectives, however, imposed after some substance taken in an oblique case, *e.g.* '*solus*'; for
'*solus*' means '*non cum alio*' ('not with another'). So in this expression
the ablative '*alio*' ('with another') is understood which signifies a different substance in an oblique case. And these types do not restrict.

---

[30]   Cf. *Tractatus* XI, cap. 4, p. 200(4-8), ed. De Rijk.

Sophisma

75   Item. Posito quod solus Sortes sciat hoc[1] enuntiabile 'equum esse animal' et ipse cum Platone et cum aliis multis sciat multa alia enuntiabilia, queritur de hoc sophismate SOLUS SORTES SCIT ALIQUOD ENUNTIABILE QUOD NON[2] OMNIS ALIUS A PLATONE IGNORAT. Probatio. Sortes scit aliquod enuntiabile quod[3] alius a Platone ignorat, quia scit equum esse animal, et hoc enuntiabile alius a Platone ignorat. Ergo[4] omnis[5] alius vel[6] non omnis alius a Platone. Si[7] omnis[8], ergo solus Sortes scit aliquod enuntiabile quod omnis alius a Platone ignorat. Ergo Sortes scit aliquod enuntiabile quod Sortes ignorat. Quod falsum est. Si non omnis, ergo solus Sortes scit aliquod enuntiabile quod non omnis alius a Platone ignorat. Et hec est prima. Contra[9]. Alius a Sorte scit aliquod enuntiabile quod non omnis alius a Platone ignorat, sicut[10] unum de communiter scitis. Non ergo solus[11] Sortes scit *etc.*

76   Solutio. Prima [*P62vb*] simpliciter vera. Et iste due 'alius a Sorte scit aliquod enuntiabile quod non omnis alius a Platone ignorat' et 'non alius a Sorte scit aliquod[1] enuntiabile quod non omnis alius a Platone ignorat' contradicunt uno modo et alio modo non, quia hoc quod dico 'aliquod[2] enuntiabile' supponit indefinite[3] per implicationem sequentem, que potest restringere[4] pro diversis, cum ponatur in ea hoc relativum diversitatis, scilicet[5] 'aliud' indefinite[6] sumptum. Unde [*T34ra*] in prima hoc quod dico 'aliquod enuntiabile' supponit solum[7] pro hoc, scilicet 'equum esse animal', et hoc relativum 'alius' tenetur pro Sorte solum. Unde concedo quod solus Sortes scit aliquod enuntiabile et nullus alius a Sorte, hoc[8] modo. Cum autem dicit 'alius a Sorte scit aliquod enuntiabile quod[9] non omnis alius a Platone ignorat', tunc hoc quod dico 'aliquod enuntiabile' non supponit pro eodem enuntiabili sed pro alio. Unde non contradicunt. Sed[10] cum pro eodem supponunt[11], tunc contradicunt.

Sophisma

75   Suppose that Socrates alone knows the stateable 'that a horse is an animal' and that along with Plato and many others he knows many other stateables, then there is a problem concerning the sophisma-sentence SOCRATES ALONE KNOWS SOME STATE-ABLE WHICH NOT EVERYONE OTHER THAN PLATO IS IGNO-RANT OF. Proof: Socrates knows some stateable which someone other than Plato is ignorant of, because he knows that a horse is an animal, and this stateable someone other than Plato is ignorant of. Therefore everyone other than or not everyone other than Plato. If everyone, therefore Socrates alone knows some stateable which everyone other than Plato is ignorant of. Therefore Socrates alone knows some stateable which Socrates is ignorant of. And this is false. If not everyone other, therefore Socrates alone knows some stateable which not everyone other than Plato is ignorant of. And this is the original sentence. There is an argument to the contrary. Someone other than Socrates knows some stateable which not everyone other than Plato is ignorant of, such as one of commonly known ones. Therefore not Socrates alone knows *etc.*.

76   Solution. The original sentence is *simpliciter* true. And the two propositions 'Someone other than Socrates knows some stateable which not everyone other than Plato is ignorant of' and 'Not someone other than Socrates knows some stateable which not everyone other than Plato is ignorant of' are contradictory in one way, whereas in another way they are not, because the expression 'some stateable' has indefinite supposition in virtue of the relative clause that follows, for the latter can restrict to diverse things, because it contains a relative of diversity, *viz.* 'someone other' taken indefinitely. Thus in the original sentence the expression 'some stateable' supposits for the stateable 'that a horse is an animal' only, and the relative 'someone other' holds for Socrates only. Thus I concede that Socrates alone knows some stateable and no one other than Socrates does, in this way. On the other hand, when someone says 'Someone other than Socrates knows some stateable of which not everyone other than Plato is ignorant', in that case the expression 'some stateable' does not supposit for the same stateable but for another one. Thus they are not contradictory, However, when they supposit for the same one, they are contradictory.

TRACTATUS QUARTUS

DE DICTIONIBUS EXCEPTIVIS

Introductio

1   Sequitur[1] de dictionibus exceptivis, ut 'preter', 'preterquam' et 'nisi'. Et primo queritur quid significet [*N55ra*] dictio exceptiva; secundo propter quid dicatur dictio exceptiva; tertio que et quot sint cause que exiguntur ad exceptionem; quarto quam habitudinem sive quam comparationem denotet dictio exceptiva; quinto cum semper excipiat partem multitudinis, a qua multitudine debeat[2] excipere; sexto utrum propositio exceptiva sit universalis vel singularis; septimo quomodo sumatur sub ea, sive quomodo sit sillogizabilis[3]; octavo et ultimo queritur de constructione ipsius.

Quid significet dictio exceptiva

2   Circa primum nota quod hec dictio 'preter' non significat exceptionem, sicut[1] quidam[2] dicunt, quia[3] neque significat[4] eam ut conceptam[5] neque ut exercitam. Quod probatur eisdem rationibus quibus[6] ostendebatur prius quod[7] hec dictio 'solus' non significat [*P63ra*] exclusionem[8] ut conceptam neque ut exercitam. Item. Ostenditur per hoc quod neutro modo significat exceptionem hec dictio 'preter', quia[9]: Nulla prepositio[10] significat affectum vel exercitium[11] sed tantum significat habitudinem casualis[12] ad actum. Ergo hec dictio 'preter' non significat exceptionem ut affectum[13] vel ut[14] exercitium. Et quod non significat eam ut conceptam[15] patet sicut prius de dictionibus exclusivis. Et sic hec dictio 'preter' nullo modo[16] significat exceptionem. Quod concedimus dicentes quod hec dictio 'preter' significat instantiam in parte sive 'non cum hoc'[17]. Et ideo dicitur dictio instantiva.

3   Sed tunc obicitur quod cum sit instantia propositio propositioni[1] contraria (ut est in *Secundo Priorum*) et hec est aut universalis aut

CHAPTER IV

ON EXCEPTIVE WORDS

1 Next we shall deal with exceptive words, *viz.* '*preter*' ('but'), '*preterquam*' ('except'), and '*nisi*' ('unless'). And *[1]* first there is a problem what an exceptive word signifies, *[2]* secondly why it is called an exceptive word, *[3]* thirdly which and how many are the causes required for an exception, *[4]* fourthly which relationship or comparison an exceptive word indicates, *[5]* fifthly, as it always excepts a part of a multitude, from what multitude it is to except, *[6]* sixthly whether an exceptive proposition is universal or singular, *[7]* seventhly in which way a conclusion can be drawn from it or how it can be used in a syllogism, *[8]* eighthly, and finally, there is a problem concerning its construction.

What an exceptive word signifies

2 *Ad [1]:* As to the first item, note that the word 'but' does not signify an exception, as some people say, for it neither signifies an exception as conceived of nor as carried out. And this is proved by the same arguments by which it was proved earlier[1] that the word 'alone' does not signify an exclusion as conceived of nor as carried out. Moreover, this is shown by the fact that the word 'but' signifies an exception in neither of these ways: no preposition signifies an affect or carrying out but merely signifies a relationship of <what is expressed in> a grammatical case to an act. Therefore the word 'but' does not signify an exception as an affect or as a being carried out. And that it does not signify an exception as conceived of is evident in the same way as for exclusive words.[2] Thus the word 'but' in no way signifies an exception. Well, we agree with this saying that the word 'but' signifies a partial counter-instance or 'not with this'. And therefore it is called a counter-instantive word.

3 However, in that case there is an argument to the contrary: because a 'counter-instance' is a proposition contrary to another

---

1 Cf. above, ch. III, cap. 4.
2 Cf. *ibid.*.

particularis, ergo contingit instantiam ferre[2] non solum in parte sed etiam in toto. Ergo sicut habemus dictionem[3] instantivam in parte, sicut 'preter'[4], ita debemus habere dictionem instantivam in toto. Quod concedimus dicentes quod dictiones exceptive (ut 'preter' et consimiles) ferunt instantiam in parte, dictiones vero exclusive (ut 'tantum', 'solus' et consimiles) ferunt instantiam in toto, quia iste removent partem a toto, ut 'omnis homo preter Sortem'[5], ille vero econtrario removent totum a parte, ut 'tantum Sortes' idest[6] *Sortes et nullus alius homo*. Et[7] sic patet primum.

Quare dictio dicatur exceptiva

4   Secundi vero patet solutio per predicta, quia hec dictio 'preter' et consimiles dicuntur exceptive non[1] ab exceptione ut[2] significata (ut obiectum est) sed ab exceptione ut[3] exercita, sicut 'tantum'[4] et 'solus' dicuntur exclusive non[5] ab exclusione ut[6] significata sed <ut> exercita.

Que et quot sint cause exceptionis

5   [*N55rb*] Circa tertium queritur[1] que et quot sint cause que exiguntur ad exceptionem. Videtur enim[2] quod sint tria[3], quia non potest fieri exceptio nisi aliquid excipiatur et ab[4] aliquo et respectu alicuius. Ut cum dicitur 'omnis homo preter Sortem currit', 'Sortes' est exceptum et hec distributio[5] 'omnis homo' est[6] id a quo [*P63rb*] excipitur, et iste actus qui[7] est 'currere' est id[8] respectu cuius excipitur. Ergo ista tria necessaria sunt ad exceptionem. Et dicendum quod quinque exiguntur[9] ad exceptionem. Unum est excipiens (et hec est anima) et alterum est instrumentum[10] excipiendi[11] (et hec est dictio exceptiva, [*T34rb*] ut 'preter' et consimiles); et etiam[12] exiguntur illa tria de quibus obicit[13], scilicet quod excipitur et a quo excipitur et respectu cuius[14]. Unde predicta tria de quibus obiciebat[15], exiguntur

proposition (as it says in Book II of the *Prior Analytics*)[3] and this is either a universal or a particular one, therefore it is possible to bring about not only a counter-instance in a part but also in a whole. Therefore just as we have a word counter-instantive in a part, *e.g.* 'but', so we must have a word counter-instantive in a whole. Well, we agree with this saying that exceptive words (*e.g.* 'but' and the like) bring about a counter-instance in a part, whereas exclusive words (*e.g.* 'only', 'alone' and the like) bring about a counter-instance in a whole. For the former remove a part from a whole, *e.g.* 'every man but Socrates', whereas the latter contrariwise remove a whole from a part, *e.g.* 'only Socrates', that is, *Socrates and no other man*. And so <the solution to> the first problem is evident.

Why a word is called exceptive

4   The solution to the second problem [*[2]*] is evident by what has been said: the word 'but' and the like are called exceptive not by an exception as signified (as was argued to the contrary) but by an exception as carried out, just as 'only' and 'alone' are called 'exclusive' not by an exclusion as signified but as carried out.

Which and how many are the causes of exclusion

5   *Ad [3]:* As to the third item, there is a problem which and how many are the causes required for an exception. For it may be argued that there are three, for one can only make an exception if there is something of which, something from which and something in respect of which an exception is made. For instance, in the expression 'Every man but Socrates is running', Socrates is the exception, the distribution 'every man' is that from which the exception is made and the act 'to run' is that in respect of which the exception is made. Therefore these three [*i.e.* causes] are necessary for an exception. The answer should be that there are five <causes> required for an exception. [1] One is an excepting entity (and this is the soul), [2] another is an instrument for excepting (and this is an exceptive word, *e.g.* 'but' and the like); and what is also required are the three things brought forward by the opponent, *viz.* [3] that which is excepted, [4] that from which an exception is made and [5] that in respect of which an exception is made. Thus the three causes

---

[3]   *Anal. Priora* II 26, 69a37.

sed non sufficiunt ad exceptionem, quia predicta quinque oportet[16] semper concurrere ad hoc quod[17] fiat exceptio.

6   Sed obicitur quod hec dictio 'preter' non semper tenetur exceptive sed quandoque tenetur diminutive, sicut quidam dicunt, quia[1]: Hec est vera 'decem preter unum sunt[2] novem'. Sed ex denario non[3] potest[4] fieri novenarius nisi per diminutionem denarii numeri[5]. Ergo oportet quod hec dictio 'preter' teneatur ibi diminutive[6]. Et sic hec dictio 'preter' equivocatur ad exceptionem et[7] diminutionem. Sed contra. Omnis pars est semper[8] in suo toto secundum habitudinem per[9] quam[10] habitudinem est pars, ut si in actu est pars, et secundum actum est in suo toto; et si in habitu est pars, et secundum habitum est in suo toto. Ergo pars[11] secundum quod est pars, non potest esse extra suum totum[12]. Ergo si ponatur extra suum totum, tunc non erit extra secundum se sed respectu alicuius alterius. Sed sicut unitas est pars denarii[13], ita unum est pars decem. Ergo unum[14] non potest[15] excipi a[16] decem nisi respectu alicuius tertii[17]. Ergo cum dicitur 'decem preter unum sunt novem', ibi est quod excipitur (quia unum) et a quo excipitur (quia decem) et respectu cuius (quia respectu huius[18] actus, scilicet 'esse novem'[19]), et etiam excipiens quod excipit (scilicet[20] intellectus) et instrumentum per quod excipit[21]. Ergo ibi sunt quinque cause predicte. Que sufficiunt ad exceptionem. Ergo tenetur ibi exceptive et non diminutive. Et sic in omnibus consimilibus. [*P63va*] Et sic[22] semper tenetur [*N55va*] exceptive. Quod concedimus.

Quam habitudinem denotet dictio exceptiva

7   Circa quartum queritur in hunc modum. Cum ubicumque est[1] exceptio, excipiatur[2] aliquid ab aliquo quod fert[3] instantiam secundum partem eius[4] a quo excipitur, necesse est ergo quod id quod excipitur sit pars eius a quo excipitur; et[5] etiam[6] sit[7] secundum actum in eo a[8] quo excipitur. Sed cum pars subiectiva et[9] pars in modo non ferant instantiam contra suum totum, quia[10] non sunt actualiter in suo toto, ideo neutra harum potest excipi a suo toto. Ergo oportet quod

brought forward by the opponent are required but do not suffice for an exception, because the five things mentioned above always need to concur in order to make an exception.

6   Now it is argued to the contrary that the word 'but' is not always taken exceptively, but sometimes diminutionally, as some people say, because the following is true: 'Ten but one are nine'. Now from a tenfold one can never make a ninefold except by diminishing the number ten. Therefore it is necessary that the word 'but' be taken in a diminutional sense in this case. And in this way the word 'but' is equivocal in relation to an exception and a diminution. However, there is an argument to the contrary. Every part is always in a whole owing to the relationship in virtue of which it is a part; for example, if it is actually a part, it is also actually in its whole, and if it is potentially a part, it is also potentially in its whole. Therefore a part *qua* part cannot have being outside its whole. Therefore if a part is posited outside a whole, then it will not be outside as such but only with respect to something else. Now just as a unity is a part of a tenfold, in the same way one is a part of ten. Therefore one can only be excepted from ten with respect to some third thing. Therefore in the expression 'Ten but one are nine', there is in this case something that is excepted (*viz.* one), something from which the exception is made (*viz.* ten) and something in respect of which the exception is made (*viz.* 'the act of being nine'), and also there is an excepting entity (*viz.* the intellect) and an instrument by means of which it makes the exception. Therefore there are in this case the five causes mentioned above. And they are sufficient for an exception. Therefore it [*i.e.* 'but'] is taken exceptively and not diminutionally. And the same goes for all similar cases. Therefore it is always taken exceptively. We agree with this.

What relationship an exceptive word indicates

7   *Ad [4]:* As to the fourth item, there is a problem of the following kind. It is on account of the fact that wherever there is an exception, something is excepted from something that forms a counter-instance in a part of that from which the exception is made, that it is therefore necessary that that which is excepted be a part of that from which the exception is made and actually be in that from which the exception is made. Now it is because a subjective part and a part in mode do not present a counter-instance against their whole, because they do not actually exist in their whole, that therefore neither of these parts can be excepted from its whole. Therefore it is necessary

dictio exceptiva dicat habitudinem partis actualiter existentis in toto[11] ad suum totum. Et ideo omnes[12] iste sunt incongrue 'homo preter Sortem currit', 'Plato preter Sortem currit', quia exceptum non est actualiter pars eius a quo fit exceptio. Et ita dictio exceptiva non repperit habitudinem ad[13] quam naturaliter[14] ordinetur[15].

8   Item. Nulla pars fert instantiam contra suum totum nisi per sui[1] negationem contradicat ei. Sed pars subiectiva per sui negationem non contradicit toti, quia Sorte non existente adhuc[2] est homo[3]. Et similiter de parte in modo. Ergo relinquitur quod partes omnes[4] aliorum generum contradicant[5] suo toti per sui negationem[6]. Sed ille[7] sunt actualiter in suo[8] toto, ut patet in toto integrali et toto in quantitate. Ergo hec dictio 'preter' solum dicit habitudinem partis actualiter existentis in suo toto ad[9] suum totum. Item[10]. Nulla pars[11] fert instantiam toti nisi sequatur ad ipsum. Sed nulla pars sequitur ad suum totum nisi actualiter sit in[12] ipso. Ergo nulla[13] pars fert instantiam contra suum totum nisi actualiter sit in ipso. Ergo hec dictio 'preter' dicit comparationem[14] partis actualiter existentis in suo toto ad suum totum. Quod concedimus.

De quibusdam regulis

9   Ex hiis patent plures regule. Prima talis est:

oportet exceptum secundum[1] naturam actualiter contineri in eo a quo fit exceptio, et removeri [T34va; P63vb] ab ipso respectu predicati vel alicuius tertii.

Ut hic[2]: 'omnis homo preter Sortem currit'. Secunda regula est talis:

quotienscumque tot excipiuntur[3] quot supponuntur, locutio est impropria[4] et falsa.

Ut 'omnis homo preter omnem [N55vb] hominem currit'[5]. Cum enim exceptum non stat[6] in ratione partis, non repperit[7] dictio exceptiva comparationem quam exigit; et sic est ibi improprietas[8]. Et cum predicatum ponatur in quolibet et removeatur[9] a quolibet, oportet ipsam esse falsam. Tertia regula talis est:

contra totam falsam non est[10] dare instantiam.

that an exceptive word indicates a relationship of a part actually existing in a whole to its whole. And therefore all the following sentences are unwell-formed: '*A man but Socrates is running', '*Plato but Socrates is running', because that which is excepted is not actually a part of that from which the exception is made. And so the exceptive word has not encountered a relationship to which it is naturally ordered.

8   Furthermore, no part presents a counter-instance against its whole unless it contradicts the latter by its being denied. Now a subjective part does not by its being denied contradict a whole, because when Socrates does not exist *man* still exists, and the same goes for a part in mode. It follows therefore that all parts of other kinds contradict their whole by their being denied. Now those parts are actually in their whole, as is evident in an integral whole and a quantative whole. Therefore the word 'but' only indicates a relationship of a part actually existing in its whole to its whole. Moreover, no part presents a counter-instance against a whole unless the former follows from the latter. Well, no part follows from its whole unless the former is actually in the latter. Therefore no part presents a counter-instance against its whole unless the former is actually in the latter. Therefore the word 'but' indicates a relationship of a part actually existing in its whole to its whole. We agree with this.

On certain rules

9   From these remarks many rules are evident. The first rule is:

> [1] It is necessary that that which is excepted is by nature actually contained in that from which the exception is made, and is removed from it with respect to the predicate or some third thing.

For example, 'Every man but Socrates is running'. The second is:

> [2] Whenever as many things are excepted as are supposited, the locution is improper and false.

For example, 'Every man but every man is running'. For because that which is excepted does not have the nature of a part, the exceptive word has not encountered the relationship it requires; and so in this case one has an improper locution. Moreover, on account of the fact that the predicate is asserted in anything whatsoever and removed from anything whatsoever, it is necessary that the locution be false. The third rule is:

> [3] Against a proposition that is wholly false one cannot give a counter-instance.

Ut 'omnis homo preter omnem hominem est lapis'. Propositio autem tota falsa est que est contraria vere , ut vult Aristotiles in *Secundo Priorum*. Ut 'omnis homo est asinus'; hec est contraria vere, idest habet falsitatem pro qualibet sui parte. Unde a tali non potest fieri exceptio, quia oporteret[11] excipere[12] quamlibet sui[13] partem. Et sic omnia[14] exciperentur quecumque supposita[15] essent. Quod est contra secundam regulam.

Sophismata

10   Secundum predicta queritur de hoc sophismate OMNE ANIMAL PRETER HOMINEM EST IRRATIONALE. Probatio. Hec est falsa 'omne animal est irrationale'. Et non est instantia nisi in[1] homine. Ergo facta exceptione pro[2] eo est vera. Ergo hec est vera 'omne animal preter hominem est irrationale'. Contra. Omne animal preter hominem est irrationale. Ergo omne animal preter hunc hominem est irrationale. Quod[3] falsum est.

11   Solutio. Prima vera. Et[1] probatio bene tenet. Sed improbatio peccat secundum figuram dictionis a simplici[2] ad personalem, quia iste accusativus 'hominem' post dictionem exceptivam habet simplicem suppositionem, cum sit terminus communis cum dicit 'omne animal preter hominem est irrationale'. Sed cum dicit 'omne animal preter hunc hominem', iste accusativus 'hunc hominem' habet personalem suppositionem[3]. Et sic est ibi figura dictionis. Item. Est ibi *consequens* ab inferiori ad superius cum distributione (sicut hic: 'omnis homo; [*P64ra*] ergo omne animal'), quia in hac propositione 'omne animal preter hominem est irrationale' ista distributio 'omne[4] animal' comprehendit in[5] se omne animal[6] aliud ab homine tantum. Sed cum dicitur 'omne animal preter hunc hominem', ista distributio 'omne animal' comprehendit in[7] se omne animal aliud ab isto homine et ita comprehendit omnia animalia que[8] prius comprehendebat, et etiam omnes homines alios ab isto homine. Et sic augmentatur[9] suppositio, sicut hic: 'omne animal aliud ab homine; ergo omne animal aliud ab isto homine'.

For example, 'Every man but every man is a stone'. A proposition that is wholly false is one that is the contrary of a true one, as Aristotle has it in Book II of the *Prior Analytics*.[4] For example, the proposition 'Every man is an ass' is the contrary of a true one, that is to say, it is false for each one of its parts. Thus from such a proposition there cannot be made an exception, because it would be necessary that every one of its parts be excepted. Thus any one of the *supposita* would be excepted. And this is contrary to the second rule.

Sophismata

10　As regards what has been said, there is a problem concerning the sophisma-sentence EVERY ANIMAL BUT MAN IS IRRATIONAL. Proof: the following is false: 'Every animal is irrational'. And the only counter-instance is man. Therefore if an exception has been made for him the sentence is true. Therefore the following is true: 'Every animal but man is irrational'. There is an argument to the contrary. Every animal but man is irrational. Therefore every animal but this man is irrational. And this is false.

11　Solution. The original sentence is true and the proof holds good. The disproof, on the other hand, commits the fallacy of figure of speech by proceeding from simple to personal supposition, because the accusative 'man' following the exceptive word has simple supposition, since it is a common term in the expression 'Every animal but man is irrational'. However, in the expression 'Every animal but this man (*preter hunc hominem*)', the accusative '*hunc hominem*' ('this man') has personal supposition. And thus one has in this case a fallacy of figure of speech. Moreover, in this case there is a fallacy of the consequent <by proceeding> from what is less general to what is more general in combination with a distribution (just as in 'Every man; therefore every animal'), because in the proposition 'Every animal but man is irrational', the distribution 'every animal' comprehends every animal other than man only. However, in the expression 'Every animal but this man', the distribution 'every animal' comprehends every animal other than this man and so it comprehends all animals it comprehended earlier, and also all men other than this man. And so the supposition is extended, just as in 'Every animal other than man; therefore every animal other than this man'.

---

[4]　*Anal. Priora* II 2, 54a4-5.

12 Idem autem est iudicium[1] de hoc sophismate OMNE ENUN-
TIABILE PRETER VERUM EST FALSUM. Et penitus[2] eadem est[3]
probatio et improbatio, et omnino eadem est solutio et de hiis OMNE
ANIMAL PRETER SANUM [*N56ra*] EST EGRUM; OMNIS QUAN-
TITAS PRETER CONTINUAM EST DISCRETA; OMNE CORPUS
PRETER INANIMATUM EST ANIMATUM.

A qua multitudine excipiat dictio exceptiva

13 Circa quintum queritur a qua [*P38vb*] multitudine habeat[1]
excipere dictio exceptiva, quia non excipit indifferenter[2] a qualibet[3]
multitudine. Nichil enim esset dictu 'homines preter Sortem currunt'. Ergo non excipit a multitudine que est in nomine pluralis
numeri. Et etiam nichil est dictu 'turba preter Sortem currit'. Ergo
non excipit a multitudine nominis collectivi.
14 Et[1] dicendum quod duplex[2] est multitudo. Quia quedam est
multitudo que est modus intelligendi. Et hec est in nomine pluralis
numeri; omnia enim accidentia partium orationis sunt modi intelligendi[3]. Et ab hac multitudine que est modus intelligendi, non excipit dictio [*T34vb*] exceptiva. Alia[4] autem est multitudo que non est
modus intelligendi sed est[5] multitudo rei. Et hec iterum[6] est duplex.
Quia est quedam potentialis. Et hec est in quolibet universali, quia
quodlibet universale potentia habet in se sua[7] individua. Et iterum
ab[8] ista non potest[9] excipere dictio exceptiva. Et ideo nichil est dictu
'homo preter Sortem currit'. Alia autem est multitudo rei que[10] est
multitudo [*P64rb*] actualis. Et hec est in toto in quantitate, quando
universale quod sumitur universaliter, continet sub se plura individua, ut 'omnis homo' vel[11] 'omne animal'. Hec[12] est etiam multitudo
que est in toto integrali et in aliis totis habentibus naturam horum.
15 Et ab hac multitudine excipit dictio exceptiva. Que est multitudo
actualis[1], quia hanc exigit[2]. Quod[3] sic[4] probatur. Dictum est enim in
predictis quod dictio exceptiva semper excipit[5] partem actualiter

12   The same judgement applies to the sophisma-sentence EVERY STATEABLE BUT THE TRUE IS FALSE. And the proof and disproof are exactly the same, and the solution to the following sophisma-sentences as well is completely the same: EVERY ANIMAL BUT THE HEALTHY IS ILL, EVERY QUANTITY BUT THE CONTINUOUS IS DISCRETE and EVERY BODY BUT THE INANIMATE IS ANIMATE.

From what multitude an exceptive word is to make an exception

13   *Ad [5]:* As to the fifth item, there is a problem from what multitude an exceptive word is to make an exception, because it does not make an exception indifferently from any multitude whatsoever. For it would make no sense to say '*Men but Socrates are running'. Therefore it does not make an exception from a multitude expressed by a noun in the plural. And it also makes no sense to say '*The mass but Socrates is running'. Therefore it does not make an exception from a multitude expressed by a collective noun.

14   The answer should be that a multitude is of two kinds. [1] One is a multitude as a mode of understanding. This kind is found in a noun in the plural; for all accidents that belong to parts of speech are modes of understanding. And from the kind of multitude that is a mode of understanding an exceptive word does not make an exception. [2] The other is the kind of multitude not taken as a mode of understanding but as a multitude of things. This kind, again, is twofold. [2.1] One is a potential multitude. This is the kind found in any universal, because any universal potentially contains its individuals. And, again, from this kind of multitude an exceptive word does not make an exception. Hence it makes no sense to say '*Man but Socrates is running'. [2.2] The second is a multitude found in a thing that is an actual multitude. And this type is found in a quantitative whole, when a universal taken universally contains under it a number of individuals, *e.g.* 'every man' or 'every animal'. Of this kind is also the multitude found in an integral whole and in other wholes that have their nature.

15   The latter [*i.e.* [2.2]] is the multitude from which an exceptive word makes an exception. It is an actual multitude, because that is what is required. And this is proved as follows. We have said in the

existentem in suo toto a[6] suo toto. Ergo cum oporteat partem aliam[7] vel alias relinqui in[8] ipso toto, quia non possunt tot excipi[9] quot supponuntur, oportet tunc quod illa alia pars vel[10] ille[11] alie partes actualiter sint in suo toto. Ergo dictio exceptiva semper exigit[12] multitudinem partium actualiter existentium in suo toto. Item. Omnes[13] partes in quas dividitur totum, ita[14] se habent ad totum quod si una est actualiter in[15] toto, et omnes alie; et si una[16] potentia[17], et omnes alie, ut patet inductive[18] in toto universali et in toto integrali et in aliis[19] totis. [*N56rb*] Sed dictio exceptiva nata est excipere partes in quas totum dividitur. Sed excipit partem actualiter existentem in toto. Ergo oportet ibi esse[20] aliam partem vel alias partes actualiter existentes[21]. Ergo dictio exceptiva exigit[22] multitudinem partium actualiter existentium in suo toto. Item. Dictio exceptiva in actu excipit. Ergo in actu invenit quod excipit a toto. Sed non inveniret[23] in actu quod exciperet[24] nisi actualiter esset in toto. Ergo quod excipit[25], actualiter est in toto. Sed nichil actualiter est in toto nisi pars actualis. Ergo dictio exceptiva semper excipit partem actualiter existentem in toto. Et[26] est idem quod prius. Quod autem dictio exceptiva excipiat[27] a quolibet toto habente in se multitudinem actualem, patet inductive[28] in quolibet toto.

De toto in quantitate, cum sophismatibus

16   Et primo patet in toto in quantitate, [*P64va*] ut 'omnis homo preter Sortem currit': hic enim a toto in quantitate excipitur pars eius. Et etiam in hoc sophismate OMNIS HOMO PRETER SORTEM EXCIPITUR, posito[1] quod omnes alii a Sorte excipiantur respectu alicuius predicati et Sortes non. Probatio prime. Hec est falsa 'omnis homo excipitur'. Et non est instantia nisi in Sorte. Ergo facta exceptione pro Sorte[2] erit vera. Ergo[3] hec est vera 'omnis homo preter Sortem excipitur'. Contra. In hac propositione dictio exceptiva

preceding[5] that an exceptive word always excepts a part actually existing in its whole from its whole. Therefore it is because it is necessary that another part or other ones remain in the whole, for one cannot except as many things as are supposited, it is necessary that this other part or the other parts actually be in their whole. Therefore an exceptive word always requires a multitude of parts actually existing in their whole. Moreover, all the parts the whole is divided into relate in such a way to their whole, that if one part is actually in its whole, so are all the others; and if one is potentially in its whole, so are all the others, as is evident from induction in case of a universal whole, an integral whole and in other wholes. Now an exceptive word has as its natural function to except the parts into which the whole is divided. Now it excepts a part existing in the whole. Therefore it is necessary that there be one part or other parts in it that actually exist. Therefore an exceptive word requires a multitude of parts actually existing in their whole. Again, an exceptive word actually excepts. Therefore it actually encounters something to except from the whole. Now it would not actually encounter something to except unless the latter actually were in the whole. Therefore what it excepts actually is in the whole. Now nothing actually is in a whole but an actual part. Therefore an exceptive word always excepts a part actually existing in the whole. And this is the same <type of argument> as before. That, however, an exclusive word makes an exception from any whole that contains an actual multitude is evident by induction in case of any whole whatsoever.

On the quantative whole, with sophismata

16   This [i.e. what has been said in cap. 15 above] is first is evident in case of a quantitative whole, e.g. 'Every man but Socrates is running': for in this case from a quantitative whole a part of it is excepted. This also happens in the sophisma-sentence EVERY MAN BUT SOCRATES IS EXCEPTED, supposing that all others than Socrates are excepted with respect to some predicate and Socrates is not. Proof of the original sentence: the proposition 'Every man is excepted' is false. And the only counter-instance is Socrates. Therefore when an exception has been made for Socrates, the proposition will be true. Therefore 'Every man but Socrates is excepted' is true. There is an argument to the contrary. In this proposition the exceptive word is adjoined to 'Socrates'. Therefore it excepts him with

---

[5]   Cf. above, capp. 7-8.

adiungitur 'Sorti'. Ergo excipit ipsum[4] respectu predicati. Ergo Sortes excipitur. Ergo prima falsa.

17   Solutio. Prima vera simpliciter[1]. Et improbatio peccat secundum quid et simpliciter, quia excipere ab exceptione non est excipere simpliciter sed secundum quid, sicut privare[2] a privatione non est privare simpliciter sed secundum quid; immo[3] potius est[4] dare habitum[5], ut privare[6] a cecitate est dare visum[7]. Ergo excipi ab exceptione non est excipi simpliciter sed secundum quid. Et ideo, licet Sortes excipiatur respectu[8] huius predicati 'excipi'[9] (sicut est in prima), non tamen excipitur simpliciter[10]. Et ideo est ibi fallacia[11] secundum quid et simpliciter. Et sic patet quod [*T35ra*] exceptio fit a toto in quantitate.

De toto integrali, cum sophismatibus

18   Patet etiam quod fit a toto integrali, ut TOTA DOMUS PRETER [*N56va*] PARIETEM EST ALBA et TOTUS SORTES PRETER PEDEM POTEST CONTINERI AB[1] ARCHA, posito quod[2] totus Sortes possit intrare archam[3], ita quod archa non possit recipere pedem eius cum eo. Probatio prime. Hec est falsa 'totus Sortes potest contineri ab archa'. Et non est instantia nisi in[4] pede[5]. Ergo facta exceptione pro pede[6] erit vera. Ergo[7] hec est[8] vera 'totus Sortes preter pedem potest contineri ab archa'. Contra. Pes Sortis potest contineri ab archa. Non ergo totus[9] Sortes preter pedem potest contineri ab archa. Ergo prima falsa.

19   Solutio. Prima vera simpliciter. Et improbatio peccat secundum accidens, quia duplici de causa pars excipitur a toto respectu predicati. Aliquando enim[1] excipitur pars [*P64vb*] a toto respectu predicati eoquod pars secundum se non vere subicitur predicato. Ut hic: 'omne animal preter hominem est irrationale': 'homo' excipitur a suo toto, quia non vere subicitur 'irrationali'[2]. Hec enim est falsa 'homo est irrationale'[3]. Aliquando autem pars excipitur a suo toto eoquod, quamvis recipiat predicatum secundum se, non tamen[4] recipit ipsum[5] prout est in suo toto. Et sic pes Sortis bene[6] potest locari in archa secundum se, sed[7] prout est unitus[8] in[9] suo toto sive cum

respect to the predicate. Therefore Socrates is excepted. Therefore the original sentence is false.

17   Solution. The original sentence is true *simpliciter* and the disproof commits the fallacy of reasoning from something taken in a certain sense to the same thing taken *simpliciter*, because to except from an exception is not to make an exception *simpliciter*, but *secundum quid*, just as to deprive of a privation is not to deprive *simpliciter*, but *secundum quid*; for rather it is to grant a possession, like to deprive of blindness is to grant sight. Therefore to be excepted from an exception is not to be excepted *simpliciter* but *secundum quid*. And therefore, although Socrates is excepted with respect to the predicate 'to be excepted' (as is the case in the original sentence), nevertheless he is not excepted *simpliciter*. Hence we have in this case a fallacy of reasoning from something taken in a certain sense to that same thing taken *simpliciter*. And thus it is evident that an exception is made from a quantative whole.

On the integral whole, with sophismata

18   It is also evident that it [*i.e.* an exception] occurs from an integral whole, *e.g.* in THE WHOLE HOUSE BUT THE WALL IS WHITE, and also in THE WHOLE SOCRATES BUT HIS FOOT FITS IN A CHEST, supposing that Socrates can enter the chest in such a way that the chest does not have room for his foot as well. Proof of the original sentence: the proposition 'The whole Socrates fits in a chest' is false, and the only counter-instance is his foot. Therefore when an exception has been made for his foot the proposition will be true. Therefore the proposition 'The whole Socrates but his foot fits in a chest' is true. There is an argument to the contrary. Socrates' foot fits in a chest. Therefore not the whole Socrates but his foot fits in a chest. Therefore the original sentence is false.

19   Solution. The original sentence is true *simpliciter* and the disproof commits the fallacy of accident, because for two reasons a part is excepted from a whole with respect to a predicate. For sometimes a part is excepted from a whole with respect to a predicate because as such it is not truly a subject of the predicate. For example, in 'Every animal but man is irrational', 'man' is excepted from its whole because it is not truly a subject of 'irrational'. For the proposition 'Man is irrational' is false. Sometimes, however, a part is excepted from its whole because although it can receive the predicate as such, it nevertheless cannot receive the latter insofar as it is in its whole. And in this way Socrates' foot by itself can well be put in a chest, but

suo toto, non[10] potest locari in archa. Unde cum dicit improbando[11] 'pes Sortis potest contineri[12] ab archa; non ergo totus Sortes preter[13] pedem potest contineri ab archa', peccat secundum accidens, quia, quamvis pes possit contineri[14] secundum[15] se, non tamen ut est[16] in suo toto. Sicut hic[17]: 'cognosco Coriscum; non ergo[18] ignoro venientem'. Licet enim cognoscam Coriscum secundum se, ignoro tamen ipsum prout[19] est veniens; et sic est ibi *accidens*.

De toto in loco et toto in tempore

20   Item. Patet quod a toto in loco potest fieri exceptio, ut 'pluit ubique preterquam hic'. Et etiam a toto in tempore, ut 'pluit[1] semper preterquam heri'.

De toto numerali, cum sophismatibus

21   Et sic patet quod dictio exceptiva[1] excipit semper a suo[2] toto habente in se multitudinem actualem[3]. Patet etiam hoc in toto numerali, ut 'decem[4] preter unum currunt'[5]. Et[6] etiam in hoc sophismate DECEM PRETER QUINQUE SUNT QUINQUE. Quod[7] sic probatur. Hec est falsa 'decem sunt quinque'. Sed[8] non est instantia nisi pro quinque. Ergo facta exceptione [*N56vb*] pro[9] quinque erit vera. Ergo hec est vera 'decem preter quinque sunt quinque'. Contra. Decem preter quinque sunt quinque. Ergo quinque non sunt quinque, quia predicatum semper removetur ab excepto.

22   Solutio. Prima est vera simpliciter. Et improbatio[1] peccat secundum accidens, quia, sicut patet, pars duobus modis causat falsitatem in oratione. Uno enim modo quia predicatum non convenit parti[2] secundum se (et sic est falsa hec 'omnis homo currit' Sorte non currente), alio autem modo causat [*P65ra*] falsitatem in oratione, quia, licet predicatum conveniat[3] parti secundum se, non tamen convenit ei ut est in suo toto (et sic est falsa hec 'totus Sortes potest locari in archa', cum pes Sortis non possit in ea esse cum Sorte). Et sicut[4] falsitas causatur per partem indifferenter, sive hoc modo sive illo, similiter[5] indifferenter contingit excipere partem a toto, aliquando hoc modo, aliquando illo, ut[6] sicut causatur falsitas[7] in

insofar as it is united in its whole or with its whole, it cannot be put in a chest. So when one says in the process of disproving 'Socrates' foot fits in a chest; therefore not the whole Socrates but his foot fits in a chest', one commits the fallacy of accident, because although by itself Socrates' foot fits in the chest, it nevertheless does not insofar as it is a part in its whole. The same goes for 'I know Coriscus; not therefore I do not know who is coming'. For although I know Coriscus as such, I do not know him insofar as he is coming; and thus we have in this case a fallacy of accident.

On the local and temporal whole

20   It is evident that from a local whole (*totum in loco*) an exception can be made, *e.g.* 'It is raining everywhere but here', and also from a temporal whole, *e.g.* 'It is always raining except for yesterday'.

On the numerical whole, with sophismata

21   And so it is evident that an exceptive word always excepts from its whole which contains an actual multitude. This is also evident in the numerical whole, *e.g.* 'Ten but one are running', and also in the sophisma-sentence TEN BUT FIVE ARE FIVE. This is proved as follows. The proposition 'Ten are five' is false. Now there is only a counter-instance for five. Therefore when an exception has been made for five, the proposition will be true. Therefore the proposition 'Ten but five are five' is true. There is an argument to the contrary. Ten but five are five. Therefore five are not five, because the predicate is always removed from what is excepted.
22   Solution. The original sentence is *simpliciter* true. The disproof commits the fallacy of accident. For, as is evident, a part in two ways causes falsity in an expression. In one way <it causes falsity> because the predicate does not come to the part as such (and in this way the proposition 'Every man is running' is false when Socrates is not running), and in another way <a part> causes falsity in an expression because although the predicate comes to the part as such, it nevertheless does not insofar as the part is in its whole (and in this way the proposition 'The whole Socrates can be put in a chest' is false, because Socrates' foot does not fit in the chest along with Socrates). And just as falsity is caused by the part, no matter whether in one way or the other, likewise one can indifferently except a part from a whole, sometimes in the one way and sometimes in the

oratione[8] per partem, ita[9] per eundem modum fiat[10] exceptio circa[11] partem.

23   Dicendum ergo[1] breviter quod prima[2] simpliciter est vera. Et improbatio peccat secundum accidens, quia 'esse quinque' predicatur de quinque secundum se (ut 'quinque sunt quinque') sed non predicatur de quinque secundum quod quinque sunt [*T35rb*] sub forma totius. Et ita peccat secundum accidens, sicut[3] prius patuit de hoc sophismate 'totus Sortes preter pedem potest locari[4] in archa'.

24   Ad[1] illud autem quod obicit quod predicatum semper[2] removetur ab excepto, dicendum quod non est verum, quia quando falsitas causatur in oratione per partem eoquod predicatum non convenit parti[3], tunc predicatum removetur ab excepto. Sed quando causatur falsitas in oratione eoquod, licet[4] predicatum conveniat parti[5] secundum se, non tamen convenit ei ut est in suo toto, tunc predicatum non contingit removeri ab[6] excepto. Et sic[7] est in proposito. Unde non sequitur 'decem preter quinque sunt quinque; ergo quinque non sunt quinque'.

Utrum exceptiva sit universalis vel singularis

25   Circa sextum sic obicitur. Propositio universalis est que omni[1] aut[2] nulli inesse significat, ut est in *Primo Priorum*. Sed propositio exceptiva non significat inesse omni aut nulli, quia ponit instantiam in aliquo[3] vel in aliquibus. Ergo propositio exceptiva non est universalis. Item ad idem. Solet dari talis[4] regula:

> *dictio exceptiva vult invenire distributionem[5] mobilem et reddere eam immobilem.*

Ergo cum dicitur 'omnis homo preter Sortem [*P65rb*] currit'[6], hec distributio 'omnis homo preter Sortem'[7] est immobilis. Ergo non stat in ratione universalis, cum contingat fieri motum sub qualibet universali. Et patet quod non est indefinita neque particularis. Ergo[8] est singularis.

other way, so that just as the falsity in an expression is caused by a part, in the same way an exception is made for a part.

23   Briefly the answer should be that the original sentence is *simpliciter* true and the disproof commits the fallacy of accident, because 'to be five' is said of five by itself (*viz.* 'five are five'), but it is not said of five insofar as five fall under the form of the whole. And so it [*i.e.* the disproof][6] commits the fallacy of accident, as has become evident before as regards the sophisma-sentence 'The whole Socrates but his foot can be put in a chest'.

24   As to the argument to the contrary[7] that a predicate is always removed from what is excepted, the answer should be that this is not true, for when falsity in an expression is caused by a part because the predicate does not come to the part, in that case the predicate is removed from what is excepted. However, when falsity in an expression is caused because, although the predicate comes to the part by itself, it nevertheless does not come to the latter insofar as it is in its whole, in that case the predicate cannot be removed from what is excepted. And this occurs in the case at issue. Hence it does not follow 'Ten but five are five; therefore five are not five'.

Whether an exceptive proposition is universal or singular

25   *Ad [6]:* As to the sixth item, there is the following argument to the contrary. A universal proposition is one that signifies something to be in all or none, as it says in Book I of the *Prior Analytics*.[8] Now an exceptive proposition does not signify something to be in all or none, because it presents a counter-instance in something or in certain things. Therefore an exceptive proposition is not universal. Again, there is an argument that yields the same conclusion. One usually presents the following rule:

> An exceptive word is designed to encounter a mobile distribution and render it immobile.

Therefore in the expression 'Every man but Socrates is running', the distribution 'every man but Socrates' is immobile. Therefore it does not have the nature of a universal because there can be movement under any universal. Also it is evident that it is not indefinite nor particular. Therefore it is singular.

---

6   Cf. above, cap. 21.
7   Cf. above, *ibid.*.
8   *Anal. Priora* I 1, 24a18.

26   Et dicendum quod propositio universalis est duplex. Quia
quedam est completa et alia incompleta. Completa est illa in qua
subiectum pro qualibet sui parte recipit predicatum, ut 'omnis homo
albus currit'; hic enim 'homo albus'[1] subicitur cursui pro quolibet
homine albo. Incompleta est illa in qua subicitur subiectum non pro
qualibet[2] sui parte sed pro quibusdam[3]. Et sic omnis exceptiva est
universalis, ut[4] 'omnis homo preter Sortem currit'. Primo autem
modo nulla exceptiva est universalis. Ad primum autem argumentum dicendum quod obicitur de propositione universali completa et
perfecta. Secundi autem argumenti patebit solutio in septima[5]
questione.

Quomodo exceptiva sit sillogizabilis

27   Circa septimum[1] sic obicitur. Cum dicitur sic 'omnis homo
preter Sortem currit; sed Plato est homo[2]; ergo Plato preter Sortem
currit', nulla est talis illatio neque sic potest fieri sillogismus. Ergo
non est sillogizabilis propositio[3] exceptiva. Item ad idem. Cum omnis
exceptiva sit immobilis (per regulam precedentem), ergo non potest
fieri sumptio sub ea[4]. Ergo non est sillogizabilis.

28   Et dicendum quod propositio exceptiva est[1] sillogizabilis[2], sic:

'omnis homo preter Sortem currit
Plato est homo
ergo Plato[3] currit',

quia ista[4] determinatio 'preter Sortem' non debet sumi ad medium
neque in conclusione, eoquod est determinatio subiecti in comparatione ad predicatum et nulla talis determinatio sumitur[5] ad medium
neque in conclusione, sed solum debet sumi determinatio eius quod
est subiectum, quia hec est absoluta, alia autem[6] est respectiva.

26   The answer should be that a universal proposition is of two
kinds: one type is complete and the other is incomplete. A complete
type is one in which the subject can receive the predicate for any of
its parts, *e.g.* 'Every white man is running'. For 'white man' is the
subject of running for any white man. An incomplete type is one in
which the subject is not made subject for any one of its parts but for
some of them. In this way every exceptive proposition is universal,
e.g. 'Every man but Socrates is running'. In the first way, however,
no exceptive proposition is universal. As to the first argument, the
answer should be that it is an argument to the contrary concerning
a complete and perfect universal proposition. To the second argument, however, the solution will become evident when discussing
the seventh item.

How an exceptive proposition can be used in a syllogism

27   *Ad [7]:* As to the seventh item, there is the following argument
to the contrary. When one says 'Every man but Socrates is running;
now Plato is a man; therefore Plato but Socrates is running', this
inference makes no sense, nor can one make a syllogism in this
way. Therefore one cannot use an exceptive proposition in a syllogism. Moreover, there is an argument that yields the same conclusion. Since every exceptive proposition is immobile (on account of
the preceding rule),[9] therefore one cannot make an assumption[10]
under it. Therefore it cannot be used in a syllogism.
28   The answer should be that an exceptive proposition can be used
in a syllogism in the following way:

'Every man but Socrates is running;
Plato is a man;
therefore Plato is running',

because the modification 'but Socrates' cannot be transferred to the
middle nor to the conclusion, because it is a modification of the subject in relation to the predicate, and no such modification can be
transferred to the middle or to the conclusion, but only a modification of that which is the subject can be transferred, because the
latter is absolute and the former relative.

---

[9]   Cf. above, cap. 25.
[10]   'To make an assumption' ('to assume') = to frame the second premise
(*'assumptio'*) of a syllogism.

29   Ad aliud autem dicendum quod propositio exceptiva est mobilis, quia est sillogizabilis, sicut dictum est, assumendo omnes partes
alias ab excepto. Unde predictam regulam dicimus esse falsam, vel[1]
saltem erit intelligenda quantum ad exceptum, hoc est quod nulla
pars potest assumi[2] cum[3] excepto. Unde non sequitur 'omnis homo
preter Sortem currit; ergo Plato preter Sortem currit; ergo Virgilius
preter Sortem currit, et sic de aliis'.

Sophisma

30   Secundum predicta queritur de hoc sophismate SORTES BIS
VIDIT[1] OMNEM HOMINEM PRETER[2] [*T35va*] PLATONEM, posito
quod Sortes una vice viderit[3] omnem hominem preter[4] Platonem et
alia vice omnem hominem. Probatio prime. Hec[5] est falsa 'Sortes bis
vidit[6] omnem hominem'[7]. Et[8] non est instantia nisi in Platone. Ergo
facta exceptione pro eo[9] erit[10] vera. Ergo hec est vera 'Sortes bis vidit
omnem hominem preter Platonem'. Contra. Sortes bis vidit omnem
hominem preter Platonem. Ergo bis non vidit Platonem. Ergo una
vice et alia vice non vidit Platonem. Quod falsum est.

31   Solutio. Prima duplex, eoquod hec dictio 'bis' potest determinare
hoc verbum 'videre' [*N57rb*] prout transit[1] supra accusativum sequentem cum sua determinatione facta per exceptionem. Et tunc est
sensus *Sortes vidit omnem hominem preter Platonem, et hoc bis*. Et tunc[2]
sequitur quod nulla vice viderit[3] Platonem. Et sic est falsa. Et sic hec
dictio 'preter' excipit ab hoc quod est 'videre omnem hominem'. Et
sic prius[4] advenit hec dictio 'preter' in oratione[5]. Alio autem modo
hec dictio 'bis' potest determinare tantum hoc quod est[6] 'videre
omnem hominem'. Et tunc hec[7] dictio 'preter' excipit ab eo quod est
'bis videre omnem hominem'. Et sic est vera, quia non bis vidit
Platonem. Et sic hec dictio 'bis' prius[8] intelligitur advenire in[9]
oratione quam hec dictio 'preter'.

29   As to the other argument to the contrary,[11] the answer should be that an exceptive proposition is mobile because it can be used in a syllogism, as has been said, by assuming all parts other than what has been excepted. Thus we say that the preceding rule[12] is false, or it is only to be taken as concerning what is excepted, that is, no part [*i.e.* no part of the universal element in the exceptive proposition] can be assumed in combination with what has been excepted. Hence it does not follow 'Every man but Socrates is running; therefore Plato but Socrates is running, therefore Virgil but Socrates is running, and so on'.

Sophisma

30   As regards what has been said, there is a problem concerning the sophisma-sentence SOCRATES HAS SEEN EVERY MAN TWICE BUT PLATO, supposing that the first time he has seen every man but Plato, whereas the second time he has seen every man. Proof of the original sentence: the proposition 'Socrates has seen every man twice' is false. And the only counter-instance is Plato. Therefore when an exception has been made for him the proposition will be true. Therefore 'Socrates has seen every man twice but Plato' is true. There is an argument to the contrary. Socrates has seen every man twice but Plato. Therefore twice he has not seen Plato. Therefore he has not seen Plato both the first and the second time. And this is false.

31   Solution. The original sentence is ambiguous, because 'twice' can modify the verb 'to see' insofar as it extends to the subsequent accusative including the modification made by the exception. And then it means *Socrates has seen every man but Plato, and he has done so twice.* In that case it follows that at no time he has seen Plato. And in this way it is false. Thus the word 'but' excepts from 'to see every man'. And so the word 'but' comes first in the sentence. In another way, however, the word 'twice' can modify the expression 'to see every man' only. In this way the word 'but' excepts from 'to see every man twice'. And thus it is true, because he has not seen Plato twice. And so the word 'twice' is understood as to come before the word 'but' in the sentence.

---

[11] Cf. above, cap. 27.
[12] Cf. above, cap. 25.

De quibusdam regulis

32   Ex predictis[1] patent plures regule. Quarum prima talis est:

cuiuslibet exceptive[2] vere sua preiacens est falsa.

Preiacens autem exceptive est illa propositio[3] a[4] qua removetur falsitas per dictionem exceptivam. Unde hic: 'omne animal est irrationale'[5] est preiacens falsa huius exceptive vere 'omne animal preter hominem[6] est irrationale'. Alia regula est talis:

si aliqua propositio est vera sine exceptione, erit falsa apposita exceptione.

Sophisma

33   [*P65vb*] Item. Queritur de hoc sophismate QUELIBET[1] VIGINTI PRETER DECEM SUNT DECEM. Probatio. Ista viginti preter decem sunt decem, illa[2] viginti preter decem sunt decem, et sic de aliis. Ergo prima vera. Contra. Preiacens est tota falsa. Ergo non potest verificari per dictionem[3] exceptivam, per hanc regulam:

contra totam falsam non est[4] dare[5] instantiam.

34   Solutio. Prima falsa simpliciter[1]. Probatio autem peccat secundum accidens, sicut in hoc sophismate OMNE COLORATUM PRETER UNUM CURRIT. Probatio. Omne album preter unum currit. Omne nigrum preter[2] unum currit. Omne medio colore coloratum preter unum currit, posito quod iste tres sunt vere. Ergo omne coloratum preter unum currit. Contra. Prima est tota falsa. Ergo non potest verificari per exceptionem[3]. Patet autem *accidens* probationis, cum quelibet premissarum non habeat instantiam nisi in uno et conclusio habeat instantiam in tribus, scilicet in uno albo et in alio nigro et in tertio[4] medio colore colorato.

On certain rules

32   From what has been said many rules are evident, of which the first is the following:

[1] Of every true exceptive proposition the basic proposition is false.

The basic proposition of an exceptive proposition is the one from which the falsity is removed by an exceptive word. Thus the proposition 'Every animal is irrational' is a false basic proposition of the true exceptive 'Every animal but man is irrational'. Another rule is:

[2] If a proposition is true without an exception, it will be false by adding an exception.

Sophisma

33   Furthermore, there is a problem concerning the sophisma-sentence ANY TWENTY BUT TEN ARE TEN. Proof: this twenty but ten are ten, that twenty but ten are ten, and so on. Therefore the original sentence is true. There is an argument to the contrary. The basic proposition is wholly false. Therefore it cannot be made true by an exception, an account of the following rule:

Against a proposition that is wholly false one cannot give a counter-instance.[13]

34   Solution. The original sentence is false *simpliciter*. The proof commits the fallacy of accident, just like in the sophisma-sentence EVERY COLOURED THING BUT ONE IS RUNNING. Proof: every white thing but one is running. Every black thing but one is running; everything of a mixed colour but one is running, supposing that these three are true. Therefore every coloured thing but one is running. There is an argument to the contrary. The original sentence is false. Therefore it cannot be made true by an exception. The fallacy of accident found in the proof, however, is evident, because both premises only have a counter-instance in one thing and the conclusion has a counter-instance in three things, namely in one white, one black and a third thing of a mixed colour.

---

[13]   Our author seems to mean 'It is useless to offer a counter-instance in order to make an exception for it', as there are only counter-instances to begin with. Or should we simply read '*exceptionem*' instead of '*instantiam*'?

De constructione dictionis exceptive

35   Circa octavum obicitur quod hec dictio 'preter' non construatur cum accusativo casu[1], quia comparatio importata per hanc dictionem 'preter' [*N57va*] est ipsius actus vel respectu actus. Ergo determinat actum. Sed actus habet significari[2] per verbum. Ergo hec dictio 'preter' determinat verbum. Ergo est adverbium. Ergo non est prepositio neque verbum, cum sint partes orationis[3] diverse[4] ab adverbio. Ergo non [*T35vb*] construitur cum accusativo.

36   Et[1] dicendum quod 'preter' non est adverbium sed prepositio, quia adverbia determinant ipsum[2] verbum ratione actus vel ratione alicuius comparationis debite ipsi actui, cum adverbium sit[3] ut *verbo adiectum*. Sed prepositiones non dicunt comparationem[4] actus, immo dicunt comparationem substantie oblique significate ad actum vel respectu actus. Et sic differunt prepositiones et adverbia. Unde non sequitur, si[5] dicat comparationem aliquam respectu actus, quod ideo[6] sit adverbium, immo potius sequitur quod non sit adverbium.

37   Item. Cum dicitur 'iste currit ibi', hoc adverbium 'ibi' dicit determinationem actus. Sed eadem determinatio significatur [*P66ra*] in hac oratione 'iste currit in illo loco'. Ergo ista prepositio 'in'[1] dicit eandem comparationem cum hoc adverbio 'ibi'. Ergo est adverbium, cum dicat eandem comparationem. Et similiter[2] de aliis prepositionibus, ut[3] 'transivit illac' idest *per illam partem*; et 'movetur sursum' idest *ad locum superiorem*; et 'currit velociter' idest *cum velocitate*; et 'factum est celitus' idest *a celo*; et 'divinitus' idest *a Deo*. Ergo prepositiones idem significant cum adverbiis, quia[4] similiter est[5] in omnibus aliis prepositionibus[6]. Ergo prepositiones non differunt ab adverbiis. Ergo hec dictio 'preter' est adverbium. Ergo non construitur cum accusativo[7].

38   Et dicendum quod hoc adverbium 'velociter' dicit velocitatem ut determinationem actus cum dico 'currit velociter'. Sed si dicam 'currit cum velocitate', hec prepositio 'cum' non dicit velocitatem ut determinationem actus sed dicit comparationem unius ad alterum, ut velocitatis[1] ad actum. Similiter hoc adverbium 'ibi' dicit locum ut determinationem actus, sed[2] hec[3] prepositio 'in' non dicit locum ut

On the construction of an exceptive word

35   *Ad [8]:* As to the eighth item, there is an argument to the contrary that the word '*preter*' cannot be construed with an accusative case, because the relationship conveyed by the word '*preter*' concerns an act or is related to an act. Therefore it modifies an act. Now an act has to be signified by a verb. Therefore the word '*preter*' modifies a verb. Therefore it is an adverb. Hence it is not a preposition nor a verb, because the latter are parts of speech that are diverse from the adverb. Therefore it is not construed with an accusative.

36   The answer should be that the word '*preter*' is not an adverb but a preposition, for adverbs modify the verb in virtue of the act or some relationship owing to this act, because an adverb is, as it were, an *adject* to a verb. Now prepositions do not indicate a relationship of an act, but rather they indicate a relationship a substance signified by an oblique case has to an act or with respect to an act. And in this way prepositions and adverbs are different. Hence it does not follow that if something indicates a relationship with respect to some act, that it should therefore be an adverb; on the contrary, it follows that it is not an adverb.

37   Again, in the expression 'He is running there', the adverb 'there' indicates a modification of the act. Now the same modification is signified in the sentence 'He is running in that place'. Therefore the preposition 'in' indicates the same relationship as the adverb 'there'. Therefore it is an adverb, because it indicates the same relationship. The same goes for other prepositions, *e.g.* 'He passed along there' (*illac*), that is, *along that way*, and 'It is moving upwards' (*sursum*), that is, *to a higher place*, and 'He is running fast', that is, *with fastness*, 'It occurred from heaven' (*celitus*), that is, *coming from heaven*, and 'by divine agency' (*divinitus*), that is, *<coming> from God*. Therefore prepositions signify the same as adverbs, because the same goes for all other adverbs. Hence prepositions do not differ from adverbs. Therefore the word '*preter*' is an adverb. Therefore it is not construed with an accusative.

38   The answer should be that the adverb 'fast' indicates fastness as the modification of an act in the expression 'He is running fast'. However, in the expression 'He is running with fastness', the preposition 'with' does not indicate fastness as the modification of an act but it indicates a relationship of the one with the other, namely of fastness with the act. Likewise the adverb 'there' indicates a place which modifies the act, but the preposition 'in' does not indicate a

determinationem actus sed dicit comparationem ipsius loci ad
actum qui fit in eo; et sic de aliis. Unde prepositiones non significant
idem cum adverbiis. [*N57vb*] Unde hec dictio[4] 'preter' non est
adverbium sed prepositio.

39   Item. Hec dictio 'preter' removet verbum personale ab excepto.
Sed verbum alicuius persone[1] non removetur nisi a nominativo.
Ergo hec dictio 'preter' construitur cum nominativo[2].

40   Et dicendum quod dupliciter removetur verbum personale ab
aliquo casuali. Quia uno modo removetur eoquod negatur compositio[1] unius ad alterum; et sic semper removetur verbum personale a
nominativo, ut 'ego non curro', 'tu non legis'[2], 'ille non disputat', et
similiter[3] in plurali[4]. Alio autem modo removetur verbum personale
ab aliquo casuali propter hoc quod illud casuale extrahitur ab aliquo
recipiente in se illum actum; et sic[5] semper removetur actus[6] ab
excepto per hanc dictionem 'preter'. Sed hoc est valde ex consequenti[7], quia primo hec dictio 'preter' extrahit partem a toto (ut
'omnis homo [*P66rb*] preter Sortem'), secundo actus ponitur in toto a
quo fit exceptio (ut 'omnis homo preter Sortem currit'), tertio quia
actus positus in toto non reperiebat[8] partem que prius remota erat a
toto respectu ipsius actus. Ideo consequebatur remotio[9] ipsius actus a
parte excepta[10]. Sicut cum vidisti pluviam venientem, primo remo-
visti librum a fenestra, secundo cecidit pluvia super fenestram,
tertio[11] sequitur[12] quod non sit recepta in libro vel quod non
ceciderit[13] supra librum.

De hiis dictionibus 'preterquam' et 'nisi'

41   Sciendum autem quod quecumque[1] sunt dicta de hac dictione
'preter', omnia debent intelligi[2] de hac dictione 'preterquam' et de
hac dictione 'nisi', secundum quod est dictio exceptiva. Excepto hoc
quod hec dictio 'preter' semper excipit in accusativo casu (ut dictum
est), sed 'preterquam' et 'nisi' semper excipiunt in eodem casu in
quo est totum a quo fit exceptio. Ut 'nullus homo currit preterquam
Sortes' vel 'nisi Sortes'; 'nullius hominis miserior preterquam Sortis'

place which modifies the act, but it indicates a relationship of that place with the act that takes place in it; and the same goes for other prepositions. Thus prepositions do not signify the same as adverbs. That is why the word '*preter*' is not an adverb but a preposition.

39 Again, the word '*preter*' removes the personal verb from what is excepted. Now the verb in some person is only removed from a nominative. Therefore the word '*preter*' is construed with a nominative.

40 The answer should be that a personal verb is removed from something expressed in a grammatical case in two ways. [1] In one way it is removed because the composition of the one with the other is denied; and in this way a personal verb is always removed from something in the nominative, *e.g.* 'I am not running', 'You are not reading', 'He is not arguing', and the same goes <for verbs> in the plural. [2] In another way the personal verb is removed from something expressed in a grammatical case because the latter is extracted from something that receives the act involved in it; and in this way an act is always removed from what is excepted by the word '*preter*'. Now this definitely occurs by consequence, because first the word '*preter*' extracts a part from a whole (*e.g.* '*omnis homo preter Sortem*' ('every man but Socrates')), secondly the act is asserted in the whole from which the exception is made (*e.g.* '*omnis homo preter Sortem currit*' ('Every man but Socrates is running')), thirdly because the act asserted in the whole did not encounter the part previously removed from the whole with respect to that act. That is why the removal of the act from the excepted part followed. It is like when you saw the rain coming, you first removed the book from the window, secondly the rain came down on the window and it follows, thirdly, that it was not absorbed by the book or that it did not end up on the book.

On the words 'preterquam' *('except') and* 'nisi' *('unless')*

41 Note that all that has been said about the word '*preter*' should also be understood about the word '*preterquam*' ('except') and the word '*nisi*' ('unless'), insofar as the latter is an exceptive word, on the proviso that the word '*preter*' always makes an exception for something in the accusative case (as has been said), whereas '*preterquam*' and '*nisi*' always make an exception for something in the same grammatical case as the whole from which the exception is made. Examples are '*nullus homo currit preterquam Sortes*' ('No man is running except Socrates') or '*nisi Sortes*' ('unless Socrates'), '*nullius hominis miserior preterquam Sortis*' ('I pity no man except Socrates'), or '*nisi*

vel 'nisi Sortis'; 'nulli[3] homini parco[4] preterquam Sorti' vel 'nisi Sorti'; 'nullum hominem video preterquam Sortem' vel 'nisi Sortem'[5]; 'a nullo homine didici preterquam a Sorte' vel 'nisi a Sorte'[6].

Sortis', '*nulli homini parco preterquam Sorti*' ('I spare no man except Socrates'), or '*nisi Sorti*', '*nullum hominem video preterquam Sortem*' ('I see no man except Socrates'), or '*nisi Sortem*', '*a nullo homine didici preterquam a Sorte*' ('I have learned from no man except Socrates'), or '*nisi a Sorte*'.[14]

---

14 In these sentences the point is that in Latin you can see that the words in question are used in constructions that are different than the ones in which the word '*preter*' occurs. All these sentences are examples of uses of '*nisi*' and '*preterquam*'.

TRACTATUS QUINTUS

DE DICTIONIBUS CONSECUTIVIS

De hac dictione 'si'

1   Dicto de dictionibus exceptivis dicendum est de dictionibus consecutivis. Et primo de hac dictione 'si'. De qua primo queritur quid significet; secundo quot sint species[1] consecutionis sive consequentie; tertio utrum in conditionali[2] contingat fieri descensum sub antecedente vel consequente; quarto qualiter[3] sumatur contradictoria[4] propositionis conditionalis; quinto utrum impossibile antecedat ad quidlibet sive ex impossibili sequatur quidlibet.

Quid significet hec dictio 'si'

2   Circa primum sic obicitur quod hec dictio 'si' non significat substantiam. Quia substantia dicitur quatuor modis; uno modo substantia dicitur materia (ut materia Sortis vel ignis[1] vel aliorum elementorum); alio autem modo substantia dicitur forma (ut forma Sortis et aliarum rerum naturalium[2]); tertio autem[3] modo substantia dicitur compositum [*P66va*] ex hiis, scilicet ex materia et forma (ut Sortes et alia individua); quarto autem modo substantia dicitur essentia dicens *quid* sive predicabile de pluribus (ut homo, animal et consimilia). Sed[4] hec dictio 'si' nullo predictorum[5] modorum significat substantiam. Ergo hec dictio 'si' substantiam non significat. Quod concedimus.

3   Item. Quidam dicunt quod hec dictio 'si' significat causalitatem, alii vero antecessionem[1], alii autem consecutionem[2]. Et videtur quod significet causalitatem, quia dicitur coniunctio causalis, et nonnisi[3] a[4] significatione[5] cause vel causalitatis. Ergo hec dictio 'si' significat causalitatem. Item. Videtur quod magis significet antecessionem quam consecutionem, quia magis se tenet cum antecedente quam cum[6] consequente a parte rei. Cuius signum est quod[7]

CHAPTER V

ON CONSECUTIVE WORDS

On the word 'if'

1   Now that we have spoken about exceptive words we must deal with consecutive words, and first we must speak about the word 'if'. Concerning this word there is *[1]* first a problem what it signifies, *[2]* secondly how many kinds of consecution or consequence there are, *[3]* thirdly whether in a conditional one can make a descent under the antecedent or consequent, *[4]* fourthly how to understand a contradictory of a conditional, *[5]* fifthly whether an impossible is an antecedent of anything whatsoever or whether from an impossible anything follows.

What the word 'if' signifies

2   *Ad [1]:* As to the first item, there is an argument to the contrary that the word 'if' does not signify substance, because 'substance' is said in four ways. [1] In one way substance indicates matter, (*e.g.* the matter of Socrates, of fire or of other elements); [2] in a second way substance indicates a form (*e.g.* the form of Socrates and other natural things); [3] in a third way substance indicates a composite thing made up of the things just mentioned, *viz.* of matter and form (*e.g.* Socrates and other individual things); [4] in a fourth way substance indicates the essence designating the 'what' or what is predicable of many things, (*e.g.* man, animal and the like). Now the word 'if' does not signify substance in any of the ways mentioned above. Therefore the word 'if' does not signify substance. Well, we agree with this.

3   Furthermore, some say that the word 'if' signifies causality, whereas others say it signifies antecedence, and others again say that it signifies consecution. It may be argued that it signifies causality, because it is called a causal conjunction, and this is only on account of the signification of cause or causality. Therefore the word 'if' signifies causality. Again, it may be argued that it rather signifies antecedence than consecution, because it is more related to the antecedent than to the consequent on the part of the state of affairs.

semper adiungitur antecedenti (et non consequenti), ut 'animal est, si homo est'. Sed semper antecessio est forma antecedentis et consecutio consequentis. Ergo magis se tenet cum antecedente[8] quam cum consequente. Ergo si[9] hec dicito 'si' significat alterum istorum, magis significat antecessionem quam consecutionem.

4   Item ad idem. 'Causa' dicitur dupliciter. Quia quedam est causa que[1] est causa rei quoad esse[2], et hec est causa essendi, ut corpus et anima sunt causa hominis quoad [*N58rb*] esse et sol lucens super terram est causa diei quoad esse. Alia autem est causa que est causa consequendi. Et sic in qualibet conditionali antecedens est causa consequentis, non essendi sed consequendi; et in quolibet argumento premisse sunt causa[3] conclusionis[4]. Et sic est causa duplex, scilicet causa essendi et causa consequendi. Sed utroque istorum modorum causa inquantum causa est antecedens, et causatum inquantum causatum est consequens. Sed hec dictio 'si' significat causam vel causalitatem. Ergo significat antecessionem et non consecutionem. Item. Videtur quod significet consecutionem, per diffinitionem coniunctionis datam a Prisciano sic: "coniunctio est pars orationis indeclinabilis coniunctiva aliarum partium vim vel ordinem demonstrans ". Et Priscianus exponit sic: vim significant ille coniunctiones [*P66vb*] que significant res aliquas simul esse (ut 'pius[5] et fortis fuit Eneas'); ordinem significant[6] coniunctiones quando monstrant[7] consequentiam aliquarum[8] rerum (ut 'si ambulat, movetur'). Sed hec dictio 'si' et consimiles significant ordinem. Ergo significant consequentias rerum sive consecutionem[9]. Non[10] ergo antecessionem.

5   Et dicendum quod hec dictio 'si' significat causalitatem sive antecessionem. Et hoc[1] non est significare plura sed unum, quia unum significat[2] in altero sive per alterum. Quia per hoc quod significat causalitatem significat[3] antecessionem, quia, sicut in omni causa intelligitur antecedens natura, cum omnis causa sit prior natura suo[4] effectu, ita[5] in causalitate intelligitur antecessio. Unde[6] hec dictio 'si' significat causalitatem secundum[7] quod in ea intelligitur antecessio. Et sic[8] significat causalitatem in[9] antecessione sive per antecessionem. Unde[10] non significat duo sed unum.

And a sign of this is that it is always adjoined to the antecedent (and not to the consequent), *e.g.* 'An animal is, if a man is'. Now antecedence is always the form of the antecedent, and consecution is the form of the consequent. Therefore it is more related to the antecedent than to the consequent. Therefore if the word 'if' signifies one of these two, it rather signifies antecedence than consecution.

4   Furthermore, there is an argument that yields the same conclusion. 'Cause' is said in two ways. [1] One is the cause that is the cause of something in terms of its being, and this is the cause of being, *e.g.* body and soul are the cause of man in terms of his being and the sun shining on the earth is the cause of a day in terms of its being. [2] The other is the cause that is the cause of consequence. In this way in any conditional the antecedent is the cause of the consequent, and not of its being but of its being consequent, and in any argument the premises are the cause of the conclusion. Thus a cause is twofold, *viz.* the cause of being and the cause of consequence. However, for both of these ways the cause *qua* cause is the antecedent, and the caused *qua* caused is the consequent. Now the word 'if' signifies cause or causality. Therefore it signifies antecedence and not consecution. Furthermore, it may be argued that it signifies consecution on account of the definition of 'conjunction' given by Priscian:[1] "A conjunction is an indeclinable part of speech that conjoins other parts of speech and displays a force or an order". Priscian explains[2] this as follows: conjunctions that signify a force are the ones that signify certain things to be simultaneous (*e.g.* 'Aeneas was pious and brave'), and those conjunctions signify an order that display a consequence of certain states of affairs (*e.g.* 'If he is walking, he is moving'). Now the word 'if' and the like signify an order. Therefore they signify consequences of states of affairs or a consecution. Hence they do not signify antecedence.

5   The answer should be that the word 'if' signifies causality or antecedence. And this is not to signify more than one thing but one, because the one is signified in the other or via the other. For it is because it signifies causality that it signifies antecedence, because just as in every cause one naturally understands the antecedent, because every cause is naturally prior to its effect, in the same way in causality one understands antecedence. That is why the word 'if' signifies causality insofar as one understands in it antecedence. Thus it signifies causality in antecedence or via antecedence. Hence it does not signify two things but one.

---

[1]   *Inst. gramm.* XVI 1, p. 93(2-3), ed. Hertz.
[2]   *Ibid.*, p. 93(4-6).

6   <Ad> argumenta autem quibus ostenditur quod[1] significat
causalitatem sive antecessionem, concedimus quod significat, sicut
dictum est, unum in altero sive per alterum. Ad argumentum autem
probans quod hec dictio 'si' significet[2] consecutionem dicendum
quod non significat consecutionem sed significat antecessionem (ut
diximus), quia[3] ad antecessionem sequitur consecutio.

7   Et nota quod 'unum sequitur ad alterum' est multiplex[1]. [*N58va*]
Quia quedam sequuntur[2] eoquod sunt essentialiter predicabilia, ut
diffinitio et[3] genus et[4] differentie[5] ad speciem. Alia autem sequuntur[6] eoquod sunt partes integrales, ut paries[7] ad domum et[8] cetere
partes eius. Alia autem sequuntur quia[9] sunt partes essentiales[10],
quamvis non sint partes integrales, ut corpus humanum et anima
intellectiva ad hominem. Et dicuntur partes integrales[11] quarum
quelibet habet quantitatem. Et ideo corpus et anima non sunt partes
integrales quia, licet corpus habeat quantitatem, tamen anima non
habet quantitatem[12]. Sed sunt partes essentiales[13] animalis vel[14]
viventis, quia anima repperitur[15] in hominibus ut intellectiva tantum[16] et in brutis ut[17] sensitiva[18] tantum[19] et[20] in terre nascentibus ut
vegetativa[21] tantum. Alia autem sequuntur[22] quia[23] sunt subiecta
propria accidentium, vel econverso quia sunt[24] propria accidentia[25]
subiectorum. Et sic sequitur linea ad rectum vel curvum, et[26]
numerus ad par vel impar, et corpus elementatum[27] ad colorem
[*P67ra*] tamquam propria subiecta, vel econverso rectum vel curvum
ad[28] lineam, et[29] par vel impar ad numerum, et color ad corpus[30] elementatum sicut accidentia[31] propria ad propria subiecta[32]. Sed nullo
predictorum modorum consecutio[33] sequitur ad antecessionem.

8   Alia autem sequuntur[1] quia dicuntur ad se invicem relative, ut
pater et filius, dominus et servus. Et hoc modo consecutio sequitur[2]
ad antecessionem. Sicut enim antecedens[3] et consequens sunt *ad
aliquid*, similiter antecessio et consecutio ad se invicem dicuntur.
Unde hec dictio 'si' significat solum[4] antecessionem. Et[5] quia omnis
antecessio[6] consecutionis[7] est antecessio, ideo ad significationem
huius dictionis 'si' sequitur consecutio relative.

6   As to the arguments,[3] however, by which it is shown that it
[*viz.* the word 'if'] signifies causality or antecedence, we agree that it
signifies, as has been said,[4] the one in the other or via the other. But
as to the argument[5] aiming to prove that the word 'if' signifies
consecution, the answer should be that it does not signify consecution, but antecedence (as we have said), because from antecedence
consecution follows.

7   Note that 'one thing follows from another' is said in many
ways. [1] Some things follow because they are essentially predicable, *e.g.* a definition, a genus and differences follow from a species. [2] Other things follow because they are integral parts, *e.g.*
'wall' from 'house', as do its other parts. [3] Other things follow because they are essential parts, although not integral ones, *e.g.* 'body'
and 'intellective soul' from 'man'. And those things are called integral parts any one of which has quantity. Hence body and soul are
not integral parts because, although the body has quantity, nonethe-
less the soul does not. Instead they are essential parts of an animal or
something that is alive, because the soul is found in men as an
intellective one only, in beasts as a sensitive one only and in the
things that grow on earth as a vegetative one only. [4] Other things
follow because they are the proper subjects of the accidents, or, conversely, because they are the proper accidents of the subjects. In this
way 'line' follows from 'straight' or 'curved', 'number' from 'even'
or 'odd' and 'body that consists of elements' from 'colour', <all> as
the proper subjects; or, conversely, 'straight' or 'curved' follows from
'line', 'even' or 'odd' from 'number' and 'colour' from 'body that
consists of elements', <all> as the proper accidents from the proper
subjects. Now in none of the ways mentioned above does consecution follow from antecedence.

8   [5] Other things again follow because they are used in a mutually relative way, *e.g.* 'father' and 'son', 'master' and 'slave'. In this
way a consecution does follow from antecedence. For just as antecedent and consequent are relatives, likewise antecedence and consecution are used in a mutually relative way. Therefore the word 'if'
signifies only antecedence, and because every antecedence is an
antecedence to a consecution, therefore the signification of the word
'if' implies consecution in the way relatives do

---

[3]   Cf. above, cap. 3.
[4]   Cf. above, cap. 5.
[5]   Cf. above, cap. 4.

Quot sint species consecutionis

9   Circa secundum[1] queritur quot sint species consecutionis[2], quia cum unum relatorum[3] exigatur ad cognitionem alterius, oportet cognoscere[4] consecutionem et modos sive[5] species consecutionis[6] ad hoc quod[7] antecessio[8] cognoscatur. Et dicendum quod consecutionis due sunt divisiones[9], excedentes et excesse. Una quidem [*N58vb*] divisio est ista: consecutionis alia est[10] simul existentium, ut 'si homo est, animal est'. Alia est existentium secundum prius et posterius; nam aliquando sequitur quod est prius, et aliquando quod est posterius. Et quod est prius, sequitur dupliciter. Quia aliquando[11] in[12] idemptitate temporis, ut 'si addiscit, ignorat'; prius[13] enim est ignorare et sequitur ad[14] addiscere, quod[15] est posterius et[16] in eodem tempore, quia quando addiscit, ignorat[17]. Nichil[18] enim addiscimus nisi quod ignoramus. Aliquando autem[19] sequitur prius[20] in diversitate temporis[21]. Et hoc dupliciter. Uno modo sequitur prius in preterito, ut 'si fumus est, ignis fuit' et 'si panis est, farina[22] fuit'; et hoc accidit[23] maxime in causis[24] non permanentibus et in causis[25] natura et tempore antecedentibus[26] suum effectum. Alio autem modo prius sequitur in tempore futuro, ut[27] 'purgatio[28] et omnia alia[29] que finaliter[30] ordinantur ad sanitatem[31] sunt[32]; ergo sanitas erit' (sanitas enim causa finalis est predictorum). Causa enim finalis semper natura prior est suo effectu; [*P67rb*] aliquando autem est[33] tempore posterior.

10   Ex predictis ergo patet quod prius aliquando sequitur in presenti, aliquando in preterito, aliquando in futuro. Hec autem diversitas consecutionis accidit eoquod causa tripliciter comparatur ad suum effectum. Aliquando enim causa est simul tempore cum suo effectu, quamvis non natura, ut sol lucens super terram cum die. Aliquando autem causa precedit effectum suum tempore et natura, ut ignis fumum et racemi vinum[1]. Aliquando autem causa antecedit suum effectum natura et est posterior tempore; et hoc maxime solet[2] accidere in causa finali. Et sic patet quod consecutionis alia est simul[3] existentium, alia[4] non simul existentium. Secunda vero divisio est

How many kinds of consecution there are

9 *Ad [2]:* As to the second item, there is a problem how many kinds of consecution there are, because since one *relatum* is required for the understanding of the other, it is necessary to acquire an understanding of consecution and the ways or kinds of consecution, in order that one may acquire an understanding of antecedence. The answer should be that of consecution there are two types of division, *viz.* the ones that exceed and the ones that are exceeded. [1] One division is the following: one type of consecution is the consecution of things that are simultaneous, *e.g.* 'If a man is, an animal is', and another type of consecution is the consecution of things that are prior and posterior, since sometimes what is prior follows, and sometimes what is posterior does. And what is posterior follows in two ways. Sometimes it happens at the same time, *e.g.* 'If he is learning, he is ignorant'; to be ignorant is prior and it follows from to learn, which is posterior and occurring at the same time, because when he is learning, he is ignorant. For we can only learn what we are ignorant of. Sometimes, on the other hand, the prior follows at a different time, and this happens in two ways. In one way the prior follows in the past, *e.g.* 'If there is smoke, there has been a fire', and 'If there is bread, there has been flour'; this mostly happens in the case of non-permanent causes and in causes that precede their effect by nature and in time. In another way the prior follows at a future time, *e.g.* 'Purification and all the other things that are ordered to health as their final cause *are*; therefore there will *be* health' (for health is the final cause of the former). The final cause in fact is always prior to its effect by nature, but sometimes it comes later in time.

10 From what has been said, therefore, it is evident that the prior sometimes follows in the present, sometimes in the past and sometimes in the future. This diversity of consecution, then, occurs on account of the fact that a cause has a threefold relation to its effect. Sometimes the cause is simultaneous with its effect, although not by nature, *e.g.* the sun shining on earth is simultaneous with daytime. Sometimes, however, the cause precedes its effect in time and by nature, *e.g.* fire precedes smoke and a bunch of grapes precedes wine. Again, sometimes the cause is antecedent to its effect by nature and comes later in time, and this chiefly tends to happen in the case of a final cause. Thus it is evident that of consecution one type is of things that are simultaneous, and the other of things that are not simultaneous. [2] The second division is the following: one

ista: consecutionis alia est simplex, alia composita, sive secundum oppositiones, ut dictum fuit[5] in tractatu *Fallaciarum*, in fallacia consequentis.

11 Hee[1] autem divisiones comparantur ad[2] se invicem ut excedentia[3] et excessa, quia utrumque membrum prime[4] divisionis repperitur in[5] simplici consequentia et in composita, et utrumque membrum secunde[6] divisionis repperitur[7] in eis que simul consequuntur et[8] in eis que consequuntur secundum prius et posterius. Ut 'si panis est, farina fuit' et 'si vinum est, racemi fuerunt'. Et hee consequuntur secundum prius et posterius et etiam ibi est simplex [*N59ra*] consequentia. Et in eisdem[9] potest formari composita[10] consequentia, ut 'si[11] vinum est, racemi fuerunt; ergo[12] si racemi non fuerunt, vinum non est'[13]. Similiter autem et in hiis terminis[14] qui simul consequuntur. Et ideo dicuntur iste divisiones excedentes et excesse quia secundum quod unum[15] membrum prime divisionis repperitur in utroque secunde[16], sic prima divisio est excedens et secunda[17] excessa; secundum autem quod unum membrum[18] secunde[19] divisionis repperitur in utroque prime, sic[20] secunda est excedens et prima[21] excessa. Et quod dico de uno membro divisionis, similiter[22] intelligatur de reliquo.

Sophisma

12 Secundum predicta queritur de hoc sophismate: SI NULLUM TEMPUS[1] EST, ALIQUOD TEMPUS EST. Probatio. Si nullum tempus est, dies non est[2]. Et si dies non est, nox[3] est[4]. Et si nox est, aliquod tempus est[5]. [*P67va*] Ergo a primo: 'si nullum tempus est, aliquod tempus est'. Contra. Ibi[6] assignatur sequi oppositum ad oppositum. Ergo locutio est impossibilis.

13 Solutio. Prima falsa simpliciter. Et dicunt quidam quod in prima conditionali probationis est locus a toto in quantitate, in secunda[1] vero conditionali est locus a contrariis immediatis, in tertia vero est locus a parte subiectiva. Et sic variatur[2] habitudo inferendi et

type of consecution is simple and another composite, or according to opposites, as been said in the treatise *On Fallacies*, in <the discussion> on the fallacy of the consequent.[6]

11   These divisions then are mutually related as what exceeds and what is exceeded, because both members of the first division are found in a simple consequence and in a composite one, and both members of the second division are found in the things that follow simultaneously and in the ones that follow as a prior and a posterior, *e.g.* 'If there is bread, there has been flour', and 'If there is wine, there has been a bunch of grapes'. The latter follow as a prior and a posterior and we have here a simple consequence as well. Also in the same cases one can form a composite consequence, *e.g.* 'If there is wine, there has been a bunch of grapes; therefore if there has been no bunch of grapes, there is no wine'. And the same goes for the terms that follow simultaneously. These divisions are called the ones that exceed and the ones that are exceeded, for the reason that according as each member of the first division is found in each of the second, thus the first division is the one that exceeds and the second the one that is exceeded. On the other hand, according as one member of the second division is found in each member of the first one, in that way the second is the one that exceeds and the first the one that is exceeded. And what I say about one member of the division, should also be understood as concerning the other one.

Sophisma

12   As regards what has been said, there is a problem concerning the sophisma-sentence IF THERE IS NO TIME, THERE IS SOME TIME. Proof: if there is no time, it is not day, and if it is not day, it is night, and if it is night, there is some time. Therefore, taking it from the beginning, if there is no time, there is some time. There is an argument to the contrary. It is said that this is a case of an opposite following from an opposite. Therefore the locution is impossible.

13   Solution: the first is false *simpliciter*. And some say that the first conditional of the proof involves the topic 'from a quantative whole', the second conditional involves the topic 'from immediate contraries' and the third the topic 'from a subjective part'. Thus there is a variety in the relationships of inference and so <an argument based on> the logical inference from the first to the last is prevented.

---

[6]   *Tractatus* VII, cap. 150, p. 169, ed. De Rijk.

ita impeditur locus a primo ad ultimum. Et ponunt ibi sophisma[3] accidentis propter variationem medii.

De duabus maximis

14 Sed[1] hoc destruitur per has duas maximas:

quicquid sequitur ad consequens[2], sequitur ad antecedens.

Ergo si ultimum consequens (scilicet[3] aliquod tempus esse[4]) sequitur ad antecedentia intermedia, et[5] antecedentia intermedia sequuntur ad primum antecedens (quod est nullum tempus esse), tunc oportet quod ultimum[6] consequens (quod est aliquod tempus esse) sequatur ad nullum tempus esse, quod est primum[7] antecedens. Et sic necesse est primam esse veram, si habitudines probationis sunt necessarie. Ergo a destructione consequentis: si prima non est vera[8], habitudines probationis non erunt necessarie.

15 Alia autem maxima est ista:

quicquid antecedit ad antecedens, [N59rb] antecedit ad consequens.

Ergo si primum[1] antecedens antecedit ad antecedentia intermedia et antecedentia intermedia antecedunt ad ultimum consequens, ergo[2] primum antecedens antecedit ad ultimum consequens. Ergo si habitudines probationis sunt necessarie, prima est vera. Nec[3] impeditur locus a primo ad ultimum propter diversas habitudines intermedias. Ergo si prima non est vera, habitudines intermedie non sunt necessarie[4]. Item ad idem. Si Sortes est animal rationale mortale, Sortes est homo (a diffinitione). Et si Sortes est homo, Sortes est animal (a specie). Et si Sortes est animal, Sortes non est lapis (ab oppositis). Ergo a primo: si Sortes est animal rationale mortale, Sortes non est lapis. Sed hoc bene sequitur et sic[5] ibi sunt diverse habitudines locales. Ergo propter[6] diversitatem habitudinum [P67vb] localium non impeditur[7] processus a primo ad ultimum. Item ad

They posit in this case a fallacy of accident caused by a variety of the middle.

On two maxims

14   However, this argument is destroyed in virtue of the following two maxims:

[1] *Whatever follows from the consequent follows from the antecedent.*

Therefore if the final consequent (*viz.* that there is some time) follows from the intermediate antecedents, and the intermediate antecedents follow from the first antecedent (*viz.* that there is no time), in that case it is necessary that the final consequent (*viz.* that there is some time) follow from the proposition that there is no time, the first antecedent. And so it is necessary that the first be true, if the logical relationships found in the proof are necessary ones. Therefore from the destruction of the consequent: if the first is not true, the logical relationships found in the proof will not be necessary ones.

15   The other maxim is the following:

[2] *Whatever is antecedent to the antecedent is antecedent to the consequent.*

Therefore if the first antecedent is antecedent to the intermediate antecedents and the intermediate antecedents are antecedent to the final consequent, therefore the first antecedent is antecedent to the final consequent. Therefore if the logical relationships found in the proof are necessary ones, the original sentence is true. Moreover, the inference from the first to the final proposition is not prevented because of diverse intermediate logical relationships. Therefore if the original sentence is not true, the intermediate relationships are not necessary ones. Furthermore, there is an argument that yields the same conclusion. If Socrates is a rational mortal animal, Socrates is a man (from the definition). Now if Socrates is a man, Socrates is an animal (from the species), and if Socrates is an animal, Socrates is not a stone (from opposites). Therefore, taking it from the beginning, if Socrates is a rational mortal animal, Socrates is not a stone. Now this is a sound inference and yet in this case diverse topical relationships are involved. Therefore it is not on account of a diversity of topical relationships that an argument from the first to the last is prevented. Again, there is an argument that yields the same conclusion. In a categorical syllogism it is not required that the

idem. In sillogismo categorico non[8] exigitur quod eadem sit
habitudo medii ad maiorem extremitatem et minorem, ut

'Nulla virtus est vitium
omnis iustitia est virtus
ergo nulla iustitia[9] est vitium'.

In hoc enim[10] sillogismo medii ad maiorem extremitatem est
habitudo contrariorum, minoris vero extremitatis ad medium est
habitudo speciei ad genus. Harum autem habitudinum localium
una facit locum intrinsecum, alia extrinsecum[11]. Ergo si inter
omnes locos maxime differunt intrinseci[12] et extrinseci sed[13] iste
non impediunt sillogismum categoricum, ergo iste[14] eedem multo-
minus impediunt sillogismum ypotheticum. Et si iste non impediunt, ergo neque alie habitudines, que[15] magis conveniunt. Et sic
arguendo[16] a primo ad ultimum non impeditur processus[17] propter[18]
diversas habitudines locales. Quod concedimus.

16 Et dicendum quod prima simpliciter est falsa. Et prima
consequentia tenet uno modo et[1] alio modo non, quia hec propositio
'dies non est' (que est primum consequens) est duplex, eoquod potest
esse negatio in genere (sive[2] negatio circa genus, quod idem est) vel
potest esse negatio simpliciter.

De negatione duplici

17 Si est negatio in genere, sic ponit subiectum suum[1], quod est
tempus communiter loquendo et[2] extenso nomine subiecti; et est
sensus istius 'dies non est' iste[3]: tempus est sed illud non est dies. Et
ita non sequitur ex primo antecedente, quia immediate contradicit
ei. Et sic non sequitur 'nullum tempus est; ergo dies non est'. Nec est
ibi locus a toto in quantitate, sed erit[4] argumentum penitus[5] dis-
parat<or>um, sicut hic: 'nullus homo currit; ergo aliquis homo
currit'[6]. Similiter est in proposito: 'nullum tempus est; ergo aliquod

logical relationship the middle term has to the major extreme is the same as the one it has to the minor one, *e.g.*

'No virtue is a vice;
every justice is a virtue;
therefore no justice is a vice'.

For in this syllogism the relationship between the middle term and the major extreme is one between contraries, whereas the relationship between the minor and the middle term is one of a species to a genus. Now of these topical relationships one forms an intrinsic topic and the other an extrinsic one. Therefore if between all topics the differences between intrinsic and extrinsic ones are the greatest and nevertheless the corresponding relationships do not prevent the formation of a categorical syllogism, therefore these same relationships will prevent the formation of a hypothetical syllogism even less. And if they do not prevent the formation of a syllogism, then other relationships, which resemble each other more, will not do so either. Thus in the argument from the first to the last an inference is not prevented because of diverse topical relationships. Well, we agree with this.

16   The answer [*viz.* to the sophisma-sentence] should be that the original sentence is *simpliciter* false and the first inference [*viz.* 'If there is no time, it is not day'] is valid in one way but not in another way: the proposition 'It is not day' (that is, the first consequent) is ambiguous, for it can be a denial within the genus[7] (or a denial that concerns the genus, which is the same) or it can be a denial *simpliciter*.

On the double negation

17   If it [*i.e.* the proposition 'It is not day'] is a denial within the genus, then it posits its subject, *viz.* time generally speaking and by extension of the noun 'subject', and the meaning of the proposition 'It is not day' is *there is time, but it is not daytime*. In this way it does not follow from the first antecedent, because it directly contradicts the latter. Thus it does not follow 'There is no time; therefore it is not day'. Nor do we have here the topic 'from a quantitative whole', but rather the argument will be one from entirely disparate things, in the same way as in 'No man is running; therefore some man is running'. The same goes for the case at issue: 'There is no time;

---

7   That is, 'only extending to the genus'.

tempus est sed illud[7] non est dies'. Si autem sit negatio simpliciter, tunc nichil ponit ista 'dies non est'. Et sic sequitur 'nullum tempus[8] est; ergo dies non est'; et sic est locus a toto in quantitate. Similem distinctionem innuit Aristotiles in *Primo Posteriorum*[9] [*P68ra*] huius quod dico 'non-par', quia si 'non-par' est negatio[10] in genere, ita[11] ponit subiectum suum, quod est numerus. Unde 'non-par'[12] ponit numerum[13], sed ille non est par. Si vero 'non-par' sit negatio simpliciter, sic nichil ponit.

18   Et sic patet quod hec est duplex 'dies non est'. Et secundum quod est negatio in genere, non sequitur ex primo antecedente. Secundum autem quod est negatio simpliciter, sic sequitur[1]. Econverso autem dicendum de secunda conditionali (scilicet de hac 'si dies non est, nox est'[2]), quia secundum quod hec 'dies non est' est negatio in genere, ita sequitur ex ea noctem[3] esse, quia destructo uno contrariorum[4] immediatorum non sequitur alterum nisi cum constantia subiecti. Unde oportet sic inferre: 'dies non est; et tempus est; ergo est nox'. Si vero hic: 'dies non est' sit negatio simpliciter, ita non sequitur ex ea noctem esse neque hoc modo est ibi locus a contrariis.

In quo sit tempus ut in subiecto

19   Item. Queritur in quo sit tempus ut in subiecto. Quia, cum omnia novem genera predicamentorum alia a substantia sint[1] accidentia <et[2] omnia accidentia> sunt in subiecto, (quia nullum accidens potest esse nisi[3] in subiecto; ut enim vult Boetius[4] accidentis esse est inesse); sed tempus est accidens (quia[5] est quantitas); ergo est in subiecto; et ideo queritur in quo subiecto sit. Et[6] dicendum quod tempus[7] est in motu primi [*N59vb*] mobilis (sive in motu Celi) ut[8] in subiecto, vel est in primo mobili inquantum mobile ut in subiecto (quia idem est dicere quod sit in primo mobili inquantum est mobile sive in motu primi mobilis), eoquod ipsius mobilis inquantum est mobile perfectio est motus, ut est in[9] tertio *Physicorum.*

therefore there is some time, but it is not day'. If, on the other hand, it is a denial *simpliciter*, then the proposition 'It is not day' posits nothing, and so it follows 'There is no time; therefore it is not day', and in this way it involves the topic 'from a quantative whole'. Aristotle suggests a similar distinction in Book I of the *Posterior Analytics*[8] as regards the expression 'non-even': if 'non-even' is a denial within the genus, then it posits its subject, *viz.* number. Hence 'non-even' posits number, but this number is not even. If, on the other hand, 'non-even' is a denial *simpliciter*, it posits nothing.

18   Thus it is evident that 'It is not day' is ambiguous, and insofar as it is a denial within the genus, it does not follow from the first antecedent, whereas insofar it is a denial *simpliciter*, it does follow from the former. However, one must say the converse of the second conditional (*viz.* 'If it is not day, it is night'), for from 'It is not day' insofar as it is a denial within the genus follows that it is night, because if one of two immediate contraries has been destroyed, the other does not follow unless the subject remains constant. Thus one must infer 'It is not day; and there is time; therefore it is night'. If, on the other hand, in 'It is not day' there is a denial *simpliciter*, then it does not follow from the former that it is night nor do we have in this way the topic 'from contraries'.

What time inheres in as in its subject

19   There is a problem what subject time inheres in as in its subject. Since all genera of the nine categories other than substance are accidents and all accidents inhere in a subject (because an accident can only be in a subject; for as Boethius has it,[9] the being of an accident is to inhere); now time is an accident (because it is a quantity); therefore it inheres in a subject,—that is why there is a problem what subject it inheres in. The answer should be that time inheres in the motion of the first moveable (or in the motion of heaven) as in its subject, or it inheres in the first moveable insofar as it is moveable as in its subject (for it is identical to say that it inheres in the first moveable insofar as it is moveable or that it inheres in the motion of the first moveable), because of this moveable insofar as it is moveable the fulfilment is motion, as it says in Book III of the *Physics*.[10]

---

[8]   *Anal. Post.* I 4, 73b20ff.

[9]   Cf. *In Categ. Arist.*, 170D-171A, ed. Migne.

[10]   *Physica* III, 201a10ff.

20   Item. Queritur, cum[1] nox et dies sint contraria immediata et
omnis contrarietas nata[2] sit fieri circa aliquod[3] idem subiectum, ergo
nox et dies erunt[4] vicissim in[5] subiecto aliquo. Et ideo quero[6] 'quid
est[7] illud'? Et dicendum quod 'nox' et 'dies' sumuntur[8] dupliciter.
Quia uno modo dicitur dies illuminatio aeris a latione, sive ex
latione, solis[9] in[10] nostro hemisperio, et nox[11] dicitur privatio illumi-
nationis aeris in nostro hemisperio, et hoc modo nox et dies sunt
contraria immediata et habent fieri vicissim circa aera ut circa
subiectum proprium et circa lationem[12] solis super terram [*P68rb*] ut
circa causam efficientem. Unde[13] sunt in aere ut in subiecto, et est
ibi quintus modus 'essendi in'. Et sunt in latione solis super terram
ut in causa efficiente; et est ibi sextus modus 'essendi in'. Alio
etiam[14] modo sumuntur 'nox' et 'dies'. Secundum quem[15] modum
dies dicitur spatium temporis[16] mensurantis lationem solis in nostro
hemisperio, ex quo sol incipit lucere in nostro hemisperio usque ad
recessum solis a[17] nostro hemisperio; et nox dicitur totum tempus
adequatum lationi solis in alio[18] hemisperio. Et sic nox et dies sunt
partes temporis. Sed magis proprie sumuntur 'nox' et 'dies' primo
modo quam secundo[19]. Hemisperium autem[20] est[21] illa medietas
celi que apparet super terram undique in circuitu. Et dicitur hemisperium ab 'hemis' (quod est 'dimidium') et 'spera, spere', quasi
'dimidia spera' vel[22] 'dimidium spere'.

De predicatione multiplici

21   Item. Queritur utrum tempus predicetur de nocte et die
secundum quod 'nox' et 'dies' sumuntur primo modo. Et dicendum
quod predicatio est[1] multis modis. Quedam enim est superioris de
inferiori: et hec est essentialis predicatio, ut 'homo est animal',
'homo[2] est risibile'[3]. Alia autem predicatio est causalis, ut quando
predicatur causa de effectu, ut 'sanitas est adequatio[4] humorum' et
'dies est sol lucens super terram'. Alia autem est accidentis de

20   Furthermore, there is a problem whether in virtue of the fact that night and day are immediate contraries and all contraries naturally happen to some one and the same subject, therefore day and night each in turn inhere in some subject. And therefore I raise the problem what this subject is. The answer should be that night and day are taken in two ways. [1] In one way day is called the illumination of air by, or from, the motion of the sun in our hemisphere, and night the elimination of the illumination of air in our hemisphere, and in this way night and day are immediate contraries and must each in turn naturally happen to air as their proper subject and to the motion of the sun across the earth as their efficient cause. Thus they inhere in air as in their subject, and in this case it is the fifth way of 'being in'. Moreover, they inhere in the motion of the sun across the earth as in their efficient cause, and in this case it is the sixth way of 'being in'. [2] 'Night' and 'day' are also taken in another way. In this way day is called the space of time that measures the motion of the sun in our hemisphere, from the moment that the sun begins to shine in our hemisphere until it disappears from our hemisphere, and night is called the whole time that equals the motion of the sun in the other hemisphere. And in this way night and day are parts of time. However, 'night' and 'day' are taken more properly in the first way than in the second. Now the hemisphere is that half of the sky that is visible above the earth from everywhere in the circuit.[11] The noun 'hemisphere' derives from '*hemis*' (which is 'half') and '*spera, -e*', which amounts to 'half a sphere' or 'half of a sphere'.

On multiple predication

21   Furthermore, there is a problem whether time is said of night and day insofar as 'night' and 'day' are taken in the first way. The answer should be that predication happens in many ways. [1] One type is <saying something> more general of something less general; and this is essential predication, *e.g.* 'A man is an animal' or 'A man is something that can laugh'. [2] Another type is causal predication, *viz.* when a cause is said of its effect, *e.g.* 'Health is the harmony of body-juices' and 'Day is the sun shining on the

---

11   Cf. Cassiodore, *Institutiones* II, cap. 7, 2, p. 154(20-3), ed. Mynors: "hemispherion est, quod est super terram, ea pars caeli quae tota a nobis videtur; hemispherion sub terra est, ut aiunt, quod videri non potest, quamdiu sub terra fuerit."

subiecto, ut 'paries est albus' et[5] 'linea est rectum[6] vel curvum'[7]. Alia est subiecti de propria[8] passione, ut 'par est numerus' et 'rectum est linea'. Et nullo istorum modorum tempus predicatur de nocte et die primo modo sumptis. Unde secundum has predicationes omnes hec est falsa 'dies est tempus' et hec similiter 'nox est tempus'. Alia predicatio est que est mensurantis, sive mensure, de mensurato, ut hic[9]: 'hoc[10] vinum est quarta una' (ibi[11] predicatur mensura de mensurato) vel 'linea est quanta' et 'numerus est quantus' et 'super-ficies est quanta'. Et sic de omnibus speciebus quantitatis predicatur hoc modo quantitas ut mensura[12], et non ut genus, quia genus non potest predicari denominative de specie. Et hoc modo tempus predicatur de nocte et die secundo[13] modo sumptis. Unde hoc modo hec est vera 'dies est tempus'. Et predicatur mensura de mensurato remoto, quia tempus primo modo mensurat motum primi mobilis et motus primi mobilis mensurat[14] motum solis. Unde ex consequenti tempus mensurat motum solis et[15] per[16] motum solis ulterius mensurat noctem et diem.

Quid sit tempus

22   Item. Queritur quid sit[1] tempus, quia[2]: Cum omne tempus constet ex priori et posteriori, sed prius et posterius debeantur motui, ergo tempus est motus (et est sillogismus in primo prime et[3] premisse intelliguntur[4] universaliter et transponuntur[5]). Et dicen-dum quod tempus ita diffinitur ab Aristotile: "tempus est numerus motus secundum prius et posterius ". Nec tamen sequitur 'ergo tempus est numerus'; nec etiam sequitur 'ergo tempus est discreta quantitas', quia ratio numeri diminuitur[6] per sibi adiunctum, quia numerare motum secundum prius et posterius hoc est mensurare ipsum <secundum prius et posterius>; sed mensurare secundum prius et posterius ponit continuitatem et non discretionem, propter hoc quod prius et posterius copulantur ad ipsum *nunc*[7]. Unde impediuntur ille due illationes per *quid et simpliciter*.

earth'.[3] Another type is saying an accident of a subject, *e.g.* 'The wall is white' or 'A line is straight or curved'. [4] Another type is saying a subject of its proper quality, *e.g.* 'Even is a number' and 'Straight is a line'. And in none of these ways time is said of night and day taken in the first way. Hence according to all these types of predication the proposition 'A day is time' is false, and likewise the proposition 'A night is time'. [5] Another type is saying what measures, or a measure, of what is measured, *e.g.* 'This wine is a quarter' (in which case a measure is predicated of something measured) or 'A line is a quantity', 'A number is a quantity' and 'A surface is a quantity'. Thus of all kinds of quantity, quantity in this way is predicated as a measure, and not as a genus, because a genus cannot be predicated denominatively of a species. Hence in this way time is said of night and day taken in the second way. Thus in this way the proposition 'A day is time' is true, and measure is predicated of what is measured in a remote way, because time in the first way measures the motion of the first moveable and the motion of the first moveable measures the motion of the sun. Hence by consequence time measures the motion of the sun and by the motion of the sun it remotely measures night and day.

What time is

22 Again, there is a problem what time is. For all time consists of a 'before' and an 'after'; now 'before' and 'after' necessarily have to do with motion; therefore time is motion (and we have here a syllogism in the first mood of the first figure, and the premises are understood universally and are transferred). The answer should be that time is defined as follows by Aristotle[12]: "Time is number of motion in respect of 'before' and 'after'". Nevertheless it does not follow 'Therefore time is a number', nor does it follow 'Therefore time is a discrete quantity' either, because the motion of number is diminished by what is adjoined to it, because to number motion in repect of 'before' and 'after' is to measure it in respect of 'before' and 'after'. Now to measure in respect of 'before' and 'after' implies continuity and not discreteness, for the reason that before and after are coupled with the *now*. Thus the two inferences mentioned above are prevented owing to the fallacy of reasoning from something taken in a certain sense to the same thing taken *simpliciter*.

---

12 *Physica* IV, 219b1-2.

De 'prius' et 'posterius'

23   Ad argumentum autem dicendum quod non est sillogismus in primo prime, sed etiam[1] paralogismus contra primum[2] prime, eoquod medium equivocatur, quia 'prius' et 'posterius' dicuntur dupliciter. Nam uno modo prius et posterius sunt partes ipsius motus et alio modo sunt[3] [*N60rb*] partes temporis. Et sicut motus[4] primus est causa temporis, ita[5] prius et posterius in motu sunt causa prioris et posterioris in tempore. Et sicut motus est subiectum temporis, ita prius et posterius in motu sunt subiectum prioris et posterioris in tempore.

De spatio, motu et tempore

24   Et nota quod tria sunt que sibi invicem proportionantur, scilicet [*P69vb*] spatium, motus et tempus. Motus enim adequatur spatio supra quod est, et tempus adequatur motui ut subiecto suo. Ut si ymagineris tres lineas equales et extensas ita quod secunda superponatur prime et tertia secunde; similiter si[1] ymagineris extensionem spatii et motum supra spatium et tempus supra motum. Sed in hoc est differentia quod extensio spatii est permanens, extensio vero motus et extensio[2] temporis sunt successive[3] neque partes aliquas habent simul. Similiter[4] si ymagineris sciphum plenum aqua et cum[5] puncto acus protrahatur[6] linea in superficie aque ab una extremitate sciphi usque ad aliam, tunc[7] de linea illa neque pars preterita[8] est (quia iam deleta est) neque pars futura est (quia neque[10] fit neque facta[11] est sed[12] fiet). Et sic de illa linea nichil est nisi illud in quo est punctus[13] acus. Similiter est[14] de motu et tempore, quia quod preteriit de utroque, iam[15] non est; quod autem futurum est[16], nondum est sed erit. Unde de utroque nulla[17] pars est neque aliquid est de ipsis nisi indivisibile. Unde[18] de tempore nichil est nisi *nunc*[19], quod neque est tempus neque pars eius sed[20] indivisibile in tempore et per hoc tempus[21] est. Et de motu nichil est nisi mobile quod fertur, quod[22] neque est motus neque pars eius <sed indivisibile in motu> et per hoc motus est.

On 'before' and 'after'

23 As to the argument, the answer should be that we do not have a syllogism in the first mood of the first figure, but we even have a fallacy contrary to this type of syllogism, because the middle term is ambiguous. For 'before' and 'after' are said in two ways. [1] In one way 'before' and 'after' are parts of motion itself and [2] in another way they are parts of time. And just as the first motion is the cause of time, in the same way 'before' and 'after' in motion are the cause of 'before' and 'after' in time. Moreover, just as motion is the subject of time, in the same way 'before' and 'after' in motion are the subject of 'before' and 'after' in time.

On space, motion and time

24 Note that the following three are things that are mutually proportionate, *viz.* space, motion and time. For motion is adapted to space on top of which it is, and time is adapted to motion as its subject, like if you imagine three equal lines extended in such a way that the second is placed on top of the first and the third on top of the second and likewise if you imagine an extension of space and motion superimposed on space and time superimposed on motion. However, there is a difference in that the extension of space is permanent, whereas the extension of motion and the extension of time are successive and the latter do not have parts at the same time. Likewise, if you imagine a mug full of water and with the point of a needle a line is drawn in the surface of the water from one end of the mug to the other, then no part of that line is a past one (because it is already deleted) nor is any part a future one (because it is not yet made nor has been made, but will be made). Thus of this line nothing exists except that part in which the point of the needle resides. The same goes for motion and time, because what has passed in time or motion has no existence any longer, and what is to come, has no existence yet, but will be. Hence of both of them [*i.e.* of time and motion] no part exists nor does there exist anything of them except something indivisible. Therefore of time nothing exists but the *now*, and this is not time nor is it a part of it, but it is something indivisible in time and that is what time owes its being to. Also of motion nothing exists but something moveable which is moving, and this is not motion nor is it a part of it, <but it is something indivisible in motion> and that is what motion owes its being to.

25 Item. Nota quod inquantum motus per suam substantiam est causa temporis et per suam quantitatem[1] dat tempori[2] quantitatem, ita[3] motus per prius est quantitas et per motum tempus est quantitas, ut est in quinto *Philosophie*[4] *prime*, in capitulo de quantitate. Sed secundum quod in tempore primo repperitur natura mensurandi et per tempus in motu, sic[5] tempus per se est quantitas et sic motus est quantitas per tempus; et hoc modo motus est quantitas per accidens.

De numero et mensura

26 Nota etiam[1] quod cum dico 'tres homines' vel 'sex'[2], duo dico, quia per hoc quod dico 'homines', dico substantias [*N60va*] hominum, per hoc autem quod dico 'tres' vel 'sex', dico mensuram eorum; et sic de omnibus aliis numeralibus. Et sic intellige quod omnis numerus et omnis quantitas uno modo est mensura et alio modo res. Quia est mensura [*P69ra*] secundum quod denominat subiectum aliquod[3], ut 'tres homines', 'quatuor[4] equi', 'homo bicubitus'[5], 'columpna tricubita'. Et res[6] est secundum quod est genus aut[7] aliqua res specialis dicens[8] *quid*. Similiter cum dico 'movetur a mane usque ad vesperam'[9], duo[10] dico, quia per hoc quod dico 'movetur' dico motum, sed per hoc quod dico 'a mane usque ad vesperam' dico mensuram motus, que est tempus. Unde quanta est extensio temporis a mane usque ad vesperam, tantum intelligo motum et extensionem eius. Et sic[11] per extensionem[12] temporis intelligo quanta est extensio motus. Et sic tempus mensurat[13] motum. Et propter hoc dicebatur prius in recta solutione[14] sophismatis quod hec negatio 'dies non est', prout est negatio in genere, ponebat subiectum suum, quod est tempus, extenso nomine subiecti, quia non solum appellatur ibi subiectum illud quod subicitur accidenti[15], sed etiam id quod est mensura alicuius accidentis[16], ut diei. Et ita nomen subiecti extenditur ad subiectum et ad mensuram; et ob hoc dicebatur[17] 'extenso nomine subiecti'.

25   Furthermore, note that insofar as motion on account of its essence is the cause of time and on account of its quantity gives quantity to time, in that way motion primarily is quantity, and on account of motion time is quantity, as it says in Book V of the *Metaphysics*, in the chapter on quantity.[13] However, according as one first encounters the nature of measuring in time and on account of time it [*i.e.* this nature of measuring] is found in motion, in that way time in itself is a quantity and thus motion is a quantity on account of time; and in this way motion is a quantity *per accidens*.

On number and measure

26   Note also that when I say 'three men' or 'six', I say two things, because by the expression 'men' I indicate the substances of men, and by the expression 'three' or 'six' I indicate their 'measure' [*i.e.* the amount] of men; the same goes for all other numerical expressions. And so understand that every number and every quantity is a measure in one way and some thing in another way: it is a measure according as it denominates some subject, *e.g.* 'three men', 'four horses', 'a bicubital man', and 'a tricubital pillar', and it is some thing according as it is some genus or some specific thing indicating an essence. Likewise when I say 'There is motion from morning until night' I say two things, because by the expression 'there is motion', I indicate motion, but by the expression 'from morning until night' I indicate the 'measure' [*i.e.* the length] of motion, *viz.* the time. Thus however long is the extension of time from morning until night, that is how long I take the motion and its extension to be. And so by the extension of time I understand how long the extension of motion is. In this way time measures the motion. And that is why it was said earlier in the <discussion of> the correct solution of the sophisma-sentence,[14] that insofar as the denial 'It is not day' is a denial within the genus, it posited its subject, *viz.* time, by extension of the noun 'subject', because in this case not only that which is the subject of an accident is named, but also that which is the measure of some accident, *viz.* day. And so the noun 'subject' is extended to include the subject and the measure; and that is why the expression 'by extension of the noun "subject"' was used.

---

[13] *Metaph.* V 13, 1020a7ff.
[14] Cf. above, cap. 17.

Sophismata

27 Item. Queritur de hoc sophismate. SI NULLA PROPOSITIO EST VERA, ALIQUA PROPOSITIO EST VERA. Probatio. Si[1] nulla propositio est vera, ista[2] propositio 'homo[3] est' non est vera (a toto in quantitate). Et[4] si ista propositio 'homo[5] est' non est vera, sua contradictoria[6] erit vera (a[7] contradictorie oppositis). Et si sua contradictoria est vera, aliqua[8] propositio est vera (a specie[9] sive a parte subiectiva[10]). Ergo a primo: si nulla propositio est vera, aliqua propositio est vera. Contra. Ibi[11] assignatur oppositum sequi ad oppositum. Ergo locutio est impossibilis.

28 Solutio. Prima, scilicet hec 'si nulla propositio est vera, aliqua propositio est vera', uno modo est vera et alio modo est falsa. Et etiam prima consequentia tenet uno modo et alio modo non, eoquod primum antecedens (scilicet 'nulla[1] propositio est vera') est duplex. Quia uno modo est negatio simpliciter. Et sic non sequitur 'si nulla propositio est vera, ista propositio "homo est " non est vera', nec est ibi locus [N60vb] a toto in quantitate, quia hoc[2] modo primum antecedens (scilicet 'nulla propositio est vera') neque[3] ponit accidens[4] (quod est 'verum') neque subiectum eius (quod est 'propositio'). Sed consequens eiusdem consequentie ponit propositionem particularem virtute demonstrationis, cum[5] dicitur 'ista propositio "homo[6] est" non est vera'. Tunc enim antecedens removet tam propositionem quam veritatem eius et consequens [P69rb] ponit propositionem virtute demonstrationis, sicut dictum est. Et sic consequens contradicit antecedenti, sicut[7] si diceretur 'si nulla propositio est neque veritas eius[8], ista propositio[9] "homo[10] est[11] " et veritas eius non est'.

29 Alio autem modo primum antecedens (scilicet 'nulla[1] propositio est vera') potest esse negatio in genere et sic ponit omnem propositionem et removet veritatem[2] ab omni propositione. Et hoc modo ponit omnes[3] contradictorias[4] simul esse falsas. Unde ex consequenti ponit omnes[5] contradictorias[6] simul esse veras, quia quandocumque una contradictoriarum[7] est falsa[8], reliqua est vera[9]. Unde[10] si hoc[11] modo est falsa, illo[12] modo est vera; et si illo[13] modo est falsa, isto[14] modo est vera. Unde si utroque[15] modo est falsa, utroque[16] modo est vera. Et sic primum antecedens ponit et removet quamlibet contradictionem[17]. Et ideo secundum quod[18] primum[19]

Sophismata

27   There is a problem concerning the sophisma-sentence IF NO
PROPOSITION IS TRUE, SOME PROPOSITION IS TRUE. Proof: if
no proposition is true, the proposition 'A man is' is not true (from a
quantative whole), and if the proposition 'A man is' is not true, its
contradictory will be true (from contradictory opposites), and if its
contradictory is true, some proposition is true (from a species or from
a subjective part). Therefore, taking it from the beginning, if no
proposition is true, some proposition is true. There is an argument to
the contrary. This is said to be a case of an opposite following from
an opposite. Therefore the locution is impossible.
28   Solution. The original sentence, *viz.* 'If no proposition is true,
some proposition is true', is true in one way and false in another
way. Furthermore, the first inference as well is valid in one way
and not in another way, because the first antecedent (*viz.* 'if no
proposition is true') is ambiguous. In one way it is a denial *simpliciter*,
and thus it does not follow 'If no proposition is true, the proposition
"A man is" is not true', nor do we have here the topic 'from a
quantative whole', because in this way the first antecedent (*viz.* 'no
proposition is true') does not posit the accident (*viz.* 'true'), nor does it
posit its subject (*viz.* 'proposition'). However, the consequent of that
same conditional asserts a particular proposition by the use of the
demonstrative pronoun in the expression 'This proposition "A man
is" is not true'. For in that case the first antecedent not only removes
this proposition, but also its truth, and the consequent asserts a
proposition by the use of the demonstrative pronoun, as was said
before. Thus the consequent contradicts the antecedent, in the same
way as if one were to say 'If no proposition nor the truth thereof
exists, the proposition "A man is" and its truth do not exist'.
29   In another way, however, the first antecedent (*viz.* 'No proposition is true') can be a denial within the genus, and thus it asserts
every proposition and removes the truth of every proposition. In this
way it asserts that all contradictories are false at the same time.
Therefore by consequence it asserts that all contradictories are true
at the same time, because whenever one of two contradictories is
true, the other is false. Hence if it [*i.e.* one of the two contradictories]
is false in this way, it is true in another way, and if it is true in the
latter way, it is false in the former way. Hence if it is false in both
ways, it is true in both ways. Thus the first antecedent both asserts
and removes any contradiction whatsoever. Therefore according as
the first antecedent is a denial within the genus, in that way the first

antecedens est[20] negatio in genere, sic bene tenet prima[21] consequentia, et omnes alie a primo ad ultimum. Et sic prima propositio
est vera, hec[22] scilicet 'si nulla propositio est vera, aliqua propositio est
vera'. Ad improbationem autem solvendum hoc modo, scilicet[23]
secundum quod primum antecedens est negatio in genere, dicendum est quod non sequitur ibi[24] oppositum ad oppositum sed sequitur
una pars [*T36ra*] contradictionis ad antecedens, quod claudit intra se
quamlibet[25] contradictionem.

30   Item. Queritur de hoc sophismate. SI TU ES UBIQUE, TU NON
ES UBIQUE. Probatio. Si tu es ubique, tu es hic (a toto in loco). Et si tu[1]
es hic[2], tu non es ibi (ab oppositis[3]). Et[4] si tu non es ibi, tu non es
ubique (a parte in loco destructive). Ergo a primo: si tu es ubique, tu
non es ubique. Contra. Ibi sequitur oppositum ad oppositum. Ergo
locutio est[5] impossibilis.

31   Solutio. Quidam dicunt quod prima est duplex, eoquod 'locus'
dicitur dupliciter, scilicet proprius et communis. Proprius autem
locus est qui adequatur rei[1] et circuit [*N61rb*] et[2] continet rem undique; et talis locus dicitur circumscriptivus[3]. Et hoc modo sumendo
'locum' impossibile est plura corpora esse in eodem loco. Communis
autem locus dicitur in quo sunt plures[4] res simul, ut plures homines
in eadem domo vel elementa et elementata[5] [*P69va*] omnia[6] intra
celum. Unde dicunt quod, si in antecedente sumatur locus communis[7] et in consequente sumatur locus circumscriptivus[8], sic prima est
vera. Si autem utrobique sumatur locus circumscriptivus[9] vel utrobique communis[10], sic est falsa. Sed hec solutio nulla est[11], quia
sumpto loco semper[12] circumscriptive[13] adhuc remanet sophisma et
procedit[14] probatio et improbatio sicut prius. Et propter hoc dicendum
quod prima est simpliciter vera, quia primum antecedens (scilicet[15]
'tu es ubique') ex duplici parte ponit contradictionem propter hoc
quod subiectum contradicit predicato (et hec est una contradictio) et
etiam ipsum predicatum ponit in se tot contradictiones quot sunt loca
circumscriptiva[16].

inference is sound, and so are all the others from the first to the last. And thus the first proposition, *viz.* 'If no proposition is true, some proposition is true', is true. As to the disproof, it can be solved in the following way: according as the first antecedent is a denial within the genus, one should say that here it is not the case that an opposite follows from an opposite, but rather that one part of a contradiction follows from the antecedent, which contains any contradiction whatsoever.

30 There is a problem concerning the sophisma-sentence IF YOU ARE EVERYWHERE, YOU ARE NOT EVERYWHERE. Proof: if you are everywhere, you are here (from a local whole), if you are here, you are not there (from opposites) and if you are not there, you are not everywhere (from a local whole, by destroying <the consequent>). Therefore, taking it from the beginning, if you are everywhere, you are not everywhere. There is an argument to the contrary. In this case an opposite follows from an opposite. Therefore the locution is impossible.

31 Solution. Some people say that the original sentence is ambiguous, because 'place' is said in two ways, namely <in the sense of> a proper place and a common place. Now a proper place is one that is equal to some one thing and surrounds and contains this thing from all sides, and this type of place is called circumscriptive. Now if one takes 'place' in this way, it is impossible that more bodies are in the same place. A common place, on the other hand, is one that includes more things at the same time, *e.g.* more men in the same house or all the elements and what is made out of them within the vaults of heaven. Thus they say that if in the antecedent 'place' is taken as common and in the consequent as circumscriptive, in that way the original sentence is true. If, on the other hand, in both antecedent and consequent 'place' is taken as circumscriptive or in both as common, in that way the original sentence is false. However, this solution is useless, because even if 'place' has always been taken circumscriptively, the sophisma still remains and the proof and disproof proceed as before. Therefore the answer should be that the original sentence is true *simpliciter*, because the first antecedent (*viz.* 'You are everywhere') from two angles asserts a contradiction, because [a] the subject contradicts the predicate (and this is one contradiction) and [b] also the predicate in itself contains as many contradictions as there are circumscriptive places.

32   Quod autem subiectum contradicat predicato patet, quia[1] per[2] hoc[3] pronomen 'tu' positum[4] in subiecto demonstrat[5] rem singularem aptam natam esse in uno loco tantum et ita non ubique[6], et predicatum[7] ponit quod ubique. Et sic est ibi[8] ubique et non ubique inter[9] subiectum et predicatum. Et sic subiectum contradicit predicato. Quod autem predicatum ponat in se contradictiones plures patet, quia, sicut impossibile est plura corpora simul[10] esse in eodem loco circumscriptive, ita impossibile est idem corpus esse[11] in diversis locis circumscriptive. Unde quod[12] est hic circumscriptive, non est ibi circumscriptive, et quod est ibi circumscriptive, non est hic circumscriptive; et sic de quolibet alio[13] loco. Unde[14] 'esse hic circumscriptive' contradicit huic quod dico 'esse ibi[15] circumscriptive' et econverso; et sic de omnibus aliis locis circumscriptivis[16]. Et sic 'esse ubique' ponit tot[17] contradictiones quot[18] sunt loca particularia circumscriptiva[19]. Patet ergo quod primum antecedens ex duplici parte ponit contradictionem. Et ideo per naturales consequentias ex[20] eo sequitur contradictio. Et propter hoc dicendum[21] est quod prima est vera. Ad improbationem dicendum quod non sequitur oppositum ad oppositum sed sequitur una pars contradictionis ad antecedens, quod claudit[22] intra se utramque et plures alias.

Utrum conditionalis sit sillogizabilis

33   [*N61rb*] Circa tertium queritur in[1] hunc modum: Sillogismorum[2] alius est categoricus, alius conditionalis[3] (categoricus est qui est ex categoricis propositionibus, conditionalis vero qui[4] est[5] ex conditionalibus propositionibus). Ergo propositio conditionalis est sillogizabilis[6]. Ergo necesse [*P69vb*] est descendere sub antecedente vel sub[7] consequente. Et dicendum quod in conditionali aliquando licet fieri descensum[8] sub antecedente, aliquando sub consequente.

De quibusdam regulis

34   Unde dantur plures regule. Et[1] prima [*T36rb*] talis est:

32 That the subject contradicts the predicate is evident: the noun 'you' placed in subject-position indicates a singular thing naturally apt to be in one place only and so not everywhere, and the predicate asserts that it is everywhere. Thus we have in this case *everywhere* and *not everywhere* between the subject and the predicate, and so the subject contradicts the predicate. That the predicate contains more contradictions is evident: just as it is impossible for more bodies to be in the same place circumscriptively, in the same way it is impossible for one body to be in different places circumscriptively. Thus what is here circumscriptively is not there circumscriptively, and what is there circumscriptively is not here circumscriptively; and the same goes for any other place. Therefore 'to be here circumscriptively' contradicts the expression 'to be there circumscriptively' and the other way round, and the same goes for all other circumscriptive places. Thus 'to be everywhere' asserts as many contradictions as there are particular circumscriptive places. It is evident, therefore, that the first antecedent from two angles asserts a contradiction, and therefore on account of the natural consequences a contradiction follows from it. And therefore one should say that the original sentence is true. As to the disproof, the answer should be that this is not a case of an opposite following from an opposite, but one part of a contradiction follows from the antececent which includes both parts and many others.

Whether a conditional sentence can be used in a syllogism

33 *Ad [3]:* As to the third item, there is a problem in the following manner. Of syllogisms one type is categorical and another conditional (a categorical syllogism is one that consists of categorical propositions, whereas a conditional syllogism is one that consists of conditional propositions). Therefore a conditional sentence can be used in a syllogism. Therefore it is necessary to make a descent under the antecedent or under the consequent. The answer should be that in a conditional sentence one can sometimes make a descent under the antecedent and sometimes under the consequent.

On certain rules

34 In this connection one presents a number of rules. The first one is the following:

si termini communes ponantur in antecedente et consequente alicuius conditionalis [2] sine distributione, sub [3] antecedente contingit fieri descensum consequente immobili permanente.

Ut 'si homo currit, animal[4] currit; ergo si Sortes currit, animal currit, et[5] si Plato currit, animal currit', et sic de aliis. Secunda regula talis est:

si termini communes ponantur cum distributione in antecedente et consequente, antecedens manet immobile et sub consequente oportet[6] fieri descensum[7].

Ut 'si omne animal currit[8], omnis homo currit; ergo si omne animal currit, Sortes currit et Plato et Cicero', et sic de aliis. Tertia regula talis est:

si aliquid[9] sequitur ad aliud, destructo consequente destruitur et[10] antecedens.

Et ob hoc semper[11] tenet argumentum a destructione consequentis, ut[12] 'si est homo, est animal; ergo si non est animal, non est homo'. Quarta regula est talis:

si aliquid[13] sequitur ad aliud, posito antecedente ponitur consequens[14].

Ut[15] 'si homo est, animal est; sed[16] homo est; ergo animal est'. Et[17] ob hoc tenet argumentum a positione antecedentis. Quinta regula est talis:

quicquid antecedit ad antecedens, antecedit ad consequens.

Ut 'si animal est, substantia est; sed si homo est, animal est; ergo[18] si homo est, substantia est'. Sexta regula talis est:

quicquid sequitur ad consequens, sequitur ad antecedens.

Ut 'si homo est, animal est; sed si animal est, substantia est; ergo si homo est, substantia est'.

[1] If common terms are placed in the antecedent and the consequent of some conditional without a distribution, one can make a descent under the antecedent while the consequent remains immobile.

For example, 'If a man is running, an animal is running; therefore if Socrates is running, an animal is running, and if Plato is running, an animal is running', and so on. The second rule is the following:

[2] If common terms are placed in combination with a distribution in the antecedent and the consequent, the antecedent remains immobile and one must make a descent under the consequent.

For example, 'If every animal is running, every man is running; therefore if every animal is running, Socrates is running and Plato and Cicero', and so on. The third rule is the following:

[3] If something follows from something else, then if the consequent is destroyed, so is the antecedent.

That is why an argument from the destruction of the consequent is always sound, *e.g.* 'If there is a man, there is an animal; therefore if there is not an animal, there is not a man'. The fourth rule is the following:

[4] If something follows from something else, then if the antecedent is asserted, so is the consequent.

For example, 'If there is a man, there is an animal; now there is a man; therefore there is an animal'. That is why an argument from the assertion of the antecedent is sound. The fifth rule is the following:

[5] Whatever is antecedent to the antecedent is antecedent to the consequent.

For example, 'If there is an animal, there is a substance; now if there is a man, there is an animal; therefore if there is a man, there is a substance'. The sixth rule is the following:

[6] Whatever follows from the consequent follows from the antecedent.

For example, 'If there is a man, there is an animal; now if there is an animal, there is a substance; therefore if there is man, there is a substance'.

Ad quid feratur negatio in conditionali

35 Circa quartum queritur[1] ad quid feratur negatio ut[2] sumatur contradictoria alicuius conditionalis. Et videtur quod[3] ad verbum consequentis, quia, ut vult Boetius[4], antecedens cedit[5] in determinationem[6] consequentis. Et ita verbum consequentis ponitur et antecedens determinat ipsum. Sed quod ponitur in affirmativa, debet negari in negativa. Ergo negatio debet ferri[7] ad verbum consequentis ut sumatur contradictoria ipsius conditionalis.

36 Sed obicitur in contrarium quia: 'Consequens' duo dicit, scilicet[1] consequens inquantum consequens et id quod est consequens, sicut 'pater' uno [*N61va*] modo dicit patrem inquantum[2] pater, et alio modo id quod est pater. Sed consequens inquantum consequens *ad aliquid[3]* est, quia[4] [*P70ra*] ad antecedens, et econverso. Et sic posito uno ponitur alterum et destructo uno destruitur reliquum, cum[5] sint relativa. Ergo non est maior ratio quare[6] negatio magis feratur ad consequens quam ad antecedens. Similiter non habet ferri[7] negatio ad id quod est[8] consequens, quia sicut hec est falsa 'si Sortes legit, Plato legit', similiter[9] hec est[10] falsa 'si Sortes legit[11], Plato non legit'. Ergo nullo modo negatio debet ferri ad consequens. Ergo non contingit contradicere conditionali[12].

De consequente triplici

37 Et dicendum quod 'consequens'[1] tribus modis dicitur[2]. Uno[3] enim modo sumitur consequens inquantum consequens; et sic est *ad aliquid* et sic correspondet cum antecedente et sic simul sunt natura consequens et antecedens, sicut pater et filius. Et hoc modo negatio non fertur ad consequens ut contradicat conditionali[4]. Alio autem modo 'consequens' dicit[5] id quod est consequens secundum se et absolute sumptum. Et neque hoc modo negatio fertur ad consequens ut contradicat conditionali. Unde sicut hec est falsa 'si homo currit[6], asinus currit', similiter et hec est falsa 'si homo currit,

What the negation in a conditional should extend to

35 *Ad [4]:* As to the fourth item, there is a problem what a negation should extend to to form the contradictory of some conditional. It may be argued that it should extend to the verb of the consequent, because, as Boethius[15] has it, the antecedent leads to the modification of the consequent, and so the verb of the consequent is asserted and the antecedent modifies it. Now what is asserted in an affirmative sentence must be denied in a negative one. Therefore a negation must extend to the verb of the consequent to form the contradictory of that conditional.

36 Now it is argued to the contrary as follows. 'Consequent' designates two things, *viz.* a consequent insofar as it is a consequent and that which is the consequent, just as 'father' in one way designates a father insofar as he is a father, and in the other way that which is the father. Now the consequent insofar as it is a consequent is a relative (*ad aliquid*), because <it is relative> to the antecedent and the other way round. In this way if the one is asserted, so is the other and if the one is destroyed, so is the other for the reason that they are relatives. Therefore there is no more reason why the negation should extend to the consequent rather than it should to the antecedent. Likewise the negation should not extend to that which is the consequent, because just as the proposition 'If Socrates is reading, Plato is reading' is false, likewise so is the proposition 'If Socrates is reading, Plato is not reading'. Therefore in no way must the negation extend to the consequent. Therefore it is impossible to form the contradiction of a conditional.

On the three types of consequent

37 The answer should be that 'consequent' is said in three ways. [1] In one way the consequent is taken insofar as it is the consequent, and in that way it is a relative and as such it corresponds with the antecedent, and in that way the antecedent and consequent are naturally simultaneous, just as father and son. In this way the negation does not extend to the consequent in order to contradict a conditional. [2] In another way 'consequent' indicates that which is the consequent by itself and taken absolutely. In this way the negation does not extend to the consequent either in order to contradict a conditional. Hence just as the proposition 'If a man is running, an

---

15 Where?

asinus non currit', quia[7] negatio fertur[8] ad consequens secundum se
sumptum. Tertio autem modo sumitur[9] id quod est consequens
secundum quod determinatur per antecedens, quia[10] in omni conditionali consequens[11] ponitur sub conditione, ut 'homo movetur, si
currit' et 'animal est, si homo est'. Et hoc modo antecedens est
determinatio consequentis.

38   Et[1] isto tertio modo negatio debet ferri ad consequens ut
contradicat ipsi conditionali. Et isto tertio modo procedit primum
argumentum, duobus autem modis aliis procedit argumentum
factum in contrarium. Unde contradictoria huius 'animal est, si
homo est' est ista 'non: animal est, si homo est'[2]; et est [*T36va*] falsa,
cum sua contradictoria sit vera. Et contradictoria istius 'si homo
currit, asinus currit' est[3] ista 'non: si homo currit, asinus currit'; et est
vera, cum sua contradictoria sit falsa[4]. Semper enim negatio debet[5]
preponi totali[6] conditionali ut contradicat ei. Unde solet dari talis
regula:

> *quotienscumque negatio preponitur alicui propositioni tam categorice quam conditionali,*
> *semper[7] contradicit ei.*

Utrum ex impossibili sequatur quidlibet

39   Circa quintum queritur utrum ex impossibili sequatur quidlibet
sive[1] impossibile[2] antecedat ad quidlibet. [*P70rb*] Et videtur quod sic,
quia: Verum et falsum sunt opposita, cum sint contraria[3]. Sed[4] unum
contrariorum destruit alterum et econverso. Ergo[5] falsum destruit
verum et econverso. Et cum[6] impossibile sit falsum, impossibile[7]
destruet[8] verum et econverso. Sed ad impossibile sequitur verum.
Ergo multo fortius ad ipsum sequitur tam falsum quam impossibile,
quia si[9] quod[10] minus videtur sequi ad[11] impossibile sequitur ad[12]
ipsum (scilicet[13] quod destruit ipsum), ergo multo fortius quidlibet
aliud[14]. Ergo ex impossibili sequitur quidlibet. Item. Omne verum
equaliter distat ab[15] impossibili, quia[16] equaliter sibi invicem[17]
repugnant. Ergo qua ratione sequitur unum verum ex impossibili, et

ass is running' is false, likewise so is the proposition 'If a man is running, an ass is not running', because the negation extends to the consequent taken by itself. [3] In the third way that which is the consequent is taken insofar as it is modified by the antecedent, for in every conditional the consequent is asserted conditionally, *e.g.* 'A man is moving, if he is running' and 'An animal is, if a man is'. In this way the antecedent is a modification of the consequent.

38 Now in this third way the negation must extend to the consequent to contradict the conditional. And the first argument[16] proceeds in this third way, whereas the argument produced to the contrary[17] proceeds in the other two ways. Hence the contradictory of the proposition 'An animal is, if a man is' is 'Not: an animal is, if a man is'; and the latter is false, because its contradictory is true. Furthermore, the contradictory of the proposition 'If a man is running, an ass is running' is 'Not: if a man is running, an ass is running'; and the latter is true because its contradictory is false. The reason for this is that the negation must always be placed before the whole conditional in order to contradict the latter. Hence one usually presents the following rule:

> *Whenever a negation is placed before some proposition, whether categorical or conditional, it always contradicts the latter.*

Whether from an impossible anything follows

39 *Ad [5]:* As to the fifth item, there is a problem whether from an impossible anything follows or whether an impossible is antecedent to anything. It may be argued that this is the case. True and false are opposites because they are contraries. Now one of two contraries destroys the other and the other way round. Therefore the false destroys the true and the other way round, and because an impossible is false an impossible destroys the true and the other way round. Now from an impossible follows the true. Therefore both the true and the false follow from it all the more, because if what is less likely to follow from an impossible follows from it (*viz.* that which destroys it), therefore anything else follows all the more. Therefore from an impossible anything follows. Again, everything true is equally remote from an impossible, because they are all equally in disagreement with it. Therefore for the very reason that one true thing follows from an impossible, any other <true thing> follows as

---

16 Cf. above, cap. 35.
17 Cf. above, cap. 36.

quodlibet aliud. Sed unum[18] verum sequitur ex impossibili, ut 'si homo est asinus, homo est animal'. Ergo quodlibet aliud verum sequitur ex impossibili.

40   Item. Probo quod ex hoc impossibili 'Sortes est homo et non est homo' sequitur quodlibet aliud impossibile, quia si Sortes est homo et non est homo, ergo[1] Sortes est homo; et est locus a toto[2], quia contradictio totum[3] est ad utramque sui partem. Sed si Sortes est homo[4], Sortes[5] est homo vel[6] asinus; et est argumentum quasi a parte subiectiva, quia totum disiunctum commune est ad utramque sui partem. Ergo a primo: si Sortes est homo et non est homo, Sortes est homo vel asinus. Sed non est homo, quia si Sortes[7] est homo et non est homo, Sortes non est homo (a toto integrali). Ergo Sortes est asinus[8]. Et sic ex hoc impossibili 'Sortes est homo et non est homo' sequitur Sortem esse asinum[9]. Et[10] eodem modo potest probari quod sequatur inde quodlibet aliud[11] impossibile. Et ita ex impossibili[12] sequitur quidlibet. Ergo impossibile[13] antecedit ad quidlibet.

41   Sed obicitur in contrarium quia: Cum conclusio sit argumento vel argumentis approbata propositio et omne argumentum sit ratio inferendi secundum aliquam vel aliquas habitudines (quia argumentum est ratio rei dubie faciens fidem et fides[1] non potest fieri de re dubia[2] nisi per habitudinem vel habitudines aliquas), necesse est ergo [*N62ra*] quod ubicumque concluditur aliquid ex altero et sequitur aliquid ex altero, quod ibi sit habitudo aliqua, vel habitudines alique, propter quam, vel propter quas, sequatur unum ex altero. Sed istius [*P70va*] impossibilis 'hominem esse asinum' non sunt habitudines alique[3], neque mediate neque immediate, ad hoc impossibile 'albedinem esse nigredinem' vel 'iustitiam esse iniustitiam'. Ergo ex hoc impossibili 'hominem esse asinum' non sequentur illa impossibilia. Non ergo ex impossibili sequitur quidlibet. Item. Oportet quod in loco a primo ad ultimum semper confirmentur[4] consecutiones intermedie per aliquos locos intrinsecos vel extrinsecos vel medios. Sed multa sunt[5] vera et multa sunt impossibilia que non possunt confirmari[6] per aliquas habitudines locales ad hoc impossibile 'hominem esse asinum'. Ergo ex hoc[7] impossibili non sequitur

well. Now one true thing follows from an impossible, *viz.* 'If a man is an ass, a man is an animal'. Therefore any other true thing follows from an impossible <as well>.

40   Furthermore, I shall prove that from the impossible 'Socrates is a man and is not a man' follows any other impossible. If Socrates is a man and is not a man, therefore Socrates is a man; and this is a case of the topic 'from a whole', because a contradiction forms a whole in relation to each one of its parts. Now if Socrates is a man, Socrates is a man or an ass, and this is an argument as it were from a subjective part, because the whole disjunct[18] is common to both of its parts. Therefore, taking it from the beginning, if Socrates is a man and is not a man, Socrates is <either> a man or an ass; now he is not a man, because if Socrates is a man and is not a man, Socrates is not a man (from an integral whole); therefore Socrates is an ass. In this way, then, from the impossible 'Socrates is a man and is not a man' follows that Socrates is an ass. In the same way one can prove that from it any other impossible follows. Thus from an impossible anything follows. Therefore an impossible is antecedent to anything.

41   Now it is argued to the contrary as follows. Since a conclusion is a proposition proved by an argument or arguments, and every argument provides the rationale for inferring it according to some logical relationship or relationships (for an argument forms the rationale which produces faith in something doubtful, and faith in something that is doubtful can only be produced by means of a logical relationship or logical relationships), therefore it is necessary that wherever something is concluded from something else and something follows from something else, that there be some logical relationship, or relationships, involved in virtue of which the one can follow from the other. Now the impossible 'that a man is an ass' has no such logical relationships, whether directly or indirectly, to the impossible 'that whiteness is blackness' or 'that justice is injustice'. Therefore from the impossible 'that a man is an ass' the impossibles mentioned will not follow. Therefore it is not the case that from the impossible anything follows. Furthermore, in an argument from the beginning to the end it is necessary that the intermediate inferences always be confirmed by certain intrinsical, extrinsical or intermediary topics. Now there are many true things and many false things that cannot be confirmed by any topical relationship with the impossible 'that a man is an ass'. Therefore it is not the case that from that impossible anything follows according to the

---

18   *i.e.* 'both disjuncts taken together'.

quidlibet per locum a primo ad ultimum neque per aliquem alium locum. Ergo non potest esse quod ex impossibili sequatur quidlibet.

De 'impossibili' tripliciter sumpto

42 Quod concedimus [*T36vb*] dicentes quod 'impossibile' tria dat intelligere. Unum est ipsum impossibile inquantum impossibile. Alterum est compositio rerum que non possunt sibi invicem[1] convenire (ut 'homo est asinus') vel divisio rerum sibi[2] invicem necessario[3] convenientium (ut 'homo non est animal'), quia ipsum impossibile inquantum est impossibile aliud est quam predicta compositio vel divisio propter hoc quod, sicut veritas et falsitas sunt circa compositionem vel divisionem sicut[4] circa subiectum extenso nomine 'subiecti' ad subiectum et ad signum rei, similiter necessitas[5] et impossibilitas sunt circa compositionem vel divisionem. Patet[6] ergo quod aliud est impossibile inquantum[7] impossibile, sive[8] ipsa impossibilitas, et aliud est compositio vel divisio circa quam[9] est. Tertium autem quod 'impossibile' dat intelligere est res ipsa que componitur vel dividitur, sive res ipse que componuntur vel dividuntur, ut homo secundum se et[10] asinus secundum se cum dicitur 'homo est asinus'.

43 Ideo ergo dicendum quod ex impossibili quoad duos primos modos nichil sequitur. Unde ex impossibili inquantum [*N62rb*] est impossibile nichil sequitur neque ex compositione vel divisione circa quam est impossibilitas aliquid sequitur. Et[1] ita nichil significant, quia[2] ipsum[3] impossibile inquantum est impossibile nichil est et ipsa compositio vel divisio circa quam est impossibilitas nichil est. Et[4] ita nichil ponunt[5]. Sed ex rebus que subiacent predicte [*P70vb*] compositioni vel divisioni sequitur aliquid[6]. Ut cum dicitur 'homo est asinus': quia illa res que est asinus, est species animalis et species semper ponit suum genus, ideo sequitur 'animal' ex 'asino'. Unde quando[7] concludit[8] sic: 'si homo est asinus, homo est animal', illud non est[9] propter impossibile inquantum impossibile neque propter compositionem circa quam est impossibilitas, sed propter habitudinem speciei ad genus, que est asini ad animal, qui[10] scilicet asinus erat res subiacens illi[11] compositioni.

topic 'from the beginning to the end', nor does it follow according to any other topic. Therefore it cannot be that from an impossible anything follows.

On 'impossible' taken in three ways

42 We agree with this, saying that 'impossible' gives to understand three things. [1] One thing is an impossible itself insofar as it is impossible. [2] Another thing is a composition of things that cannot be mutually in agreement (*e.g.* 'A man is an ass') or the division of things that necessarily are mutually in agreement (*e.g.* 'A man is not an animal'). For an impossible itself insofar as it is impossible is something other than the composition or division mentioned above, for the reason that, just as truth and falsity concern a composition or division as their subject by extension of the noun 'subject' to include the subject and the sign of something, likewise necessity and impossibility concern a composition or division. It is evident therefore that it is one thing to be an impossibile insofar as it is impossible, or an impossibility itself, and it is another thing to be the composition or division the impossibility concerns. [3] The third thing 'impossible' gives to understand is the thing itself that is combined or divided, or the things themselves that are combined or divided, *e.g.* man in himself or ass in itself in the expression 'A man is an ass'.

43 Hence the answer should therefore be that from an impossible in terms of the first two ways nothing follows. Thus from an impossible insofar as it is impossible nothing follows nor does something follow from the composition or division the impossibility concerns. Thus they [*i.e.* these two types of 'impossible'] do not signify anything, because an impossible insofar as it is impossible is nothing, and the composition or division the impossibility concerns is nothing either. Thus they assert nothing. However, from the things that are the subject of the composition or division just mentioned something does follow. For example, in the expression 'A man is an ass', it is in virtue of the fact that *ass* is a species of *animal* and a species always implies its genus, that 'animal' follows from 'ass'. Thus when one concludes 'If a man is an ass, a man is an animal', this is not on account of an impossible insofar as it is impossible nor on account of the composition the impossibility concerns, but on account of the logical relationship a species has with its genus, *viz.* of *ass* with *animal*, if in fact *ass* was the thing that was the subject of this composition.

44   Dicendum ergo breviter quod ex impossibili quoad duos primos modos nichil[1] sequitur. Sed ex impossibili quoad istum tertium modum sequuntur tantum[2] ista[3] vera vel illa impossibilia cum quibus[4] habet[5] aliquam habitudinem. Ut 'si homo est asinus, homo est animal': sequitur[6] verum[7] isto tertio modo; et est locus a specie. Et 'si homo est asinus, homo est animal rudibile'[8]: sequitur impossibile[9] predicto tertio modo; et est locus a descripto[10]. Et similiter intelligendum est de quolibet alio impossibili[11]. Et ita patet quod ex impossibili non sequitur quidlibet.

45   Ad prima duo argumenta dicendum quod non sequitur verum ex impossibili inquantum est impossibile, sicut dictum fuit prius. Sed sequitur ex rebus quarum compositio vel divisio est impossibilis, sicut dictum fuit prius. Sed hoc modo, quamvis impossibile perimat verum et econverso, tamen[1] res que subiacet[2] compositioni vel divisioni impossibli, non perimit[3] verum nec econverso, sed potius ponit ipsum. Et etiam[4] hoc modo non omnia vera equaliter distant ab impossibili, quia magis distant illa vera que nullam habent habitudinem ad ipsum impossibile, et minus distant illa vera que habent aliquam habitudinem[5], vel aliquas habitudines, cum rebus subiacentibus compositioni vel divisioni impossibili.

46   Ad tertium dicendum quod bene tenet argumentum[1] usque ad illationem que fit a primo ad ultimum dicendo sic: 'ergo[2] a primo: si Sortes est homo et[3] non est homo, ergo Sortes est homo vel asinus'. Sed sequens[4] illatio non tenet, [*N62va*] quia non interimit[5] hanc 'Sortes est homo', quod[6] oporteret ad hoc quod sequeretur Sortem esse asinum, cum hec sit vera 'Sortes est homo vel asinus', quia predicta contradictio, scilicet[7] 'Sortes est homo et non est homo', equaliter interimit[8] et ponit hanc [*T37ra*] scilicet 'Sortes [*P71ra*] est homo'. Et ita non[9] magis interimit quam ponit eam[10]. Et propter hoc non interimit alteram partem disiunctive. Et ob hoc non est locus a divisione, et ideo[11] non sequitur argumentum. Argumenta vero

44   Briefly then one should say that from an impossible in terms of the first two ways nothing follows, but from an impossible in terms of the third way only those true things or those impossibles follow with which that impossible has some logical relationship. For example, in 'If a man is an ass, a man is an animal', something true follows in this third way; and it involves the topic 'from a species'. Also in 'If a man is an ass, a man is an animal that can bray', an impossible follows in the third way mentioned above; and it is a case of the topic 'from what is described' [the '*descriptum*']. Likewise one should understand this as concerning any other impossible. Thus it is evident that it is not the case that from an impossible anything follows.

45   As to the first two arguments,[19] the answer should be that something true does not follow from an impossible insofar as it is impossible, as has been said before. Rather it follows from the things the composition or division of which is impossible, as has been said before. Now in this way, although an impossible annihilates something true and the other way round, nevertheless the thing that can be the subject of an impossible composition or division does not annihilate something true nor the other way round, but rather they assert it. Moreover, in this way not all true things are equally remote from an impossible, because the true things that have no relationship with the impossible are more remote from it, and the things that do have some such relationship, or relationships, with the things that are the subject of an impossible composition or division are less remote from it.

46   As to the third,[20] the answer should be that the argument is valid up to the inference that takes place from the beginning to the end, by saying 'Therefore, taking it from the beginning, if Socrates is a man and is not a man, therefore Socrates is <either> a man or an ass'. However, the subsequent inference is not valid, because it does not annihilate the proposition 'Socrates is a man', something it should have done in order for it to follow that Socrates is an ass, because the proposition 'Socrates is <either> a man or an ass' is true; for the contradiction we started off with, *viz.* 'Socrates is man and is not a man', both annihilates and asserts the proposition 'Socrates is a man'. Thus it does not annihilate the latter more than it asserts it, and that is why it does not annihilate one part of the disjunction. Therefore it is not a case of the topic 'from division', and therefore the argument is not valid. On the other hand, we agree with the

---

[19] Cf. above, cap. 39.
[20] Cf. above, cap. 40.

probantia quod ex impossibili non sequitur quidlibet, concedimus; et procedunt.

Sophismata

47   Secundum predicta queritur de hoc sophismate SI NICHIL EST, ALIQUID EST. Probatio. Si nichil est, nichil esse est verum (et est locus a[1] causa, quia res est causa veritatis orationis[2], ut est in *Predicamentis*[3]). Sed si nichil esse est verum, hoc enuntiabile, scilicet 'nichil esse'[4], est verum (a convertibili sive a pari). Et[5] si hoc enuntiabile est verum[6], aliquid est verum (a parte subiectiva). Et si aliquid est verum, aliquid est[7] (a convertibili sive a pari, quia 'esse' et 'esse verum' convertuntur in eis que sunt complexa). Ergo a primo: si nichil est, aliquid est. Contra. Ibi assignatur[8] sequi oppositum ad oppositum. Ergo locutio est impossibilis.

48   Solutio. Quidam dicunt quod prima est simpliciter falsa. Et dicunt quod prima consequentia non tenet propter hoc quod, cum[1] ista propositio[2] 'nichil est' omnia removeat[3] et sic non relinquat[4] artes aliquas neque scientias neque principia aliqua neque maximas neque locos neque causas aliquas neque effectus aliquos, ideo non est ibi locus a[5] causa neque aliquis alius. Et ideo non tenet ista[6] consequentia 'si nichil est, nichil esse est verum'. Sed hoc nichil est, quia posito quod nichil sit de rebus creatis[7] (sicut erat ante rerum creationem[8]) et ista distributio 'nichil' non comprehendat[9] sub se nisi res creatas, tunc hec est vera 'nichil est', loquendo de rebus creatis; et etiam hec 'nichil esse est verum'. Et una non potest intelligi sine altera nec econverso. Ergo necessario una sequitur ad alteram et econverso.

49   Alii autem dicunt quod prima ponit impossibile et ex impossibili sequitur quidlibet. Et ita ex prima sequitur aliquid esse. Sed hoc nichil est, quia ostensum est prius quod ex impossibili non[1] sequitur quidlibet. Alii autem dicunt quod prima interimit[2] seipsam. Et ideo ponit suum oppositum [*N62vb*] (scilicet aliquid esse), quia

arguments[21] meaning to prove that it is not the case that from the impossible anything follows; and these arguments obtain.

Sophismata

47 As regards what has been said, there is a problem concerning the sophisma-sentence IF NOTHING IS, SOMETHING IS. Proof: if nothing is, it is true that nothing is (and this is a case of the topic 'from a cause', because a *pragma* is the cause of the truth of a proposition, as it says in the *Categories*).[22] Now if it is true that nothing is, the stateable 'that nothing is' is true (from a convertible or from an equal), and if that stateable is true, something is true (from a subjective part), and if something is true, something is (from a convertible or an equal, because 'to be' and 'to be true' are convertible in complex expressions). Therefore, taking it from the beginning, if nothing is, something is. There is an argument to the contrary. This is said to be a case of an opposite following from an opposite. Therefore the locution is impossible.

48 Solution. Some say that the original sentence is *simpliciter* false. They say that the first inference [*viz.* 'If nothing is, it is true that nothing is'] does not hold in virtue of the fact that because the proposition 'Nothing is' removes everything and thus leaves no arts, objects of knowledge, principles, maxims, topics, causes, and effects, therefore there is no topic 'from a cause' in this case or any other one. Hence the inference 'If nothing is, it is true that nothing is' does not obtain. However, this is nonsense, because supposing that there are no created things (just as it was the case before the creation of things) and the distribution 'nothing' only extends to created things, in that case the proposition 'Nothing is' is true, when speaking of created things, and so is the proposition 'It is true that nothing is'. And <then> the one cannot be understood without the other nor the other way round. Therefore the one necessarily follows from the other and the other way round.

49 Others say that the first <part of the conditional> asserts an impossible and from an impossible anything follows. Thus from the first part follows that something is. However, this is nonsense, because it was shown earlier that it is not the case that from an impossible anything follows. Others say that the first <part of the conditional> destroys itself. Therefore it asserts its opposite (*viz.* that

---

[21] Cf. above, cap. 41.
[22] *Categ.* 5, 4b8-10; 12, 14b21-2.

prima removet omnes res nature³ et moris et rationis. Et sic removet omnem sillogismum et omnem propositionem, cum sint res rationis. Sed si removet et perimit omnem propositionem, ergo et seipsam. Et ita interimit seipsam. Et ita sequitur ex ea et⁴ nichil esse et aliquid esse. [*P71rb*] Sed hoc nichil est, quia sumpta distributione pro rebus creatis (sicut dictum fuit prius), tunc hec est vera 'nichil est', loquendo de statu qui erat ante rerum creationem. Ergo neque interimit se neque ponit suum oppositum.

50   Ad hoc autem quod obiciunt¹ quod antecedens prime conditionalis removet res nature et res moris et res rationis; unde removet omnem sillogismum et omnem propositionem, ergo seipsam, — dicendum quod non sequitur, immo² est ibi *quid et simpliciter*, quia removet omnem sillogismum et omnem propositionem ut sunt res. Ergo³ illa propositio 'nichil est' non⁴ sumitur ut res sed sumitur ut signum rei vel sicut via⁵ in rem. Et sic nichil negat de se sed de rebus intellectis per ipsam. Simile autem est hic: posito quod omnes propositiones destruantur et nulla remaneat, tunc si aliquis dicat 'nulla propositio est', verum dicit et tamen ipse profert propositionem, hanc scilicet 'nulla propositio est'. Nec ex hoc sequitur quod aliqua propositio sit, quia hec⁶ propositio quam ipse profert (scilicet 'nulla [*T37rb*] propositio est') non sumitur ut res sed sumitur ut signum⁷ et ut via ad omnes alias propositiones. Unde esse istius⁸ non est nisi per esse illarum. Et ideo non facit numerum in esse cum illis. Et ideo non sequitur quod aliqua propositio sit.

51   Et propter hoc dicendum quod prima est falsa, hec scilicet 'si nichil est, aliquid est'. Et prima consequentia bene tenet, hec scilicet 'si nichil est, nichil esse est verum', quia ex impossibili¹ aliquo² bene sequitur aliquod³ aliud impossibile, dum⁴ habuerit aliquam habitudinem ad ipsum. Et est ibi locus ab effectu, quia veritas propositionis ponit veritatem dicti, sicut effectus ponit causam. Et etiam secunda consequentia bene tenet, hec scilicet 'si nichil esse est verum, hoc enuntiabile⁵ est verum'. Sed tertia consequentia⁶ peccat⁷ secundum

something is), because the first part removes all things that belong to nature, custom and reason. Thus it removes every syllogism and every proposition, because they are things of reason. Now if it removes and destroys every proposition, it therefore destroys itself as well. Thus it does away with itself. And so from it follows both that nothing is and that something is. However, this is nonsense, because by taking the distribution to extend to created things (as has been said before), then the proposition 'Nothing is' is true when speaking of the state that existed before the creation of things. Therefore the proposition neither does away with itself nor asserts its opposite.

50   As to the argument to the contrary that the antecedent of the first conditional removes things that belong to nature, custom and reason, and thus removes every syllogism and every proposition and therefore itself,—the answer should be that this does not follow: rather in this case one commits the fallacy of reasoning from something taken in a certain sense to the same thing taken *simpliciter*, because it [*i.e.* the antecedent] removes every syllogism and every proposition taken as things. Therefore the proposition 'Nothing is' is not taken as a 'thing' but as a sign of a 'thing' or a way to a 'thing'. Thus it does not deny anything of itself, but rather of the things understood by it. We have a similar case in the following: supposing that all propositions are destroyed and none remains, then if someone says 'No proposition is', he says something true and nevertheless he pronounces the proposition himself, *viz.* the proposition 'No proposition is'. And from this it does not follow that some proposition is, because the proposition he pronounces himself (*viz.* 'No proposition is') is not taken as a 'thing' but is taken as a sign and as a way to all other propositions. Hence this proposition only has being via the being of the former [*i.e.* all other propositions]. Therefore it cannot be summed up with them in the <domain of> being. That is why it does not follow that some proposition is.

51   This is why the answer should be that the original sentence is false, *viz.* 'If nothing is, something is'. The first inference is valid, *viz.* 'If nothing is, it is true that nothing is', because from some impossible indeed follows some other impossible, as long as the former has some relationship to the latter. In that case one has the topic 'from an effect', because the truth of a proposition posits the truth of the *dictum*, in the same way as an effect posits its cause. The second inference is also valid, *viz.* 'If it is true that nothing is, this stateable is true'. In the third inference, however, one commits the fallacy of reasoning from something taken in a certain sense to the

quid et simpliciter, hec scilicet 'si hoc enuntiabile est verum, aliquid est verum', [*N63ra*] quia[8] enuntiabile[9] non ponit esse[10] simpliciter, sed iste terminus 'aliquid' ponit ens simpliciter. Et ideo incidit[11] *quid et simpliciter*. Patet etiam hoc aliter, quia cum dicit 'si hoc enuntiabile est verum, aliquid est verum', per hoc pronomen 'hoc'[12] demonstrat[13] hoc enuntiabile 'nichil esse', quod[14] nichil ponit in esse sed omnia removet. Et per[15] hoc consequens [*P71va*] 'aliquid est verum' ponit rem simpliciter esse. Et sic ponit ens simpliciter. Unde si aliquis[16] recte inspexerit[17] tertiam[18] conditionalem, videbit quod consequens eius contradicit antecedenti ipsius. Et ideo aut[19] nulla est ibi[20] apparentia, aut, si est, incidit *quid et simpliciter*.

52   Item. Queritur de hoc sophismate SORTES DICIT VERUM, SI SOLUS PLATO LOQUITUR, posito quod Sortes dicat solum Platonem loqui. Probatio[1] prime. Sortes dicit solum Platonem loqui. Sed solum Platonem loqui est verum, si solus Plato loquitur. Ergo Sortes dicit verum si solus Plato loquitur. Contra. Si solus Plato loquitur, nullus alius a Platone loquitur (a diffinito vel a descripto). Et si nullus alius a Platone loquitur, Sortes non loquitur (a toto in quantitate). Et si Sortes non loquitur, Sortes[2] non dicit verum (a genere, quia loqui superius est ad dicere verum et ad[3] dicere falsum et ad omnes locutiones speciales). Non ergo dicit Sortes verum, si solus Plato loquitur.

53   Solutio. Prima est simpliciter falsa. Et probatio peccat secundum *accidens*, quia, quamvis[1] Sortes dicat solum Platonem loqui et illud sit verum, si solus Plato loquitur, non tamen dicit verum, si solus Plato loquitur. Sicut quamvis cognoscat eum qui est coopertus, ut Coriscus[2], non tamen cognoscit coopertum[3], sed est sophisma accidentis. Et similiter in proposito, quia, sicut coopertum accidit Corisco, similiter verum accidit ei quod est 'solum Platonem loqui'. Unde prima est simpliciter falsa et ponit contradictionem, quia ponit solum Platonem loqui et non solum Platonem loqui, et Sortem dicere verum et[4]

same thing taken *simpliciter*, that is, 'If this stateable is true, something is true', because the stateable does not posit a being *simpliciter*, but the term 'something' posits a being *simpliciter*. That is why there happens to be a fallacy of reasoning from something taken in a certain sense to the same thing taken *simpliciter*. This is also evident in another way, because in the expression 'If this stateable is true, something is true', the pronoun 'this' refers to the stateable 'that nothing is', which posits nothing in <the domain of> being but removes all things <from it>. And owing to the consequent 'something is true', the expression asserts that a thing is *simpliciter*. Thus it posits a being *simpliciter*. Hence if someone has looked at the conditional in the right way, he will see that its consequent contradicts its antecedent. Thus either there is no evidence in this case, or, if there is any, there happens to be a fallacy of reasoning from something taken in a certain sense to the same thing taken *simpliciter*.

52   Furthermore, there is a problem concerning the sophisma-sentence SOCRATES SAYS SOMETHING TRUE, IF PLATO ALONE IS SPEAKING, supposing that Socrates says that Plato alone is speaking. Proof of the original sentence: Socrates says that Plato alone is speaking. Now that Plato alone is speaking is true, if Plato alone is speaking. Therefore Socrates says something true, if Plato alone is speaking. There is an argument to the contrary. If Plato alone is speaking, no one other than Plato is speaking (from what is defined or from what is described), and if no one other than Plato is speaking, Socrates is not speaking (from a quantative whole), and if Socrates is not speaking he does not say something true (from a genus, because to speak is more general than to say something true and to say something false and more general than all specific locutions). Therefore it is not the case that Socrates says something true, if Plato alone is speaking.

53   Solution. The original sentence is *simpliciter* false and the proof commits the fallacy of accident. For although Socrates says that Plato alone is speaking and this is true, if Plato alone is speaking, nevertheless he does not say something true if Plato alone is speaking. Just as although someone knows the person who is disguised, namely Coriscus, nevertheless he does not know the disguised, for this is a fallacy of accident. And the same goes for the case at issue, for just as 'the disguised' is an accident of Coriscus, likewise 'some thing true' is an accident of 'Plato alone is speaking'. Thus the original sentence is *simpliciter* false and it asserts a contradiction, because it asserts that Plato alone is speaking and that not Plato alone is speaking, and that Socrates says something true and does not say some-

non dicere verum, cum omnes alii a Platone excludantur respectu huius actus 'loqui'. Unde probatio non probat eam.

54   Quidam tamen dicunt[1] quod, sicut prima ponit contradictionem, similiter positio quam facit, ponit contradictionem. Unde non est mirum si ex una contradictione vere[2] sequatur altera. Sed isti decepti [*N63rb*] sunt per *quid et simpliciter*, quia cum taceo et nichil dico, interroganti quid dicam vere respondeo 'nichil dico'. Et ex hoc non [*P71vb*] sequitur 'ergo dico aliquid', immo est *quid et simpliciter*, quia dictio mea non sumitur ut res que significetur[3] vel dicatur per [*T37va*] seipsam, sed sumitur ut signum aliarum rerum[4]. Similiter est[5] quod solo[6] Platone loquente Sortes bene potest hoc significare et dicere 'solus Plato loquitur'. Nec ponit ista positio contradictionem, quia dictio Sortis sumitur ut signum aliarum dictionum, unde non facit numerum cum aliis dictionibus. Et ideo non sequitur 'ergo alius a Platone loquitur'.

55   Item. Queritur de hoc sophismate SI TU SCIS TE ESSE LAPIDEM, TU NON SCIS TE ESSE LAPIDEM. Probatio. Si tu scis te esse lapidem, te esse lapidem[1] est verum, quia[2] nichil scitur nisi verum. Sed si[3] te esse lapidem est verum, tu es lapis (per locum a convertibili, quia dictum convertitur cum propositione). Et si tu es lapis, tu nichil scis (ab oppositis). Et si[4] nichil scis, tu non scis te esse lapidem (a[5] toto in quantitate). Ergo a primo: si tu scis te esse lapidem, tu non scis te esse lapidem. Contra. Ibi sequitur oppositum ad oppositum. Ergo locutio est impossibilis.

56   Solutio. Prima est simpliciter vera, quia consequens necessario sequitur ex antecedente per locales habitudines, sicut probatio manifestat. Ad improbationem autem solvendum per interemptionem[1], quia non sequitur ibi oppositum ad oppositum, sed sequitur una pars contradictionis ad antecedens quod claudit intra se utramque[2], quia hoc antecedens 'tu scis te esse lapidem' ratione[3] rei[4] huius verbi

thing true, because all other than Plato are excluded with respect to the act 'to speak'. That is why the 'proof' does not prove the original sentence.

54   Nevertheless some say that, just as the first asserts a contradiction, likewise the position it produces asserts a contradiction. Hence it is no wonder that from one contradiction truly follows the other. However, these people are deceived by the fallacy of reasoning from something taken in a certain sense to the same thing taken *simpliciter*, because when I remain silent and say nothing, I truly respond 'I am saying nothing' to the person who asks me what I am saying, and from that it does not follow 'Therefore I am saying something', for rather this is a fallacy of reasoning from something taken in a certain sense to the same thing taken *simpliciter*, because my utterance is not to be taken as something that is signified or is said by itself, but it is taken as a sign of other things. Likewise, when Plato alone is speaking, it can well be that Socrates is referring to that and says 'Plato alone is speaking', and this does not imply a contradiction, because Socrates' utterance is taken as a sign of other utterances; hence it is not included in the collection of the other utterances, and therefore it does not follow 'Therefore someone other than Plato is speaking'.

55   Furthermore, there is a problem concerning the sophisma-sentence IF YOU KNOW THAT YOU ARE A STONE, YOU DO NOT KNOW THAT YOU ARE A STONE. Proof: if you know that you are a stone, it is true that you are a stone, because one only knows something true. Now if it true that you are a stone, you are a stone (by the topic 'from a convertible', because the *dictum* is convertible with the proposition), and if you are a stone, you know nothing (from opposites), and if you know nothing, you do not know that you are a stone (from a quantitative whole). Therefore, taking it from the beginning, if you know that you are a stone, you do not know that you are a stone. There is an argument to the contrary. In this case an opposite follows from its opposite. Therefore the locution is impossible.

56   Solution. The original sentence is *simpliciter* true, because the consequent necessarily follows from the antecedent in virtue of topical relationships, as the proof displays. As to the disproof, it can be solved by destroying it altogether, because in this case an opposite does not follow from an opposite, but one part of a contradiction follows from the antecedent, which includes both parts: on account of the meaning of the verb 'to know', the antecedent 'You know that you are a stone' posits knowledge in the subject, whereas on account

'scire' ponit scientiam in subiecto, sed ratione obiecti eiusdem verbi
(quod scilicet obiectum est[5] te esse lapidem) privat scientiam a
subiecto. Et ita ponit subiectum scire et[6] non scire, et esse lapidem et
non esse lapidem, et[7] scire se esse lapidem et non scire se esse lapidem. Et omnes istas contradictiones[8] habet in se antecedens inte-
grantes[9] ipsum[10], sicut totum integrale habet in se suas partes integrales[11]. Unde ex primo antecedente sequitur quelibet[12] istarum[13]
contradictionum[14] per locales habitudines et non propter [*P72ra*] hoc
quod ex[15] impossibili sequitur [*N63va*] quidlibet, sicut ex toto integrali sequitur quelibet eius pars secundum consequentiam naturalem.

of the meaning of the object of that very verb (*viz.* the object that you are a stone), the antecedent removes knowledge from the subject. Thus it asserts that the subject has knowledge and is ignorant, that it is a stone and is not a stone, and knows that it is a stone and does not know that it is a stone. And the antecedent contains all these contradictions it forms in the manner of an integral whole, in the same way as an integral whole contains all its integral parts. Hence from the first antecedent any of the contradictions mentioned follow on account of topical relationships and not because from the impossible anything follows, just as from an integral whole any of its parts follow in accordance with natural consequence.

TRACTATUS SEXTUS

DE HIIS VERBIS 'INCIPIT' ET 'DESINIT'

Introductio

1   A[1] quibus dependet cognitio[2] rei priora sunt re. Sed cognitio[3] horum verborum 'incipit', 'desinit' dependet[4] a rebus permanentibus et a successivis, quia si hec verba[5] adiungantur rebus permanentibus et successivis habebunt secundum hoc diversas rationes. Et ideo dicturi[6] de hiis verbis 'incipit'[7] et 'desinit' primo queremus[8] que est differentia successivorum et[9] permanentium[10]; secundo que sint rationes horum verborum 'incipit'[11] et 'desinit' cum rebus[12] permanentibus et successivis; tertio utrum motus incipiat vel desinat et[13] qualiter, et quid sit motus; quarto utrum tempus incipiat vel desinat, et quid sit tempus et cuius sit[14] mensura et in quo sit ut in subiecto; quinto utrum potentia incipiat vel desinat et quot modis dicatur 'potentia'; sexto utrum termini habeant differentem suppositionem cum hiis verbis[15] a parte post et cum aliis verbis.

Que sit differentia inter successiva et permanentia

2   Circa primum sic obicitur. Cum successiva non habeant esse nisi a[1] permanentibus, ergo non habebunt rationem sive[2] diffinitionem nisi ab eis, quia a [*T37vb*] quo est esse[3], et est ratio. Ergo ratio successivorum non differt a ratione permanentium. Sed quorum rationes[4] non sunt differentes, ipsa non sunt differentia. Ergo successiva et permanentia non differunt.

CHAPTER VI

ON THE VERBS 'BEGINS' AND 'CEASES'

Introduction

1   The things on which the knowledge of something depends are prior to it. Now the knowledge of the verbs 'begins' and 'ceases' depends on permanent things and on successive things, because if these verbs are added to permanent things and successive things, they will have different meanings accordingly [*i.e.* corresponding to these uses]. Hence being on the verge of discussing the verbs 'begins' and 'ceases', *[1]* the first problem we are to consider is what the difference is between successive things and permanent things, *[2]* secondly what are the meanings of the verbs 'begins' and 'ceases' in combination with permanent things and successive things, *[3]* thirdly whether motion begins or ceases and in what way, and what motion is, *[4]* fourthly whether time begins or ceases, what time is, what it measures and what it inheres in as its subject, *[5]* fifthly whether a potency begins or ceases and in how many ways the word 'potency' is said, and *[6]* sixthly whether terms have a different supposition in combination with these verbs placed after them than they have in combination with other verbs.

What the difference is between permanent and successive things

2   *Ad [1]:* As to the first item, there is an argument to the contrary as follows. It is because successive things derive their being from permanent things only, that they therefore owe their descriptive account or definition to those things only, because what something derives its being from, it also derives its description from. Therefore the description of successive things is no different from the description of permanent things. Now the things of which the descriptions are not different, these things themselves are no different. Therefore successive things and permanent things are not different.

De rebus permanentibus et rebus successivis

3   Et dicendum (ut tactum est) quod rerum alie sunt permanentes,
alie successive. Et differunt a se invicem[1] multipliciter. Prima differentia est quod res permanentes dicuntur quarum esse est totum
simul, ut sunt homo, lapis, lignum, aer, terra. Res autem successive
dicuntur quarum esse non est totum simul sed est in successione, ut
sunt motus et tempus. Secunda autem differentia est[2] quoniam partes
permanentium simul sunt omnes (ut partes hominis, lapidis et
aeris) et non est una post alteram. Successivarum[3] vero partes non
sunt simul omnes[4] sed una est post alteram successive. [*N63vb*] Ut
partes motus et partes temporis, quia post unam partem motus sequitur altera et non sunt due partes motus eiusdem simul. Neque[5] due
partes temporis sunt simul sed est una post alteram successive;
impossibile enim[6] est plura tempora [*P72rb*] simul esse. Tertia vero
differentia est quoniam[7] permanentia natura priora sunt successivis
et successiva natura sunt posteriora permanentibus[8]; permanentia
enim sunt causa successivorum. Quarta differentia est quia[9] res
permanentes sunt in se terminate[10], quecumque habent terminos,
sed res successive non[11] habent in se terminos, ut motus qui terminatur ad res permanentes, ut alteratio ad qualitatem, augmentum
et diminutio ad quantitatem et sic de aliis. Quinta differentia est
quia[12] res permanentes sunt in sui principio et in sui fine, ut patet in
substantia et in accidentibus[13] permanentibus, ut in lapide[14] et in
albedine et nigredine. Res vero successive neque sunt in sui principio neque in sui fine, ut postea patebit de motu.

Que sint rationes horum verborum cum illis

4   Circa secundum obicitur quia[1]: Cum[2] motus habeat rationem a
suis terminis: quamvis magis a termino ad quem quam a termino a
quo quia motus fere omnes diffiniuntur per[3] terminum ad quem
(nam dealbatio est motus ad albedinem, denigratio vero motus ad

On permanent and successive things

3   The answer should be (as has been touched upon)[1] that of things some are permanent and some successive. These things are different from each other in many ways. [1] The first difference is that those things are called permanent of which the being is complete at the same time, as there are a man, a stone, a line, the air, and the earth, whereas things are called successive of which the being is not complete at the same time but only in succession, as there are motion and time. [2] The second difference is that the parts of permanent things all have being at the same time (*e.g.* the parts of a man, a stone and the air) and one does not come after another, whereas the parts of successive things do not all have being at the same time, but one part succeeds another, *e.g.* the parts of motion and the parts of time, because after one part of motion another follows, and there are not two parts of the same motion at the same time. Nor are there two parts of time at the same time, but one succeeds the other; for it is impossible that there be many instances of time at the same time. [3] The third difference is that permanent things are naturally prior to successive things and successive things are naturally posterior to permanent things; for permanent things are the cause of successive things. [4] The fourth difference is that permanent things that are limited have their limits in themselves, whereas successive things do not have their limits in themselves, *e.g.* motion has its limit in the permanent things [it belongs to], as change in the quality [involved in the alteration], and growth and diminution in a quantity, and so on. [5] The fifth difference is that permanent things exist at their beginning and at their end, as is evident in substance and permanent accidents, *e.g.* in a stone, in whiteness and in blackness, whereas successive things do not exist at their beginning nor at their end, as will become evident later in the section on motion.

What the meaning of these verbs are in combination with things

4   *Ad [2]:* As to the second item, there is an argument to the contrary as follows. Motion is defined by its limits, albeit rather by the limit *towards which* than by the limit *from which*, because almost all types of motion are defined by the limit *towards which* (for 'whitening' is a motion towards whiteness, 'blackening' is a motion

---

1   Cf. above, cap. 1.

nigredinem, augmentum vero motus est ad maiorem quantitatem, generatio vero est motus[4] ad substantiam); et sic omnis[5] motus diffinitur[6] per terminum finalem, preter corruptionem, que[7] diffinitur per terminum a quo (quia corruptio est mutatio a substantia); igitur omnis motus habet rationem a suis terminis, quamvis magis a termino ad quem quam a termino a quo, — igitur cum 'incipit' et 'desinit' dicant motum, vel modum motus, respectu termini a quo vel respectu termini ad quem, tunc oportet quod si termini sunt specie differentes, quod et rationes horum verborum 'incipit'[8] et 'desinit' sint specie differentes, si talibus terminis adiungantur. Sed successiva et permanentia sunt specie differentia. Ergo hoc verbum desinit si adiungatur permanentibus et successivis, habebit secundum[9] hoc rationes specie differentes. [*N64ra*] Et similiter hoc verbum 'incipit'.

5 Quod concedimus dicentes quod ratio huius verbi 'incipit' cum permanentibus est ista, scilicet *est et ante hoc non fuit*, ut 'incipit esse albus': *est albus et ante hoc non fuit albus*. Unde hoc modo hoc verbum [*T38ra*] 'incipit' dicit positionem[2] presentis cum privatione preteriti. [*P72va*] Vel etiam sic: 'incipit': *nunc primo est*. Cum rebus autem successivis exponitur sic: *nunc primo est*[3]; vel sic: *non est sed post hoc erit*[4] (ut 'incipit moveri': *non*[5] *movetur sed post hoc movebitur*); tunc privat presens et ponit futurum. Sed hoc verbum 'desinit' cum permanentibus exponitur sic: *nunc*[6] *ultimo est* vel sic: *est et de cetero non erit* (ut 'desinit esse albus': *nunc ultiọmo est albus* vel sic: *est albus et de cetero non erit albus*); et sic ponit presens et privat futurum. Cum rebus autem successivis exponitur sic: *nunc ultimo fuit* vel sic: *non est sed ante hoc fuit* (ut[7] 'desinit currere': *non currit sed ante hoc cucurrit*) et sic privat[8] presens et ponit preteritum[9].

6 Item. Queritur, cum diversa tempora intelligantur per ista verba 'incipit' et 'desinit', utrum intelligantur ibi[1] equaliter vel unum per prius et alterum per posterius. Et dicendum quod ista verba 'incipit' et 'desinit' dicunt inceptiones vel desitiones[2] rerum. Sed inceptiones et desitiones non sunt nisi in terminis initialibus et finalibus. Sed ultra terminum[3] finalem nichil est de re neque ante terminum initialem aliquid est de re, eoquod tota res infra suos

towards blackness, growth is a motion towards greater quantity, and generation is a motion towards substance). Thus all motion is defined by its limit *towards which*, except corruption, which is defined by the limit *from which* (because corruption is a change starting from a substance). Thus every motion derives its definition from its limit, albeit rather from the limit *towards which* than from the limit *from which*. Hence in virtue of the fact that 'begins' and 'ceases' indicate motion, or a mode of motion, with respect to the limit *from which* or with respect to the limit *towards which*, it is necessary that if these limits are specifically different, that the meanings of the verbs 'begins' and 'ceases' be specifically different if they are connected with such limits. Now successive things and permanent things are specifically different. Therefore if the word 'ceases' is connected with permanent things and with successive things, it will have specifically different meanings accordingly. The same goes for the word 'begins'.

5   We agree with this, saying that the meaning of the word 'begins' in combination with permanent things is *it is and before this it was not*, e.g. 'It begins to be white' means *it is white and before this it was not white*. Hence in this way the verb 'begins' indicates the assertion of the present with the elemination of the past, or we can even put it like this: 'it begins' is *it is now for the first time*. In combination with successive things, on the other hand, it is analysed as *it is now for the first time* or *it is not but after this it will be* (e.g. 'It begins to move' means *it is not moving but after this it will move*). In that case eliminates the present and asserts the future. Now in combination with permanent things the verb 'ceases' is analysed as *it is now for the last time* or *it is and it will no longer be* (e.g. 'It ceases to be white' is *it is now white for the last time* or *it is white and it no longer will be white*), and in this way it is asserts the present and eliminates the future. In combination with successive things, on the other hand, it is analysed as *it has been now for the last time* or *it is not but before this it has been* (e.g. 'It ceases to run' means *it is not running but before this it has been running*), and this way it eliminates the present and asserts the past.

6   Furthermore, since diverse times are understood by the verbs 'begins' and 'ceases', there is a problem whether in this case they are understood equally or whether one is understood primarily and the other secondarily. The answer should be that the verbs 'begins' and 'ceases' indicate beginnings and endings of things. Well, beginnings and endings are only found in the initial and final limits of things. Now beyond the final limit there is nothing left of that thing nor is there anything of that thing before the initial limit,

terminos continetur. Ideo est quod cum hoc verbum 'desinit' dicat terminum finalem rei,[4] per prius dat intelligere presens et consequenter[5] privationem futuri, eoquod ultra terminum finalem nichil est de[6] re (et loquor in permanentibus). Unde hoc modo ista expositio *nunc ultimo est* rectior est quam ista *est et de cetero non erit*. Cum successivis autem hec est rectior *nunc ultimo fuit* quam sic: *non*[7] *est sed ante hoc fuit*[8]. Unde per[9] prius ponitur[10] ibi preteritum [*N64rb*] terminatum[11] ad presens et consequenter[12] privatio presentis. Sed per hoc verbum 'incipit' adiunctum permanentibus per[13] prius datur[14] intelligi presens et consequenter privatio preteriti, quia res permanentes sunt in sui principio et ante ipsum[15] nichil est de hiis. Unde hoc modo rectius exponitur sic[16]: *nunc primo est* quam sic: *est et ante hoc non fuit*. Sed cum[17] successivis per[18] prius intelligitur positio futuri terminati[19] ad presens et per posterius [*P72vb*] privatio presentis propter hoc quod res successive non sunt in sui principio sed post principium.

De 'tempore' dupliciter sumpto

7   Et nota quod hoc verbum 'incipit' non semper[1] est diversorum temporum, quia 'tempus' dicitur dupliciter. Uno enim modo tempus est mensura primi[2] motus ut motus primi mobilis; et est species quantitatis continue et sic est tempus secundum veritatem temporis. Et tempus[3] isto modo non accidit verbo. Et sic dantur intelligi diversa tempora per illa verba 'incipit' et 'desinit'. Sed non a parte consignificationis eorum sed a parte terminorum[4] suorum significationum principalium[5]; qui quidem[6] termini sunt causa[7] eorum quorum est desitio vel inceptio. Alio autem modo tempus dicitur non mensura primi motus neque tempus secundum veritatem temporis, sed dicitur modus temporis. Et hoc modo tempus accidit verbo. Et[8] sic 'incipit' et 'desinit' sunt[9] presentis temporis. Et sic intelliguntur [*T38rb*] in eis diversa tempora a parte significationis principalis et intelligitur in eis unum solum tempus a parte consignificationis[10]. Et predicta distinctio temporis est similis distinctioni generis, quod similiter dicitur dupliciter. Uno enim modo genus dicitur secundum

because the whole thing is confined within its own limits. Therefore it happens that in virtue of the fact that the verb 'ceases' indicates the final limit of something, it primarily gives to understand the present and consequently an elimination of the future, because beyond the final limit there is nothing left of that thing (and I am speaking of permanent things). Hence in this way the analysis *it is now for the last time* is more correct than *it is and it will no longer be.* On the other hand, in combination with successive things the analysis *it has been now for the last time* is more correct than *it is not but before this it has been.* Hence what is primarily asserted in this case is the past ending at the present and consequently an elimination of the present. However, adjoined to permanent things the verb 'begins' primarily gives to understand the present and consequently an elimination of the past, for permanent things exist at their beginning and before that there is nothing of these things. Hence in this way the analysis *it is now for the first time* is more correct than *it is and before this it has not been.* However, when added to successive things it primarily gives to understand an assertion of the future ending at the present and secondarily an elimination of the present, for the reason that successive things do not exist at their beginning but after their beginning.

On 'time' taken in two ways

7   Note that the verb 'begins' is not always of diverse times, because 'time' is said in two ways. [1] In one way time is the measure of the first motion, taken as the motion of the first moveable, and it is a species of continuous quantity and thus it is time in the sense of its true nature. In this way time is not an accident of the verb, and thus diverse times are understood by the verbs 'begins' and 'ceases'. However, <this diversity> is not on account of the consignification of these verbs, but on account of the principle significative meanings of the terms they are adjoined to; indeed, these terms are the cause of that which comes to an end or has a beginning. [2] In another way time does not indicate the measure of the first motion nor does it indicate time in the sense of its true nature, but rather it indicates the mode of time. In this way time is an accident of the verb, and thus 'begins' and 'ceases' are of the present time. In this way diverse times are understood in them on account of their principle signification, but only one time on account of their consignification. The distinction between the different types of time just mentioned is similar to the distinction between different types of gender, which is likewise said in two ways. [1] In one way 'gender' indicates

veritatem generis; et hoc modo non sunt nisi duo genera reperta in natura rerum, scilicet masculinum et femininum et[11] hoc[12] modo genus tantum est in animalibus ut in maribus[13] et feminis. Alio autem modo genus dicitur modus generis; et sic repperitur genus in rebus[14] insensibilibus[15]; et sic dicitur 'lapis' masculini generis et 'petra' feminini. Unde sicut genus dicitur uno modo veritas[16] generis et alio modo modus generis, similiter tempus dicitur uno modo veritas temporis[17] [*N64va*] (et sic non accidit verbo) et alio modo dicitur modus temporis (et sic accidit verbo).

Utrum motus incipiat et desinat

8   Circa tertium obicitur[1] quia: Vult Aristotiles quod si aliquis[2] movetur, movebitur et movebatur. Sed[3] si movebitur — simus in illo futuro —, tunc verum est dicere quoniam movetur. Ergo iterum: movebitur et movebatur. Illud iterum futurum accipiatur et verum erit in illo dicere quoniam movetur. Ergo iterum: movebitur et[4] in alio futuro. Et sic contingit moveri in infinitum. Ergo motus non potest desinere. Eodem autem[5] modo probatur quod non potest incipere, quia: Si [*P73ra*] movetur[6], movebitur et movebatur. Sed[7] si movebatur — simus in illo preterito—, et[8] verum erit dicere in illo preterito quoniam[9] movetur. Ergo movebatur prius in alio preterito. Et si iterum illud preteritum accipiatur, verum erit in illo dicere quoniam movetur. Ergo movebatur in alio priori preterito[10]. Et sic contingit abire in infinitum a parte ante sicut a parte post, sive a parte preteriti sicut a parte futuri. Sed impossibile est abire in infinitum, quia infinita non possunt pertransiri. Ergo impossibile est quod motus incipiat. Et sic motus non potest incipere neque[11] desinere. Et sicut obicitur de motu, similiter potest[12] obici de cursu quod non possit[13] incipere neque desinere, quia si currit[14], cucurrit et curret;

gender in the sense of its true nature, and in this way there are only two types of gender found in nature, *viz.* the male and the female, and this type of gender is only found in animals, *viz.* males and females. [2] In another way 'gender' indicates a mode of gender, and in that way one finds it in inanimate things; thus '*lapis*' (stone) is called masculine and '*potra*' (rock) is called feminine. Hence just as in one way 'gender' indicates gender in the sense of its true nature and in the other way it indicates a mode of gender, likewise 'time' in one way indicates time in the sense of its true nature (in in this way it is not an accident of the verb) and in the other way it indicates a mode of time (and in the latter way it is an accident of the verb).

Whether motion begins and ceases

8   *Ad [3]:* As to the third item, there is an argument to the contrary. Aristotle says[2] that if someone is moving, he will be moving and was moving. Now if he will be moving (let us find ourselves in that instant in the future), in that instant it is true to say 'He is moving'. Therefore, once again, he will be moving and was moving. Let us once again take this instant in the future, it will also be true to say in that instant 'He is moving'. Therefore, once again, he will be moving at some other instant in the future as well. Thus it happens that he moves *ad infinitum.* Therefore motion cannot cease. In the same way one proves that motion cannot begin. If someone is moving, he will be moving and was moving. Now if he was moving (let us find ourselves in that instant in the past), it will be true in that instant in the past as well to say 'He is moving'. Therefore he was moving earlier at some other past instant. And if once again we take that instant in the past, it will be true in that instant to say 'He is moving'. Therefore he was moving at some earlier instant in the past. Thus one can go on *ad infinitum* backwards and forwards, or in the past and in the future. Now it is impossible to go on *ad infinitum*, because infinite things cannot be transgressed. Therefore it is impossible that motion begins. And so motion can neither begin nor cease. And in the same way as one argues against motion, one can likewise argue against running that it can neither begin nor cease, because if someone is running, he was running and will run; and so we will have the same argument as

---

[2]   Cf. *Physica* IV 11, 219b16-8.

et[15] inde ut prius. Eodem autem modo potest obici de quolibet alio[16] successivo quod non possit incipere neque desinere.

9   Et dicendum quod motui rerum inferiorum et[1] cuilibet successivo debetur[2] principium et finis, ut patet in motu alterativo[3], qui est ab uno termino[4] in alterum (ut[5] ab una qualitate[6] contraria[7] in alteram vel[8] in mediam; et augmentum[9] ab una quantitate[10] ad[11] alteram et motus secundum locum[12] ab uno loco in alterum[13]). Et sic omnes motus inferiores incipiunt et desinunt.

Quod 'infinitum' dicatur tripliciter

10   Ad illud[1] autem quod obicit[2] de infinitatione[3] motus dicendum quod 'infinitum' proprie dicitur tripliciter. Scilicet divisione, ut linea dicitur infinita [N64vb] divisione et quodlibet continuum; omne enim continuum est divisibile in[4] infinitum. Alio autem modo dicitur infinitum appositione, ut numerus; omnis enim numerus augmentabilis est[5] in infinitum. Tertio autem modo dicitur[6] infinitum utroque modo, ut motus[7] et tempus. Utrumque enim[8] est infinitum divisione, cum sit continuum, et est[9] infinitum appositione, [T38va] cum post unum tempus[10] sit aliud[11] tempus et post unum motum sit alius motus in infinitum. Et sic est infinitas utroque modo, scilicet appositione et divisione. Dicendum ergo breviter quod infinitum isto triplici modo est[12] tantum[13] in potentia et non in actu. Et ideo bene[14] potest pertransiri[15], eoquod[16] infinitum in potentia bene potest pertransiri, infinitum autem in actu non potest. Unde quia obiectiones volebant reducere potentiam infiniti[17] ad actum dividendo motum, ideo sequebatur infinitas. Quod autem[18] niteatur[19] reducere [IP73rb] infinitum divisione ad[20] actum patet, quia cum dicit[21] 'si[22] movetur, movebitur et movebatur', iam dividit motum per partes suas. Et cum[23] iterum sumit[24] preteritum vel futurum dicens quod si movetur[25] in illo, ergo movebitur et movebatur, patet quod adhuc dividit partes motus. Et sic potentiam[26] divisionis infinite nititur reducere[27] in actum divisionis. Unde licet motus[28] sit infinitus reducendo aptitudinem[29] infinite divisionis in[30] actum, non[31] propter hoc sequitur

before. In the same way one can argue against any other successive thing whatsoever that it can neither begin nor cease.

9 The answer should be that the motion of sublunary things as well as any successive thing must have a beginning and an end, as is evident in the case of motion found in change, which occurs from one limit to another (*e.g.* from one contrary quality to the other contrary or to the mediary quality, the increase from one quantity to another and the motion from one place to another). Thus all sublunary motions begin and cease.

That 'infinite' is said in three ways

10 As to the argument to the contrary[3] concerning the infinitation of motion, the answer should be that 'infinite' properly speaking is said in three ways. These ways are [1] by division, *e.g.* a line is called infinite by division and so is any other continuum, for every continuum is divisible *ad infinitum*. [2] In another way 'infinite' is said by apposition, *e.g.* a number, for any number can increase *ad infinitum*. [3] In the third way 'infinite' is said in both ways, *e.g.* motion and time. For both are infinite by division, because they are a continuum, and both are infinite by apposition, because after one time comes another and after one motion comes another *ad infinitum*. In this way we have infinity in both ways, namely by apposition and by division. Briefly one should say, therefore, that something that is infinite in this threefold way only exists potentially but not actually. Therefore it can well be transgressed, because something potentially infinite can well be transgressed, whereas something actually infinite cannot. Hence it is on account of the fact that by dividing motion, the arguments to the contrary intended to reduce the potency of infinity to an act, that therefore infinity followed. Now that the opponent attempts to reduce something infinite by division to an act is evident, because when he says 'If he is moving, he will be moving and was moving', he is already dividing the motion into its parts, and when once again he takes the past or the future, saying that if he is moving at that time, therefore he will be moving and was moving, it is evident that he is still dividing the parts of the motion. Thus he attempts to reduce the potency of an infinite division to an actual division. Hence although motion is infinite by reducing the aptitude of an infinite division to its actual being, it does not therefore follow that motion is infinite *simpliciter*,

---

[3] Cf. above, cap. 8.

quod motus sit infinitus simpliciter, sed est ibi[32] fallacia secundum *quid et simpliciter.*

11   Si queratur ubi debeat[1] resistere obiectionibus dicendum quod ultime illationi debet resistere, quia bene probat quod contingit[2] abire in infinitum a parte ante et a parte post, dividendo motum a parte principii sive a parte finis. Sed ex hoc non sequitur 'ergo[3] motus non potest incipere neque[4] desinere', quia[5] motus secundum se finitus est, divisione autem infinitus. Unde omnis motus inferior incipit et desinit.

12   Item. Obicitur quod motus primi mobilis sive celi est infinitus, quia una revolutio[1] naturaliter est post aliam, sicut unus homo [*N65ra*] ex[2] alio homine generatur. Ergo non fuit prima[3] revolutio celi, quia si fuisset prima, tunc[4] illa non fuisset post aliam. Ergo motus celi non incepit. Ergo fuit ab eterno. Ergo et[5] celum ab eterno. Ergo[6] plura ab[7] eterno, quod est impius[8] error. Similiter autem[9] videtur[10] motus primus[11] a parte post[12] infinitus, quia post unam revolutionem[13] celi naturaliter sequitur altera. Ergo non est sumere ultimam revolutionem[14] celi. Ergo motus celi est infinitus a parte post[15]. Item. Similiter[16] obicitur quod generatio hominum sit infinita a parte ante et a parte post, et plantarum et aliorum generabilium et corruptibilium, quia hoc est principium in natura: homo ex homine generatur et equus ex equo, leo ex leone, planta ex planta. Ergo non est sumere primum[17] hominem, quia si sumas[18] aliquem, ille erit[19] ex alio secundum viam nature et ille alius ex alio priori. Et sic in infinitum in hominibus et ceteris animalibus et in plantis.

13   Et dicendum quod motus primus[1] et generatio omnium inferiorum, ut animalium et plantarum, possunt sumi dupliciter, quia uno modo secundum viam nature et secundum principia[2] nature et alio modo secundum [*P73va*] comparationem ad principium[3] quod est supra naturam ut ad[4] Causam Primam. Et secundum primum modum non est repperire primam revolutionem celi neque ultimam,

but rather in this argument one commits the fallacy of reasoning from something taken in a certain sense to the same thing taken *simpliciter*.

11   If one were to ask at what stage one must reject the arguments to the contrary,[4] the answer should be that one must do so at the last inference, because he correctly proves that one can go on *ad infinitum* backwards and forwards by dividing motion at its beginning or at its end. However, from this it does not follow 'Therefore motion cannot begin or cease', because motion in itself is finite whereas by division it is infinite. Hence all sublunary motion begins and ceases.

12   Again, there is an argument to the contrary that the motion of the first moveable or of heaven is infinite, because one revolution naturally comes after another, just as one man is begotten by another man. Therefore there has not been a first revolution of heaven, because if there had, in that case it would not have come after another one. Therefore the motion of heaven did not have a beginning. Therefore it has been from eternity. Therefore heaven also has been from eternity. Therefore there will have been more than one thing[5] from eternity, and this is an impious error. Likewise it may be argued that the first motion will never end, because after one revolution of heaven another naturally follows. Therefore one cannot assume a final revolution of heaven. Therefore the motion of heaven will never end. Furthermore, a similar argument to the contrary is that the generation of men never had a beginning nor will ever end, and the same goes for plants and other things that can be generated and perish. The reason for this is that nature has the following principle: a man is begotten by a man, a horse by a horse, a lion by a lion, and a plant by a plant. Therefore one cannot assume a first man, because if one were to do so, this man would owe his existence to another man, according to the course of nature, and this other one would owe his existence to another earlier one, and so on *ad infinitum* in the case of men, other animals and plants.

13   The answer should be that the first motion and the generation of all sublunary things, such as animals and plants, can be taken in two ways. [1] In one way they can be taken according to the course of nature and according to the principles of nature, and [2] in another way according to the relationship they have to the principle which surpasses nature, *viz.* the First Cause. According to the first way one cannot find a first revolution of heaven nor a final one, nor

---

4   Cf. above, *ibid.*.

5   *i.e.* not only God.

neque primum hominem vel[5] primum animal [*T38vb*] vel primam plantam, quia natura non potuit facere primum hominem neque primum leonem neque primam plantam neque primam revolutionem. Sed modo secundo fuit repperire[6] primum hominem et primam generationem in omnibus generabilibus[7], quia principium[8] quod est supra naturam ut[9] Causa Prima, ex sua summa potentia potuit facere quidlibet ex nichilo, quod natura non potuit.

14   Item. Eodem modo obicitur quod motus non sit[1] in sui[2] principio neque in sui fine, sicut obiciebatur quod non poterat[3] incipere neque desinere, quia si aliquis in principio motus movetur, ergo movebatur [*N65rb*] prius. Non ergo erat in principio. Et si aliquis movetur in fine, ergo movebitur[4] post; non ergo erit in fine. Ergo motus non erat[5] in sui[6] principio neque[7] erit in suo fine. Quod concedimus.

Quid sit motus

15   Habito quod omnis motus incipiat et desinat et etiam qualiter incipiat et desinat, quia motus inferiores[1] nature incipiunt et desinunt per principia[2] nature, motus autem superior[3], et etiam tota generatio continua inferiorum, incipit et desinit per[4] principium[5] supra naturam, — sciendum quod motus diffinitur sic: motus est existentis in potentia perfectio secundum quod[6] huiusmodi. Quod patet sic quia: Mobile et solum[7] mobile est in potentia passiva ad motum. Sed omnis potentia perficitur per suum actum, ut potentia ad calefaciendum per calefieri[8] et potentia ad dealbandum per albationem[9] et sic de aliis. Ergo cum 'mobile' dicat potentiam ad motum, ideo mobilis[10] inquantum est mobile perfectio est motus. Et ideo perficitur mobile inquantum est mobile cum movetur, ut visibile inquantum est visibile cum videtur, et augmentabile inquantum[11] est augmentabile cum augmentatur, et alterabile inquantum[12] est alterabile cum alteratur. Ergo simpliciter mobile inquantum est

can one find a first man, a first animal or a first plant, because nature has not been able to produce a first man, a first lion, a first plant or a first revolution. In the second way, however, one can find a first man and a first generation in all things that can be generated, for the principle that surpasses nature, *viz.* the First Cause, has been able to produce from its highest power anything whatsoever out of nothing, something that nature was not able to do.

14   Furthermore, in the same way there is an argument to the contrary that motion does not exist at its beginning nor at its end, just as it was argued to the contrary that motion could begin nor cease, for if someone is moving at the beginning of the motion, therefore he was moving earlier. Therefore it [*i.e.* the motion] did not exist at its initial stage. Again, if someone will be moving at the end <of the motion>, therefore he will be moving later on; therefore it [*i.e.* the motion] will not exist at its final stage. Therefore motion did not exist at its initial stage nor will it exist at its final stage. We agree with this.

What motion is

15   Now that we have said that all motion begins and ceases and also in what way it begins and ceases, for sublunary motions begin and cease according to the principles of nature, whereas superior motion, and also the total continuous generation of sublunary things, begins and ceases according to the principle that surpasses nature,—note that motion is defined[6] thus: motion is the fulfilment of what exists potentially insofar as it exists potentially. This is evident as follows: something moveable and only something moveable is in a passive potency with respect to motion. Now every potency is fulfilled by its act, *e.g.* the potency to become warm is fulfilled by becoming warm and the potency to be white is fulfilled by whiteness, and so on. Therefore since 'moveable' indicates a potency to motion, therefore the fulfillment of something moveable insofar as it is moveable is motion. That is why something moveable insofar as it is mobveable is fulfilled when it moves, just as something visible insofar as it is visible is fulfilled when it is seen and something increasible insofar as it is increasible when it increases and something changeable insofar as it is changeable when it changes. Therefore something that is *simpliciter* moveable insofar as it is moveable is fulfilled when it moves. Now something moveable

---
6   Aristotle, *Physica* III 1, 201a10-1.

mobile perficitur cum movetur. Sed mobile inquantum est mobile existit in potentia, ut dictum est. Ergo motus est existentis in potentia perfectio secundum quod huiusmodi, quia est perfectio mobilis quod[13] existit in potentia inquantum est mobile.

Utrum tempus incipiat vel desinat

16 Circa quartum obicitur quia[1]: Ut vult Aristotiles in quarto[2] *Phisicorum*, sicut punctus continuat duas partes linee [*P73vb*] et est indivisibile[3] in linea, similiter *nunc* est indivisibile[4] in tempore et continuat duas partes temporis, ut tempus prius tempori posteriori. Et ideo dicit[5] quod *nunc* est semper finis temporis precedentis[6] et principium subsequentis[7]. Ergo impossibile est repperire primum[8] *nunc* in tempore, quia quodcumque[9] *nunc* accipiatur[10], semper erit finis unius temporis et principium alterius. Ergo ante illud *nunc* erit[11] accipere aliud tempus prius et ante illud[12] tempus erit accipere aliud *nunc*[13] quod erat[14] principium[15] illius[16] et finis iterum [*N65va*] alterius temporis precedentis. Ergo non est[17] sumere primum tempus. Ergo tempus non incepit[18]. Ergo tempus est ab eterno.

17 Et dicendum sicut dictum est[1] de motu circulari et de motu generativo[2] quod 'tempus' potest sumi secundum[3] duas comparationes, scilicet secundum comparationem ad naturam et secundum comparationem ad Causam Primam. Si autem sumatur[4] secundum[5] comparationem ad naturam, sic[6] tempus[7] non potuit incipere[8], quia natura non potuit facere primum tempus. Unde tempus secundum viam nature procedit in[9] infinitum a[10] parte ante et[11] a parte post. Si autem sumatur 'tempus' per[12] comparationem ad [*T39ra*] Causam Primam, sic[13] incepit[14] tempus, quia incepit[15] cum motu et cum mobili primo. Quid autem sit tempus et cuius sit mensura (quia[16] est mensura primi motus sive motus primi mobilis) et in quo sit ut in subiecto (quia[17] in motu circulari primo[18]), dictum est in tractatu huius dictionis[19] 'si'.

insofar as it is moveable exists potentially, as has been said. Therefore motion is the fulfilment of what exists potentially insofar as it exists potentially, because it is a fulfilment of something moveable which exists potentially insofar as it is moveable.

Whether time begins or ceases

16   *Ad [4]:* As to the fourth item, there is an argument to the contrary that, as Aristotle says in Book IV of the *Physics*,[7] just as a point is a continuation of two parts of a line and is indivisible in the line, likewise the *now* is indivisible in time and is the continuation of two parts of time, namely of an earlier time and a later time. That is why he says[8] that the *now* is always the end of a preceding time and the beginning of a subsequent time. Therefore it is impossible to find a first *now* in time, because whatever *now* one takes, it will always be the end of one time and the beginning of another. Therefore before this *now* one will have to accept another earlier time and before that time one will have to accept another *now* which was the beginning of the former and the end of yet some other preceding time. Therefore one cannot assume a first time. Therefore time did not begin. Therefore time exists from eternity.

17   The answer should be like what has been said[9] about circular motion and the motion of generation that time can be considered according to two relationships, *viz.* according to its relationship to nature and according to its relationship to the First Cause. Now if one considers it according to its relationship to nature, in that way time could not have had begun, because nature could not have produced a first time. Hence according to the course of nature time proceeds *ad infinitum* both backwards and forwards. If, on the other hand, one considers time according to its relationship it has to the First Cause, in this way time did begin, because it began together with motion and the first moveable. As to the question what time is and what it measures (for it measures the first motion or the motion of the first moveable), and what it inheres in as in its subject (for it is found in the first circular motion), this has been discussed in the chapter on the word 'if'.

---

[7]   *Physica* IV 11, 220a9-11.
[8]   *Physica* IV 13, 222a33-b1.
[9]   Cf. above, cap. 13.

Utrum potentia incipiat vel desinat

18   Circa quintum queritur utrum potentia incepit[1] vel non. Et
videtur quod non incepit, quia: Si potentia incepit, possibile incepit.
Sed si possibile incepit, ergo non erat[2] possibile antequam inciperet[3],
sicut non erant[4] res antequam[5] inciperent[6]. Ergo ex[7] non-possibili
factum est possibile. Sed[8] 'non-possibile' et[9] 'impossibile' equipollent[10]. Ergo ex impossibili factum est possibile. Quod videtur inconveniens. Ergo possibile non incepit. Ergo neque potentia ipsius possibilis incepit. Sed contra sic[11] obicitur quia: Si possibile non incepit,
ergo fuit ab eterno. Et sic sequitur heresis dicentium[12] quod non
solum Deus fuit ab eterno, sed etiam[13] materia prima fuit ab eterno
cum[14] Deo, quod est error non solum in fide sed etiam in scientia
naturali, quia ponitur esse materia sine forma[15] et separata a
sensibus[16]. Ergo necesse est possibile incepisse. Ergo et[17] potentiam[18]
ipsius.

Quot modis dicatur 'potentia'

19   Et dicendum quod duplex est potentia. Quia est quedam
potentia[1] rerum creatarum[2], que dividitur per potentiam activam
creatam[3] et per[4] potentiam passivam[5]. Et illa incepit esse et utraque
pars eius. Alia autem est potentia que[6] est potentia increata[7], et hec est
potentia Cause Prime sive primi agentis. Et ista[8] non incepit esse sed
est ab eterno. Et sic potentia passiva[9] incepit et possibile incepit et
etiam[10] potentia activa rerum creatarum[11] incepit.
20   Ad illud autem quod obicit [*N65vb*] quod si possibile incepit,
ergo ex[1] non-possibili factum est possibile; ergo[2] ex impossibili
factum est possibile, cum 'non-possibile' et 'impossibile' equipolleant[3], — dicendum quod hoc non est inconveniens uno modo et
alio modo sic, quia inconveniens est quod[4] aliquod[5] agens naturale
ex impossibli faciat possibile in natura. Sed de agente quod est supra
naturam ut Causa Prima, non est inconveniens quod ex impossibli

Whether a potency begins or ceases

18 *Ad [5]:* As to the fifth item, there is a problem whether a potency has begun or not. And it may be argued that it did not begin, because if it did, the possible has had a beginning. Now if the possible has had a beginning, then there was no possible before it began, just as there were no things before they began. Therefore out of the non-possible the possible has been produced. Now 'non-possible' and 'impossible' are equivalent. Therefore out of the impossible the possible has been produced. And this is clearly absurd. Therefore the possible has had no beginning. Therefore the potency of the possible has had no beginning either. However, there is the following counter-argument. If the possible has had no beginning, therefore it has been from eternity. In this way the heresy follows of the people who say that not only God has existed from eternity, but also prime matter has existed with God from eternity. Now this is an error not only against faith but also against natural science, because it implies that there is matter without form and separated from the senses. Therefore it is necessary that the possible has had a beginning, and hence its potency has had a beginning as well.

In how many ways one says 'potency'

19 The answer should be that a potency is twofold. [1] One is the potency found in created things, which is divided into active created potency and passive potency. This type of potency has begun to be, and this applies to both subtypes. [2] The other is increated potency, and this is the potency of the First Cause or the first agent. This potency has not begun to be but exists from eternity. Thus passive potency as well as the possible and also active potency found in created things had a beginning.

20 As to the argument to the contrary[10] that if the possible has had a beginning, therefore out of the non-possible the possible has been produced; therefore out of the impossible the possible has been produced, because 'non-possible' and 'impossible' are equivalent,— the answer should be that this is not absurd in one way but is in another way: it is absurd that some natural agent should produce something possible in nature out of the impossible. However, as regards the agent that surpasses nature as the First Cause, it is not absurd that it produces something possible in nature out of the

---

[10] Cf. above, cap. 18.

faciat[6] possibile in natura, quia natura non potuit[7] facere aliquid ex
nichilo, sed Causa Prima potuit[8]. Et ita[9] ex impossibili in[10] natura
potuit[11] facere possibile Causa Prima.

21   Item. Nota, sicut dictum est, quod quedam est potentia increata[1],
et hec est activa semper[2] a se et a[3] nullo alio. Et hec[4] est Cause Prime,
ut diximus, que[5] nullo modo mota[6], neque per se neque per accidens[7], movet[8] omnia creata. Alia autem est potentia creata[9] que incepit esse, ut diximus, cum rebus creatis[10]. Huius[11] autem potentie[12]
alia est activa[13], que mota movet (et hec est cuiuslibet agentis naturalis); alia autem dicitur potentia passiva; et hec potentia passiva est
materie prime et eorum que consequuntur[14] materiam primam.

22   Item. 'Potentia passiva' sumitur[1] tripliciter. Quia[2] est quedam
potentia passiva[3] que est semper[4] finibilis[5] et potest habere totum
actum suum simul. Ut potentia que est in[6] materia aeris ad hoc ut ex
aere fiat ignis, simpliciter[7] est[8] perfecta quando ignis generatus est
in eadem materia; et potentia que est in ligno ut ex eo fiat archa,
simpliciter[9] est[10] perfecta quando[11] facta est archa. Alia autem est
potentia passiva que est perfectibilis semper[12] secundum partem et
numquam secundum[13] totum. Ut potentia dividendi in infinitum;
ut[14] in continuis particulares[15] divisiones perficiunt partem[16] illius
potentie, quia quoad [*T39rb*] hoc quod[17] iam divisum[18] est continuum in aliquam vel[19] in aliquas partes, secundum hoc[20] finita est
illa[21] potentia. Sed quia impossibile est omnes divisiones continui
simul esse, ideo impossibile est illam potentiam[22] perfici secundum
totum. Tertia autem potentia passiva est que[23] non potest finiri[24]
neque secundum partem neque secundum [*N66ra*] totum. Et hec est
in ceco et in animali mortuo, quia in oculo manet materia in qua
fuit visus et in homine mortuo manet materia in qua fuit vita. Ergo
cum[25] materia non [*P74rb*] possit esse sine potentia, necesse est quod
ibi remaneat potentia, sed aliter quam prius, quia prius[26] potentia[27]
poterat finiri[28], modo autem non potest, eoquod a privatione non est
regredi in[29] habitum per naturam. Et hec potentia passiva dicitur
infinita.

impossible, for nature cannot have produced something out of nothing, but the First Cause has been able to do so. Therefore the First Cause has been able to produce something possible in nature out of the impossible.

21   Furthermore, note that, as has been said, there is one increated potency and this potency is active by itself and not owing to anything else. It is the potency of the First Cause, as we have said, which, while it is not moved in any way itself, neither *per se* nor *per accidens*, moves all created things. The other potency, however, is a created one which began to be, as we have said, together with created things. Of this potency one is active which, when being moved itself, moves <other things> (and this is the potency found in every natural agent), whereas the other one is called a passive potency; and the latter passive potency is found in prime matter and in those things that follow from prime matter.

22   Again, passive potency is considered in three ways. [1] One type of passive potency is one that can always come to an end and that can have its whole actuality simultaneously. For example, the potency found in the matter of air in order that out of air a fire starts, is *simpliciter* fulfilled when fire is generated in that same matter, and also the potency found in wood in order that from this wood a chest is produced, is *simpliciter* fulfilled when the chest has been produced. [2] Another type of passive potency is one that can always be fulfilled in part but never completely. Such is the potency to divide <something> *ad infinitum*; for example, in the case of continuums the particular divisions make part of this potency fulfilled, because insofar as a continuum is already divided into a part or parts, to that extent this potency has come to an end. Now because it is impossible that all divisions of an indivisible whole exist at the same time, therefore it is impossible that this potency be completely fulfilled. [3] The third type of passive potency is one that cannot come to an end, neither completely nor in part. This type is the potency found in a blind and in a dead animal, because in the eye remains the matter that had contained sight, and in a dead man remains the matter that had contained life. Therefore it is because matter cannot be without a potency, it is necessary that the potency remain in it, but in another way than before, because earlier the potency could come to an end, whereas now it cannot, since in the course of nature there is no return from a privation to the quality <involved>. This type of passive potency is called endless.

Sophismata

23   Item. Posito quod Sortes sit albissimus hominum qui modo sunt
et post hoc instans nascatur quidam[1] albior eo, queritur de hoc
sophismate SORTES DESINIT ESSE ALBISSIMUS HOMINUM.
Probatio[2]. Sortes est albissimus hominum. Et de cetero non erit albissimus hominum. Ergo Sortes desinit[3] esse albissimus hominum.
Contra. Sortes desinit esse albissimus hominum. Ergo hominum qui
sunt vel[4] hominum qui non sunt. Quorum utrumque est falsum.

24   Et dicendum quod prima est vera. Et[1] probatio bene tenet, sed
improbatio non valet[2]. Et dicunt quidam quod ibi[3] est figura[4] dictionis a simplici suppositione[5] ad personalem. Et[6] dicunt quod iste[7]
genitivus 'hominum'[8] tenetur simpliciter in prima, sed cum infert
'ergo hominum qui sunt vel hominum qui non sunt', personalem
habet suppositionem. Alii dicunt quod est ibi figura dictionis ab
ampliata suppositione ad restrictam, quia iste genitivus 'hominum'
in prima tenetur pro quolibet alio homine[9] a Sorte, sed cum dicitur
'ergo[10] hominum qui sunt vel hominum[11] qui non sunt', iste genitivus 'hominum' restringitur[12] ad existentes ex una parte et ad non-
existentes ex alia[13] per implicationes circa ipsum factas. Vel dicendum quod improbatio peccat secundum accidens, quia desitio significatur respectu hominum simpliciter, non tamen respectu hominum qui sunt vel respectu[14] hominum qui non sunt, quia non est
necesse quod si aliquid accidat[15] antecedenti[16], quod propter hoc
accidat consequenti.

25   Item. Posito quod Sortes sciat[1] tria enuntiabilia necessario[2] (et
nominentur *a, b,* et *c*[3]) et *d*[4] sit quartum enuntiabile quod scit[5] modo
Sortes et de cetero non sciat[6] ipsum, [*N66rb*] queritur de hoc sophismate SORTES DESINIT SCIRE QUICQUID IPSE SCIT. Probatio.
Sortes scit quicquid ipse scit. Et de cetero non sciet quicquid ipse scit.
Ergo desinit scire quicquid ipse scit. Contra. Sortes desinit scire
quicquid ipse scit. Sed scit *a*. Ergo desinit scire *a*[7].

26   Solutio. Prima[1] falsa. Et probatio non valet, quia minor est
duplex, eoquod negatio potest precedere distributionem[2]. [*P74va*] Et
sic est vera hec 'de cetero non quicquid ipse scit sciet'. Et sic facit

Sophismata

23   Supposing that Socrates is the whitest of the men who exist now and that after this instant another one whiter than he is born, there is a problem concerning the sophisma-sentence SOCRATES CEASES TO BE THE WHITEST OF MEN. Proof: Socrates is the whitest of men, and afterwards he will not be the whitest of men. Therefore Socrates ceases to be the whitest of men. There is an argument to the contrary. Socrates ceases to be the whitest of men. Therefore he ceases to be the whitest of men who exist or of men who do not exist. Both of these are false.

24   The answer should be that the original sentence is true and that the proof is valid whereas the disproof is not. And some say that we have here a figure of speech from simple to personal supposition. They say that the genitive 'of men' (*hominum*) has simple supposition in the original sentence, whereas if one infers 'Therefore of men who exist or of men who do not exist', it has personal supposition. Others say that we have here a figure of speech from ampliated to restricted supposition, because the genitive 'of men' in the original sentence applies to any man other than Socrates, whereas in the expression 'Therefore of men who exist or of men who do not exist', the genitive 'of men' is restricted to existing ones in one part and non-existing ones in the other on account of the relative clauses that are added to it. Or the answer could be that the the disproof commits the fallacy of accident, because the ceasing is signified with respect to men *simpliciter*, but not with respect to men who exist or with respect to men who do not exist, because it is not necessary that if something is an accident of the antecedent, that it therefore be an accident of the consequent.

25   Furthermore, supposing that Socrates knows only three stateables necessarily (and let them be called *a*, *b* and *c*) and that *d* is a fourth stateable which Socrates now knows and afterwards will not know, there is a problem concerning the sophisma-sentence SOCRATES CEASES TO KNOW ALL THAT HE KNOWS. Proof: Socrates knows all that he knows and afterwards he will not know all that he knows. Therefore he ceases to know all that he knows. There is an argument to the contrary. Socrates ceases to know all that he knows. Now he knows *a*. Therefore he ceases to know *a*.

26   Solution. The original sentence is *simpliciter* false and the proof is not valid. The minor is ambiguous in that the negation can <either> precede the distribution, and in that way the proposition 'and afterwards he will not know all that he <now> knows' is true,

distributionem teneri[3] particulariter. Et sic est vera, sed sic non sequitur conclusio[4]. Vel negatio potest sequi distributionem sic: 'de cetero quicquid scit non sciet'. Et sic est falsa, quia sensus est 'de cetero nichil eorum que scit, sciet', quod falsum est. Et sic sequitur conclusio.

27 Et nota quod 'incipit' et 'desinit' cum adiunguntur[1] multitudini vel nomini[2] pluralis numeri, debent[3] exponi removendo [*T39va*] totam multitudinem vel unumquodque de[4] multitudine, ut 'Sortes scit quicquid ipse scit et[5] de cetero nullum eorum sciet'. Et similiter hic: 'Sortes videt omnem hominem et de cetero nullum videbit[6] hominem; ergo DESINIT VIDERE OMNEM[7] HOMINEM'; posito quod Sortes videat semper omnem hominem alium a Platone et modo videat Platonem et de cetero non videbit[8]. Et probatio et improbatio fiunt[9] omnino similiter sicut in precedenti sophismate.

28 Item. Posito quod Sortes[1] sciat tria enuntiabilia necessario et semper sciat ea (scilicet *a, b, c*) et cum illis[2] sciat hoc enuntiabile, scilicet 'se nichil desinere scire', et post hoc instans non[3] sciat illud, queritur de hoc sophismate SORTES DESINIT SCIRE SE NICHIL DESINERE SCIRE. Probatio. Sortes scit se nichil desinere scire. Et de cetero non sciet se nichil desinere scire. Ergo Sortes[4] desinit scire se nichil desinere scire. Contra. Sortes desinit scire se nichil desinere scire. Ergo[5] Sortes[6] scit se nichil desinere scire. Sed quicquid scitur est verum, quia[7] nichil scitur nisi verum. Ergo Sortem nichil[8] desinere scire est verum. Ergo nichil[9] desinit scire (a dicto [*N67ra*] ad propositionem sive[10] a convertibili). Ergo non desinit scire hoc enuntiabile, scilicet se nichil desinere scire.

29 Solutio. Prima[1] vera. Et probatio bene[2] tenet, sed improbatio peccat secundum *quid et simpliciter* in hoc argumento 'nichil desinit scire; ergo non desinit scire hoc enuntiabile se[3] nichil desinere scire', quia sciendo[4] hoc enuntiabile non propter hoc augmentatur scientia sua, eoquod scire hoc enuntiabile nichil aliud est nisi quod

and thus it causes the distribution to be taken particularly [as opposed to universally] only. In that way the minor is true but then the conclusion does not follow. Or the negation can follow the distribution like this: 'all that he knows he will not know afterwards'. In this way the minor is false, because it means 'nothing of what he knows he will know afterwards', which is false. In this way the conclusion follows.

27 Note that whenever 'begins' and 'ceases' are adjoined to a group of things or a plural noun, they must be analysed by removing the whole group or every single member of the group, *e.g.* 'Socrates knows all that he knows and afterwards he will know none of these things'. The same goes for the proposition 'Socrates sees every man and afterwards he will see no man; therefore HE CEASES TO SEE EVERY MAN', supposing that Socrates always sees every man other than Plato, that he sees Plato now and will not see him afterwards. Both the proof and the disproof are completely the same as in the preceding sophisma-sentence.

28 Furthermore, supposing that Socrates knows three stateables necessarily and that he always knows them (*viz. a, b* and *c*), and that along with them he knows the stateable 'that there is nothing he ceases to know', and that after this instant he does not know the latter, there is a problem concerning the sophisma-sentence SOCRATES CEASES TO KNOW THAT THERE IS NOTHING HE CEASES TO KNOW. Proof: Socrates knows that there is nothing he ceases to know, and afterwards he will not know that there is nothing he ceases to know. Therefore Socrates ceases to know that there is nothing he ceases to know. There is an argument to the contrary. Socrates ceases to know that there is nothing he ceases to know. Therefore Socrates knows that there is nothing he ceases to know. Now whatever one knows is true, because one only knows what is true. Therefore that there is nothing Socrates ceases to know is true. Therefore there is nothing he ceases to know (from the *dictum* to the proposition or from a convertible). Therefore he does not cease to know the stateable that there is nothing he ceases to know.

29 Solution. The original sentence is true and the proof holds good, whereas the disproof commits the fallacy of reasoning from something taken in a certain sense to something taken *simpliciter* In the argument 'There is nothing he ceases to know; therefore he does not cease to know the stateable that that there is nothing he ceases to know', for by knowing this stateable his knowledge is not therefore increased, because to know this stateable is nothing other

ipse [*P74vb*] sciat se[5] scire illa tria enuntiabilia. Et de cetero non sciet
se scire ea, sicut accidit quando[6] dormit. Unde[7] sicut homo non
plura scit in habitu cum vigilat quam cum dormit, similiter non
plura scit sciendo hoc enuntiabile quam non sciendo ipsum. Cuius
causa est[8] quia hoc enuntiabile[9] ponit reflectionem[10] actus sciendi
supra seipsum, ut[11] sciat illa tria et sciat se scire ea. Et ita[12] sciet[13]
quod nullius[14] eorum obliviscatur. Et propter hoc scit se nichil
desinere scire. Sed sive scientia reflectatur sive non reflectatur, non
propter hoc augmentatur[15] neque[16] diminuitur, sed modus est alius.
Sicut cum videt coloratum et videt se videre coloratum, non propter
hoc plura videt quam si videret[17] coloratum tantum ita quod non ad-
vertat[18] se videre. Unde sicut hic est *quid et simpliciter*. 'nichil videt;
ergo non videt tenebram', eoquod[19] licet tenebra sit aliquid, tamen
nichil est in videndo, similiter in proposito, ut[20] 'nichil desinit scire;
ergo non desinit scire hoc enuntiabile, scilicet se nichil desinere
scire'.

30 Item. Posito quod Sortes[1] sit in penultimo[2] instanti vite sue,
queritur de hoc sophismate SORTES DESINIT ESSE NON DESI-
NENDO ESSE. Probatio[3]. Sortes est non desinendo esse. Et[4] de cetero
non erit non desinendo esse. Ergo Sortes[5] desinit esse non desinendo esse. Contra. Sortes desinit esse non desinendo esse. Ergo Sortes[6]
desinit esse dum desinit esse, vel si[7] non desinit esse, vel quia[8] non
[*T39vb*] desinit esse: gerundium[9] enim in '-do' resolvitur[10] per
'dum' vel per 'si' vel per 'quia'. Quorum unumquodque est impossibile.

31 Solutio. Prima duplex[1], eoquod hec determinatio 'non desinendo esse' potest determinare hoc verbum 'desinit' vel hoc verbum
'esse' quod immediate sequitur. Si vero determinet hoc verbum
'desinit', sic falsa est et opposita ponuntur circa idem. Unde sensus
est 'desinit quia[2] non desinit vel[3] dum non desinit vel si non desinit'; et secundum hoc improbat. Si autem determinet hoc verbum
'esse', sic est vera et est sensus 'Sortes desinit esse non desinendo
esse' idest 'Sortes desinit esse [*P75ra*] indesinens'[4] vel 'esse sine

than that he knows that he knows these three stateables. Afterwards he will not know that he knows these stateables, as it happens when he is asleep. Hence just as a man does not know more things in the state when he is awake than when he is asleep, likewise he does not know more when he knows the stateable in question than when he does not know it. The reason for this is that this stateable merely imposes a reflexive act of knowing on itself, so that he knows these three stateables and he knows that he knows them. Hence he will know that he will not forget any of them. And that is why he knows that there is nothing he ceases to know. Now whether this knowledge is or is not reflected on, it is not therefore increased or diminished, but the mode is different, just as when one sees something coloured and sees that he sees something coloured, one does not therefore see more than if one would see something coloured only, so that one pays no attention to his act of seeing. Hence just as we have a fallacy of reasoning from something taken in a certain sense to the same thing taken *simpliciter* in 'He sees nothing; therefore he does not see the darkness', because although darkness is something, nevertheless it is nothing in relation to seeing, the same happens in the case at issue, *viz.* 'There is nothing he ceases to know; therefore he does not cease to know the stateable that there is nothing he ceases to know'.

30 Again, supposing that Socrates is at the penultimate instant of his life, there is a problem concerning the sophisma-sentence SOCRATES CEASES TO BE NOT CEASING TO BE. Proof: Socrates *is*, not ceasing to be and afterwards he will not be not ceasing to be. Therefore Socrates ceases to be not ceasing to be. There is an argument to the contrary. Socrates ceases to be not ceasing to be. Therefore Socrates ceases to be *while* he does not cease to be, or *if* he does not cease to be or *because* he does not cease to be, for the gerund in ' ing' is resolved into 'while', 'if' or 'because'. Each one of these is impossible.

31 Solution. The original sentence is ambiguous in that the determining expression 'not ceasing to be' can determine the verb 'ceases' or the verb 'to be' which follows directly. Now if it modifies the verb 'ceases', in that case the proposition is false and opposites are asserted as concerning one and the same thing. Thus the meaning is 'he ceases, because he does not cease or while he does not cease or if he does not cease', and the disproof runs along these lines. If, on the other hand, it determines the verb 'to be', in that case it is true and it means 'Socrates ceases to be not ceasing to be', that is, *Socrates ceases to be unceasing or to be without cessation*. Hence he does not

desitione'. Unde non desinit esse simpliciter sed esse tale, scilicet esse indesinens vel sine desitione, quia usque modo habuit esse indesinens vel esse sine desitione et de cetero non habebit tale esse, immo habebit esse desinens et cum desitione. Et primo modo est composita et falsa, secundo vero divisa et vera. Unde est ibi sophisma compositionis[5].

Quam suppositionem habeant termini cum 'incipit' et 'desinit'

32 Circa ultimum queritur utrum termini habeant eandem suppositionem cum hiis verbis 'incipit' et 'desinit' et cum aliis verbis vel diversam. Et videtur quod eandem[1], quia bene sequitur 'Sortes est homo; et de cetero non erit homo qui est; ergo desinit esse homo'. Sed posito quod nullus sit color nisi albedo et corrupta albedine statim erit nigredo et non erit[2] nisi in Sorte, tunc non sequitur 'Sortes est coloratus; et de cetero non erit coloratus colore qui est; ergo desinit esse coloratus'. Non ergo similem habent suppositionem termini substantiales et termini accidentales cum istis verbis 'incipit' et 'desinit'. Item. Bene sequitur 'Sortes incipit esse homo; ergo incipit esse animal'; sed non sequitur 'incipit esse albus; ergo incipit esse coloratus'. Quod concedimus dicentes[3] quod[4] aliam habent suppositionem termini substantiales et aliam termini accidentales cum hiis verbis[5]. Cuius causa est quod forme accidentales sunt transmutabiles circa idem[6], forme vero essentiales non, quia in accidentibus potest fieri transmutatio ab una in aliam, in essentialibus vero non.

33 Item. Bene sequitur 'est albus; ergo est coloratus'. Sed non sequitur 'incipit esse albus; ergo incipit esse coloratus'. Ergo termini non habent [*N67ra*] eandem suppositionem cum hiis verbis 'incipit' et 'desinit' et[1] cum aliis verbis. Quod concedimus. Cuius causa est quod in accidentibus manente genere species transmutatur circa idem, ut Sorte[2] manente, vel[3] corpore solo, color transmutari[4] potest ab albedine in nigredinem[5] vel in aliam speciem coloris. Sed in substantialibus impossibile est.

cease to be *simpliciter*, but to be in that particular way, *viz.* to be unceasing or without cessation, for until now he has had unceasing being or being without cessation, and afterwards he will not have that particular being, rather he will have ceasing being and being with cessation. In the first way the sentence is compounded and false, whereas in the second way it is divided and true. Thus we have here a fallacy of composition.

What supposition terms have in combination with 'begins' and 'ceases'

32 *Ad [6]:* As to the sixth item, there is a problem whether terms have the same supposition in combination with the verbs 'begins' and 'ceases' as they have in combination with other verbs, or <whether they have> a different supposition. It may be argued that <they have> the same, because the inference 'Socrates is a man and afterwards will not be a man who is; therefore he ceases to be a man' is sound. Now supposing that there is no other colour than whiteness and that as soon as whiteness has been destroyed there will be blackness and that it will only inhere in Socrates, then it does not follow 'Socrates is coloured and afterwards he will not be coloured by a colour that exists; therefore he ceases to be coloured'. Therefore substantial terms and accidental terms do not have the same supposition in combination with the verbs 'begins' and 'ceases'. Furthermore, it follows 'Socrates begins to be a man; therefore he begins to be an animal', but it does not follow 'He begins to be white; therefore he begins to be coloured'. We agree with this saying that substantial terms have another supposition than accidental terms in combination with the verbs 'begins' and 'ceases'. The reason for this is that accidental forms can change in the same thing whereas substantial forms cannot, because in accidental forms a change can take place from one form to another, whereas in essential forms there cannot.

33 Again, it follows 'It is white; therefore it is coloured', but it does not follow 'It begins to be white; therefore it begins to be coloured'. Therefore terms do not have the same supposition in combination with the verbs 'begins' and 'ceases' as they have in combination with other verbs. We agree with this. The reason for this is that in the case of accidents while the genus remains, a species can change in the same thing; for example, while Socrates remains, or only his body, his colour can change from whiteness to blackness or to some other species of colour. In the case of substantial forms, however, this is impossible.

34   Item. Ex predictis patet quod cum dicitur 'Sortes incipit esse coloratus', iste terminus 'coloratus' non solum copulat[1] pro colore qui est sed etiam pro colore qui fuit. Et cum dicitur 'Sortes desinit esse coloratus', non solum [*P75rb*] copulat pro colore qui est sed etiam pro colore qui erit. Et hoc est ex natura horum verborum 'incipit' et 'desinit', que[2] non solum ponunt albedinem in presenti[3], sed etiam unum eorum [*T40ra*] privat albedinem in preterito et alterum[4] in futuro in[5] predictis orationibus et consimilibus. Sed contra. Forma minus communis restringit ad pauciora quam forma magis communis, ut 'album' ad pauciora quam 'coloratum'. Sed 'desinit' est minus commune quam 'est', quia[6] sequitur 'desinit; ergo est' et non econverso. Ergo[7] 'desinit' restringit ad pauciora quam hoc verbum 'est'. Sed hoc verbum 'est' restringit ad ea que sunt. Ergo hoc verbum 'desinit' restringit ad pauciora. Ergo non faciet[8] terminum copulare pro colore qui est et qui non est.

35   Et dicendum quod termini accidentales significantes[1] res permanentes[2] cum adiunguntur istis verbis 'incipit' et 'desinit' dicunt[3] positionem[4] rei in presenti et ideo copulant pro presentibus. Sed quia ista verba dicunt inceptiones vel[5] desitiones rerum[6], ideo dicunt terminum initialem vel finalem. Et ante terminum initialem nichil est de[7] re; et similiter post terminum finalem nichil[8] est de[9] re. Ideo[10] consequitur[11] ad hoc verbum 'desinit' privatio[12] rei permanentis[13] in futuro ratione termini finalis. Et ad hoc verbum 'incipit' consequitur privatio rei permanentis in preterito ratione termini initialis[14]. Dicendum ergo breviter quod hec verba per suam significationem[15] faciunt predictos [*N67rb*] terminos copulare pro presentibus. Et copulatio pro preteritis vel futuris consequitur ad hec verba ratione terminorum quos dicunt.

36   Ex predictis autem patet quod[1] si quis querat propter quid alia verba non amplient terminos[2] sicut ista, causa eius[3] est quod ista verba dicunt terminos rerum, ut dictum est, alia autem verba non. Et hec est eadem causa quare ista verba ponuntur sincategoreumata et alia[4] non. Ad argumentum <in contrarium> autem dicendum quod

34   From what has been said it is evident that in the expression 'Socrates begins to be coloured', the term 'coloured' must not only have copulation[11] for a colour that is, but also for a colour that has been. Also in the expression 'Socrates ceases to be coloured', the term 'coloured' must not only have copulation for for a colour that is, but also for a colour that will be. This occurs on account of the nature of the verbs 'begins' and 'ceases', which not only assert whiteness in the present, but also one of them eliminates whiteness in the past and the other whiteness in the future in the expressions just mentioned and similar ones. However, there is an argument to the contrary. A form less common restricts to fewer things than a form more common, *e.g.* 'white' restricts to fewer things than 'coloured'. Now 'ceases' is less common than 'is', because it follows 'It ceases; therefore it is' and not the other way round. Therefore 'ceases' restricts to fewer things than the verb 'is'. Now the verb 'is' restricts to the things that are. Therefore the verb 'ceases' restricts to fewer things. Therefore it will not make a term have copulation for a colour that is and a colour that is not.

35   The answer should be that when accidental terms that signify permanent things are adjoined to the verbs 'begins' and 'ceases', they indicate an assertion of something in the present and therefore they have copulation for present things. Now these verbs indicate beginnings and endings of things, and this is why they indicate an initial or final limit. Now before the initial limit there is nothing of the thing and likewise after the final limit there is nothing of the thing. Therefore from the verb 'ceases' follows an elimination of a permanent thing in the future owing to the final limit, and from the verb 'begins' follows an elimination of a permanent thing in the past owing to the initial limit. Briefly then one should say that owing to their signification these verbs make the terms mentioned above have copulation for present things, and the copulation for past or future things follows from these verbs owing to the limits they indicate.

36   From what has been said it is evident that if one raises the problem why other verbs do not ampliate terms in the same way as the verbs in question, the reason is that these verbs indicate limits of things, as has been said, whereas other verbs do not. And for the same reason these verbs are asserted <to be> syncategorematic terms and other verbs are not. As to the argument to the contrary,[12] the

---

[11] 'Copulation' is the logical property adjectival nouns have in virtue of their being 'coupled' to nouns (either predicatively or attributively).

[12] Cf. above, cap. 34.

'forma minus communis' est[5] duplex. Quia uno modo fit minus commune per differentiam advenientem magis communi, ut 'album' per 'disgregativum visus' adveniens 'colorato'. [*P75va*] Alio autem modo forma minus communis fit[6] per privationem advenientem rei. Et ita fiunt[7] ista verba 'incipit' et 'desinit'. Et primo modo forma minus communis restringit ad pauciora, secundo autem modo non. Unde hoc adiectivum 'albus' restringit ad pauciora quam hoc adiectivum 'coloratus' et hec[8] verba 'incipit' et 'desinit' non[9] restringunt ad pauciora quam hoc verbum 'est'.

answer should be that 'a form less common' is ambiguous: in one way something is less common on account of a difference that comes to the more common, e.g. 'white' is less common on account of the difference 'that which makes sight discern'[13] that comes to 'coloured'; in another way a form less common occurs on account of a privation that comes to something, and this is the way in which the verbs 'begins' and 'ceases' occur. In the first way a form less common restricts to fewer things, whereas in the second way it does not. Thus the adjective 'white' restricts to fewer things than the adjective 'coloured', and the verbs 'begins' and 'ceases' do not restrict to fewer things than the verb 'is'.

---

[13]   Cf. Aristotle, *Topica* III 5, 119a30.

DE HIIS DICTIONIBUS 'NECESSARIO' ET 'CONTINGENTER'

Introductio

1   Finito tractatu horum verborum 'incipit' et[1] 'desinit' dicendum[2] est de hiis dictionibus 'necessario', 'contingenter'. Circa[3] quas primo queritur quid sit necessarium et quid contingens; secundo autem quot modis dicantur, sive que sint divisiones[4] eorum; tertio utrum determinent[5] compositionem vel non, et[6] qui modi faciant[7] propositionem[8] modalem; quarto utrum iste dictiones habeant vim ampliandi; quinto autem queritur quomodo propositiones de contingenti et necessario convertantur.

Quid sint necessarium et contingens

2   Circa primum ergo[1] sciendum quod necessarium diffinitur sic 'necessarium est ens non potens aliter se habere'. Et[2] per hoc patet quod male dicunt diffinientes sic: 'necessarium est quod[3] non potest nec potuit nec[4] poterit aliter se habere', quia sic nichil esset necessarium per se nisi Causa Prima, quia[5] omnia alia ceperunt esse et ita exierunt a[6] non esse [*T40rb*] in esse. Sciendum autem quod [*N67va*] 'contingens' simpliciter dicitur equivoce. Et ideo non potest diffiniri, quia nullum equivocum diffinitur.

Quot modis 'necessarium' et 'contingens' dicantur

3   Circa secundum sciendum[1] quod 'necessarium' dicitur duobus modis sicut[2] et 'necessitas'[3]. Quia est quedam necessitas[4] modi[5] et

CHAPTER VII

ON THE WORDS 'NECESSARILY' (*NECESSARIO*) AND 'CONTINGENTLY' (*CONTINGENTER*)

Introduction

1   Now that we have concluded the chapter on the verbs 'begins' and 'ceases', we must discuss the words 'necessarily' and 'contingently'. Concerning these words, there is *[1]* first a problem what is 'necessary' and what is 'contingent', *[2]* secondly in how many ways they are said, or what their divisions are, *[3]* thirdly whether they modify a composition or not and what moods produce a modal proposition, *[4]* fourthly whether these words have ampliative force, and *[5]* fifthly there is a problem in what way propositions *de contingenti* [*i.e.* propositions that contain the mode 'contingent'] and propositions *de necessario* [*i.e.* propositions that contain the mode 'necessarily'] are convertible.

What are necessary and contingent

2   *[Ad [1]:* As to the first item, one should know that 'necessary' is defined as follows: 'Something necessary is a being that cannot be otherwise', and therefore it is evident that they do not speak well defining it thus: 'Something necessary is what cannot be otherwise now, in the future or in the past', because in that case nothing would be necessary in itself except the First Cause, for all other things have begun to be and thus have transgressed from non-being to being. One should know, however, that 'contingent' absolutely speaking is said equivocally. Hence it cannot be defined, for nothing equivocal has a definition.

In how many ways 'necessary' and 'contingent' are said

3   *Ad [2]* As to the second item, one should know that 'necessary' is said in two ways, as is 'necessity': one type is necessity of mode

alia rerum. Necessitas autem modi[6] et[7] non rerum significatur per hanc dictionem 'necessario' et hec[8] ponitur sine necessitate rerum[9]. Unde hec propositio 'Sortes necessario currit' est de necessario sed non necessaria, immo est contingens. Necessitas autem rerum significatur per ipsas [*P75vb*] res, non apposito modo necessitatis. Unde hec propositio est necessaria 'homo est animal', sed non est de necessario, cum sit de inesse et non sit modalis.

4   Item. Necessitas rerum est duobus[1] modis. Quia una est necessitas intentionum communium logicalium[2], ut 'de[3] quocumque predicatur species, et genus', 'de quocumque predicatur diffinitio, et[4] diffinitum', quia[5] genus, species, diffinitio et diffinitum, totum et pars[6] sunt intentiones communes dialetice. Alia autem est necessitas non rerum que sunt intentiones, sed rerum specialium quarum sunt intentiones, que, scilicet res speciales, considerantur in aliqua scientia speciali. Et talis necessitas est hic: 'omnis numerus est par vel impar'; et pertinet specialiter ad arismeticam. Et similiter hic: 'omnis triangulus habet tres angulos equales duobus rectis'; et hec necessitas non pertinet nisi ad geometriam specialiter. Et quot modis dicitur 'necessitas', tot modis et eisdem dicitur 'necessarium'.

5   'Contingens' autem dicitur primo duobus modis. Quia est quoddam contingens quod opponitur necessario; et istud contingens diffinitur sic: 'contingens est quod potest esse et non esse'. Alio autem modo dicitur contingens quod predicatur de necessario et de isto contingenti quod opponitur necessario. Unde est quasi[1] commune ambobus, scilicet necessario et contingenti quod opponitur necessario. Verbi gratia hominem esse animal est necessarium, et hominem crescere[2] vel augeri vel canescere est contingens quod opponitur necessario. Et possum[3] dicere quod hominem esse[4] animal est contingens: contingit enim hoc esse, quia[5] est et hominem canescere[6] est contingens quia potest [*N67vb*] esse. Et sic contingens predicatur de necessario et de[7] contingenti quod necessario opponitur.

6   Item. 'Contingens quod[1] opponitur necessario'[2] dicitur tribus modis. Quia est quoddam contingens quod dicitur contingens ad

and the other is necessity of 'things'.[1] Now the necessity of mode and not the necessity of things is signified by the word 'necessarily' and this is asserted without necessity of things. Hence the proposition 'Socrates necessarily is running' is a proposition *de necessario*, but it is not a necessary one, rather it is a contingent. However, the necessity of things is designated by the things themselves, not by adding a mode of necessity. Thus the proposition 'A man is an animal' is necessary, but it is not *de necessario*, because it is a *de inesse* and not a modal proposition.

4   Furthermore, necessity of things occurs in two ways. [1] One type is the necessity of common logical intentions, *e.g.* 'Of whatever the species is predicated, the genus is predicated as well' and 'Of whatever the definiens is said, the definitum is said as well', because genus and species, definiens and definitum and whole and part are common intentions of logic. [2] The other type is the necessity of things that are not intentions, but of specific things the intentions concern, namely specific things that are considered in a specific science. This type of necessity is found in the proposition 'Every number is even or odd', and it specifically pertains to mathematics. <This type of necessity> is likewise found in the proposition 'Every triangle has three angles equal to two right ones', and this type of necessity pertains specifically to geometry only. Now in as many ways 'necessity' is said, in so many and in the same ways 'necessary' is said.

5   'Contingent' is first said in two ways. [1] One type is a contingent opposite to the necessary, and this type of contingent is defined thus: 'Contingent is what can both be the case and not be the case'. [2] In another way that is called contingent which is predicated of the necessary and of the contingent opposite to the necessary. Hence it is, as it were, common to both, *viz.* the necessary and the contingent opposite to the necessary. For example, that a man is an animal is necessary, and that a man is running, is growing or is turning grey, is a contingent opposite to the necessary. We can also say that that a man is an animal is contingent, for it is contingent that this is the case because it *is* the case, and that a man turns grey is contingent because it *can be* the case. Thus 'contingent' is said of the necessary and of the contingent which is opposite to the necessary.

6   Furthermore, 'the contingent which is opposite to the necessary' is said in three ways. [1.1] One type of contingent is what is

---

[1]   The word '*res*' used by Peter is translated into 'thing', but as we shall see, the term covers intentions (*i.e.* concepts) and states of affairs as well.

utrumlibet. Et illud equaliter se habet ad partem affirmativam et
negativam. Et diffinitur sic: 'contingens ad utrumlibet est quod equaliter potest esse et non esse, sicut accidit in motibus et in operationibus[3] voluntariis[4]. Unde de se tale contingens non determinatum[5] est magis ad esse quam ad non esse, sed per causam suam
quandoque[6] magis determinatur ad unum quam ad alterum. Item.
[*P76ra*] Contingentis oppositi necessario alia pars est que[7] dicitur
contingens natum. Et diffinitur sic: 'contingens natum est quod
magis se habet ad esse quam ad non esse', ut hominem canescere
in senectute. Et istud etiam contingens dicitur contingens ut[8] in
pluribus vel frequenter. Tertia vero pars eius est contingens in
paucioribus[9] vel raro. Et diffinitur sic: 'contingens in paucioribus vel
raro est [*T40va*] quod minus se habet ad esse quam ad non esse'.
Exemplum autem Aristotilis est hoc ut bonum in paucioribus est vel
raro, malum[10] autem in pluribus vel frequenter; et ideo mali homines sunt ut in pluribus, boni vero[11] ut in paucioribus.

7   Sciendum autem quod predicte divisiones[1] necessarii et contingentis sunt divisiones[2] vocis in significationes, non secundum
quod[3] dictio equivoca plura significet equaliter, sed secundum quod
dictio equivoca plura significat secundum prius et posterius, ut 'ens'
aut 'bonum' aut 'medicinale' aut 'sanativum' aut 'expediens'[4].

Utrum hee dictiones determinent compositionem

8   Habito quot modis dicitur 'necessarium' et 'contingens' consequenter obicitur circa tertiam questionem[1] quia: Habitudines rerum
causantur a rebus, ut habitudo generis a genere et speciei[2] a specie et
sic de aliis. Ergo habitudines rerum non habent esse nisi a rebus.
Ergo neque necessitatem[3] habent nisi a rebus. Ergo necessitas per
prius est in rebus quam in habitudinibus rerum. Ergo cum nulla
compositio[4] propositionis sit necessaria nisi propter necessariam

called contingent as regards either of two outcomes. This contingent is equally related to an affirmative and a negative part, and it is defined thus: 'Contingent as regards either of two outcomes (*contingens ad utrumlibet*) is what can both be the case and not be the case', as it happens in motions and in operations of the will. Hence in itself such a contingent is not more determined towards being than towards non-being, but owing to its cause it is sometimes more determined towards the one than towards the other. [1.2] Another type of the contingent opposite to the necessary is what is called a contingent naturally bound to occur (*contingens natum*) and it is defined thus: 'A contingent naturally bound to occur is what is more related to being than to non-being', *e.g.* that a man turns grey in old age. This type of contingent is also called a contingent in most cases or frequently occurring. [1.3] A third type of contingent is a contingent in a few cases or rarely occurring, and it is defined thus: 'The contingent in a few cases or rarely occurring is what is less related to being than to non-being'. Aristotle's example[2] is the following, that the good is in a few cases or occurs rarely, whereas the bad is in most cases or occurs frequently; so bad men are in the majority, whereas good men are in the minority.

7   One should know that the divisions of 'necessary' and 'contingent' mentioned above are divisions of the words into different meanings, but not according as an equivocal word signifies many things equally, but according as an equivocal word signifies many things in the order of prior and posterior, such as 'being', 'good', 'medicinal', 'restorative', or 'expedient'.

Whether these words modify a composition

8   [*Ad [3]*:] Now that we have discussed in how many ways 'necessary' and 'contingent' are used, there is next an argument to the contrary that concerns the third problem. The relationships things have are caused by things, just as the relationship a genus has is caused by the genus and the one the species has is caused by the species and so on. Therefore the relationships things have do not have being except owing to the things. Therefore they [*i.e.* the relationships things have] do not have necessity either except owing to the things. Therefore necessity is found rather in things than in their relationships. Hence it is because a composition found in a proposition is necessary only because of the necessary relationship

---

2   Where?

habitudinem predicati ad subiectum, ergo per prius erit necessitas in re que subicitur et in re que predicatur et per posterius in compositione. [*N68ra*] Ergo hec dictio 'necessario' per prius debet[5] determinare subiectum vel predicatum et per posterius[6] compositionem. Et ita[7] primo et[8] proprie non debet[9] determinare compositionem, sed subiectum et[10] predicatum.

9 Et dicendum quod necessitas est duplex, quia est quedam necessitas substantiarum et alia actuum[1]. Quamvis enim necessitas actus[2] non [*P76rb*] causetur nisi a[3] necessitate substantie, ut necessitas primi motus non causatur nisi a[4] necessitate motoris[5] et mobilis, tamen[6] necessitas ipsius actus sive motus alia est a necessitate substantie. Et sicut est duplex necessitas, ita[7] est duplex signum necessitatis. Quoddam enim signum necessitatis est quod significat necessitatem[8] ut dispositionem[9] substantie, ut hoc[10] nomen 'necessarius, necessaria, necessarium'. Alio autem modo est signum necessitatis quod significat necessitatem ut dispositionem actus, ut hoc adverbium 'necessario'. Et propter hoc istud signum debet[11] determinare compositionem, et[12] non rem subiectam[13] vel predicatam.

10 Ad illud autem quod obicit quod non est necessitas in compositione neque in habitudine predicati ad subiectum nisi per ipsum predicatum et per ipsum subiectum, dicendum quod verum[1] est. Sed tamen alia est necessitas compositionis (quia hec necessitas est inherentie ipsius actus ad substantiam) et alia est necessitas rei que subicitur vel predicatur[2]. Et ideo sicut sunt diverse necessitates, ita sunt diversa signa dicentia[3] dispositiones unius et alterius, ut dictum est. Et sic hec dictio 'necessarium'[4] determinat compositionem; unde[5] facit propositionem modalem.

11 Item. Cum subiectum et predicatum sint principales partes[1] propositionis, ergo qua ratione propositio dicitur modalis a dispositionibus predicati, eadem ratione debet dici modalis a dispositionibus subiecti. Et sic modi facientes propositionem[2] modalem erunt plures quam illi sex quos determinat Aristotiles in *Secundo Perihermeneias* et quos habent pueri in *Modalibus* suis.

between the subject and the predicate, that therefore necessity primarily occurs in the thing that is the subject and the thing that is the predicate and secondarily in the composition. Hence the word 'necessary' must primarily modify the subject or the predicate and secondarily the composition. Thus primarily and properly speaking it must not modify the composition, but rather the subject and predicate.

9   The answer should be that necessity is twofold: [1] one is necessity of substances and [2] the other is necessity of acts. For although the necessity of an act is only caused by the necessity of a substance, as the necessity of the first motion is only caused by the necessity of a mover and something moveable, nevertheless the necessity of that act, *viz.* motion is different from the necessity of a substance. And just as necessity is twofold, so is the sign of necessity. [1] One sign of necessity is that which signifies necessity as a disposition of a substance, *e.g.* the noun 'necessary' (*necessarius, necessaria, necessarium*). [2] In another way a sign of necessity is that which signifies necessity as the disposition of an act, *e.g.* the adverb 'necessarily'. That is why the latter sign of necessity should modify the composition, and not the thing that is made subject or made predicate.

10   As to the argument to the contrary[3] that there is only question of necessity in the composition and in the relationship between the subject and the predicate owing to the subject itself and the predicate itself, the answer should be that this is true. Nevertheless the necessity of a composition is one thing (because this type of necessity belongs to the inherence of the act in a substance) and the necessity of the thing that is made subject or predicate is another. Hence, just as there are diverse types of necessity, in the same way there are diverse signs that indicate dispositions of the one and the other, as has been said. Thus the word 'necessarily' modifies the composition, which is why it produces a modal proposition.

11   Again, it is because the subject and the predicate are the main parts of the proposition, that therefore for the very reason that the proposition is called modal after the dispositions of the predicate, for the same reason it is called modal by the dispositions of the subject. Thus the modes that produce modal propositions will be more than the six Aristotle defines[4] in Book II of the *Perihermeneias* and the ones the juniors have in their treatises *De modalibus*.

---

[3]   Cf. above, cap. 8.
[4]   *De interpr.* 12; cf. Petrus Hispanus, *Tractatus* I, cap. 19, p. 11(25)-12(2), ed. De Rijk.

12 Et dicendum quod sicut subiectum et predicatum sumuntur dupliciter (uno enim modo sumitur subiectum inquantum est subiectum et predicatum [*T40vb*] inquantum est predicatum et alio modo 'subiectum' dicit id quod est subiectum et 'predicatum' id quod est predicatum), similiter est duplex dispositio subiecti et predicati. Quia quedam sunt dispositiones eius quod subicitur et eius [*N68rb*] quod predicatur, alie autem sunt dispositiones que sunt predicati inquantum est predicatum et subiecti inquantum est subiectum. Et dispositiones[1] que[2] sunt subiecti inquantum est subiectum et predicati inquantum est predicatum [*P76va*] denominant[3] propositionem[4], alie autem[5] non. Verbi gratia[6] 'omnis homo albus necessario currit velociter'; ista determinatio 'albus' est eius[7] quod est subiectum, ut hominis secundum se; hec autem determinatio 'velociter' est eius quod est predicatum, ut ipsius cursus secundum se. Et[8] neutra harum denominat[9] propositionem; unde nichil est dictu 'hec propositio est alba' vel 'velox'. Hec autem dispositio 'omnis' est subiecti inquantum est subiectum et denominat[10] propositionem, quia ab hac dispositione propositio dicitur universalis. Hec autem dispositio 'necessario' est predicati inquantum est predicatum. Unde denominat[11] propositionem, cum ab ea dicatur propositio modalis[12].

13 Et nota quod dispositiones subiecti inquantum est subiectum denominant propositionem a parte quantitatis, cum ab eis[1] dicatur universalis vel particularis vel indefinita vel singularis. Dispositiones autem predicati inquantum est predicatum denominant ipsam a parte qualitatis, cum ab illis dicatur propositio affirmativa vel negativa vel modalis vel de inesse. Sicut enim dicitur negativa quia predicatum negatur de subiecto (et hoc est predicatum inquantum est predicatum), similiter dicitur affirmativa quando[2] predicatum affirmatur de subiecto: affirmatio enim[3] ipsius predicati est, sicut et negatio. Et sicut a modo determinante compositionem et per compositionem determinantem predicatum dicitur propositio modalis[4], similiter a sola inherentia predicati in subiecto dicitur propositio de inesse. Item. Sicut bene dicitur[5] 'Sortem currere est contingens' vel 'Sortem currere est necessarium'[6], similiter bene dicitur[7] 'Sortem currere est bonum', 'Sortem currere est malum'. Et sicut iste due

12 The answer should be that just as 'subject' and 'predicate' are taken in two ways (in one way the subject is taken insofar as it is the subject and the predicate insofar as it is the predicate, and in the other 'subject' indicates that which is the subject and 'predicate' that which is the predicate), in the same way the disposition of the subject and the predicate is twofold. Some are dispositions of that which is made subject and that which is made predicate, whereas others are the dispositions that are of the subject insofar as it is the subject or of the predicate insofar as it is the predicate. Well, the dispositions of the subject insofar as it is the subject and of the predicate insofar as it is the predicate denominate the proposition, whereas the others do not. For example, in 'Every white man necessarily runs fast', the modification 'white' belongs to that which is the subject, namely the man in himself, whereas the modification 'fast' belongs to that which is the predicate, namely that which is the running in itself, and neither of these denominate the proposition. Therefore it is nonsense to say 'This proposition is white' or 'fast'. However, the disposition 'every' belongs to the subject insofar as it is the subject and it denominates the proposition, because after this disposition the proposition is called universal. The disposition 'necessarily', on the other hand, is a disposition that belongs to the predicate insofar as it is the predicate. That is why it denominates the proposition, because by that disposition the proposition is called modal.

13 Note that the dispositions of the subject insofar as it is the subject denominate the proposition on the part of its quantity, because after these ones the proposition is called universal, particular, indefinite, or singular. The dispositions of the predicate insofar as it is the predicate, on the other hand, denominate the proposition on the part of its quality, because after these ones the proposition is called affirmative, negative, modal, or *de inesse*. For just as a proposition is called negative because the predicate is denied of the subject (and this is the predicate insofar as it is the predicate), likewise it is called affirmative when the predicate is affirmed of the subject. The affirmation indeed concerns the predicate, as does the negation. Also just as after the mode that modifies the composition and owing to the composition modifying the predicate the proposition is called modal, likewise after the mere inherence of the predicate in the subject the proposition is called *de inesse*. Furthermore, just as it is correct to say 'That Socrates is running is contingent' or 'That Socrates is running is necessary', likewise it is also correct to say 'That Socrates is running is good' or 'That Socrates is running is

premisse sunt modales, similiter[8] et due sequentes. Et[9] sic erunt plures modi modificantes propositionem.

14 Et dicendum quod 'contingens' et 'necessarium' et consimilia, quamvis sint in predicato, disponunt[1] tamen compositionem et[2] dicunt comparationem[3] unius ad alterum. Sed 'bonum' et 'malum' predicantur de eo quod est *Sortem currere* [*N68va*] effective[4] vel causaliter, et non propter hoc quod disponant compositionem. Quando[5] enim Sortes currit, causatur in [*P76vb*] eo sanitas vel egritudo vel commodum vel incommodum aliquod. Et ideo dicitur 'bonum' vel 'malum' de eo quod est *Sortem currere* effective vel[6] causaliter.

Utrum naturam habeant ampliandi

15 Circa quartum queritur utrum iste dictiones 'necessario', 'contingenter' naturam habeant ampliandi quia: Cum dicitur 'homo necessario est animal' vel 'homo potest esse Antichristus', utrobique ampliantur termini non solum ad presentia sed etiam ad futura. Ergo tam 'necessario' quam 'contingenter' habent naturam ampliandi, quia 'contingenter' et 'possibiliter' equipollent. Quod concedimus. Utrumque enim ampliat ad ea que sunt et ad ea que erunt[1].

16 Item. Queritur utrum natura ampliandi sit in eis eadem[1] vel diversa. Et quod eadem sit videtur per hoc quod dictum est quod utrumque ampliat ad futura. Ergo est eadem. Et dicendum quod non est eadem natura [*T41ra*] ampliandi in utroque, quia iste dictiones 'contingens' et 'contingenter' non habent naturam ampliandi nisi propter[2] potentiam que in eis intelligitur, que (scilicet potentia) ordinabilis est ad actum per quem perficitur, ut 'homo potest legere', 'homo potest currere', 'homo potest sedere'[3], quia potentia ad[4] legendum perficitur per[5] ipsum legere et potentia ad[6] currendum per[7] ipsum currere et[8] potentia ad sedendum per[9] ipsum sedere et sic de aliis. Sed iste dictiones 'necessarium', 'necessario'[10], 'necesse' non dicunt potentiam vel possibilitatem[11] sed perpetuitatem ipsius esse, quia perpetuitas ipsius esse se extendit ad omne tempus. Et[12] ideo iste dictiones[13] ampliant non solum ad presentia sed etiam ad futura. Et sic patet quod 'contingens' et 'contingenter' ampliant propter[14] potentiam vel possibilitatem ordinatam ad aliquem actum. Sed iste dictiones 'necessarium', 'necessario', 'necesse' ampliant propter

bad'. Therefore just as the two propositions presented first are modal ones, likewise the two that follow are modal ones as well, and so there will be more modes that modify a proposition.

14 The answer should be that 'contingent' and 'necessary' and the like, although they are in predicate-position, are dispositions of the composition and indicate the relation of the one to the other. However, 'good' and 'bad' are only said of *that Socrates is running* by way of an effect or by way of a cause, and not because they are dispositions of the composition. For when Socrates is running, health or illness or something good or bad is caused in him, and therefore 'good' or 'bad' is said of 'that Socrates is running' by way of an effect or a cause.

Whether they have an ampliative nature

15 *Ad [4]:* As to the fourth item, there is a problem whether the words 'necessarily' and 'contingently' have an ampliative nature. For in the expression 'A man is necessarily an animal' or 'A man can be the Antichrist', in both propositions the terms are not only ampliated to include present cases, but also to include future ones. Therefore both 'necessarily' and 'contingently' have an ampliative nature, because 'contingently' and 'possibly' are equivalent. We agree with this, for each word ampliates <the terms involved> to include things that are and things that will be.

16 Furthermore, there is a problem whether the ampliative nature in these words is the same or different. That it is the same may be argued on account of what has been said that both ampliate to include future cases. Therefore it is the same. The answer should be that the ampliative nature in each one is not the same, because the words 'contingent' and 'contingently' only have an ampliative nature owing to the potency understood in each of them, which (*viz.* the potency) can be ordered towards the act by which it is fulfilled, *e.g.* 'A man can read', 'A man can run' and 'A man can be seated', because the potency to read is fulfilled by reading, the potency to run is fulfilled by running and the potency to sit is fulfilled by sitting and so on. On the other hand, the words 'necessary' (*necessarium, necesse*) and 'necessarily' do not indicate a potency or possibility, but they indicate a perpetuity of being itself, because the perpetuity of being itself extends to all times. Therefore these words do not ampliate to include present cases only but to include future ones as well. Therefore it is evident that 'contingent' and 'contingently' ampliate owing to the potency or possibility ordered towards some act, whereas the words 'necessary' and 'necessarily'

perpetuitatem[15] ipsius esse completi, quia in necessariis non est possibilitas respectu ipsius esse completi et perfecti secundum speciem aut, si est, simul est cum ipso esse. Et ideo dicit [*P77ra*] Aristotiles in tertio *Physicorum* quod in perpetuis[16] non differt [*N68vb*] esse et posse.

Qualiter convertantur propositiones de necessario et contingenti

17 Circa quintum queritur qualiter convertantur propositiones de necessario et contingenti. Et[1] dicendum quod propositiones de necessario convertuntur sicut ille de inesse, quia universalis negativa et particularis affirmativa convertuntur simpliciter in utrisque. Ut 'nullus homo est lapis': 'nullus[2] lapis est homo'; 'quidam homo est animal': 'quoddam animal est homo'; similiter in illis de necessario, ut[3] 'nullus homo necessario est lapis': 'nullus lapis necessario est homo'; 'quidam homo necessario est animal': 'quoddam animal necessario est homo'. Universalis[4] vero affirmativa convertitur secundum partem (idest convertitur in particularem) in utrisque. Particularis vero negativa non convertitur in hiis de necessario, sicut neque in illis[5] de inesse. Hec enim[6] est vera 'quoddam animal non est homo', hec autem falsa 'quidam homo non est animal'; et ideo non convertitur. Et eadem est causa in illis de necessario.
18 Item. Nota quod non omnes propositiones de contingenti similiter convertuntur cum predictis. Omnes enim propositiones affirmative de contingenti, tam universales quam particulares, similiter convertuntur, sed negative non similiter convertuntur. Unde nota quod negative de contingenti quod dicitur de necessario et negative de illo contingenti quod opponitur necessario, similiter[1] convertuntur[2], ut 'nullum hominem contingit esse equum'[3]; 'nullum equum contingit esse hominem'. Iste enim propositiones sunt de contingenti dicto de necessario; inde dicuntur contingere quia sunt necessarie[4]. Item. 'Nullam tunicam contingit esse albam':

ampliate owing to the perpetuity of complete being itself, because in necessary things there is no question of possibility with respect to complete and perfect being with respect to a species, or, if there is, this possibility is simultaneous with that being itself. That is why Aristotle says in Book III of the *Physics*[5] that in perpetual things there is no difference between being possible and existing.

In what way propositions de necessario *and* de contingenti *are convertible*

17   *Ad [5]:* As to the fifth item, there is a problem in what way propositions *de necessario* and *de contingenti* are convertible. The answer should be that propositions *de necessario* like the ones *de inesse* are convertible, for the universal negative and particular affirmative are convertible *simpliciter* in both, *e.g.* 'No man is a stone' and 'No stone is a man', 'Some man is an animal' and 'Some animal is a man'. The same goes for the propositions *de necessario, e.g.* 'Necessarily no man is a stone' and 'Necessarily no stone is a man', 'Necessarily some man is an animal' and 'Necessarily some animal is a man'. On the other hand, a universal affirmative proposition is partly convertible (that is, it is convertible into a particular one) in both groups of propositions. A particular negative proposition, however, is not convertible in the case of propositions *de necessario*, just as it is not convertible in the case of propositions *de inesse*. For 'Some animal is not a man' is true, whereas 'Some man is not an animal' is false, and that is why it is not convertible. And the same goes for propositions *de necessario*.

18   Again, note that not all propositions *de contingenti* are convertible in the same way as the ones above. For all affirmative propositions *de contingenti*, both universal and particular ones, are convertible in the same way, whereas negative ones are not convertible in the same way. Hence note that negative propositions that deal with a contingent said of the necessary and negative propositions that deal with a contingent opposed to the necessary are convertible in the same way, *e.g.* 'It is contingent that no man is a horse', 'It is contingent that no horse is a man'. For these propositions are of a contingent said of something necessary. They are said to be contingent precisely because they are necessary. The same goes for the propositions 'It is contingent that no tunic is white' and 'It is

---

5   *Physica* III 4, 203b30.

'nullum album contingit esse tunicam'. Et iste sunt de contingenti quod opponitur necessario; inde dicuntur contingere in[5] eo quod non ex necessitate insunt[6].

19 Item. Propositiones de contingenti ad utrumlibet et propositiones[1] de contingenti nato[2] sive ut[3] in pluribus convertuntur secundum oppositas qualitates. Sed[4] differenter, quia propositiones de contingenti ad utrumlibet (sive de contingenti[5] infinito, quod idem est) convertuntur equaliter ab affirmatione in negationem et econverso (ut si nullum hominem contingit currere, omnem hominem contingit currere, et econverso), quia cum istud contingens [*N69ra*] equaliter se habeat ad esse et ad non esse, ergo sicut contingit esse, ita contingit non esse. Propositiones vero de contingenti nato sive ut in pluribus convertuntur <secundum[6] quod 'contingit esse' equivalet> ei[7] quod est 'non necesse est esse', ut si contingit hominem [*T41rb*] canescere, non necesse est hominem canescere. Et nota [*P77rb*] quod omnes propositiones de contingenti ad utrumlibet et de contingenti nato sunt affirmative. Quod patet per hoc quod convertuntur secundum oppositas qualitates. Et hec est causa quare non contingit[8] ex eis sillogizare in secunda figura, quia ex affirmativis in secunda figura nichil sequitur[9].

Sophismata

20 Hiis[1] habitis queritur de hoc sophismate OMNIS HOMO NECESSARIO EST ANIMAL. Probatio. Hec[2] est necessaria 'omnis homo est animal'. Ergo modificata modo[3] necessitatis erit vera. Ergo[4] hec est vera 'omnis homo necessario[5] est animal'. Contra[6]. Omnis homo necessario est animal. Sed[7] Sortes est homo. Ergo Sortes necessario est animal (in tertio prime). Sed conclusio est falsa. Ergo aliqua premissarum est falsa. Non[8] minor. Ergo maior. Sed hec est prima[9]. Ergo prima[10] falsa.

21 Solutio. Prima vera simpliciter. Et improbatio peccat secundum accidens, quia sub terminis[1] simpliciter non sunt sumendi termini

contingent that no white thing is a tunic', and these are of a contingent as opposed to something necessary. Hence they are said to be contingent precisely because they do not obtain of necessity.

19 Furthermore, propositions that deal with what is contingent as regards both outcomes and with a contingent naturally bound to occur or in most cases are convertible according to opposite qualities. However, this happens in different ways, because propositions that deal with what is contingent as regards both outcomes (or an infinite contingent, which is the same), are equally convertible from an affirmation into a negation and the other way round (*e.g.* 'If it is contingent that no man is running, it is contingent that every man is running', and the other way round), for since this contingent is equally related to being and non-being, therefore just as it is contingent that it is the case, in the same way it is contingent that it is not. On the other hand, propositions that deal with a contingent naturally bound to occur or in most cases are convertible according as 'is contingent to be' is equivalent to 'is not necessary to be', *e.g.* 'If it is contingent that a man turns grey, it is not necessary that a man turns grey'. Also, note that all propositions that deal with what is contingent as regards both outcomes and the ones that deal with a contingent naturally bound to occur are affirmative. This is evident from the fact that they are convertible according to opposite qualities. That is the reason why it is not possible to form a syllogism from them in the second figure, because from affirmative propositions in the second figure nothing follows.

Sophismata

20 Now that we have discussed these matters there is a problem concerning the sophisma-sentence EVERY MAN NECESSARILY IS AN ANIMAL. Proof: the proposition 'Every man is an animal' is necessary. Therefore when modified by a mode of necessity, it will be true. Therefore the proposition 'Every man necessarily is an animal' is true. There is an argument to the contrary. Every man necessarily is an animal. Now Socrates is a man. Therefore Socrates necessarily is an animal (in the third mood of the first figure). However, the conclusion is false. Therefore one of the premises is false. Now the minor is not false; hence the major is false. Now the major is the original sentence. Therefore the original sentence is false.

21 Solution. The original sentence is true *simpliciter* and the disproof commits the fallacy of accident, because under terms taken

ut nunc. Et dicuntur termini simpliciter qui[2] habent[3] esse[4] a natura; termini autem ut nunc dicuntur[5] qui aliquando sunt, aliquando non[6].

22 Item. Queritur de hoc sophismate ANIMA ANTICHRISTI NECESSARIO ERIT. Probatio. Anima Antichristi erit. Et quando erit, necessario erit. Ergo anima Antichristi necessario erit. Contra. Anima Antichristi necessario erit. Ergo animam Antichristi necessarium est fore. Ergo est[1] in quolibet futuro. Ergo erit hodie et etiam[2] cras, quod falsum est.

23 Et dicendum quod prima est duplex, eoquod hec dictio 'necessario' potest determinare compositionem vel predicatum. Si autem[1] determinet compositionem[2], sic modificat eam et ampliat[3] ad quodlibet futurum. Et sic poneretur[4] anima Antichristi esse hodie et cras et in quolibet alio futuro. Et sic prima[5] falsa. Si autem determinet predicatum[6], tunc est sensus 'anima Antichristi necessario erit': 'erit ens necessario'. Et sic non determinat compositionem nec prima est modalis. [N69rb] Et sic prima[7] vera, quia quelibet anima humana[8] est ens necessario. Ad probationem autem dicendum quod peccat secundum *quid et simpliciter.* Sicut enim non sequitur 'Sortes[9] quando currit necessario currit; ergo Sortes necessario[10] currit' (sed est ibi *quid et simpliciter*), similiter[11] in proposito 'anima Antichristi quando[12] erit necessario[13] erit; ergo anima Antichristi necessario[14] erit'. Unde est ibi[15] *quid et simpliciter,* secundum quod est propositio modalis.

24 Item. Queritur de hoc sophismate SI SORTES NECESSARIO EST MORTALIS, SORTES NECESSARIO[1] EST IMMORTALIS. Probatio. [P77va] Si Sortes necessario est mortalis, Sortes necessario est aliqualis. Et si Sortes necesssario est aliqualis, Sortes necessario est. Et si Sortes necessario est, Sortes necessario[2] est immortalis. Ergo a

simpliciter one may not take terms *as of now* (*ut nunc*). Now those terms are called *simpliciter* that <signify things that> have necessary being and terms as of now are ones that <signify things that> sometimes are and sometimes are not.

22   Furthermore, there is a problem concerning the sophisma-sentence THE SOUL OF THE ANTICHRIST NECESSARILY WILL BE. Proof: the soul of the Antichrist will be, and when it will be, it necessarily will be. Therefore the soul of the Antichrist necessarily will be. There is an argument to the contrary. The soul of the Antichrist necessarily will be. Therefore it is necessary that the soul of the Antichrist will be. Therefore it will be at any future time whatsoever. Therefore it will be today and also tomorrow. And this is false.

23   The answer should be that the original sentence is ambiguous in that the word 'necessarily' can modify the composition or the predicate. Now if it modifies the composition it then modifies it and ampliates it to include any future thing whatsoever. Thus it would be asserted that the soul of the Antichrist be today, tomorrow and at any other future time whatsoever. In this way the original sentence is false. On the other hand, if it modifies the predicate, then 'The soul of the Antichrist necessarily will be', means 'It will be a being necessarily'. In this way it does not modify the composition nor is the original sentence a modal one. Thus the original sentence is true, because any human soul is a being necessarily. As to the proof, the answer should be that it commits the fallacy of reasoning from something taken in a certain sense to the same thing taken *simpliciter*. For just as it does not follow 'When Socrates is running he is necessarily running; therefore Socrates is running necessarily' (but in that case one commits the fallacy of reasoning from something taken in a certain sense to the same thing taken *simpliciter*), the same applies to the case at issue, 'When the soul of the Antichrist will be it will be necessarily; therefore the soul of the Antichrist will be necessarily'. Therefore in that case one commits the fallacy of reasoning from something taken in a certain sense to the same thing taken *simpliciter* according as it is a modal proposition.

24   Furthermore, there is a problem concerning the sophisma-sentence IF SOCRATES NECESSARILY IS MORTAL, SOCRATES NECESSARILY IS IMMORTAL. Proof: if Socrates necessarily is mortal, Socrates necessarily is something of a certain kind, and if Socrates necessarily is something of a certain kind, Socrates necessarily is. Now if Socrates necessarily is, Socrates necessarily is immortal. Therefore, taking it from the beginning, if Socrates

primo: si Sortes necessario est mortalis, Sortes necessario[3] est immortalis. Contra. Ibi[4] assignatur sequi oppositum ad oppositum. Ergo locutio est impossibilis[5].

25 Solutio. Prima conditionalis est duplex, eoquod antecedens eius est duplex (scilicet istud 'Sortes necessario est mortalis'), eoquod[1] hec dictio 'necessario' potest determinare compositionem vel predicatum. Si vero determinet compositionem, sensus est: 'hec propositio est necessaria "Sortes est mortalis"'. Et sic[2] hoc predicatum 'mortale' ponitur semper[3] et[4] de necessitate[5] inherere[6] Sorti vel csse in Sorte. Et[7] similiter[8] Sortes ponitur semper[9] et de necessitate. Et sic ponitur mortalis et immortalis Sortes[10]. Et sic ponuntur[11] opposita in[12] eodem subiecto. Si autem hec dictio 'necessario'[13] determinet hoc predicatum 'mortale'[14], adhuc [*T41va*] est duplex, quia hec differentia[15] 'mortale' duplicem habet comparationem. Unam ad illud cuius est vel in quo ponitur, ut ad Sortem, et aliam ad actum ad quem ordinatur sive respectu cuius dicit aptitudinem, ut ad istum actum qui est mori. Unde hec dictio 'necessario' potest determinare differentiam in comparatione ad substantiam in qua est; et est sensus 'Sortes[16] necessario est mortalis' idest 'mortale de necessitate est in Sorte'. Et sic[17] ponuntur opposita in eodem sicut[18] prius[19], scilicet quod Sortes simul[20] sit mortalis et immortalis.

26 Unde hiis duobus modis predictum[1] antecedens est falsum[2] et impossibile, sed conditionalis est vera. Nec sequitur oppositum ad oppositum, sed sequitur una pars contradictionis[3] ad antecedens quod claudit[4] intra se utrumque. Et licet predicti duo sensus sequantur ad [*N69va*] se invicem conversim, tamen diversi sunt, quia aliud est quod hec dictio 'necessario' determinet compositionem[5] et aliud quod determinet predicatum. Si autem hec[6] dictio 'necessario'[7] determinet[8] hanc differentiam 'mortale' in comparatione ad actum suum, qui est mori, tunc est sensus 'Sortes necessario est mortalis' idest 'Sortes de necessitate morietur'. Et sic propositio que est antecedens, vera est et prima conditionalis est falsa.

27 Ad probationem autem[1] dicendum hoc modo quod peccat secundum *quid et simpliciter* hic[2]: 'si Sortes necessario[3] est mortalis[4], Sortes necessario est aliqualis', quia non sequitur 'Sortes morietur de necessitate; ergo Sortes[5] de necessitate est aliqualis', immo potius

necessarily is mortal, Socrates necessarily is immortal. There is an argument to the contrary. This is said to be a case of an opposite following from an opposite. Therefore the locution is impossible.

25 Solution. The original conditional is ambiguous in that its antecedent is ambiguous (*viz.* 'Socrates necessarily is mortal'), because the word 'necessarily' can modify the composition or the predicate. If it modifies the composition, it means 'The following proposition is necessary: "Socrates is mortal"' and the predicate 'mortal' is asserted to inhere or to be in Socrates always and of necessity. Likewise Socrates is posited always and of necessity. Thus Socrates is posited both mortal and immortal, and so two opposites are posited in the same subject. If, on the other hand, the word 'necessarily' modifies the predicate 'mortal', in that case it is still ambiguous, because the difference 'mortal' has a double relationship. It has [1] a relationship to that to which it belongs or that in which it is asserted, namely to Socrates, and it has [2] another to the act towards which it is ordered or in respect of which it indicates the aptitude, namely the act of dying. Hence the word 'necessarily' can modify the difference in relation to the substance to which it belongs, and the proposition 'Socrates necessarily is mortal' means '*mortal' of necessity inheres in Socrates*. In this way two opposites are posited in one and the same thing just as before, *viz.* that Socrates is mortal and immortal at the same time.

26 Hence in these two ways the antecedent mentioned above is false and impossible, but the conditional is true. Nor is it the case that an opposite follows from an opposite, but one part of the contradiction follows from the antecedent which contains both parts of the contradiction. And although the two meanings follow from each other in both ways, nevertheless they are diverse, for it is one thing that the word 'necessarily' modifies the composition and another that it modifies the predicate. If, however, the word 'necessarily' modifies the difference 'mortal' in relation to its act, *viz.* the act of dying, then the proposition 'Socrates is necessarily mortal' means *Socrates will die of necessity* and thus the proposition which is the antecedent is true and the original conditional is false.

27 As to the proof,[6] one should say that it commits the fallacy of reasoning from something taken in a certain sense to the same thing taken *simpliciter*, in 'If Socrates necessarily is mortal, Socrates necessarily is something of a certain kind', because it does not follow 'Socrates will die of necessity; therefore Socrates is something

---

[6] Cf. above, cap. 24.

sequitur oppositum, quia si[6] Sortes[7] morietur de necessitate, ergo non necessario est aliqualis. Sicut non sequitur hic: 'est homo mortuus; ergo est homo', immo potius [*P77vb*] sequitur oppositum, scilicet 'ergo non est homo'.

28   Item. Posito quod sint tres anime et sint necessario iuste[1] et cras creetur una iniusta[2], queritur de hoc sophismate OMNIS ANIMA NECESSARIO EST IUSTA[3]. Probatio. Hec anima necessario est iusta[4] et illa et tertia. Et non sunt plures, quia illa que erit, nondum est. Ergo omnis anima necessario[5] est iusta. Contra. Hec propositio[6] est[7] falsa, scilicet[8] 'omnis anima est iusta'. Ergo nunc[9] modificata modo necessitatis est falsa.

29   Solutio. Prima duplex[1], eoquod hec dictio 'necessario' potest determinare compositionem vel predicatum. Si vero determinet compositionem, sic ponitur esse falsa, quia tunc ampliat compositionem et mediante compositione subiectum et predicatum ad omne tempus. Et sic pro futuro tempore 'anima' comprehendit sub se animam contingenter iustam. Si autem determinet predicatum, ita[2] ponitur esse vera. Et tunc non est modalis sed est de inesse, quia compositio[3] non determinatur per modum aliquem. Et est sensus 'omnis anima necessario est iusta' idest 'omnis anima est ens iusta necessario', ita quod ista dictio 'necessario' ponatur super hoc quod dico 'ens iusta' et non ponatur super hoc verbum 'est' secundum quod stat in ratione compositionis.

De quibusdam regulis

30   Item. Dari solent tales regule harum dictionum 'necessario', 'contingenter':

> *quotienscumque [N69vb] due determinationes compositionis ponuntur in eadem oratione, duplex est oratio eoquod una potest esse materialis respectu alterius, vel[1] econverso.*

Ut 'Sortes non currit necessario' vel 'Sortes non currit contingenter'. Iste enim propositiones sunt duplices, eoquod negatio potest negare necessitatem vel contingentiam aut econverso necessitas vel contingentia potest cadere super[2] negationem. Item. Alia regula est talis:

of a certain kind of necessity'. Indeed, rather the opposite follows, for if Socrates will die of necessity, therefore he is not necessarily something of a certain kind, just as it does not follow 'He is a dead man; therefore he is a man'; in fact, rather the opposite follows, *viz.* 'therefore he is not a man'.

28   Again, supposing that there are three souls and they are necessarily just, and tomorrow one unjust one will be created, then there is a problem concerning the sophisma-sentence EVERY SOUL NECESSARILY IS JUST. Proof: this soul necessarily is just and that one and the third one, and there are no more, because the one that will be, is not as yet. Therefore every soul necessarily is just. There is an argument to the contrary. The proposition 'Every soul is just' is false. Therefore when modified by the mode of necessity it is false <as well>.

29   Solution. The original sentence is ambiguous in that the word 'necessarily' can modify the composition or the predicate. Now if it modifies the composition, then it [*i.e.* the proposition] is asserted to be false, for in that case it [*i.e.* 'necessarily'] ampliates the composition and by means of that composition it ampliates the subject and predicate to include every time. Thus for a future time 'soul' contains a soul that is contingently just. If, on the other hand, it modifies the predicate, then it [*i.e.* the proposition] is asserted to be true. In that case it is not a modal proposition but a proposition *de inesse*, because the composition is not modified by some mode. And in that case the proposition 'Every soul necessarily is just' means *every soul is a just being necessarily*, so that the word 'necessarily' is asserted to extend to the phrase 'a just being' and not to extend to the verb 'is', according to which it would be an essential part of the composition.

On certain rules

30   One usually presents the following rules that concern the words 'necessarily' and 'contingently':

[1] *Whenever two modifications of the composition are placed in one and the same expression, the expression is ambiguous, because the one can be the matter extended to by the other, or the other way round.*

For example, 'Socrates is not running necessarily' or 'Socrates is not running contingently'. For these propositions are ambiguous in that the negation can deny the necessity or contingency, or, conversely, the necessity or contingency can extend to the negation. Another rule is the following:

> *quotienscumque hec dictio 'necessario' ponitur in consequenti alicuius conditionalis,*
> *duplex est oratio.*

Ut 'si Sortes currit, necessario movetur', [*T41vb*] eoquod potest dicere necessitatem consequendi (et est sensus 'si Sortes currit, necessario sequitur quod moveatur'), vel potest dicere necessitatem propositionis que est consequens[3] (et est sensus 'si Sortes currit, hec propositio "Sortes movetur" est necessaria', quod falsum est). Item. Alia regula est talis:

> *quotienscumque hec dictio 'necessario' ponitur in propositione disiunctiva[4] contra-*
> *riorum[5] vel contradictorie oppositorum, duplex[6] est oratio, eoquod potest esse necessitas*
> *disiunctionis [P78ra] vel partium disiunctarum[7].*

Ut 'omnis numerus necessario[8] est par vel impar' et 'Sortem necessario sedere est[9] verum vel falsum' et 'Sortes necessario currit vel non currit'. Alia regula est talis:

> *quotienscumque hoc verbum 'contingit' adiungitur terminis accidentalibus, duplex est*
> *oratio, eoquod potest dicere contingentiam predicati et non subiecti vel potest dicere*
> *contingentiam utriusque.*

Ut 'omne album contingit currere'. Si dicat contingentiam[10] predicati tantum, talis est sensus 'omne quod est[11] album, contingit currere'. Si[12] autem dicat contingentiam utriusque, talis est sensus 'omne quod[13] contingit esse album, contingit currere'. Et sic reduplicatur modus ad subiectum. Et ideo distinguit Aristotiles in libro *Priorum* istam 'omne b contingit esse a', quia uno modo significat hoc[14] 'omne quod est b, contingit esse a'; alio autem modo est[15] sensus 'omne quod contingit esse b, contingit esse[16] a'.

[2] Whenever the word 'necessarily' is placed in the consequent of some conditional, the expression is ambiguous.

For example, 'If Socrates is running, he necessarily is moving', for it can indicate the necessity of the inference (meaning 'If Socrates is running, it necessarily follows that he is moving'), or it can indicate the necessity of the proposition that is the consequent (meaning 'If Socrates is running, the proposition "Socrates is moving" is necessary', which is false). Furthermore, another rule is the following:

[3] Whenever the word 'necessarily' is placed in a proposition disjunctive of contraries or contradictory opposites, the expression is ambiguous, because there can be necessity of the disjunction or of the disjuncts.

For example, 'Every number necessarily is even or odd', 'That Socrates is necessarily sitting is true or false' and 'Socrates necessarily is running or not running'.

[4] Whenever the expression 'is contingent' is added to accidental terms, the expression is ambiguous, because it can indicate the contingency of the predicate and not of the subject, or it can indicate the contingency of both.

For example, 'Every white thing can run'. If this expression indicates the contingency of the predicate only, it means 'Every thing that is white can run'. If, on the other hand, it indicates the contingency of both, it means 'Every thing that can be white can run'. In the latter way the mode is repeated to apply to the subject as well. That is why in the *Prior Analytics* Aristotle[7] makes a distinction in the proposition 'Every b can be a', because in one way it means 'All that is b, can be a' and in the other way it means 'All that can be b, can be a'.

---

[7] *Anal. Priora* I 13, 32b25-9.

TRACTATUS OCTAVUS

DE CONIUNCTIONIBUS

Introductio

1 Genera coniunctionum sunt plura[1]. Quia quedam sunt dubitative et quedam[2] interrogative secundum Priscianum, ut '-ne', 'an' [*N70ra*] et 'utrum'. Et hoc genus coniunctionum comprehendit Donatus sub disiunctivis. Sed obmissis[3] aliis interrogativis et[4] dubitativis coniunctionibus de hac coniunctione 'an' adpresens intendimus.

A. DE HAC CONIUNCTIONE 'AN'

2 Circa quam primo queritur que sit differentia inter interrogationem factam per nomen[1] et interrogationem factam per adverbium et interrogationem[2] factam per coniunctionem; secundo queritur quid significet hec dictio 'an'; tertia[3] questio est qualiter differat hec coniunctio 'an' ab aliis coniuctionibus interrogativis, ut ab hiis coniunctionibus[4] '-ne' et 'utrum'; quarta[5] questio est, cum habeat in se naturam disiunctionis, inter[6] que[7] habeat disiungere; quinta[8] questio est, cum exerceat tres actus (quia[9] importat disiunctionem et[10] interrogationem et[11] dubitationem), utrum equaliter se habeat ad omnes istos[12] actus vel non.

Que sit differentia inter interrogationes diversimode factas

3 Circa primum obicitur quia[1]: Quicquid est, aut est substantia aut accidens. Sed omnis[2] dubitatio est de re aliqua. Ergo est de substantia vel de accidente. Sed[3] omnis interrogatio est de re dubitata[4]. Ergo omnis interrogatio est de substantia vel de accidente. Sed omnis interrogatio de substantia fit per hec interrogativa 'quis', 'que', 'quod'

CHAPTER VIII

ON CONJUNCTIONS

Introduction

1   There are many kinds of conjunctions. [1] There are dubitative ones, and [2] there are interrogative ones, according to Priscian,[1] *e.g.* '*-ne*', '*an*' ('whether', 'or') and '*utrum*' ('whether'). Donatus arranges[2] this type of conjunction under the disjunctive ones. However, leaving out the other interrogative and dubitative conjunctions, at present we wish to concentrate on the conjunction '*an*'.

A. ON THE CONJUNCTION '*AN*'

2   As to the word '*an*', there is *[1]* first a problem what the difference is between a question expressed by a noun, a question expressed by an adverb and a question expressed by a conjunction, *[2]* secondly what the word '*an*'signifies, *[3]* thirdly there is a problem in what way the word '*an*' differs from other interrogative conjunctions, *e.g.* from '*-ne*' and '*utrum*', *[4]* fourthly there is a problem that because this word has the nature of a disjunction, what the things are it is to disjoin between, *[5]* fifthly there is a problem that because this word carries out three acts (for it brings about a disjunction, a question and a doubt), whether it is equally related to all these acts or not.

What the difference is between questions made in different ways

3   *Ad [1]:* As to the first item, there is an argument to the contrary. Whatever is, is either a substance or an accident. Now every doubt concerns some thing. Therefore it concerns either a substance or an accident. Now every question concerns some doubted thing. Therefore every question concerns a substance or an accident. Now every question that concerns a substance is expressed by the

---

[1]   Cf. *Inst. gramm.* XVI 12, p. 101, (9-10; 16), ed. Hertz.
[2]   Donatus, *Ars minor*, p. 364(37), ed. Keil.

vel 'quid'. Et[5] hec sunt nomina. Sed[6] interrogatio de accidente, cum accidens significetur vel per[7] nomina quedam vel per adverbia, fiet[8] per nomina (ut 'qualis', 'quantus', 'quotus', 'quotennis'[9]) vel per adverbia (ut 'cur', 'quare', 'quando', 'ubi' et consimilia). Ergo omnis[10] interrogatio fit per nomen vel per [*P78rb*] adverbium. Ergo omnis dictio[11] interrogativa est nomen vel adverbium. Ergo nulla coniunctio est dictio interrogativa.

4   Et dicendum quod quandoque contingit [*T42ra*] dubitare de re significata[1] per nomen, sive significetur per modum substantie sive per modum accidentis. Et[2] de huiusmodi re queritur per nomina interrogativa (ut 'quis', 'que', 'quod' vel 'quid', 'qualis', 'quantus'[3], 'quotus', 'quotennis') secundum diversitatem substantie et[4] eorum que accidunt substantie. Quandoque autem dubitatur de actu speciali. Et tunc queritur de ipso per hoc [*N70rb*] interrogativum 'quid'[5] additum actui generali, ut 'quid[6] agit?': 'sedet' vel 'dormit' vel 'disputat' vel[7] 'legit' et sic de aliis. Et sic hiis duobus modis queritur per nomen de re dubitata[8]. Quandoque autem dubitamus de hiis que[9] debentur actui, ut de causa actus, ut cum[10] legit: 'quare legit?' vel[11] de tempore in quo fuit actus, ut 'quando cucurrit[12]?' vel 'quando[13] curret?' vel de loco comparato ad actum secundum quod actus sumitur in loco vel de loco vel ad locum vel per locum, ut 'ubi est?', 'ubi fecit[14] hoc?', 'unde venit?', 'quo vadit?', 'qua transivit?'; et sic[15] de omnibus queritur[16] per adverbia localia. Et sic patet quod de omnibus predictis que debentur actui, queritur per adverbia. Quandoque[17] autem dubitamus de inherentia vel de compositione actus cum substantia. Et[18] tunc queritur de ipsa inherentia vel compositione per coniunctiones interrogativas, ut per has coniunctiones '-ne', 'an' et 'utrum'.

5   Et ideo interrogativa rerum dubitatarum[1] sunt tribus modis. Quia quedam sunt nomina et quedam sunt[2] adverbia, alia vero

interrogatives '*quis*' ('who') '*que*', '*quod*', or '*quid*' ('what'), and these are nouns. On the other hand, it is because an accident is signified by nouns or adverbs, that a question concerning an accident will occur by means of nouns (such as '*qualis*' ('of what kind'?), '*quantus*' ('of what size?)' and '*quotus*' ('of what position in the series?'), '*quotennis*' ('how many years?')) or by adverbs (such as '*cur*' ('why?'), '*quare*' ('for what reason?'), '*quando*' ('when?'), '*ubi*' ('where?'), and the like). Therefore every question occurs by means of a noun or by an adverb. Therefore every interrogative word is a noun or an adverb. Therefore no conjunction is an interrogative word.

4   The answer should be that sometimes it happens to doubt something signified by a noun, whether signified in the manner of a substance or in the manner of an accident. Then one phrases a question regarding something of this type by using interrogative nouns (such as '*quis*', '*que*', '*quod*' or '*quid*', '*qualis*' '*quantus*', '*quotus*', '*quotennis*'), according to the diversity of the substance and the things that are accidents of the substance. Sometimes, on the other hand, there is a doubt concerning a specific act. In that case one phrases a question about it by using the interrogative '*quid*' ('what') added to a general act, *e.g.* 'What is he doing?', <the answer being> 'sitting', 'sleeping', 'arguing' or 'reading', and so on. In these two ways one phrases a question about something doubted by using a noun. Sometimes, however, we are in doubt about things that pertain to an act, *e.g.* the cause of an act, such as when he is reading, saying 'Why is he reading?' or the time at which an act has taken place, as in 'When was he running?' or 'When will he run', or the location in relation to the act according as the act is understood <as taking place> in a location, as concerning a location, towards a location, or through a location, *e.g.* 'Where is he?', 'Where did he do that?', 'Where does he come from?', 'Where is he going?', 'Where did he pass through?'; and in this way one phrases a question about all of these things by using adverbs of location. Thus it is evident that about all the things mentioned, which pertain to an act, one phrases a question by using adverbs. Sometimes, however, we are in doubt about the inherence or about the composition of an act with a substance. In that case one phrases a question about the inherence or composition involved by using interrogative conjunctions, *viz.* the conjunctions '*-ne*', '*an*' and '*utrum*'.[3]

5   Hence the interrogatives concerning things there are doubts about are of three kinds: some are nouns, some are adverbs and

---

3   all meaning 'whether' or just introducing a question.

coniunctiones. Et hec differentia sumpta est a parte ipsorum dubitabilium[3] que sunt obiecta dubitationis. Ad argumentum[4] dicendum
quod omnis dubitatio[5] est de substantia vel de accidente, extendendo
'accidens' ad ipsum accidens et ad adherentiam[6] ipsius[7] accidentis
cum subiecto[8] vel ipsius actus cum substantia. Et tunc interrogatio de
accidente aliquando[9] fit per quedam[10] nomina interrogativa[11] (ut
'qualis', 'quantus' et consimilia), aliquando per adverbia, aliquando
per coniunctiones. Et ita[12] insufficienter dividit[13] interrogationem[14]
accidentis opponendo.

Quid significet hec dictio 'an'

6   Circa secundum[1] queritur quid significet hec dictio 'an'. Et
dicunt quidam quod significat disiunctionem cum electione. Sed
quod hec dictio 'an' non significet electionem probo[2] quia: Hec[3] est
dictio[4] interrogativa et ita importat[5] interrogationem. Sed omnis
interrogatio causatur ex dubitatione. Ergo hec dictio [*N70va*] 'an'
importat dubitationem. Sed dubitatio contraria est electioni, quia[6] qui
dubitat nescit eligere inter[7] ea de quibus dubitat. Ergo hec dictio 'an'
non importat electionem[8]. Item ad idem. Si hec dictio 'an' significet
electionem, aut significat eam ut conceptam[9] vel[10] ut affectum[11]. Sed
non[12] ut conceptam[13] quia: Cum omnis[14] electio sit actus anime[15] et
nullus actus anime possit significari ut conceptus[16] nisi per nomen
vel[17] verbum vel participium, ergo si hec dictio 'an' significet electionem ut[18] conceptam, oportet quod sit nomen vel verbum vel
participium. Quod falsum est. Si autem significet eam per modum
affectus: Sed affectus anime non significatur per modum affectus[19]
nisi per quedam adverbia et per interiectiones et per modos verborum. Ergo si hec dictio 'an' significet electionem per modum affectus[20], oportet quod sit adverbium vel interiectio vel accidat verbo
[*T42rb*] tamquam modus. Quod est impossibile. Ergo impossibile est
quod hec dictio 'an' significet electionem per modum conceptus vel
per[21] modum affectus.

7   Quod concedimus dicentes quod hec dictio 'an' significat
disiunctionem cum dubitatione sub modo interrogandi[1]. Et quia[2]
quicumque[3] interrogat petit certificari inquantum interrogat, ideo[4]

others are conjunctions. The difference between them derives from the doubtful things themselves that are the objects of doubt. As to the argument,[4] the answer should be that every doubt concerns a substance or an accident, by extension of 'accident' to include the accident itself, and the adherence of the accident in a subject or of an act in the substance. In that case one sometimes phrases a question about an accident by using interrogative nouns (*e.g. 'qualis', 'quantus'* and the like) sometimes by using adverbs and sometimes by using conjunctions. So it is evident that in his objection he insufficiently divides the questions concerning an accident.

What the word 'an' signifies

6   *Ad [2]*: As to the second item, there is a problem what the word '*an*' signifies. Some say that it signifies a disjunction in combination with a choice. However, I shall prove that the word '*an*' does not signify a choice as follows. It is an interrogative word and so it conveys a question. Now every question is caused by a doubt. Therefore the word '*an*' conveys a doubt. Now a doubt is contrary to a choice, because the person who doubts does not know how to choose between the things he is in doubt about. Therefore the word '*an*' does not convey a choice. There is an argument that yields the same conclusion. If the word '*an*' signifies a choice, it either signifies that choice as conceived of or as an affect. Now it does not signify a choice as conceived of, for it is because every choice is an act of the soul and an act can only be signified as conceived of by a noun, a verb or a participle, that therefore if the word '*an*' signifies a choice as conceived of, it is necessary that it be a noun, a verb or a participle; and this is false. If, on the other hand, it signifies a choice in the manner of an affect: Now affects of the soul are only signified in the manner of an affect by some adverbs, by interjections and by moods of the verb. Therefore if the word '*an*' signifies a choice in the manner of an affect, it is necessary that it be an adverb, an interjection or that it be an accident of a verb in the form of a mood; and this is impossible. Therefore it is impossible that the word '*an*' signifies a choice in the manner of a concept or an affect.

7   We agree with this saying that the word '*an*' signifies a disjunction in combination with a doubt under the mode of questioning. And it is because whoever asks a question requests to be

---

4   Cf. above, cap. 3.

ad interrogationem sequitur petitio certificationis[5] de re dubitata. Et
ideo quia hec dictio 'an' interrogat disiungendo[6] inter aliqua, propter
hoc[7] per ipsam importatur petitio alterius[8] disiunctorum[9]. Quod
autem hec dictio[10] 'an' significet disiunctionem patet per hoc quod
est[11] coniunctio disiunctiva. Quod[12] autem importet[13] dubitationem
patet per hoc quod est dictio interrogativa et ulterius ad interrogationem sequitur petitio alterius disiunctorum[14], ut dictum est.

Qualiter differat ab aliis coniunctionibus interrogativis

8   [*P78vb*] Circa tertium queritur que sit differentia huius
dictionis 'an' ad alias coniunctiones[1] interrogativas (que sunt '-ne' et
'utrum') quia: Si nulla est differentia, ergo una earum sufficit. Ergo
alie superfluunt. Et dicendum quod iste[2] tres coniunctiones 'utrum',
'an', '-ne' conveniunt [*N70vb*] in hoc quod interrogant de compositione actus cum substantia, ut dictum est. Sed differunt in hoc quod
hec coniunctio '-ne' magis se tenet cum actu, iste vero coniunctiones
'an' et 'utrum' magis se tenent a parte suppositi[3]. Et[4] differunt iste due
(scilicet 'an' et 'utrum') hoc modo quia hec coniunctio 'utrum' numquam geminatur sine <alia> disiunctiva[5] coniunctione, sed[6] exigit
secum coniunctionem aliam disiunctivam[7], ut 'utrum Sortes currat
vel Plato'. Sed ista coniunctio 'an' quandoque[8] geminatur sine altera
coniunctione, ut 'tu scis an Sortes currat an Plato'. Et ex hoc patet alia
differentia, scilicet quod coniunctio ista '-ne' non potest recipere
supra se transitionem alterius actus propter[9] hoc quod se tenet cum
actu; actus enim non transit supra alium actum sed supra aliquod
casuale. Unde nichil est dictu 'tu vides curritne Sortes', sed 'tu vides
Sortem currentem'[10]. Alie vero due recipiunt supra se transitionem
actus propter hoc quod magis se tenent cum substantia sive cum
supposito, ut 'tu scis an Sortes currat' et 'tu vides utrum Plato legat'.
Tertia differentia est quod hec coniunctio '-ne' semper est interrogativa, alie autem due aliquando[11] tenentur tantum disiunctive, ut

certified insofar as he is asking, that therefore from a question follows a request to be certified about that which the doubt concerns. Hence in virtue of the fact that the word '*an*' expresses a question by making a disjunction between certain things, for that reason it conveys a claim for one of two disjuncts. Now that the conjunction '*an*' signifies a disjunction is evident in virtue of the fact that it is a disjunctive conjunction. That it conveys a doubt is evident in virtue of the fact that it is an interrogative word and ultimately the question is followed by a claim for one of the disjuncts, as has been said.

In what way it differs from other interrogative conjunctions

8   *Ad [3]:* As to the third item, there is a problem what the difference is between the word '*an*' and other interrogative conjunctions (which are '*-ne*' and '*utrum*'). If there is no difference, then one of them would suffice. Therefore the other ones would be superfluous. The answer should be that the three conjunctions '*utrum*', '*an*' and '*-ne*' are in agreement in that they convey a question concerning the composition of an act with a substance, as has been said.[5] However, they differ in that the conjunction '*-ne*' rather relates to the act, whereas the conjunctions '*an*' and '*utrum*' rather relate to the *suppositum*. The latter (*viz.* '*an*' and '*utrum*') are different in the sense that the conjunction '*utrum*' is never used in a paired expression without a disjunctive conjunction, but it needs to be combined with another disjunctive conjunction, *e.g.* '*utrum Sortes currat vel Plato*' ('whether Socrates is running or Plato'). On the other hand, the conjunction '*an*' is sometimes used in a paired expression without another conjunction, *e.g.* '*tu scis an Sortes currat an Plato*' ('You know whether Socrates is running or Plato'). Also from this discussion another difference is evident, *viz.* that the conjunction '*-ne*' cannot receive a transition of another act on account of the fact that it relates to the act. For an act does not extend to another act but to an inflection. Thus it makes no sense to say '**tu vides curritne Sortes*', but <one should say> '*tu vides Sortem currentem*' ('You see Socrates running'). The other two receive a transition of an act on account of the fact that they relate more to the substance or the *suppositum, e.g.* '*tu scis an Sortes currat*' ('You know whether Socrates is running') and '*tu vides utrum Plato legat*' ('You see whether Plato is reading'). The third difference is that the conjunction '*ne*' is always interrogative, whereas the other two are sometimes merely used disjunctively, *e.g.* '*ego bene*

---

5   Cf. above, cap. 5.

'ego bene[12] scio utrum Plato legat vel non' et 'bene scio an legat an non legat'.

Inter que habeat disiungere

9   Circa quartum queritur, cum hec coniunctio 'an' sit coniunctio disiunctiva, inter que habeat[1] disiungere. Et de hoc talis datur regula:

> quotienscumque hec dictio[2] 'an' semel ponitur, disiungit inter dicta[3] contradictorie[4] opposita[5]; quando vero bis ponitur, disiungit inter dicta inventa.

Quod autem prima pars regule sit vera probo[6] quia: In omni interrogatione supponitur aliquid commune ad id quod queritur, ut cum querit[7] aliquis 'quis disputat?', supponit hominem in[8] communi disputare et vult certificari de particulari homine qui disputat; [*P79ra*] et similiter in qualibet alia interrogatione. Ergo in omni interrogatione [*N71ra*] supponitur aliquid[9] commune sive universale ad id quod queritur. Ergo in hac interrogatione 'tu scis an Sortes currat' supponitur aliquid[10] commune ad id quod queritur. Sed non queritur nisi[11] altera pars contradictionis, quia de illa [*T42va*] solum dubitatur. Ergo supponitur <aliquid> commune ad illam. Sed nichil est commune ad partes[12] contradictionis nisi disiunctio[13]. Ergo supponitur ibi disiunctio inter partes contradictionis. Sed non est ibi aliquid[14] per quod supponatur ista disiunctio nisi per hanc con-iunctionem[15] 'an'. Ergo hec coniunctio 'an' disiungit inter partes[16] contradictionis. Sed hoc modo semel ponitur. Ergo quando semel ponitur, disiungit inter dicta contradictorie opposita. Quod concedimus.

10   Sed contra. Omnis disiunctio est adminus inter duo. Unde[1] nichil est dictu 'Sortes currit vel', quia deficit[2] alterum extremorum. Ergo nichil est dictu 'tu scis an Sortes currat', cum deficiat alterum extremorum. Solutio. Non est simile de hac dictione 'an' et de hac dictione 'vel', quia hec dictio 'an' est dictio interrogativa et dis-

scio utrum Plato legat vel non' ('I know perfectly well whether Plato is reading or not') and *'bene scio an legat an non legat'* ('I know perfectly well whether he is reading or not').

What it is to disjoin between

9   *Ad [4]:* As to the fourth item, there is a problem, because the conjunction *'an'* is a disjunctive conjunction, what it is is to disjoin between. As regards this problem one presents the following rule:

> *Whenever the word 'an' occurs once, it forms a disjunction between two contradictory opposites, but when it occurs twice, it forms a disjunction between the* dicta *it encounters.*

I shall prove that the first part of the rule is true. In every question something that is general in relation to what is asked is assumed, *e.g.* when someone asks 'Who is arguing?', one assumes that a man in general is arguing and one wishes to certified about the man in particular who is arguing, and the same goes for any other question. Therefore in every question one assumes something that is general or universal in relation to what is asked. Therefore in the question 'You know if Socrates is running'[6] one assumes something general in relation to what is asked. Now there is only a question concerning one part of a contradiction, because that is the only part one is in doubt about. Therefore one assumes something that is general in relation to it. Now nothing is general in relation to the parts of a contradiction except a disjunction. Therefore in that case one assumes a disjunction between the parts of a contradiction. Now the only thing by means of which one assumes this disjunction is the conjunction *'an'*. Therefore the conjunction *'an'* disjoins between the parts of a contradiction. Now in this way it is used once. Therefore when it is used once, it disjoins between contradictory opposite *dicta*. Well, we agree with this.

10   However, there is an argument to the contrary. Every disjunction concerns at least two things. Therefore it makes no sense to say '**Sortes currit vel*' ('*Socrates is running or'), because one of the extremes is missing. Therefore it makes no sense to say '*tu scis an Sortes currat*' ('You know whether Socrates is running'), because one of the extremes is missing. Solution. The situation as regards the conjunction *'an'* and the one as regards the word 'or' is not alike,

---

6   This is a so-called oblique question. It equals '*tu scis an Sortes currat vel non currat*'.

iunctiva. Et ideo ratione interrogationis adiuncte disiunctioni, quando adiungitur uni parti contradictionis[3], dat intelligere alteram, quia qui dubitat de uno oppositorum, dubitat de reliquo. Sed hec dictio 'vel' tantum est disiunctiva et non interrogativa. Et ideo non dat intelligere alterum[4] extremorum.

11 Item. Obicitur circa[1] secundam partem regule quia: Multorum non est dubitatio una sed plures, nisi illa multa opponantur aliquo genere oppositionis. Sed cum dicitur 'tu scis an Sortes currat an Plato disputet', ista[2] scilicet 'Sortem[3] currere' et 'Platonem disputare' non opponuntur aliquo genere oppositionis. Ergo non est eorum dubitatio una. Ergo hec dictio 'an' non disiungit inter ea. Ergo non disiungit inter dicta inventa quando bis ponitur. Sed contra. Omne illud quod[4] queritur per[5] interrogationem[6], solvitur[7] <per> illud quo in responsione dato questio[8] terminatur. Sed dato utrolibet predictorum enuntiabilium questio terminatur. Ergo indifferenter queritur hoc vel illud. Ergo hec dictio 'an' disiungit inter ea, quia[9] solum disiungit [*N71rb*] inter ea de quibus querit. Sed hec sunt dicta inventa. Ergo[10] quando bis ponitur, [*P79rb*] disiungit inter dicta[11] inventa. Quod concedimus.

12 Ad hoc quod obicit in contrarium, dicendum quod 'dubitatio una' et 'interrogatio[1] una' et 'responsio una' sunt dupliciter. Quia uno modo est responsio una simpliciter, ut quando queritur unum de uno secundum se et absolute (ut cum queritur[2] 'curritne Sortes?' et[3] respondetur 'sic' vel 'non'). Alio autem modo est[4] responsio una non simpliciter sed per suppositionem, ut cum queritur[5] 'curritne Sortes vel Plato?'; hic enim oportet supponere quod alter[6] istorum currat ad hoc ut detur responsio una. Et similiter 'dubitatio una'[7] et etiam 'interrogatio una' sunt dupliciter, scilicet simpliciter et per suppositionem. Ut cum queritur 'tu scis an Sortes currat an Plato disputet', non est interrogatio una neque dubitatio simpliciter sed per suppositionem, ut quod uterque[8] illorum sit[9] et[10] quod respondens sciat de altero[11] illorum.

because the word '*an*' is an interrogative and disjunctive word. Hence in virtue of the question added to the disjunction when it is added to one part of a contradiction, it gives to understand the other part, because whoever is in doubt about one opposite, is in doubt about the other. The word '*vel*' ('or'), on the other hand, is only disjunctive and not interrogative. Therefore it does not give to understand the other of the extremes.

11 Again, there is an argument to the contrary that concerns the second part of the rule. If there are doubts about many things, the doubt is not a single one but a multiple one (*plures*), unless these many doubts are opposed in some kind of opposition. Now in the expression 'You know whether Socrates is running or Plato is arguing', the phrases 'that Socrates is running' and 'that Plato is arguing' are not opposed in some kind of opposition. Therefore the doubt concerning these things is not a single one. Therefore the word '*an*' does not disjoin between the two. Therefore it does not disjoin between the *dicta* it encounters when it is used twice. There is an argument to the contrary. Everything that is asked by means of a question is solved by that which, once it has been given in answer, terminates the question. Now when either of the stateables mentioned is given as an answer, the question is terminated. Therefore the question is neutral as regards this or that answer. Therefore the word '*an*' disjoins between them, because it only disjoins between the things about which there is a question. Now these things are the *dicta* it encounters. Therefore when it is used twice, it disjoins between the *dicta* it encounters. Well, we agree with this.

12 As to the argument to the contrary, the answer should be that 'single doubt', 'single question' and 'single answer' are ambiguous. [1] In one way an answer is a single one *simpliciter*, namely when there is one question about something that is one in itself and absolutely (*e.g.* when one asks 'Is Socrates running?', and the answer is 'Yes' or 'No'). [2] In another way an answer is not a single one *simpliciter*, but by assumption, (*e.g.* when one asks 'Is Socrates running or Plato?'), for in this case it is necessary to assume that one of them is running in order to give a single answer. In the same way the expressions 'single doubt' and 'single question' are ambiguous as well, *viz.* <single> *simpliciter* and <single> by assumption. For example, in the question 'You know whether Socrates is running or Plato is arguing', there is not a single question or a single doubt *simpliciter* but by assumption, *viz.* that either one of them exists and that the answerer has knowledge as regards one of them.

Utrum equaliter se habeat ad omnes suos actus

13   Circa quintum obicitur[1] quod hec dictio 'an' non debeat exercere istos tres actus qui sunt disiungere[2], interrogare et dubitare, quia
unius actus unum est instrumentum proprium et econverso. Ergo si
hec dictio 'an' est instrumentum interrogandi, non erit[3] instrumentum dubitandi neque disiungendi[4]. Et dicendum quod instrumentum idem secundum [*T42vb*] substantiam et secundum rationem
non potest esse instrumentum diversorum actuum sese non conse-
quentium[5]. Sed instrumentum idem secundum substantiam et
diversum secundum rationem potest esse actuum simpliciter diversorum. Unde sicut[6] pulmo est instrumentum temperandi calorem
cordis per respirationem (et hoc[7] secundum quod est attractivus
aeris) et etiam[8] est instrumentum loquendi repercutiendo[9] aera ad
vocalem[10] arteriam (et hoc[11] inquantum est expulsivus et repercussivus[12] aeris); et ita secundum aliud[13] est instrumentum temperandi
calorem cordis et secundum aliud est instrumentum loquendi, —
similiter hec coniunctio 'an' secundum quod disiungit, continetur
sub specie disiunctivarum coniunctionum[14], secundum autem quod
per ipsam[15] interrogamus, continetur sub specie interrogativarum
coniunctionum; secundum autem quod per ipsam dubitamus,
[*N71va*] continetur sub[16] specie dubitativarum. [*P79va*] Et sic semper
est coniunctio eadem secundum substantiam, differt[17] autem secundum rationem et speciem, cum sit[18] diversarum specierum secundum quod per[19] ipsam exercemus tres predictos[20] actus.

14   Et nota quod per prius est disiunctiva et per posterius[1] interrogativa et dubitativa, quia semper disiungit sed non semper interrogat
vel dubitat. Et nota quod hec dictio 'an' petit[2] alteram partem determinate eorum inter que disiungit. Et propter hoc solet dici quod[3]
oportet quod respondens sciat[4] alteram partem determinate. Quod[5]
probatur sic. Respondens[6] magis certus[7] debet[8] esse de questione
quam interrogans, quia respondens debet certificare interrogantem
de questione. Sed interrogans[9] scit alteram partem in[10] genere sive
in communi. Ergo oportet quod[11] respondens sciat alteram partem
specialiter[12] et determinate. Quod concedimus.

15   Sed contra. Sicut contingit scire universale ignorando particulare (ut scio hominem in universali esse in Yspania[1], tamen[2] nullum
particularem scio[3] ibi esse), — similiter contingit scire disiunctum

Whether it is equally related to all its acts

13   *Ad [5]:* As to the fifth item, there is an argument to the contrary that the word '*an*' should not carry out the three acts of disjoining, asking and doubting, because one act has one proper instrument and the other way round. Therefore if the word '*an*' is an instrument for asking, it will not be an instrument for doubting or disjoining. The answer should be that an instrument that is identical *qua* substance and *qua* definition cannot be an instrument for diverse acts that do not follow from each other. However, an instrument that is identical *qua* substance and diverse *qua* definition can be an instrument for acts *simpliciter* diverse. Thus just as the lungs are an instrument for tempering the heart's heat by means of respiration (and this is because they attract air) and also an instrument for speaking by thrusting air to the vocal artery (and they have this function insofar as they discharge and thrust air), and so in one way they are an instrument for tempering the heart's heat and in another way an instrument for speaking,—likewise insofar as it disjoins the conjunction '*an*' is contained under the species of disjunctive conjunctions, whereas insofar as we use it to ask a question it is contained under the species of interrogative conjunctions, and insofar as we use it to express a doubt, it is contained under the species of dubitative conjunctions. Thus it is always the same conjunction *qua* substance, but it differs *qua* definition and species, because it belongs to diverse species insofar as we use it to carry out the three acts mentioned above.

14   Note that it is primarily disjunctive and secondarily interrogative and dubitative, because it always disjoins, whereas it does not always have the function of asking or doubting. Also note that the word '*an*' aims at one part determinately of the things between which it disjoins. This is why one usually says that the answerer must know one part determinately. And this is proved as follows. The answerer must be more certain about the question than the questioner, because the answerer must certify the questioner as regards the question. Now the questioner knows one part in general or generally. Therefore it is necessary that the answerer know one part specifically and determinately. Well, we agree with this.

15   However, there is an argument to the contrary. Just as it can happen that one knows something general while not knowing something particular (*e.g.* I know in general that there are human beings in Spain, yet I do not know anyone in particular to be there),—likewise it can happen that one knows a 'disjunct' or a

sive disiunctionem ignorando quamlibet partem disiunctionis.
Probatio. Scio astra esse paria vel imparia, tamen neque[4] scio hanc
partem neque illam. Ergo cum dico 'tu scis an Sortes currit an Plato
disputet', non[5] oportet quod respondens sciat alteram partem
determinate. Et dicendum quod hoc[6] ultimum argumentum non
tenet. Si enim hec dictio 'an' esset tantum disiunctiva, bene oporteret[7]. Sed quia non solum est disiunctiva sed etiam interrogativa,
ideo non tenet, quia[8] quicumque interrogat petit[9] certificari eo ipso
quod interrogat[10]. Et ideo cum hec dictio 'an' sit interrogativa alterius
disiunctorum[11], oportet quod importet petitionem alterius disiunctorum[12]. Et propter huiusmodi[13] petitionem oportet quod respondens
sciat alteram partem determinate. Et ita argumentum predictum
impeditur propter interrogationem huius dictionis 'an'.

Sophismata

16   Queritur de hoc sophismate[1] TU SCIS AN OMNIS HOMO[2] SIT[3]
SORTES AN DIFFERAT AB[4] ILLO. Probatio. Tu scis an Sortes sit
Sortes an [*P79vb*] differat [*N70vb*] ab illo. Tu scis an Plato[5] sit Sortes
an differat ab illo et sic de singulis[6]. Ergo prima vera. Contra. Tu scis
an omnis homo sit Sortes an differat ab illo[7]. Ergo tu scis omnem
hominem esse Sortem an[8] omnem hominem differre a[9] Sorte; quorum utrumque est falsum.
17   Solutio. Prima falsa simpliciter. Et probatio peccat secundum
consequens ab insufficienti, quia in hac propositione[1] 'tu scis an
omnis homo sit Sortes an differat ab [*T43ra*] illo' est duplex universa-
litas, quoniam[2] in una parte disiunctionis est una distributio et alia
in altera. Unde sensus est[3] 'tu scis an omnis homo sit Sortes[4] an
omnis[5] homo differat a Sorte'. Sed non sumuntur omnes singulares
harum duarum distributionum in ipsa probatione[6], quia preter illas[7]
quas sumit, deberet[8] sumere istas 'tu scis an Sortes sit Sortes an
omnis homo differat a Sorte', 'tu scis an Plato sit Sortes an omnis
homo differat a Sorte' (et hec disiunctiva est falsa, quia utraque pars
eius est falsa) et similiter[9] omnes alie que relinquuntur[10]. Et hoc

disjunction while not knowing any one member of the disjunction. Proof: I know that the number of stars is even or odd, yet I do not know this member or that one. Therefore when I say 'You know whether Socrates is running or Plato is arguing', it is not necessary that the answerer know one member determinately. The answer should be that the final argument is not valid. For if the word 'whether' (*an*) were a disjunctive only, it would be valid. However, it is not only disjunctive but also interrogative, and that is why the argument is not valid, because whoever asks a question requests to be certified by the mere fact that he is asking. Hence it is because the word '*an*' is interrogative as regards one of the disjuncts, that it is necessary that it conveys a request for one of the disjuncts, and it is on account of such a request [*viz.* the request for being certified about one of the disjuncts], that it is necessary that the answerer know one member determinately. So the argument just mentioned is prevented because of the the interrogative nature of the word '*an*'.

Sophismata

16 There is a problem concerning the sophisma-sentence YOU KNOW WHETHER EVERY MAN IS SOCRATES OR DIFFERS FROM HIM. Proof: you know whether Socrates is Socrates or differs from him, you know whether Plato is Socrates or differs from him and so on. Therefore the original sentence is true. There is an argument to the contrary. You know whether every man is Socrates or differs from him. Therefore you know that every man is Socrates or that every man differs from Socrates, and each one of these is false.

17 Solution. The original sentence is false *simpliciter*, and the proof commits the fallacy of the consequent by proceeding from an insufficient <enumeration>, because in the proposition 'You know whether every man is Socrates or differs from him' there is a two-fold universality, because there is one distribution in one member of the disjunction and another in the other. Therefore it means 'You know whether every man is Socrates or whether every man differs from Socrates'. Now the proof does not take all the singular propositions of these two distributions, because besides the ones it does take it should <also> take 'You know whether Socrates is Socrates or every man differs from Socrates' and 'You know whether Plato is Socrates or every man differs from Socrates' (and the latter disjunctive is false because both members are false), and likewise all the other ones that remain. In this way one should take all the

modo deberet[11] sumere omnes particulares[12] prime distributionis secunda[13] distributione[14] integra[15] permanente. Et etiam deberet econverso sumere omnes particulares[16] secunde distributionis ita quod prima distributio integra permaneat[17]. Ut 'tu scis an omnis homo sit Sortes an Sortes differat a Sorte'[18] et 'tu scis an omnis homo sit Sortes an Plato differat a Sorte' et sic de aliis. Alio[19] etiam[20] modo deberet sumere particulares[21], scilicet accipiendo singulares[22] unius cum omnibus singularibus alterius, ut 'tu scis an Sortes[23] sit Sortes an Sortes differat a Sorte' et 'tu[24] scis an Plato sit Sortes an Sortes differat a Sorte' et sic de aliis. Sed harum omnium nullam accepit[25]. Et ita procedit ab insufficienti. Unde peccat secundum consequens[26].

18   Item. Posito quod Sortes vel Plato mentiatur[1] sed tu nescias uter[2] eorum mentiatur, queritur de hoc sophismate TU SCIS AN DE MENTIENTE SIT FALSUM SORTEM ESSE ILLUM. Probatio. Hec negativa[3] est vera 'non de[4] mentiente est falsum Sortem esse[5] illum' utroque [*N72ra*] casu contingente, scilicet sive Sortes mentiatur sive Plato. Quia Sorte mentiente hec est vera [*P80ra*] 'non de mentiente est falsum Sortem esse illum' (idest 'Sortem esse mentientem'), immo est verum de Sorte. Item Platone mentiente hec est vera 'non de mentiente est falsum Sortem esse illum' (idest 'Sortem esse Platonem mentientem'), quia[6] licet sit falsum Sortem esse Platonem, non tamen est[7] falsum de Platone, quia non est enuntiabile de eo. Unde neque verum neque falsum de eo est[8], propter hoc[9] quod enuntiabile dicitur[10] semper de re subiecti termini, sive de eo quod subicitur, et non de eo quod predicatur, ut[11] 'hominem esse lapidem' est enuntiabile de homine et non de lapide, sed 'lapidem esse hominem' est enuntiabile de lapide et non de homine. Et sic patet quod utroque casu contingente hec est vera 'non de mentiente est falsum Sortem esse illum'. Et hoc scis[12] et etiam scis ex ypothesi quod plures casus non possunt contingere[13]. Ergo tu scis hanc, scilicet[14] 'non[15] de mentiente est[16] *etc.*'. Et hec est altera pars prime disiunctive, quia hec dictio 'an' semel[17] posita disiungit inter opposita. Ergo hec est vera 'tu scis an de mentiente sit falsum Sortem esse illum an non de

particular propositions of the first distribution while the second distribution remains untouched. Moreover, one should, conversely, take all the particular propositions of the second distribution so that the first distribution remains untouched, *viz.* 'You know whether every man is Socrates or Socrates differs from Socrates' and 'You know whether every man is Socrates or Plato differs from Socrates' and so on. One should take the particular propositions in yet another way as well, namely by taking the singular propositions of the one [*i.e.* distribution] in combination with all the singular propositions of the other, *viz.* 'You know whether Socrates is Socrates or Socrates differs from Socrates', 'You know whether Plato is Socrates or Socrates differs from Socrates' and so on. Now the argument to the contrary did not take any one of all these propositions, and so it proceeds from an insufficient enumeration. Hence it commits the fallacy of the consequent.

18   Again, supposing that Socrates or Plato is lying but you do not know which one of the two is lying, there is a problem concerning the sophisma-sentence YOU KNOW WHETHER OF THE ONE WHO IS LYING IT IS FALSE THAT SOCRATES IS HE. Proof: the negative proposition 'It is not the case that of the one who is lying it is false that Socrates is he' is true if either case applies, *viz.* whether Socrates is lying or Plato. For if Socrates is lying, the proposition 'It is not the case that of the one who is lying it is false that Socrates is he' (that is, that Socrates is lying) is true, for it is true of Socrates. Furthermore, if Plato is lying, the proposition 'It is not the case that of the one who is lying it is false that Socrates is he' (that is, that Socrates is the lying Plato) is true, for although it is false that Socrates is Plato, it is nevertheless not false of Plato, because the stateable involved is not about him. Thus it is neither true nor false of him, because a stateable is always said of the thing signified by the subject term, or of that which is made subject, and not of that which is made predicate, *e.g.* 'that a man is a stone' is a stateable about a man and not about a stone, whereas 'that a stone is a man' is a stateable about a stone and not about a man. Thus it is evident that in either case, the proposition 'It is not the case that of the one who is lying it is false that Socrates is he' is true, and you know this, and by assumption you also know that more than one cases cannot apply. Therefore you know the proposition 'It is not the case that of the one who is lying, *etc.*', and this is one member of the first disjunctive, because the word 'whether' (*an*) used once disjoins between opposites. Therefore the proposition 'You know whether of the one who is lying it is false that Socrates is he or that it is not the case that of the

mentiente sit falsum Sortem esse illum', quia huius disiunctive[18] altera pars est vera.

19   Contra. Tu scis an de mentiente sit falsum Sortem[1] esse illum. Ergo tu scis an de mentiente sit falsum illum esse Sortem (per locum a convertibili, ut 'si Sortes est ille, ille est Sortes', sicut[2] 'si homo est animal, et animal est homo'). Sed conclusio est dubia et non[3] certa, quia Sorte mentiente hec negativa[4] est vera 'non de mentiente est falsum illum[5] esse Sortem', idest 'mentientem[6] esse Sortem'. Sed Platone mentiente falsa est, quia sensus est 'non[7] de mentiente est falsum illum[8] esse Sortem' (idest 'Platonem esse Sortem'), quia hoc est falsum de mentiente, eoquod 'Platonem esse Sortem' est falsum de [*T43rb*] Platone. Ergo predicta negativa est dubia, cum sit vera uno casu[9] contingente et alio[10] falsa et nescis[11] quis casus debeat contingere[12]. Ergo sua opposita est dubia, quia quisquis[13] dubitat de uno oppositorum, necesse est ipsum de reliquo dubitare. Ergo hec est falsa 'tu scis an de mentiente sit falsum [*N72rb*] illum[14] esse Sortem. Ergo prima[15] est falsa ex[16] qua sequitur.

20   Solutio. Prima est simpliciter vera, hec scilicet 'tu scis an de mentiente sit falsum Sortem esse illum'. Et probatio bene tenet. Sed primum argumentum improbationis peccat secundum sophisma accidentis. Sicut hic[1]: 'tu scis quod[2] de homine [*P80rb*] est enuntiabile hominem esse substantiam; ergo tu scis quod de homine est enuntiabile[3] substantiam esse hominem'. Quod[4] falsum est, quia[5] licet[6] 'hominem esse substantiam' et 'substantiam esse hominem' convertantur, non tamen quod subicitur in uno[7], subicitur[8] in reliquo[9]. Unde[10] est unum enuntiabile de homine et non de substantia (quia homo subicitur in eo) et alterum est enuntiabile de substantia et non de homine, quia substantia subicitur in eo[11].

B.   DE HAC CONIUNCTIONE 'VEL'

21   Habito[1] de hac coniunctione disiunctiva[2] 'an' consequenter queritur[3] de hac dictione 'vel'. Circa quam primo queritur quid significet hec dictio[4] 'vel'; secundo autem[5] queritur utrum suum

one who is lying it is false that Socrates is he' is true, because of this disjunctive one member is true.

19   There is an argument to the contrary. You know whether of the one who is lying it is false that Socrates is he. Therefore you know whether of the one who is lying it is false that he is Socrates (on acount of the topic 'from a convertible', *e.g.* 'If Socrates is he, he is Socrates', in the same way as 'If a man is an animal, an animal is a man'). Now the conclusion is doubtful and not certain, because if Socrates is lying the negative proposition 'It is not the case that of the one who is lying it is false that he is Socrates', that is, 'that he who is lying is Socrates', is true. However, if Plato is lying it is false, for it means 'It is not the case that of the one who is lying it is false that he is Socrates' (that is, 'that Plato is Socrates'), because this is false of the one who is lying, since 'that Plato is Socrates' is false of Plato. There fore the negative just mentioned is doubtful, because it is true if one case applies and is false if the other case applies and you do not know which case must apply. Therefore its opposite proposition is doubtful, because whoever is in doubt about one opposite, necessarily must be in doubt about the other one. Therefore 'You know whether of the one who is lying it is false that he is Socrates' is false. Therefore the original sentence from which it follows is false.

20   Solution. The original sentence, *viz.* 'You know whether of the one who is lying it is false that Socrates is he', is true *simpliciter*, and the proof[7] holds good. However, the first argument of the disproof commits the fallacy of accident, just as 'You know that of a man there is a stateable that a man is a substance; therefore you know that of a man there is a stateable that a substance is a man', which is false, because, although 'that a man is a substance' and 'that a substance is a man' are convertible, nevertheless it is not the case that what is made subject in the one is made subject in the other. That is why the one is a stateable about a man and not about a substance (because a man is made subject in it) and the other is a stateable about a substance and not about a man (because a substance is made subject in it).

B. ON THE CONJUNCTION '*VEL*' ('OR')

21   Now that we have discussed the disjunctive conjunction '*an*', we must next deal with the word '*vel*' ('or'). As regards this word there [1] first is a problem what the word '*vel*' signifies, [2] secondly

---

7   Cf. above, cap. 18.

significatum[6] sit[7] ens simpliciter vel non; tertio utrum res huius dictionis 'vel' sit in genere vel non; quarto qualiter differat ab aliis coniunctionibus disiunctivis; quinto utrum disiunctio[8] faciat terminum[9] disiunctum[10] predicabilem[11] de pluribus.

Quid significet hec dictio 'vel'

22   Circa primum queritur[1] quia: Ut patet per diffinitionem coniunctionis, hec coniunctio 'vel' significat comparationem que est secundum simul aut secundum prius et[2] posterius. Sed non significat comparationem que est[3] secundum prius et[4] posterius, quia sic esset dictio consecutiva[5]. Ergo significat comparationem que est secundum simul. Ergo significat res simul esse. Sed contra. Dicit[6] Boetius quod hoc sapit disiunctiva coniunctio quod ea[7] inter que coniungit simul esse non permittit[8]. Ergo hec coniunctio[9] 'vel' non ponit res simul esse. Ergo non significat comparationem que[10] est secundum simul. Item ad idem. Priscianus diffinit coniunctionem disiunctivam dicens[11] "disiunctive coniunctiones sunt que, quamvis dictiones coniungant, sensus tamen disiungunt et alteram quidem rem esse, alteram vero non esse significant"[12]. Sed diffinitio superioris convenit cuilibet [*N72va*] inferiori. Ergo oportet quod hec[13] diffinitio intelligatur in hac coniunctione 'vel'. Ergo hec coniunctio 'vel' non ponit res simul esse. Ergo non significat comparationem que est secundum simul.

23   Et dicendum quod hec coniunctio 'vel' significat comparationem rerum[1] simul existentium disiungendo. Et hec comparatio est disiunctio[2] ipsorum disiunctorum equaliter se habens ad utrumque, quia hec coniunctio 'vel' non magis se habet ad unum disiunctorum [*P80va*] quam ad alterum quantum est de se, ut cum dicitur 'Sortes vel Plato'. Ad illud autem quod obicit per Boetium, dicendum quod ubicumque[3] est disiunctio, duo exiguntur, scilicet

there is a problem whether its significate is a being *simpliciter* or not, *[3]* thirdly whether the 'thing' signified by this word belongs to a category or not, *[4]* fourthly in what way it differs from other disjunctive conjunctions, and *[5]* fifthly whether a disjunction makes a disjoined term be predicable of many.

What the word 'vel' signifies

22   *Ad [1]:* As to the first item, there is a problem: as is evident from the the definition of the conjunction, the conjunction '*vel*' signifies a relationship in the sense of a being at the same time or in the sense of a being prior and posterior. Now it does not signify a relationship in the sense of a being prior and posterior, because in that way it would be a consecutive word. Therefore it signifies a relationship in the sense of a being together. Therefore it signifies things to be at the same time. However, there is an argument to the contrary. Boethius says[8] that the disjunctive conjunction displays its cleverness in that it does not allow the things it conjoins to be at the same time. Therefore the conjunction '*vel*' cannot signify things to be at the same time. Therefore it does not signify a relationship in the sense of a being at the same time. Again, there is an argument that yields the same conclusion. Priscian defines[9] a disjunctive conjunction saying: "Disjunctive conjunctions are the ones that, although they conjoin words, they disjoin meanings, and they signify that a certain one thing is, whereas the other is not". Now the definition of something more general agrees with whatever is less general. Therefore it is necessary that this definition be understood in the conjunction '*vel*'. Therefore the conjunction '*vel*' does not assert things to be at the same time. Therefore it does not signify a relationship in the sense of a being at the same time.

23   The answer should be that the conjunction '*vel*' signifies a relationship between things existing at the same time in that it disjoins <them>. This relationship amounts to a disjunction of these disjuncts which is equally related to both, because the conjunction '*vel*' is not more related to one of the disjuncts than to the other taken as such, *e.g.* in the expression 'Socrates or Plato'. As to the argument to the contrary brought about by <referring to> Boethius, the answer should be that wherever there is a disjunction, two things are

---

[8]   Cf. Boethius, *De hyp. syll.* III 11, p. 388(56-7) (ed. Obertello – 876C 8-9 ed. Migne): "coniunctio quae disiunctiva ponitur sentit simul eas esse non posse."
[9]   *Inst. gramm.* XVI 7, p. 97(17-8), ed. Hertz.

ea que disiunguntur et illud respectu cuius est disiunctio. Unde[4] cum dicitur 'Sortes vel Plato currit'[5] Sortes vel Plato sunt disiuncta et disiunguntur respectu huius actus 'currit'. Unde hec coniunctio 'vel' ponit ipsa[6] disiuncta simul esse et illud respectu cuius est disiunctio, non ponit simul[7] esse in eis. Unde Sortes et Plato simul ponuntur secundum se, non tamen simul ponuntur sub cursu. Et ideo quod dicit Boetius, intelligendum est quoad illud respectu cuius est [*T43va*] disiunctio. Ad illud autem quod obicit de diffinitione coniunctionis disiunctive, dicendum quod 'simul' est duobus modis. Quia uno modo est simul contra[8] prius et posterius in consequendo. Et sic omnes coniunctiones disiunctive dicunt res simul esse, eoquod non[9] ponunt unum tamquam antecedens et reliquum tamquam consequens. Alio autem modo dicitur 'simul' secundum participationem unius rei, ut si Sortes et Plato participant albedinem, dicuntur esse simul in participatione albedinis. Et hoc modo dicit Priscianus quod[10] coniunctiones disiunctive disiungunt sensus et alteram quidem rem esse, alteram vero non esse significant.

Utrum suum significatum sit ens simpliciter

24   Circa secundum queritur[1] quia: Quod importatur per hanc dictionem 'vel' repperitur in ente[2] (ut 'homo vel asinus') et in non-ente (ut 'chimera vel hircocervus'). Ergo non est ens simpliciter. Item ad idem. Quicquid est ens simpliciter, aut est substantia aut quantitas et sic de aliis. Sed hec coniunctio 'vel' non [*N72vb*] significat substantiam neque quantitatem et sic de aliis. Ergo significatum[3] eius non est ens simpliciter sed quodammodo. Quod concedimus dicentes quod significat respectum quendam repertum tam in ente quam in[4] non-ente.

required, namely the things that are disjoined and that in respect of which there is a disjunction. Hence in the expression 'Socrates or Plato is running', Socrates and Plato are the disjuncts and they are disjoined in respect of the act 'is running'. That is why the disjunction '*vel*' asserts the disjuncts to be at the same time, and as for that in respect of which there is a disjunction, the disjunction '*vel*' does not assert it to be in the disjuncts at the same time. Hence Socrates and Plato are posited at the same time as such, nevertheless they are not posited at the same time under the aspect of running. So what Boethius says should be understood as concerning that in respect of which there is a disjunction. As to the argument to the contrary concerning the definition of a disjunctive conjunction, the answer should be that 'at the same time' is twofold. [1] In one way 'at the same time' is opposed to 'prior' and 'posterior' in an inference. In this way all disjunctive conjunctions indicate things to be at the same time, because they do not posit one thing as antecedent and the other as consequent. [2] In the other way 'at the same time' is said in the sense of participating in one <and the same> thing, *e.g.* if Socrates and Plato participate in whiteness they are said to be at the same time in participating in whiteness. In this way Priscian says[10] that disjunctive conjunctions disjoin meanings, and they signify that one thing is and the other thing is not.

Whether its significate is a being simpliciter

24   *Ad [2]:* As to the second item, there is a problem: what is conveyed by the word 'or' is found in <the domain of> being (*e.g.* 'a man or an ass') and in <the domain of> non-being *e.g.* ('a chimaera or a goatstag'). Therefore it is not a being *simpliciter*. Again, there is an argument that yields the same conclusion. Whatever is a being *simpliciter* is either a substance or a quantity, and so on. Now the conjunction '*vel*' does not signify a substance or a quantity and so on. Therefore its significate is not a being *simpliciter* but a being in a certain sense. Well, we agree with this saying that it signifies a kind of 'bringing together' concerning <the domains of> both being and non-being.

---

10   *Inst. gramm.* XVI 7, p. 97(17-8), ed. Hertz.

Utrum res huius dictionis 'vel' sit in genere vel non

25   Circa tertium obicitur[1] quia: Cum omnes relationes sint[2] in *Ad aliquid* (sive in predicamento Relationis), sed hec dictio 'vel' non dicit rem absolutam sed respectivam (quia nichil est dictu 'Sortes currit vel' propter hoc quod deficit [*P80vb*] alterum extremorum), ergo dicit relationem. Ergo est in[3] *Ad aliquid* (sive in predicamento Relationis). Item. Hec dictio 'vel' equaliter se habet quantum est de se ad utrumque extremorum. Sed[4] dicit comparationem unius ad alterum. Ergo dicit relationem secundum equiparantiam. Ergo est in genere Relationis. Sed obicitur in contrarium quod nulla comparatio que est secundum simul aut[5] secundum prius et posterius, est in aliquo predicamento[6]. Sed omnis res cuiuslibet coniunctionis est comparatio que est secundum simul aut[7] secundum[8] prius et[9] posterius. Ergo nulla res alicuius[10] coniunctionis est in aliquo predicamento (et est sillogismus in secundo prime). Ergo significatum[11] huius dictionis 'vel' non est in aliquo genere. Quod concedimus.

26   Ad primum autem quod obicit dicendum quod 'comparatio' sive 'respectus' est duplex. Quia quedam sunt comparationes que sunt res simpliciter existentes ut pater—filius, duplum—dimidium. Et tales comparationes sunt in predicamento Relationis, eoquod sunt[1] relationes. Alie autem sunt comparationes que non sunt res simpliciter existentes, eoquod sunt tam existentium quam non-existentium. Et huiusmodi comparationes non sunt in genere Relationis. Et[2] tales sunt significationes coniunctionum disiunctivarum. Unde non sequitur quod quamvis hec coniunctio 'vel' dicat rem respectivam, quod propter hoc sit in *Ad aliquid* (sive in genere Relationis).

27   Ad aliud dicendum quod 'comparatio secundum equalitatem' est duplex. Quia quedam est que[1] est ab anima tantum dum anima apprehendit significata partium orationis. Et talis comparatio secundum equalitatem non est in *Ad aliquid*, quia non est ens simpliciter sed [*N73ra*] quodammodo, cum sit ipsorum significatorum[2] et contingat significare tam ens quam non-ens. Ergo comparationes[3] significatorum non possunt esse simpliciter entes[4]. Ergo non sunt in

Whether the 'thing' signified by the word 'vel' belongs in a category or not

25 *Ad [3]:* As to the third item, there is an argument to the contrary. All relations are relatives (or belong in the category of 'relation'). Now the word 'vel' does not indicate an absolute thing but a respective one (because it makes no sense to say '*Socrates is running or' since the other extreme is missing). Therefore it indicates a relation. Therefore it is a relative (or belongs in the category of 'relation'). Furthermore, the word 'vel' is in itself equally related to each one of the extremes. Now it indicates a 'bringing together' of the one and the other. Therefore it indicates a relationship in terms of comparable qualities (*secundum equiparantiam*). Therefore it belongs to the category of 'relation'. However, there is an argument to the contrary that no 'bringing together' <of things> in the sense of their being at the same time or in the sense of their being prior and posterior belongs in a category. Now every 'thing' signified by whatever conjunction is a 'bringing together' <of things> in the sense of their being at the same time or in the sense of their being prior and posterior. Therefore no 'thing' of whatever conjunction belongs in some category (this is a syllogism in the second mood of the first figure). Therefore the significate of the word 'vel' does not belong in some category. Well, we agree with this.

26 As to the first argument to the contrary, the answer should be that 'bringing together' or 'relation' is twofold. [1] One type of things brought together are things *simpliciter* existing, *e.g.* father-son and double-half, and these things brought together belong in the category of 'relation' because they are relations. [2] The other type of things brought together are not things *simpliciter* existing, because they belong to both existing and non-existing things, and relationships of this kind do not belong in the category of 'relation'. The significations of disjunctive conjunctions are of the latter type. Hence although the conjunction 'vel' indicates a respective thing, it does not follow that it is therefore a relative (or belongs in the category of 'relation').

27 As to the other argument to the contrary, the answer should be that 'relationship in terms of equality' is twofold. [1] There is one type that derives from the mind only, when the mind apprehends the significates of parts of speech, and this type of relationship in terms of equality does not belong to the category of 'relation', because it is not a being *simpliciter* but in a certain sense, because it belongs to the significates themselves and it may signify both being and non-being. Therefore the relationships between the significates

genere[5]. Et huiusmodi comparatio significatur per coniunctionem
disiunctivam. Alia autem est comparatio secundum equalitatem que
solum [*T43vb*] sequitur rem completam et perfectam in esse, ut ami-
cus—vicinus[6], similis—equalis. Et huiusmodi comparatio secundum equalitatem est equiparantia[7]. Et est[8] species Relationis. Unde
est in genere Relationis.

Qualiter differat ab aliis coniunctionibus disiunctivis

28   Circa quartum obicitur quia[1]: Si iste coniunctiones[2] 'vel', '-ve',
'aut', '-ne', 'an', 'utrum' non superfluunt, oportet eas differre a se
invicem, [*P81ra*] aut si non differunt, oportet quod alique earum
superfluant. Et propter hoc queritur qualiter hec coniunctio[3] 'vel'
differat ab aliis coniunctionibus disiunctivis. Et dicendum quod iste
coniunctiones 'vel', '-ve', 'aut'[4] differunt ab istis tribus, scilicet 'an'[5],
'-ne', 'utrum', per hoc quod iste tres possunt esse medium per[6] quod
unus actus transit[7] supra alium actum[8], ut 'scio an Sortes currat' et[9]
'scis[10] utrum[11] Sortes currat' et 'scit utrum Sortes currat' et 'putasne
Sortes currat'. Sed 'vel' et '-ve' et 'aut' non possunt esse medium quo
unus actus possit[12] transire supra alium actum[13]. Nichil enim[14] est
dictu 'scis[15] vel Sortes currit', 'scisve Sortes currit' et[16] 'scis aut Sortes
currit', ut actus sciendi intelligatur transire supra hoc quod dico
'Sortem currere', sicut ex alia parte bene[17] dicebatur 'tu scis an Sortes
currat' idest 'tu scis Sortem currere vel non currere'. Alia etiam est
differentia quia ille tres sunt interrogative, sed 'vel', '-ve' et 'aut' non
sunt interrogative, immo tantum disiunctive.

29   Item. Hec coniunctio 'vel' disiungit res que debent movere
intellectum speculativum vel quamlibet aliam virtutem cognosciti-
vam[1] non[2] motam ab affectu vel ab appetitu, sed prout[3] est cognosci-
tiva[4] tantum. Sed hec coniunctio[5] 'aut' disiungit res motivas[6] practici
intellectus vel ipsius affectus vel etiam motivas[7] ipsius appetitus
sensibilis. [*N73rb*] Item. Hec coniunctio '-ve' differt ab hiis[8] duabus,
scilicet 'vel' et 'aut', quia hec est disiunctiva encletica, ille[9] vero non,
sed sunt tantum disiunctive. Enclesis autem est inclinatio; unde

cannot be beings *simpliciter*. Therefore they do not belong in a category. A relationship of this kind is signified by a disjunctive conjunction. [2] The other type is a relationship in terms of equality that is only connected with something complete and perfect in being, *e.g.* 'friend-neighbour' and 'similar-equal'. Well, this kind of relationship in terms of equality is one that occurs by way of the capacity for being compared. It is a species of relation and hence it belongs to the category of 'relation'.

In what way it differs from other disjunctive conjunctions

28   *Ad [4]:* As to the fourth item, there is an argument to the contrary. If the conjunctions '*vel*', '*-ve*', '*aut*', '*-ne*' '*an*', and '*utrum*' are not superfluous, it is necessary that they differ from one another, or if they do not differ, it is necessary that some of them be superfluous. This is why there is a problem in what way the conjunction '*vel*' differs from the other disjunctive conjunctions. The answer should be that the conjunctions '*vel*', '*-ve*' and '*aut*' are different from the three '*an*', '*-ne*' and '*utrum*' in that the latter three can be the intermediary by which one act has another act as its object, *e.g.* 'I know whether (*an*) Socrates is running', 'You know whether (*an*) Socrates is running', 'He knows whether (*utrum*) Socrates is running', and 'Do you believe (*putasne*) that Socrates is running?'. Now '*vel*', '*-ve*' and '*aut*' cannot be the intermediary by which one act can have another act as its object, for it makes no sense to say '*You know or (*vel, -ve, aut*) Socrates is running', so that an act of knowing is understood to have the *dictum* 'that Socrates is running' as its object, in the same way as on the other hand it was correct to say 'You know whether Socrates is running', that is, *you know that Socrates is running or not running*. There is another difference in that the former are interrogative, whereas '*vel*', '*-ve*' and '*aut*' are not, rather they are merely disjunctive.

29   Furthermore, the conjunction '*vel*' disjoins between things that must move the speculative intellect or any other cognitive faculty not moved by an affect or by a desire, but insofar as it is cognitive only. Now the conjunction '*aut*' disjoins between things that move the practical intellect, an affect or even things that move the sensory desire. Moreover, the conjunction '*-ve*' differs from the other two, *viz.* '*vel*' and '*aut*', because it is an enclitic disjunctive, whereas the others are not, as they are merely disjunctive. Now '*enclesis*' means 'inclination', hence 'enclitic' (*encleticum*) is 'inclinative' (*inclinativum*).

'encleticum'[10] idest 'inclinativum'[11]. Et sic iste tres differunt inter se et ab hiis[12] tribus interrogativis.

30 Item. Hec coniunctio '-ve' differt ab hiis duabus 'an' et 'utrum' quia '-ve'[1] est interrogativa encletica, 'an' vero et 'utrum' non sunt encletice. Enclesis autem in solis tribus repperitur coniunctionibus que dicuntur encletice '-que', '-ne', '-ve'. Et quia attrahunt accentum precedentis dictionis ad ultimam sillabam (ut 'putasne'[2], 'dixitve', 'amavitque'[3]), ideo sequuntur semper primam dictionem illius clausule in qua ponuntur. Et ideo dicuntur[4] a gramaticis subiunctive.

Utrum disiunctio faciat terminum disiunctum predicabilem de pluribus

31 Circa quintum obicitur quod terminus disiunctus[1] predicatur de utraque sui parte, ut 'Sortes est Sortes vel Plato' et 'Plato est Sortes vel Plato'. Ergo terminus disiunctus est terminus communis ad utrumque disiunctorum. Ergo est predicabilis de pluribus. Sed obicitur in contrarium quia: Quicquid predicatur de pluribus est genus vel [*P81rb*] species vel[2] differentia vel proprium vel accidens vel[3] diffinitio. Sed terminus disiunctus nullum istorum est, quia omnia[4] ista sunt entia[5], terminus vero[6] disiunctus repperitur tam in ente quam in non-ente. Ergo terminus disiunctus non est predicabilis de pluribus.

32 Solutio. Communitas predicationis[1] est duobus modis. Quia uno modo est quando res [*T44ra*] una participata a pluribus predicatur de pluribus vel substantialiter vel accidentaliter. Et tunc oportet quod sit unum de quinque predicabilibus vel diffinitio[2]. Alio autem modo communitas predicationis est quando non predicatur res una, sed[3] complexio plurium rerum indifferenter[4] ponendo unum et removendo reliquum. Et hoc modo terminus disiunctus est predicabilis de pluribus, ut 'Sortes vel Plato' et sic de aliis. Et quia hec coniunctio 'vel' de natura[5] sua indeterminate[6] ponit unum disiunctorum et removet reliquum respectu alicuius[7] tertii (et sic est[8] disiunctiva), ideo proprie sumitur cum disiunctive tenetur, minus [*N73va*] vero proprie quando tenetur subdisiunctive; et dicitur subdisiunctive teneri quando utraque pars disiunctionis est vera.

33 Item. Videtur quod terminus disiunctus debeat esse aliquod[1] de quinque predicabilibus[2] quia: Quicquid recipit supra se distributionem, est unum de quinque predicabilibus. Sed terminus disiunctus

This is the way the three words differ from each other and from the three interrogative ones.

30   Furthermore, the conjunction '*-ve*' differs from the two '*an*' and '*utrum*', because '*-ve*' is an enclitic interrogative, whereas '*an*' and '*utrum*' are not enclitic. *Enclesis* is only found in the three conjunctions that are called enclitic, *viz.* '*-que*', '*-ne*' and '*-ve*', and it is because they draw the accent of the preceding word to the last syllable (*e.g.* '*putasne*', '*dixitve*' and '*amavitve*'), that they therefore always come after the first word in the phrase they are used in. And that is why grammarians call them 'subjunctive'.

Whether a disjunctive word makes a disjoined term predicable of many

31   *Ad [5]:* As to the fifth item, there is an argument to the contrary that a disjoined term is predicated of each one of its members, *e.g.* 'Socrates is Socrates or Plato' and 'Plato is Socrates or Plato'. Therefore the disjoined term is common to each one of its disjuncts. Therefore it is predicable of many. However, there is an argument to the contrary. Whatever is predicated of many is a genus, a species, a difference, a proprium, an accident, or a *definiens*. Now a disjoined term is none of these, because all of these are beings, whereas a disjoined term is found in both being and non-being. Therefore a disjoined term is not predicable of many.

32   Solution. The commonness of predication occurs in two ways. [1] One way is when one thing participated by many is predicated of many either substantially or accidentally. In that case it is necessary that it be one of the five predicables or a *definiens*. [2] In another way there is commonness when not one thing is predicated, but a complex of more things by indifferently positing the one and removing the other. In this way a disjoined term is predicable of many things, *e.g.* 'Socrates or Plato' and so on. Well, it is because the conjunction '*vel*' by its nature indeterminately posits one of the disjuncts and removes the other with respect to some third thing (and thus it is disjunctive), that it is therefore properly taken when it is taken disjunctively, whereas it is taken less properly when it is taken subdisjunctively; and it is said to be taken subdisjunctively when each member of the disjunction is true.

33   Again, it may be argued that a disjoined term should be one of the five predicables, because whatever is susceptible of a distribution is one of the five predicables. Now a disjoined term is susceptible of

recipit supra se distributionem. Ergo terminus disiunctus est unum de quinque predicabilibus. Maior patet quia[3]: 'Omnis' et[4] 'nullus' et[5] consimilia universaliter[6] consignificant. Sed nichil sumitur universaliter nisi universale. Ergo tantum sunt dispositiones universalis. Sed[7] universale dividitur per quinque predicabilia. Ergo quicquid recipit supra se distributionem *etc.* Et hec fuit maior. Minor vero[8] patet, quia aliter non esset hec vera 'omne rationale vel irrationale est animal' et econverso.

34 Solutio. In termino disiuncto[1] duo sunt: unum est ipsa disiunctio et aliud ipsi termini qui disiunguntur. Unde terminus disiunctus ratione disiunctionis[2] numquam potest recipere distributionem[3]. Sed ratione terminorum qui disiunguntur, aliquando potest, aliquando non, quia[4] quando termini disiuncti sunt singulares non potest[5] recipere distributionem; nichil enim est dictu 'omnis Sortes vel[6] Plato'. Quando autem termini qui disiunguntur sunt universales, tunc terminus disiunctus potest recipere distributionem, ut 'omnis homo vel[7] asinus est homo'. Sed tunc oratio est duplex, eoquod potest recipere distributionem pro altera parte tantum. Et sic est vera hec 'omnis homo vel asinus [*P81va*] est homo', et hic[8] est sensus: 'omnis homo est homo vel omnis asinus est homo'; et sic est propositio disiunctiva. Alio autem modo potest recipere distributionem pro utraque parte[9] simul. Et sic est falsa hec 'omnis homo vel asinus est homo'; et est categorica et est sensus: 'tam homo quam asinus universaliter est homo'. Tertio autem modo totum disiunctum potest recipere distributionem supra[10] se, prout[11] convenit utrique parti disiunctionis. Et sic hec est vera 'omne rationale vel irrationale est animal', quia[12] natura animalis adequatur cum disiuncto quod est 'rationale vel irrationale'. Et sic [*N73vb*] patet qualiter terminus disiunctus sive[13] totum disiunctum potest recipere supra se distributionem et qualiter non. Patet etiam quod in sillogismo quem[14] facit maior et minor sunt duplices.

Sophismata

35 Secundum predicta queritur de hoc sophismate QUICQUID EST VEL NON EST, EST. Probatio. 'Quicquid est, est'; hec est vera. Sed verum potest disiungi[1] a quolibet alio[2] a vero. Ergo prima vera. Contra. Quicquid est vel non est, est. Sed Cesar est vel non est. Ergo

a distribution. Therefore a disjoined term is one of the five pre-dicables. The major is evident: 'every', 'no' and the like signify <that something be taken> universally. Now only a universal is taken universally. Therefore they [*i.e.* 'every', 'no' and the like] are only dispositions of a universal. Now a universal is divided into the five predicables. Therefore whatever is susceptible of a distribution, *etc..* Now this was the major. The minor is evident, because otherwise 'Every rational or irrational thing is an animal' and the converse would not be true.

34   Solution. In a disjoined term there are two things: one is the disjunction itself and the other consists in the terms that are dis-joined. Hence on account of the disjunction a disjoined term can never receive a distribution, but on account of the terms that are disjoined it sometimes can and sometimes cannot. For when the disjoined terms are singular, they cannot receive a distribution, for it makes no sense to say '*every Socrates or Plato'. On the other hand, when the terms that are disjoined are universal, in that case a disjoined term can receive a distribution, *e.g.* 'Every man or ass is a man'. However, in that case the expression is ambiguous, because it can receive the distribution for one member only. In that way the proposition 'Every man or ass is a man' is true, and it means 'Every man is a man or every ass is a man', and thus it is a disjunctive proposition. In another way it can receive a distribution for both parts at the same time. In that way the proposition 'Every man or ass is a man' is false, and it is a categorical one and means 'Both man and ass are all of them a man'. In the third way a whole disjunct can receive a distribution, insofar as it comes to each member of the disjunction. In that way the proposition 'Every rational or irrational thing is an animal' is true, because the animal nature equals the disjunct 'rational or irrational'. Thus it is evident in which way a disjoined term or a whole disjunct can receive a distribution and in which way it cannot. It is also evident that in the syllogism he [the opponent] produces the major and minor are ambiguous.

Sophismata

35   As regards what has been said, there is a problem concerning the sophisma-sentence WHATEVER IS OR IS NOT, IS. Proof: the expression 'Whatever is, is' is true. Now something true can be dis-joined from anything other than what is true. Therefore the origi-nal sentence is true. There is an argument to the contrary. What-ever is or is not, is. Now Caesar is or is not. Therefore Caesar is.

Cesar est. Solutio. Prima duplex, eoquod potest esse divisa; et est sensus: 'quicquid est, est vel quicquid [*T44rb*] non est, est'. Et sic est vera, quia[3] pro altera parte; et sic est disiunctiva. Vel[4] potest esse composita, et est sensus 'quicquid[5] est vel non est, est' idest 'tam omne illud quod est quam omne illud quod non est, est'. Et sic est falsa et sic est categorica. Unde est ibi sophisma compositionis, quia composita est falsa.

36   Item. Queritur de hoc sophismate OMNIS PROPOSITIO VEL EIUS CONTRADICTORIA EST VERA. Probatio. Ista propositio[1] 'Sortes currit' vel eius contradictoria est vera. Et illa propositio 'Plato disputat' vel eius contradictoria est vera, et sic de aliis[2]. Ergo omnis propositio vel eius contradictoria est[3] vera. Contra. Omnis propositio vel eius contradictoria est[4] vera. Sed non omnis propositio est vera. Ergo omnis eius contradictoria est vera. Quod falsum est.

37   Solutio. Prima duplex, eoquod distributio potest cadere supra propositionem sumptam[1] absolute. Et sic distribuit ipsam pro qualibet particulari propositione; et sic est falsa et divisa, quia hec est disiunctiva cuius utraque pars est falsa. Vel distributio potest cadere supra propositionem non[2] absolute sumptam sed comparatam ad suam contradictoriam. Et hoc modo adhuc est duplex. Quia uno modo iste terminus disiunctus[3] 'propositio vel eius contradictoria' potest subici predicato pro utraque parte universaliter, sicut in hiis 'omne rationale vel irrationale est animal' et econverso; 'omne par vel impar est numerus' vel econverso; 'omne rectum [*P81vb*] vel curvum est linea' et econverso. Et sic[4] prima adhuc est falsa, quia hoc modo sensus est 'omnis propositio vel eius contradictoria est vera' idest 'omnes propositiones et earum[5] contradictorie[6] [*N74ra*] sunt vere insimul'[7], quod est impossibile. Alio autem modo iste terminus disiunctus[8] 'propositio vel eius contradictoria'[9] subicitur huic predicato, scilicet 'esse verum', non pro utraque parte disiunctionis insimul et universaliter, sed pro utraque indeterminate, ita quod aliquando sit veritas pro aliquibus singularibus unius partis disiunctionis, aliquando[10] pro singularibus[11] alterius[12] partis disiunctionis; et sic est vera. Ut si[13] stent sex propositiones, scilicet 'Deus est', 'homo est lapis', 'Sortes est asinus', et[14] cum istis sint earum contradictorie, tunc cum dicitur 'hec propositio "Deus est" vel eius contradictoria est vera, illa propositio, scilicet "homo est lapis" vel eius contradictoria est vera'

Solution. The original sentence is ambiguous. It can <either> be divided, and it means 'Whatever is, is, or whatever is not, is' and in this way it is true, because it is true for one part, and thus it is disjunctive, or it can be compounded, and the proposition 'Whatever is or is not, is' means 'Both all that is and all that is not, is', and in this way it is false and it is a categorical proposition. Hence we have here a fallacy of composition, because the compounded proposition is false.

36 Again, there is a problem concerning the sophisma-sentence EVERY PROPOSITION OR ITS CONTRADICTORY IS TRUE. Proof: the proposition 'Socrates is running' or its contradictory is true, the proposition 'Plato is arguing' or its contradictory is true, and so on. Therefore every proposition or its contradictory is true. There is an argument to the contrary. Every proposition or its contradictory is true. Now not every proposition is true. Therefore every proposition contradictory to it is true. And this is false.

37 Solution. The original sentence is ambiguous, because the distribution can extend to the proposition taken absolutely. In that way it distributes the proposition for any particular one, and thus it is false and divided, because this is a disjunctive proposition of which both parts are false. In another way the distribution can range over the proposition not taken absolutely but in relation to its contradictory. In this way it is still ambiguous, because in one way the disjoined term 'a proposition or its contradictory' can be made subject to the predicate for each part universally, just as in 'Every rational or irrational thing is an animal' and the other way round, 'Every even or odd thing is a number' or the other way round and 'Every straight or curved thing is a line' and the other way round. In this way the original sentence is still false, because in this way 'Every proposition or its contradictory is true' means 'All propositions and their contradictories are true at the same time', which is impossible. In another way the disjoined term 'a proposition or its contradictory' is made subject of the predicate 'to be true' not for every part of the disjunction at the same time and universally, but for each part indeterminately, so that sometimes the truth applies to the singular instances of one part of the disjunction, and sometimes to the singular instances of the other part of the disjunction. In this way it is true. For example, if there were six propositions, viz. 'God is', 'A man is a stone' and 'Socrates is an ass' and their contradictories, then when one says 'The proposition "God is" or its contradictory is true', the proposition "A man is a stone" or its contradictory is true' (and so on

(et sic de aliis tam affirmativis quam negativis, ut quelibet illarum sex accipiatur tam affirmativa[15] quam negativa in disiunctione ad suam oppositam), — aliquando est veritas ex una[16] parte disiunctionis, aliquando ex altera. Et sic probat. Et sic distribuitur 'propositio'[17] pro omni affirmativa[18] in disiunctione ad suam negativam et pro omni negativa in disiunctione ad suam affirmativam. Unde tres sunt sensus in predicta oratione[19]. Et secundum primum est ibi[20] sophisma divisionis, quia[21] tunc[22] est divisa et falsa (et[23] est tunc propositio disiunctiva). Aliis autem duobus modis est categorica. Et primo[24] eorum est falsa, secundo[25] vera.

C. DE CONIUNCTIONE COPULATIVA

38 In precedentibus dictum est de coniunctionibus[1] interrogativis et disiunctivis. Nunc autem dicendum est de hac coniunctione 'et'. Circa quam primo queritur quid significet; secundo utrum res eius sit[2] ens simpliciter vel non; tertio utrum res eius sit [*T44va*] in genere vel non; quarto queritur cuiusmodi unitas fiat[3] per hanc coniunctionem copulativam 'et'; quinto[4], cum habeat copulare diversa, queritur que sint illa[5] diversa; sexto queritur[6] propter quid, quando preponitur, geminatur.

Quid significet hec coniunctio 'et'

39 Circa primum queritur quid significet hec coniunctio 'et' quia[1]: Hec coniunctio 'et' dicitur copulativa ab actu copulandi quem exercet. Sed nulla dictio significat actum quem exercet, sicut nullum instrumentum significat actum suum. Ergo cum hec dictio 'et' exerceat copulationem, [*N74rb*] (vel actum copulandi), tunc hec coniunctio 'et' non potest significare copulationem. [*P82ra*] Item ad idem[2]. Hec coniunctio 'et' est pars orationis reperta ad copulandum ceteras partes orationis[3]. Sed cum dico quod est pars orationis reperta ad copulandum alias partes, in hoc attribuo[4] ei duo: unum est[5] quod est pars orationis, aliud est quod habet[6] ex natura sua copulare ceteras partes. Sed sua[7] significatio debetur ei per hoc quod est pars orationis,

with both the affirmative and the negative ones, so that whichever of these six is taken both as an affirmative and as a negative in disjunction with its opposite),—then sometimes the truth derives from one member of the disjunction and sometimes from the other. In this way it is proved, and 'proposition' is distributed for every affirmative one in disjunction with its negative and for every negative one in disjunction with its affirmative. Hence the expression mentioned above has three meanings: in the first sense there is a fallacy of division, because in that case it is divided and false (and then it is a disjunctive proposition), whereas in the other two ways it is a categorical proposition, and in the first way it is false, and in the second way it is true.

C. ON THE COPULATIVE CONJUNCTION

38   In the preceding we have discussed interrogative and disjunctive conjunctions. We must now discuss the conjunction '*et*' ('and'). As regards this word, there is *[1]* first a problem what it signifies, *[2]* secondly whether the 'thing' it signifies is a being *simpliciter* or not, *[3]* thirdly whether the 'thing' it signifies belongs in some category or not, *[4]* fourthly there is a problem what kind of unity is produced by the copulative conjunction 'and', *[5]* fifthly, since it must couple diverse things, there is a problem what these diverse things are, and *[6]* sixthly there is a problem why it is repeated when it is placed before one <extreme>.

What the conjunction 'and' signifies

39   *Ad [1]:* As to the first item, there is a problem what the conjunction 'and' signifies. The conjunction 'and' is called 'copulative' after the act of coupling it carries out. Now no word signifies the act it carries out, just as no instrument signifies its act. Therefore in virtue of the fact that the word 'and' carries out a coupling (or an act of coupling), therefore this conjunction cannot signify a coupling. Again, there is an argument that yields the same conclusion. The conjunction 'and' is a part of speech invented to couple the other parts of speech. Now when I say 'that is a part of speech invented to couple other parts', in that phrase I attribute two things to it: one is that it is a part of speech and the other is that by its nature it must couple the other parts. Now its signification comes to it on account of

copulatio vero[8] debetur ei ratione finis[9] ad quem est[10] et propter quem[11] inventa fuit[12]. Qui[13] scilicet finis est copulare partes alias. Ergo significatio huius[14] coniunctionis[15] 'et' non est copulatio[16]. Ergo non significat copulationem. Quod[17] concedimus.

40   Ad illud quod queritur[1], dicendum quod hec coniunctio 'et' significat comparationem[2] que[3] est <secundum> simul sive secundum[4] simultatem[5]. Et ad istam simultatem sequitur copulatio, sicut ad hoc quod dico 'non cum alio' sequitur exclusio. Unde cum dico 'Sortes et Plato sunt albi', hec[6] coniunctio 'et' dicit simultatem vel unitatem eorum[7] in albedine, et ideo copulat istos[8] respectu albedinis. Et nota quod hec coniunctio[9] 'et' non dicit simul[10] in tempore, quia sic esset hec falsa 'Adam et Noë fuerunt homines'[11], quia non fuerunt in eodem tempore, quia neque in tempore Ade[12] neque in tempore Noë[13]. Ergo non[14] dicit simul in tempore. Item ad idem. Bene[15] dicitur[16] 'ille cucurrit[17] heri et currit modo et[18] curret cras'. Sed cursus[19] hesternus[20] et hodiernus et crastinus non sunt in eodem tempore. Ergo hec coniunctio 'et' non dicit[21] simul in tempore. Quod concedimus dicentes quod hec coniunctio[22] 'et' dicit primo et per se simultatem[23] plurium subiectorum in uno accidente de pari[24] quantum est de se, vel plurium accidentium in uno subiecto, ut 'Sortes et Plato sunt albi' vel[25] 'Sortes sedet[26] et disputat'. Circa secundum et circa tertium queratur et solvatur sicut prius de hac coniunctione 'vel'.

Cuiusmodi unitas fiat per hanc coniunctionem 'et'

41   Circa quartum obicitur quia[1]: Omne[2] totum habet in se aliquam unitatem. Sed omnis terminus copulatus (ut 'Sortes et Plato') est quoddam totum. Ergo habet in se aliquam unitatem (in primo prime[3]). Sed obicitur [N74va] in contrarium quod[4] non est unum[5] genere neque unum specie neque unum numero (quia neque unum nomine vel diffinitione) neque unum proprio neque unum accidente.

its being a part of speech, whereas the coupling comes to it in virtue of the end for which and because of which it is invented. Now this end is to couple other parts. Therefore the signification of the conjunction 'and' is not to couple. Therefore it does not signify a coupling. Well, we agree with this.

40 As to the problem, the answer should be that the conjunction 'and' signifies a relationship in terms of a 'together' or togetherness, and from this togetherness follows a coupling, just as from the expression 'not with another' follows an exclusion. Hence in the expression 'Socrates and Plato are white', the conjunction 'and' indicates a togetherness or unity of them in whiteness, and therefore it couples them in respect of whiteness. Note that the conjunction 'and' does not indicate a simultaneity, because in that case the expression 'Adam and Noah were men' would be false, because they were not at the same time, that is, neither in the time of Adam nor in the time of Noah. Therefore it does not indicate a simultaneity. Again, there is an argument that yields the same conclusion. It is correct to say 'He ran yesterday, he is running now and he will run tomorrow'. However, yesterday's, today's and tomorrow's running do not occur at the same time. Therefore the conjunction 'and' does not indicate simultaneity. Well, we agree with this, saying that the conjunction 'and' primarily and in itself indicates a togetherness of more subjects in one accident on an equal level as far as it itself is concerned, or of many accidents in one subject, *e.g.* 'Socrates and Plato are white' or 'Socrates is sitting and arguing'. *Ad [2], [3]:* As to the second and third items, there may be a problem that can be solved in the same way as before regarding the conjunction '*vel*'.[11]

In what way the conjunction 'and' produces a unity

41 *Ad [4]:* As to the fourth item, there is an argument to the contrary. Every whole contains some unity. Now every coupled term (*e.g.* 'Socrates and Plato') is some sort of whole. Therefore it contains some unity (in the first mood of the first figure). There is an argument to the contrary, however, that it [*i.e.* a coupled term] is not something one *qua* genus, nor something one *qua* species, nor something numerically one (since it is not something one *qua* name or *definiens*) nor something one *qua* proprium, nor something

---

[11] Cf. above, capp. 24-27.

Ergo non habet in se aliquam unitatem. Omnes enim premisse per
se manifeste sunt. Et ideo supponantur[6].

42   Et dicendum quod 'unum' dicitur multipliciter. Quia est quoddam unum quod est[1] ex materia et forma, ut homo est ex corpore
[*T44vb*] humano (quod est eius materia) et ex anima intellectiva
(que est eius forma). Alio autem modo est unum continuatione[2], ut
linea, superficies, tempus et quodlibet continuum. Tertio autem
modo est unum insertu[3], ut in arbore ex ramo[4] unius arboris et
trunco alterius arboris fit unum per[5] insertionem. Alio autem modo
est unum contiguatione[6], sicut sunt duo corpora inter que non est
medium, sicut contiguatur digitus digito quando[7] nichil[8] est in
medio. Alio autem modo est unum aggregatione, ut acervus lapi-
dum. Alio autem modo est unum collatione[9], sicut ex carne et osse
fit unum per quoddam medium quod non[10] est omnino caro neque
omnino os, sicut sunt nervi et cartillagines. Dico ergo quod hec
coniunctio 'et' facit unitatem aggregationis et non aliam ex predictis.
Unde terminus copulatus[11] est unum aggregatione[12].

43   Ad illud autem quod obicit[1] in contrarium (dividendo unum
per unum genere et unum specie et sic de aliis), dicendum quod
unum[2] ibi non dividitur quoad omnes suas significationes, sed
tantum quoad illas[3] secundum quas sumuntur[4] quatuor predicata[5] in
Topicis, et annexa eorum. Quatuor autem predicata de quibus agitur
in *Topicis* hec sunt: diffinitio, proprium, genus, accidens; annexa
eorum sunt alia predicata reducibilia ad hec. Ut 'idem genere'
reducitur ad genus et etiam differentia reducitur ad genus; comparationes vero accidentis[6] (ut 'melior', 'fortior', 'iustior', 'utilior' et 'peior',
et sic[7] de aliis) reducuntur ad predicatum de accidente; idem autem
simpliciter et diversum reducuntur ad predicatum [*N74vb*] de[8] diffinitione.

44   [*P82va*] Item. Nota quod licet hec coniunctio 'et' debeat
copulare diversa, non tamen copulat quelibet diversa, quia non potest
copulare adiectivum substantivo nec econverso (ut 'homo et albus

one *qua* accident. Therefore it does not contain some unity. For all premises are clear in themselves. That is why they should be assumed.

42   The answer should be that 'one' is said in many ways. [1] One type is something one that consists of matter and form, *e.g.* a man consists of a human body (which is his matter) and of an intellective soul (which is its form). [2] In another way there is something one by continuation, *e.g.* a line, a surface, time, and any other continuum. [3] In a third way there is something one by insertion, *e.g.* the branch of one tree and the trunk of another tree is made into one thing by insertion [grafting]. [4] In another way there is a something one by proximity, such as there are two bodies between which there is nothing in between and a finger is proximate to a finger when there is nothing in between. [5] In another way there is something one by joining together, *e.g.* a heap of stones. [6] In another way there is something one by a bringing together, such as from flesh and bones one thing is made through some intermediary thing which is neither entirely flesh nor entirely bone, such as muscles and cartilages. Well, I say that the conjunction 'and' produces a unity by a bringing together [[6]] and not in any other of the ways mentioned above. Therefore a coupled term is one by a bringing together.

43   As to the argument to the contrary[12] (by dividing something one into something one *qua* genus, something one *qua* species and so on), the answer should be that in that argument 'one' was not divided according to all its significations, but only those according to which the four predicates in the *Topica* and the ones adjoined to them are taken. The four predicates the *Topica* deals with are: *definiens*, proprium, genus, and accident;[13] the ones adjoined to them are other predicates reducible to the four predicates mentioned. For example, 'the same *qua* genus' is reduced to 'genus' and also 'difference' is reduced to 'genus'; the comparatives of an accident (*e.g.* 'better', 'stronger', 'more just', 'more useful', 'worse', and so on) are reduced to the predicate that contains the accident in question; 'the same *simpliciter*' and 'diverse' are reduced to the predicate that contains the *definiens* in question.[14]

44   Furthermore, note that although the conjunction 'and' must couple diverse things, it nevertheless does not couple just any kind of diverse things, because it cannot couple a substantive to an

---

[12] Cf. above, cap. 41.
[13] Aristotle, *Topica* VI, IV and II, respectively.
[14] Cf. Aristotle, *Topica* VII.

currit') propter hoc quod de¹ se dicit associationem aliquorum de²
pari. Unde equaliter respicit utrumque extremorum. Et ideo primo et
per se vel copulat duas substantias³ uni accidenti vel duo⁴ accidentia
uni substantie, ut 'Sortes et Plato sunt⁵ albi', 'homo⁶ legit et disputat'⁷.

Quam diversitatem exigat hec coniunctio 'et'

45 Circa quintum queritur quia: Videtur iam¹ ex predictis quod
hec coniunctio 'et' non possit copulare quelibet diversa, quia non
potest copulare adiectivum substantivo², ut prius patuit. Ergo non
copulat quelibet diversa. Et propter hoc queritur quam diversitatem
exigat hec³ coniunctio⁴ 'et'. Et dicendum, sicut iam patet ex⁵ predictis, quod exigit⁶ diversitatem substantiarum de⁷ pari se habentium
vel etiam⁸ accidentium⁹ vel habitudinum. Et universaliter debet
copulare diversa de¹⁰ pari se habentia, ut 'Sortes et Plato' vel¹¹ 'albus
et niger', vel 'ab illo et¹² in illo'; et sic de aliis habitudinibus, acciden-
tibus¹³ et substantiis.

46 Sed tunc queritur utrum sufficiat ei diversitas suppositorum
cum unitate significationis, ut 'homo et homo currunt'¹. Et videtur
quod sic quia: Omne² plurale geminat singulare in terminis [*T45va*]
communibus (ut removeantur signa universalia, nam 'omnis' non
geminat suum singulare). Sed bene dicitur 'homines sunt'. Ergo
bene dicitur³ 'homo et homo sunt'. Et similiter bene dicitur 'homines currunt'. Ergo bene dicitur³ 'homo et homo currunt'; et sic de
aliis⁴. Item ad idem. Dicit Boetius in libro suo *De Trinitate* quod talia
sunt predicata qualia subiecta permiserint. Quod probat quia: Cum
dicitur 'homo est iustus', 'Deus⁵ est iustus', hoc nomen 'iustus' predicat de homine iustitiam accidentalem, de⁶ Deo autem predicat
divinam⁷ essentiam. Econverso tamen potest dici quod talia sunt⁸
subiecta qualia permiserint predicata. Sed cum dicitur 'homo et
homo currunt', predicatum exigit quod iste terminus 'homo' inde-
finite⁹ sumptus teneatur pro diversis. Sed si pro diversis teneatur,
bene dicitur. [*N75ra*] Ergo¹⁰ recte dicitur 'homo et homo currunt'.

adjective nor the other way round (*e.g.* '*A man and white is running', and the reason for this is that in itself it indicates an association of things on an equal level. Thus it is equally related to both extremes. Hence primarily and in itself it couples either two substances to one accident or two accidents to one substance, *e.g.* 'Socrates and Plato are white' and 'A man is reading and arguing'.

What diversity the conjunction 'and' requires

45 *Ad [5]:* As to the fifth item, there is a problem. It may be clear already from what has been said that the conjunction 'and' cannot couple just any kind of diverse things, because it cannot couple an adjective to a substantive, as has become evident earlier. Therefore it does not couple just any kind of diverse things, and that is why there is a problem what diversity the conjunction 'and' requires. The answer should be, as is already evident from what has been said, that it requires a diversity of substances that are on an equal level or even of accidents or of relationships. Generally speaking it must couple diverse things that are on an equal level, *e.g.* 'Socrates and Plato', 'white and black' or 'from him and in him', and so on as regards other relationships, accidents and substances.

46 However, then there is a problem whether a diversity of *supposita* together with a unity of signification is sufficient for this, *e.g.* 'A man and a man are running'. It may be argued that this is the case, because every plural doubles its singular as far as common terms are concerned (to remove universal signs, for 'every' does not double its singular). Now it is correct to say 'Men are'. Therefore it is correct to say 'A man and a man are'. Likewise it is correct to say 'Men are running'. Therefore it is correct to say 'A man and a man are running' and so on. Again, there is an argument that yields the same conclusion. Boethius says[15] in his book *On the Trinity* that such are the predicates as the subjects allow for. He proves this as follows. In the expressions 'A man is just' and 'God is just', the noun 'just' predicates accidental justice of a man, whereas of God it predicates the divine essence. Conversely, however, one can say that such are the subjects as the predicates allow for. Yet in the expression 'A man and a man are running', the predicate requires that the term 'man' taken indefinitely apply to diverse ones. Now if it applies to diverse ones, therefore the expression is in order. Therefore it is correct to say 'A man and a man are running'. Well, we agree with this.

---

15 Boethius, *De trinitate*, p. 156(4-5), ed. Peiper (=1252A5-6 ed. Migne).

Quod concedimus. Sciendum[11] autem quod convenientius copulat
diversa supposita[12] et diversa significata de[13] pari se habentia [*P42vb*]
(ut 'homo et equus currunt') quam diversa supposita cum unitate
significationis (ut 'homo et homo currunt').

Propter quid, quando preponitur, geminetur

47 Circa sextum queritur quia[1]: Omnis copulativa coniunctio, nisi
sit encletica, equaliter se habet ad utrumque extremorum. Ergo[2] hec
coniunctio 'et' equaliter se habet ad utrumque extremorum. Sed
quando preponitur uni, magis se habet ad illud cui preponitur. Ergo
numquam debet[3] preponi. Sed si non preponitur, non geminatur.
Ergo numquam debet geminari. Et dicendum quod hec[4] coniunctio
'et' equaliter respicit[5] utrumque extremorum. Et ideo quando[6] preponitur uni extremorum: quia[7] magis se habet ad illud cui preponitur,
propter[8] hoc oportet quod preponatur alteri, ut equaliter se habeat ad
utrumque extremorum. Et hec est[9] causa propter[10] quam quando
preponitur, geminatur.

Sophismata

48 Secundum predicta queritur de hoc sophismate OMNE NON-
ANIMAL QUOD ET SORTES SUNT DUO, NON EST SORTES.
Probatio. Hoc non-animal quod et Sortes sunt duo, non est Sortes
(demonstrato ligno). Illud non-animal quod et Sortes sunt duo, non
est Sortes (demonstrato lapide), et sic de aliis. Ergo omne non-
animal quod et Sortes sunt duo, non est Sortes. Contra. Omne non-
animal quod et Sortes sunt duo, non est Sortes. Ergo omne aliud
quam animal quod et Sortes sunt duo, non est Sortes (locus[1] a
convertibili, quia 'non-animal' et 'aliud quam animal' equipollent).
Sed Sortes est aliud quam animal quod et Sortes sunt duo. Ergo Sortes
non est Sortes (in quarto prime).

Nevertheless, one should know that it couples diverse *supposita* and diverse significates that are on an equal level more harmoniously (*e.g.* 'A man and a horse are running') than it couples diverse *supposita* that are one in their signification (*e.g.* 'A man and a man are running').

Why the copulative conjunction is repeated when it is placed before one extreme

47 *Ad [6]:* As to the sixth item, there is a problem. Every copulative conjunction, unless it is enclitic, is equally related to both extremes. Therefore the conjunction 'and' is equally related to both extremes. Now when it is placed before one extreme, it is more related to the one before which it is placed. Therefore it must never be placed before one extreme. Now if it is not placed before one extreme, it is not repeated. Therefore it must never be repeated. The answer should be that the conjunction 'and' equally relates to both extremes. Therefore, when it is placed before one of the extremes, <it should be said that> because it relates more to the one before which it is placed, it is therefore necessary that it be placed before the other one <as well> so that it equally relates to both extremes. This is the reason why, when it is placed before <an extreme>, it is repeated.

Sophismata

48 As regards what has been said, there is a problem concerning the sophisma-sentence EVERY NON-ANIMAL WHICH WITH SOCRATES CONSTITUTE TWO, IS NOT SOCRATES. Proof: this non-animal which with Socrates constitute two, is not Socrates (pointing to a piece of wood), this non-animal which with Socrates constitute two, is not Socrates (pointing to a stone), and so on. Therefore every non-animal which with Socrates constitute two, is not Socrates. There is an argument to the contrary. Every non-animal which with Socrates constitute two, is not Socrates. Therefore everything other than an animal which with Socrates constitute two, is not Socrates (the topic 'from a convertible', because 'non-animal' and 'something other than an animal' are equivalent). Now Socrates is something other than an animal which with Socrates constitute two. Therefore Socrates is not Socrates (in the fourth mood of the first figure).

49 Solutio. Prima simpliciter est vera. Et improbatio non valet. Nec est sillogismus[1] quem facit, sed[2] paralogismus, quia maior et minor sunt duplices. Quia hec[3] propositio que erat maior (scilicet[4] 'omne aliud quam animal quod et Sortes sunt duo, non est Sortes') est duplex, eoquod hoc relativum 'quod' potest referre hunc terminum 'aliud' vel hunc terminum 'animal'. Si autem referat istum[5] terminum 'aliud'[6], sic est maior vera et est sensus: 'omne aliud ab animali quod (scilicet aliud ab animali) et Sortes sunt duo, non est Sortes'. Et hoc est verum, quia nichil est aliud[7] ab animali nisi lapis et lignum et cetera inanimata omnia, quorum nullum [*N75rb*] est Sortes. Si autem referat istum terminum 'animal'[8], sic maior est falsa et est sensus: 'omne aliud quam animal quod (scilicet animal) [*P83ra*] et Sortes sunt duo, non est Sortes'. Hoc autem[9] falsum est, quia Sortes non facit numerum secum, sed omnis alii homines faciunt numerum cum Sorte, et alia animalia. Et ita Sortes est aliud a quolibet [*T45rb*] animali faciente numerum cum Sorte. Et sic Sortes[10] comprehenditur in[11] hac distributione 'omne aliud quam animal quod (scilicet animal[12]) *etc.*', secundum quod hoc relativum 'quod' refert istum terminum 'animal'. Unde hoc modo maior dicit quod Sortes non est Sortes. Econverso autem dicendum est de minori. Et[13] ut melius pateat falsitas maioris in sensu secundo, ponatur quod Sortes sit et nullum aliud animal sit[14] nisi Plato et unus equus. Tunc nullum aliud animal est quod[15] faciat numerum cum Sorte nisi Plato et ille equus. Et Sortes aliud est ab illis duobus. Et sic hec est falsa 'omne aliud quam illa[16] duo animalia que (scilicet animalia[17]) faciunt numerum cum Sorte, non est Sortes'.

50 Item. Queritur de hoc sophismate OMNE[1] ENUNTIABILE DIFFERT AB ALIQUO ET SUUM OPPOSITUM EST COMPONIBILE[2] ILLI. Probatio. Hoc enuntiabile 'Sortem esse' differt ab aliquo et suum oppositum est componibile illi, quia differt ab hoc enuntiabili 'equum currere' et suum oppositum, scilicet 'Sortem non esse', est componibile illi, quia potest stare cum illo: simul enim possunt esse vera hec dua enuntiabilia, scilicet 'Sortem non esse' et 'equum currere'. Istud enuntiabile, scilicet 'hominem legere', differt ab aliquo et suum oppositum est componibile illi, et sic de aliis. Ergo prima vera. Contra. Hec est quedam copulativa cuius utraque pars est falsa. Ergo[3] ipsa[4] est falsa. Solutio. Prima falsa. Et probatio peccat

49   Solution. The original sentence is *simpliciter* true. The disproof
is not valid, nor is it a syllogism it produces, but rather a paralogism,
because the major and the minor are ambiguous. The proposition
that was the major (*viz.* 'Everything other than an animal which
with Socrates constitute two, is not Socrates') is ambiguous, because
the relative 'which' can refer to the word 'animal' or the word
'other'. Now if it refers to the word 'other', the major is true and it
means 'Everything other than an animal which [*viz.* that thing
other than an animal] with Socrates constitute two is not Socrates'.
This is true, because there is nothing other than an animal except a
stone or a piece of wood and all other inanimate things, not one of
which is Socrates. If, on the other hand, it refers to the term
'animal', in that way the major is false and it means 'Everything
other than an animal which [*viz.* that animal] with Socrates constitute two, is not Socrates'. This, however, is false, because Socrates
does not constitute a multitude with himself, but all other men
constitute a multitude with Socrates, and so do all other animals.
Thus Socrates is something other than any animal whatsoever
which constitutes a multitude with Socrates. In this way Socrates is
understood in the distribution 'Everything other than an animal
which (*viz.* an animal) *etc.*', insofar as the relative 'which' refers to
the term 'animal'. Hence in this way the major indicates that Socrates is not Socrates. The opposite goes for the minor, however. And, in
order that the falsity of the major in the second sense be more
evident, let us suppose that Socrates exists and that there is no other
animal than Plato and one horse, in that case there is no other
animal that constitutes a multitude with Socrates than Plato and that
horse, and Socrates is something other than these two. Thus the
proposition 'Every animal other than these two animals that constitute a multitude with Socrates, is not Socrates' is false.

50   Furthermore, there is a problem concerning the sophisma-
sentence EVERY STATEABLE DIFFERS FROM SOME STATEABLE
AND ITS OPPOSITE CAN BE UNITED WITH IT. Proof: the stateable
'that Socrates is' differs from some stateable and its opposite can be
united with it, because it differs from the stateable 'that a horse is
running', and its opposite, *viz.* 'that Socrates is not', can be united
with it, because it can obtain with it: for the two stateables 'that Socrates is not' and 'that a horse is running' can be true at the same time.
The stateable 'that a man is reading' differs from some stateable and
its opposite can be united with it, and so on. Therefore the original
sentence is true. There is an argument to the contrary. This is a
copulative proposition of which each part is false. Therefore it is false

secundum figuram dictionis a pluribus <suppositionibus> determinatis ad unam[5] huius termini 'aliquo'. Et etiam est ibi *accidens* per
quandam regulam in *Distributionibus* habitam quia, quamvis hec
distributio 'omne enuntiabile' secundum se convertibiliter sequatur
ad suas partes singulares omnes, tamen secundum quod partes stant
sub hoc predicato quod est 'differre ab aliquo', sic non sequitur ad
illas, sed est ibi *accidens*.

D DE HAC DICTIONE 'NISI'

Introductio

51 Loquentes communiter ponunt quod hec dictio[1] 'nisi' per se et
proprie tenetur consecutive et non exceptive. [*N75va*] Et [*P83rb*] ideo
circa hanc dictionem 'nisi' primo queratur utrum possit teneri exceptive vel non; secundo queratur utrum hec dictio 'nisi' et hec oratio 'si non' equipolleant ad invicem, cum hec dictio 'nisi' compona-
tur ex 'si' et 'non'; tertio queritur quot sint genera dictionum instantivarum et qualiter differant in genere; quarto queritur quare potius ex
hoc adverbio negandi 'non' per compositionem fiat dictio instantiva
que[2] est exceptiva quam alia dictio instantiva alterius generis; quinto
queritur quare hec dictio 'nisi', secundum quod est consecutiva, vult
semper adiungi verbo subiunctivi modi.

Utrum hec dictio 'nisi' possit teneri exceptive

52 Circa primum obicitur quod[1] aliquando teneatur exceptive quia:
Instantia[2] aliquando fit in toto, ut 'Sortes currit', 'nullus homo currit';
hic enim[3] fit instantia in toto contra partem; aliquando[4] fit instantia
in parte contra[5] totum, ut[6] cum dicitur 'omnis homo currit', 'Sortes
non currit' vel 'quidam homo non currit'; hic enim fertur instantia

itself. Solution. The original sentence is false and the proof commits the fallacy of figure of speech by reasoning from many determinate suppositions to one determinate supposition of the term 'some stateable'. Moreover, it commits the fallacy of accident on account of a rule discussed in *On distributions:*[16] although the distribution 'every stateable' as such convertibly follows from all its singular parts, nevertheless insofar as its parts fall under the predicate 'to differ from some stateble', in that way it does not follow from them, but in that case there is a fallacy of accident.

D. ON THE WORD '*NISI*' ('EXCEPT', 'UNLESS')

Introduction

51   According to common usage, one asserts that the word '*nisi*' as such and is properly understood consecutively and not exceptively. And therefore regarding the word '*nisi*' one should *[1]* first raise the problem whether it can be understood exceptively or not, *[2]* secondly whether the word '*nisi*' and the expression 'if not' (*si non*) are mutually equivalent, since the word '*nisi*' is a combination of '*si*' ('if') and '*non*' ('not'), *[3]* thirdly there is a problem how many are the kinds of counter-instantive words and how they differ in kind, *[4]* fourthly there is a problem why from the adverb of negation '*non*' used in combination rather a counter-instantive word is made that is exceptive, than another counter-instantive word of another kind, *[5]* fifthly there is a problem why the word '*nisi*', insofar as it is consecutive, always wishes to be adjoined to a verb in the subjunctive mood.

Whether the word 'nisi' can be taken exceptively

52   *Ad [1]:* As to the first item, there is an objection that sometimes it is understood exceptively. A counter-instance is sometimes produced in <adducing> a whole, *e.g.* <against> 'Socrates is running': 'No man is running', for this type of counter-instance is produced in <adducing> a whole against the part, whereas sometimes a counter-instance is produced in <adducing> a part against the whole, *e.g.* <against> 'Every man is running': 'Socrates is not running' or 'Some man is not running', for here the counter-instance is produced in

---

[16]   See Petrus Hispanus, *Tractatus* XII, capp. 11-12, pp. 217(17)-218(5), ed. De Rijk.

in parte contra totum. Sed posito quod Sortes currat et nichil aliud, tunc hec est vera 'nullus homo currit nisi Sortes'. Sed ibi est instantia extrahendo[7] partem a toto. Sed non est possibile ferre instantiam extrahendo[8] partem a toto nisi per dictionem exceptivam. Ergo hec dictio 'nisi' in predicta oratione tenetur exceptive. Item[9] ad [*T45va*] idem. Cum dicitur 'nullus homo currit nisi iste[10] asinus', hec oratio est impropria. Sed si hec dictio 'nisi' teneatur consecutive, esset propria sed esset falsa. Ergo hec dictio 'nisi' non tenetur ibi consecutive. Sed tenetur consecutive vel exceptive. Ergo tenetur exceptive. Item ad idem. Consequentia est duplex[11]. Quia[12] quedam est consequentia simplex[13], ut 'si homo currit, animal currit'. Alia autem est consequentia *ut nunc*, ut 'si veneris mecum[14], ibo ad ecclesiam'. Sed ex nulla earum licet inferre[15] consequens vel[16] antecedens. Quia ex prima consequentia non sequitur 'ergo homo currit' (quod est antecedens) neque sequitur 'ergo animal currit' (quod est consequens). Et ex altera consequentia, que est consequentia *ut nunc*, non[17] sequitur 'ergo venies[18] mecum' (quod est antecedens) neque[19] sequitur 'ergo ibo ad ecclesiam' (quod est consequens). Ergo ex nulla earum sequitur consequens neque antecedens. Sed cum dicitur 'nullus homo currit[20] nisi Sortes', [*N75vb*] ex hac bene sequitur 'ergo Sortes currit'. Ergo hec dictio 'nisi' non tenetur ibi consecutive. Et tenetur[21] consecutive vel exceptive. Ergo tenetur exceptive.

53   Quod concedimus dicentes quod [*P83va*] aliquando tenetur exceptive, ut in predictis orationibus et consimilibus, et non semper[1] tenetur consecutive. Sed contra. Hec dictio[2] 'nisi' componitur ex 'si' et 'non'. Sed neque 'si' neque 'non' sunt dictiones exceptive neque habent naturam[3] exceptionis. Ergo hec[4] dictio 'nisi' non habebit naturam[5] exceptionis, cum compositum non habeat naturam aliquam[6] nisi a suis componentibus. Ergo hec[7] dictio 'nisi' numquam tenetur exceptive. Et tenetur exceptive vel consecutive. Ergo tenetur consecutive. Item. Omnis dictio exceptiva dicit habitudinem partis ad totum. Sed nulla coniunctio dicit habitudinem partis ad totum.

\<adducing\> a part against the whole. Now supposing that Socrates is running and nothing else, then the proposition 'No man is running except (*nisi*) Socrates' is true. Now in this case there is a counter-instance by extracting a part from a whole. Now it is only possible to produce a counter-instance by extracting a part from a whole by an exceptive word. Therefore the word '*nisi*' in the sentence just mentioned is understood exceptively. Again, there is an argument that yields the same conclusion. When one says 'No man is running except that ass', the expression is improper. Now if the word '*nisi*' were understood consecutively, it would be proper, but false. Therefore the word '*nisi*' is not understood consecutively in this case. Now it is \<either\> understood consecutively or exceptively. Therefore it is understood exceptively. Again, there is an argument that yields the same conclusion. There are two kinds of consequence: one is an absolute consequence, *e.g.* 'If a man is running, an animal is running'; the other is a consequence *as-of-now*, *e.g.* 'If you will come with me, I will go to church'. Now from none of these one is allowed to infer the consequent or the antecedent. For from the first consequence it does not follow 'Therefore a man is running' (which is the antecedent) nor does it follow 'Therefore an animal is running' (which is the consequent), and from the other consequence, which is a consequence *as-of-now*, it does not follow 'Therefore you will come with me' (which is the antecedent) nor does it follow 'Therefore I will go to church' (which is the consequent). Therefore from none of these does the consequent or the antecedent follow. On the other hand, when one says 'No man is running except Socrates', from this 'Therefore Socrates is running' is a good inference. Therefore in this case the word '*nisi*' is not understood consecutively. Now it is understood \<either\> consecutively or exceptively. Therefore it is understood exceptively.

53   Well, we agree with this saying that sometimes it is understood exceptively, as in the propositions mentioned above and in similar ones, and so it is not always understood consecutively. However, there is an argument to the contrary. The word '*nisi*' is a combination of '*si*' and '*non*'. Now '*si*' and '*non*' are not exceptive words, nor do they have the nature of an exception. Therefore the word '*nisi*' will not have the nature of an exception, since a combination only has some feature from its components. Therefore '*nisi*' is never understood exceptively. Now it is \<either\> understood exceptively or consecutively. Therefore it is understood consecutively. Furthermore, every exceptive word indicates a relationship of a part to a whole. Now no conjunction indicates a relationship of a part to a

Ergo nulla coniunctio est dictio exceptiva (in secundo secunde). Ergo hec dictio 'nisi' non est dictio[8] exceptiva. Sed[9] est exceptiva vel consecutiva. Ergo est consecutiva.

54   Et dicendum, sicut dictum est prius[1], quod hec dictio 'nisi' aliquando tenetur exceptive, aliquando consecutive. Ad illud autem quod obicit in contrarium, dicendum quod, sicut obicit[2], hec dictio 'nisi' componitur ex 'si' et 'non'. Sed hoc adverbium 'non' semper fert instantiam ei[3] cui adiungitur, cum semper[4] contradicat ei. Et sic est dictio instantiva et fert instantiam aliquando in toto, aliquando in parte, sicut diximus prius. Sed per compositionem[5] trahitur[6] ad instantiam que est in parte, extrahendo partem a toto. Et hoc sufficit ad dictionem exceptivam, ut 'nullus homo[7] nisi Sortes'. Et ideo hec dictio 'nisi' aliquando tenetur exceptive, aliquando consecutive. Et sic patet quod, quamvis hoc adverbium 'non'[8] non[9] sit dictio exceptiva, habet tamen naturam instantie[10], que (scilicet natura instantiva) per compositionem[11] trahitur[12] ad naturam[13] dictionum exceptivarum in hac dictione 'nisi'. Ad secundum quod obicit in contrarium, dicendum quod non sillogizat in secundo secunde, sed potius paralogizat, quia minor paralogismi predicti est [*N76ra*] duplex, scilicet hec 'nulla coniunctio dicit habitudinem partis ad totum', eoquod quedam sunt coniunctiones que habent in se naturam duplicem. Sicut ille coniunctiones que sunt composite ex coniunctione et ex aliis partibus orationis, ut hec coniunctio 'quapropter', que est composita ex hoc nomine 'qua' et ex hac prepositione 'propter'; et sic intellectus eius constituitur ex intellectibus illarum[14] dictionum. Hec autem coniunctio 'nisi' composita est, ut dictum est, ex 'non' et 'si'. Unde habet in se naturam instantie que est secundum partem, ut dictum fuit prius. [*T45vb*] Et per[15] hoc dicit habitudinem[16] partis ad totum[17]. Et sic habet in se duplicem naturam, scilicet[18] naturam instantivam ratione[19] adverbii ex quo componitur, et naturam consecutivam[20] ratione coniunctionis, unde dicitur coniunctio consecutiva[21].

whole. Therefore no conjunction is an exceptive word (and this is a syllogism in the second mood of the second figure). Therefore the word '*nisi*' is not an exceptive word. Now it is <either> exceptive or consecutive. Therefore it is consecutive.

54 The answer should be, as was said before, that the word 'except' is sometimes understood exceptively and sometimes consecutively. As to the argument to the contrary, the answer should be that, just as it was argued to the contrary, the word '*nisi*' is a combination of '*si*' and '*non*'. Now the adverb '*non*' always produces a counter-instance against that to which it is adjoined, because it always contradicts it. In this way it is a counter-instantive word and it sometimes produces a counter-instance in <adducing> a whole, and sometimes in <adducing> a part, as we have said before. Now in virtue of the combination it is reduced to <be> a counter-instance which adduces a part, by extracting a part from a whole, and this suffices for there being an exceptive word, *e.g.* 'No man except Socrates'. Therefore the word 'except' is sometimes understood exceptively, sometimes consecutively. Thus it is evident that, although the adverb 'not' is not an exceptive word, it nevertheless has a counter-instantive nature, which (*viz.* the counter-instantive nature) in the word '*nisi*' via the combination is confined to the nature that belongs to exceptive words. As to the second argument to the contrary, the answer should be that it is not a syllogism in the second mood of the second figure, but rather it is a paralogism. For the minor of the paralogism just mentioned, *viz.* 'No conjunction indicates a relationship of a part to a whole', is ambiguous, because there are some conjunctions that have a twofold nature. This is the case in the ones that are combinations of a conjunction and other parts of speech, *e.g.* the conjunction '*quapropter*' ('wherefore'), which is a combination the word '*qua*' ('which') and '*propter*' ('in view of'), and so its notion is constituted of the notions of these words. Now the conjunction '*nisi*' is a combination of '*non*' and '*si*', as has been said. Hence it has the nature of a counter-instance that concerns a part, as has been said before. That is why it indicates a relationship of a part to a whole. Thus it has in it a double nature, *viz.* a counter-instantive nature on account of the adverb it is made up of, and a consecutive nature *qua* conjunction, on account of which it is called a consecutive conjunction.

Utrum 'nisi' et 'si non' equipolleant ad invicem

55 Circa secundum nota quod, sicut patet ex predictis[1], hec dictio 'nisi' aliquando tenetur exceptive, aliquando consecutive. Et secundum quod tenetur consecutive, hec dictio[2] 'nisi' et hec oratio 'si non' equipollent, ut 'non currit nisi moveatur' idest 'non currit si non moveatur'. Secundum autem quod hec dictio 'nisi' tenetur exceptive, tunc[3] significat aliud quam hec oratio 'si non' et non significat idem, cum tunc significet habitudinem partis ad totum, ut 'non cum[4] hoc'; sicut enim dictio exclusiva significat hoc <totum> 'non cum alio', similiter econverso dictio exceptiva significat hoc[5] totum 'non cum hoc'.

Quot sint genera dictionum instantivarum

56 Circa tertium nota quod tria sunt genera dictionum instantivarum. Quia quedam sunt exclusive; et iste instant excludendo. Alie sunt exceptive; et iste instant excipiendo. Alie sunt contradictorie sive contradicentes; et per istas fit instantia contradicendo. Nota etiam quod in genere sic differunt[1] quia[2] exclusive instant semper in toto excludendo[3] ipsum (ut 'solus Sortes'[4]), exceptive vero instant semper in parte, extrahendo[5] partem a toto (ut 'nullus homo nisi Sortes'); contradictorie vel contradicentes instant [*N76rb*] indifferenter aliquando in parte, aliquando in toto, removendo aliquid a toto[6] vel a parte[7] (ut 'quidam homo currit, nullus homo currit'; 'omnis homo currit; quidam homo non currit').

De compositione huius dictionis 'nisi'

57 Circa quartum obicitur quia[1]: Cum hec dictio 'non' intelligatur in qualibet dictione instantiva (ut in exclusivis et in exceptivis dictionibus et[2] in contradicentibus) et ita[3] sit principium[4] omnium earum, ergo, sicut per compositionem[5] ex[6] ea fit dictio exceptiva, sic[7]

Whether 'nisi' and 'si non' are mutually equivalent

55 *Ad [2]:* As to the second item, note that, as is evident from what has been said above,[17] the conjunction '*nisi*' is sometimes understood exceptively and sometimes consecutively. According as it is understood consecutively, the word '*nisi*' and the expression '*si non*' are equivalent, *e.g.* 'He is not running unless (*nisi*) he is moving', that is, 'He is not running if he is not (*si non*) moving'. However, according as the word '*nisi*' is understood exceptively, then it signifies something other than the expression '*si non*' and it does not signify the same, since in that case it signifies a relationship of a part to a whole, *e.g.* 'not with this'. For just as an exclusive word signifies the whole expression 'not with another', likewise an exceptive word signifies the whole expression 'not with this'.

How many are the kinds of counter-instantive words

56 *Ad [3]:* As to the third item, note that there are three kinds of counter-instantive words. [1] Some are exclusive, and these produce a counter-instance by excluding. [2] Others are exceptive, and these produce a counter-instance by making an exception. [3] Others are contradictory or contradicting, and these produce a counter-instance by contradicting. Note also that they are generically different to the extent that exclusives always produce a counter-instance in <adducing> a whole by excluding it (*e.g.* 'only Socrates'), exceptives always produce a counter-instance in <adducing> a part by excluding a part from a whole (*e.g.* 'no man except Socrates') and contradictory or contradicting words produce a counter-instance in either way, sometimes in <adducing> a part and sometimes in <adducing> a whole, by removing something from a whole or a part (*e.g.* 'Some man is running'–'No man is running' and 'Every man is running'–'Some man is not running').

On the composition found in the word 'nisi'

57 *Ad [4]:* As to the fourth item, there is an argument to the contrary. It is because the word 'not' is understood in any counter-instantive word whatsoever (*viz.* in exclusive, exceptive and contradicting words) and thus is the principle of them all, that therefore,

---

17 Cf. above, capp. 53-54.

etiam ex ea debet fieri dictio instantiva alterius generis, ut exclusiva. Et dicendum quod non est idem modus intelligendi hanc dictionem 'non' in qualibet[8] dictione instantiva. Unde non est uno modo principium omnium dictionum instantivarum. [*P84ra*] Quia dupliciter est una dictio principium alterius, quia uno modo per impositionem, alio[9] modo per compositionem. Unde dico quod in dictionibus exclusivis per impositionem earum intelligitur negatio, quia 'tantum' et 'solus' ex sua impositione significant 'non[10] cum alio'. Et ita[11] iste dictiones exceptive 'preter', 'preterquam' similiter habent per[12] impositionem negationem[13] de intellectu suo. Sed iste dictiones[14] contradicentes 'nullus', 'nichil', 'neuter' et etiam hec dictio[15] exceptiva 'nisi' per compositionem habent negationem[16] de intellectu suo. Et sic patet quod non est idem modus cointelligendi[17] negationem in omnibus dictionibus instantivis. Unde non oportet, si in quibusdam est per compositionem, quod[18] in aliis sit similiter per compositionem.

58 Item. Queritur quare ex hoc adverbio 'non' et ex hac coniunctione 'si' potius[1] fiat dictio exceptiva per compositionem quam exclusiva, cum hoc adverbium 'non'[2] sit instantivum[3] et instantia repperiatur tam in exclusivis[4] quam in exceptivis[5], quamvis differenter[6]. Et dicendum quod hoc adverbium 'non' negativum est, quod[7] negat; et[8] per ordinationem[9] ipsius [*T46ra*] ad[10] hanc dictionem 'si' intelligitur adversatio. Unde[11] in hac dictione 'nisi' intelligitur negatio et adversatio. Et propter[12] hoc est dictio exceptiva, quia adversatur preiacenti[13] in aliqua parte ipsius.

59 Item. Cum hec[1] dictio 'nisi' semper sit composita ex 'non'[2] et 'si' et [*N76va*] aliquando sit exceptiva, aliquando vero consecutiva, oportet ergo quod diversimode fiat compositio huius dictionis 'nisi' ex suis componentibus. Quod concedimus dicentes quod quando hec dictio 'nisi' est consecutiva, consecutio cadit supra negationem; et tunc consecutio est completiva huius dictionis 'nisi'. Et tunc hec dictio 'nisi' secundum Priscianum continetur sub coniunctione continuativa[3] et secundum Donatum sub coniunctione causali. Ut 'non

just as by combining it an exceptive word is produced, in the same way a counter-instantive word of another kind, *viz.* an exclusive, must be produced from it. The answer should be that the way of understanding this word [*viz.* '*non*'] is not the same in any counter-instantive word whatsoever. Hence it is not in one way the principle of all counter-instantive words. For one word is the principle of another in two ways: in one way by imposition and in another way by combination. Hence I say that in exclusive words one understands a negation in virtue of their imposition, for it is in virtue of their imposition that 'only' and 'alone' signify 'not with another', and likewise the word '*preter*' and '*preterquam*' ('except') have a negation as part of their notion in virtue of their imposition. On the other hand, the contradicting words '*nullus*' ('no one'), '*nichil*' ('nothing'), '*neuter*' ('neither') and also the exceptive word '*nisi*' have a negation as part of their notion in virtue their being combined. Thus it is evident that the way of co-understanding a negation is not the same in all counter-instantive words. Hence if it [*i.e.* a negation] is found in certain words in virtue of their being combined, it is not necessary that it likewise be found in others in the same way in virtue of their being combined.

58   Furthermore, there is a problem why by combining the adverb '*non*' and the conjunction '*si*' one produces an exceptive word rather than an exclusive word. For the adverb '*non*' is counter-instantive, and a counter-instance is found in both exclusive and exceptive words, although in different ways. The answer should be that the adverb '*non*' is negative and denies; and it is by arranging it with the word '*si*' that one understands a negation and an opposition. Hence in the word '*nisi*' one understands a negation and an opposition. And that is why it is an exceptive word, because it is opposite to its basic proposition[18] in some part of it.

59   Again, it is because the word '*nisi*' is a combination of '*non*' and '*si*' and it sometimes is exceptive and sometimes consecutive, that it is therefore necessary that the combination of the word 'except' (*nisi*) out of its components occurs in different ways. We agree with this saying that when the word 'except' is a consecutive word, the consecution extends to the negation, and in that case the consecution completes the word '*nisi*'. In that case, according to Priscian[19] the word '*nisi*' falls under the continuative conjunctions and according to Donatus[20] under the causal conjunctions. For example, 'He is not

---

18   *i.e.* the foregoing proposition that is contradicted.
19   Cf. *Inst. gramm.* XVI 2, p. 94(12ff.), ed. Hertz.
20   *Ars minor*, pp. 364(39)-365(2), ed. Keil.

currit nisi[4] moveatur' idest 'si[5] non moveatur, non currit'. Quando autem est exceptiva, tunc negatio cadit supra consecutionem. Et sic negatio transmutat[6] compositionem in alteram speciem, quia[7] in dictionem exceptivam. Et sic secundum diversos modos compositionis est hec dictio 'nisi' alterius et alterius speciei.

60 Si[1] autem queratur utrum instantia repperiatur equaliter in tribus[2] predictis generibus dictionum[3] instantivarum, dicendum[4] quod non, quia per prius est instantia in dictionibus instantivis[5] contradicentibus (quia[6] hic[7] maxima[8] est oppositio, cum ibi sit contradictio) et per posterius instantia repperitur in dictionibus exceptivis. [*P84rb*] Et tamen in hiis plus est de instantia quam in exclusivis, quia quamvis exceptum[9] non immediate contradicat suo toti, tamen bene[10] sequitur contradictio. Ut 'omnis homo preter Sortem currit'; ex hoc sequitur quod Sortes non currat[11] et[12] ulterius sequitur quod homo[13] non[14] currat, quia si Sortes non[15] currit, homo[16] non currit (et est locus a parte subiectiva). Sed in dictionibus exclusivis id quod excluditur non contradicit ei a quo fit exclusio. Ut 'solus Sortes currit' idest 'Sortes currit[17] et nullus alius a Sorte currit'; iste enim due 'Sortes currit', 'nullus alius a Sorte currit' non contradicunt neque primo neque ex consequenti. Et ideo minus est de instantia in dictionibus exclusivis et plus in dictionibus exceptivis, et maxime in contradicentibus[18].

Quare hec dictio consecutiva 'nisi' vult semper adiungi verbo subiunctivi modi

61 Circa quintum obicitur sic. Coniunctio nata est coniungere ceteras partes orationis. Ergo tam nomina quam verba et sic de aliis partibus, et quoslibet numeros et quaslibet[1] personas et quelibet[2] tempora et quoslibet[3] modos et sic de aliis accidentibus sub hiis partibus et sub aliis. Ergo hec dictio 'nisi' secundum [*N76vb*] quod est coniunctio[4] consecutiva, male determinatur tantum[5] ad modum

running unless he is moving', that is, 'If he is not moving, he is not running'. On the other hand, when it is exceptive, then the negation extends to the consecution. In that case the negation changes the combination into another species, viz. into an exceptive word. Thus in accordance with the different modes of combination, the word '*nisi*' sometimes belongs to one, and sometimes to another species.

60 Now if one asks whether a counter-instance is found equally in the three kinds of counter-instantive words mentioned above,[21] the answer should be that that is not the case, because a counter-instance is primarily found in contradicting counter-instantive words (for this is where the opposition is the greatest, since this is where there is a contradiction), and secondarily a counter-instance is found in exceptive words. Nevertheless one finds more of a counter-instance in these words than in exclusive words, for although the excepted thing does not inmediately contradict its whole, nevertheless a contradiction does follow. For instance, from 'Every man except Socrates is running' it follows that Socrates is not running and eventually it follows that some man is not running, because if Socrates is not running, a man is not running (and this is a case of the topic 'from a subjective part'). However, in the case of exclusive words, that which is excluded does not contradict that from which the exclusion is made. For example, in 'Socrates alone is running', that is, 'Socrates is running and no one other than Socrates is running', the two propositions 'Socrates is running' and 'No one other than Socrates is running' do not contradict each other either primarily or by consequence. Hence there is less of a counter-instance in exclusive words, more in exceptive words and the most in contradicting words.

Why the consecutive word 'nisi' *always wishes to be adjoined to a verb in the subjunctive mood*

61 *Ad [5]:* As to the fifth item, there is the following argument to the contrary. A conjunction is by nature apt to conjoin the other parts of speech. Therefore it conjoins both nouns and verbs, and the same goes for other parts of speech, and also any numbers whatsoever and any person, any tenses and any moods whatsoever, and the same goes for the other accidents that fall under these parts of speech and under other ones. Therefore insofar as the word '*nisi*' is a consecutive word it is erroneously limited to the subjunctive mood.

---

[21] Cf. above, cap. 57.

subiunctivum[6]. Et dicendum quod negatio[7] que est in hac[8] dictione 'nisi', non est negatio absoluta sed respectiva, secundum quod hec dictio 'nisi' est dictio consecutiva. Et huius causa est quia negatio et consecutio uniuntur in[9] intellectu uno huius dictionis 'nisi'. Et[10] quia intellectus est in consecutione, ideo negatio est in consecutione, quia unitur[11] in intellectu uno cum ipsa consecutione, ut diximus. Et ideo[12] negatio non est ibi absoluta sed respectiva. Unde cum negatio debeat determinare verbum, ideo[13] negatio absoluta debet[14] determinare verbum absolutum et negatio respectiva[15] determinabit[16] verbum respectivum. Et ideo, quia inter omnes modos verborum solus modus subiunctivus dicit rem suam respectivam[17], sive in respectu sive in comparatione ad aliud, ideo hec dictio[18] 'nisi', secundum quod est consecutiva, debet adiungi verbo subiunctivi[19] modi.

Sophismata

62   Secundum predicta queritur de hoc sophismate NICHIL EST VERUM [*T46rb*] NISI IN HOC INSTANTI. Probatio. Quicquid est verum, est verum in hoc instanti. Ergo nichil est verum nisi in hoc instanti. Contra. Nichil est verum nisi in hoc instanti. Ergo te esse asinum non est verum[1] nisi in hoc instanti. Ergo te [*P84va*] esse asinum est verum in hoc instanti. Ergo tu es asinus. Vel sic potest probari. Hec est falsa 'nichil est verum'. Et non est instantia nisi pro vero[2] in hoc instanti. Ergo facta exceptione pro illo erit vera. Ergo hec est vera 'nichil est verum nisi in hoc instanti'.

63   Solutio. Prima duplex, eoquod hec dictio 'nisi' potest teneri exceptive vel consecutive. Et utroque modo est vera sumpto 'instanti' communiter ad ipsum instans, sive ad ipsum *nunc,* et ad tempus presens. Sed tunc[1] distinguenda est prima, quia aliter et aliter respondendum est ad argumenta sequentia improbationis[2]. Prius[3] autem videndum[4] est utrumque sensum prime quam respondeamus improbationi[5]. Unde sensus[6] prime secundum quod est exceptiva, est talis 'nichil est verum nisi in hoc instanti' idest 'nichil est verum

The answer should be that the negation found in the word 'nisi' is not an absolute but a respective one, insofar as the conjunction 'nisi' is a consecutive word. The reason for this is that the negation and the consecution are united in the one notion of the word 'nisi'. Now in virtue of the fact that its notion consists in consecution, therefore the negation concerns the consecution, because it [i.e. the negation] is united in one notion with that consecution, as we have said. Therefore the negation in this case is not absolute but respective. Hence, it is because the negation must determine the verb, that therefore an absolute negation must determine the verb in its absolute signification and a relative negation must determine the verb in its respective signification.[22] And so, in virtue of the fact that among all moods of verbs the subjunctive mood alone indicates its *pragma* (*res*) respective, *i.e.* in relation to something else, therefore insofar as the word 'nisi' is consecutive, it must be adjoined to a verb in the subjunctive mood.

Sophismata

62   As regards what has been said, there is a problem concerning the sophisma-sentence NOTHING IS TRUE EXCEPT IN THIS INSTANT. Proof: whatever is true, is true in this instant. Therefore nothing is true except in this instant. There is an argument to the contrary. Nothing is true except in this instant. Therefore that you are an ass is not true except in this instant. Therefore that you are an ass is true in this instant. Therefore you are an ass. Or it can be proved as follows. The proposition 'Nothing is true' is false, and there is no counter-instance except for what is true in this instant. Therefore if one makes an exception for this it will be true. Therefore the proposition 'Nothing is true except in this instant' is true.

63   Solution. The original sentence is ambiguous because the word 'except' can be understood exceptively or consecutively. Now in both ways it is true if one understands 'instant' commonly for the specific instant involved (that is, for the *now*) and for the present time. However, a distinction must be then be made in the original sentence, because one should respond in different ways to the arguments that follow in the disproof. Now before we can answer the disproof, we must first consider each sense of the original sentence. Well, insofar as it is exceptive, the meaning of the original sentence is 'Nothing is true except in this instant', that is, 'There is nothing

---

22   *i.e.* its consignification.

preter verum in hoc [*N77ra*] instanti'. Et hoc modo est vera sumpto
'vero' communiter ad verum quod est in[7] hoc instanti et ad verum
quod est in tempore, sicut 'instans' sumebatur communiter ad instans et ad tempus[8]. Si autem teneatur consecutive prima, tunc est
sensus 'nichil est verum nisi in hoc instanti' idest 'nichil est verum
si non est verum in hoc instanti'. Et iterum[9] hoc modo prima est
vera.

64 Habita ergo distinctione[1] prime[2] respondeo[3] improbationi[4]
dicendo[5] quod, prout prima est exceptiva, sic primum argumentum
improbationis non tenet, hoc scilicet 'nichil est verum nisi in hoc
instanti; ergo[6] te esse asinum non est verum nisi in hoc instanti',
quia est ibi sophisma accidentis (sicut hic 'nullus homo preter
Sortem currit; ergo Plato preter Sortem non[7] currit'), quia hoc modo
prima est categorica et hec distributio 'nichil' comprehendit sub[8] se
tam vera quam falsa, tam complexa quam imcomplexa. Unde
verum in hoc instanti excipitur ab illa distributione[9] sic sumpta.
Unde verum in hoc instanti est pars illius distributionis[10]. Sed non
est pars huius quod dico[11] 'te esse asinum' (sicut Sortes erat[12] pars
huius distributionis 'nullus homo' sed non erat pars Platonis). Si
autem prima teneatur consecutive, tunc primum argumentum
improbationis[13] bene tenet, hoc scilicet 'nichil est verum nisi[14] in
hoc instanti; ergo te esse asinum non est verum nisi in hoc instanti',
quia sensus est 'nichil est verum, si[15] non est verum in hoc instanti;
ergo te esse asinum non est verum, si non est verum in hoc
instanti'. [*P84vb*] Sed aliud[16] quod sequitur non tenet, hoc scilicet 'te
esse asinum non est verum nisi in hoc instanti; ergo te esse asinum
est verum in hoc instanti', quia sensus est 'te esse asinum non est
verum si non est verum in hoc instanti; ergo te esse asinum est
verum in hoc instanti', quia vel nulla est ibi apparentia et argumentum est penitus disparatum, vel est ibi *quid et simpliciter* propter
hoc quod ex nulla conditionali licet inferre antecedens vel consequens. Ut 'si homo currit, animal[17] currit'; ex hac non sequitur
[*T46va*] 'ergo homo[18] currit' vel 'ergo[19] animal currit'. Similiter non
sequitur 'te esse asinum non[20] est verum si[21] non est verum in hoc

true except what is true in this instant'. In this way it is true, when 'true' is taken commonly for what is true in this instant and what is true in time, in the same way as 'instant' was taken commonly for an instant and for time. If, on the other hand, the original sentence is taken consecutively, then 'Nothing is true except in this instant' means 'Nothing is true if it is not true in this instant', and again in this way the original sentence is true.

64 Now that I have dealt with the distinction in the original sentence, I shall answer to the disproof by saying that insofar as the original sentence is exceptive, in that way the first argument of the disproof is not valid, *viz.* 'Nothing is true except in this instant; therefore that you are an ass is not true except in this instant', in this case we have a fallacy of accident (in the same way as in 'No man except Socrates is running; therefore Plato except Socrates is not running'). For in this way the original sentence is categorical, and the distribution 'nothing' includes under it both what is true and what is false, and both what is complex and what is incomplex. Hence what is true in this instant is excepted from that distribution taken in this way. Hence what is true in this instant is part of that distribution. However, it is not part of 'that you are an ass' (in the same way as Socrates was part of the distribution 'no man', but was not a part of Plato). If, on the other hand, the original sentence is taken consecutively, in that case the first argument of the disproof *viz.* 'Nothing is true except in this instant; therefore that you are an ass is not true except in this instant' is a good inference, because it means 'Nothing is true, if it is not true in this instant; therefore that you are an ass is not true, if it is not true in this instant'. However, the other thing that is inferred, *viz.* 'That you are an ass is not true except in this instant; therefore that you are an ass is true in this instant' does not follow, for it means 'That you are an ass is not true if it is not true in this instant; therefore that you are an ass is true in this instant'. For in this case there is either no evidence whatsoever and the argument is completely disparate,[23] or we have here the fallacy of reasoning from something taken in a certain sense to the same thing taken *simpliciter*, in virtue of the fact that from no conditional one is allowed to infer the antecedent or the consequent. For example, from 'If a man is running, an animal is running' it does not follow 'Therefore a man is running' or 'Therefore an animal is running'. Likewise it does not follow 'That you are an ass is not true, if it is not true in this instant; therefore that you are an ass is true in

---

[23] This is because its premises are completely disparate ('incommensurable'), because 'except' does not equal 'if not'.

instanti; ergo[22] te esse asinum est verum in hoc instanti', quia ponit ibi antecedens[23], et sic[24] est ibi *quid et simpliciter*. Potes tamen[25] dicere quod[26] nulla est ibi[27] apparentia, quia ex negativo[28] antecedente et negativo[29] consequente infert antecedens affirmatum. Ut 'si[30] non est animal, non est homo; ergo[31] est animal'; in hoc enim argumento aut nulla est apparentia, ut diximus, aut[32], si est ibi[33] apparentia, est ibi[34] *quid et simpliciter*.

65   Item. Queritur de hoc sophismate NULLUS HOMO LEGIT PARISIUS NISI IPSE SIT ASINUS. Probatio. Hec est falsa 'aliquis[1] homo legit Parisius nisi ipse sit asinus'. Ergo sua contradictoria est vera, hec scilicet 'non aliquis homo legit Parisius nisi ipse sit asinus'. Sed 'non aliquis' et 'nullus' equipollent. Ergo prima vera. Contra. Nullus homo legit Parisius nisi ipse sit asinus. Ergo (a destructione consequentis) si aliquis homo legit Parisius, ipse est asinus. Quod falsum est. Ergo prima falsa.

66   Solutio. Prima simpliciter est falsa. Et hec est duplex 'non aliquis homo legit Parisius nisi ipse sit asinus', eoquod negatio potest determinare verbum consequentis secundum se et absolute, quod est 'legit'. Et sic est falsa. Et sic equipollet prime, quia hoc[1] modo 'non aliquis' et 'nullus' equipollent. Sed[2] in[3] hoc sensu ista propositio 'non aliquis homo legit Parisius *etc.*' non contradicit huic 'aliquis homo legit Parisius *etc.*', quia[4] utraque[5] est[6] falsa. Vel negatio potest determinare verbum consequentis, quod est 'legit', non[7] secundum se et absolute sed in comparatione ad antecedens. Et sic est vera et contradicit huic 'aliquis homo legit Parisius *etc.*'. Sed[8] hoc modo non equipollet prime.

67   Item. Queritur de hoc sophismate NULLUS HOMO MORITUR NISI UNUS SOLUS HOMO MORIATUR. Probatio. Hec est falsa [*P85ra*] 'aliquis homo moritur nisi unus solus homo moriatur'. Ergo sua contradictoria erit vera, hec scilicet 'non aliquis homo moritur *etc.*'. Sed 'non aliquis' et 'nullus' equipollent. Ergo prima vera. Contra. Antecedens est possibile[1] et[2] consequens impossibile. Ergo

this instant', because it asserts the antecedent, and thus we have here a fallacy of reasoning from something taken in a certain sense to the same thing taken *simpliciter*. Nevertheless you can say that there is no evidence here whatsoever, because from the negative antecedent and the negative consequent one infers the antecedent affirmed. For example, in the argument 'If it is not an animal, it is not a man; therefore it is an animal', there is no evidence whatsoever, as we have said, or if there is, it is in this case a fallacy of reasoning from something taken in a certain sense to the same thing taken *simpliciter*.

65   Furthermore, there is a problem concerning the sophisma-sentence NO MAN IS READING IN PARIS UNLESS HE IS AN ASS. Proof: the proposition 'Some man is reading in Paris if he is not an ass' is false. Therefore its contradictory opposite, *viz.* 'Not some man is reading in Paris if he is not an ass' is true. Now 'not some' and 'no' are equivalent. Therefore the original sentence is true. There is an argument to the contrary. No man is reading in Paris if he is not an ass; therefore (by destroying the consequent) if some man is reading in Paris, he is an ass. And this is false. Therefore the original sentence is false.

66   Solution. The original sentence is *simpliciter* false. Also the proposition 'Not some man is reading in Paris if he is not an ass' is ambiguous, for the negation can modify the verb of the consequent, *viz.* 'is reading', in itself and absolutely. In this way it is false and thus it is equivalent to the original sentence, for in this way 'not some' and 'no' are equivalent. However, in this sense the proposition 'Not some man is reading in Paris *etc.*' does not contradict 'Some man is reading in Paris *etc.*', because both [being two sub-contrary propositions] are false. Or the negation can modify the verb of the consequent, *viz.* 'is reading', not in itself and absolutely, but in relation to the antecedent.[24] And in this way it is true and contradicts 'Some man is reading in Paris *etc.*'. However, in this way it is not equivalent to the original sentence.

67   Furthermore, there is a problem concerning the sophisma-sentence NO MAN IS DYING UNLESS ONE MAN ALONE IS DYING. Proof: the proposition 'Some man is dying unless one man alone is dying' is false. Therefore its contradictory opposite, *viz.* 'Not some man is dying, *etc.*', is true. Now 'not some' and 'no' are equivalent. Therefore the original sentence is true. There is an argument to the contrary. The antecedent is possible and the consequent is

---

[24]   reading: 'Not: some man is reading in Paris *etc.*'.

conditionalis est falsa. Quod autem antecedens sit possibile[3] [*N77va*] patet per hoc quod habet duas causas veritatis, vel plures, quia unum solum hominem non[4] mori est verum si duo moriuntur vel[5] si plures moriuntur quam duo vel etiam si omnes[6] moriuntur. Et semper[7] consequens est falsum, scilicet 'nullus homo moritur'. Solutio est eadem que[8] in precedenti sophismate.

E. DE CONIUNCTIONE REDUPLICATIVA

De hac reduplicatione 'in eo quod'

68   Modus reduplicationis diversificatur secundum diversitatem causarum. Et ideo dicitur communiter quod hec[1] reduplicatio 'in eo quod' habet diversas intentiones[2] secundum diversitatem causarum. Et propter hoc circa eam queritur primo de distinctione ipsius[3] secundum diversa genera causarum; secundo queritur utrum reduplicatio debeat poni ad subiectum vel ad predicatum in propositione; tertio queritur ad quid ponatur in sillogismo, videlicet utrum ad maiorem extremitatem[4] vel ad minorem[5] vel[6] ad medium.

De distinctione ipsius secundum diversa genera causarum

69   Circa primum sciendum est, sicut [*T46vb*] communiter solet dici, quod hec reduplicatio 'in eo quod' aliquando dicit causam efficientem. Ut 'Sortes et Plato in eo quod sunt albi, sunt similes', quia albedo in diversis subiectis[1] est causa efficiens similitudinis[2] eorum; et 'in eo quod sol lucet super terram, est dies' et 'in eo quod terra est obiecta inter solem et lunam, est eclipsis'. Aliquando dicit causam[3] materialem. Ut 'corpus rerum animatarum in eo quod est corpus organicum, est perfectibile per animam'. Aliquando[4] dicit causam formalem. Ut 'anima in eo quod est anima, est perfectio corporis[5] organici potentia vitam habentis' et 'Sortes in eo quod albedo est in ipso, est albus'; anima enim forma est instrumentalis corporis potentia vitam habentis et albedo forma est albi. Aliquando autem[6] dicit causam finalem. Ut 'sanitas in eo quod sanitas, finis est medicine et omnium[7] eorum que ordinantur ad ipsam' et[8] 'virtus in eo quod imponit[9] necessitatem operationibus[10] precedentibus, [*P85rb*] finis est earum'[11].

impossible. Therefore the conditional is false. Now that the antece
dent is possible is evident in virtue of the fact that it has two causes of
truth, or even more, because that one man alone is not dying is true
if two are dying or more than two or even if all are dying. And the
consequent, *viz.* 'No man is dying', is always false. The solution is
the same as in the preceding sophisma-sentence.

E. ON THE REDUPLICATIVE CONJUNCTION

On the reduplication 'eoquod' *('insofar as')*

68   The mode of reduplication is diversified according to the diversity of causes. Hence it is commonly said that the reduplication
'insofar as' has different meanings according to the diversity of
causes. It is on account of this fact that as regards this expression
there is *[1]* first a problem concerning the distinction in this expression according to the diverse kinds of causes, *[2]* secondly there is a
problem whether the reduplication should be added to the subject or
to the predicate in the proposition, *[3]* thirdly there is a problem to
what it is added in a syllogism, namely to the major extreme, the
minor extreme or the middle term.

On the distinction in that expression according to the diverse kinds of causes

69   *Ad [1]:* As to the first item, one should know that, as one
commonly says, the reduplication 'insofar as' sometimes indicates
an efficient cause. An example is 'Insofar as they are white, Socrates
and Plato are alike', because whiteness in diverse subjects is the
efficient cause of their likeness; the same goes for 'Insofar as the sun
shines on earth, it is day' and 'Insofar as the earth is a screen between the sun and the moon, there is an eclipse'. Sometimes it indicates a material cause, *e.g.* in 'Insofar as it is an organic body, the
body of animate things can receive its perfection by the soul'. Sometimes it indicates a formal cause. Examples are 'The soul, insofar as
it is the soul, is the perfection of an organic physical body that potentially has life' and 'Insofar as there is whiteness in him, Socrates is
white', for the soul is the instrumental form of a body that potentially has life and whiteness is the form of something white. Sometimes, however, it indicates a final cause, *e.g.* 'Insofar as it is health,
health is the end of medicine and all things ordered to it' and
'Insofar as it imposes necessity on preceding operations, virtue is the
end of these operations'.

Sophismata

70   Secundum predicta queritur de hoc sophismate ALIQUA IN EO QUOD CONVENIUNT, DIFFERUNT[1]. Probatio. Aliqua in eo quod conveniunt, sunt. In eo quod sunt, sunt multa. In eo quod sunt multa, differunt. Ergo a primo: aliqua[2] in eo quod conveniunt, differunt. Contra[3]. Convenire et differre sunt opposita. Ergo unum non est causa alterius. Ergo prima est falsa, quia hec reduplicatio 'in eo quod' dicit quod convenire est causa eius quod est differre.

71   Solutio. Prima simpliciter est falsa. Et solvendum est ad probationem per interemptionem[1] huius 'in eo quod sunt, sunt multa', quia falsa[2] est. Quod patet quia: Sicut omnes particulares homines in eo quod sunt homines, participant naturam unam et reducuntur ad[3] unitatem speciei (unde[4] dicit Porphirius quod participatione speciei plures homines[5] unus homo), similiter aliqua, sive[6] omnia, in eo quod sunt[7], participant naturam entis et reducuntur ad unitatem entis. Et ita in eo quod sunt, non sequitur quod sint multa, sed potius sequitur quod sint unum in eo[8] quod sunt.

72   Si quis[1] obiciat quod impossibile est convenire nisi ea que differunt quia[2]: Convenientia est secundum quod multa. Et[3] inter se differentia participant naturam aliquam[4] unam eis communem. Ergo necesse est[5] si conveniunt, quod differant. Ergo aliqua in eo quod conveniunt, differunt, — dicendum quod, sicut obicit, hec est vera 'si aliqua conveniunt, differunt', nec tamen prima est vera, quia conditio[6] non dicit causam, sed hec determinatio 'in eo quod' dicit causam et convenientia non est causa differentie, ut dictum est. Unde sicut hec est vera 'si Sortes est, risibile est' et tamen hec est falsa 'Sortes in eo quod Sortes[7], risibile est'[8], immo in eo quod homo,

Sophismata

70   As regards what has been said there is a problem concerning the sophisma-sentence INSOFAR AS THEY ARE IN AGREEMENT, SOME THINGS ARE DIFFERENT. Proof: insofar as they are in agreement, some things are. Insofar as they are, they are many. Insofar as they are many, they are different. Therefore, taking it from the beginning, insofar as they are in agreement, some things are different. There is an argument to the contrary. To be in agreement and to differ are opposites. Therefore the one is not the cause of the other. Therefore the original sentence is false, because the reduplication 'insofar as' indicates that being in agreement is the cause of being different.

71   Solution. The original sentence is *simpliciter* false. One can solve the proof by getting rid of the proposition 'Insofar as they are, they are many', because it is false. This is evident: just as insofar as they are men, all particular men partake of one nature and are reduced to the unity of a species (which is why Porphyry says[25] that by partaking of a species many men are one man), likewise insofar as they are, some things (or all things) partake of the nature of being and are reduced to the unity of being. Hence insofar as they are, it does not follow that they are many, but rather it follows that they are one insofar as they are.

72   If someone argues to the contrary that it is impossible to be in agreement except for things that are different, reasoning as follows: Agreement exists insofar as there is a multitude. Well, mutually different things partake of some one nature common to them. Therefore it is necessary that, if they are in agreement, they are different. Therefore insofar as they are in agreement, some things are different,—the answer should be that, as the argument to the contrary[26] says, the proposition 'If some things are in agreement, they are different' is true. Nevertheless it is not the case that the original sentence is true as well, for a condition does not indicate a cause, whereas the modification 'insofar as' does, and agreement is not a cause of difference, as has been said.[27] Hence, just as the proposition 'If Socrates is, he is something that can laugh' is true, and nevertheless the proposition 'Insofar as he is Socrates, he is something that can laugh' is false, because rather <this is the case> insofar as he is a

25 *Isag.* (transl. Boethii), p. 12(18-9), ed. Minio-Paluello (Aristoteles latinus I 6).
26 Cf. above, cap. 70.
27 Cf. above, *ibid.*.

— similiter hec est vera 'si aliqua conveniunt, differunt', tamen hec est falsa 'aliqua in eo quod conveniunt, differunt.

73   Item. Queritur de hoc sophismate EQUIVOCA IN EO QUOD EQUIVOCA, SUNT UNIVOCA. Probatio. Equivoca in eo quod equivoca, participant nomen 'equivoci' et rationem eius. Sed quecumque participant nomen et rationem alicuius[1], univocantur [*N78ra*] in eo. Ergo equivoca in eo quod equivoca, univocantur in equivoco[2]. Sed quecumque [*P85va*] univocantur in[3] aliquo, [*T47ra*] sunt univoca. Ergo equivoca in eo quod equivoca, sunt univoca. Contra. Equivocum et univocum sunt opposita. Sed nullum oppositum[4] est causa alterius. Ergo hec est falsa 'equivoca in eo quod equivoca, sunt univoca', quia hec determinatio 'in eo quod' significat quod subiectum eius[5] est causa predicati. Quod falsum est.

74   Solutio. Prima simpliciter est falsa. Et concedo quod equivoca in eo quod equivoca, univocantur in equivoco. Nec tamen sequitur ex hoc quod sint[1] univoca neque quod univocentur[2] in aliquo[3], quia univocari[4] in equivoco non est univocari[5] simpliciter sed secundum quid. Et ideo probatio[6] peccat secundum *quid et simpliciter*. Quod[7] autem univocari[8] in equivoco non sit univocari[9] simpliciter sed secundum quid[10], patet quia[11]: Quecumque univocantur[12], participant nomen unum et rationem unam; et hoc est univocari simpliciter. Sed quecumque univocantur in equivoco, participant[13] nomen unum et rationes diversas. Et ideo univocari in equivoco non est univocari simpliciter, sed potius equivocari.

Utrum reduplicatio debeat poni ad subiectum vel ad predicatum

75   Circa secundum nota quod reduplicatio in propositione secundum se, et ut magis proprie dicam[1:] in enuntiatione, debet[2] poni ad subiectum, cum subiectum sit causa predicati vel[3] habeat in se causam predicati, ut 'Sortes in eo quod homo est risibile' et 'triangulus in eo quod triangulus habet tres angulos equales duobus rectis' et 'animal[4] in eo quod habet pulmonem[5], respirat' et 'animal[6] in eo quod habet cor, habet sanguinem'.

man, —likewise the proposition 'If some things are in agreement, they are different' is true, and nevertheless the proposition 'Insofar as they are in agreement, some things are different' is false.

73 Furthermore, there is a problem concerning the sophisma-sentence INSOFAR AS THEY ARE EQUIVOCAL EQUIVOCALS ARE UNIVOCAL. Proof: insofar as they are equivocal, equivocals partake of the name 'equivocal' and its definition. Now whatever things partake of a name and definition of something, are univocal in that respect. Therefore, insofar as they are equivocal, equivocals are univocal in their being equivocal. Now whatever things are univocal in some respect, are univocal. Therefore insofar as they are equivocal, equivocals are univocal. There is an argument to the contrary. 'Equivocal' and 'univocal' are opposites. Now no opposite is the cause of the other. Therefore the proposition 'Insofar as they are equivocal, equivocals are univocal' is false, because the modification 'insofar as' signifies that its subject is the cause of the predicate. And this is false.

74 Solution. The original sentence is *simpliciter* false and I concede that insofar as they are equivocal, equivocals are univocal in their being equivocal. Nevertheless from this it does not also follow that they are univocal, nor that they are univocal in some respect. For to be univocal in being equivocal is not to be univocal *simpliciter* but in a certain sense. Hence the argument commits the fallacy of reasoning from something taken in a certain sense to the same thing taken *simpliciter*. Now that to be univocal in being equivocal is not to be univocal *simpliciter* but in a certain sense is evident, because whatever things are univocal partake of one name and one definition, and this is to be univocal *simpliciter*. Now whatever things are univocal in being equivocal partake of one name and diverse definitions. Hence to be univocal in being equivocal is not to be univocal *simpliciter*, but rather to be equivocal.

Whether a reduplication should be added to the subject or to the predicate

75 *Ad [2]:* As to the second item, note that a reduplication in a proposition in itself, and, to put it more properly, in an enunciation, must be added to the subject, because the subject is the cause of the predicate or contains the cause of the predicate, *e.g.* 'Insofar as he is a man, Socrates is something that can laugh', 'Insofar as it is a triangle, a triangle has three angles equal to two right ones', 'Insofar as it has lungs, an animal can breathe' and 'Insofar as it has a heart, an animal has blood'.

Ad quid reduplicatio ponatur in sillogismo

76   Circa tertium vero nota[1] quod reduplicatio in sillogismo debet
poni ad maiorem extremitatem et non ad medium neque ad
minorem extremitatem[2], ut 'omnis homo est risibile in eo quod
homo; sed Sortes est homo; ergo Sortes est risibile in eo quod homo'.
Exemplum[3] autem Aristotilis est hoc 'cuiuslibet boni est disciplina
in eo quod bonum; sed omnis iustitia est bonum[4]; ergo iustitie[5] est
disciplina [*N78rb*] in eo quod bonum' (in primo prime). Et sic[6]
reduplicatio solum ponitur ad maiorem extremitatem et non ad
medium. Et subiungit causam dicens[7] "nam bonum in eo quod
bonum predicari[8] de iustitia est falsum et non[9] intelligibile", quia
propter hoc quod ponitur idem esse causa sui ipsius[10] est falsum et
quia intellectus non [*P85vb*] potest comprehendere[11] idem in essentia esse diversum in essentia et prius et posterius natura[12] seipso, ideo
est non intelligibile. Et hec omnia sequuntur inconvenientia ex hac
propositione 'iustitia est bonum in eo quod bonum', ut reduplicetur
predicatum[13] ad seipsum, quia termini communes predicantur[14]
ratione essentie et subiciuntur ratione substantie. Ut 'homo est
homo': 'homo' enim in predicato dicit essentiam, ut vult ars[15], in
subiecto dicit substantiam[16]. Eadem[17] autem essentia non potest esse
causa sui ipsius, quia[18] sic esset in seipsa eadem et diversa et prior et
posterior natura, quia esset[19] causa et effectus.

77   Quod autem terminus dicens[1] *quid* ut[2] 'homo', 'animal' et
consimiles predicentur[3] ratione essentie et subiciantur[4] ratione substantie, patet per ordinationem[5] predicamentalem[6] secundum rec-
tam lineam. Quia[7] secundum quod homo ordinatur in linea[8] pre-
dicamentali[9] supra Sortem et Platonem et supra alia individua, sic[10]
[*T47rb*] nominat essentiam et ratione illius predicatur. Sed secundum quod homo inclinatur ad[11] individua in quibus est, sic nominat
substantiam, sicut hoc[12] individuum vagum quod est aliquis homo.
Et ideo quando 'homo' subicitur ratione alicuius inferiorum, tunc[13]
dicitur subici ratione substantie.

What a reduplication must be added to in a syllogism

76   *Ad [3]*: As to the third item, note that a reduplication in a
syllogism must be added to the major extreme and not the middle
or the minor extreme, *e.g.* 'Insofar as he is a man, every man is
something that can laugh; now Socrates is a man; therefore insofar
as he is a man, Socrates is something that can laugh'. The example
brought forward by Aristotle[28] is the following: 'There is a discipline
of every good insofar as it is a good; now every justice is a good;
therefore there is a discipline of justice insofar as it is a good (in the
first mood of the first figure). Thus the reduplication is only added
to the major extreme and not to the middle. And he adds[29] the
reason <for this being the case>, saying "For to predicate the good
insofar as it is good of justice is false and not intelligible". For owing
to the fact that it asserts that the same thing is the cause of itself, it is
false, and because the intellect cannot apprehend what is the same
in essence to be diverse in essence and both prior and posterior to
itself in nature, therefore it is not intelligible. Well, all these absur-
dities follow from the proposition 'Justice is good insofar as it is a
good', so that the predicate is reduplicated in relation to itself, because common terms are predicated in virtue of the essence and are
made subject in virtue of the substance. An example is 'A man is a
man': 'man' in the predicate indicates the essence, as the art <of
logic> has it, and in the subject it indicates the substance. Now the
same essence cannot be the cause of itself, for in that case it would
be in itself both the same and diverse, and prior and posterior in nature, because it would be <both> cause and effect.
77   That terms indicating an essence (*quid*), *e.g.* 'man', 'animal'
and the like, are predicated in virtue of the essence and made subject in virtue of the substance, is evident by the categorial arrange-
ment in the straight line. For according as 'man' is arranged in the
categorial line above Socrates, Plato and other individuals, it thus
names the essence and it is predicated in virtue of that <essence>.
On the other hand, according as 'man' has an inclination towards
the individuals in which it inheres, it thus names a substance,
namely this indeterminate individual which is some man. Therefore whenever 'man' is made subject in virtue of its containing its
inferiors, then it is said to be made subject in virtue of its being a
substance.

---

28   *Anal. Priora.* I 38, 49a12-9.
29   *Ibid.*, 49a21-2.

F. DE HAC CONIUNCTIONE 'QUIN'

Introductio

78   Numerus coniunctionum in[1] specie secundum Donatum est quinarius, secundum Priscianum vero multo plures sunt[2] species coniunctionum. Inter[3] quas numerantur species causalium tam a Prisciano quam a Donato et species rationalium, quas Priscianus appellat collectivas sive rationales. Sed secundum Donatum hec dictio[4] 'quin' continetur sub causalibus, secundum[5] Priscianum vero continetur sub[6] collectivis sive[7] sub rationalibus. Hanc autem diversitatem adpresens obmittamus[8], quia pertinet [*N78va*] ad gramaticum. Unde primo intendimus querere circa hanc coniunctionem[9] 'quin' utrum significet consequentiam; secundo[10] autem, habito quod significet consequentiam, queritur[11] utrum significet consequentiam aliquam an[12] consequentiam communiter ad omnes[13] consequentias; tertio autem queritur utrum hec dictio 'quin' sit[14] composita ex hiis dictionibus 'quod', 'non'; quarto queritur utrum equipolleat eis sive convertatur cum[15] illis; quinto autem queritur quare hec dictio[16] 'quin' coniungatur semper verbo subiunctivi[17] modi.

Utrum significet consequentiam

79   Circa primum obicitur[1] quia: Ut vult Priscianus, omnis coniunctio significat vim vel ordinem; et[2] coniunctiones significant vim quando res aliquas significant simul esse (ut 'pius et fortis fuit Eneas'); ordinem autem significant [*P86ra*] coniunctiones[3] quando consequentiam[4] aliquarum[5] rerum demonstrant[6] (ut 'si ambulat, movetur'). Sed hec coniunctio 'quin' non significat res simul esse. Ergo significat consequentiam[7] aliquarum rerum. Ergo hec con-

F. ON THE CONJUNCTION '*QUIN*' ('BUT THAT')

Introduction

78   The number of specific conjunctions, according to Donatus,[30] is five, whereas according to Priscian,[31] there are many more species of conjunction. Among these species both Priscian[32] and Donatus[33] enumerate the species of causal conjunction and the species of rational conjunction, which Priscian[34] calls 'inferential' or 'rational'. Now according to Donatus,[35] the conjunction '*quin*' falls under the species of causal conjunctions, whereas according to Priscian,[36] it falls under the species of inferential or rational conjunctions. Let us leave this diversity for the present, however, for it concerns the grammarian. Hence we *[1]* first intend to discuss the problem concerning the conjunction '*quin*', whether it signifies a consequence, *[2]* secondly, after we have decided that it signifies a consequence, there is a problem whether it signifies a certain consequence or a consequence taken commonly for all other consequences, *[3]* thirdly there is a problem whether the word '*quin*' is a combination of the words '*quod*' and '*non*', *[4]* fourthly there is a problem whether the former is equivalent to or convertible with the latter ones, *[5]* fifthly there is a problem why the conjunction '*quin*' is always connected with a verb in the subjunctive mood.

Whether it signifies a consequence

79   *Ad [1]:* As to the first item, there is an argument to the contrary. As Priscian[37] has it, every conjunction signifies a force or an order, and conjunctions signify a force when they signify things to be simultaneous (*e.g.* 'Aeneas was pious and brave'); on the other hand, conjunctions signify an order when they display a consequence of certain states of affairs (*e.g.* 'If he is walking, he is moving'). Now the conjunction '*quin*' does not signify things to be simultaneous. Therefore it signifies a consequence of certain states of affairs. Therefore the conjunction '*quin*' signifies a consequence.

---

30   *Ars minor*, p. 364(34-5), ed. Keil.
31   *Instit. gramm.* XVI 1, p. 93(13-6), ed. Hertz.
32   *Ibid..*
33   *Ars minor*, p. 364(39), ed. Keil.
34   *Instit. gramm.* XVI 11, p. 100(15), ed. Hertz.
35   *Ars minor*, p. 365(1), ed. Keil.
36   Cf. *Instit. gramm.* XVI 11, p. 100(15-6), ed. Hertz.
37   *Inst. gramm.* XVI 1, p. 93(1-6), ed. Hertz.

iunctio 'quin' significat consequentiam. Item ad idem. Hec est vera
'non est[8] homo quin sit animal'. Et in hac oratione significatur quod
non potest esse homo ita quod non sit animal. Ergo significatur quod
homo non potest[9] esse sine animali. Sed[10] si homo non potest esse
sine animali, tunc animal de necessitate sequitur ad hominem[11].
Ergo significatur ibi quod animal de necessitate sequitur ad hominem. Sed hec coniunctio 'quin' non potest significare hoc nisi sit
dictio[12] consecutiva. Et sic significat consequentiam. Ergo hec coniunctio 'quin' significat consequentiam. Item ad idem. Dicit Priscianus quod collective coniunctiones sive rationales sunt[13] que per
illationem colligunt supradictum[14]. Et exemplificat de[15] istis 'ergo',
'igitur', 'itaque', 'quin' et de pluribus aliis. Ergo hec dictio 'quin' est
illativa[16]. Sed in omni illatione intelligitur consequentia. Ergo in
hac dictione 'quin' intelligitur consequentia. Sed obicitur in contrarium quia: Communiter recipiuntur iste propositiones 'iste non audit
lectionem[17] quin dormiat', 'iste non comedit quin bibat' et consimiles. Sed in eis unum non de necessitate sequitur ad alterum.
Ergo hec dictio 'quin' non significat consecutionem[18].

80   Et dicendum quod hec dictio 'quin' dicit consecutionem
illationis. Unde est[1] dictio consecutiva sive illativa. Et concedimus
omnes rationes ad hoc. Ad illud autem quod obicit[2] in contrarium
(quod communiter ponitur[3] esse vera[4] hec 'iste non audit lectionem[5]
quin [*T47va*] dormiat', et consimiles), dicendum quod duplex est
consequentia: una est consequentia simplex[6] (ut 'si homo est, animal
est'), alia est[7] consequentia *ut nunc* (ut 'si veneris ad me, ibo[8] tecum').
Et hoc secundo modo non sequitur[9] de necessitate unum ad alterum.

81   Item. Videtur quod non significet consecutionem, quia est
collectiva sive rationalis secundum Priscianum. Ergo significat illationem. Ergo non significat consecutionem. Et dicendum quod
omne illatum inquantum est illatum, sequitur et omne inferens
inquantum est inferens, antecedit. Unde in omni illatione consecutio[1] et antecessio intelliguntur. Et ideo hec dictio 'quin' significat

Furthermore, there is an argument that yields the same conclusion. The proposition 'He is [or: 'there is'] not a man, but that (*quin*) he is an animal' is true. In this proposition what is meant is that a man cannot be such that he is not an animal. Therefore it means that there cannot be man without animal. Now if man cannot be without animal, then animal necessarily follows from man. Therefore what is meant in this case is that animal necessarily follows from man. Now the conjunction '*quin*' cannot have this meaning unless it is a consecutive word. Thus it signifies a consequence. Therefore the expression '*quin*' signifies a consequence. Furthermore, there is an argument that yields the same conclusion. Priscian says[38] that inferential or rational conjunctions are ones that bring together what has been said before [*i.e.* the premises] by way of an inference. As examples of these <words> he adduces '*ergo*' and '*igitur*' ('therefore'), '*itaque*' ('and so'), '*quin*', and many others. Therefore the word '*quin*' is inferential. Now in every inference one understands a consequence. Therefore in the word '*quin*' one understands a consequence. However, there is an argument to the contrary. One commonly accepts the following propositions: 'He does not hear a lecture but that he sleeps' and 'He does not eat but that he drinks' and the like. Now in these propositions one thing does not follow from the other of necessity. Therefore the word '*quin*' does not signify a consecution.

80   The answer should be that the conjunction '*quin*' indicates a consecutive inference. Hence it is a consecutive or inferential word, and we agree with all the arguments induced to that end. As to the argument to the contrary (that the propositions 'He does not hear a lecture but that he sleeps' and the like are commonly stated to be true), the answer should be that there are two types of consequence: one type is the absolute consequence (*e.g.* 'If a man is, an animal is') and the other the consequence *as-of-now* (*e.g.* 'If you will come to me, I will go with you'). In this second way one thing does not follow from the other of necessity.

81   Again, it may be argued that it does not signify a consecution, because it is inferential or rational according to Priscian.[39] Therefore it signifies an inference. Therefore it does not signify a consecution. The answer should be that everything that is inferred, insofar as it is inferred, follows, and everything that implies, insofar as it implies, is antecedent. Hence in every inference one understands consecution and antecedence. That is why the word '*quin*' signifies

---

[38] *Inst. gramm.* XVI 11, p. 100(15-7), ed. Hertz.
[39] *Inst. gramm.* XVI 11, p. 100(15-6), ed. Hertz.

consecutionem per illationem sive in illatione. Et ita[2] significat[3]
unum per alterum sive [*P86rb*] in altero. Et ideo hoc[4] non est significare plura sed unum.

82   Item. Cum hec dictio 'quin' sit illativa et in omni illatione per
prius intelligatur antecessio quam consecutio (quia inferens causat
ex se illatum, et non econverso), ergo hec dictio 'quin' per prius
significabit antecessionem quam consecutionem. Et dicendum quod
hec dictio 'quin' per prius significat consecutionem, antecessionem
vero[1] non significat nisi ex consequenti, propter hoc quod consecutio[2] non potest esse sine antecedente[3]. Ad aliud autem quod obicit[4]
(quod in illatione per prius est antecessio et per posterius consecutio),
dicendum quod verum est. Tamen dictiones illative magis se
habent ad consecutionem quam ad antecessionem, eoquod illatio
respicit conclusionem[5] ut obiectum sive ut[6] terminum ad quem et
respicit premissas ut ex quibus est[7] sive ut terminum a quo. Et quia
motus magis habet rationem et speciem a[8] termino ad quem est
quam a termino a quo est, ideo illatio essentialius[9] comparatur ad id
quod infertur sive ad conclusionem[10] quam ad illud quod infert[11]
sive ad premissas, propter[12] hoc quod conclusio[13] est ut[14] completivum [*N79ra*] et[15] perfectivum[16] illationis. Et propter hoc hec[17] dictio
'quin', cum sit illativa, magis se habet[18] ad consecutionem[19] quam
ad[20] antecessionem.

83   Et[1] nota quod premisse quoad cognitionem[2] suam sunt causa
efficiens cognitionis[3] ipsius conclusionis. Sed ipse[4] premisse quoad
substantiam suam[5] sunt uno modo causa materialis substantie conclusionis et alio modo quoad substantiam suam sunt causa efficiens
substantie[6] conclusionis, quia eedem premisse quoad extremitates
suas sunt materia conclusionis: descinditur[7] enim[8] maior extremitas
a[9] premissis et etiam minor ut ex[10] eis fiat coniunctio[11] tamquam ex
materia[12]. Sed premisse, quoad <ad>[13] medium ordinatur utraque extremitas, secundum suam substantiam sunt causa efficiens substantie conclusionis, propter hoc quod medium est tota virtus premissarum, per quam virtutem educitur[14] substantia conclusionis a
non[15]-esse in esse. Et sic patet quod premisse uno modo sunt

consecution via an inference or in an inference. Thus it signifies the one via the other or the one in the other. Hence this is not to signify many things but one.

82   Furthermore, it is because the word '*quin*' is an inferential word and in every inference antecedence is understood prior to consecution (for that which implies as such causes what is inferred, and not the other way round), that therefore the word '*quin*' will signify antecedence prior to consecution. The answer should be that the word '*quin*' primarily signifies consecution, whereas it only consequently signifies antecedence, in virtue of the fact that a consecution cannot be without antecedence. As to the other argument to the contrary (that in every inference one primarily understands antecedence and secondarily consecution), the answer should be that this is true. Nevertheless, inferential words are more related to consecution than to antecedence, in virtue of the fact that an inference relates to the conclusion as its object or the *term towards which* and it relates to the premises as to what it starts from or the *term from which*. Well, it is because a motion takes its rationale and kind more after the *term towards which* it is aimed than from the *term from which* it starts, that therefore an inference more essentially relates to that which it infers or the conclusion than to that which infers or the premises, on account of the fact that the conclusion completes the inference and makes it perfect. That is why the word '*quin*', because it is inferential, relates more to consecution than to antecedence.

83   Note that as far as their knowledge is concerned, the premises are the cause of the knowledge of the conclusion as such. However, as far as their material side is concerned, the premises themselves are in one way the material cause of the substance[40] of the conclusion, and in another way, as far as their material side is concerned, they are the efficient cause of the substance of the conclusion. For the same premises, as far as their extremities are concerned, are the matter of the conclusion: for the major extreme is cut out from the premises, and so is the minor, so that from them a combination is made as from their matter. However, insofar as each extremity is ordered towards the middle, as regards their substance the premises are the efficient cause of the substance of the conclusion, in virtue of the fact that the middle constitutes the whole efficacy of the premises, on the basis of which efficacy the substance of the conclusion is led from non-being to being. Thus it is evident that in one way the premises are the matter of the conclusion and in two ways

---

[40]   *i.e.* of their material(ly) being.

materia[16] conclusionis et duobus modis[17] sunt causa efficiens. Nota
etiam quod in sillogismis disparatis (ut 'omnis homo est lapis;
omnis capra[18] est homo[19]; ergo omnis capra est lapis') et universaliter in quolibet sillogismo ex falsis, premisse non [*P86va*] sunt causa
efficiens quoad cognitionem[20], [*T47vb*] sed sunt[21] causa efficiens
quoad substantiam et etiam sunt causa materialis, sicut dictum est.

Utrum significet consequentiam communiter dictam

84   Circa secundum obicitur quod cum hec dictio 'quin' dicat comparationem unius ad alterum tantum, sed[1] in comparatione unius ad
alterum est tantum[2] consecutio simplex[3] et non composita, ergo hec
dictio 'quin' solum dicit consecutionem[4] simplicem, sive consequentiam simplicem, et non compositam. Quod concedimus dicentes quod consecutionis alia est simplex (ut 'si homo est, animal est'),
sicut dictum fuit in fallacia consequentis; alia[5] est composita sive
plures, ut illa que est secundum oppositiones, sicut illa que est *in ipso*
sive *econtrario*[6]. Unde dicimus quod hec dictio 'quin' non significat
consequentiam[7] communiter ad simplicem et ad compositam, sed
tantum significat illam que est simplex. Huius[8] autem que est simplex, alia est[9] consequentia sive[10] consecutio simplex (ut dictum est
prius), alia vero[11] *ut nunc*. Unde hec dictio 'quin' [*N79rb*] non significat consequentiam communiter ad omnes alias[12] consequentias,
sed tantum significat consequentiam[13] simplicem. Et ideo[14] aliquando dicit consequentiam simplicem, aliquando[15] *ut nunc*.

Utrum sit composita ex 'quod' et 'non'

85   Circa tertium obicitur quod[1], si hec dictio 'quin' est composita
ex hac dictione 'quod' et hoc adverbio 'non', ergo est composita ex[2]
nomine et adverbio[3]. Ergo debet esse nomen vel adverbium, cum
omnis dictio[4] composita[5] trahat[6] significationem a[7] suis componentibus. Et dicimus[8] quod hec dictio[9] 'quin' est dictio[10] simplex (sicut

thcy are the efficient cause. Note also that in the case of a disparate syllogism (*e.g.* 'Every man is a stone; every goat is a man; therefore every goat is a stone') and generally speaking in any syllogism whatsoever that consists of false propositions, the premises are not the efficient cause as far as knowledge is concerned, but they are the efficient cause as far as the material side is concerned and they are also the material cause, as has been said.

Whether it signifies a consequence commonly said

84   *Ad [2]:* As to the second item, there is an argument to the contrary. It is because the word '*quin*' indicates a relationship of one 'thing' to another, and in a relationship of one thing to another there is only a simple consecution and not a composite one, that therefore the word '*quin*' only indicates a simple consecution or a simple consequence, and not a composite one. We agree with this saying that of consecution one type is simple (*e.g.* 'If a man is, an animal is'), as has been said in the discussion on the fallacy of the consequent,[41] and the other type is composite or multiple (*plures*), *viz.* the type that is based on oppositions, like the consequence *in itself* (*in ipso*) or the consequence *by contraposition* (*econtrario*). Hence we say that the conjunction '*quin*' does not signify a consequence common to the simple and to the composite, but it merely signifies the one which is simple. Now of the simple consequence one type is an absolute consequence or consecution, as has been said before, and the other is a consequence *as-of-now*. Hence the word '*quin*' does not signify a consequence taken commonly for all consequences, but it merely signifies a simple consequence. Thus it sometimes indicates an absolute consequence, and sometimes a consequence *as-of-now*.

Whether it is a combination of 'quod' *and* 'non'

85   *Ad [3]:* As to the third item, there is an argument to the contrary that if the word '*quin*' is a combination of the word '*quod*' and the adverb '*non*', therefore it is a combination of a noun and an adverb. Therefore it must be either a noun or an adverb, because every composite word draws its signification from its components. Well, we say that the word '*quin*' is a simple word (as I believe), that

---

[41]   *Tractatus* VII, cap. 150, p. 169(11-5), ed. De Rijk.

ego credo) habens de intellectu suo consecutionem cum negatione
ex natura sue impositionis[11]. Sed quia communiter dicitur quod est
composita ex hac dictione 'quod' et ex[12] hoc adverbio 'non', ideo
sustinendo illorum positionem respondendum est aliter. Unde[13]
dicimus[14] quod hec dictio 'quin' est coniunctio et est composita[15] ex
hoc nomine infinito 'quod' et ex hoc adverbio 'non'. Sed[16] coniunctiones composite diversas habent compositiones[17]. Quedam
enim componuntur ex aliis coniunctionibus (ut 'atque', 'etenim',
'siquidem' et consimiles); alie vero componuntur ex pronominibus
(ut 'ideo'); alie vero ex nomine et prepositione (ut[18] 'quapropter'); alie
ex pluribus nominibus cum prepositione (ut 'quamobrem'); alie ex[19]
verbis (ut 'videlicet', 'scilicet'); alie ex adverbio electivo (ut
'quamquam'); alie ex adverbio et verbo[20] (ut 'quamvis'). Hoc[21] etiam
videtur innuere Priscianus in *Maiori*[22] *Volumine,* in tractatu *De coniunctione,* determinando de specie coniunctionis sive potestate dicens
"inveniuntur nomina vel pronomina vel prepositiones[23] vel adverbia
que[24] loco causalium[25] accipiuntur coniunctionum".

86   Ad illud autem quod obicit (quod dictio composita trahit significationem[1] suam a suis componentibus, ergo [*P86vb*] hec[2] dictio
'quin' erit nomen vel adverbium), dicendum quod non sequitur
quod propter hoc sit nomen vel adverbium, quia[3] dictio composita
multipliciter[4] trahit significationem a suis componentibus. Quia
aliquando ex partialibus intellectibus componentium[5] fit unus intellectus compositus in eodem genere (ut 'magnanimus', 'omnipotens'); aliquando autem componentia [*N79va*] sunt diversorum
generum, compositum autem manet in genere alterius eorum (ut
'quisque'; hoc est [*T48ra*] nomen compositum[6] ex nomine et coniunctione); aliquando autem dictio composita est[7] alterius generis
quam utrumque compositorum (ut 'quare'[8] est[9] compositum ex duobus nominibus). Et hoc est propter hoc quod aliquando alterum componentium[10] est completivum significationis dictionis composite (et
tunc compositum manet in eodem genere cum suo completivo, ut
'magnanimus'[11], 'centimanus'); aliquando vero intellectus dictionis

from the nature of its imposition has consecution as part of its notion in combination with negation. However, since one commonly says that it is a combination of the word '*quod*' and the adverb '*non*', therefore in sustaining the position of these people one must answer in another way. Hence we say that the word '*quin*' is a conjunction and it is a combination of the indefinite noun '*quod*' and the adverb '*non*'. Now composite conjunctions have diverse combinations, for some are a combination of other conjunctions (*e.g.* '*atque*' ('and also'), '*etenim*' ('and indeed'), '*siquidem*' ('if indeed'), and the like), whereas others are a combination of pronouns (*e.g.* '*ideo*' ('on account of which'), others are a combination of a noun and a preposition (*e.g.* '*quapropter*' ('on account of which')), others are a combination of several nouns and a preposition (*e.g.* '*quamobrem*' ('for that reason')), others are a combination of verbs (*e.g.* '*videlicet*' ('as one can see'), '*scilicet*' ('as one can know')), others consist of <a repetition of> the elective[42] adverb (*e.g.* '*quamquam*' ('however' in the sense of 'although')), and others again are a combination of an adverb and a verb (*e.g.* '*quamvis*' ('although')). Priscian[43] also appears to suggest this in the major volume of his treatise '*On the conjunction*', when he describes the species of conjunction or their function with the words "One finds nouns, pronouns, prepositions, or adverbs, which are taken in lieu of causal conjunctions".

86   As to the argument to the contrary (that a composite word draws its signification from what its components, therefore the word '*quin*' will be a noun or an adverb), the answer should be that it does not follow that therefore it is a noun or an adverb, because a composite word draws its signification from its components in many ways. For sometimes the partial notions of the components form one composite notion in the same genus (*e.g.* 'magnanimous', 'omnipotent'); sometimes the components belong to diverse genera whereas the composite remains in the genus of one of them (*e.g.* '*quisque*' ('whoever')); this is a combination of a noun and a conjunction); sometimes a composite word belongs to another genus than either of the components (*e.g.* '*quare*' ('wherefore')) is a combination of two nouns). The reason for this is that sometimes one of the components completes the signification of the composite word (and in that case the composite remains in the same genus as that which completes it, *e.g.* 'magnanimous', 'hundredhanded'), and sometimes the

---

42   This etymology is quite mistaken, of course, because '*quamquam*' is actually a repetition of the exclamative '*quam*', indicating admiration or indignation. Thus it litterally means 'however much (badly *etc.*)'.

43   *Inst. gramm.* XVI 5, 95 (26-7), ed. Herz.

composite non fit ex intellectibus partialibus componentium[12], sed fit ex habitudinibus[13] aut ex[14] comparationibus componentium. Unde quia isti duo[15] ablativi 'qua' et 're' dicunt[16] habitudinem cause ratione[17] sue causalitatis[18] et preterea iste ablativus 'qua' est interrogativum, ideo ex hiis duabus comparationibus, scilicet ex interrogatione et causalitate, constituitur unus intellectus adverbialis[19] per compositionem[20] illorum ablativorum. Et sic[21] fit adverbium interrogativum cause[22] quod est 'quare'. Et sic dictio composita multipliciter[23] trahit significationem suam[24] a suis componentibus. Et ideo[25] non sequitur quod dictio composita semper sit eiusdem generis cum suis componentibus. Similiter dico quod huic nomini 'quod'[26] aliquando accidit relatio, aliquando interrogatio, aliquando infinitatio. Unde ex[27] eo secundum quod est nomen infinitum, et ex negatione constituitur unus intellectus ordinativus vel coniunctivus plurium dictionum vel orationum. Et sic fit coniunctio.

87   Item ad idem. Nomen significat substantiam. Coniunctio[1] vero dicit associationem[2] que est secundum simul vel que est secundum prius et posterius. Hec autem associatio est tam substantiarum[3] quam accidentium quam omnis eius quod significatur[4], sive sit ens sive non-ens. Sed ex substantia non potest fieri respectus sive associatio predicta. Ergo hec coniunctio[5] 'quin' non est composita ex hoc[6] nomine infinito 'quod' et ex hoc adverbio 'non'. Solutio autem patet ex predictis. Quia[7] compositio huius coniunctionis[8] 'quin', que[9] est [N79vb] ex hoc nomine infinito 'quod' et ex hoc adverbio 'non', non[10] est ratione substantie significate per hoc nomen 'quod', immo[11] ratione[12] comparationis[13] ut[14] ratione infinitatis que accidit ipsi[15] substantie, sicut dictum fuit prius de hoc adverbio 'quare' et de consimilibus (ut 'quamobrem', 'cotidie', 'pridie', 'impresentiarum'[16] et consimilia). [P87ra] Et sic aliquando fit compositio ex significationibus componentium, aliquando non[17] ex significationibus componentium[18] sed ex habitudinibus eorundem.

notion of the composite word is not a combination of the partial notions of the components, but it is a combination of the types of reference the components have. Hence it is because the type of reference the two ablatives '*qua*' and '*re*' indicate is a reference in terms of cause in virtue of their causality, and, moreover, the ablative '*qua*' is interrogative, that therefore from these two types of reference, *viz.* from interrogation and causality, one adverbial notion is constituted by combining these ablatives. Thus an interrogative adverb is produced, namely '*quare*'. This is how a composite word draws its signification from its components in many ways. Therefore it does not follow that a composite word always belongs to the same genus as its components. In the same way I say that the noun '*quod*' sometimes has the feature of a reference, sometimes that of an interrogation and sometimes that of an indefiniteness. Hence from its being an indefinite noun and from its being a negation one notion is constituted that orders or conjoins a plurality of words or sentences. Thus a conjunction is made.

87   Again, there is an argument that yields the same conclusion. A noun signifies a substance. A conjunction indicates an association <of things> that is one in terms of simultaneousness or according to 'prior' and 'posterior'. Now this association is not only one of substances, but also of accidents and of everything that is signified, whether it be being or non-being. Now from a substance one cannot produce a reference or the association just mentioned. Therefore the conjunction '*quin*' is not a combination of the indefinite noun '*quod*' and the adverb '*non*'. The solution is evident from what has been said. The combination found in the conjunction '*quin*', which is one of the indefinite noun '*quod*' and the adverb '*non*', does not have being in virtue of the substance signified by the noun '*quod*', but it has being in virtue of the reference, *viz.* in virtue of the indefiniteness that belongs to this substance, in the same way as has been said before about the adverb '*quare*' and the like (*e.g.* '*quamobrem*' ('for that reason'), '*cotidie*' ('every day'), '*pridie*' ('the day before yesterday'), '*impresentiarium*' ('in the present circumstances'), and the like). Thus sometimes a combination is made of the significations of the components and sometimes it is not made of the significations of the components, but of the relationships they have.

Utrum equipolleat eis sive convertatur cum eis

88 Circa quartum obicitur quod hoc nomen 'quod' significat substantiam infinitam cum articulo subiunctivo secundum Priscianum, quia[1] 'qui' apud nos idem[2] est quod 'ostis'[3] apud Grecos; et[4] 'os' est articulus subiunctivus et 'tis'[5] est nomen infinitum. Sed omnis articulus significat[6] relationem, nulla autem coniunctio significat relationem. Ergo nulla coniunctio habet naturam articuli (in secundo secunde). Ergo ad hanc[7] coniunctionem 'quin' non sequitur 'quod non'. Non[8] ergo convertuntur, quia antecedens semper ponit consequens et ita[9] supponit[10] semper naturam sui consequentis. Et[11] dicendum quod[12] 'quin' et 'quod non' non[13] convertuntur, quia ad 'quin' sequitur 'quod non' et non econverso. Cuius causa est quia 'quin' dicit consequentiam inter negationes sive unius negative ad alteram[14] (ut[15] 'non currit quin moveatur'), sed 'quod non' aliquando adiungitur affirmativis (ut 'iste dicit [*T48rb*] tibi quod non venias', quod[16] non potest facere 'quin'; nichil enim est dictu 'iste dicit tibi quin venias'). Aliquando autem[17] adiungitur negativis, ut 'iste non currit quod non moveatur' et 'non est homo quod[18] non sit animal'. Et hoc secundo modo 'quod non' et 'quin' equipollent et convertuntur, ut 'si non est homo quod non sit animal, ergo non est homo quin sit animal' et econverso.

89 Ad illud autem quod obicit, dicendum quod relatio significata per articulum alia est et diversa a relatione significata per nomina vel per[1] pronomina relativa, quia relatio nominis vel pronominis vult quod aliquod[2] antecedens precedat[3] cuius [*N80ra*] fiat recordatio[4] per relativum[5], ut 'Sortes currit et ille disputat'. Et sic relativum nominis vel[6] pronominis numquam ordinatur simul cum suo antecedente sed semper posterius naturaliter ordinatur. Relatio autem articuli alterius generis est, quia articulus vult adiungi suppositis[7] ponendo quandam discretionem[8] circa supposita, sicut sillabice adiectiones que ponunt quandam discretionem circa pronomina, ut 'egomet', 'tutemet'. Sed in hoc differunt quod articulus non post-

Whether it is equivalent with those words or whether they are convertible

88 *Ad [4]:* As to the fourth item, there is an argument to the contrary that according to Priscian[44] the noun '*quod*' ('that which') signifies an indefinite substance in combination with a subjunctive article. For '*qui*' ('he who') in our language signifies the same as '*ostis*' for the Greeks, and '*os*' is a subjunctive article and '*tis*' is an indefinite noun. Now every article signifies a reference, whereas no conjunction signifies a reference. Therefore no conjunction has the nature of an article (in the second figure of the second mood). Therefore from the conjunction '*quin*' does not follow '*quod non*'. Therefore they are not convertible, because an antecedent always posits the consequent and so it always assumes the nature of its consequent. The answer should be that '*quin*' and '*quod non*' are not convertible, because from '*quin*' follows '*quod non*' and not the other way round. The reason for this is that '*quin*' indicates a consequence between denials or from one negative proposition to another (*e.g.* 'He does not run but that (*quin*) he moves'), whereas '*quod non*' is sometimes adjoined to affirmative propositions (*e.g.* 'He is telling you not to come', a function '*quin*' cannot carry out, for it makes no sense to say '*He is telling you but that (*quin*) you come'). Sometimes, however, '*quod non*' is adjoined to negative propositions (*e.g.* 'He does not run that does not (*quod non*) move' and 'He is not a man that is not (*quod non*) an animal'). In this second way '*quod non*' and '*quin*' are equivalent and convertible, *e.g.* 'He is not a man that is not (*quod non*) an animal; therefore he is not a man but that (*quin*) he is an animal' and the other way round.

89 As to the argument to the contrary, the answer should be that the reference signified by an article is other than and diverse from a reference signified by nouns or by relative pronouns. For the reference signified by a noun or pronoun requires that some antecedent precedes, the recollection of which occurs by means of the relative, *e.g.* <in> 'Socrates is running and he is arguing'. Thus the reference signified by a noun or pronoun is never construed with its antecedent, but is always naturally construed later. Now the reference signified by an article is of another kind, because an article should be adjoined to *supposita* by asserting a certain discreteness concerning the *supposita*, just as syllabic adjuncts that assert a certain discreteness concerning pronouns, *e.g.* '*egomet*' ('I myself') and '*tutemet*' ('you yourself'). However, they are different

---

[44] Cf. *Inst. gramm.* XIII 17, p. 11 (28-9), ed. Hertz.

ponitur supposito, sicut sillabica adiectio pronomini, immo articulus preponitur suppositis. Et etiam ex articulo et supposito non fit dictio una, sicut ex illa parte. Unde articulus simul sumitur cum supposito[9]. Dico ergo quod articulus nichil dicit de relatione nisi in hoc quod simul sumitur[10] cum supposito et significat discretionem quandam fieri circa ipsum[11]. Et quia discretio non est neque intelligitur sine eo[12] cuius est discretio, ideo discretio suppositi[13] non potest esse neque intelligi nisi per suppositum. Et ideo articulus dicit relationem ad ipsum suppositum[14]. Et sic patet quod alia est relatio articuli et alia nominis vel pronominis. [*P87rb*] Quod autem[15] articulus simul sumatur cum supposito patet in lingua materna (in qua habemus articulos, quamvis non habeamus eos in latina), quia[16] in ea semper articuli coniunguntur[17] suppositis. Et ideo relatio importata per articulum non[18] impedit compositionem[19] huius coniunctionis 'quin' neque[20] convertibilitatem eius cum[21] hac oratione[22] 'quod non', sicut diximus.

90 Item. Probo quod relatio articuli alia[1] est a relatione huius nominis 'qui' (non prout[2] sumitur relative), quia: Hoc nomen 'qui' secundum quod tenetur infinite (ut 'qui tirannum[3] interficiet, premium[4] accipiet') non tenetur relative neque dicit relationem ad aliquod antecedens, sed adhuc habet de intellectu suo articulum. Sed articulus dicebat[5] relationem suppositi. Ergo relatio articuli separatur a relatione que est recordatio rei predicte. [*N80rb*] Ergo relatio articuli alia est et diversa a relatione nominis vel pronominis. Quod concedimus.

Quare semper coniungatur verbo subiunctivi modi

91 Circa quintum obiciebatur[1]. Et solvatur[2] sicut prius de hac coniunctione[3] 'nisi' propter quid adiungitur semper verbo subiunctivi modi quando erat[4] dictio consecutiva. Item. Nota quod hec dictio 'quin' sive hec oratio 'quod non' prout convertuntur, dicunt consecutionem unius negative ad alteram[5] negativam, propter hoc quod de intentione earum est quod ponunt unum universaliter in

in that an article is not placed after a *suppositum*, as is the syllabic adjunct after the pronoun, rather it is placed before the *supposita*. Moreover, from an article and a *suppositum* one does not produce one word, as in the other case. Hence the article is taken together with the *suppositum*. I therefore say that an article indicates nothing of a reference except to the extent that it is taken together with the *suppositum* and it signifies that a certain discreteness occurs as regards that *suppositum*. Well, it is because the discreteness has no being and is not understood without that which the discreteness is concerned with, that therefore the discreteness belonging to a *suppositum* can only have being and be understood via the *suppositum*. Hence an article indicates a reference to that *suppositum*. Thus it is evident that the reference signified by an article is other than the reference signified by a noun or of a pronoun. That the article is taken together with the *suppositum* is evident in the mother tongue in which we have articles, although we do not have them in Latin, because in the former articles are always connected with *supposita*. Hence the relation designated by the article does not prevent the combination found in the conjunction '*quin*' nor its convertibility with the expression '*quod non*', as we have said.

90 Furthermore, I shall prove that the reference signified by an article is other than the reference signified by the noun '*qui*' (not insofar as it is taken relatively). Insofar as the noun '*qui*' is taken indefinitely (*e.g.* in 'He who will kill the tyrant will receive a reward'), it is not taken relatively nor does it indicate a reference to some antecedent. However, it still has an article as part of its notion. Now an article indicated a reference of a *suppositum*. Therefore the reference signified by an article is separated from the reference that consists in the recollection of the thing mentioned before. Therefore the reference signified by an article is other than and diverse from the reference signified by a noun or pronoun. We agree with this.

Why it is always connected with a verb in the subjunctive mood

91 *Ad [5]:* As to the fifth item, there was an argument to the contrary. Let it be solved in the same way as the question before regarding the conjunction '*nisi*' was solved, why it is always added to a verb in the subjunctive mood, when it was a consecutive word. Again, note that insofar as the word '*quin*' or the expression '*quod non*' are convertible, they indicate a consecution of one negative proposition to another negative one. This is because it is part of their intention that they assert one thing universally in the other in an

altero affirmative, vel[6] affirmatio unius sequitur ad affirmationem
alterius. Ut[7] 'non est homo quin sit animal; ergo quilibet homo est
animal' vel 'si est homo, est animal'; et 'non est domus quin sit
paries; ergo si domus est, paries est'. Sed cum[8] affirmatio sequitur[9] ad
affirmationem, per consequentiam econtrario[10] negatio sequitur ad
negationem, ut 'si est homo, est animal; ergo non est homo, si non
est animal' vel 'non est homo quin sit animal'.

Sophismata

92 Secundum predicta queritur de hoc sophismate TU NON
POTES VERE NEGARE TE NON ESSE ASINUM. Probatio. Te non
esse asinum est necessarium. Sed tu non potes vere negare necessarium. Ergo tu non potes vere negare te non esse asinum. Contra.
Tu non potes vere negare te non esse asinum. Ergo tu[1] non potes
vere negare quod non sis[2] asinus. Ergo[3] tu non potes vere negare
quin sis asinus. Ergo tu es asinus. Solutio. Prima duplex secundum
communiter[4] loquentes. Dicunt[5] enim quod 'negare'[6] equivocum est
in hac oratione. Unde unus sensus est 'tu non potes vere negare *etc.*'
idest 'tu non potes vere[7] negationem[8] huius proferre (sive negationem hanc dicere, quod idem est) '"te non esse asinum"'. Et[9] sic est
falsa, quia vere tu potes dicere hanc negationem 'te non esse asinum'. Alius sensus est 'tu non potes vere negare te non esse asinum'
idest 'tu non [*P87va*] potes vere negationem[10] huius proferre', quia[11]
negatio huius 'te non esse asinum' hec est 'non: tu non es asinus',
que equipollet huic 'tu es asinus'. Et hoc non potes vere dicere. Et sic
[*N80va*] est vera.

93 Sed hec[1] solutio nulla est, quia negare est actus egrediens ab
hac potentia[2] activa que est negativum[3]. Sed sicut potentia[4] activa duplicem habet comparationem, unam scilicet ad illud a quo est (sive
ad illud per quod est ut ad ipsum agens), alia vero[5] ad illud ad quod
est ut ad ipsum obiectum in[6] quod transit actio[7] illius, similiter actus
ipsius[8] potentie duas habet comparationes et etiam easdem[9] non
alias. Ergo ad idem obiectum[10] comparatur actus ad quod potentia

affirmative way, or the affirmation of the one follows from the affirmation of the other. For example, in 'There is not a man but that there is an animal; therefore any man whatsoever is an animal' or 'If there is a man, there is an animal', and 'There is not a house but that there is a wall; therefore if there is a house, there is a wall'. Now when an affirmation follows from an affirmation, then by contraposition a negation follows from a negation, *e.g.* in 'If there is a man, there is an animal; therefore there is not a man, if there is not an animal' or 'There is not a man but that there is an animal'.

Sophismata

92   As regards what has been said, there is a problem concerning the sophisma-sentence YOU CANNOT TRULY DENY THAT YOU ARE NOT AN ASS. Proof: that you are not an ass is necessary. Now you cannot truly deny something necessary. Therefore you cannot truly deny that you are not an ass. There is an argument to the contrary. You cannot truly deny that you are not an ass. Therefore you cannot truly deny that you are not an ass. Therefore you cannot truly deny but that you are an ass. Therefore you are an ass. Solution. The original sentence is ambiguous according to people following common usage. For it says that 'to deny' is equivocal in the sentence in question. Therefore one meaning of the proposition 'You cannot truly deny *etc.*' is *you cannot truly enunciate the denial of this* <*proposition*> (or express this denial, which is the same) '*that you are not an ass*'. In this way it is false, because you can truly express the denial 'that you are not an ass'. The other meaning of the proposition 'You cannot truly deny that you are not an ass' is *you cannot truly enunciate the denial of that proposition*, for the denial of 'that you are not an ass' is 'Not: you are not an ass', which is equivalent to 'You are an ass', and you cannot truly say this. In this way it is true.

93   However, this solution is useless, for denying is an act that comes from the potency that is effective of denying.[45] Now just as an active potency has a double relation, *viz.* one to that from which it originates (or to that by means of which it exists, *viz.* to the agent), and the other to that towards which it is aimed, *viz.* to the object the act of that potency proceeds to, likewise the act of that potency has two relations, and in fact it has these same ones and not other ones. Therefore the act is related to the same object as to which the active

---

45   For this meaning of '*negativum*' cf. '*significativum*', '*completivum*', '*perfectivum*', '*sanativum*' etc..

activa. Ergo cuiuscumque[11] obiecti est hec potentia activa[12] que est negativum[13], eiusdem obiecti est actus iste qui[14] est negare. Sed ista potentia[15] que est negativum, est ipsius predicati a subiecto, quia[16] negativum semper est negativum alicuius et ab aliquo. Ergo iste actus qui est negare, semper erit[17] ipsius predicati et a subiecto. Ergo semper est eiusdem rationis. Ergo univocum[18]. Ergo nichil dicunt. Item ad idem. Sicut iste actus qui est videre[19], non est[20] equivocum ad visionem[21] albedinis et ad visionem nigredinis, quamvis sint opposita, similiter 'negare' non est equivocum ad negare[22] quod-libet[23] predicatum, sive fuerit prius affirmatum sive negatum, quia, sive fuerit tale sive tale, semper removetur a subiecto. Ergo negare non equivocatur ad dicere negationem hanc[24] 'tu non es asinus', in qua negabatur[25] predicatum prius[26] affirmatum, et ad dicere negatio-nem huius 'tu non es asinus', in[27] qua removebatur[28] predicatum[29] negatum sic: 'ergo[30] non tu non es asinus'. Ergo[31] nichil dicunt[32]. Item ad idem. Aristotiles docet repperire multiplicitatem in[33] casi-bus. Ut si 'sanativum' dicitur multipliciter de effectivo, conservativo et preparativo, ergo[34] et 'sanare' dicitur multipliciter de[35] effectivo, conservativo et preparativo. Et[36] econverso: si 'sanare' dicitur multi-pliciter de effectivo, conservativo, preparativo, et 'sanativum'[37] eodem modo dicetur[38] multipliciter de eisdem[39]. Ergo si unum casualium[40] non[41] dicitur multipliciter, neque reliquum (a [N80vb] destructione consequentis). Sed[42] 'negativum'[43] non dicitur[44] multipliciter. Ergo[45] neque 'negare' (a[46] casibus). Item ad[47] idem. Sumatur oratio[48] in secundo[49] sensu quem ponunt. Et sic[50] adhuc remanet [T48vb] pro-batio et improbatio. Ergo non[51] solvunt.

94 Quod concedimus dicentes predictam solutionem nullam esse. Unde dicimus[1] quod prima est vera simpliciter, sed conclusio immediate sequens est duplex secundum amphiboliam, hec scilicet 'tu non potes vere negare quod non sis asinus', eoquod hoc verbum

potency is related. Therefore to whichever object this potency, which is effective of denying, is related, to the same object the act of denying is related. Now the active potency, which is effective of denying, concerns denying the predicate of the subject, because effective of denying is always effective of denying something, and of something. Therefore the act of denying will always be <to deny> the predicate and <to deny> of the subject. Therefore it will always have the same definition. Therefore it is univocal. Therefore they [*i.e.* the people following common usage] say nothing. Again, there is an argument that yields the same conclusion. Just as the act of seeing is not equivocal in relation to seeing whiteness and to seeing blackness, although they are opposites, in the same way 'to deny' is not equivocal in relation to denying any predicate, whether it would have been affirmed or denied previously. For whether it would have been so or so, it is always removed from the subject. Therefore denying is not equivocal in relation to expressing the denial 'You are not an ass', in which a predicate previously affirmed is denied, and in relation to expressing the denial of 'You are not an ass', in which a denied predicate is removed thus, 'Therefore not: you are not an ass'. Therefore they say nothing. Furthermore, there is an argument that yields the same conclusion. Aristotle teaches[46] us to discover the existence of multiplicity in cases. For example, if 'sanative' is said in many ways, *viz.* of that which causes, that which conserves and that which prepares health, therefore '*sanare*' ('to heal') is also said in many ways, *viz.* of that which causes, that which conserves and that which prepares health. Conversely, if 'to heal' is said in many ways, *viz.* of that which causes, that which conserves and that which prepares health, in the same way 'sanative' will also be said in many ways, *viz.* of the same things. Therefore, if one of the inflections is not said in many ways, neither is the other (by destroying the consequent). Now 'effective of denying' is not said in many ways; therefore 'to deny' is not either (from cases). Furthermore, there is an argument that yields the same conclusion. Let the proposition be taken in the second sense in which they use it. In that way as well the proof and disproof still remain. Therefore they do not solve it.

94   Well, we agree with this saying that the solution just mentioned is useless. Hence we say that the original sentence is *simpliciter* true. However, the conclusion that immediately follows, *viz.* 'You cannot truly deny that you are not an ass', is ambiguous

---

46   *Topica* I 15, 106b33-7.

'negare' habet constructiones[2] secundum diversas habitudines cum hoc quod sequitur, scilicet 'quod non sis asinus'. Quia hoc quod dico 'quod non sis asinus' potest esse obiectum supra quod transit ipsum negare (et est sensus 'tu non [*P87vb*] potes vere negare quod non sis asinus' idest 'tu non potes vere negare istud necessarium quod non sis asinus'); et sic est vera. Alio autem modo construitur[3] cum hoc verbo 'negare' non in[4] ratione obiecti sed in[5] ratione finis (et est sensus 'tu non potes vere negare quod non sis asinus' idest 'tu non potes vere negare aliquid propter quod[6] non sis asinus'); et sic est falsa, quia sive[7] te neges esse irrationale vel te esse brutum[8], ex hoc[9] sequitur quod non sis asinus. Et sic est ibi amphibolia ex diversa[10] ratione construendi unum cum altero.

95   Sed ad illud[1] argumentum quod sequitur (scilicet 'tu non potes vere negare quod non sis asinus; ergo tu non potes vere negare quin sis asinus') potest dici quod non sequitur, quia 'quin'[2] et 'quod non' non[3] convertuntur, sicut[4] dictum est prius, nisi secundum quod dicunt consecutionem[5]. Sed[6] ego dico hanc conclusionem[7] secundam, scilicet 'tu non potes vere negare quin sis asinus' esse[8] duplicem, sicut et predictam[9], eadem duplicitate. Unde secundum quod 'quin' et 'quod non' dicunt consecutionem[10] et convertuntur in ratione finis, sic bene sequitur 'tu non potes vere negare quod[11] non sis asinus; ergo tu[12] non potes vere negare quin sis asinus; ergo[13] [*N81ra*] tu es asinus'. Sed ille sunt false, sicut dictum est. Et ex falso[14] bene[15] sequitur falsum. Et non sequitur ad primam illo modo, sicut[16] dictum est. Si autem fiat[17] constructio[18] in ratione obiecti, tunc vere sunt ille[19] due sequentes conclusiones[20], ut dictum est, sicut et prima. Sed ultimum argumentum non valet, hoc scilicet 'tu non potes vere negare quin sis asinus; ergo tu es asinus'. Et[21] hoc modo nulla est ibi habitudo, sicut neque hic 'tu non potes vere negare hominem non[22] esse asinum; ergo homo est asinus', immo potius sequitur oppositum sic: 'ergo homo non est asinus'. Et similiter in proposito, quia sicut 'hominem non[23] esse asinum' est obiectum ipsius negare, similiter 'quin sis[24] asinus' est obiectum eiusdem[25] negare[26] illo respectu[27].

according to a fallacy of amphibology, for the verb 'to deny' is construed with that which follows, *viz.* that you are not an ass, according to diverse relations. For the expression 'that you are not an ass' can be the object the denial extends to (and then the proposition 'You cannot truly deny that you are not an ass' means *you cannot truly deny the necessary <state of affairs> that you are not an ass*), and in this way it is true. In another way, however, it [*i.e.* what follows] is construed with the verb 'to deny' not in terms of an object, but in terms of an end (and then the proposition 'You cannot truly deny that you are not an ass' means *you cannot truly deny something in order not to be an ass*), and in this way it is false. For whether you deny that you are irrational or that you are a beast, from this it follows that you are not an ass. Thus in this case there is question of a fallacy of amphibology that derives from the diverse sense in which one construes the one with the other.

95 However, as to the argument that follows (*viz.* 'You cannot truly deny that you are not an ass; therefore you cannot truly deny but that you are an ass'), one can say that this does not follow, because '*quin*' ('but that') and '*quod non*' ('that not') are not convertible, as has been said before,[47] unless insofar as they indicate a consecution. However, I say that the conclusion 'You cannot truly deny but that you are an ass' is ambiguous, just like the one mentioned above, owing to the same duplicity. Hence insofar as '*quin*' and '*quod non*' indicate a consecution and are convertible in terms of an end, in that way 'You cannot truly deny that you are not an ass; therefore you cannot truly deny but that you are an ass; therefore you are an ass' is a good inference. However, these are false, as has been said, and from something false something false indeed follows. Also it does not follow from the original sentence in that way, as has been said. If, on the other hand, there is a construction in terms of an object, then these two conclusions that follow are true, as has been said, just like the original sentence is as well. However, the final argument, *viz.* 'You cannot truly deny but that you are an ass; therefore you are an ass' is not valid. And in this way there is no relationship involved, just as there is not in 'You cannot truly deny that a man is not an ass; therefore a man is an ass' either, for rather the opposite follows in this way: 'Therefore a man is not an ass'. The same goes for the case at issue, for, just as 'that a man is not an ass' is the object of the denying, likewise 'but that you are an ass' is the

---

[47] Cf. above, cap. 88.

Unde deberet[28] inferre oppositum eius quod infert[29], sic 'ergo tu non[30] es asinus'.

96   Item. Probo[1] quod prima est falsa quia: Hec est vera 'tu[2] non potes vere enuntiare te esse asinum; ergo tu non potes vere negare te esse[3] asinum' (a genere, quia 'vere enuntiare' commune est ad 'vere affirmare' et ad 'vere negare'). Sed si[4] tu non potes vere negare te esse asinum, ergo tu potes vere[5] negare suum oppositum, idest 'te non esse asinum'. Ergo hec est vera 'tu potes[6] vere negare te non[7] esse asinum'. Ergo eius contradictoria est falsa, hec scilicet 'tu non potes vere negare te non[8] esse asinum'. Sed hec est prima. Ergo prima falsa.

97   Solutio. Prima est vera simpliciter. Et ratio sua peccat in prima illatione[1]. Neque est ibi locus a genere, quia quamvis 'vere[2] enuntiare' sit commune ad 'vere affirmare'[3] et[4] ad 'vere negare'[5], tamen 'vere enuntiare te esse asinum' non est commune, quia enuntiare[6] te esse asinum hoc[7] est affirmare[8], eoquod enuntiare contrahitur per obiectum. [*T49ra*] Unde sicut nullum est argumentum 'tu non potes vere [*P88ra*] affirmare[9] te esse[10] asinum; ergo tu non potes vere negare illud[11] idem' neque est ibi aliqua apparentia, quia oppositum deberet[12] [*N81rb*] inferre, — similiter in proposito nullum est argumentum neque aliqua apparentia inferendo sic: 'tu non potes vere enuntiare te esse asinum; ergo tu non potes vere negare[13] te esse[14] asinum'. Quod autem enuntiare[15] contrahatur[16] per obiectum ad affirmare, patet quia: Actus dupliciter contrahitur. Uno enim modo per differentias sumptas a parte agentis, alio autem modo per differentias sumptas a parte obiecti. Ut sentire visu[17] idem est quod videre, sentire vero[18] auditu idem est quod audire et sentire gustu[19] idem est quod gustare, et sic de aliis; ergo contrahitur actus[20] per differentias sumptas a parte agentis. A parte vero obiecti contrahitur sic: sentire coloratum idem est quod videre, sentire vero sonum idem est quod audire, et sic de aliis; ergo contrahitur actus a parte obiecti. Ergo omnis actus[21] habens obiectum dupliciter contrahitur, ut[22] dictum est. Ergo enuntiare contrahitur dupliciter[23] quia enuntiare affirmative[24] idem est quod affirmare et enuntiare negative[25] idem est quod negare; et sunt iste differentie sumpte a parte agentis. Item[26] enuntiare hominem esse animal idem est quod affirmare

object of the same denying in that sense. Hence one should infer the opposite of what one infers, *viz.* 'Therefore you are not an ass'.

96 Furthermore, I shall prove that the original sentence is false. The proposition 'You cannot truly enunciate that you are an ass; therefore you cannot truly deny that you are an ass' is true (from a genus, because 'to truly enunciate' is common to 'to truly affirm' and 'to truly deny'). Now if you cannot truly deny that you are an ass, therefore you can truly deny its opposite, *viz.* 'that you are not an ass'. Therefore the proposition 'You can truly deny that you are not an ass' is true, and therefore its contradictory opposite, *viz.* 'You cannot truly deny that you are not an ass' is false. Now this is the original sentence. Therefore the original sentence is false.

97 Solution. The original sentence is true *simpliciter* and its reasoning [*i.e.* the argument just dealt with] commits a fallacy in the first inference. Also there is no topic 'from a genus' in this case, for although 'to truly enunciate' is common to 'to truly affirm' and to 'to truly deny', nevertheless 'to truly enunciate that you are an ass' is not common. For 'to truly enunciate that you are an ass' is to affirm, because the enunciating is restricted by its object. Hence just as 'You cannot truly affirm that you are an ass; therefore you cannot truly deny the same thing' is a useless argument, there is not any evidence in it either, for one should infer the opposite,—likewise in the case at issue the argument is useless nor is there any evidence by inferring thus, 'You cannot truly enunciate that you are an ass; therefore you cannot truly deny that you are an ass'. Now that the enunciating is restricted to affirming by the object is evident. For an act is restricted in two ways. [1] In one way it is restricted by the differences taken from the part of the agent and [2] in another way by the differences taken from the part of the object. For instance, to perceive by sight is the same as to see, to perceive by hearing is the same as to hear and to perceive by taste is the same as to taste, and so on; therefore the act is restricted by the differences taken from the part of the agent. From the part of the object, on the other hand, an act is restricted thus: to perceive something coloured is the same as to see and to perceive sound is the same as to hear, and so on; therefore the act is restricted from the part of the object. Therefore every act that has an object is restricted in two ways, as has been said. Therefore to enunciate is restricted in two ways, for to enunciate affirmatively is the same as to affirm and to enunciate negatively is the same as to deny; and these are differences taken from the part of the agent. Again, to enunciate that a man is an animal is the same as to affirm it, and to enunciate that a man is not a stone is

ipsum et enuntiare hominem non esse lapidem idem est quod negare; et est ista contractio facta[27] a parte obiecti.

98   Item. Queritur de hoc sophismate IN NULLO[1] TEMPORE ALIQUID EST VERUM QUIN IPSUM[2] SIT NECESSARIUM[3]. Probatio. In nullo[4] tempore 'deum esse' est verum quin ipsum sit necessarium[5]. Ergo prima vera. Contra. In nullo tempore aliquid est verum quin ipsum sit necessarium. Ergo in quocumque[6] tempore aliquid est verum, et[7] ipsum est necessarium. Ergo in quocumque[8] tempore te sedere est verum, et[9] ipsum est necessarium. Quod falsum est.

99   Solutio. Prima est simpliciter falsa. Quia sensus est: 'in nullo[1] tempore aliquid est verum, si[2] non sit necessarium'. Hec autem falsa est, quia ad[3] antecedens non sequitur consequens, eoquod ad negationem speciei non sequitur negatio generis; necessitas autem est species veritatis. Probatio autem peccat secundum consequens, quia bene sequitur 'in nullo tempore deum esse est verum quin ipsum[4] sit necessarium', et econverso: 'si Deum esse non est necessarium, in nullo tempore est verum'. Unde vera est [*N81va*] illa propositio[5] quam primo[6] sumit, scilicet[7] hec 'in nullo tempore Deum esse est verum quin ipsum sit necessarium', quia veritas in Deo convertitur cum sua necessitate. Sed in aliis veritas et necessitas non convertuntur, sed veritas est in plus quam necessitas. Unde est ibi *consequens* ab inferiori ad superius negando[8], sicut hic 'in nullo tempore est homo quin sit risibile; ergo in nullo tempore est animal quin sit risibile'.

the same as to deny it. And this second restriction derives from the part of the object.

98 Furthermore, here is a problem concerning the sophisma-sentence AT NO TIME SOMETHING IS TRUE BUT THAT IT IS NECESSARY. Proof: at no time 'that God exists' is true but that it is necessary. Therefore the original sentence is true. There is an argument to the contrary. At no time something is true but that it is necessary. Therefore at whatever time something is true, it is also necessary. Therefore at whatever time it is true that you are sitting, it is also necessary. And this is false.

99 Solution. The original sentence is *simpliciter* false. For it means 'At no time something is true, if it is not necessary'. However, this is false, because the consequent does not follow from the antecedent since from the negation of a species the negation of the genus does not follow, and necessity is a species of truth. The disproof commits the fallacy of the consequent, for 'At no time it is true that God exists but that it is necessary' is a good inference, and conversely 'If that God exists is not necessary, at no time it is true'. Hence the proposition the opponent starts off with, *viz.* 'At no time that God exists is true but that it is necessary' is true, because in God truth is convertible with his necessity. However, in other things truth and necessity are not convertible, but truth is more extensive than necessity. Hence we have here a fallacy of the consequent in proceeding negatively from something less general to something more general, just as in 'At no time there is a man but that there is something that can laugh; therefore at no time there is an animal but that there is something that can laugh'.

DE 'QUANTO', 'QUAM' ET 'QUICQUID'

A. DE HAC DICTIONE 'QUANTO'

Introductio

1   Obmissis dubitationibus que[1] incidunt circa hanc dictionem 'quanto' videnda est eius multiplicitas. Sciendum ergo[2] quod hec dictio 'quanto' aliquando tenetur interrogative, ut 'quanto[3] profecisti hodie?', cui[4] respondetur 'multum' vel 'parum' vel cum[5] notatione 'istarum[6] rerum'. Aliquando tenetur relative[7], ut 'tanto[8] profeci[9] hodie in hac lectione quanto [*P88rb*] tu in eadem'[10]. Aliquando tenetur infinite, ut 'quanto[11] volueris, tanto proficiam'[12]. Et nullo[13] istorum trium[14] modorum intendimus hic de hac dictione 'quanto'. Alio autem modo hec dictio 'quanto' dicit causam, ut 'quanto calor[15] intensior est, tanto fortius calefacit'. Nota quod hec dictio 'quanto' aliquando[16] dicit causam efficientem, ut in predicto exemplo; calor[17] enim causa est efficiens calefaciendi[18], ut calor intensior intensius[19] [*T49rb*] calefacit. Aliquando dicit causam materialem, ut 'quanto corpus citius fit organicum, tanto citius recipit animam'. Aliquando dicit causam formalem, ut 'quanto anima citius[20] est infusa, tanto corpus organicum citius est perfectum': anima enim intellectiva infusione fit; creando enim infunditur[21] et infundendo creatur. Aliquando dicit causam finalem, ut 'quanto premium[22] maius, tanto labor[23] facilius toleratur'.

Sophismata

2   Secundum predicta queritur de hoc sophismate QUANTO[1] MAGIS ADDISCIS[2], TANTO MINUS SCIS. Posito quod tu addiscas duo enuntiabilia (ut 'hominem esse animal' et 'aliquid esse') et scias unum (ut 'hominem esse gramaticum'). Inde sic. Quanto id quod tu

CHAPTER IX

ON '*QUANTO*', '*QUAM*' AND '*QUICQUID*'

A. ON THE WORD '*QUANTO*'

Introduction

1   Leaving aside the problems concerning the word '*quanto*', we must take a look at its multiplicity. One should know, then, that the word '*quanto*' is [1] sometimes taken interrogatively, *e.g.* 'How much (*quanto*) have you progressed today?' to which one answers 'much' or 'too little' or adding the explanation 'in those things'. [2] Sometimes, on the other hand, it is taken relatively, *e.g.* 'I have made as much progress today in this lecture as (*quanto*) you have in it'. [3] Sometimes it is taken indefinitely, *e.g.* 'As much as (*quanto*) you have wished, that much I shall progress'. Now in none of these three ways do we wish to consider the word '*quanto*'. [4] In another way, however, '*quanto*' indicates a cause, *e.g.* 'The more (*quanto*) intense the heat, the more strongly it heats'. Note, therefore, that the word '*quanto*' sometimes indicates an efficient cause, as in the example mentioned above; for heat is the efficient cause of heating, as <indeed> a more intense heat heats more intensely. Sometimes, however, it indicates a material cause, *e.g.* 'The faster a body becomes organic, the faster it receives a soul'. Sometimes, however, it indicates a formal cause, e.g. 'The faster the soul is infused, the faster the organic body receives its perfection'. For the intellective soul comes into existence by infusion; by creating it is infused and by infusing it is created. Sometimes it indicates a final cause, *e.g.* 'The greater the reward, the more easily the labour is borne'.

Sophismata

2   As regards what has been said, there is a problem concerning the sophisma-sentence THE MORE YOU LEARN, THE LESS YOU KNOW. <Proof:> supposing that you learn two stateables (*e.g.* 'that a man is an animal' and 'that something exists)', and you know one, *e.g.* 'that a man is a grammarian', hence there is the following

addiscis est maius eo quod tu scis, tanto id quod tu scis est minus eo quod addiscis. Ergo quanto magis addiscis, tanto minus scis. Contra. Quanto magis addiscis, tanto magis augmentatur[3] scientia in te (per locum a causa efficiente). Sed quanto magis augmentatur[3] scientia in te, tanto magis scis (iterum[4] a causa efficiente). Ergo a primo: quanto magis addiscis, tanto magis scis. Non ergo minus.

3   Solutio. Prima simpliciter est falsa, quia[1] hec dictio 'quanto' significat in prima quod[2] magis addiscere sit[3] causa efficiens sciendi minus. Quod est impossibile, cum sit causa proxima efficiens sui oppositi, scilicet sciendi magis, quia eadem causa proxima non potest esse oppositorum (quamvis remota possit[4]; ut est in secundo *Phisicorum*: sicut[5] nauta causa est efficiens salutis navis et submersionis[6] eius, sed[7] nauta per sui presentiam est causa proxima salutis navis et per sui absentiam est causa remota[8] submersionis[9] eius[10]). Et improbatio bene tenet. Sed probatio peccat secundum figuram dictionis procedendo ab una specie huius predicamenti quod[11] est Relatio, ad alteram speciem eiusdem, quia 'maius'[12] et 'minus' dicunt relationes causatas a quantitatibus[13], 'magis'[14] et 'minus' dicunt relationes causatas a[15] qualitatibus. Unde sicut fit figura dictionis[16] mutando[17] modum quantitatis[18] in modum qualitatis[19] (ut *quantum*[20] in *quale* vel econverso), similiter fit figura dictionis procedendo a relatione causata a quantitate ad relationem causatam a qualitate vel econverso.

4   [*P88va*] Item. Queritur de hoc sophismate QUANTO ALIQUID MAIUS EST, TANTO MINUS VIDETUR. Probatio. Quanto aliquid maius est, tanto a remotiori videtur. Sed[1] quanto a remotiori videtur, tanto minus videtur. Ergo a primo: quanto aliquid maius est, tanto minus videtur. Contra[2]. Ibi assignatur[3] causa predicati quod[4] non est causa. Ergo oratio[5] est impossibilis.

5   Solutio. Prima est simpliciter falsa, quia esse[1] maius non est causa eius quod est maius[2] videre [*N82va*] neque etiam est causa eius quod est magis videri[3]. Quia ad ipsum videre et ad ipsum videri

argument. By how much what you learn is more than what you know, by that much what you know is less than what you learn. Therefore the more you learn, the less you know. There is an argument to the contrary. The more you learn, the more your knowledge in you is growing (by the topic 'from an efficient cause'). Now the more your knowledge grows in you, the more you know (again by the topic 'from an efficient cause'). Therefore, taking it from the beginning, the more you learn, the more you know, and not therefore the less you know.

3   Solution. The original sentence is *simpliciter* false. For the word '*quanto*' in the original sentence means that to learn more is the efficient cause of knowing less. And this is impossible, because it [*i.e.* to learn more] is the proximate efficient cause of its opposite, *viz.* of knowing more. For the same proximate <efficient> cause cannot be of two opposites (although a remote one can, as it says in Book II of the *Physics*:[1] just as the sailor is the <remote> efficient cause of the safety of the ship and its submergence, whereas by his presence the sailor is the proximate cause of the safety of the ship but by his absence he is the remote and not the proximate cause of its submergence). Now the the disproof is valid. The proof, on the other hand, commits the fallacy of figure of speech by proceeding from one species of the category 'relation' to another species of the same category. For 'larger' and 'smaller' indicate relations caused by quantities, whereas 'more' and 'less' indicate relations caused by qualities. Thus just as there is a figure of speech by changing the mode of quantity to the mode of quality (*viz.* from 'of what size' to 'of what kind' or the other way round), likewise there is a figure of speech when proceeding from a relation caused by quantity to a relation caused by quality, and the other way round.

4   Furthermore, there is a problem concerning the sophisma-sentence THE LARGER SOMETHING IS, THE SMALLER IT IS SEEN AS. Proof: the larger something is, the more it is seen from a distance. Now the more it is seen from a distance, the smaller it is seen as. Therefore, taking it from the beginning, the larger something is, the smaller it is seen as. There is an argument to the contrary. In this case one assigns as the cause of the predicate what is not its cause. Therefore the sentence is impossible.

5   Solution. The original sentence is *simpliciter* false, because being larger is not the cause of seeing something larger, nor is it the cause of being seen more. For in order for there to be 'seeing' and

---

[1]   *Physica* II 3, 195a11-4.

exigitur visus[4] tamquam virtus et exigitur coloratum[5] tamquam obiectum et exigitur lucidum[6] a parte obiecti sive illuminatio obiecti; et etiam exigitur medium, quod est aer[7] vel aqua (videmus enim mediante aere vel[8] aqua). Et cum hiis etiam exigitur distantia debita. Quia si minima[9] fuerit distantia, non videtur visibile, ut si ponatur visibile supra visum sive supra oculum[10]; aliquando[11] etiam si distantia fuerit maxima, non poterit res videri; et ideo necessario exigitur debita distantia. Et hec quinque insimul congregata[12] sunt causa efficiens eius quod est videre et videri, quia per 'virtutem visivam' supponimus organum sive instrumentum videndi. Unde maius[13] non est causa eius quod est videre nec eius quod est videri. Ad probationem autem solvendum est per interemptionem, quia hec est falsa 'quanto aliquid maius est, tanto a remotiori videtur', quia ut est in libro *De visu*, unumquodque visorum habet spatium quo facto non amplius videbitur; idest unumquodque quod est visibile est elongabile in tanta distantia ultra debitam[14] in qua distantia si ponatur[15], non amplius videtur. Unde hec est falsa 'quanto aliquid maius est, tanto a remotiori videtur'.

B. DE HAC DICTIONE 'QUAM'

Introductio

6 Plures autem[1] dubitationes incidunt circa hanc dictionem 'quam'. Prima est de distinctione[2] ipsius; secunda[3] qualiter importet[4] comparationem; tertia[5] que sit comparatio ipsius ad nomen[6] comparativi gradus; quarta[7] que sit comparatio eius ad nominativum sequentem (ut 'Sortes est fortior[8] quam Plato'); quinta vero propter quid sequatur nominativus, quando[9] hec dictio 'quam' coniungitur comparativo[10]; sexta questio[11] est propter quid comparativus construatur aliquando[12] cum ablativo, aliquando[13] cum nominativo interposita 'quam'[14].

'being seen' what is required is sight as a capacity, something coloured as an object and brightness on the part of the object or illumination of the object; also what is required is a medium, *viz.* air or water (for we see owing to the intermediacy of air and water). Moreover, in addition to these things what is required is an appropriate distance. For if the distance is too small, the visible is not seen, as if the visible is superimposed on sight, *viz.* on the eye; sometimes if the distance is too great, one will not be able to see the thing either; and this is why an appropriate distance is indispensably required. And these five requirements taken together form the efficient cause of seeing and to be seen, for by 'the capacity to see' we understand an organ or instrument for sight. Hence something larger is not the cause of seeing nor of being seen. As to the proof, it should be solved by destroying it altogether, because the proposition 'The larger something is, the more it is seen from a distance' is false, for as it says in the book *On sight,*[2] each thing that is seen knows of a spatial distance which being reached it will no longer be seen, that is, each visible thing can be moved away at such a distance beyond the appropriate one, and, if it is placed at that distance, it is no longer seen. Hence the proposition 'The larger something is, the more it is seen from a distance' is false.

B. ON THE WORD '*QUAM*' ('THAN' OR 'AS')

Introduction

6   There are many problems that occur concerning the word '*quam*'. *[1]* The first concerns its distinction, *[2]* the second in what way it conveys a comparison, *[3]* the third is what its relationship is to a noun in the comparative degree, *[4]* the fourth is what its relation is to the nominative that follows (*e.g.* 'Socrates is stronger than Plato'), *[5]* the fifth is why does a nominative follow whenever the word '*quam*' is connected with a comparative, *[6]* the sixth problem is why a comparative is sometimes construed with an ablative and sometimes with a nominative by placing '*quam*' in between.

---

[2] Cf. Aristotle, *De sensu et sensato*, cap. 7, 449a22-5.

De distinctione huius dictionis 'quam'

7 [*N82rb*] Circa primum ergo nota quod hec dictio 'quam' aliquando est adverbium similitudinis, ut 'iste fecit[1] hoc tam quam prudens' et 'tam iste quam ille [*P88vb*] currit'. Aliquando est adverbium comparandi, ut 'Sortes est fortior quam Plato'. Aliquando est adverbium admirandi, ut 'quam felix!', 'quam preclara!'[2] et 'quam bonus Deus[3] Israel!'; aliquando indignandi, ut 'quam turpe factum!' et 'quam abhominabile scelus!'. Preter hoc etiam est coniunctio electiva. Que[4] sic diffinitur a Prisciano "coniunctio electiva est quando[5] diversis propositis aliquid[6] ex eis nos eligere ostendimus", ut 'dives[7] esse volo quam pauper': divite et paupere positis[8] eligit se esse[9] divitem relinquendo[10] alterum. Et hic similiter[11]: 'bonum est confidere in Domino quam confidere in homine'; hic[12] hec dictio 'quam' est coniunctio electiva. Et sic patet multiplicitas huius dictionis 'quam'.

Qualiter importet comparationem

8 Circa secundum nota quod ad comparationem quinque exiguntur. Unum est quod comparatur; aliud est in quo comparatur sive in quo est comparatio; tertium autem est excessus in eo in quo est comparatio; quartum vero est illud cui comparatur; quintum vero est respectus[1] medius inter comparatum[2] et illud cui[3] comparatur. Verbi gratia cum dico 'Sortes est fortior quam Plato', Sortes est illud[4] quod comparatur et 'fortior'[5] dicit fortitudinem in qua est comparatio et etiam excessus ipsius fortitudinis, quia Sortes habet fortitudinem et etiam habet eam in excessu respectu Platonis; Plato vero est illud cui comparatur; et[6] hoc adverbium 'quam' dicit respectum[7] medium inter ipsum comparatum[8] et illud cui comparatur. Unde[9] hoc adverbium 'quam' nichil habet[10] de comparatione nisi predictum respectum[11]. Nota etiam quod aliquando ponitur sextum in comparatione, quod est mensura ipsius[12] excessus[13]. Et tunc comparativus gradus construitur cum duplici ablativo[14], ut 'Sortes est maior Platone uno pede', vel construitur cum uno ablativo et cum nominativo inter-

On the multiplicity in the word 'quam'

7 *Ad [1]:* As to the first item, note that the word '*quam*' is some-times an adverb of similitude, *e.g.* 'He did this as a prudent man' and 'Both this one as well as that one are running'. Sometimes it is an adverb of comparison, *e.g.* 'Socrates is stronger than Plato'. Some-times it is an adverb of admiration, e.g. 'How fortunate!', 'How excellent!' and 'Truly God of Israel is good'. Sometimes it is an adverb of indignation, *e.g.* 'What a disgraceful deed!' and 'What an abominable crime!'. Besides this it is also an elective conjunction. It is defined thus by Priscian:[3] "A conjunction is elective when after diverse things have been proposed we choose one of them", *e.g.* 'I would rather be rich than poor', <in which case> when wealth and poverty have been proposed one chooses to be rich, relinquishing the other alternative. And likewise in 'It is good to trust in the Lord rather than in man', the word '*quam*' is an elective conjunction. Thus the multiplicity found in the word '*quam*' is evident.

In what way it conveys a comparison

8 *Ad [2]:* As to the second item, note that for a comparison five things are required: [1] One thing is that which is compared, [2] the second is that in which the comparison is found or that in which there is a comparison, [3] the third is the excess in that in which the comparison is found, [4] the fourth is that to which <something> is compared, [5] the fifth is an intermediary reference between what is compared and that to which <something> is compared. For ex-ample, in the expresssion 'Socrates is stronger than (*quam*) Plato', Socrates is that which is compared, 'stronger' indicates the strength in which there is a comparison and also the excess of the strength involved, because Socrates has strength and also has it in excess with respect to Plato, and Plato is that to which he is compared; the adverb '*quam*' indicates an intermediary reference between that which is compared and that to which he is compared. Hence the adverb '*quam*' has nothing to do with a comparison except the rela-tionship just mentioned. Note also that sometimes one assumes a sixth element in a comparison, *viz* the measure of the excess. In that case a comparative degree is construed with a double ablative, *e.g* '*Sortes est maior Platone uno pede*' ('Socrates is taller than Plato by one foot'), or it is construed with an ablative and a nominative with

---

[3] *Inst. gramm.* XVI 9, p. 98(25-6), ed. Hertz.

posita 'quam', ut 'Sortes est maior quam Plato uno pede'. Et sic[15] (sicut[16] diximus) Sortes est excedens sive quod comparatur et[17] illud comparativum 'maior' dicit [*N82va*] illud in quo excedit sive illud in quo est comparatio, et etiam dicit excessum ipsius maioritatis[18], et 'Plato' dicit quod exceditur sive cui comparatur; et hoc adverbium 'quam'[19] dicit respectum[20] medium (ut diximus) inter excedens[21] et illud quod exceditur sive illud cui comparatur; et iste ablativus 'uno pede' dicit quantus est excessus maioritatis[22] in Sorte respectu Platonis et ita dicit mensuram ipsius excessus. Unde quotienscumque volumus significare mensuram [*P89ra*] excessus significati per comparativum[23], predicta sex exiguntur ad comparationem. Quotienscumque vero volumus significare comparationem sine[24] mensura excessus, sufficiunt predicta quinque. Patet ergo quod hoc adverbium 'quam' importat comparationem in hoc quod dicit respectum medium inter excedens[25] comparatum et illud[26] quod exceditur a[27] comparato, ut diximus.

Que sit comparatio ipsius ad nomen comparativi gradus

9   Circa tertium nota quod hoc adverbium 'quam' habet rationem termini cum nominativo[1] sequente in respectu ad comparativum[2], quia omne comparativum dicit excessum respectu alicuius[3] termini sive respectu eius quod exceditur; et nominativus non potest esse terminus illius excessus nisi mediante hoc adverbio 'quam'.

Que sit comparatio eius ad nominativum sequentem

10   Circa quartum vero nota quod hoc adverbium 'quam' est ratio, per quam rationem nominativus terminat respectum[1] comparativi, quia nominativus secundum se non potest[2] terminare[3] respectum comparativi; unde habet rationem[4] termini per hoc adverbium 'quam'. Unde hoc adverbium 'quam' est ratio nominativi inquantum nominativus est terminus comparativi. Et sic comparatur ad ipsum nominativum ut[5] ratio eius inquantum terminat respectum comparativi.

'*quam*' in between, *e.g.* '*Sortes est maior quam Plato uno pede*' ('Socrates is taller than Plato by one foot'). Thus (as we have said) Socrates is the exceeding entity or that which is compared, the comparative 'taller' indicates that in which he exceeds or that in which there is a comparison and also it indicates the excess of that 'being taller', 'Plato' indicates that which is exceeded or to which there is a comparison, the adverb '*quam*' indicates the interrelationship (as we have said) between the exceeding entity and that which is exceeded or that to which there is a comparison, the ablative 'by one foot' indicates how much the excess of 'being taller' in Socrates is with respect to Plato, and so it indicates the measure of the excess. Hence whenever we wish to express the measure of excess signified by a comparative, the six things mentioned before are required for the comparison. Whenever, on the other hand, we wish to express the comparison without the measure of excess, the five things mentioned earlier suffice. Hence it is evident that the adverb '*quam*' conveys a comparison because it indicates an interrelationship between the compared exceeding entity and that which is exceeded by the the entity compared, as we have said.

What its relation is to a noun of a comparative degree

9 *Ad [3]:* As to the third item, note that in combination with the nominative that follows the adverb '*quam*' has the nature of a termination with respect to the comparative. For every comparative indicates an excess with respect to some term or with respect to that which is exceeded. And the nominative can only be the termination of that excess owing to the intermediacy of the adverb '*quam*'.

What its relation is to the nominative that follows

10 *Ad [4]:* As to the fourth item, note that the adverb '*quam*' is the rationale owing to which a nominative terminates the relationship signified by a comparative, because the nominative by itself cannot terminate a relationship signified by a comparative. Hence it has the nature of a termination owing to the intermediacy of the adverb '*quam*'. Hence the adverb '*quam*' is the rationale of the nominative insofar as the nominative is the termination of the comparative. Thus it stands in relation to the nominative as such *qua* its rationale insofar as it terminates the relationship signified by the comparative.

Propter quid sequatur nominativus

11 Circa quintum nota quod substantia sumitur ut agens in
nominativo, in obliquis autem sumitur ut patiens, quia nominativus
dicit modum agentis, obliqui vero dicunt modum patientis. Et quia
hec dictio 'quam' facit illud quod exceditur retorqueri ad alium
actum et actus semper est ab[1] aliquo agente sive[2] ab aliquo quod habet
modum agentis, modus autem agentis est in nominativo (ut [*N82vb*]
diximus), — ideo quando hoc adverbium 'quam' adiungitur comparativo, oportet quod sequatur nominativus qui comparatur[3] ad alium[4]
actum, ut 'Sortes est fortior quam Plato' idest 'quam Plato sit'.

Propter quid comparativus diversimode construatur

12 Circa sextum nota quod illud quod exceditur per comparativum,
duobus modis potest significari. Quia uno modo inquantum exceditur[1] solum, alio autem modo inquantum exceditur et etiam ordinatur[2] ad alium actum. Si autem sumatur solum inquantum est res
excessa ab ipso[3] comparato sive per ipsum comparativum[4], sic stat in
ratione eius a quo removetur excessus qui significatur per comparativum. Excessus enim est in ipso comparato[5] respectu rei excesse et
non est in re[6] excessa sed aufertur ab ea. Et sic res excessa stat[7] ut[8] in
ratione eius a quo[9] aliquid[10] aufertur. Sed comparatio ista que est
termini[11] a quo, est solum reperta in ablativo. Et ideo quando[12] significatur res excessa inquantum[13] est excessa solum, tunc oportet quod
ponatur [*P89rb*] in ablativo. Et ideo comparativum isto modo semper
construitur cum ablativo. Quando autem res excessa significatur
inquantum est excessa et etiam[14] inquantum comparatur ad alium[15]
actum: quia comparatio ad alium[16] actum advenit[17] supra primam[18]
comparationem (scilicet inquantum est excessa), ideo comparatio ad
alium actum est quasi completiva prime comparationis, et ideo
ordinat rem excessam ad alium actum. Et quia actus, ut diximus, est
semper[19] ab aliquo quod stat[20] sub modo agentis, ideo sequitur

Why a nominative follows

11   *Ad [5]*: As to the fifth item, note that the substance in the nominative is understood as active, but in an oblique case as passive. For the nominative indicates the mode of an agent, whereas oblique cases indicate the mode of a patient. Well, it is because the word '*quam*' makes that which is exceeded to be referred to another act, and the act always derives from some agent or from something that has the mode of an agent, and the mode of an agent is in the nominative (as we have said) that therefore when the adverb '*quam*' is adjoined to a comparative, it is necesary that the nominative follow which is compared to the other act, *e.g.* 'Socrates is stronger than Plato', that is, 'than Plato is'.

Why a comparative is construed in different ways

12   *Ad [6]*: As to the sixth item, note that that which is exceeded, expressed by a comparative, can be signified in two ways: [1] in one way insofar as it is exceeded only, and [2] in the other way insofar it is exceeded and also ordered to a second act.[4] Now if it is signified only insofar as it is the thing exceeded by the thing compared or is expressed by the comparative, in that way it is indicated as that from which the excess signified by the comparative is removed. For the excess is in the compared thing itself with respect to the thing exceeded, and it is not in the exceeded thing but rather removed from it. Thus the exceeded thing is part of its essence, as that from which something is removed. Now that comparative relation which belongs to the *term from which* is only found in the ablative. Therefore when the thing exceeded is signified only insofar as it is exceeded, then it is necessary that it be expressed in the ablative. Hence the comparative in this way is always construed with an ablative. When, on the other hand, the exceeded thing is signified insofar as it is exceeded and also insofar as it is compared to a second act, it is because the comparison to the other act goes beyond the first comparison (*viz.* insofar as it [*i.e.* the thing] is exceeded), that therefore the comparison to that other act completes, as it were, the first comparison, and therefore it orders the exceeded thing relative to the other act. And it is because the act, as we have said, always derives from something which stands in the mode of an

---

4   What is meant here is not some other act, but rather the same act as performed by a second subject, *e.g.* 'Tom runs faster than Dick runs'.

nominativus. Et hoc modo comparativus semper construitur cum nominativo interposita 'quam'. Et[21] sic[22] patet propter quid[23] comparativus[24] aliquando construitur cum ablativo, aliquando vero cum nominativo interposita 'quam'. Et patet etiam quando comparativus[25] debet construi cum uno et quando cum alio. Patet etiam quando[26] comparativus debet construi cum duplici ablativo et <quando> cum uno[27] ablativo et cum nominativo interposita 'quam'.

Sophismata

13   Secundum predicta queritur de hoc sophismate IMPOSSIBILE EST TE SCIRE PLURA QUAM SCIS. Probatio. Hec est impossibilis 'tu scis plura quam scis'. Ergo dictum eius est impossibile. Ergo hec est vera 'impossibile est [*N83ra*] te scire plura quam scis'. Contra. Tu potes addiscere plura quam scis. Ergo[1] tu potes scire plura quam scis. Ergo prima[2] falsa.

14   Solutio. Prima est duplex. Quia sicut 'possibile' dicit relationem (quia omnis potentia[1] est eorum que sunt *ad aliquid* secundum Aristotilem), similiter 'impossibile' dicit relationem, quia[2] impotentia privat potentiam ab aliquo et respectu alicuius[3], sicut potentiam dicit[4] 'possibile' in aliquo et respectu alicuius, quia[5] respectu actus essentialis[6], ut[7] respectu forme completive, vel respectu actus accidentalis, ut respectu comparationis egredientis[8] ab ipsa forma, quia agere est forme. Dico ergo quod prima est duplex, eoquod hec dictio 'impossibile' potest ponere rem[9] suam in re dicti accusativi[10] (et sic[11] prima[12] est falsa et est sensus 'tu non potes scire plura quam scis') vel potest[13] ponere rem suam supra totum dictum; et sic prima est vera[14] et est sensus 'te scire plura quam scis est impossibile', quia in nullo tempore scies[15] plura quam scis[16] in eodem.

15   Item. Queritur de hoc sophismate IMPOSSIBILE EST ALIUD QUAM ASINUM[1] GENUISSE TE. Probatio. Hominem esse asinum est impossibile. Et[2] est aliud quam asinum genuisse te. Ergo

agent that therefore a nominative follows. In this way a comparative is always construed with a nominative with '*quam*' placed in between. Thus it is evident why a comparative is sometimes construed with an ablative, and sometimes with a nominative with '*quam*' placed in between. It is also evident when the comparative must be construed with the one and when it must be construed with the other. It is also evident when the comparative must be construed with a double ablative, and when it must be construed with one ablative and a nominative with '*quam*' placed in between.

Sophismata

13 As regards what has been said, there is a problem concerning the sophisma sentence IT IS IMPOSSIBLE THAT YOU KNOW MORE THAN YOU KNOW. Proof: the proposition 'You know more than you know' is impossible. Therefore its *dictum* is impossible. Therefore the proposition 'It is impossible that you know more than you know' is true. There is an argument to the contrary. You can learn more than you know. Therefore you can know more than you know. Therefore the original sentence is false.

14 Solution. The original sentence is ambiguous. For just as 'possible' indicates a relationship (because every potency falls under the things that are relative, according to Aristotle),[5] likewise 'impossible' indicates a relationship. For an impotency deprives something of a potency and this with respect to something, just as 'possible' asserts a potency in something and this with respect to something, *viz.* with respect to an essential act, *e.g.* with respect to a consummative form, or with respect to an accidental act, *e.g.* with respect to a relationship originating from the form itself, because to act belongs to a form. I therefore say that the original sentence is ambiguous, because the word 'impossible' can assert its content in the content of the *dictum* expressed in the accusative (and in this way the original sentence is false and means *you cannot know more than you know*) or it can assert its content to extend to the whole *dictum*, and thus the original sentence is true and means *that you know more than you know is impossible*, because at no time will you know more than you know at that same time.

15 Furthermore, there is a problem concerning the sophisma-sentence AN IMPOSSIBLE IS SOMETHING OTHER THAN AN ASS HAS BEGOTTEN YOU. Proof: that a man is an ass is impossible and it is other than that an ass has begotten you. Therefore an impossible

---

[5] Cf. *Categ.* 7, 6b33-6.

impossibile est aliud quam asinum genuisse te. Contra. Impossibile est aliud quam asinum genuisse te. Ergo asinus genuit te.

16 Solutio. Prima duplex, eoquod hoc relativum[1] diversitatis 'aliud'[2] potest referri ad hunc terminum 'asinum'; et sic hoc relativum 'aliud' est accusativi casus. Et est sensus [*P89va*] 'impossibile est <aliud quam asinum genuisse te' idest: 'impossibile est> rem[3] aliquam aliam ab asino genuisse te': et sic est falsa. Vel hoc relativum 'aliud' potest referre totum dictum (scilicet 'asinum genuisse te') et tunc hoc relativum 'aliud' est nominativi[4] casus. Et est sensus 'impossibile est aliud quam asinum genuisse te' idest[5] 'aliud est impossibile quam hoc impossibile quod est "asinum genuisse te"', ut 'hominem esse lapidem' est impossible aliud ab illo impossibili, scilicet 'asinum genuisse te'. Et sic est vera.

C. DE HAC DICTIONE 'QUICQUID'

Introductio

17 Quia hec dictio 'quicquid' uno modo importat distributionem, ideo[1] quoad hoc de ipsa debet determinari[2] in *Distributionibus*. Sed quoad[3] hoc quod importat consecutionem[4] cum disiunctione[5], debet determinari de[6] ipsa in [*N83rb*] *Sincategoreumatibus*. Circa hanc ergo dictionem 'quicquid' primo queritur quid significet; secundo utrum sit dictio equivoca vel non; tertio autem utrum importet relationem vel non.

Quid significet hec dictio 'quicquid'

18 Circa primum[1] nota quod quatuor sunt de intellectu huius dictionis 'quicquid' sive de sua significatione. Unum est distributio. Alterum vero est materia sue distributionis, quia, sicut hec dictio 'quilibet'[2] habet in se distributionem et rem distributam per[3] suam distributionem, similiter et 'quicquid'[4]. Tertium autem est[5] consecutio. Quartum vero disiunctio, quia cum dicitur 'quicquid currit, movetur', sensus est 'sive[6] hoc currit, movetur, sive illud'[7]. Et sic est ibi consecutio[8] et disiunctio[9]. Et ista quatuor sunt de significatione huius dictionis 'quicquid'.

is something other than an ass has begotten you. There is an argument to the contrary. An impossible is that something other than an ass has begotten you. Therefore an ass has begotten you.

16   Solution. The original sentence is ambiguous because the relative of diversity 'other' (*aliud*) can refer to the term 'ass' and thus the relative 'other' is in the accusative case, and 'An impossible is: something other than an ass has begotten you' means *(an) impossible is that another thing than an ass has begotten you*, and thus it is false. Or the relative 'other' can refer to the whole *dictum* (*viz.* that an ass has begotten you) and in that case the relative 'other' (*aliud*) is in the nominative case, and 'An impossible is something other than: an ass has begotten you' means *something other is impossible than the impossible 'that an ass has begotten you'*, e.g. 'that a man is a stone' is an impossible other than the impossible 'that an ass has begotten you'. In this way it is true.

C.   ON THE WORD '*QUICQUID*' ('WHATEVER')

Introduction

17   It is because the word '*quicquid*' in one way conveys a distribution, that therefore to that extent it must be laid down in <the treatise> *On distributions*. However, to the extent that it conveys a consecution in combination with a disjunction, it must be determined in <the treatise> *On syncategorematic words*. So on the word '*quicquid*' there is *[1]* first a problem what it signifies, *[2]* secondly whether it is equivocal or not, *[3]* thirdly whether it conveys a relation or not.

What the word 'quicquid' *signifies*

18   *Ad [1]:* As to the first item, note that there are four elements in the notion of the word '*quicquid*' (or in its signification). [1] One is a distribution. [2] The other is the content of the distribution, for just as the word '*quilibet*' ('whoever') contains a distribution and something distributed by the distribution, likewise so does '*quicquid*'. [3] The third is a consecution. [4] The fourth is a disjunction, for when one says 'Whatever is running is moving', the meaning is 'If this is running, it is moving, or if that'. Thus we have in this case a disjunction and a consecution. And these four elements belong to the signification of the word '*quicquid*'.

Utrum sit dictio equivoca vel non

19   Circa[1] secundum nota quod, quamvis diversa intelligantur[2] in significatione[3] huius dictionis 'quicquid', non tamen est dictio equivoca, quia significat illa plura per modum unius, eoquod distributio significatur in suo subiecto sive in re distributa mediante consecutione[4]. Et propter hoc semper[5] redditur ei unum verbum quod est antecedens et aliud quod est consequens, ut 'quicquid currit, movetur'.

Utrum importet relationem vel non

20   Circa tertium obicitur quia[1]: Sensus istius 'quicquid currit, movetur' est iste 'omne quod currit, movetur'. Sed hic est relatio. Ergo in prima est relatio. Ergo hec dictio 'quicquid' importat relationem. Et[2] dicendum quod hec dictio 'quicquid' non importat relationem nec est dictio relativa, sed est nomen distributivum et infinitum significans illud[3] quod diximus. Et componitur per geminationem[4] huius nominis 'quid' secundum quod hoc nomen 'quid'[5] simpliciter est infinitum, et non secundum quod[6] est interrogativum[7] vel etiam[8] relativum. Argumentum autem peccat secundum accidens, quia non oporteret[9] si in uno convertibilium intelligitur relatio, quod in altero intelligatur[10]. Verbi gratia iste due convertuntur [*P89vb*] 'homo albus currit' et 'homo qui est albus, currit' et in una intelligitur relatio, in altera vero non.

Sophisma

21   Secundum predicta queritur de hoc sophismate QUICQUID DEUS SCIVIT, SCIT. Probatio. Deus scivit[1] omnia. Et nichil oblitus est. Ergo quicquid Deus scivit, scit[2]. Contra[3]. Quicquid Deus scivit, scit. Sed scivit[4] te esse[5] nasciturum. Ergo scit[6] te[7] esse nasciturum[8]. Ergo tu es nasciturus.

22   Solutio. Prima simpliciter vera, quia scientia Cause Prime semper[1] est eadem nec recipit in se aliquam transmutationem[2]; unde de rebus omnibus scientiam habet immobilem[3]. Et[4] ideo de

Whether it is an equivocal word or not

19   *Ad [2]:* As to the second item, note that, although diverse things are understood in the signification of the word '*quicquid*', nevertheless it is not an equivocal word. The reason for this is that it signifies the many things in the manner of one thing, for it signifies a distribution in its subject or in the thing that is distributed by means of a consecution. It is on account of this that one verb is always construed with it which is antecedent and another which is consequent, *e.g.* 'Whatever is running is moving'.

Whether it conveys a relation or not

20   *Ad [3]:* There is an argument to the contrary that the meaning of 'Whatever (*quicquid*) is running is moving' is 'Everything that is running is moving'. Now this is a relative construction. Therefore in the first sentence there is question of a relation. Hence the word '*quicquid*' conveys a relation. The answer should be that the word '*quicquid*' does not convey a relation nor is it a relative word, but it is a distributive and indefinite noun that signifies what we have said. It consists in a duplication of '*quid*', that is, insofar as the word '*quid*' is merely indefinite, and not insofar as it is interrogative or even relative. The argument then commits the fallacy of accident, because it is not necessary that if a relative construction is understood in one convertible, that it <also> be understood in the other. For example, the two propositions 'A white man is running' and 'A man who is white is running' are convertible, and in one of them a relative construction is understood whereas in the other there is not.

Sophisma

21   As regards what has been said, there is a problem concerning the sophisma-sentence WHATEVER GOD HAS KNOWN HE KNOWS. Proof: God has known everything and He has forgotten nothing. Therefore whatever God has known He knows. There is an argument to the contrary. Whatever God has known He knows. Now He has known that you will be born. Therefore He knows that you will be born. Therefore you will be born.
22   Solution. The original sentence is *simpliciter* true, because the knowledge possessed by the First Cause is always the same and it does not receive in it any kind of change; hence It has an

rebus corruptibilibus scientiam habet immobilem[5]. Cuius causa hec
est. Omne cognoscens cognoscit secundum modum suum[6] et
secundum virtutem sue cognitionis, et non secundum modum
cogniti sive rei cognite. Unde quia virtus cognitiva Cause Prime non
dependet a rebus (sed res dependent ab Ipsa[7] tamquam a sua causa),
cognitio autem nostra dependet a rebus cognitis et perficitur ab eis,
ideo sciendum[8] quod nostra cognitio et scientia est permutabilis
secundum rerum permutationem; scientia[9] vero Cause Prime non
est permutabilis secundum mutationem rerum.

23   Improbatio autem peccat secundum[1] figuram dictionis ex com-
mutatione[2] predicamenti, quia mutatur *quid* in *quando*. Hec enim
distributio 'quicquid' dicit *quid*, 'nasciturus' autem dicit *quando*. Et sic
mutatur *quid* in *quando*, assumendo[3] 'nasciturum' sub eo quod est
'quicquid'[4]. Et etiam[5] est ibi sophisma accidentis[6]. Quia *quid*[7] et
quando possunt accipi uno modo inquantum significantur per dictionem; et sic peccatum est in eis secundum figuram dictionis propter
principium motivum[8] quod est in dictione. Alio autem modo
possunt sumi *quid*[9] et *quando*, scilicet[10] a parte rei sive ut sunt modi
rerum circumscripto[11] sermone; et sic error in eis facit sophisma
accidentis propter principium motivum in[12] re. Universaliter enim
dico quod[13] ubicumque est figura dictionis, ibi semper est sophisma
accidentis, et non econverso. Sed hoc est propter causas diversas,
sicut tetigimus, quia modi rerum predicamentalium[14] [*T50va*]
sunt[15] diversi. Si[16] accipiantur inquantum per dictionem significantur, sic[17] fit figura dictionis. Si autem isti[18] idem modi accipiantur a
parte rei sive[19] ut sunt modi rerum, sic fit *accidens* in eis, quia primo
modo est principium motivum in dictione, secundo vero[20] in re.

immutable knowledge of all things. Therefore it has an immutable knowledge of corruptible things. The reason for this is the following. Everything that has knowledge has knowledge in its own way and according to the power of its own cognition, and not according to the mode of what is known or the thing *qua* known. Hence as the cognitive power of the First Cause does not depend upon things (but rather the things depend upon It as their cause), whereas our knowledge does depend upon the things known and is achieved by them, therefore one should know that our cognition, and our knowledge, is mutable in accordance with the mutation of things. The knowledge possessed by the First Cause, on the other hand, is not mutable according to the mutation of things.

23   The disproof[6] goes astray according to the fallacy of figure of speech, by changing one category into another, because a 'what' is changed into a 'when'. For the distribution '*quicquid*' designates a *what* and 'will be born' designates a *when*. Thus a 'what' is changed into a 'when' by taking 'will be born' as falling under '*quicquid*' ('whatever'). Moreover, there is in this case a fallacy of accident. For 'what' and 'when' can be taken in one way insofar as they are signified by a word, and thus there is a fallacy of figure of speech on account of the principle that is active in language. In the other way 'what' and 'when' can be taken from the viewpoint of the thing <signified> or insofar as they are modes of things quite apart from their verbal expression. In the latter way the error in them produces a fallacy of accident on account of the principle that is active in the thing <signified>. For generally I say that wherever there is question of a figure of speech, in that case there is always question of a fallacy of accident, and not the other way round. Now this is due to diverse causes, as we have mentioned, because the modes of things signified by the categories are diverse. If they are taken insofar as they are signified by a word, a figure of speech occurs. If, on the other hand, these modes are taken from the viewpoint of the thing or insofar as they are modes of things, then there occurs in them a fallacy of accident, because in the first way the principle that is active occurs in language, whereas in the second it occurs in the thing <involved>.

---

6   Cf. above, cap. 21.

TRACTATUS DECIMUS

DE RESPONSIONIBUS

De interrogatione et responsione

1   Responsio sequitur[1] interrogationem, quia interrogatio est petitio responsionis. Et est ab interrogantc[2] [*N83vb*] ut[3] a causa efficiente.
Quia ergo interrogatio[4] per interrogantem[5] cognoscitur sicut per
suam[6] causam, sciendum quod bene interrogans[7] quinque debet
facere. Primum est[8] invenire locum a quo [*P90ra*] sive per quem
debet arguere. Secundum est[9] formare[10] interrogationes[11] sive propositiones secundum[12] locum prius repertum. Tertium autem est
ordinare eas ad se invicem. Quartum est proponere eas ad alterum,
ut ad[13] respondentem. Quintum autem est ut cogat ipsum respondentem dicere improbabilia[14]. Unde si bene vis opponere oportet te
facere[15] predicta quinque, vel saltem quatuor priora ex eis. Hec
autem quinque determinat Aristotiles in octavo *Topicorum*; quatuor
quidem in principio octavi, quintum autem in capitulo *De responsione*.

De modis solutionis

2   Sequitur autem videre modos solutionis[1] in genere. Solutionum[2] ergo alia est[3] recta, alia vero[4] apparens. Apparens[5] quidem
solutio fit multis modis. Quia quedam est ad[6] interrogantem, ut[7]
quando interrogans[8] impeditur ne procedat ad suam conclusionem,
quamvis veram habeat rationem. Alia autem est solutio ad[9] tempus,
ut[10] quando solutio que datur ad propositum, indiget maiori inqui-
sitione et maiori tempore quam ipsum[11] propositum; hec autem que
eget[12] pluris temporis quam propositum, est pessima[13] omnium solutionum. Et utraque istarum solutionum[14] apparentium[15] dicitur *ad
hominem*.

CHAPTER X

ON ANSWERS

On question and answer

1   An answer follows after a question because a question is a request for an answer, and the latter derives from a questioner as from its efficient cause. It is because the question is known via the questioner as its cause, that therefore one should know that a good questioner must do five things. [1] The first is to find a topic from which or by means of which he should form his argument. [2] The second is to frame questions or propositions in terms of the topic discovered earlier. [3] The third is to arrange them in a consistent order. [4] The fourth is to propose them to the partner, *viz.* the respondent. [5] The fifth is that he force the respondent to pronounce improbable things. Hence if you intend to be a good opponent, it is necessary that you do the five things just mentioned, or at least the first four of them. It is these five things that Aristotle lays down in the Book VIII of the *Topics*, four of them in fact at the beginning of the eighth book[1] and the fifth in the chapter *On answer.*[2]

On the modes of solution

2   Next we shall consider the ways of solution in general. Of solutions, then, some are correct and some are apparent. Now in fact an apparent solution occurs in many ways. [1] For one relates to the questioner, *e.g.* when he is prevented from proceeding to his conclusion, even though he may have a true argument. [2] Another solution is related to time, *e.g.* when a solution given to what has been proposed requires a greater investigation and more time than has been proposed. Now this solution, which requires more time than what has been proposed, is the worst of all solutions. And both these apparent solutions are called *ad hominem.*

---

[1] *Topica* VIII 1, 155b3-7.
[2] *Ibid.* 4, 159a18-20.

3   Recta vero solutio[1] dicitur solutio ad orationem. Et diffinitur etiam[2] sic in secundo *Elenchorum*: "recta quidem solutio est manifestatio falsi sillogismi et propter quid[3] est falsus". Species autem sive partes recte solutionis sunt due, quia[4] alia est per interemptionem, alia vero[5] per divisionem[6]. Solutio quidem per interemptionem est quando interimitur aliqua premissarum propter sui falsitatem. Solutio autem per divisionem est quando manifestatur quod conclusio non sequitur ex premissis propter aliquam fallaciam in dictione vel extra dictionem. Unde[7] solutio per interemptionem debetur orationi que[8] procedit ex falsis[9]; [*N84ra*] solutio[10] per divisionem[11] debetur[12] orationi peccanti[13] secundum aliquam fallaciam in dictione vel extra dictionem.

4   Quotienscumque ergo vis orationem[1] aliquam solvere, sive in sophismatibus sive in aliis, primo considera utrum conclusio sit vera vel falsa. Quoniam[2] si est falsa, non potest probari nisi sophistice; et sic[3] ad probationem solvendum est per divisionem. Aut probabitur[4] per fallaciam[5]; et tunc ad ipsam probationem solvendum per interemptionem; improbatio autem vera debet esse. Si autem conclusio vera sit, tunc recta debet esse probatio, sed improbatio peccabit secundum aliquam fallaciam; et tunc solvendum est per divisionem. Aut[6] accipiet aliquod falsum; et[7] tunc solvendum per interemptionem.

De divisione sillogismorum a parte conclusionis

5   [*P90rb*] Terminatis[1] sincategoreumatibus et habitis eis que[2] exiguntur ad oppositionem in genere et visis modis solutionum in communi, consequenter dicendum est de divisione sillogismorum a parte conclusionis. Sciendum ergo [*T50vb*] quod sillogismorum alii sunt universales, alii particulares. Universales autem dicuntur[3] qui habent conclusionem universalem, sicut patet in primo et secundo[4] prime figure et etiam[5] in primo et secundo secunde[6] figure. Particulares autem dicuntur qui habent conclusionem particularem, sicut patet in reliquis sillogismis omnium figurarum.

3   A correct solution, on the other hand, is called *ad orationem*. It is also defined[3] in the second book of *On Sophistical Refutations* thus: "A correct solution is the exposure of a false syllogism and the reason why it is false". The kinds or parts of a correct solution are two. [3] One is by way of destruction and the other by way of division. Now a solution by way of destruction occurs when some one of the premises is destroyed on account of its falsity, whereas a solution by way of division occurs when one makes clear that the conclusion does not follow from the premises owing to some fallacy dependent on language or independent of it. Hence a solution by way of destruction pertains to a proposition that follows from what is false, whereas a solution by way of division pertains to a proposition erring according to some fallacy dependent on language or independent of it.

4   This is why whenever you wish to solve some proposition, whether this be in the case of sophismata or in others, the first thing to do is to consider whether the conclusion is true or false. For if it is false it can only be proved in a sophistical way, and then as to the proof, the solution should be produced by means of division. Or it will be proved via a fallacy, and then as to the proof, the solution should be produced by destruction. The disproof, then, must be true. If, on the other hand, the conclusion is true, in that case the proof must be correct whereas the disproof will err according to some fallacy, and in that case it must be solved by division. Or one [*i.e.* the interlocutor] will accept something false, and in that case it can be solved by destruction.

On the division of syllogisms from the viewpoint of the conclusion

5   Now that we have ended our discussion on syncategorematic words and have dealt with the things required for opposition in general and seen the ways of solution in general, we must next speak about the division of syllogisms from the viewpoint of the conclusion. One should know, therefore, that of syllogisms some are universal and others particular. Now those are called universal that contain a universal conclusion, as is evident in the first and the second mood of the first figure and also in the first and second mood of the second figure. Those are called particular that contain a particular conclusion, as is evident in the remaining syllogisms of all figures.

---

[3] *Soph. El.* 18, 176b29-30; 24, 179b23-4.

6   Nota ergo quod universales semper plura sillogizant sive plures habent semper conclusiones, quia habent suam propriam[1] conclusionem et etiam concludunt conversam[2] sue conclusionis; et etiam concludunt particularem proprie conclusionis; preter autem has tres conclusiones sillogismi universales negativi concludunt quartam conclusionem; et hec est[3] particularis propositio converse sue proprie conclusionis. Verbi gratia secundus prime infert[4] suam propriam conclusionem sic[5]: 'nullum[6] animal est lapis; omnis homo est animal; ergo nullus homo est lapis'. Et concludit conversam sue conclusionis sic: 'ergo nullus lapis est homo'. Et concludit particularem sue[7] proprie[8] conclusionis sic: 'ergo quidam homo non est lapis'. Et concluditur particularem sue converse proprie conclusionis sic: 'ergo quidam lapis non est homo'.

7   Et iste quatuor conclusiones sequuntur [*N84rb*] ex duabus premissis in predicto sillogismo positis[1]. Et sic omnes universales negativi[2] quatuor habent conclusiones. Sed universales affirmativi[3] habent tres, scilicet propriam conclusionem universalem[4] et suam[5] particularem et suam conversam. Unde[6] nota quod quintus prime continetur sub primo, quia nichil aliud concludit[7] nisi[8] conversam conclusionis primi. Et sextus prime continetur sub secundo, quia nichil concludit nisi conversam conclusionis secundi. Eadem[9] ratione septimus continetur sub tertio. Unde intellige quod Aristotiles non separavit quintum[10] a primo neque sextum a secundo neque septimum a tertio, sed Boetius. Unde Aristotiles in primo[11] *Priorum*, ubi[12] determinat generationem sillogismorum, nullam facit mentionem de illis tribus, scilicet de quinto et sexto et septimo, sed solum dicit in principio[13] secundi *Priorum* quod universales[14] sillogismi omnes[15] semper plura[16] sillogizant, idest[17] plures habent conclusiones, ut diximus. Et ab illo loco extraxit eos[18] Boetius. Item. Particularium sillogismorum affirmativi plures habent conclusiones, quia suam propriam[19] conclusionem et conversam eius. Et ideo, sicut diximus, septimus[20] prime continetur sub tertio. Sed particulares negativi unam solam habent conclusionem, [*P90va*] eoquod particularis[21] negativa non convertitur.

6 Note, therefore, that the universal ones always give more than one result, *i.e.* they have many conclusions, for they have their proper conclusion and they also conclude to the converse of their conclusion; in addition they conclude to the particular of the proper conclusion. And apart from these three conclusions universal negative syllogisms also have a fourth conclusion, *viz.* the particular proposition of the converse of its proper conclusion. For example, the second mood of the first figure draws its proper conclusion thus: 'No animal is a stone; every man is an animal; therefore no man is a stone'. It also concludes the converse of the conclusion thus: 'Therefore no stone is a man'; it concludes the particular proposition of its proper conclusion: 'Therefore some man is not a stone', and likewise it concludes the particular proposition of the converse of its proper conclusion thus: 'Therefore some stone is not a man'.

7 And these four conclusions follow from the two premises that are part of the syllogism mentioned above. Thus all universal negatives have four conclusions. Universal affirmative ones, on the other hand, have three, *viz.* the proper universal conclusion, its particular and its converse. Hence note that the fifth mood of the first figure is contained under the first mood because it concludes nothing other than the converse of the conclusion of the first mood. The sixth mood of the first figure is contained under the second mood, because it concludes nothing other than the converse of the conclusion of the second mood. For the same reason the seventh is contained under the third. So understand that it is not Aristotle who has separated the fifth from the first mood nor the sixth from the second nor the seventh from the third, but Boethius. That is why in his *Prior Analytics*, where he deals with the generation of syllogisms,[4] Aristotle makes no mention of these three moods, that is, the fifth, the sixth and the seventh, but he only says[5] at the beginning of the Book II of the *Prior Analytics* that all univeral syllogisms always give more than one result, that is, they have many conclusions, as we have said. It is Boethius who has extracted[6] them from this work. Furthermore, of particular syllogisms the affirmative ones have many conclusions, because they have their proper one and its converse. Therefore, in the same way as we have said, the seventh mood of the first figure is contained under the third. Particular negative syllogisms, however, have one conclusion only, because a particular negative proposition cannot be converted.

---

[4] *Anal. Priora* I 27, 43a20ff.
[5] *Anal. Priora* II 1, 53a4-5.
[6] *De categ. syll.* II, 810D-821A.

De ostensione sillogismorum

8   Visa[1] divisione[2] sillogismorum a parte conclusionis[3] quoad quantitatem[4] et qualitatem in precedenti lectione[5] (non[6] quoad principia sillogismorum, que sunt modus et figura, quia[7] divisio sillogismorum a[8] parte figurarum et modorum habita fuit[9] prius in *Tractatu sillogismorum*, assignando figuras tres et modos proprios eorundem[10]), — consequenter sciendum quod omnis sillogismus ostenditur duobus modis, quia ostenditur convertendo et etiam ducendo[11] ad impossibile (sive[12] per sillogismusm conversivum et per sillogismum ad impossibile).

9   Notandum etiam[1] quod eodem modo ordinantur termini[2] et propositiones in sillogismo conversivo et in sillogismo ad impossibile. [*N84va*] Sed differunt duobus modis. Prima differentia est in hoc quod sillogismus conversivus fit alio[3] sillogismo prius facto, sumendo oppositum conclusionis cum altera premissarum ad interimendum reliquam, sed aliquando maiorem, aliquando vero[4] minorem. Verbi gratia si accipiatur[5] oppositum conclusionis cum minori, interimit[6] maiorem. Ut 'omne animal est substantia; omnis homo est animal; ergo omnis homo est substantia'. Oppositum autem[7] conclusionis est hoc 'quidam homo non est substantia'. Ex[8] hoc ergo cum minori [*T51ra*] potes[9] interimere maiorem sillogizando in quinto tertie sic: 'quidam homo non est substantia; omnis homo est animal; ergo quoddam animal non est substantia'; et hec conclusio contradicit maiori alterius sillogismi. Si vero accipiatur[10] idem oppositum cum maiori, interimit minorem sillogizando in quarto secunde sic: 'omne animal est substantia; quidam homo non est substantia; ergo quidam homo non est animal'; et[11] hec conclusio interimit minorem primi sillogismi. Et sic sillogismus conversivus fit semper sillogismo[12] alio[13] prius facto. Sed[14] sillogizando ad impossibile non est necesse alium prius facere sillogismum, sed solum sumpta aliqua propositione[15]: si[16] ex ea ducat[17] <respondentem> ad maius inconveniens quod[18] sit cognitum esse falsum (unde[19] suum oppositum erit manifeste verum), et propter hoc

On the demonstration of syllogisms

8   Now that we have looked at the division of syllogisms from the
viewpoint of the conclusion as far as quality and quantity are concerned in the preceding lecture[7] (not as far as the principles of syllogisms, *viz.* mood and figure, are concerned, because the division of
syllogisms from the viewpoint of figures and mood has been discussed in the treatise *On syllogisms,*[8] by assigning three figures and
the moods proper to them),— next one should know that every syllogism is demonstrated in two ways, because it is demonstrated by
conversion and also by reducing it to an impossible (or by a conversive syllogism and by a syllogism *ad impossibile*).

9   One should also note that terms and propositions in a conversive syllogism and in a syllogism *ad impossibile* are placed in the
same position. However, they are different in two ways. [1] The first
difference is that a conversive syllogism is formed after another
syllogism has previously been formed by taking the opposite of the
<latter's> conclusion in combination with one of its premises in or-
der to destroy the remaining one, and sometimes this is the major
and sometimes the minor. For example, if one takes the opposite of
the conclusion in combination with the minor, one destroys the
major, as in 'Every animal is a substance; every man is an animal;
therefore every man is a substance'. Now the opposite of the conclusion runs 'Some man is not a substance'. Therefore if you take this
in combination with the minor you can destroy the major by producing a syllogism in the fifth mood of the third figure as follows:
'Some man is not a substance; every man is an animal; therefore
some animal is not a substance'. The latter conclusion contradicts
the major premise of the former syllogism. If, on the other hand,
one takes the same opposite <conclusion> in combination with the
major, one destroys the minor by producing a syllogism in the
fourth mood of the second figure as follows: 'Every animal is a
substance; some man is not a substance; therefore some man is not
an animal'. The latter conclusion destroys the minor of the original
syllogism. And in this way a conversive syllogism is always
formed after some other syllogism has previously been formed.
Now in producing a syllogism *ad impossibile* it is not necessary to
previously produce another syllogism, but merely by taking a
proposition: if from it one leads the respondent to an even more
absurd one, which is known to be false (hence its opposite will be

---

[7] Cf. above, capp. 5-7.
[8] *Tractatus* IV, pp. 44(7)-51(13), ed. De Rijk.

interimat[20] propositionem[21] quam prius sumebat, — tunc erit sillogismus ad impossibile. Ut[22] si tu[23] des propositionem hanc scilicet
quod 'arbores non habent animam' et[24] ex hoc concludat[25] impossibile[26] magis manifestum sic: 'ergo arbores non nutriuntur[27] neque
augmentantur'; sed hoc est impossibile; ergo impossibile est arbores
[*P90vb*] non habere animam, — sic factus est sillogismus ad impossibile. Secunda autem differentia est quod sillogismus conversivus
est ad ostendendum illationem[28] esse necessariam; sillogismus
vero[29] ad impossibile est ad ostendendum propositum esse falsum;
unde ex consequenti est ad[30] ostendendum oppositum propositi[31] esse
verum.

10   Sciendum ergo[1] quod quilibet sillogismus cuiuslibet figure
potest ostendi quoad[2] suam illationem per [*N84vb*] sillogismum conversivum, ut diximus, et etiam quelibet conclusio cuiuslibet sillogismi potest ostendi quoad suam veritatem per sillogismum ad impossibile, ut dictum est. Si autem aliquis in[3] istis voluerit esse promptus,
oportet eum frequenter exercitari[4] in huiusmodi sillogismis.

manifestly true), and therefore one destroys the proposition which was previously accepted,—in that case one will have a syllogism *ad impossibile*. For instance, if you present the proposition 'Trees do not have a soul', and <the opponent> concludes from it what is more manifestly impossible as follows, 'Therefore trees are not nourished nor do they grow; now this is impossible; therefore it is impossible that trees do not have a soul,—thus a syllogism *ad impossibile* has been produced. [2] The second difference is that a conversive syllogism is meant to demonstrate that an inference is necessary, whereas a syllogism *ad impossibile* is meant to demonstrate that what has been proposed is false, and, consequently, to show that the opposite of what has been proposed is true.

10   One should know, therefore, that any syllogism whatsoever, regardless the figure, can be demonstrated as regards its inferential force by means of a conversive syllogism, as we have said, and also any conclusion whatsoever of whatever syllogism can be demonstrated as regards its truth by means of a syllogism *ad impossible*, as has been said. However, if anyone wants to be quick in these syllogisms, it is necessary that he frequently exercise in syllogisms of this type.

CRITICAL APPARATUS

INTRODUCTIO

1

   1 solus nisi] *codd.* solum nichil *H*
   2 consimilibus] *codd.* consimilia *H*
   3 predicabilium] *codd.R^c* predicatum *R*

2

   1 ut ... equus] *codd.* quia est quedam res subicibilis ut homo vel equus
NH
   2 ambulat vel currit] *NC* vel currit *P* currit *TRH*
   3 est] *codd.* dicitur *RC*
   4 subicibilis vel predicabilis] *codd.* subiecti et predicati *P* subiecti aut
predicati *H*
   5 item] *codd.* iterum *H* est duplex *add.P*
   6 dispositio] *codd.* res *T*
   7 id] *codd.* ad *C*
   8 ita ... econverso] *codd.* *om. H*
   9 subiectum] *codd.* dicitur *add. PC*
   10 ut] *codd.* sicut *PN*
   11 alia] *codd.* autem *add. P*
   12 vel] *codd.* et alia est dispositio *C*
   13 necessario] *TP* necessarium *cett.*
   14 ipsius] *codd.* dispositiones *P*
   15 in comparatione] *codd.* compositiones *C*
   16 dicunt] *codd.* dant *H*
   17 comparationes] *codd.* compositiones *C*
   18 subiecti] *RC* subicibilis *cett.*
   19 predicati] *RC* predicabilis *cett.*
   20 dicitur sincategoreuma] *codd.* dicuntur sincategoreumata *H*
   21 predicativum] *TNH* predicamentum *P* predicatum *R* predicabilis *C*

3

   1 et sic] *codd.* sicut *R*
   2 nunc] *T^cPCH* tunc *TR* tamen *N*
   3 earum] *codd.* *om.TC*
   4 vult] *codd.* dicit *R*
   5 dictionibus] *TC* *om. cett.*
   6 non] *codd.* *om. N*

4

   1 ad] *codd.* hoc *add. T*

2 per se] *codd.* *om. TC*
3 sciendum] *codd.* autem *add. N*
4 diffinitione] *codd.* alicuius *add. PCH*
5 de diffinito] *codd.* *om. T* et etiam diffinitio *add. PCH*
6 enim] *codd.* equum *(!)N*
7 animal ... ut] *codd. P^c om. P*
8 de] *codd.* suo *add. R^m*
9 punctum] *codd.* punctus *P*
10 rectis] *codd. T^rH^c om. TH*
11 modo] *codd. R^c om. R*
12 per se] *TPN* proprium *cett.*
13 sua diffinitione] *codd.* subiecto diffiniendo *CH*
14 omne] *codd.* esse *CH*
15 obiectu] *codd.* subiectu *(!)N*
16 per se ... passio] *NR* accidens per se ... passio *T* per se proprium accidens ... passio *P* propria passio sive proprium accidens *CH*
17 par vel impar] *codd.* pars par et impar *N*
18 recta vel curva] *codd.* curva vel recta *P*
19 et] *codd.* *om. P*
20 divisibilis] *codd.* divisus *P*
21 rectum] *codd.* recta *R*
22 est] *codd.* *om. N*
23 par vel impar] *codd.* *hic incipit codex Eporedianus (E)*
24 quia] *codd.* *om. T*
25 propria] *T* *om. cett.*
26 premissarum] *codd. R^c* principiorum *R*
27 lumine] *codd. P^c* *om. P*

5

1 dictionibus] *codd.* diffinitionibus *(!)C*
2 sive] *codd.* in *add. TNC*
3 solus] *NECH* solum *TPR*
4 nunc] *codd.* nunc et *R* non *(!)E*
5 est] *codd.* illud *(!)E*
6 aliis] *P* *om. cett.*
7 et] *codd.* quia *add. E*
8 est] *codd.* *om. N*
9 prior] *codd.* prima *R*
10 esse] *codd. H^c* *om. H* prior *add. R*
11 negatione] *T* *om. cett.*
12 intelligitur ... negatione] *T* et etiam quia in negatione intelligitur affirmatio *cett.*

6

1 ergo] *codd.* *om. P*
2 est] *codd.* per prius significat *add. N* per prius *add. N^c*
3 compositionem] *codd.* quandam compositionem *P*
4 consignificat] *codd.* significat *PH*
5 etiam] *RC* *om. cett.*

TRACTATUS PRIMUS

DE COMPOSITIONE

1

  1 est quod] *TP*   est *N*   ergo quod *cett.*
  2 quare] *codd.*   quia *T*
  3 relationis] *codd.*   relatorum *N*
  4 dividitur autem] *T*   dividitur *P*   dividatur autem *N*
  5 primo] *codd.*   om. *T*
  6 compositionis ... modorum] *codd.*   causa compositionis est alia rerum alia modorum *E*
  7 compositio ... significandi] *codd.*   om. *P*
  8 gramaticum] *codd.*   gramaticos *H*
  9 nomine] *codd.*   homine *E*
  10 et in verbo] *C*   om. *cett.*
  11 compositio] *P*   om *cett.*

2

  1 accidentis cum] *codd.*   cum accidens *EH*
  2 subiecto] *codd.*   substantia *T*
  3 anime] *codd.*   om. *P*
  4 anima] *codd.*   differentia *(!)E*
  5 cum] *TP*   in *N*   cum suo *cett.*
  6 speciei] *T*   specierum *cett.*
  7 mathematicum] *codd.*   metaphisicum *E*   metaphisicam *T*
  8 logicum] *codd.*   logicam *T*
  9 est] *codd.*   compositio *add. cett.*
  10 nomine] *TN*   om. *cett.*
  11 dicemus] *TNER*   dicimus *P*   dicetur *C*   dicemdum *H*

3

  1 ergo] *codd.*   enim *P*
  2 homo] *codd. Tᶜ*   om. *T*
  3 nomen] *codd.*   om. *RC*
  4 homo] *codd.*   hoc *N*
  5 eo] *codd.*   ipso *H*

4

  1 circa] *codd.*   contra *CH*
  2 et] *codd.*   om. *T*
  3 significet] *codd.*   significat *T*
  4 qualitate] *codd.*   et *C*   ergo *H*   nomen significat substantiam cum qualitate *add. CH*

5 omne] *codd.* om. *CII*
6 sillogismus] *codd.* om. *C*
7 et hoc] *T* quod *cett.*

5

1 modis] *codd.* om. *N*
2 contingit significare] *codd.* significari *H*
3 eandem] *codd.* unam *C*
4 primo] *codd.* modo *add. R*
5 diversa] *codd.* divisa *R* sequitur rasura in *P*
6 eandem dictionem] *P* dictionem eandem *Rᶜ* dictionem *R* eam *cett.*
7 hoc] *codd.* om. *CH*
8 quod] *P* et *cett.*
9 secundum] *Tᶜ* sed et *T* per *H* et *cett.*
10 et similiter] *codd.* sicut *E*
11 tertio] *codd.* autem *add. PNERCH*
12 significatur] *codd.* om. *N*
13 ex ... significat] *codd.* om. *N* ex transsumptione *TP* in transsumtione *ER* transsumptive *CH*
14 significat] *TPR* om. *cett.*
15 transsumptive] *codd.* transsumptione *E*
16 diversa] *codd.* plura *E*
17 sive ... alterum] *codd. Tᶜ* om. *T*
18 intelligendi] *codd.* it cuius est et cognoscendi ipsum *add. C*
19 intelligendi] *codd.* inferendi *R*
20 illud] *codd.* id *T* illius *H*
21 ut figura triangularis] *codd.* triaregulim (!)*E*
22 cultellum] *codd.* cutelum *E*

6

1 modo] *codd.* om. *T*
2 et suam substantiam] *codd.* cum sua substantia *E*
3 qualitas] *codd.* om. *T*
4 vero] *codd.* non *H*
5 quia unum] *TPNE* quia nomen *RC* primum *H*
6 ibi] *codd.* in *N*
7 significandi] *codd.* generandi (!)*E*
8 cum] *codd.* si *T* om. *R*
9 magnitudinem] *codd.* ymaginatam (!)*P*
10 quia color] *codd.* quare *E*
11 videndi] *codd.* intendi *N*
12 magnitudinem] *codd.* ymaginem *P*
13 ideo] *T* propter hoc *cett.*
14 antiquum] *coni.* quod *post lacunam Tᵗ* est quia *R* est quod *cett.*
15 alterum] *codd.* ibi *add. PNRᶜCH*
16 est] *codd.* Regula *add. Pᵐ*

7

1 sit] *codd.*   est *P*
2 aliquid] *codd.*   unde locus *add. E*
3 substantia] *codd.*   *sequitur lacuna septem litterarum in T*
4 sed] *T*   et *cett.*
5 debet dici] *TNER*   oportet dicere *PCH*
6 et compositionem] *codd.*   cum compositione *C*

8

1 rem] *codd.*   tria vero secundum rationem *add. H*
2 tria ... qualitas] *codd.*   *om. H*
3 scipsa componitur] *codd.*   seipsam componit *N* cum seipsa componit *E*
4 et etiam] T^cPNERH^c etiam et *T*   etiam *CH*
5 id] *codd.*   illud *R*
6 nisi] *codd.*   ibi *sic saepius R*
7 quod accidentis ... inesse] *TPNR*   quod accidens esse est inesse *H*
quod accidens est inesse *E*   quia quod accidit esse est inesse *C*
8 alio] *codd.*   quo *E*
9 esse] *codd.*   omne *E*
10 materia] *codd.*   modo *E*
11 ratione] *codd.*   oratione *E*
12 autem] *codd.*   *om. PN*
13 cum] *codd.*   est *R*
14 sint] $TECH^c$ sunt *PRH*   sit *N*
15 rem] *codd.*   et substantiam *add. P*
16 et] *codd.*   non *N*
17 extremorum] *TR*   extremum *PN*   ex oppositorum *(!)E*   diversa est ab
eis *add.* H^m *sequitur lacuna decem litterarum in T*
18 alterius rationis est] *codd.* T^c *om. T*   altera rationis est *E*
19 dixi] *codd.*   diximus *T*
20 erant] *codd.*   non sunt nisi *E*
21 loquitur] *codd.* H^c *om. H*
22 rebus] *codd.*   tribus *N*
23 dicitur ... et] *N*   debet dici ... et *TRE*   *om. PCH*
24 non] *codd.* H^c *om. H*
25 nomen] *codd.*   quando *R*

9

1 sit illa]   est illa *T*   sit *cett.*
2 non est aliquid] *P*   nichil est *cett.*
3 abire] *codd.*   ire *P*
4 oporteret enim] *TR* oporteret etiam *PNC*   oportet etiam H^c etiam *H*
5 aut] *T*   om *cett.*
6 vel qualitas] *codd.*   cum qualitate *R*
7 sic] *R*   om. *cett.*
8 sic] *T*   similiter *cett.*
9 questio] *TE*   querendum *cett.*
10 illa] *TNR*   ipsa *CH*   ista *PE*

10

1 substantia in] II^c *om.* H *cett.*
2 scilicet unita] *codd.* ut vita (!)E
3 cum substantia] R *om. cett.*
4 distantis] $PNER^cC^c$ distans TRC
5 quia videtur quod] TPR quod videtur quia *cett.*
6 sit] T est *cett.*
7 ut] T *om. cett.*
8 aliquando] *codd.* est *add.* N
9 quando] TN quia *cett.*
10 subiecto] *codd.* substantia E
11 in predicato] T predicatur PNH in predicato ponitur RC
12 debet esse] TPN esset *cett.*
13 qualitatis] *codd.* actus P

11

1 dicitur dupliciter] T debet esse duplex *cett.*
2 sumitur] T *om. cett.*
3 ad ... inclinationem] *codd. om.* EC
4 que ... predicantur] *codd.* que de altero dicuntur N quod ... predicatur R
5 illa] *codd.* prima N
6 ut] *codd.* non ut R
7 a substantia] T *om cett.*
8 eam] *codd.* causam E
9 predicatum] *codd.* predicantur E
10 sed] *codd.* scilicet N

12

1 quod] *codd.* quia TP
2 dico] T dicendum *cett.*
3 quia ... unita] *codd. om.* H
4 essentialis] *codd.* esse naturalis R
5 et ... qualitatem] $TPEH^c$ *om.* NRCH
6 loquimur] *codd.* loquitur T
7 non] $TPNEH^c$ *om.* RCH
8 homini] TPNEC hominis RH
9 neque est] *codd.* inest E
10 hominem] *codd.* homo R
11 propositum] *codd.* presens propositum H oppositum (!)E
12 hac] *codd.* alia TH
13 vero] *codd.* enim T
14 est] *codd.* H^c *om.* H
15 tamen] *codd.* cum P
16 propositum] *codd.* oppositum E

13

1 dicto] *codd.* iam *add.* R

2 alia] *codd.* una *H*
3 item] *codd.* iterum *N*
4 subdividebatur] *codd. T^c* subdividitur *T*
5 quoniam] *T* quia *cett.*

14

1 ergo] *codd.* igitur *P* vero *T*
2 cum ... actus] *codd. om. R*
3 uniti] *codd.* unita *E*
4 alia] *codd.* vero est actus *add. P*
5 actus] *N om. P* ut *cett.*
6 distantis] *codd.* distans *TE*
7 uniti] *codd.* cum substantia *add. CH*
8 substantia] *codd.* subiecto *T*
9 actionem vel] *codd. om. T*
10 quare] *codd.* quia *NE*
11 substantie] *codd.* in (?*pro* cum) substantia *T*
12 hoc] *codd. om. T*
13 inductive] *PN* inductione *cett.*
14 qui ... quare] *codd.* quid substantia infinita que est *E*
15 quare] *codd.* quia *P*
16 sunt] *codd.* in eo *add. R*
17 substantia] *codd.* infinita *add. H^c*
18 simpliciter] *codd.* specialiter sive simpliciter *H*
19 ut ... quod] *codd. om. H* distantis a substantia patet per hoc quod *H^c*
20 semper] *codd. om. C*
21 dicam] *T* dicatur *cett.*
22 ut] *codd.* et *T*
23 predicatum determinatum] *T* predicatur *R* predicatum *cett.*

15

1 a se invicem] *TP* ab invicem *R* ad invicem *cett.*
2 suam] *codd. om. N*
3 perfectionis] *PNRC* perfectiones *TH* perficiens *E*
4 quare] *T* quod *H* quia *cett.*
5 qualitas] *T* qualitas nominis *cett.*
6 complet ... nominis] *codd. R^c om. R*
7 perfectio unitur] *codd.* perficiuntur *E*
8 perfectibili] *codd. R^c* perfectibile *RH*
9 sit] *codd.* fit *NC*
10 actus] *TPR^cC om. NERH*
11 sicut] *codd.* ut *P*
12 subiecto] *codd.* verbo *E*
13 est de altero] *codd.* dicitur de aliquo *T*
14 predicatum] *codd.* predicatur *EC*
15 et sic] *codd.* sic *TH*

16

1 autem aliquis] *T* quis *cett.*
2 non] *codd.* om. *E*
3 compositiones] *codd.* sed differunt *add. T*
4 compositio] *codd.* om. *N* est positis (*!*)*E*
5 simpliciter] *codd.* in quolibet modo *T*

17

1 compositione] *codd.* appositione *N*
2 quantum ... modum] *codd.* quoniam est in indicativo *T*
3 quantum ad] *TPN* quod *cett.*
4 tres modos] *codd.* omnes *H*
5 importatur] *codd.* interpretatur *E*
6 cum] *codd.* om. *TN*
7 habeat] *PCH* habet *TNR* habebat *E*
8 idem ... simili] *coni.* idem videtur similiter *T* a simili videtur idem *cett.*
9 quia] *codd.* quod *T* om. *N*
10 similiter fit] *coni.* fit *T* similiter significatur *cett.*
11 significetur] *codd.* significatur *PH*
12 queritur] *codd.* queratur *PN*
13 per] *codd.* alterum quod est *add. H*
14 utrumque] *codd.* extremorum *add. PER*

18

1 ad primum] *TPN* om. *cett.*
2 subiectum] *NERH* substantiam *TPC*
3 obiectum ... obiecta] *coni.* obiecta *T* obiectum *cett.*
4 visio] *TR* visus *cett.*
5 scilicet] *codd.* sicut *T*
6 suum] *codd.* visionis *N*
7 scilicet] *coni.* scilicet ad *P* om. *cett.*
8 compositio ... ipsa composita]compositio duplicem habet comparatio-nem unam ad suum componens scilicet animam aliam ad suum obiec-tum scilicet quod est ipsa composita *P* compositio] *codd. T^c* om. *T* incli-natio *E*
9 suum] *codd.* om. *N*
10 ipsum componens] *N* compositiones *R* componens *cett. R^c*
11 suum ... ipsa composita]sive ad obiecta que sunt ipsa composita vel opposita *T* suum quod est ipsa composita *NC* suum sive ad obiecta quod est (*!*) ipsa composita *E* sive ad obiecta quod est (*!*) ipsa composita *RH*
12 composita] *codd.* compositio (*!*)*N*
13 recipiunt] *codd.* accipiunt *H*
14 comparationem] *codd.* compositionem *R*
15 ad] *codd.* om. *R*
16 sed secundum] *codd.* secundam *P*
17 cum] *codd. T^c* om. *T*
18 ipsum] *codd.* om. *N*

19 in] *codd.*   *om. P*
20 compositio] *codd.*   *om. NR*
21 est] *codd. T^c*   *om. T*
22 subiecto] *codd.*   suo *add. N*

19

1 compositio] *codd.*   per quam actus est de altero ut predicatum de subiecto *add. R^mC*
2 inclinatio] *codd.*   ipsius actus *add. C^cH*   ipsius *add. cett.*
3 inclinatio compositionem] *codd.*   inclinatio compositioni *H   om. P*
4 et ... compositionem] *P   om. cett.*
5 vel a subiecto] *codd.   om. R*
6 proprium ... inesse] *P*   accidens proprium substantie *cett.*
7 etsi] *codd.*   etiamsi *C*
8 ei] *codd.*   tamen habet naturalem inclinationem ad substantiam *add.P*
9 cum unitur] *codd.*   si uniatur *C*
10 ergo] *codd.*   et *add. N*
11 natura] *codd.*   non *E*

20

1 est] *codd. R^c   om. NR*
2 natura] *T   om. cett.*
3 accidens et non] *codd.*   accidentalis et non est *E*
4 ipsi] *codd. H*   ideo ipsi *H^c*
5 precedit compositionem] *codd.*   precedat compositionem *P*   procedit (!) compositioni *H*
6 accidens] *T*   actus *NC   om. cett.*
7 non] *codd.*   nisi *add. N*
8 prout] *codd.*   ut *T*
9 inclinat se] *codd.*   inclinatur *C*
10 enuntiandum] *codd.*   determinandum *E*
11 compositionem] *codd.*   compositioni *H*
12 et] *codd. H^c   om. H*   quod *add. RCH*
13 altera] *codd.*   alterum *T*
14 naturam] *codd.*   vel natura *add. C*

21

1 operationes] *codd.*   comparationes *N*
2 similitudines] *codd.*   similitudinem *H*
3 prius] *codd.   sequitur rasura sex litterarum in T*
4 cognoscit] *codd.*   cognoscunt *N*
5 anima] *codd.   om. H*   natura *H^c* omnia *E*
6 consentiat] *codd.*   sentiat *C*
7 aliam] *codd.*   alteram *P*   alteram vel aliam *H*   rem *add. T*
8 rei] *codd.   om. TP*
9 actus] *codd.   om. N*
10 accidens] *codd. T^c*   actus *T*
11 anima] *codd.*   aliam *N*
12 actus] *codd.*   cum substantia *add. P^m*

22

1 hoc] *codd.* om. *T*
2 verbum] *codd.* verbo *N*
3 debebat] *coni.* debeat *codd.*
4 apprehenderat] *coni.* apprehendiderat *(!)H* apprehendebat *TNR* apprehendit *PC*
5 afficiebatur] *TNH* efficiebatur *PERC*
6 istum] *codd.* primum *N*
7 inclinabatur] *codd.* inclinatur *C*
8 ipsum] *codd.* actum *N* om. *H*
9 enuntiabat] *codd.* enuntiabit *C*
10 est] *codd.* intra se *add. N*
11 anime] *codd.* ipsius anime *R*
12 istum] *codd.* ipsum *T*
13 affectum] *codd.* effectus *P*
14 enuntiandum] *codd.* ipsum de substantia *add. Hᵐ*
15 istam] *codd.* ipsam *N*
16 indicatio] *codd.* inclinatio et indicatio *N*
17 indicatio] *codd.* sive modus *add. N*
18 ordinentur] *codd.* intus *add. N*
19 tamen actu] *coni.* se(?) tamen *N* tamen *TPERᶜ* non *R* cum *H*
20 et] *TPNE* ut *R* om. *CH*
21 quod] *codd. TᶜHᶜ* om. *TH*
22 dat] *codd.* dant *PE*
23 intelligere] *codd.* quasi intelligere *P* ipsum signum *add. H*
24 quasi accidentia] *codd.* quasi accidentalia *T* accidentalia *P*
25 affectus] *codd.* actus *E*
26 proxima] *codd.* prima *N* immediata *add. H*
27 affectu] *codd.* effectu *T*
28 remota] *codd.* om. *N*
29 vel initiali] *codd.* et universali *P* in universali *E*

23

1 sunt] *codd.* varie *add. H*
2 predicatur] *codd.* ponitur *N*
3 sicut] *codd.* tamquam *N*
4 et] *codd.* ad *N*
5 tamquam] *codd.* sicut *N*
6 effectus] *codd.* affectus *R* suam *add. H*
7 sumpto] *codd.* et non contracto *add. Pᶜ*
8 et contracto] *T* et econverso *E* seu contracto *cett.*

24

1 significati] *codd.* signi et *E*
2 ut] *codd.* ubi *E*
3 dicendum] *codd.* sciendum *sic saepius H*
4 hec] *codd. Hᶜ* om. *PH*

5 male intellecta] *T^c* non intellecta *TPN* sive eoquod non intelligit ea que predicta sunt *add. TNR* sive eoquod non intelligat ea que predicta sunt *add. P* sive eoquod predicta non intelliguntur *add. CH* sive et quod non intelligat ea que predicta sunt *add. E*
6 essent] *codd.* erant *NR*
7 ut ... actus] *codd.* om. *N*
8 substantia] *codd.* subiecto *H*
9 autem] *codd.* enim *P*
10 in] *codd.* om. *P*
11 actus] *R* om. *codd.*
12 orationis] *codd.* et per istam secundam inclinationem reperitur modus in verbo *add. T^mECH*

25

1 illa] *codd.* ipsa *H*
2 quam] *PN* quia *codd.*
3 sine] *codd.* suis *add. T*
4 est] *codd.* et propter quod est *add. R*
5 alio] *codd.* om. *TC*
6 abire] *codd.* ire *P*
7 ipsam] *T* om. *cett.*
8 per illud] *TPNR* om. *cett.*
9 per illud] *TPNR* om. *cett.*
10 subiectum suum] *codd.* substantiam suam *PH*
11 que] *codd.* qui *R*
12 consignificatur] *PNR* significatur *cett.*
13 consignificat] *codd.* significat *TH* assignat consignificat *(!)N*
14 est] *codd.* erit *R*
15 verbi] *codd.* ipsius verbi *P*
16 est] *codd.* om. *N*

26

1 etiam quod] *codd.* quod etiam *H*
2 suam] *PN* om. *cett.*
3 re] *codd.* ut in subiecto *add. P*
4 sicut] *codd.* sequitur *(!) C*
5 veritatem] *codd.R^c* virtutem *R*
6 ut ... signo] *codd.* sicut in suo subiecto et est in urina sicut in signo *T*
7 compositio] *codd.* que *add. H*
8 substantie] *T* om. *cett.*
9 et precedit] *codd.* procedit *H*
10 aliquo] *codd.* alio *PN*
11 prius] *codd.* om. *T*

27

1 utrum] *codd.* om. *N*
2 ens simpliciter] *codd.* ens *P* specialiter ens *N*
3 non ens] *codd.* ens *N*

4 repertum in] *codd.* om. *N*
5 priorum] *codd. H* primorum *(!)C* secundi priorum *H*^c
6 consequitur] *codd.* assequitur *R*
7 aliqua] *codd.* alia *EC*
8 diversa] *codd.* divisa *R*
9 consequatur] *TNEC* sequatur *P* sequitur *R* consequitur *H*
10 ergo ... sequitur eis quodammodo] *codd.* om. *H*
11 primo] *NERC* om. *TP*
12 est] *codd.* om. *N*
13 ad compositionem] *PNRC* om. *TEH*
14 primo] *PNC* prius *TER* per prius *H*

28

1 posterius] *T* posterius compositioni *cett.*

29

1 videtur quod] *codd. R*^c quod videtur *R*
2 compositio] *codd.* verbalis *add. R*
3 conveniat] *R* convenit *cett.*
4 ponantur] *codd.* inesse *add. H*^c
5 et] *codd.* ergo et *H*^c
6 sequitur] *codd.* om. *H*
7 non ens ... est] *codd.* om. *N*
8 ergo chimera est] *codd.* om. *NH*
9 sint entia] *codd.* sicut causa sua *E*
10 quodammodo] *codd. sequitur rasura quindecim litterarum in T* et non simpliciter *add. H*^c
11 erit] *P* est *cett.*
12 cum ... homo] *codd.* om. *N*
13 sit] *codd.* est *T* similiter *E*
14 et ... homo quodammodo] *codd. R*^c om. *PNR*

30

1 eius] *codd.* in communi *add. T*
2 similiter] *codd.* simpliciter *N* in communi *add. NRC*
3 entia] *codd.* essentia *N*
4 eius que] *codd.* entium eius quod *H*
5 entium] *codd.* om. *H*
6 est ens simpliciter] *codd.* simpliciter est ens *N*
7 sed simpliciter] *codd.* om. *R*
8 hec] *codd.* antichristus est homo *add. TERCH*

31

1 illud] *codd.* aliud *sic saepius TH*
2 dicimus] *NE* dicendum *cett.*
3 ut] *TERC* unde *PNH*
4 sunt] *codd.* est *R*
5 propter hoc] *T* tamen *cett.*

6 sint] *codd. T^c* sint sibi invicem convenientia *T*
7 non tamen] *TCH* neque *cett.*
8 ista] *P* om. *cett.*
9 et] *codd.* om. *R*
10 extremorum ... compositionis] *codd. T^c* compositionis extremorum est causa *T*

32

1 se ... non entium] *T* predicetur de compositione entium et de compositione non entium *PNEC* predicatur de compositione entium et [*R^c om. R*] non entium *RH*
2 et] *TC* om. *cett.*
3 est non ens] *TPNR* non est ens *cett.*
4 ergo ... ens] *codd.* om. *N*
5 est ens simpliciter] *T* simpliciter est ens *cett.*
6 in utraque] *N* utriusque *cett.*
7 altera vero] *codd.* altera vero compositio *P* alia vero compositio *H*
8 non entium] *codd.* est entium *N*
9 unam] *codd.* partem *add. R^cH*

33

1 illud autem] *PER* aliud autem *TH* illud *C*
2 quod] *codd.* quod cum *H*
3 est] *TP* sit *cett.*
4 earum simpliciter est] *codd.* est simpliciter earum *N*
5 est] *codd.* om. *N*
6 per] *codd.* om. *N*
7 vera] *codd. T^cH^c* om. *TH*
8 hic] *TN* om. *cett.*
9 erit] *TPN* est *cett.*
10 extremorum] *P^cER^cH^c* om. *TPNRH*
11 vel] *TPNR* ad *add. HC* per repugnantiam ad *add. H^c*
12 propter] *T* per *cett.*
13 alteram] *codd.* partem *add. R^cC*
14 immo sunt non entia] *TPNR^cC* immo non entia *H^c* om. *H* immo non sunt entia *ER*
15 ita] *codd.* ideo *T*
16 quodammodo] *codd.* Capitulum de negatione *add. P* de negatione *add. N* Sequitur de negatione *add. RC*

TRACTATUS SECUNDUS

DE NEGATIONE

1

1 cum] *codd.* autem *add.* C
2 est] *codd.* om. P
3 modo] *codd.* negatio *add.* PN
4 enuntiationis] *codd.* enuntiationum P
5 autem alia] *TPNH* alia autem R alia EC
6 oratio affirmativa] T affirmativa *PNEH* affirmatio RC
7 alia] *codd.* alia est N
8 negativa] *codd.* negatio RC
9 homo currit[T om. cett.
10 ab] *TPNC* de *ERH*
11 negatio] *codd.* om. P
12 tripliciter] *codd.* dupliciter H
13 negatio] *codd.* negativo N
14 negatio] T om. cett.
15 ut ... participio] T ut in verbo et participio H ut in verbo et in participio N ut in participio vel in verbo C in verbo et in participio *PR*
16 et] *codd.* ex (!)T et in P
17 modis] *codd.* om. T

2

1 affectus] *codd.* sive exercitus *add.* C
2 conceptus] *codd.* conceptio E
3 aliquam] *codd.* exteriorem *add.* RCH
4 cogito] *codd. sequitur rasura quinque litterarum in* T
5 hominibus] *codd. T*ᶜ hominibus tunc T
6 autem] *codd.* enim C
7 exercitio] E exercito (!)R exercitium T exercitus *cett.*
8 dicitur esse] *codd.* efficiens ER
9 afficiens] *codd.* efficiens ER
10 cursus] *codd.* cur (!)P
11 exercitus] *TPNH* exercito (!)R exercens *Rᶜ*C om. E
12 et] TPN om. cett.

3

1 isto] *codd.* in N
2 termini] *codd.* nisi (!)N
3 vel ... infinito] *codd. T*ᶜ om. T
4 termino] N om. cett.
5 nomen] *codd. T*ᶜ om. T

6 privativum] *TPRC* privatum *NEH*
7 sive privativum] *TPNR* sive privatum *EH* *om. C*

4

1 accidentalis] *codd.* *om. H*
2 possint] *N* possunt *RC* possit *TPH*
3 quia] *codd.* que *N*
4 diversa] *T* huiusmodi *cett.*
5 sunt] *codd.* sibi invicem *add. H^c*
6 est *codd.* sunt *CH*
7 sunt] *T* et *cett.*
8 et] *codd.* similiter *add. PN*
9 significari] *T* significare *cett.*
10 unum] *codd.* nomen *R*
11 vel] *codd.* vel est *R^{c}C*
12 sortes] *codd.* est *add. ERC*
13 potest] *codd.* *om. N*
14 predicari] *codd.* impediri *(!)E*
15 alio ... altero] *codd. P^c* *om. P*
16 significari] *T* significare *cett.*
17 denominative] *codd.* denominate *C*
18 albus] *codd.* album *P*
19 non] *T* non denominative *cett.*
20 studiosus] *codd.* et *add. N*
21 dicuntur] *codd.* dicitur *R*
22 cursor et pugillator] *codd.* *om. H* et consimilia *add. RC*

5

1 ad substantiam] *codd.* cum substantia *P*
2 substantie cum] *codd.* *om. T*
3 cum] *codd. T* sit de *T^e*
4 trium] *codd.* *om. P*
5 opponatur] *codd.* apponatur *R*
6 et sic erit] *coni.* et sic est *T* ergo sic erit *R* ergo sit est *C* ergo erit *PNH*
7 quare] *T* ergo *cett.*
8 quod] *T* *om. cett.*
9 negatio ut est] *T* quia ut est negatio *R* quod negatio ut est *cett.*
10 ut afficiens] *T* efficiens *N* afficiens *cett.*
11 in genere] *N* *om. cett.*
12 alia vero] *T* et alia *cett.*
13 quia] *T* *om. cett.*
14 illa est in specie] *T* illa in specie est *PH* illa in specie sumpta est *NR* sumpta in specie est *C*
15 quadruplex] *codd.* duplex *P* quadruplex *(!)P^c*
16 termini] *codd.* tripliciter *add. H*
17 quedam ... que] *T* quia est negatio termini *PN* quia est quedam negatio termini *cett.*
18 non asinus] *T* non equus *cett.*

19 unitum] *codd. R^c om. PR*
20 intra] *codd. R^c* unita *R*
21 non laborat] *codd.* non legit *H*
22 partes tres] *TN* tres partes *cett.*

6

1 obicit] *codd.* obicitur *N*
2 actus scilicet] *TN* actus *PR om. cett.*
3 dicendum] *codd. T^c om. T*
4 dividit] *codd. T^c* dividit dicendum quod verum est *T*
5 intra] *codd.* unita *H*
6 sint] *TPNH* sunt *cett.*
7 quedam] *codd.* compositio *add. H*
. 8 qualitatis] *codd.* qualitas *R*
9 infinitum] *codd.* esse infinitum *CH*
10 vero] *T* vero compositio *cett.*
11 a] *codd.* etiam *N*
12 eadem] *TPER om. NCH*
13 et] *codd.* eadem *add. N*
14 intra] *codd. R^c* unita *R*
15 sic] *codd. bis in P*
16 insufficienter] *codd. T^c* sufficienter *T*

7

1 scilicet] *TC* scilicet substantie *cett.*
2 suppositum] *codd. E^c* oppositum *E* subiectum *R*
3 infinite] *codd.* indefinite *C*
4 et] *codd. om. P*
5 currens] *codd.* cursus *N*
6 ipse] *codd.* ille *P*
7 vero] *TNR^cC om. cett.*
8 interius] *codd.* intus *E* ulterius *(!)C*

8

1 et] *E om. cett.*

9

1 sicut dicitur] *T* ut est *PN*
2 predicatur] *codd.* ponitur *TR*
3 predicatur] *codd.* ponitur *TE*
4 predicatur] *PNCH* ponitur *TE*
5 aliquid] *codd.* aliud semper *R*
6 tunc] *codd.* hinc *H*
7 quod] *codd. om. N*
8 affirmatur] *codd. T^c* affirmatur compositio *TN*
9 neque negatur compositio *T^cERC* neque negatur *TN* non enim negatur compositio *P* et non negatur compositio *H^c* non negatur compositio *H*
10 quod ... non est] *TPN* etc. *cett.*

10

1 negationem] *T* privationem *cett.*
2 privationem] *T* negationem *cett.*
3 quam] *TPNE* quam negatio ergo mortuum plus participat de ente quam *R* quam negatio *H* quam negatio scilicet *H*
4 quare] *codd.* ergo *P^c* quam *P*
5 nomen infinitum] *T* terminus infinitus *cett.*
6 etiam de] *PNER* de *TH^c* om. *H*
7 terminos] *codd. T^c* terminos nominis *T*
8 homo] *codd.* om. *R*
9 omne] *codd.* om. *N*
10 bene] *codd.* om. *R*
11 sequitur] *N* sequitur *cett.*

11

1 solutio solet dici quod] *coni.* Item *codd.*
2 quedam est] *T* est enim in eo *P* est in eo quedam *NER* est in eo *H*
3 vere] *codd.* ut in hiis que sunt nature *add. R*
4 proportionaliter] *codd.* ut in hiis que sunt rationis *add. R*
5 homine] *codd.* nomine *N*
6 cum] *T* cum suo *cett.*
7 cum] *TH* cum suo *cett. H^c*
8 subalternis] *codd.* alterius (!)*N*
9 sicut] *codd.* sunt *add. PN*
10 sunt] *T* om. *cett.* sunt ... per quas] differentie que [sunt *T^c*] secundum rationem finis vel cause alicuius per quas differentias addicuntur (!) enti *T*
11 que] *codd. T^c* que sunt *T*
12 alterius] *coni.* alicuius *codd.*
13 differentias] *coni.* coll. *T*
14 genera] *R* om. *cett.*
15 differunt ... generalissima] *codd.* om. *N*
16 ente] *codd. R^c* esse *R*
17 ut patet] *codd.* patet enim *P*
18 se] *codd.* existens *add. P*
19 substantie] *codd.* *T^c* om. *T*
20 qualitas] *codd.* qualitatis *N*
21 vel] *TNR* et *P* substantie vel *ECH*
22 qualificativum] *TP* qualitativum *cett.*
23 vero] *codd.* autem *P* om. *H*
24 comparativum ... ens] *codd.* om. *N*
25 hec] *codd.* de hac *N*
26 sev *codd.* existens *add. P*
27 genera generalissima] *R^c* genera *R* generalissima *cett.*

12

1 formetur] *TPNE* formatur *cett.*
2 opponitur] *TPNR* oppositio *H* respondet *E*

3 ergo ... negatio] *codd.* *om.* P
4 existcnti] *codd.* existente R
5 que est] *TPNR* *om. cett.*
6 removeatur] *codd. T^c* removeatur pro una vel pro pluribus *TERCH^c*
7 unaqueque earum] *T^cPR* unaqueque *TNE* unumquodque *CH*
8 omnibus] *codd.* animabus (!)E
9 removeatur] *codd.* rcmoveretur P
10 iam] *codd.* inde E *om.* H
11 negativus] *codd.* negationis T
12 de] *codd.* *om.* P
13 et ... duplex] *codd. T^c* *om.* T
14 est duplex] *codd.* sumitur dupliciter P

13

1 quia] *codd.* *om.* P
2 infinitari] *codd.* *sequitur lacuna quattuor litterarum in* T
3 negativus] *codd.* et sic non homo nichil ponit *add.* N
4 et] *codd.* *om. ER*
5 ct] *codd.* *om. E*
6 quia] *codd.* quod R
7 et] *codd.* *om.* N
8 et] N *om. cett.*
9 non ente] T eo quod non est *cett.* nullus terminus infinitus potest predicari de eo quod non est *add.* N
10 enim] *codd.* *om.* N
11 terminus] T terminus communis *cett.*
12 cuius] *codd. T^cP^c* cuius ad TP
13 removetur] *codd.* negatur P

14

1 negatio] *codd.* negativa T
2 et sic] *T^cPNR* unde *TECH*
3 quod] *codd.* quia H
4 nomen ... est] *TNCH* nomen infinitum dicitur *PE* potest nomen infinitari dupliciter R
5 quod] *TPE* eoquod *cett.*
6 rectum curvum] T *om.* P rectum *cett.*
7 ut ... econverso] *codd.* *om.* P
8 est non] *codd.* non est R
9 dicendo] *codd. T^c* ct dicendum est T
10 sibi] *TPN* se *cett.*
11 sicut] *codd.* et sic E
12 hoc] *codd.* licet E
13 dicit] *codd.* dicitur T
14 equale] *codd. T^c* equale ut dictum est T
15 vel] *codd.* *om.* T
16 predicetur] *codd.* predicatur *CH*
17 dicut] *codd.* dicitur P
18 principio secundi] *PNR* principio T secundo *T^cECH*

19 quod]*codd.* quia *P*
20 converterentur]*codd.* convertentur *(!)N* intellige *add. P*
21 isto modo]*codd.* ista materia *E*
22 de accidentali]*codd.* de termino accidentali infinito *H*
23 non iustum]*TNCH* non iustus *PR* non rectum *E*

15

1 ponitur]*codd.* predicatur *R*
2 remaneat] removeat*(!)E* remanet *cett.*
3 hoc]*codd. om. T*
4 quia]*codd.* quod *R*
5 modo]*codd.* peccat *add. EH*
6 non iustus]*T* non iustum *PNRH* non rectum *E*
7 quod]*codd.* quia *N*
8 et]*codd.* quod *R*
9 modo]*codd. om. N*
10 aut]*codd.* sive *R*
11 rem]*P* rationem *cett.*
12 unde]*codd.* verum *R*
13 sit ... affirmata]*TNRC* sit ... affirmativa *EH* affirmata est ibi compositio *P*
14 tamen]*codd. om. H*
15 ibi]*codd. om. T*
16 diminutum]*codd.* diminute *N*
17 ibi]*TR^c om. cett. R*
18 affirmata]*codd.* affirmativa *EH*
19 cum diminuatur]*TPR* cum *ante lacunam in N* diminutum *H* quia est ibi diminutum *H^c*
20 est]*codd. om. N*

16

1 autem]*codd.* tertio*(!)H*
2 terminus]*codd. om. N*
3 subicibile vel predicabile]*TN* sit subicibile vel predicabile *PRH* sit subicibilis vel predicabilis *C*
4 et ideo]*codd.* unde *P*

17

1 speciali]*codd. om. H*
2 faciente verbum infinitum]*T* infinitatem (!) verbum *H* infinitante verbum *cett.*
3 est]*codd. om. TN*
4 est]*codd. om. TN*
5 omni eo]*TPN* eo *R* quolibet *ECH*
6 similiter]*codd.* simpliciter *H*
7 affirmatam]*TPNR* affirmativam *cett.*
8 substantia de qua]*codd.* subiecto de quo *N*
9 secundum quod non currit]*codd. om. R*
10 affirmata]*TPNC* affirmativa *ERH*

18

1 infinitum] *TPNE om. cett.*
2 non] *codd. P^c om. P*
3 quia ... alia] *TPNE* quoniam ... alia *R^c* est una ... alia *R* quia verbum pars una est orationis et negatio alia *CH*
4 quia] *codd.* sed *P*
5 negative] *codd.* negate *C*
6 in eis] *codd. om. TPN*
7 eos] *P* eas *cett. P^c*
8 affirmata] *TPNC* affirmativa *ERH*

19

1 illud] *codd.* aliud *P*
2 affirmata] *codd.* affirmativa *HE*
3 ad compositionem] *codd. om. H*
4 neque ... et ita] *codd. om. H*
5 affirmate] *TPNR* affirmative *ECH*
6 est affirmata] *TPNR* est affirmativa *E* affirmata *C* affirmatur *H*
7 ponitur] *codd.* ponit *H*
8 predicati] *codd.* compositionis *H*
9 est ens] *codd. om. R*
10 simpliciter ... est ens] *codd. T^c om. T* simpliciter ponit ens ... est ens *R*
11 ponitur] *codd.* ponit *H*
12 predicatum est] *codd.* predicatur *R*
13 vel] *codd.* ens *add. R*
14 ideo] *codd. om. H*
15 non currit est] *om. P* non] *NECH* currit *R om. T*

20

1 et] *TPN om. cett.*
2 nichil ... sunt] *codd.* et est sicut termini negativi secundum quod verbum participium (!)*E*
3 sic] *TRCH* et sic *E om. PN*
4 et hoc] *codd.* hoc etiam *H* et *T*
5 negatione] *codd.* autem *add. H*
6 et ideo relinquatur] *T om. E* relinquitur *cett.*

21

1 negatione orationis] *codd.* negationibus (? *pro* negativis) orationibus *H*
2 precedit] *codd.* suum *add. C*
3 unde] *codd. R^c* ut *E om. R*
4 vel ... precedit] *codd.* et precedit *P* et procedunt *H*
5 contradictionem] *T^c om. T*
6 quod] *codd.* ut *H*
7 compositionem] *codd.* eam *R*
8 aut ... aut] *codd.* est causa vel *P* est substantia vel *P^c*

9 nonnisi] *TPN*   non est nisi *cett.*
10 eam] *codd.*   esse *N*
11 Item cum] *TPNE*   item *P^c*   cum *cett.*
12 quia] *codd.*   quod *N*
13 principium principiorum] *TE*   primum principium *cett.*   de quolibet affirmatio vel negatio *add. P^m*
14 oratio negativa] *codd.*   negativa *T*   negatio *N*
15 neque] *codd.*   modi *add. ER*
16 locus] *codd.*   et est locus *R*   *om. NE*
17 oratio] *codd.*   *om. TN*
18 in ... falsum] *codd.*   illa verum vel falsum significat *H*   illa que verum vel falsum significat *H^c*   verum vel falsum *E*

22

1 generalem] *codd.*   singularem *N*
2 et ... est] *HE*   et specialem universalis *(!)* significatio est *C*   ut *TPNR*
3 specialis vero] *ECH*   specialem vero ut *TPN*   et specialem ut *R*   est *add. E*   ut *add. H*
4 sicut] *PNER*   sic *TCH*
5 et ... est] *codd.*   *om. N*
6 generalis] *codd.*   *om. E*   significatio *add. P*
7 vero] *codd.*   significatio *add. P*
8 actum] *codd.*   locum *(!)N*
9 duplex ... specialis] *codd.*   dicendum est quod est compositio generalis vel specialis *H*
10 scilicet] *codd.*   et *P*   *om. E*
11 generalis autem] *codd.*   unde genera vel *(!)C*
12 consignificat] *TPEC*   significat *RH*   consignificant *N*
13 compositionem] *codd.*   *om. P*
14 vel illam sed] *codd.*   *om. H*   vel illam sed dicimus *H^c*
15 generalis] *codd.*   et debetur ipsi agere vel pati in genere communiter sumpto sicut dictum est prius *add. NC*   que debetur ipsi agere et pati in genere communiter sumpto *add. P^c*
16 adhuc] *codd.*   ad hoc *N*   et huic *(!)H*
17 contingit] *codd.P^c*   *om. P*

23

1 solet dici] *codd.*   dicitur *T*
2 affirmationi] *codd.*   uni *add. H^c*
3 negationi] *codd.*   uni negationi *H*
4 et videtur quod] *T*   quod videtur quia *cett.*
5 destruere] *codd.*   removere *NH*
6 repperit] *codd.*   deperit *(!)E*
7 actus] *codd.H*   accidens actus et *(!)H^c*
8 aliquando negatio negatur] *T^cN^cH*   et ideo aliquando negatio negatur *H^c*   aliquando negatur *TCE*   aliquando negatur negatio *R*   aliquando negatio negatio *(!)*   negatur *P*
9 et ... negationem] *TPNE*   *om. cett.*
10 ideo] *E^cR*   et ideo non *N*   et ideo *cett. E*

11 quia ... affirmatio] *codd. H^c* *om. NH*
12 vel negationem] *codd. R^c* *om. N* afirmatio *R*
13 affirmatio autem] *codd.* *om. N* affirmatio *R*
14 destruere] *codd.* differre (!)*N*
15 ipsum potius] *T* potius *R* ipsum *cett.*
16 affirmata] *codd.* affirmatur *E*
17 affirmationis] *codd.* ponit ipsum et conservat *add. P* quod del *P^c*
18 non removeatur] *codd.* notetur (!)*R*
19 ob] *codd.* et ob *R*

24

1 et] *R* *om. cett.*
2 comparationes] *codd.* compositiones *R*
3 diversimode] *codd.* diversis modis *R*
4 aliam vero habet] *TPNE* alio vero est *cett.*
5 non] *codd. T^c* *om. T*
6 compositio eius] *R^c* *om. cett. R*
7 ei que] *RC* quod *H* ei quod *cett. H^c*
8 compositionis] *TRC* oppositionis *PNEH*
9 semper] *R* *om. cett.*
10 sicut] *codd. T^c* sicut negatio *T*
11 negabat] *codd.* negat *NR*
12 affirmatio] *codd.* negatio *P*
13 affirmat] *codd.* ut dictum est *add. E*
14 ad ... affirmationem] *codd.* et negatione *H*
15 per] *TNH* propter *cett.*

25

1 dicit ... quod] *codd. T^c* *om. TN* sicut dicit aristotiles in secundo topicorum scilicet *P*
2 affirmari] *R* negari *cett.*
3 poterit] *H* potest *cett.*
4 negari] *R* affirmari *cett.*
5 non] *codd. T^c* *om. T*

26

1 negatio] *codd.* *om. H*
2 aliquid] *TR* *om. cett.*
3 scilicet de] *P* sive de *TNER* sive *H*
4 participat] *codd.* aliquo modo *add. R*
5 sic] *codd.* sicut *N*
6 quamvis] *codd.* quam *H*
7 supra] *codd.* in *N*
8 sicut ... agendo in se] *codd. T^c* *om. T*
9 caliditas] *codd.* ignis *add. P*
10 causata] *codd.* causatur *P*
11 in] *codd.* *om. R*
12 cognoscendo] *codd.* cogitando *T*

13 iudicando de]*PNEH* videndo de *TR* udicando*(!)* de *T^c* videndo *C*
14 que]*codd.R^c* quia *R*
15 causatum]*codd.* causa tamen *NE*
16 reflecti ... negationem]*codd.* fieri ... negationem sive reflecti *R*
17 sive]*codd.P^c* om. *P*
18 negatam]*codd.* agendo in eam *add. PR* agendo in ipsam *add. RH*
19 aristotilis]*codd.* in secundo topicorum *add. H*
20 currit]*codd.* et *add. P*
21 sed ... aristotiles]*ERCH* sed aristotiles dicit contrarium *T^c* sed aristotiles *T* sed dicit aristotiles *PN*

27

1 dupliciter fit]*codd.* duplex est *H*
2 sortes non currit]*codd.R^c* et hec illi affirmative primo opponitur *add. H*
3 sed]*codd.* et *H*
4 contradicit ... non currit]*TPNER* om. *CH* ex consequenti *H^c*
5 ista]*codd.* prima *N*
6 primo]*C* om. *P* prima *cett.*
7 altera negatio]*T* altera est negatio et altera est affirmatio *PNE* alia est negatio et altera affirmatio *RCH*
8 aristotiles]*codd.* om. *T*

28

1 postposita]*codd.R^c* apposita *R*
2 sortes ... sortes currit]*codd.* non sortes currit et sortes non currit *H* sortes non currit *N*
3 indefinita]*codd.* de infinita *(!)C*
4 non]*codd.P^c* om. *P*
5 est ... currit]*codd.* om. *H* non homo currit universalis negativa *H^c*
6 neque]*codd.* hoc *P*
7 in]*codd.* ei *R* om. *H*
8 quod]*codd.* quia *R*
9 et intelligatur]*coni.* et idem intelligit *R* et intelligit *TN* quia intelligit *C* quia intelligit hoc *H*
10 intellexit]*P* om. *CH* intelligit *cett.*
11 dictione ... predicabilis]*codd.* dictionibus subicibilibus et predicabilibus *H*
12 est]*codd.* om. *T*
13 predicabilis]*codd.* ut homo est animal *add. T^mRH* ut animal est homo *add. C*
14 vel ... predicabilis]*codd.T^c* om. *TP* vel illis que sunt dispositiones subiecti et predicati *H*
15 intellexit]*P* intelligit *cett.*
16 ad]*codd.H* per comparationem ad *H^c*
17 universalia]*codd.* universalium *P*
18 de]*codd.* ab *P*
19 respectu]*codd.* comparatione *PH*

29

1 erit] R est *cett.*
2 sed] *codd.* om. P
3 currit] *codd.* om. P
4 currit vel] *codd.* om. PN vel P^c

30

1 quia] *codd.* et P
2 ista] *codd.* probatio *add.* H
3 per quam probat] *codd.* secundum quam probas P
4 et est duplex] R *om. cett.*
5 primo modo equipollet] TNR^c primo equipollet P primo equipollet modo R prima equipollet H
6 compositione] *codd.* comparatione R
7 nullo] $TPNR$ nullus *cett.*
8 uno] TPN eodem *cett.*
9 fertur] $TPNRC$ potest ferri H
10 et ita] *codd.* ergo P
11 et] *codd.* om. P
12 non] *codd.* T^c om. T
13 aliquo] *codd.* obliquo N
14 etc.] *codd.* om. T
15 hoc] *codd.* etiam *add.* PN

31

1 probatio] T^c om. T
2 prima ... ergo] *codd.* om. N
3 esse] *codd.* om. TNE
4 ergo] *codd.* nichil *add.* R
5 est] *codd.* om. P
6 et] *codd.* om. P

32

1 regulam] *codd.* equipollentiarum *add.* R
2 eadem] *codd.* una P aliqua H
3 et alterum] *codd.* reliquum PH
4 hic est] *codd.* est hoc H

33

1 videtur ibi esse] N videtur ibi T^c videtur T hic sit P
2 dicendum] *codd.* sciendum *sic saepius* H
3 fallacia secundum consequens] *coni.* locus consequens secundum (!) H locus secundum consequens *cett.*
4 apponitur] *codd.* opponitur N
5 negatum] *codd.* negant N
6 a subiecto] P *om. cett.*
7 in eodem affirmatum] T affirmatum in eodem $PNEC$ predicatum affirmatum in eodem genere R affirmativum (!) in eodem H

8 omnis] *TPNE* quilibet *RCH*
9 aliquod ... omnis homo] *codd.* *om. E*
10 risibile] *codd.* rationale *E*
11 risibile] *codd.* rationale *E*
12 et] *RCH* *om. cett.*
13 nullus homo] *TPE* nullum animal *cett.*
14 risibile] *codd.* rationale *E*

34

1 et] *codd.* *om. PN*
2 ergo ... nichil] *codd.* *om. R*
3 erit] *codd.* est *T*

35

1 reducere] *codd.* totum *add. H*
2 subiectum] *codd.* substantiam *E*
3 ens] *codd.* nulla *add. E*
4 istarum] *codd.R^c* regularum *R*
5 eius] *codd.* eiusdem *R*
6 aliud] *codd.H^c* *om. TH*

TRACTATUS TERTIUS

DE DICTIONIBUS EXCLUSIVIS

1

1 de ... affirmatione] *T* de negatione et de affirmatione *NE* de affirmatione et de negatione *RCH* de affirmatione et negatione *P*
2 quas] *codd.* que *H*
3 secundo] *codd.* queritur *add. P*
4 quot et que] *T* que et quot *cett.*
5 sint] *P* sunt *cett.*
6 exclusionis] *codd.* et *add. NH*
7 tertio] *codd.* que *add. R*
8 partes sive species] *TPNR* species sive partes *CH*
9 quarto] *codd.* autem *add. P*
10 descendendo] *codd. H^c* dicendo *H*
11 que] *codd.* et quas *H*
12 sint] *N* sunt *cett.*

2

1 ergo] *codd.* om. *P*
2 ut ... actum quem exercet] *codd. T^c* om. *T*
3 et ... aliis] *codd.* om. *PR*
4 sed ... de aliis] *codd. T^c* om. *TH*
5 dictio] *codd.* exclusiva *add. H*
6 est] *codd.* om. *P*
7 enumeratis] *codd.* numeratis *P*
8 exercent] *codd.* significant *N*
9 significant] *codd.* exercent *N*

3

1 ut] *codd.* om. *R*
2 conceptus] *codd. T^cP^c* om. *TP*
3 aliter] *codd.* aliquando *P*
4 cum] *codd.* om. *N*
5 aliquis] *codd.* homo *add. H*
6 in] *N* om. *cett.*
7 sicut] *codd.* et sic intelligitur *P*

4

1 eam ... illo] *P* hoc modo vel illo *R* ut conceptam aut ut exercitam *cett.*
2 sed si] *P* si *codd. R^c* sed *R*
3 eam] *codd.* exclusionem *PN*

4 et exclusus]*codd.T^c om. TN*
5 neque]*codd.* significant eam *add. P*
6 qui est significare]*codd.T^c* quam exercet *T*
7 similiter ... ergo hec]*PR* dictio specialis non significat actum suum proprium sed exercet ipsum ergo hec *N om. cett.*
8 dictio ... ergo]*codd.T^c om. T*
9 specialis solus]*codd.T* specialis *T^{c}R* solus *CH*
10 ipsam]*T* eam *codd.*
11 ut ... exclusionem]*codd. om. H*
12 exercitam]*codd.* conceptam *P*
13 conceptam]*codd.* exercitam *P*

5

1 significent]*RCH* significant *T* significat *P*
2 tantum]*codd.* et *add. PNR*
3 sicut ... significata]*codd. om. H*
4 sicut homo hominem]*codd. om. T*
5 homo]*codd.* significat *add.P*

6

1 autem]*codd. om. R*
2 queritur]*codd.* querit *N*
3 sive]*codd.* aut *R*
4 idest sortes currit]*codd.R^c* idest sortes *P om. R*
5 nichil]*codd.* non *R*
6 quilibet ... aliud]*coni.* quilibet... quilibet alius *T* quidlibet aliud ... quilibet alius homo *P* quilibet alius *N alii aliter*
7 alius]*codd.* a sorte *add. H*
8 ita]*codd. om. NR*
9 associatur]*NC* consociatur *TPR* sociatur *H*
10 associationem]*codd.* associatonis *P*
11 suam]*R om. cett.*
12 dicitur]*codd.* dicit *P* dicuntur *H*
13 proprius]*codd.* per prius *H*
14 patet]*codd.T^c om. T*

7

1 opponuntur]*codd.* apponuntur *R*
2 hunc] hoc *codd.*
3 illam]*P* illa *cett.*
4 ad]*codd. om. N*
5 associetur]*NR* associatur *cett.*

8

1 scilicet]*TPNR* id *CH*
2 a quo ... quartum]*codd. om. N*
3 excluditur]*TR om. cett.*
4 est]*TPR om. cett.*

5 gratia] *codd.* cum dicitur *add. P*
6 ut a] *codd.R^c* et a *P* ut *R*
7 excludendi] *TPNR* exercendi *CH*
8 importatur] *codd. T^c* om. *T*
9 semper] *P* simpliciter *cett.*

9

1 que talis est] *codd.* om. *N*
2 exclusio fit] *codd.* excluditur *R*
3 excluduntur] *codd.* excludantur *P*
4 ut ... excluduntur] *codd.* om. *N*
5 est risibile] *codd.* om. *P*

10

1 predictis ... alia] predictis patet quedam *T* predictis patet alia *NR* predictis sequitur alia *CH* lilis autem alia patet *P*
2 in] *codd.* ex *P*
3 illa] *codd.* om. *P*
4 ut] *codd.* sicut *P*
5 sortes ... tantum] *codd.* om. *P*
6 autem] *codd.* eius *add. P*
7 ut ... homo currit] *TPN* ut sortes currit *C* ut tantum sortes currit ergo sortes currit *R* om. *H*

11

1 secundum ... sophismate] *codd.* om. *H*
2 non ergo] *codd.* ergo non *R^c* ergo *R*
3 dicit] *codd.* vult *PR^c* om. *R*
4 simulac] *codd.* simul et postquam ac (!)*N*
5 unum] *codd.* quia unum *P*
6 dicit] *TP* om. *cett.*
7 quia] *TPNR* quod *CH*
8 unum ... unum] *T* si unum numero est unum est *PNR* quicquid est unum numero est unum *CH*
9 unumquodque ... unum est] *TR* etc. *N* om. *CH*
10 est unum] *TR* quod est unum est *PN* om. *cett.*
11 idem patet] *T* om. *N* item ad idem *cett.*
12 per ... talis est] *codd.* om. *N*
13 convertibilium ... altero] *codd.* dicitur de altero convertibiliter *PN*
14 vere] *codd.* om. *PN*
15 currit] *TP* om. *cett.*
16 adiungatur] *codd.* addatur *N*
17 enti et uni] *codd.* uni et enti *RH* ente (!) et uni *P* et econverso *add. TPCH*
18 est] *codd.N^c* om. *N*

12

1 in esse] *codd.* om. *H*

2 rei in] *TR^cH*   rei *PNR*   rerum in *C*
3 distinguendo] *codd.*   diffiniendo primo *N*
4 sua] *codd.*   *om. H*
5 etiam] *T^cNH*   ipse *RC*   ipse etiam *T*   etiam ipse *P*
6 et] *TPNR*   et sic *CH*
7 numeri] *codd.*   *om. H*
8 numeratur] *codd.*   enumeratur *C*
9 nisi] *codd.*   quam *H^c*   *om. H*
10 unitatibus] *codd.*   unitate *P*

13

1 etiam] *P*   *om. cett.*
2 ut] *codd.*   sicut *P*
3 sicut] *codd.*   sic *TN*
4 unitas ... accipiatur] *codd. T^c*   *om. T*
5 essentialis ... essentiale] *codd. T^c*   accidentalis ... accidentale *N*
6 essentiale ... accipiatur] *codd. T^c*   *om. TC*
7 unitas ... unum] *codd.*   *om. C*
8 exclusiva] *codd. P^c*   *om. P*
9 suum] *R^c*   *om. R cett.*
10 similiter] *codd.*   et sic *R*
11 est *T*   currit *P*   *om. cett.*
12 duo ... ergo] *codd.*   *om. CH*

14

1 hec ... unum est] *codd.*   *om. P*
2 et ... vera] *codd.*   *om. P*
3 potest fieri exclusio] *codd.*   *om. P*
4 et ... vera] *codd.*   *om. P*
5 sequitur] *codd.*   tantum unum est *add. R^cCH*
6 meliorem] *codd.*   veriorem *N*

15

1 probationem] *codd.*   autem *add. P*
2 secundum] *codd. P^c*   *om. P*
3 quoniam] *codd.*   quia *N*
4 completivum] *P*   complementum *cett.*
5 ut] *TPNR*   sicut *CH*
6 a ... re] *codd.*   *om. N*
7 autem] *codd.*   *om. P*
8 quod] *codd.*   vera sunt quia *add. R^cCH*
9 unum] *TPNR*   *om. cett.*
10 unitatem essentialem] *PCH*   essentiale *TNR*
11 et] *codd.*   *om. R*

16

1 est] *codd.*   *om. CH*
2 accipiendo ... unum est] *codd. T^c*   *om. T*

3 unum secundum] *coni.* ens secundum T^c *om. T cett.*
4 hec ... currit] R *om. cett.*
5 enim] PNR *om. cett.*
6 currit] *codd.* hec autem falsa *add. N*
7 ibi] R^c *om. R cett.*
8 sicut] TNR ut P sicut iam CH
9 circa] *codd.* supra R
10 accidens] $TPNR$ fallacia accidentis CH
11 adiungatur] *codd.* adiungantur N
12 ut] *codd.* P^c *om. P*
13 vere] TCH *om. PNR*
14 numeralem] *codd.* terminalem R^c talem R
15 de hoc uno] *codd.* hoc modo R
16 est] TPN *om. RCH*
17 ascendendo ... aliis] *codd.* *om. CH*
18 unum] *codd.* est *add. PR*
19 tria] *codd.* neque quatuor *add. P*
20 eius] PR rei N *om. cett.*
21 respectu esse] *codd.* T^c *om. T*
22 communiter inesse] *coni.* inesse P communiter R convenire *cett.*

17

1 illud] PNR id CH aliud T
2 per regulam] *codd.* de regula P
3 regula] *codd.* *om. P*
4 et omnes alie regule] PNR et ille regule omnes T alie regule omnes CH
5 sit] *codd.* *om. P*
6 quicquid] *codd.* enim *add. N*
7 quod est] TCH *om. PNR*

18

1 exclusionis] *codd.* sive species *add. P*
2 due] *codd.* tantum *add. P*
3 quia ... exclusio] *codd.* *om. H*
4 enim] *codd.* est *add. H*
5 generalis] *codd.* enim *add. P* est illa *add. CH*
6 exclusio] *codd.* que *add. CH*
7 specialis] *codd.* vero *add. NR* autem *add. CH*
8 genere] *codd.* genera R
9 diversa] *codd.* excluditur diversum NR
10 excluduntur] *codd.* *om. NR*
11 tertia exclusio] P alia exclusio *cett.* scilicet *add. CH*
12 erunt] *codd.* *om. CH*

19

1 partes] *codd.* sive species *add. P*
2 cum eo] *codd.* *om. T*

3 ad]*codd.* ut ad *CH*
4 sicut in]*TP* ut in *N* in *RC* sub *H*
5 unde ... aliud ens]*codd.* *om. P* et ... aliud *Pᶜ*
6 quando]*codd.* quia *PR*
7 in ... sive]*codd.* *om. N*
8 alia]*codd.* *om. T*
9 si autem]*T* si *N* sed si *cett.*

20

1 prius datam]*PN* datam *T* prius dictam *cett.*
2 relinquit]*codd.* ponit *P*
3 veram]*codd.* *om. P*
4 tunc]*codd.* sic *Tᶜ* *om. T*
5 excluderetur risibile]*codd.* *Tᶜ* *om. T*
6 et ... mortale]*codd.* *om. R*
7 sed]*codd.* *om. T*
8 secundum hoc]*T* hic *P* sic *cett.*
9 et]*codd.* dicitur quod *add. H*
10 fieri]*codd.* esse *PR*

21

1 quod cum] cum *TN* quod *cett.*
2 genere]*codd.* *om. PN*
3 generali]*PN* alia *T* *om. cett.*
4 ad]*codd.* *Tᶜ* *om. T*
5 que sunt]*RC* *om. cett.*
6 quod]*N* quia *T* quare *cett.*
7 scilicet]*codd.* *om. N*
8 exclusio]*codd.* *Rᶜ* *om. NR*

22

1 ut]*codd.* non *N*
2 semper] *T* quia semper *cett.*
3 huiusmodi]*codd.* hec *P*
4 vera]*TP* falsa *NHRC*
5 autem]*P* est *N* *om. TR*
6 homo]*codd.* *R* solus homo *Rᶜ*
7 quia]*codd.* quod *N*
8 sortes]*codd.* *om. N*
9 argumentum]*TPNR* *om. CH*
10 quod]*codd.* *Rᶜ* quando *R*
11 in se claudit]*TN* claudit intra se *P* concludit in se *RC*
12 nullum aliud animal]*codd.* *N* nullus alius currit *Nᶜ*
13 negativas]*PNR* negativam *T*
14 ibi]*TP* *om. NR*
15 et ... inferius]*codd.* *om. N*

23

1 generali] *codd.* autem *add. N*
2 datur] *codd.* solet dari *PN*
3 duas] *codd. T^c* om. *TP*
4 duas] *T^{c}NR* om. *cett.*
5 sed] *codd.* om. *N*
6 affirmativarum] *TNR^c* affirmationis *PH* affirmarum *(!)R*
7 sequitur] *codd.* ut *add. PR*
8 negativarum] *codd.* negationis *P*
9 ergo] *codd.* et *N*

24

1 circa] *T* quantum est de quo *E* quantum de quo *cett.*
2 descendendo] *TE* erat descendo *(!)N* erat descendendo *cett.*
3 excluditur] *codd.* excludebatur *C*
4 et] *TNEH* unde *PRC*
5 queritur] *codd.* om. *N*
6 excluditur] *TNE* debet excludi *PRC*
7 illa] *codd.* prima *N*
8 continet ... septem] *TPEC* habet in se alias *N* septem habet alias *R* continet sub se alias *H*
9 prima est] *codd.* unde prima *H*
10 utrum] *TPNE* an *RCH*
11 enti] *codd.* ente *PH*
12 est ... est] *C* et nichil aliud est *T* et nichil aliud *NERH* ergo nichil aliud *P*
13 et] *codd.* om. *N*
14 isti] *codd.* ista *T*
15 aliquid] *codd.* quid *P*
16 utrum] *codd.* dictio exclusiva *add. PRC*
17 uni] *codd.* om. *H*
18 alia] *TPNE* aliud *RCH*
19 quantitas] *codd.* qualitas *H*
20 omnibus] *codd.* om. *C*
21 albedo] *codd.* aut econverso *add. PC*
22 quarta] *codd. R^c* versata *(!)R*
23 alicui] *codd.* om. *N*
24 alias] *codd.* ceteras *R*
25 predicamento] *codd.* predicamentorum *P* predicato *E*
26 omnibus] *codd.* aliis *add. PC*
27 substantialibus] *codd.* specialitus *C* et *add. P*
28 sive ... quid] *T* sive in situm *(!)* quid predicantibus *N* sive in quid predicantibus *ERH* sive que predicantur in quid *PC*
29 species et genera] *codd.* sunt genera et species *PC*
30 predicamenti] *codd.* predicatum *E* om. *H*
31 termino] *codd.* om. *N*
32 alios] *codd.* aliquos *N*
33 sonorum] *codd.* sanum *T* scientiarum *(!)E*
34 alterum] *TPEH* reliquum *NR*

35 ut ... album] *codd.* om. *C*
36 cecum] *codd.* cecus *T*
37 parti ... totum] *coll. infra capite 58* toti ... partem *codd.*
38 et utrum] *NRC* vel *cett.*
39 maiori ... minorem] *T* minori ... maiorem *cett.*
40 vel] *codd.* et *PN*
41 et] *codd.* vel *P* ut *N*
42 tria ... duo] *T* duo ... tria *cett.*

25

1 primum] *codd.* sic *add. P*
2 enti vel] *codd.* enti et *T^c* om. *T*
3 communicare] *codd.* convenire *N*
4 a] *codd.* ex *R*
5 fit] *codd.* excluditur *H* excluditur vel *H^c*
6 in aliquo] *codd.* om. *PN*
7 communicare] *codd.* convenire *N*
8 aliquo generali] *codd.* alio quia nichil est supra ens *add. R*
9 sive ... ens] *codd.* sive speciali *P* om. *R*
10 scilicet vel *PN* vel *cett.*
11 excludi] *TPNR* excludere *ECH*
12 item] *TP* item ad idem *cett.*
13 non] *TE* nichil *cett.*
14 nichil] *codd.* non *N*

26

1 potest excludi [*T* excluditur *cett.*
2 quod est] *TN* vel *EH* om. *P*
3 quoad] *codd.* quod ad (!) *T*
4 suppositionem] *codd. T^{c}R^c* om. *TER*
5 homo] *codd. T^c* om. *T*
6 aliquid] *codd.* illud *R* quod *add. H*
7 sumpto] *codd.* om. *N*
8 nichil] *codd.* non *N*
9 suppositionem] *codd.* naturaliter enim supponuntur per terminum tam entia quam non entia unde exclusio non solum est de ente sed etiam de non ente quoad naturalem suppositionem *add. T   del. T^c*
10 et] *TP* om. *cett.*
11 excludi] *codd.* excludere *R*
12 item] *codd.* ad idem *add.N*
13 quicquid ... ens] *codd.* quod est ens *T* quod est ens est *T^c*
14 dictu tantum est] *PNRH* dictu tantum esse *T* dictu *C* determinato (!) est *E*
15 nec aliquid ... dictu] *codd.* om. *C*
16 dictu tantum ens] *TH* deum timetis (!)*E* est *add. PNRC*

27

1 alia] *codd.* om. *N* que *add. NEH*

2 que] *TPR^c* *om. NERH*
3 naturaliter ... de non ente] *codd. T^c om. TE* quoad naturalem suppositionem sed ab ente simpliciter sumpto nichil est diversum *add. T^r*
4 supponuntur] *codd.* supponitur *R*
5 entia] *codd.* essentia *N*
6 est] *codd. om. N*
7 est] *codd. om. N*

28

1 quod ... dicendum] *TN* autem dicendum primo dici (!)*P* quod obicit primo dicendum *H* quod obicitur primo dicendum *E* quod primo dicitur dicendum *R*
2 quare convertit] *coni.* convertit enim *P* quia convertit *cett.*
3 hic] *TPER^c om. NRCH*
4 oportet] *codd.* dicere *add. R^c*
5 est] *codd.* sit *P*
6 quod] *codd. H^c om. PH*
7 sicut] *codd.* sortes (!)*P*
8 animal] *codd. om. P*
9 est] *codd.* est animal *P*
10 excludi] *codd.* exclusio *NR*
11 est] *codd. om. TNR*
12 in] *codd. om. T*
13 in non] *codd.* non in *P*
14 speciali] *codd.* in aliquo speciali *P*
15 quare] quia *codd.*

29

1 dicendum] *codd.* dicimus *H*
2 non] *PN* nichil *cett.*
3 terminum] *codd.* cui adiungitur *add. RC*
4 multiplex] *codd.* multipliciter *TP*
5 quia] *codd. om. P*
6 equi] *codd.* hominis *P*
7 hominis] *codd.* equi *P* est essentia hominis *N*
8 continetur] *codd.* convertatur *R*
9 entium quam non entium] *codd.* entia quam non entia *H*
10 essentias] *codd.* essentiales *T* essentiam *E*
11 non] *codd. om. N*
12 quoad ... terminum] *codd. om. H*
13 naturales] *TE om. cett.*
14 dico quod licet] *codd.* licet dico quod *T*
15 quia ... extra ens] *codd. om. N*
16 essentia] *codd.* esse natura (!)*T*
17 est] *codd. om. C*

30

1 solvendum] *codd.* dicendum *P*

2 comprehendit] *codd.* apprehendit *N*
3 omnem ... antecedens] *codd.* quodlibet aliud accidens *P* esse aut actu sicut ... antecedens *N*
4 ideo] *codd.P^c* om. *P*
5 non] *codd.P^c* om. *P*
6 suppositum] *codd.* supposita *H*
7 sua] *codd.* entia *P*
8 quia supposita] *codd.* omnia sumpta *N*
9 ideo] que *H* et ideo *cett.*
10 possunt] *codd.* potest *P*
11 quoad] *codd.* naturalem *add. R*
12 ita] *codd.* prima *N*
13 si currit] *codd.* sicut *N*
14 est] *codd.* om. *NC*
15 est] *codd.* et sic de aliis *add. PNERCH*

31

1 secundum] *codd.* secundam questionem *H*
2 sic] *codd.* om. *P*
3 diversum] *codd.* diversa *P*
4 suppositionem] *codd.P^c* om. *P*
5 et sic] *codd.* om. *NR*
6 ergo] *codd.* et sic *NR*
7 a subiecto *H^c* subiecto *TNRCH* ab eo *PE*
8 generalissima] *codd.* genera *P*
9 semper] *PNR* om. *cett.*

32

1 quod] *codd.* illud quod *P*
2 in subiecto] *codd.T^c* om. *T*
3 currit] *RECH* om. *cett.*
4 currit] *ECH* om. *cett.*
5 gramaticum] *codd.* grammatica *N*
6 dat] *codd.T^c* non dat *T*
7 excludit substantiam] *PNR* potest excludere substantiam vel non excludit *cett.*
8 ergo] *codd.* non ergo dictio exclusiva *N*
9 omnis] *codd.* omnis propositio *R*
10 exclusiva] *codd.* exclusiva vera *CH*
11 preiacentem] *codd.* veram *add. NRCH*
12 ideo] *codd.* non *N*
13 alia] *codd.* om. *R* generalissima alia *R^c*
14 est] *codd.* om. *N*
15 uni] *codd.* generalissimo *add. PNR*

33

1 ordinatione] *TER^cCH* coordinatione *PNR*
2 quolibet] *codd.* alio *add. C*

3 in]*codd.* de *PN*
4 que]*TECII* et *PNR*
5 habent]*codd.* habet *PR*
6 comparationem secundum]*codd.* om. *T*
7 subiecta in quibus]*PNRH* substantiam in qua *T* substantiam in quibus (!)*EC*
8 essentie]*TEC* substantie *PNR* om. *H*
9 sive per]*codd.* super (!)*N*
10 quod]*P* que *E* qui *cett.*

34

1 generalissimo]*codd.* om. *P*
2 quia superficies]*codd.R^c* om. *NR*
3 faciant]*codd.* facerent *CH*
4 sed ... comparationem]*codd.* secundum autem comparationem *P* om. *N*
5 ad subiectum]*T* om. *cett.*
6 uni]*codd.* generalissimo add. *NR*
7 alterum]*TPN* reliquum *cett.*
8 unde]*TPNH* ut *ERC*
9 sequitur]*codd.* ergo add. *PC*
10 musicum ... tricubitum]*add.* musicus vel bicubitus vel tricubitus *C* musicum vel tricubitum *R*
11 vel homo]*codd.* om. *N*
12 quia sortes quia]*T^{c}NE* vel sortes quia sortes *TRCH* vel quasi sortes *P*
13 et]*TPH* om. *cett.*
14 et]*NR* vel *cett.*
15 unde dicendum]*TPHC* dicendum ergo *NR* unde dicendum ergo *E*
16 sumantur]*codd.* sumatur *RE*
17 uni ... adiuncta]*codd.* om. *C* uni]*codd.* generalissimo add. *R*
18 sumantur]*codd.* sumatur *E*
19 uni]*codd.* generalissimo add. *RC*
20 unum]*codd.R^c* om. *R* ut dictum est add. *PNRCH*

35

1 ad... unum]*codd.T^c* om. *T* ad]*codd.* aliquid *N*
2 dicendum]*codd.T* om. *E* dicendum est *T^c*
3 secundum quod generalissima]*R* sed si *E* si *cett.*
4 et ... excludit]*coni.* et exclusio non excludit *T* et exclusio non excludit illud *T^c* et tale non excluditur *PNE* tale vero non excluditur *cett.*
5 alio]*T* aliud(!) autem *N* alio autem *cett.*
6 concretum dat]*codd.T^o* dat concretum *T*
7 album]*codd.* albus *T*
8 corpore]*codd.* subiecto *T*
9 sive]*codd.* si *CH*
10 accipiam]*codd.* accipias *P* accipiat *N*
11 similiter est]*TPNR* similiter *CH* sic est *E*

12 intelligantur abstracta]*codd.* accipiantur in abstractione *NR*
13 et ... aliis]*codd.* *om.P*
14 sive ... aliis]*codd.* *om. CH*
15 concreta]*codd.* in concretione *R*
16 dant]*codd.* dat *N*
17 concreto ... abstracto]*codd.P^c* *om. P*
18 unde]*T* ut *cett.*
19 est]*codd.* non tantum quantitas *add. N*
20 dicendo]*T* dico *cett.*
21 alicuius ... unum]*codd.* *om. N*
22 vel]*TPE* et *N* sive *cett.*

36

1 dicimus]*TECH* dicendum *PNR*
2 omnis]*codd.* propositio *add. R*
3 exclusiva]*codd.* exclusio *T* vera *add. R^cCH*
4 preiacentem]*codd.* veram *add. R^c*
5 et ... exclusiva]*codd.* *om. N* et]*codd.* ad *R*
6 ipsam]*T* eam *cett.*
7 hec propositio]*codd. T^c* *om. T*
8 est]*codd. T^c* *om. T*
9 substantiam]*codd.* in esse *add. R^c*

37

1 addita]*T* adiuncta *cett.*
2 gratia huius]*T* *om. cett.*
3 generibus]*codd.* predicamentis *T*
4 quam]*codd.* etiam *R* etiam quam *R^c*
5 multo]*codd.H^c* *om. TH*

38

1 ad quod]*T* item *E* et *cett.*
2 ea]*codd.* *om. P*
3 est]*codd.* *om. N*
4 diversa]*codd.* diversum *P*
5 ibi]*codd.* ubique *P*
6 tempore]*codd.* tempus *H*
7 est]*PNRC* *om. cett.*
8 a]*codd.* ex *N*
9 ut]*codd.* unde *T*
10 ergo]*codd.* est *add. PNERCH*
11 ita]*codd.* tamen *C*
12 non insit]*codd.H^c* non sit *T^c* sit *T* non *H*
13 sortes est tantum]*T* tantum sortes est *cett.*
14 tantum]*codd.* tantum sortes *P* tamen *(!)C*
15 legit]*codd.* non ergo disputat *add. TPNEH*
16 quia ... quantus]*codd.* *om. H*
17 coloratum]*codd.* coloratus *NR*

18 neque ... movetur]*codd. om. C*
19 inest per alterum]*ECH* est per alterum *T* est in altero *PNR*
20 in altero]*TECH* per alterum *NR* in altero per alterum *P*
21 et]*codd.* in *E*
22 quinque modis]*codd.* patet quinque modis quod *P*
23 diversum]*codd.* diversis *E*
24 exclusivam]*codd.* et non diversa unde non excluditur superficies
per hanc tantum sortes est albus *add. E*

39

1 predictis]*TPE* hiis *cett.*
2 diversa]*codd.* diversum *H*
3 hanc]*codd.* dictionem *add. H* dictionem tantum ut tantum *add. PN*
dictionem tantum cum dicitur tantum *add. R* dictionem tantum ut
cum dicitur tantum *CH^c*
4 sortes]*codd.* homo *N*
5 ita]*codd.* prima *N*
6 predicamenti]*codd.* predicati *E*
7 alias ... unius predicamenti excludit]*codd. om. E*
8 vel]*TP* sive *N* vel dum *cett.*
9 argumenti]*codd.* predicamenti *P*
10 exclusiva]*codd. om. N*
11 aliquo]*codd.* ab aliquo *R*
12 tentum]*coni.* tantum *codd.*

40

1 excludat]*TPN* concludit *H* excludit *cett.*
2 comparetur]*PNR* comparatur *cett.*
3 alteram]*T* aliam *cett.*
4 disparata]*codd. T^c* disparatas *T*
5 non ... est]*TE* ergo linea non est *PNRH*
6 similiter]*T om. cett.*
7 unde bene sequitur]*codd.* bis in *P*
8 quia]*codd. om. N*
9 ille]*codd. om. CH*
10 disparate]*TEH* disparata *PNR*

41

1 prius]*codd. om. N*
2 sive disparatum]*codd.* sive separatum *T* separatum *E*
3 vel ... unum]*codd. om. T*
4 faciat]*codd. R^c* faciant *R* faciunt *N*
5 sortes est tantum]*coni.. coll. capite 32°* tantum sortes est *codd.*
6 sortes est tantum]*coni..* tantum sortes est *codd.*
7 coloratus]*TPNR* coloratum *cett.*
8 quantus *TP* quantum *cett.*
9 coloratum]*codd.* coloratus *N*
10 in]*codd. om. PR*

11 quantus *TNR* quantum *cett.*
12 album]*N* album est *cett.*
13 unum]*codd.* coloris *add. P*

42

1 adiuncta ... dictio exclusiva]*codd.* *om. E*
2 uni]*codd.* vim *(!)R*
3 diversa]*codd.* diversum *P*
4 unum sed diversa]*TPER* sed diversa N   unum *CH*
5 alio]*TP* altero *cett.*
6 excludit]*codd.* excludit *PN*

43

1 quam verum]*codd.* *om. N*
2 quia]*codd.* falsam quia *add. P*
3 frigidum]*codd.* opponuntur *add. N* opponuntur et multa alia *add. R*

44

1 improbatio]*codd.* in probatione *CH*
2 opponi simpliciter]*T* opponi sive *P* oppositio veri *R* opponi *R^c cett.*
3 in]*codd.* *om. CH*

45

1 quia]*codd.* quod *N*
2 unde]*T* ut *cett.*
3 omnis]*PNRCH^c* *om. TEH*
4 dictio]*codd.R^c* *om. R* divisio *(!)N*

46

1 illa]*codd.* prima *N*
2 quia]*codd.* quod *N*
3 secundum]*codd.T^cE^c* et secundum *TPE*
4 ideo]*NR* et ideo *cett.*
5 est]*codd.* *om. T*
6 sed]*codd.* scilicet *CH*
7 est]*codd.* *P* est quia *P^c*
8 est ad]*codd.* autem et *N*
9 et]*codd.* *om. N*
10 exclusionis]*codd.* dictionis exclusive *P*
11 quia]*codd.* quod *sic saepius N*
12 quia ponit]*codd.* scilicet *P*
13 et ... non esse]*codd.* *om. P*

47

1 est]*codd.* *om. P*
2 et ... est]*codd.* *om. N*
3 aliud]*codd.* alius *N*
4 assignatur]*coni.* significatur *codd.*

48

1 ad] *codd.* Solutio ad *P*
2 tripliciter] *codd.* simpliciter tripliciter *N*
3 quia album] *codd.* album enim *P*
4 nominat] *codd. R^c* *om. ER*
5 et ... dictu] *T^c P* et hoc est *TNE* hoc est dictum *CH* *om. R*
6 hoc quod est subiectum] *CH* hoc est subiectum *P* hoc subiectum *R*
subiectum *N*
7 substantia] *codd.* res *NR*
8 alio] *TECH* tertio *PNR*
9 album] *codd.* est quod *add. P*
10 alio] *codd.* autem *add. P*
11 materia et forma] *T* subiecto et accidente *cett.*
12 in] *T* *om. cett.*
13 correlativorum] *codd.* correlative oppositorum *H*
14 alio] *codd.* altero *P*
15 unum] *codd.* unum correlativorum *R*

49

1 excludat] *codd.* excludit diversa *P*
2 diversa] *codd.* *om. P*
3 et] *TECH* sed *N* *om. PR*
4 faciant] *P* possint facere *CH* possunt facere] *TNER*
5 unum *T* unum sed diversa *cett. T^c*
6 sunt] *codd.* *om. T*
7 nec] *codd. T^c* ne *T*
8 aliquo alio] *PN* in aliquo alio *R* aliquo *TE* alio *CH*
9 tunc] *PNR* *om. cett.*
10 quod] *codd.* ut *P*
11 solutio ... dicendo] *NR* solutio autem recta est dicendo *P* solutio
recta est dicendum *T* solutio et recte est dicendum *E* solutione recta est
dicendum *H*
12 est] *codd.* pater est et cum *add. N*
13 ponitur] *codd.* *om. CH*
14 que] *TNER* quia *P* *om. CH*
15 omne] *codd.* esse *NE*
16 sic] *T* ita *cett.*
17 filium] *codd.* scilicet a parte exclusionis *add. E*
18 hoc relativum] *codd.* hic tantum (!)*E*
19 quod] *TH* quia *PNER*
20 una] *codd.* alia *N* natura (!)*E*
21 parte] *codd.* sue *add. P*
22 ipsum] *codd.* filium *P*
23 sui] *codd.* *om. T*

50

1 quia] *codd.* quod *N*
2 ibi] *codd.* *om. T*
3 claudit] *codd.* claudunt *N* cludit (!)*T*

4 ad]*codd.* suum *add. PH*
5 ergo ... currit]*codd. om. PE*
6 sortes]*codd.* non *add. R*
7 est]*codd.* ibi *add. P*
8 contradictio enim]*codd.* prima enim contradictio *P*
9 ex suis partibus]*TP* sicut domus ex suis partibus *P^c* ex suis partibus duabus sicut domus ex suis partibus *N* ex duabus suis partibus sicut domus ex suis partibus *R* ex hiis duabus partibus sicut domus ex suis partibus *H* ex suis partibus sicut domus ex suis *E*
10 affirmationem quam negationem]*codd.* affirmativam quam negativam *P* affirmatio quam negatio *R*

51

1 tantum]*codd. T^c om. T*
2 hominem]*codd.* cecum *add. P del. P^c*
3 tantum]*codd. H^c* solum *R om. EH*
4 tantum]*codd. T^c om. T*
5 hominem]*codd.* cecum *add. P del. P^c*
6 videntem se]*codd.* videntem *T* videns se *E*
7 sortes videt]*codd.* sortem videre *PH*
8 tantum]*T^cH om. TPNRE*
9 se]*codd. om. P*
10 tunc]*codd. P* tunc quero *P^c*
11 se]*codd. om. P*
12 non]*codd. om. E*
13 et ... videns se]*codd. om. N*
14 videbat]*codd.* videt *H*
15 quemlibet]*codd.* quemquem *T*
16 sed]*codd. om. E*
17 talem]*codd.* tale *EH*
18 se]*codd. om. T*
19 quoniam]*TPRE* quia *cett.*

52

1 omnem]*codd. R^c om. R*
2 se]*codd.* et omnis propositio implicans contradictionem est impossibilis propositio *add. T^m*
3 probatio]*codd.* autem *add. TNR* vero *add. P*
4 procedendo]*codd. om. T*
5 distributione ... exclusiva]*codd.* dictione exclusiva et etiam cum distributione *P*
6 omne]*codd.* omnis *H*
7 est]*codd. om. P*
8 est]*codd.* ut *N*
9 se]*codd.* nec tamen est cecus *add. PNERCH*
10 vigilans]*codd. R^c* videns *R*
11 oculos habens]*N* oculos *TP* est (?*pro* cum) habet oculo*s E* habens oculos *T^c cett.*
12 causos (!)*E*

53

1 quod] *T* autem *add. cett.*
2 tantum] *codd. T^c om. T*
3 habeat] *codd.* habeant *N*
4 scilicet] *codd. om. P*
5 et] *codd.* sortes *add. NRH*
6 hominem] *codd. T^c* hominem tantum *T*
7 expositive] *codd.* de expositione *N* composite vel exposite *H*
8 videntem] *codd. T^c* non videntem *T*
9 non] *codd. T^c om. T*
10 ergo] *codd.* sortes *add. N*
11 sortes] *TE* ergo sortes *cett.*
12 quia] *codd.* ille *add. R^c*
13 affirmationes] *codd. T^c* distributiones *T*
14 earum] *codd. om. TE*
15 ut] *codd. om. N*
16 et] *codd.* si *add. N*
17 necessario] *TPR^c* necesse *E om. NRC*
18 sortes] *codd. om. P*
19 a] *codd. om. N*
20 non videt se] ergo non videt se *PR* ergo sortes non videt se *R^c cett.*
21 et] *codd. om. P*
22 altera] *codd.* alia *TE*
23 altera] *codd.* parte *add. P*
24 et] *TECH om. PNR*
25 modo] *codd.* sequitur *add. H*
26 non] *codd. T^c om. T*
27 hic] *TPE* hec *cett.*
28 est] *codd. om. NR*
29 et ita] *PE* et quia *T* ergo ista *NRH^c* ergo una *H*
30 claudit intra] *TNH* claudit in *E* prima cludit (!)*P* prima claudit *R*

54

1 illud idem] *TN* idem *H* illud *P* ad illud *R* ad idem *E*
2 quia] *codd.* sequitur *add. REH*
3 videntem] *codd.* non videntem *R*
4 videret] *RE* videt *cett.*
5 iam] *NRH* ergo *PE om. T*
6 videns se] *codd. T^c om. T*
7 videretur] *P* videtur *cett.*
8 nullus] *codd.* homo *add. PE*
9 hominem] *codd.* non *add. T del. T^c*
10 sic habetur] *codd.* hec est *P*
11 alia] *codd.* altera *P*
12 in] *codd.* intra *P*

55

1 probo quod] *T* probatio *H* probatio quod *cett.*

2 ponatur]*codd.* enim *add. R*
3 homines]*T om. cett.*
4 videant se]*codd.H* se videant *Hᶜ*
5 et tunc]*T* et cum *E* tunc *cett.*
6 videns se non videt]*coni.* videt se *N* ut videt se *R* non videns se *cett.*
7 singularibus]*codd.* ut *add. N*
8 plato]*TPE* cicero *cett.*
9 cicero]*TPE* plato *cett.*
10 tres]*codd.* omnes *CH*
11 sequitur]*codd. om. N*
12 sed]*codd.Rᶜ* se *R* scilicet *N*
13 videt]*codd.Rᶜ* neque *R*
14 tantum]*codd.* omnes *CH*
15 se]*codd.Tᶜ om. T*
16 et est locus]*TPE* per locum *cett.*
17 sortes]*codd.* ergo sortes *R*
18 omnem]*codd. om. R*
19 se]*codd. om. CH*
20 omnis]*codd. om. P*
21 se]*codd.Pᶜ om. P*
22 tantum]*TᶜPN om. T cett.*
23 est]*codd.* et *N*
24 tantum]*TᶜPNERᶜ om. TRCH*

56

1 Solutio]*codd.* ergo *N*
2 sicut]*T* ut *cett.*
3 primam autem positionem]*codd.* primum autem positum *H*
4 incompossibilia]*TᶜCH* impossibilia *TPN* possibilia *(!)R*
5 quod]*codd.* quia *sic saepius N*
6 sed ... secundum se]*codd.Tᶜ om. T*
7 insimul]*codd.* simul sumpta *P*
8 incompossibilia]*codd.* impossibilia *RE*
9 secundum]*codd.* per *N*
10 illo]*codd. om. P*
11 homines]*TP om. cett.*
12 incompossibilia']*TᶜR* impossibilia *PECHᶜ* possibilia *H*
13 isti tres tantum]*P* isti tres *TE* isti tantum tres *R* tantum isti tres *cett.*
14 sint]*TER* sunt *cett.*
15 se]*codd.Tᶜ om. T*
16 se]*codd. om. N*
17 videat]*codd.* se cum non sit de illis ita ponit quod sortes videat *add. Hᶜ*
18 non]*codd.Tᶜ om. T*
19 ponit ... et ita]*codd. om. H*
20 se]*codd.Rᶜ om. PR*
21 duo]*codd.* dictio *(!)R*
22 posita]*codd.Rᶜ* ponit *R* sumpta posita *H*

23 ita] *T*   ideo *cett.*
24 incompossibilia | *codd.*   impossibilia *TP*

57

1 aliud] *TEH*   illud autem *PR*   alius autem *N*
2 dicendum | *codd.*   *om. T*
3 similiter] *TPE*   *om. cett.*
4 scilicet] *TER^c*   hic *P*   *om. R cett.*
5 possibile] *codd. R^c*   *om. R*
6 tantum] *PNER*   *om. cett.*
7 cecum] *codd.*   cecum tantum *T*
8 homine] *codd.*   hoc *E*   omni homine *H*
9 vidente] *codd.*   videntes (!) *E*
10 sortes | *codd.*   *om. N*
11 et] *TPE*   *om. cett.*
12 removetur] *codd.*   enim removetur *NR^c*   removetur enim *R*
13 sic] *codd.*   conclusio *H*
14 iterum] *T^{c}PNE*   tantum *TR*   idem *H*
15 se] *codd.*   *om. P*
16 se] *codd.*   *om. P*
17 si premissa] *TPNER*   si *R^c*   sed conclusio *CH*
18 positione] *codd.*   propositione *N*

58

1 vel] *codd.*   et *P*
2 vel] *codd.*   et *P*
3 excludat] *TE*   possit excludere *cett.*
4 tantum] *codd. H^c*   *om. TII*
5 libras] *codd.*   marcas *N*
6 ut] *codd.*   si *add. PNER*
7 albus] *codd.*   alba *E*
8 exclusiva] *codd.*   semper *add. NER*
9 sed ... colorata] *codd.*   *om. N*
10 paries] *codd.*   ergo paries *PE*
11 quia coloratus] *codd. T^c*   *om. T*
12 paries | *codd.*   ergo paries *NR*
13 coloratus] *codd. E^c*   colorata *E*
14 toti] *codd.*   parti *T*
15 partem] *codd.*   totum *T*   totum partem (!) *E*

59

1 tantum] *codd.*   *om. TPE*
2 ex] *codd.*   in *N*
3 et habere] *codd.*   he (?) *T*
4 omnes] *codd.*   essentiales *H*
5 integralis] *codd.*   *om. E*
6 ipsius] *TP*   *om. cett.*
7 hominis] *codd. H^c*   *om. CH*

8 sed]*codd.* est pars *add.* P pars *add.* NRCH
9 centum]*codd.* tantum centum *TE*
10 libras convenit]*codd.* marcas *N*
11 ita toti quod]*TPR* in toto quod *E* toti et *CH*
12 autem]*TPE om.* NR
13 tantum parti]*TE* parti et non toti *NCH* tantum parti et non toti *R*
14 minus]*codd. T^c om. TE*
15 videlicet]*T* ut *P* et *N* vel *cett.*
16 partialitas]*codd.* particulari *(!)C*
17 alii quanto]*TPNE* alii *C* alii quantitati *R* quanto *cett.*
18 ad]*codd. om. N*
19 modo]*codd. om. N*
20 toti et parti]*codd.* parti et toti *P*
21 calidum frigidum]*codd.* frigidum calidum *TP*
22 accidentis]*T* accidentium *cett.*
23 libras]*codd.* marcas *N*
24 in]*TP* et in *cett.*
25 semper]*codd. om. P*

60

1 circa predicta]*PE* secundum predicta *T* item *cett.*
2 probatio ... sortis]*codd. T^c om. T*
3 et]*codd. om. P*
4 alio]*codd.* quoniam *add. R*
5 a solo ... prima vera]*P* a solo sorte etc. *TN* a solo sorte differt etc. quia si ab alio differt illud sit illud plato et procedatur sic a solo platone differt quicquid non est sortes vel pars sortis ergo sortes non differt a platone et hoc est impossibile ergo prima vera *H*
6 contra]*codd.* sed contra *RCH*
7 nec]*TP* vel *cett.*

61

1 probativa]*TPE* probantium *cett.*
2 alio]*codd.* aliquo *P*
3 ab alio]*codd.* ab aliquo *P^c* aliquo *P*
4 aliquis]*codd. om. P*
5 sicut ... pluribus]*codd. T^c om. T*
6 equum ... homo]*codd.* omnis homo videt equum *N*
7 tamen]*codd.* tantum *N*
8 iste equum]*T^c* terminus equum *TP* iste accusativus equum *NER* iste accusativus *cett.*

62

1 maiori numero]*PNE* minori numero *T* maiori *cett.*
2 minorem]*codd.* maiorem *T*
3 numeri]*N* minores numeri *codd.*
4 ternarius ... aliis]*P* quinarius ternarius et sic de aliis *T* ternarius quaternarius et sic de aliis *NE*

5 quia] *codd.* que *N*
6 condividentes] *codd.* dividentes *P*
7 uni] *codd.* speciei *add.* P^c speciei numeri *add. NRH*
8 alias] *codd.* alios *P*
9 maiori] *TPNR om. H*
10 excludet] *TP* excludit *cett.*
11 quamlibet unitatem] *TE om. cett.*
12 quemlibet minorem speciem] *codd. om. TE*
13 quia ... minorem speciem] *codd. om. N*
14 quinario] *codd.* binario *R*
15 quamlibet aliam | *codd.* quaternarium *H*
16 suum preiacentem] *T* suam partem *cett.*
17 si ... esse] *T* si ... est *PE* quod si duo sunt unum est *NR*
18 ergo] *codd.* et ideo *P*

63

1 sicut] *TPE* et similiter *NR*
2 quod idem est] *TPER^c om. R cett.*
3 numero] *codd.* non *add. T del. T^c*
4 quemlibet minorem] *PNR* quemlibet numerum minorem *E*
quemlibet numerum *H* minorem numerum quemlibet *T*
5 decem] *codd. om. N*
6 octo] *codd.* sunt paria *add. NRH*
7 etiam] *codd.* ita *R*
8 superiores] *codd.* maiores *C*
9 sic] si *TR om. cett.*
10 undecim neque] novem neque *T om. cett.*
11 ascendendo] *codd.* ostendendo(!) *T*
12 non] *codd.* in *T*
13 est] *TE* constat *cett.*
14 ex quibus] *codd. om. N*
15 immo] *codd.* unde *P*
16 ponet] *P* ponit *cett.*
17 non ergo novem] *P* ergo octo non *TEH* non ergo octo *N*
18 septem] *TP^cE* novem *P* sex *N*
19 oppositum] *codd.* quantum *T*
20 quia] *codd.* quod *N*
21 si] *codd. T^c om. T*
22 sequitur ... currant] *TN* non sequitur ergo novem non currunt *P*
23 et currant] *NRE om. T* et etiam quod octo non currant *P*
24 minor] *codd.* maiori *C*

64

1 unde] *TP om. cett.*
2 parte] *codd. om. T*
3 excepto] *codd.* ex *E*
4 toto] *codd. om. T*

65

1 duo prima argumenta]*TE* duo argumenta predicta *P* ad argumenta predicta *NRH*
2 facilis]*codd.* talis *R*
3 solutio]*codd.* solum *N*
4 suarum totalitatum]*TPE* sue totalitatis *NRH*
5 aggregationum]*TPE* sive ratione sue aggregationis *NRH*
6 uni]*codd.* speciei numeri *add. NRH*
7 autem]*codd.* argumentum *add. NRH*
8 accepit]*E* accipit *cett.*
9 sunt]*TPE* est numerus *NR* fit numerus *H*

66

1 et]*codd.* *om. N*
2 a]*TPE* quoniam *R* quam *cett.*
3 duo]*codd.* *om. T*
4 pauciora]*TPE* ergo prima vera *add. P*
5 contra ... pauciora]*codd.* *om. N*

67

1 exponi]*codd.* [excludi] exponi *T*
2 dictionem exclusivam]*T* exclusionem *cett.*
3 obliquo]*codd.* rectitudine*T*
4 probatur]*PE* improbatur *T* *om. cett.*
5 et ... vera]*codd.R^c* *om. TP*
6 et est sensus ... aliis a tribus]*P^c* *om. P cett.*
7 pauciora]*P^c* tribus *add. et del. P^c*
8 rectitudine ... probatur]*codd.* obliquo et sic improbatur *T*
9 et ... falsa]*P^c* et sic est vera *T* *om. cett.*
10 et est sensus ... tribus sunt pauciora]*P^c* *om. P cett.*
11 ideo]*TPE* sic *NH* tunc *R*
12 exponentibus]*codd.* componentibus *H*
13 falsa]*codd.* vera et altera falsa *T*
14 hec scilicet]*codd.* *om. E*
15 cum ... sunt pauciora]*codd.* *om. E*

68

1 seipsa ... locutio]*PNER* multiplex est locutio seipsa est (!) attingentia *T*
2 quia]*TP* ex eo quod *N* eoquod *RCH*
3 poterat]*TPE* potest *NR*
4 reliquum vel econverso] *T* alium vel *R* alterum vel *cett.*
5 aut ... ab eo]*codd.* *om. PN* aut]*TE* vel *cett.*

69

1 ascensus]*codd.* assensus *P*
2 augmenti]*codd.* argumenti *R*
3 in quantilate]*TPE* quantitates *NH*

4 loquendo]*PN om. cett.*
5 ascensu]*codd.* accensu *T*
6 minores]*TPE* omnes minores *NRCH*
7 causa maiorum]*TPE* cause maiorum numerorum *NRCH*
8 est]*codd. om. P*
9 est]*codd. om. P*
10 intantum ... causa]*TE* Inquantum est prior est causa *NREH*
11 et ... est]*T om. E* et omnis causa superiori prior et superior *P* et omnis causa superiori et prior *N^c* et omnis causa superior est et prior *R* et omnis causa superior et prior est *H*
12 a]*TPE* sic a *R* sic de *NR^cH*
13 quemlibet]*TPEH om. NR*
14 est descendere]*P* descendere *T* aut descendere *E* autem est descendere *NR*
15 loquendo]*codd. om. NH*
16 quantitatis ... qualitatis]*codd.* augmenti sive quantitatis *P*
17 hunc]*codd. om. T*
18 maiores ... superiores]*codd.* superiores ... maiores *T*
19 eoquod]*TPE* et ideo quia *NH*
20 maioribus]*TPE* est *NR*
22 descensus]*TE* autem descensus *P* autem est descensus *NR* est autem descendendo *H*
23 fiunt]*codd.* fuit *E*
24 numeri]*T* minorum *PE* numerorum *NRH*

70

1 quartam]*codd.* quandam *P*
2 principio huius]*codd.* primo *P*
3 scilicet ... differant]*TPE* de differentia harum dictionum solus tantum *NRCH*
4 casuali]*codd.R^c* causali *sic saepius ER*
5 sortes]*codd.* currit *add. N*
6 do]*TPE* ego do *NRH*
7 vel ... currit]*codd. om. P*
8 alius]*codd.* homo *add. P* currit *add. NRH*
9 idest ... facit]*codd.* et nichil aliud *NII*
10 natum]*codd.* aptum natum *P*

71

1 substantie]*codd. om. P*
2 similiter]*codd.* sic *N*
3 et absolute]*codd. om. N*
4 actum]*codd.* verbum sive actum *PR^c*
5 dispositio]*codd. om. P*
6 solum]*NRH om. TPE* solus *P^c*
7 aliquando ... absolute]*codd. om. P*
8 vero]*TE om. NRH*
9 actu ... ipso casuali]*codd. om. N*

10 vel aliquo casuali] *TP* ab aliquo casuali R^c ab aliquo causali *E* *om.*
cett.
11 ipso]*P* aliquo *cett.*
12 ut]*codd.* actu (!)*add. N*
13 predictis]*T* supradictis *cett.*

72

1 item]*codd.* postea *P*
2 alius]*codd.* excludatur *add. NRH*
3 quedam propositio]*TPE* propositio *RH* probatio *N*

73

1 excludi]*TNH* excludendi *PRE*
2 a privatione]*TPR^c* privationem *NER*
3 ut]*codd.* sicut *N*
4 cecitatem]*codd.* cecum *N*
5 sed]*codd.* sed etiam *N*
6 privare privationem]*TP* privari privatione *NRH* privari privationem
(!)*E*

74

1 solus]*codd. T^c* *om. T*
2 vim]*TPE* naturam *cett.*
3 sed hec dictio]*codd.* *om. T*
4 debet ... restringere]*codd.* restringit *P*
5 terminum]*codd.* *om. T*
6 cui adiungitur]*codd.* *om. P*
7 regula]*codd.* illa *N* hec *R*
8 adiectivis]*codd.* obiectivis (!)*N*
9 ut]*codd.* sunt *add. NRH*
10 adiectivis]*codd.* adiectis (!)*N*
11 minus]*codd.* unius (!)*N*
12 ab albedine]*codd.* albedine *N* albedinem (!)*E*
13 in eo]*codd. T^c* *om. T*
14 diversam]*codd.* *om. N*

75

1 hoc enuntiabile]*codd. T^c* *om. TE*
2 non]*codd.* *om. E*
3 alius]*codd.P* non omnis alius P^x
4 ergo]*codd.* quero an *add.* P^x
5 omnis alius]*TPEH* vel omnis alius *R* *om. N*
6 vel ... alius]*TNRH* *om. P* an non omnis alius P^x vel non alius *E* a
platone *add. H*
7 si]*codd.* scilicet *E*
8 omnis]*codd.* alius *add. NRH*
9 contra]*codd.* *om. N*

10 sicut ... scitis]*codd. T^c* om. *T*
11 solus]*codd.* sicut *(!)* solus *N*

76

1 aliquod]*codd.* hoc *R*
2 aliquod]*codd.* om. *N*
3 indefinito]*codd.* infinite *NE*
4 restringere]*codd. R^c* intelligere *R*
5 scilicet]*codd.* quod est *N*
6 indefinite]*codd.* infinite *NH*
7 solum]*codd.* tenetur *add. P*
8 hoc modo]*codd.* om. *NCH*
9 quod ... dico]*codd.* om. *T*
10 cum]*T* si *cett.*
11 supponunt]*T* supponerent *NERH* contradicerent *NER*

TRACTATUS QUARTUS

DE DICTIONIBUS EXCEPTIVIS

1

1 Sequitur] *codd.* Dicto de dictionibus exclusivis sequitur autem *N*
2 debeat] *codd.* habeat *P*
3 sillogizabilis] *codd.* sillo dictionem *(!)N*

2

1 sicut] *codd.* ut *P*
2 quidam] *codd.* quidem *N*
3 quia] *codd. Rᶜ om. NR*
4 significat eam] *codd. om.N*
5 conceptam] *codd.* exceptam *E*
6 quibus ... prius] *codd.* sicut prius ostensum est *P*
7 quod] *codd.* quia *PR*
8 exclusionem] *codd.* exceptionem *N*
9 quia] *codd. Tᶜ om. T*
10 prepositio] *TRCH* propositio *PNE*
11 exercitium] *T* exercitum *cett.*
12 casualis] *TPE* casualem *cett.*
13 affectum] *codd.* affectam *T*
14 ut exercitium] *coni.* exercitum *N* ut exercitam *T* ut exercitum *cett.*
15 conceptam] *codd.* conceptum *EH*
16 modo] *codd. om. N*
17 hoc] *TNCH* alio *PER*

3

1 propositioni contraria ut] *codd.* propositionem ut *(!)R*
2 ferre] *PEH* inferre *T* fieri *N* versari *Rᶜ* sive *R*
3 dictionem instantivam] *codd.* instantiam *N*
4 preter] *TNER* patet *P*
5 sortem] *codd.* currit *add. NR*
6 idest sortes] *TPEH om. NR*
7 et ... primum] *codd. om. T*

4

1 non] *codd. om. TE*
2 ut] non *TP om. cett.*
3 ut] *P om. cett.*
4 tantum et solus] *TE* solus et tantum *cett.*
5 non] *CH om. cett.*
6 ut] *T* non *PᶜER om. PNCH*

5

1 queritur] *codd.* quantum *N*
2 enim] *codd.* autem *P*
3 tria] *codd.* tres *P* tota *N*
4 ab aliquo] *codd.* ab alio *E*
5 distributio] *codd.* dictio *P*
6 est id] *TᶜE* id *T* est aliquid *P* est illud *cett.*
7 qui] *codd.* que *N* quod *H*
8 id] *T* *om. E* illud *sic saepius cett.*
9 exiguntur] *codd.* sunt necessaria *N*
10 instrumentum] *codd.Rᶜ* inscitum *R* instetimento *(!)E*
11 excipiendi] *codd.* accipiendi *N*
12 etiam] *codd.* *om. C*
13 obicit] *TPE* obiciebatur *cett.*
14 cuius] *codd.* excipitur *add. EH* accipitur *add. R*
15 obiciebat] *TPE* obiciebatur *cett.*
16 oportet semper] *TPRᶜ* oportet *NRH* debent semper *C* species debet *(!)E*
17 quod] *codd.* ut *P*

6

1 quia] *PR* quod *NE* secundum quod *CH* sed *T*
2 sunt] *codd. Tᶜ* *om. T*
3 non] *codd.* numquam *H*
4 potest fieri] *codd.* fit *P*
5 numeri] *codd. Tᶜ* termini *R* *om. T*
6 diminutive] *codd.Nᶜ* diminutionem *N*
7 et] *TP* et ad *cett.*
8 semper] *codd.* *om. NE*
9 per] *codd.* secundum *P*
10 quam] *codd.* habitudinem *add. T*
11 pars] *codd.* et pars *P*
12 suum] *TPE* *om. NRH*
13 denarii] *codd.* numeri *add. NR*
14 unum] *codd.* tantum *R*
15 potest] *codd.* unum *add. R*
16 a decem] *codd.* adesse *E*
17 tertii] *TPERᶜ* *om. NRH*
18 huius actus] *T* huiusmodi *N* huius *cett.*
19 novem] *codd.* decem *N*
20 scilicet intellectus] *TRᶜ* idest intellectus *N* *om. cett.*
21 excipit] *TPN* excipitur *cett.* scilicet preter *add. Rᶜ*
22 et sic] *Tᵉ* ergo *cett.*

7

1 est] *codd.* sit *P*
2 excipiatur] *codd.* excipitur *EC* semper *add. PE*
3 fert] *codd.R* ferat *C* infert *Rᶜ*

4 eius]*RC* ei *cett.*
5 et ... excipitur]*codd.* *om.* E
6 etiam]*TPNR* *om. cett.*
7 sit]*TPN* fit R sic *CH*
8 a quo ... cum]*codd.* ergo oportet quod *C*
9 et ... totum]*codd.* non ferat instantiam in totum et pars in modo *TC*
10 quia non]*codd.* neque P
11 toto]*codd.* suo toto *PR* vel *add.* R
12 omnes]*T* omnis E orationes *PCH* omnes orationes R omnes dictiones N
13 ad ... naturaliter]*codd.* *om.* E
14 naturaliter]*codd.* actualiter P
15 ordinetur]*TCH* ordinatur *PNER*

8

1 sui]*codd.* suam *TN* *om.* E
2 adhuc]*codd.* ad hoc *TN*
3 homo]*codd.* ergo pars subiectiva non infert(!) instantiam contra suum totum *add.* R
4 omnes]*TPE* omnium *NRCH* omnes omnium R^c
5 contradicant]*codd.H* non contradicant H^c
6 negationem]*codd.* que fuerat contra suum totum *add.* R
7 ille]*codd.* que *add. NRCH*
8 suo]*codd.* *om.* N
9 ad suum totum]*TPER* *om. NCH*
10 item ... ipsum]*codd.T^c* *om.* T
11 pars fert instantiam]*codd.* sunt instantia E
12 in ipso]*codd.T^{c}R^c* ipso T expositio R
13 nulla ... ergo]*NR* *om. cett.*
14 comparationem]*codd.* compositionem R

9

1 secundum ... actualiter]*codd.R^c* *om. NR*
2 hic]*codd.* *om.* N
3 excipiuntur quot supponuntur]*TNER* supponuntur quod (!) excipitur P excipiuntur quot relinquuntur H
4 impropria et falsa]*codd.* impossibilis et falsa N impropria et falsa et impossibilis P
5 currit]*codd.* *om.* N
6 stat]*E* est T sic (!)N stet *cett.*
7 repperit]*codd.* repit *NR*
8 improprietas]*codd.T^c* proprietas T
9 removeatur]*codd.P^c* ponatur P
10 est]*TNER* contingit *cett.*
11 oporteret]*TNR* oportet *cett.*
12 excipere]*codd.* accipere N
13 sui]*T* *om. cett.*
14 omnia]*codd.* supposita *add.T*
15 supposita]*PNER* sumpta *CH* *om.* T

10

1 in] *codd.* pro *NR*
2 pro eo] *codd. Tᶜ om. T* pro homine *P*
3 quod falsam est] *PR om. cett.*

11

1 et] *codd. om. P*
2 simplici] *codd. Pᶜ* speciali *P*
3 suppositionem] *codd. Tᶜ om. T*
4 omne animal] *codd. om. N*
5 in] *codd.* sub *PE*
6 animal aliud ab homine] *TᶜPE* aliud animal ab homine *TN*
7 in] *codd.* sub *CH*
8 que] *codd.* qui *E* alia quam que *P*
9 augmentatur] *codd.* argumentatur *E* arguitur *R*

12

1 iudicium] *codd.* videndum *E*
2 penitus] *codd.* ponitur *E*
3 est] *PR om. TNE*

13

1 habeat excipere] *TPE* debeat excipere *NR* excipiat *H*
2 indifferenter] *codd. om. N*
3 qualibet] *TPE* quacumque *NR* excipiat *H*

14

1 et] *codd. om. T*
2 duplex] *codd. Rᶜ* dupliciter *PR*
3 intelligendi] *codd.* et hec in homine ut genus numerus singularitas *add. R*
4 alia ... preter sortem currit] *codd. om. R*
5 est] *codd. om. P*
6 iterum] *codd.* multitudo *add. N*
7 sua individua] *codd.* omnia individua sua *P*
8 ab ista] *codd. om. P*
9 potest excipere] *TPE* excipit *cett.*
10 que est multitudo] *codd. om. T* que est *Tᶜ*
11 vel omne animal] *codd.* est animal *N*
12 hec ... que est] *P* hec etiam multitudo est *NRH* hec est multitudo que est *T* et est multitudo que est *C* hec etiam multitudo *E*

15

1 actualis] *codd.* accidentalis *N*
2 exigit] *codd.* suppositionem *add. Rᶜ*
3 quod] *codd.* et *PN*
4 sic] *codd.* aliud *add. Rᶜ*

5 excipit] *codd.P^c* exigit *P*

6 a suo toto] *PCH habet ea verba post* Ergo cum *T* que vero debet *T^c om. cett.*

7 aliam vel alias] *codd.* aliquam vel aliquas *P*

8 in ipso toto] *codd. T^c* in toto *T om. P*

9 excipi] *codd.* accipi *N*

10 vel] *codd.* et *N*

11 ille] *codd. om. P*

12 exigit multitudinem] *codd.* excipit a multitudine *H*

13 omnes] *T^cR^c om. cett.*

14 ita] *TPCH* in *NER*

15 in toto] *codd. om. N*

16 una] *codd.* est *add. N*

17 potentia] *codd.* potentialiter *R*

18 inductive] *codd.* inductione *TE*

19 aliis totis] *T* quolibet alio toto *cett.*

20 esse] *TP om. cett.*

21 existentes] *P* existere *T^ccett. om. T*

22 exigit ... exceptiva] *codd. om. E* exigit] *codd.P* excipit *P^c*

23 inveniret] *codd.* inveniet *E*

24 exciperet] *PN* excipit *TE*

25 excipit] *codd.* incipit *(!)N*

26 et ... prius] *T* et idem ut prius *PE* et ita idem quod prius *N* et idem quod prius *R* et sic est idem prius *CH^c* et est idem prius *H*

27 excipiat] *codd. om. C*

28 inductive] *codd.* inductione *C*

16

1 posito quod] *codd.* plato quia *(!)E*

2 sorte] *TPEC* illo *NRH*

3 ergo ... vera] *codd. om. C*

4 ipsum] *codd.* eum *P*

17

1 simpliciter] *codd. om. P*

2 *bis* privare] *P* privari *cett.*

3 immo] *codd.R^c* in modo *R*

4 est] *codd. om. N*

5 potius] *codd.* privatio *C*

6 privare] *PERC* privari *cett.*

7 visum] *codd.* habitum *P*

8 respectu huius predicati] *TPEC* ab hoc predicato *cett.*

9 excipi] *codd.* excipitur *P*

10 simpliciter] *T om. cett.*

11 fallacia secundum] *codd. om. NR*

18

1 ab archa] *codd.* in archa *sic semper P*

2 quod ... sortes] *codd.* *om. N*
3 archam] *codd.* in archam *TR*
4 in] *TPE* de *cett.*
5 pede] *PE* sortis *add. cett.*
6 pede] *P* eo *T* illo *cett.*
7 ergo ... vera] *codd.* *om. N*
8 est] *codd.* erit *P*
9 totus sortes] *codd.* sortes *T* totus *P*

19

1 enim] *codd.* autem *P*
2 irrationali] *codd.* irrationalibus *P*
3 irrationale] *codd.* et ideo homo excipitur a suo toto *add. CH*
4 tamen] *NE* *om. cett.*
5 ipsum] *TP* eum *E* *om. cett.*
6 bene ... sortis] *codd.* *om. E*
7 sed] *codd.* sed non *T* non tamen *P*
8 unitus] *codd.* vinctus *P*
9 in suo toto] *T* suo toti *cett.*
10 non] *codd.* *om. P*
11 improbando] *TPNR^c* improbatio *R* in probatione *CH^c* probatione *H*
12 contineri ab] *codd.* locari in *P*
13 preter ... ab archa] *codd.* potest locari in archa etc. *P*
14 contineri] *codd.* ab archa *add. NRCH*
15 secundum se] *codd.* *om. T*
16 est in suo toto] *codd.* in toto *T* est in toto *E*
17 hic] *codd.* *om. N*
18 ergo] *codd.* ego *E*
19 prout est] *T* ut ens *E* ut est *cett.*

20

1 pluit] *T* currit *H* cucurrit *H^c cett.*

21

1 exclusivaceptiva *(!)N*
2 suo] *T* *om. cett.*
3 actualem] *codd.* actualiter *P* partium *add. H^c*
4 decem] *codd.* novem *P*
5 currunt] *codd.* currit *P* sunt novem *R*
6 et etiam] *codd.* querunt et *C*
7 quod] *codd.* et *P*
8 sed] *codd.* et *N*
9 pro] *codd. P^c* *om. P*

22

1 improbatio] *codd.* in probatione *sic saepius H*
2 parti] *codd.* subiecto *P*
3 conveniat ... partem] *codd.* *om. N*

4 sicut] *TP* sic *cett.*
5 similiter] *codd.* om. *T*
6 ut] *codd.* et *NR*
7 falsitas] *codd. T*^c om. *T*
8 oratione] *codd.* dictione *N*
9 ita] *codd.* om. *P*
10 fiat] *TPE* fit *cett.*
11 circa]*P* contra *cett.*

23

1 ergo] *codd.* om. *PR*
2 prima] *codd.* illa *sic saepius N*
3 sicut prius patuit] *T*^c sicut prius *T* ut prius patuit *P* sicut patuit prius *NER*
4 locari in]*TE* contineri in *PR* contineri ab *cett.*

24

1 ad illud]*codd.* ad aliud *T* solutio ad illud *P*
2 semper] *codd.* om. *P*
3 parti] *codd.* subiecto sive parti *P*
4 licet] *codd.* om. *N*
5 parti] *codd. P*^c subiecto parti*P*
6 ab excepto] *codd.* [a subiecto] ab excepto *P*
7 sic] *codd.* sicut *N*

25

1 omne] *codd.* convenit *add.P*
2 aut] *codd.* vel *T*
3 aliquo] *codd.* obliquo *N*
4 talis] *codd.* om. *N*
5 distributionem] *codd.* distributivam *T*
6 currit] *codd.* om. *P*
7 sortem]*P* sortem currit *cett.*
8 ergo est] *TNR*^c*CH* ergo *PR* neque *E*

26

1 albus] *codd.* currit hic enim homo albus *add. N*
2 qualibet sui parte] *codd.* quolibet suo supposito *C*
3 quibusdam] *codd.* subicitur predicato *add. NRH* recipit predicatum *C*
4 ut ... universalis] *codd.* om. *P* ut] *codd.* non *C*
5 septima] *codd.* sequenti *R* sumpta *(!)E*

27

1 septimum] *codd.* septimam *P*
2 homo] *codd.* preter sortem *add. P*
3 propositio] *codd.* dictio *T*
4 ea] *codd.* ipsa *P*

28

1 est]*codd.* non est *C*
2 sillogizabilis]*codd.* subicibilis *E*
3 plato]*codd. sequitur rasura in T*
4 ista]*codd.* hec *P*
5 sumitur]*codd.* debet sumi *P*
6 autem est]*codd.* vero *P*

29

1 vel ... intelligenda]*codd. bis in P* vel solum esse intelligendam *NH*
2 assumi]*codd. P^c* sumi *P* accipi *T*
3 cum]*codd.* sub *CH*
4 ergo ... currit]*codd. om. EC*

30

1 vidit]*codd.* videt *NC*
2 preter ... hominem]*codd. om. N*
3 viderit]*TRH* videat *PE^cC om. E*
4 preter ... hominem]*TE* et alia [alia *om. P*] vice omnem hominem
preter platonem *cett.*
5 hec est falsa]*codd. om. T*
6 vidit]*codd.* videt *PC*
7 hominem]*codd.* hec est falsa *add. T*
8 et]*codd.* sed *P*
9 eo]*TE* ipso *P* illo *cett.*
10 erit]*codd.* est *TR*

31

1 transit]*codd. P^c* fert *P*
2 tunc]*codd.* sic *C om. E*
3 viderit]*NERC* vidit *TH* videt *P*
4 prius]*codd.* primum *H*
5 oratione]*codd.* dictione *N*
6 est]*codd.* dico *H*
7 hec]*codd.* est *N*
8 prius]*codd.* primo *C*
9 in oratione]*codd. P^cH^c om. PH*

32

1 predictis]*codd.* patet solutio *add. et del. P*
2 exceptive]*TPNE* exceptiva *cett.*
3 propositio]*TE om. cett.*
4 a]*codd.* in *P*
5 irrationale]*codd.* risibile *P*
6 hominem]*codd.* omnem hominem *R*

33

1 quelibet] *codd.* quodlibet *R* quolibet *E*
2 illo ... decem] *codd.H^c* om. *PH*
3 dictionem exceptivam] *TPE* exceptionem *NRCH*
4 est] *codd.* vere *add. P*
5 dare instantiam] *codd.* instantia *N*

34

1 simpliciter] *codd.* om. *P*
2 preter unum] *codd.P^c* om. *P*
3 exceptionem] *codd.* dictionem exceptivam *P*
4 tertio ... colorato] *P* alio ... colorato *T* tertio quod [que *N*] ... coloratum *cett.*

35

1 casu] *codd.* om. *PE*
2 significari] *codd.* determinari *R*
3 orationis] *codd.* om. *N*
4 diversa ab] *codd.* divise *R* divise ab *R^c*

36

1 et] *codd.* solutio *P*
2 ipsum] *codd.* om. *P*
3 sit ut verbo adiectum] *coni.* sit in verbi adiectum *TPR* sit verbi adiectum *E* sit ut verbi adiectivum *H^c* sic vi verbi adiectivum *NCH*
4 comparationem ... dicunt] *codd.* om. *N* comparationem] *codd.* comparationes *P*
5 si] *codd.* sic *RH*
6 ideo ... quod] *codd.* om. *N*

37

1 in dicit] *codd.* indicit *(!)R*
2 similiter] *codd.* sic *R*
3 ut] *codd.* et *E*
4 quia ... adverbiis] *codd.H^c* om. *EH*
5 est in omnibus] *TP* est in *R* est cum omnibus *H* de *N*
6 prepositionibus] *codd.* quoniam sic est in aliis prepositionibus *add. N*
7 accusativo] *codd.* casu *add. R*

38

1 velocitatis] *TPNR* velocitas *EH*
2 sed] *codd.* si dicam in loco *add. P*
3 hec] *PNER* om. *cett.*
4 dictio] *TEH* prepositio *PNR*

39

1 persone] *codd.* personale *H*
2 nominativo] *codd.* accusativo *P*

40

1 compositio] *codd.* comparatio *R*
2 legis] *TE* curris *cett.*
3 similiter] *TPE* sic *cett.*
4 plurali] *codd.* personali *H*
5 sic] *codd.* om. *N*
6 actus] *codd.* om. *P*
7 consequenti] *codd.* consequente *P*
8 repperiebat] *codd.* repperiet *R*
9 remotio ipsius] *T* prius remotio *N* remotio *cett.*
10 excepta] *TH* exceptiva *cett.*
11 hic tertio] *codd.* *hic desunt duo folia in T*
12 sequitur] *PNR* consequitur *EH*
13 ceciderit] *codd.* cecidit *N*

41

1 quecumque] *codd.* quicumque *N*
2 intellige] *codd.* dici *P*
3 nulli ... nisi sorti] *codd.* om. *N*
4 parco] *H* loquor *PER*
5 sortem] *codd.* nulli homini loquor preterquam sorti vel nisi sorti *add.* *N*
6 sorte] *codd.* de dictionibus exceptivis dicta sufficiant *add. NRH*

TRACTATUS QUINTUS

DE DICTIONIBUS CONSECUTIVIS

1

  1 species] *codd.* partes species *E*
  2 conditionali contingat] *codd.* conditionalibus licet *P*
  3 qualiter] *codd.* quomodo *P*
  4 contradictoria] *codd.* contradictio *N*

2

  1 ignis] *codd. R^c* lignum *R*
  2 naturalium] *codd.* materialium *E*
  3 autem] *codd.* vero *P*
  4 sed] *codd.* et *N*
  5 predictorum] *codd.* istorum *P*

3

  1 antecessionem] *codd.* consecutionem *P*
  2 consecutionem] *codd.* antecessionem *P*
  3 nonnisi] *codd. P^c* non *P*
  4 a] *codd.* om. *N*
  5 significatione] *codd.* consignificatione *NR*
  6 cum] *PR^c* om. *R cett.*
  7 quod] *NE* quia *cett.*
  8 antecedente quam cum consequente] *codd.* antecessione quam cum consecutione *E*
  9 si ... si] *codd.* si *P* om. *E*

4

  1 que est causa] *NRH* om. *PE*
  2 esse] *codd.* rem *E*
  3 causa] *PRCH* cause *NE*
  4 conclusionis] *PR^{c}H* illa conclusionis *R* illationis *N* contribulonis (!)*E*
  5 pius et fortis] *codd.* fortis et pius *P*
  6 significant coniunctiones] *P* significet coniunctio *N* significat coniunctio *cett.*
  7 monstrant] *P* determinat *E* demonstrat *cett.*
  8 aliquarum] *TPE* aliarum *cett.*
  9 consecutionem] *codd.* consecutiones *N*
  10 non ergo] *P* sive *E* ergo non *cett.*

5

1 hoc non] *codd. P^c* non *P* hoc *H*
2 significat]*E* significatur *cett.*
3 significat]*codd.* sive *E*
4 suo]*codd.* om. *P*
5 ita]*codd.* prima sic saepius *N* et ita *P*
6 unde ... si]*codd.* et sic *P*
7 secundum ... causalitatem]*codd.* om. *N*
8 sic]*codd.* om. *H*
9 in antecessione]*codd.* in antecedendo *H* et antecessionem *C*
10 unde]*codd.* unum *N*

6

1 quod ... est]*CH* sicut dictum est quod significat *cett.*
2 significet]*N* significat *cett.*
3 quia]*P* sed *cett.*

7

1 multiplex]*PN* multipliciter *ERCH*
2 sequuntur]*PN* consequuntur *ERCH*
3 et]*PE* ?est *H^c* om. *NRCH*
4 et]*PER* om. *NCII*
5 differenter *PER* differentia *NCH*
6 sequuntur]*N* consequuntur *cett.*
7 paries]*codd.* domus add. *P*
8 et ... eius]*codd.* om. *P*
9 quia]*ECH* eoquod *P*
8 et ... eius]*codd.* om. *P*
9 quia]*ECH* eoquod *P* que *NR*
10 essentiales]*PE* essentiales rerum *P^c* essentiales rei *RCH*
efficientes rem *N*
11 integrales]*codd.* quia licet add. et del. *N*
12 quantitatem]*codd.* aliquam add. *PH^c*
13 essentiales]*codd.* efficientes *N*
14 vel viventis]*E* et iumentis (!)*N* viventis *cett.*
15 repperitur]*codd.* invenitur *P*
16 tantum]*P* om. *cett.*
17 ut]*codd.* ut in *N*
18 sensitiva]*codd.* sensibilis *P*
19 et]*PER* om. *NCH*
20 vegetativa]*codd.* vegetiva (!)*E* vegetatilia (!)*R*
21 sequuntur]*codd.* consequuntur *E*
22 quia]*codd.* que *N*
23 sunt]*codd. H^c* om. *EH*
24 accidentim]*codd.* accidentium *P*
25 et]*codd.* et sic *NR*
26 elementatum]*PNER* coloratum *CH*
27 ad lineam]*codd.* de linea *P*

28 et] *codd.* ad *N*
29 corpus elementatum] *NER* corpora elementata *P* corpus coloratum
CH
30 accidentia ... ad] *codd.* *om.* *P*
31 subiecta] *codd.* substantia *R*
32 consecutio] *codd.* consequentia *N*

8

1 sequuntur] *NC* consequuntur *cett.*
2 sequitur] *PNRC* consequitur *NH*
3 antecedens] *codd.* accidens *E*
4 solum] *codd.* solam *E*
5 et] *codd.* *om.* *NR*
6 antecessio] *codd.* et *add.* *N*
7 consecutionis] *codd.* consequens *E*

9

1 secundum] *codd.* sic proceditur primo *add.* *P*
2 consecutionis] *codd.P^c* equivocationis *P*
3 relatorum] *codd.* relativorum *NR*
4 cognoscere] *codd.* ad *add.* *P*
5 sive] *codd.* et *P*
6 consecutionis] *codd.P* antecessionis *P^c*
7 quod] *NER* ut *PH*
8 antecessio] *codd.* consecutio *P*
9 divisiones] *codd.P^c* species *R* dictiones divisiones *(!)N* scilicet *add.*
R ante *(!) add. E*
10 est] *codd.* *om.* *P*
11 aliquando] *codd.* est *add.* *P*
12 in idemptitate] *codd.* in deitate *(!)E*
13 prius ... ignorare] *RCH^c* prius est ignorare *H* et prius est ignorare *E*
prius enim est addiscere *P* posterius est ignorare *N*
14 ad addiscere] *NCH* addiscere *ER* ignorare *P*
15 quod] *codd.* et quod *E*
16 et] *codd.* *om.* *P*
17 ignorat] *codd.* ignorabat *P*
18 nichil] *codd.* non *E*
19 autem] *PECH^c* *om.* *NRH*
20 prius] *codd.* *om.* *P*
21 temporis] *codd.* *om.* *C*
22 farina fuit] *PCH* et aqua *add.* *P* farina et aqua fuerunt *NER*
23 accidit maxime] *codd.* maxime contingit *P*
24 causis non] *codd.P^c* causis *P*
25 causis] *codd.* causatis *P*
26 antecedentibus] *codd.* *om.* *R* precedentibus *R^c*
27 ut] *codd.* si *add.* *P*
28 purgatio] *codd.R^c* purgatio est *PR*
29 alia] *PE* *om.* *cett.*
30 finaliter] *codd.* simul *P* similiter *E*

31 sanitatem] *codd.* et finaliter *add. P*
32 sunt] *RCH om. PNE*
33 est] *codd. om. P*

10

1 vinum] *codd.* unium (!)*E*
2 solet] *codd.* aliquando *add. N*
3 simul] *codd.* tempore *add. E*
4 alia ... existentium] *codd. om. N*
5 fuit] *codd.* est *N*
6 tractatu ... consequentis] *coni.* tractatu fallaciarum fallacie
consequentis *E* tractatu fallacie *PNR* in fallacia consequentis *CH*

11

1 hee] *C* hec *cett.*
2 ad se invicem] *codd.* adinvicem *E* sibi adinvicem *CH*
3 excedentia] *codd.* existentia *E*
4 prime ... membrum] *codd. om. N* prime] *codd.Pᶜ om. P*
5 in simplici] *codd.Pᶜ om. P*
6 secunde] *codd.Pᶜ om. P* nec (!)*N*
7 repperitur] *codd. om. C*
8 et ... consequuntur] *PNERᶜC om. RH*
9 eisdem]*E* eis *P* eadem etiam *cett.*
10 composita] *codd.* et *add. N*
11 si] *codd. om. P*
12 ergo] *codd.* et *P*
13 est] *codd.* fuit *P*
14 terminus qui]*P* qui *N* que *cett.*
15 unum]*ER* utrumque *cett.*
16 secunde] *codd.* secundum se *E*
17 secunda] *codd.* est *add. NR*
18 membrum] *codd.* membrorum *N*
19 secunde] *codd.Pᶜ om. P*
20 sic] *codd.* sed *P* similiter *N*
21 prima] *codd.* est *add. NR*
22 similiter] *codd.* supra *E*

12

1 tempus] *codd.* tempestas *H*
2 est] *codd.* a toto in quantitate *add. EH*
3 non] *codd.Pᶜ om. P*
4 est] *codd.* a contrariis immediatis *add. PERᶜCHᶜ*
5 est] *codd.* a specie sive a parte subiectiva *add. PERᶜCHᶜ*
6 ibi assignatur sequi] *coni.* ibi significatur sequi *PNCHᶜ* significatur
sequi *H* denotatur ibi sequi *R* ibi sequitur *E*

13

1 secunda] *codd.* falsa *N*

2 variatur] *codd. P^c*   numeratur *P*
3 sophisma accidentis] *NER*   fallaciam accidentis *cett.*   sive sophisma *add. CH*

14

1 sed] *codd.*   et *N*
2 consequens ... ad] *codd.*   om. *N*
3 scilicet] *PE*   quod est *NRCH*
4 esse] *codd.*   est *N*
5 et sequuntur] *codd. P^c*   om. *P*
6 ultimum] *codd.*   nullum *E*
7 primum] *PNR*   prius *CH*   ipsum *E*
8 vera] *PCH*   necessaria *NER*

15

1 primum] *codd.*   ipsum *E*
2 ergo ... consequens] *codd. P^c*   om. *PE*
3 nec] *codd.*   ergo non *P*
4 necessario] *PNER*   vere *CH*
5 sic] *PE*   om. *cett.*
6 propter] *codd.*   om. *N*
7 impeditur] *codd.*   ibi add. *P*
8 non] *codd.*   quod *N*
9 iustitia] *codd. P^c*   iustus *P*
10 enim] *codd.*   autem *P*
11 extrinsecum] *codd.*   locum extrinsecum *P*
12 intrinseci] *codd.*   loci intrinseci *P*
13 sed] *codd.*   et *N*
14 iste eedem] *codd.*   iste eodem *E*   om. *P*
15 que ... habitudines] *codd.*   om. *E*
16 arguendo] *coni.*   argumentum *PR^c*   in argumento *H^c*   om. *NRH*
17 processus] *codd.*   om. *R*
18 propter] *codd.*   per *P*

16

1 et] *codd.*   om. *P*
2 sive ... est] *P^c*   sive extra genus negatio quod idem est *P*   sive circa genus quod idem est *N*   sive negatio circa genus aliquod quod idem est *R*   vel extra genus *H*

17

1 suum] *codd.*   in esse *add. R*
2 et] *PER*   om. *NH*   cum *H^c*
3 iste ... illud] *NE*   idest tempus est sed illud <tempus *R^c*> *R*   et aliquod tempus sed illud *P*   istud tempus est si illud *H*
4 erit] *N*   est *PE*   om. *H*
5 penitus] *PNR*   potius *H*   om. *E*
6 currit] *codd.*   om. *P*

7 illud] *codd.* aliud *N*
8 tempus est] *codd.* om. *N*
9 posteriorum] *codd.* topicorum *E*
10 negatio] *codd.P^c* om. *P*
11 ita] *codd.* sic *P*
12 non par] *codd.P^c* par *P*
13 numerum] *codd.* subiectum suum *P* subiectum suum idest numerum *N*

18

1 sequitur] *codd.* ex eo *add. NRH^c* ex primo antecedente *add. P*
2 est] *codd.* non est *E*
3 noctem] *codd.* necesse est *N*
4 contrariorum] *codd.* oppositorum *P*

19

1 sint] *codd.* sunt *P* sicut *N*
2 et ... accidentia] *suppl.* ergo *PNRH^c* om. cett.
3 nisi in] *NR* sine *PEH*
4 boetius] *codd.* aristotiles et boetius *P*
5 quia est quantitas] *codd.* quantitalis *E*
6 et] *codd.* solutio *P*
7 tempus] *add.* accidentis *add. E*
8 ut ... est mobile] *codd.* om. *N*
9 in tertio] *codd.* intentio *E*

20

1 nox et dies] *codd.* dies et nox *P*
2 nata sit] *codd.* habet *P*
3 aliquod idem] *coni.* aliquod *PNER* idem *H*
4 erunt] *codd.* habent fieri *P*
5 in subiecto aliquo] *PNER* circa idem subiectum vel in eodem subiecto *H*
6 quero] *codd.* querunt *R*
7 est] *codd.* sit *P*
8 sumuntur] *codd.* dicuntur *P*
9 solis] *codd.* super terram *add. R*
10 in] *codd.* a *N*
11 non ... et] *codd.* om. *N*
12 lationem] *codd.* locationem *R*
13 unde] *codd.P^c* ut *P*
14 etiam] *coni.* autem] *codd.*
15 quem] *codd.* quod *NR*
16 temporis] *codd.* om. *P*
17 a ... solis] *codd.* om. *N*
18 alio] *codd.* aliquo *E*
19 secundo] *codd.* modo *add. N*
20 autem] *codd.* enim *P*

21 est]*PE* dicitur *cett.*
22 vel dimidium spere]*codd.* om. *NR*

21

1 est]*codd.* dicitur *P*
2 homo est]*codd.* om. *N*
3 risibile]*P* rationale *cett.*
4 adequatio]*codd.* aut equatio *N*
5 et]*P* vel *cett.*
6 rectum]*PER* recta *R^c cett.*
7 curvum]*PE* curva *cett.*
8 propria]*codd.* om. *N*
9 hic]*E* in hoc *P* om. *cett.*
10 hoc vinum]*codd.* unum *E*
11 ibi]*codd.* hic *NR*
12 mensura]*codd.* mensuratum *N*
13 secundo]*codd.* primo *ER*
14 mensurat]*codd.* per *add. N*
15 et ... solis]*codd.* om. *P*
16 per]*codd.* post *N*

22

1 sit]*codd.* om. *P*
2 quia]*codd.* om. *N*
3 et]*E* quia et *H* quia *PR^cCH^c* qui *R* cum *N*
4 intelliguntur]*codd.* intelligantur *N*
5 transponuntur]*codd.* transponantur *N*
6 diminuitur]*codd.* dimitantur *(!)E*
7 nunc]*codd.* numerum *E*

23

1 etiam]*E* om. *cett.*
2 primum]*codd.* ipsum *E*
3 sunt]*codd.* om. *P*
4 motus]*codd.* motum *N*
5 ita]*codd.* prima *sic saepius N*

24

1 si]*PN* om. *cett.*
2 extensio]*codd.* om. *P*
3 successive]*codd.* successiva *P*
4 similiter]*PE* si *N* om. *R*
5 cum puncto]*NR* cum pucto *(!)P* om. *E*
6 protrahatur]*codd.* pertrahatur *P*
7 tunc]*codd.* se *(!)E*
8 preterita]*codd.* preternita *(!)E* preterea *N*
9 deleta]*codd.* delata *E* debita *N*
10 neque]*codd.* iam non *H^c* iam *H*

11 facta ... sed] *codd.* om. *N*
12 sed fiet] *codd.* om. *E*
13 punctus] *EH* puctus *(!)P* punctum *NR*
14 est] *codd.* om. *N*
15 iam] *codd.* et quod *E*
16 est] *codd.* om. *N*
17 nulla] *codd.* illa *E*
18 unde] *NR* ut *cett.*
19 nunc] *codd.* indivisibile *add. P^c*
20 sed ... tempore] *codd.* om. *E*
21 tempus] *codd.E^c* motus *E*
22 quod] *NE* quia *cett.*

25

1 quantitatem] *codd.* naturam *P^c* substantiam *P*
2 tempori] *codd.R^c* temporis *ER*
3 ita] *codd.* et ita *P*
4 philosophie prime ... repperitur] *codd.* om. *N*
5 sic] *codd.* similiter *NR*

26

1 etiam] *codd.* om. *NR*
2 sex] *codd.* quinque *P*
3 aliquod] *NR* om. *cett.*
4 quatuor] *codd.* decem *E* om. *N*
5 bicubitus] *codd.* biasticus *(!)E*
6 res est] *codd.* est modus *N*
7 aut] *codd.* ut *E*
8 dicens quid] *NER* dicta quid *P* dictus secundum quid *H*
9 vesperam] *PE* vesperum *NR*
10 duo ... vesperam] *codd.* om. *P*
11 sic] *codd.* om. *N*
12 extensionem] *codd.* eius scilicet *add. P*
13 mensurat motum] *codd.* et mensura motus *PN*
14 solutione] *codd.* ratione *P*
15 accidenti] *NER* actui *cett.*
16 accidentis] *codd.* actus vel accidentis *H*
17 dicebatur] *ER* dicebat *PN* dicebam *H*

27

1 si nulla] *codd.* om. *N*
2 ista] *codd.* et ista *N*
3 homo] *codd.* locutio *E*
4 et] *codd.* tunc *N*
5 contradictoria] *codd.* contraria *P*
6 a ... vera] *codd.* om. *N*
7 aliqua] *codd.* et aliqua *N*
8 specie sive a] *codd.* om. *P*

9 subiectiva]*codd.* subiective *N* subiecta *E*
10 ibi assignatur sequi]*coni.* ibi significatur sequi *ER* hic videtur sequi *P* ibi sequitur *N*

28

1 nulla]*PEH* si nulla *NRH^c*
2 hoc]*codd.* uno *ER*
3 neque]*codd.* non *N*
4 accidens]*coni.* antecedens *codd.* hoc antecedens *NR^c*
5 cum]*codd.* ut cum *E*
6 homo est]*NR^cCH om. R cett.*
7 sicut si]*NE* similiter si *PR* similiter cum *H*
8 suis]*ER* eius est *PR^cH om. N*
9 propositio]*codd.* est *add. NR*
10 homo est]*codd. om. N*
11 est]*codd. om. NR*

29

1 nulla]*ERCH* si nulla *PR^c om. N*
2 removet]*codd.* omnem *add. P*
3 omnes]*NRH om. PE*
4 contradictorias]*codd.P^c* contrarias *P*
5 omnes]*codd.* aliquas *E*
6 contradictorias]*codd.H^c* contrarias *P om. H*
7 contradictoriarum]*codd.* contradictoria *N*
8 falsa]*NR* vera *cett.*
9 vera]*NR* falsa *cett.*
10 unde]*codd.* ut *E*
11 hoc modo est]*PEH* modo hec est *NR* hec hoc modo est *H^c*
12 illo modo est]*PNE* illa est modo *R* illa modo est *H* illa hoc modo est *H^c*
13 illo modo]*PER^c* illa *RH* illa modo *H^c*
14 isto modo est]*PE* isto modo *R* ista modo *N* ista est *H* ista modo est *H^c*
15 utroque ... falsa]*R^c* utraque modo est vera *P* utraque modo est falsa *R cett.*
16 utroque ... vera]*ER^c* utroque (!) est modo vera *R* utraque est modo falsa *P* utraque est modo vera *cett.*
17 contradictionem]*codd.* propositionem *P*
18 quod]*codd. om. N*
19 primum]*codd. om. P*
20 est]*codd.* primo est *P*
21 prima]*codd.* ipsa *P* prime *N*
22 hec ... vera]*codd. om. N*
23 scilicet]*codd. om. P*
24 ibi]*P om. cett.*
25 quamlibet contradictionem]*TNER* utramque partem contradictionis *P* totam contradictionem *CH*

30

1 tu] *codd.* om. *T*
2 hic] *codd. P^c* om. *P*
3 oppositis] *codd.* sive a disparatis *add. H^m*
4 et] *PEH* om. *cett.*
5 est] *codd.* om. *N*

31

1 rei] *codd.* locate *add. R^c*
2 et continet] *codd.* om. *N*
3 circumscriptivus] *codd.* circumscriptus *N* circumscriptio *H*
4 plures res simul] *codd.* rei *(!)N*
5 elementata] *codd. P^c* elementra *(!)P*
6 omnia] *codd.* om. *P*
7 communis ... autem ... locus] *codd.* om. *N* communis] *codd.*
communiter *R*
8 circumscriptivus] *P* circumscriptive *cett.*
9 circumscriptivus] *P* circumscriptive *cett.*
10 communis] *P* communiter *cett.*
11 est quia] *codd.* est *E* et *N*
12 semper] *codd.* om. *P*
13 circumscriptive] *codd.* sic prima est vera sed *add. R^c*
14 procedit] *codd.* proce oportet *(!)E*
15 scilicet] *codd.* si *P* scilicet si *NR*
16 circumscriptiva] *codd.* circumscripta *N*

32

1 quia] *codd.* quod *N*
2 per] *codd.* om. *NR*
3 hoc] *codd. T* quod *add. T^c*
4 positum] *codd.* ponit *TN*
5 demonstrat rem] *codd. R^c* demonstro rem *RH* demonstrationem *T*
6 ubique] *codd.* ponit *add. N*
7 predicatum] *TE* predicatam *cett.*
8 ibi] *T^c NR* om. *T cett.*
9 inter] *codd.* intra *P*
10 simul] *codd. H^c* om. *PH*
11 esse] *codd.* simul esse *NR*
12 quod ... hic circumscriptive] *codd.* econverso *P*
13 alio loco] *codd.* om. *N* alio modo *E*
14 unde] *codd.* ut *P*
15 ibi] *codd.* in *N* et econverso] *codd.* econverso *P^c* om. *P*
16 circumscriptivis] *codd.* circumscriptive *N*
17 tot] *codd.* om. *P*
18 quot] *codd.* quod *sic saepissime P*
19 circumscriptiva] *codd.* et sic de quolibet alio loco circumscriptivo
add. R^c
20 ex eo] *TP* ex ipso *cett.* eorum eo *N*

21 dicendum] *T*   dictum *cett.*
22 claudit] *codd.*   concludit *T*

33

1 in] *codd.*   al *N*
2 sillogismorum alius est] *TNR*   cum sillogismorum alius sit *cett.*
3 conditionalis] *codd.*   ypotheticus sive *PN*
4 qui] *codd.*   ille qui *P*   om. *T*
5 est] *E*   om. *cett.*
6 sillogizabilis] *codd.*   fallaciter (!)*R*
7 sub consequente] *codd.*   subsequente *E*
8 descensum] *TPN*   descensus *cett.*

34

1 et] *T*   om. *cett.*
2 conditionalis] *codd.*   contradictionis conditionalis *E*
3 sub] *codd.*   in *N*
4 animal currit] *codd.*   et sic de aliis *N*
5 et ... aliis] *codd.*   om. *N*
6 oportet] *TER*   operi (!)*N*   debet *CH*   licet *P*
7 descensum] *TPN*   descensus *cett.*
8 currit] *codd.*   est *N*
9 aliquid] *codd.*   quid *N*
10 et] *TR*   om. *cett.*
11 semper] *codd.*   om. *T*
12 ut ... non est homo] *codd.*   om. *N*
13 aliquid] *codd.*   quid *N*
14 consequens] *codd.*   et propter hoc tenet argumentum a positione antecedentis *add. R*
15 ut ... antecedentis] *codd.*   om. *N*
16 sed] *codd.*   sed si *P*
17 et ... antecedentis] *codd.*   om. *R*
18 ergo ... substantia est] *codd.*   om. *N*

35

1 queritur] *codd.*   hoc modo *add. T*
2 ut] *codd.*   si *add. T*
3 quod] *codd.*   debet ferri *add. R*
4 boetius] *codd.*   locus (!)*T*
5 cedit] *codd.*   cadit *TE*
6 determinationem] *codd.*   terminationem *N*   determinatione *T*
7 ferri] *codd.*   fieri *E*

36

1 scilicet consequens] *codd.*   om. *T*
2 inquantum pater] *codd.*   in eo quod pater *E*   om. *T*
3 aliquid] *codd.*   aliud *N*
4 quia] *T*   quod est *N*   quia est *cett.*

5 cum sint relativa] *codd. P^c* om. *P*
6 quare] *codd.* quia *P*
7 ferri] *codd.* vel ferri fieri (!)*E*
8 est] *T^cPNR* om. *TH*
9 similiter ... non legit] *T^c* om. *T*
10 est falsa] *codd.* om *N*
11 legit] *codd.* non legit *NR*
12 conditionali] *codd.* in conditionali *TR^c*

37

1 consequens] *codd.* antecedens *C*
2 dicitur] *T* sumitur *cett.*
3 uno] *codd.* primo *C*
4 conditionali] *codd.* aliquid *N*
5 dicit id quod est] *codd. T^c* dicitur *T*
6 currit] *codd. T^c* non currit *TNR*
7 quia] *codd.* quare *T*
8 fertur] *codd.* non fertur *T^cNR*
9 sumitur] *codd.* sumitur consequens *P*
10 quia] *codd.* et *P*
11 consequens] *codd. P* antecedens *P^c*

38

1 et ... conditionali] *codd. T^c* om. *T*
2 est] *codd. T^c* non est *T*
3 est ista] *codd.* om. *N*
4 falsa] *codd.* ut si homo currit asinus currit add. *R^m*
5 debet preponi] *codd.* preponitur *P*
6 totali] *PR* toti *cett.*
7 semper] *codd* om. *P*

39

1 sive] *TNR* vel *cett.*
2 impossibile] *codd.* antecedens add. *P*
3 contraria] *codd.* contradictoria *P*
4 sed] *codd.* et *TNR*
5 ergo ... impossibile ... ergo] *T^cNR* cum ergo *cett.*
6 cum] *T^cNR* om. *cett.*
7 impossibile] *T^cNR* tunc impossibile *cett.*
8 destruet ... impossibile] *codd.* om *N*
9 si] *R^c* om. *R. cett.*
10 quod] *codd. T^c* om. *T*
11 ad impossibile] *T* om. *cett.*
12 ad ipsum] *codd.* om. *T*
13 scilicet ... ipsum] *T* om. *H* scilicet verum add. *P*
14 aliud] *codd.* sequitur rasura duarum litterarum in *T*
15 ab] *codd.* ex *P*
16 quia ... ex impossibili] *codd. P^c* om. *P* quia] *codd.* om. *E*

17 invicem] *codd.*　*om. N*
18 unum] *codd.R^c*　*om. NR*

40

1 ergo] *codd.*　sed *E*　*om. H*
2 toto] *codd.*　integrali *add. PNRH^c*
3 totum] *TPR*　tota *E*　totius *H*　totum integrale *R^c*
4 sed] *codd.P^x*　ergo a primo *P*
5 homo] *codd.*　et non est homo *add. R^c*
5 sortes] *codd.P^x*　et non *P*
6 vel] *codd.*　et *N*
7 est ... et non est homo] *codd.*　*om. N*　est] *codd.*　*om. P*
8 asinum] *codd.*　a divisione *add. P*
9 asinum] *codd.*　a divisione *add. R^c*
10 et] *codd.*　*om. N*
11 aliud] *codd.*　*om. P*
12 impossibili] *codd.P^x*　possibili *P*
13 impossibile ... quidlibet] *codd.*　ad impossibile sequitur quidlibet *E*

41

1 fides] *codd.*　argumentum *E*
2 dubia] *codd.*　*om. N*
3 aliqui] *codd.*　*om. N*
4 confirmentur] *codd.*　affirmentur *N*
5 sunt] *codd.*　contraria *add. N*
6 confirmari per aliquas] *codd.*　consequi secundum aliquas *T*
7 hoc] *codd.R^c*　*om. NR*

42

1 invicem] *codd.*　necessario *add. R^c*
2 sibi invicem] *codd.H^c*　sibi *TH*　supra (!)*E*
3 necessario] *PER^cH*　*om. NR*
4 sicut] *codd.*　sic *T*
5 necessitas] *codd.*　veritas *NE*
6 patet ... aliud] *codd.P^x*　*om. P*
7 inquantum impossibile] *codd.H^c*　*om. TEH*
8 sive] *codd.*　unde *P*
9 est] *codd.*　illud impossibile *add. C*
10 et ... se] *codd.P^x*　*om. PE*　et] *codd.*　vel *T*

43

1 et ... et] *codd.*　*om. NR*
2 quia] *codd.*　quod *N*
3 ipsum] *NR*　*om. cett.*
4 et ... ponunt] *codd.*　*P^cH^c*　*om. TPEH*
5 ponunt] *codd.R^c*　ponit *R^c*
6 aliquid] *codd.*　aliud *C*
7 quando] *codd.R^c*　quomodo *E*　*om. NR*

8 sic]*codd.* om. *NR*
9 est]*codd.* sequitur *NRC*
10 qui]*NER* quia *cett.*
11 illi]*codd.* om. *P*

44

1 nichil sequitur]*codd.* non sequitur *T* sicut dictum est *add. R*
2 tantummodo]*T* terra (!)*E* tantum *cett.*
3 vera vel illa impossibilia]*P^x* ista vera *TPN* ista vera et impossibilia *R*
ista vera et illa impossibilia *C* illa *E*
4 quibus]*codd.* quilibet (!)*E*
5 habet]*codd.R^c* habent *NR*
6 sequitur ... animal]*codd.* om. *C*
7 verum]*codd.* vero *N*
8 rudibile]*PCH* risibile *ER* rationale *N*
9 impossibile]*codd.* om. *N*
10 descripto]*codd.* specie *T*
11 impossibili]*codd.* inquantum impossibile *add. PCH*

45

1 tamen ... econverso]*codd.* om. *N*
2 subiacet]*PR* subiacent *ECH*
3 perimit]*P^xER* permutat *P* perimunt *CH* potuit *T*
4 etiam]*codd.* om. *NR*
5 habitudinem]*codd.* om. *P*

46

1 argumentum]*codd.R^c* om. *NR*
2 ergo a primo]*codd.P^x* om. *P*
3 et ... homo]*codd.* om. *N*
4 sequens]*codd.* consequens *P*
5 interimit]*codd.* interiit *P*
6 quod]*codd.* consequens *P*
7 scilicet]*codd.* om. *N*
8 interimit]*codd.* interiit *P*
9 non magis]*codd.P^x* non si *P* magis non *E*
10 eam]*codd.* om. *N*
11 ideo]*codd.* om. *T*

47

1 a causa]*codd.* ab effectu *PE*
2 orationis]*codd.* vere *add. N*
3 predicamentis]*codd.* predictis *E*
4 esse]*codd.* est verum (!)*N*
5 et ... pari]*codd.T^c* om. *T*
6 verum]*codd.* om. *P* nichil esse est verum *add. P^m*
7 est]*codd.* verum *add. E*
8 assignatur] significatur *codd.*

48

  1 cum] *codd.* *om. N*
  2 propositio] *codd.* compositio *E*
  3 removeat] *codd.* removet *N* removerat *(!)E*
  4 relinquat] *T* relinquit *cett.*
  5 a causa] *codd.* ab effectu *P*
  6 ista] *TPR* ibi *ECH* ibi prima *H^c*
  7 creatis] *codd.* causatis *sic saepius TPR*
  8 creationem] *codd.* causationem *sic semper R*
  9 comprehendat] *codd.* comprehendit *NR*

49

  1 non] *codd.P^c* *om. PE*
  2 interimit] *codd.* interiit *P*
  3 nature] *codd.* veras *E*
  4 et] *TECH* *om. cett.*

50

  1 obiciunt] *NE* obicitur *cett.*
  2 immo] *codd.* ut *E*
  3 ergo] *codd.* sed *N* ergo si *H^c*
  4 non] *codd.* ut *E*
  5 via in] *codd.* signans *(!)T*
  6 hec] *codd.* *om. P*
  7 signum] *codd.* signum rei *P*
  8 istius] *codd.* ipsius *R* ad istius *(!)N*

51

  1 impossibili] *codd.* possibili *P*
  2 aliquo] *codd.* *om. P*
  3 aliquod] *codd.* aliquando *P*
  4 dum] *codd.* cum *PN* dummodo *P^c*
  5 enuntiabile] *codd.* nichil esse *add. P^m* nichil esse est verum *add. T^m*
  6 consequentia] *codd.* consequens *N* *om. P*
  7 peccat ... scilicet] *codd.* dicitur *N*
  8 quia ... aliquid est verum] *codd.* *om. N*
  9 enuntiabile] *codd.* hoc enuntiabile *P*
  10 esse] *P* aliquid esse *cett.*
  11 incidit] *codd.* dicit *R*
  12 hoc] *codd.* hic *P*
  13 demonstrat] *PCH* demonstratur *NER*
  14 quod] *codd.* quia *TR*
  15 per] *codd.* *om. P*
  16 aliquis] *codd.* quis *P*
  17 inspexerit] *codd.* inspiciat *N*
  18 tertiam conditionalem] *TPER* *om. N*
  19 aut] *codd.* *om. P*
  20 ibi] *P* *om. cett.*

52

1 probatio ... verum] *codd. P^c* om. P
2 sortes] T om. cett.
3 et ad dicere] *TNR* et P vel ad dicere *CH* et ad rem (!)E

53

1 quamvis] *codd. P^c* quam P
2 coriscus] *TCH* coriscum *PNR*
3 coopertum] *codd.* coriscum N
4 et ... verum] *PNR* om. cett.

54

1 dicunt] *codd.* debent N
2 vere] *NER* vera P om. cett.
3 vel dicatur] *TERH* et dicatur N sive dicitur P
4 rerum] *codd.* unde cum profero hoc scilicet nichil dico non profero illud ut rem de qua loquor sed ut rem per quam loquor sicut signum et quia signum semper est aliud a significato et diversum ideo ista propositio non continetur in suppositione huius quod dico aliquid unde non est ita restrictio sicut solet dici in insolubilibus *add. alii aliter PERCH^c desunt haec verba in TNH*
5 est] *codd.* hic *add. P^c*
6 solo] *codd.* solutio N

55

1 lapidem] *codd. P^c* om. P
2 quia ... verum] *codd.* om. N
3 si] *codd.* om. N
4 si] *codd. P^c* om. P
5 a ... non scis te esse lapidem] *codd.* om. P etc. *P^c*

56

1 interemptionem] *codd.* intentionem E
2 utramque] *codd.* partem contradictionis *add. P^c*
3 ratione ... lapidem] *codd.* om. R ratione ... eiusdem verbi] *codd.* retinet vim unius verbi N
4 rei] *codd.* verbi (!)E om. T
5 est] *codd.* om. N
6 et non scire] *codd.* om. N
7 et ... *alterum* lapidem] *codd.* om. T
8 contradictiones] *codd. P^c* conditionales P
9 integrantes] *codd.* integratas E
10 ipsum] *codd.* ipsam E in ipsa N
11 integrales] *codd. P^c* om. P
12 quelibet] *codd.* quidlibet P
13 istarum] *codd.* aliarum P
14 contradictionum] *codd. P^c* conditionalium P
15 ex impossibili] *codd.* de possibili N

TRACTATUS SEXTUS

DE HIIS VERBIS 'INCIPIT' ET 'DESINIT'

1

1 A] *TECH* Ea a *PNR^c* Ea *R*
2 cognitio] *PNEH^c* consignificatio *RC* *om. H*
3 cognitio] *codd.* consignificatio *C*
4 dependet] *codd. P^c* *om. P*
5 verba] *codd.* incipit et desinit *add. N*
6 dicturi] *TER^c* dicatur *P* dicetur *N* cum dicatur *C* cum dicitur *R* ante *H* antequam determinemus *H^c*
7 incipit] *codd.* scilicet incipit *P*
8 queremus] *TNE* queramus *P* queritur *RC* *om. H*
9 et] *codd.* *om. N*
10 permanentium] *codd.* prius queremus *add. H^c*
11 incipit et desinit] *codd.* *om. NR*
12 rebus] *T^cCH* *om. PNR*
13 et qualiter] *codd.* qualiter *E* equaliter *(!)NR*
14 sit ... quo] *codd.* *om. N*
15 verbis] *codd.* incipit et desinit a parte ante et *add. H^c*

2

1 a] *codd.* *om. NR*
2 sive] *codd. R^c* suum *R* sui *E*
3 esse] *codd.* rei ab eo *add. P^c*
4 rationes] *codd.* vel diffinitiones *add. P*

3

1 invicem] *codd.* *om. P*
2 est quoniam] *ECH* est quando *T* quoniam *E* est quod *NR* quod *P*
3 successivarum vero partes] *T* sed partes successivorum *cett.*
4 omnes] *codd.* *om. NR*
5 neque] *codd. P^c* *om. P*
6 enim est] *codd.* est causa *N*
7 quoniam] *TE* quod *PNR* quia *CH*
8 permanentibus] *H^c* *om. H cett.*
9 quia] *T* quod *cett.*
10 terminate] *codd.* terminare *E*
11 non habent ... terminos] *TE* non habent omnes in se terminos *P* non habent in se terminari *N* non omnes habent in se terminari *R* in aliis et ad alia terminantur quecumque habent terminos *H*
12 quia] *T* quod *cett.*

13 accidentibus]*codd.* et *add. N*
14 lapide et in]*codd. om. E*

4

1 quia]*ER* quod *cett.*
2 cum]*codd. om. E*
3 per terminum]*PNRII* om. TEH*
4 motus]*codd.P*^{c} mutatio *TPR*
5 omnis]*P* omnes *cett.*
6 diffinitur]*P* diffiniuntur *cett.*
7 que]*codd.* qui *P*
8 incipit et desinit]*codd. om. N*
9 secundum hoc|*codd. om. PM*

5

1 quod ... incipit]*codd. om. N*
2 positionem]*codd.* propositionem *N*
3 est]*codd.* erit *C* est idest erit *P*
4 erit]*codd.* est *T*
5 non]*codd.* cum *E*
6 nunc ... est]*codd.P*^{c} ponit *P*
7 ut]*codd.* vel *N*
8 privat]*codd.P*^{c} ponit *P*
9 preteritum]*codd.P*^{c} presens et preteretum *P* futurum *E*

6

1 ibi ... posterius]*codd.P*^{c} per prius et de altero per posterius *P*
2 desitiones]*codd.P*^{c} diffinitiones *PE*
3 terminum ... aliquid]*codd.* initialem nichil *(!)E*
4 rei ... finalem]*codd. om. E*
5 consequenter privationem]*P* consequenter privatio *(!)E* consequitur privatio *TR* sequitur privatio *cett.*
6 de re]*codd.* dicere *R*
7 non]*codd.* nunc *NR*
8 fuit]*codd.R*^{c} non fuit *NR*
9 per]*codd. om. NR*
10 ponitur]*codd.* ponit in tempore *C*
11 terminatum]*codd.* terminorum *E*
12 consequenter]*coni.* consequitur]*codd.*
13 per prius]*codd.H*^{c} om. *EH*
14 datur]*codd.* dat *P*
15 ipsum]*codd.* principium *NR*
16 sic]*codd.H*^{c} om. *EH*
17 cum]*codd.* in *P*
18 per prius]*P*^{c} om. *P* prius *cett.*
19 terminati]*codd.P*^{c} termini *P* determinati *NR*

7

1　semper] *TE*　propter hoc *cett.*
2　primi mobilis] *codd.*　primobilis *(!)N*
3　tempus illo] *codd.*　primo *N*
3　tempus illo] *codd.*　primo *N*
4　terminorum suorum] *TN*　suorum terminorum *E*　suarum *P*
terminorum suarum *cett.*
5　principalium] *codd. H^c*　terminorum principalium *P*　om. *H*
6　quidem] *codd.*　quid *E*
7　causa eorum] *coni.*　eorum *H*　ea *cett.*
8　et sic] *codd.*　om. *N*
9　sunt] *codd.*　et sunt *P*
10　consignificationis] *codd.*　cognitionis *T*
11　et] *codd.*　quia *NR*
12　hoc] *T*　hoc modo *cett.*
13　maribus et feminis] *codd.*　feminis et maribus *P*
14　rebus] *codd.*　om. *P*
15　insensibilibus] *codd.*　sensibilibus *T*
17　veritas] *codd.*　mensura *E*
17　temporis] *codd.*　generis et alio modo modus generis similiter [*N 64 va*] dicitur uno modo veritas temporis *(!)N*

8

1　obicitur] *codd.*　queritur *P*
2　aliquis] *codd.*　quid *N*
3　sed si] *codd. R^c*　ut si *N*　sed *ER*
4　et] *PH^c*　om. *cett.*
5　autem] *codd.*　om. *P*
6　movetur] *codd.*　modo *E*
7　sed si movebatur] *codd.*　om. *N*
8　et] *codd.*　om. *E*
9　quoniam] *NR*　quod *cett.*
10　preterito] *codd.*　om. *N*
11　neque] *codd.*　vel *P*
12　potest obici] *codd.*　obicitur *PN*
13　possit *EH*　potest *cett.*
14　currit] *codd.*　quod *add. P^c*
15　et inde] *codd.*　et idem *NR*　unde *E*
16　alio] *TNER*　om. *cett.*

9

1　et ... successivo] *codd.*　om. *E*
2　debetur] *codd.*　debet autem *N*
3　alterativo] *coni.*　alterato *E*　alteratio *TC*　alterationis *cett.*
4　termino] *codd.*　tempori *C*　om. *P*
5　ut] *codd.*　vel *C*
6　qualitate ... una] *codd.*　om. *C*
7　contraria] *codd. P^c*　om. *PR*

8 vel in mediam]*codd.* secundum (!) in mediam *P* contrariam vel intermediam *R*

9 augmentum]*codd.* argumentum *E*

10 quantitate]*codd.* qualitate *E*

11 ad]*TNH* in *cett.*

12 locum]*codd.* motum *N*

13 alterum]*codd.* alium *P*

10

1 illud]*codd.* id *E* aliud *P*

2 obicit]*TCH* obicitur *cett.*

3 infinitatione]*codd.* infinitate *NR*

4 in]*codd.* et *N*

5 est]*codd.* om. *T*

6 dicitur infinitum]*codd.Hᶜ* om. *TH*

7 motus]*codd.Pᶜ* modus *P*

8 enim]*N* om. *cett.*

9 est]*codd.* om. *P*

10 tempus]*codd.* om. *P*

11 aliud tempus]*TPR* om. *N* aliud *cett.*

12 est]*codd.* om. *T*

13 tantum]*codd.Hᶜ* om. *TH*

14 bene]*codd.* om. *P*

15 bis pertransiri]*codd.* transiri *N*

16 eoquod]*codd.* quia *P*

17 infiniti]*codd.* infinitum *P*

18 autem]*codd.* om. *N*

19 nitentur] niteretur *TEH* nitentur *PR* videntur *N*

20 ad]*T* in *cett.*

21 dicit] dicitur]*codd.*

22 si]*codd.* om. *P*

23 cum]*TNE* tunc *PH* sic *R*

24 sumit]*codd.* fuerit *N*

25 movetur]*codd.* movebatur *T*

26 potentiam]*codd.Hᶜ* potentia *R* ponam *N* om. *H*

27 reducere]*codd.Pᶜ* ducere *P* reduce (!)*T*

28 motus sit]*codd.* si motus *N*

29 aptitudinem]*codd.* habitudinem *N*

30 in]*codd.* ad *P*

31 non]*codd.* non tamen *NR*

32 ibi]*codd.* om. *P*

11

1 debeat]*codd.* debebat *N*

2 contingit abire in]*PNCHᶜ* ire contingit in *R* in *T* om. *H*

3 ergo]*codd.* quod *PE*

4 neque]*codd.* vel *P*

5 quia]*codd.* quod *NCH*

12

1 revolutio]*codd.* revelatio *E* celi *add. P^cH*
2 ex alio homine]*codd.* ex alia *P* materialiter ex alia *P^c* naturaliter
add. R
3 prima]*codd.H^c* om. *TH*
4 tunc]*codd.* om. *TR*
5 et celum]*codd.* et motus celi fuit *P*
6 ergo plura]*T* et multa *P* ergo plura sunt *NER* ergo plura fuerunt *H^c*
7 ab eterno]*codd.* om. *P*
8 impius]*codd.* maximus *P* om. *E*
9 autem]*codd.* iam *N*
10 videtur]*codd.* quod *add. PN*
11 primus]*NER* primi *PH^c* om. *TH*
12 post]*codd.* est *add. PR* sit *add. N* positione *add. P^c*
13 revolutionem]*codd.* remotionem *R*
15 post]*codd.* ante et a parte post *P*
16 similiter]*codd.* sic *T*
17 primum hominem]*codd.* principium hominum *N*
18 sumas]*NR* sumeret *P* sumat *cett.*
19 erit]*codd.* exiret *P^c* exit *P*

13

1 primus]*codd.* primi mobilis *N*
2 principia]*codd.* principium *E*
3 principium]*codd.* primum *TE*
4 ad]*NC* om. *cett.*
5 vel]*codd.* neque *T*
6 repperire]*codd.* repire *(!)NR*
7 generalibus]*TPE* generationibus *RC* generalibus *NH*
8 principium]*codd.* primum *TE*
9 ut]*codd.* vel *C*

14

1 sit]*codd.* possit esse *P*
2 sui]*codd.R^c* suo *NR*
3 poterat]*codd.* potuit *P*
4 movebitur]*codd.* novebatur *N* movetur *R*
5 erat]*codd.* est *P*
6 sui]*codd.* suo *N* om. *T*
7 neque ... fine] neque in sui fine *PE* neque in fine *NRCH* om. *T*

15

1 inferiores]*codd.* inferioris *N*
2 principia]*NR* principium *PCE* primum *TH*
3 superior]*codd.* superiores *E*
4 per]*codd. P^c* et *P*
5 principium]*NECH* primum *TPR*
6 quod]*codd.* et *add. N*

7 solum] *codd.* solummodo *E* solis *N*
8 calefieri] *codd.* calefactionem *R*
9 albationem]*R* albedinem *cett.* album fieri *P^c*
10 mobilis] *codd.* mobile *NR*
11 inquantum est augmentabile]*NER om. cett.*
12 inquantum est alterabile]*NR om. cett.*
13 quod existit] *codd.* existentis *E*

16

1 quia] *codd.* quod *N*
2 quarto]*TPER* quinto *NCH*
3 indivisibile] *codd. T^cR^c* divisibile *TR*
4 indivisibile] *codd.R^c* divisibile *R*
5 dicit ... est] *codd. T^c om. T*
6 precedentis] *codd.* preteriti *E*
7 subsequentis] *codd.* consequentis *N*
8 primum] *codd.* principium *R*
9 quodcumque]*codd.* quicumque *N* quod oportet (!)*E*
10 accipiatur] *codd.* accipiantur *N*
11 erit] *codd.* est *TR*
12 illud] *codd. om. T*
13 nunc] *codd.* tempus nunc *R*
14 erat]*R* est *T* erit *cett.*
15 principium] *codd.* primum *P*
16 illius] *codd.* nunc illius *E*
17 est sumere] *codd.* accipe (!)*N*
18 incepit] *codd.* incipit *TE*

17

1 est] *codd.* fuit *N*
2 generativo]*uni.* generationis *NF* generabili *PRC* generali *TH*
3 secundum] *codd.* per *C*
4 sumatur] *codd.* tempus *add. PNR*
5 secundum] *codd.* per *NR*
6 sic] *codd.* sicut *E* scilicet *H*
7 tempus] *codd.* tempora(!)*C*
8 incipere ... potuit] *codd. om. N* incipere] *codd.* incidere *R*
9 in] *codd. om. TRH*
10 a] *codd.* sive a *E*
11 et] *codd.* sive *E*
12 per] *codd.* secundum *NR*
13 sic] *codd.* sicut *E*
14 incepit] *codd.* incipit *ER*
15 incepit] *codd.* incipit *ER*
16 quia ... mensura] *codd. om. N*
17 quia] *codd.* ut *P*
18 primo] *codd.* est primo *R* prius *P*
19 dictionis se] *codd.* divisionis si *N* divisionis *E*

18

1   incepit] *codd.*   incipit *sic semper E*
2   erat] *codd.*   erit *E*
3   inciperet] *codd.P^c*   tempus *P*
4   erant] *codd.*   erat *ER*
5   antequam] *codd.*   aliquam *N*
6   inciperent] *codd.*   inciperet *ER*
7   ex non possibili] *codd.R^c*   ex non impossibili *R*   ex impossibili *R*   non ex impossibili *E*
8   sed ... possibile] *codd.H^c*   *om. H*   sed] *PNRCH^c*   quia *TE*
9   et] *codd.*   est *E*
10   equipollent] *codd.*   et convertuntur *add. T*   cum convertantur *add. R*
11   sic] *codd.*   *om. NR*
12   dicentium] *codd.*   dicens *E*   dicendum *N*
13   etiam] *T^c*   *om. T cett.*
14   cum deo] *codd.*   *om. NE*
15   forma] *codd.*   distincta *add. N*
16   sensibus] *E*   sensibilibus *P*   sensibilibus passionibus *P^c*   passionibus *T (in rasura) NR^{c}CH*   possibilibus *R*
17   et] *codd.T^{c}H^c*   *om. TH*
18   potentiam] *codd.*   potentia esse *E*

19

1   potentia] *codd.*   *om. E*
2   creatarum] *codd.*   causatarum *TR*
3   creatam] *codd.P^c*   causatam *TR*   *om. P*
4   per] *codd.*   *om. P*
5   passivam] *codd.*   incausata *TR*
8   illa] *codd.*   ita *E*   prima *N*
9   passim] *codd.*   *om. P*
10   etiam] *P*   *om. cett.*
11   creatarum] *codd.*   causatarum *TR*

20

1   ex non] *codd.R^c*   non ex *N*   non *R*
2   ergo ... possibile] *codd.*   *om. CH*
3   equipolleant] *codd.*   equipollent *P*
4   quod] *codd.P^c*   *om. P*
5   aliquod agens] *codd.*   aliquid agens *N*
6   faciat] *codd.R^c*   fiat *R*
7   potuit] *codd.*   *R* potest *NR^c*
8   potuit] *codd.*   potest *NR*
9   ita] *P*   ideo *cett.*
10   in] *codd.*   ut *N*
11   potuit] *codd.*   potest *R*

21

1 increata] *codd.* incausata *R*
2 semper] *P* simpliciter *cett.*
3 a nullo] *codd.* in *E*
4 hec est] *E* om. *T* est *cett.*
5 que] *P* quia *cett.*
6 mota] *codd. T^c* vita (!) *E* om. *TP*
7 accidens] *codd.* movetur *add. P^c* cum *add. P* autem *add. H^c*
8 movet] *codd.* tamen *R*
9 creata] *codd.* causata *R*
10 creatis] *codd.* causatis *R*
11 huius] *codd.* huiusmodi *P*
12 potentie] *codd.* potentia *P* possibile *E*
13 activa] *codd. R^c* accidentium *R*
14 consequuntur] *TPCH* sequuntur *NE* sequitur *R*

22

1 sumitur] *codd.* est *R* om. *N*
2 quia] *codd.* que *N*
3 passiva] *codd.* om. *N*
4 semper] *P* simpliciter *cett.*
5 finibilis] *H* finalis *NER* terminabilis *TP* vel initiabilis *add. H*
6 in] *codd.* om. *N*
7 simpliciter] *codd.* Simpliciter autem *TP*
8 est] *codd.* om. *T*
9 simpliciter ... archa] *codd. H^c* om. *NH*
10 est] *codd.* autem *TP*
11 quando] *codd.* ex ea *add. NERH*
12 semper] *codd.* simpliciter *R*
13 secundum] *codd.* om. *P*
14 ut] *codd.* om. *N*
15 particulares] *codd.* autem *add. T* enim *add. TH*
16 partem] *P* partes *cett.*
17 quod] *codd. T^c H^c* om. *TH*
18 divisum] *codd.* divisivum *N*
19 in] *codd.* om. *P*
20 hoc] *codd.* totum *add. T* partes *add. N* tantum *add. cett.*
21 illa] *codd.* om. *T*
22 potentiam] *T^c R^c* om. *TR cett.*
23 que] *codd. T^c* quia *T*
24 finiri] *TP^c NE* fieri *P cett.*
25 cum materia] *codd.* materia cum *E*
26 prius] *codd.* primo *N*
27 potentia] *NR* om. *cett.*
28 finiri] *TPE* fieri *cett.*
29 in] *codd.* ad *PE*

23

1 quidam]*codd.* infans alius *add. H*
2 probatio ... hominum]*codd.* *om. N*
3 desinit ... ergo]*codd.* *om. E*
4 vel]*codd.* et *T*

24

1 et probatio]*codd.* improbatio *N*
2 valet]*codd.* tenet *E*
3 ibi]*codd.* *om. N*
4 figura]*codd.* fallacia figure *P*
5 suppositione]*NE om. cett.*
6 et]*codd.* quia *P* que *N*
7 iste]*codd.* est *E*
8 hominum]*codd.P^c om. P*
9 homine]*codd.* *om. P*
10 ergo]*codd.* alio *N*
11 hominum qui]*codd.* *om. P*
12 restringitur]*codd.* restringit *P*
13 alia]*TE* altera *cett.*
14 respectu]*TPE om. cett.*
15 accidat]*codd.* accidit *P*
16 antecedenti]*codd.* accidenti *P*

25

1 sciat]*codd.P^cH^c* sciat tantum *PH*
2 necessario]*codd.* et semper sciat ea *add. PR^c*
3 c]*codd.* et c *T*
4 d et sit]*R* scit *(!)P* de sit *cett.*
5 scit]*codd.* sciat *PR* sit *H*
6 sciat]*codd.* sciet *N*
7 a]*codd.* quod falsam est *add. H^c*

26

1 prima]*codd.* est *add. P* est simpliciter *add. H^c*
2 distributionem]*codd.* affirmationem *E*
3 teneri particulariter]*TER* tantum particulariter teneri *P* tantum particulariter *NH*
4 conclusio]*codd.* consequentia *P*

27

1 adiunguntur]*codd.* adiungantur *NR*
2 nomini]*codd.* nominis *N*
3 debent]*codd.* debet *ER*
4 de multitudine]*codd.* multitudinis *N*
5 et]*codd.T^cH^c om. TEH*
6 videbit hominem]*codd.R^c* eorum videbit *N* videbit *R*
7 omnem]*codd.* *om. E*

8 videbit] *codd.* eum *add.* P*cH*c
9 [iunt] *coni.* sunt *CH* fit *PNER* sit *T*

28

1 sortes] *codd.* om. *N*
2 illis] *codd.* aliis *P*
3 non sciat] *codd.* nesciat *T*
4 sortes] *TH* om. *cett.*
5 ergo ... scire] *codd.* om. *N*
6 sortes] *T* om. *cett.*
7 quia ... verum] *P* om. *cett.*
8 nichil] *codd.* scire nichil *E*
9 nichil] *codd.* non *P*
10 sive a convertibili] *codd.* om. *T*

29

1 prima] *codd.* est *add.* P
2 bene tenet] *codd.* bona *E*
3 se] *codd.* sed *add.* N
4 sciendo] *codd.* in sciendo *N*
5 se] *codd.* de (!)*N*
6 quando] *codd.* homo *add.* P
7 unde ... dormit] *codd.* om. *N*
8 est] *codd.* solum *add.* E
9 enuntiabile] *codd.* solum *add.* H*c*
10 reflectionem] *codd.* restrictionem *R*
11 ut sciat] *TRH* cum scit *N* cum sciebat *P* cum sciat *E*
12 ita] *codd.* ideo *N*
13 sciet] *T* sciat *cett.*
14 nullius eorum] *codd.* nullius *N* ulterius eorum non *P*
15 augmentatur] *codd.* augetur *N*
16 neque] *codd.* vel *T*
17 videret] *E* videat *cett.*
18 advertat] *codd.* videat *E*
19 eoquod] *codd.*P*c* eoquod haberet *P* quia *H*
20 ut] *codd.* si *add.* N
21 scilicet se] *codd.* sed *NE*

30

1 sortes] *codd.* om. *N*
2 penultimo] *codd.* ultimo *T*
3 probatio ... esse] *codd.* om. *N*
4 et] *codd.* om. *P*
5 sortes ... esse] *codd.* prima vera *PN*
6 sortes] *TH* om. *cett.*
7 si] *codd.* quia *NH*
8 quia] *codd.* si *H*

   9 gerundium]*EH* gerundivum *cett.*
  10 resolvitur]*codd.* habet resolvi *N*

31

   1 duplex]*codd.* dividitur *E*
   2 quia .. si non desinit]*codd.* *om. N*
   3 vel ... si non desinit]*codd.* *om. E*
   4 indesinens]*sic semper P* indeficiens *sic semper cett.*
   5 compositionis]*codd.* divisionis *E*

32

   1 eandem]*coni.* diversam]*codd.*
   2 erit]*codd.* erunt *T* est *E*
   3 dicentes]*R^cH^c om. RH cett.*
   4 quod]*TPE* quorum *N* quia *R*
   5 verbis]*codd.* incipit et desinit *add. PEH^c*
   6 idem]*codd.* substantiam *P*

33

   1 et ... verbis]*codd.* *om. P*
   2 sorte]*codd.* sortes *NR*
   3 vel corpore solo color]*E* color *TPR* colore *N* colorato color *H^c*
colorato *H*
   4 transmutari]*codd.* transsumi *T* mutari *R*
   5 nigredinem ... in]*codd.* *om. P*

34

   1 copulat]*codd.* supponit *H*
   2 que]*codd.* quia *NR*
   3 presenti]*codd.* subiecto presenti *P*
   4 alterum]*codd.* alter *N*
   5 in]*codd.P* ut patet in *P^c*
   6 quia sequitur]*codd.* sicut enim *E* si *add. PNR^c*
   7 ergo]*codd.P^c om. P*
   8 faciet]*PN* facit *cett.*

35

   1 significantes]*codd.* significant *P*
   2 permanentes]*codd.* dicunt positionem rei in presenti et ideo *add. H^c*
   3 dicunt]*codd.* que dicunt *P*
   4 positionem]*P* compositionem *cett.*
   5 vel]*TN* et *cett.*
   6 rerum]*RH^c* earum *P* eorum *NE om. TCH*
   7 de re]*codd.* dicere (!)*E*
   8 nichil ... re]*codd.* *om. P*
   9 de re]*codd.* *om. N* dicere *E*
  10 ideo]*codd.* item *NC*
  11 consequitur]*codd.* sequitur *T*

12 privatio] *codd.P*[c] *om. P*
13 permanentis in futuro] *codd.* de futuro permanentis *T*
14 initialis] *codd.* accidentalis initialis *N*
15 significationem] *codd.* consignificationem *P*

36

1 quod] *codd.P*[c] *om. PNR*
2 terminos] *codd.* rerum *add. H*[c]
3 eius] *R* enim *TH* non *P* *om. EN*
4 alia non] *coni.* non alia *codd.*
5 est duplex] *codd.* dicitur dupliciter *P*
6 fit] *codd.* habet fieri *H*[c] *om. H*
7 fiunt] *TPNE* sunt *R* faciunt *H*
8 hec verba] *codd.* hoc verbum *N*
9 non] *codd.* *om. P*

TRACTATUS SEPTIMUS

DE HIIS DICTIONIBUS 'NECESSARIO' ET 'CONTINGENTER'

1

   1 et] *codd.* om. *P*
   2 dicendum] *codd.* consequenter dicendum *N*
   3 quas] *codd.* que *H*
   4 divisiones] *codd.* dictiones *NH*
   5 determinent] *codd.* desinent *R*
   6 et] *codd.* vel *C*
   7 faciant] *PR* faciunt *cett.*
   8 propositionem] *codd.P^c* compositionem *P*

2

   1 ergo] *codd.* om. *P*
   2 et per hoc] *codd.* et propter hoc *C* quare per hoc *P*
   3 quod] *codd.* ens quod *P*
   4 nec poterit] *codd.* om. *N*
   5 quia] *codd.* a qua *C*
   6 a non] *codd.* ante *NE*

3

   1 sciendum] *codd.* dicendum sive sciendum *E*
   2 sicut et] *TPEH* sicut *C* et *N* et sicut *R*
   3 necessitas] *codd.* necessitatis *N*
   4 necessitas] *codd.* om. *P*
   5 quia ... diffinitum] *codd.* om. *P*
   6 pars] *codd.* et consimilia *add. ER*

4

   1 duobus] *codd.* ex duobus *N*
   2 logicalium] *TRCH* logyce *E* loycum *P* logicarum *N*
   3 de ... predicatur] *codd.* om. *P*
   4 et] *codd.* om. *P*
   5 quia ... diffinitum] *codd.* om. *P*
   6 pars] *codd.* et consimilia *add. ER*

5

   1 quasi] *codd.* quoddam *P*
   2 crescere] *coni.* currere *codd.*
   3 possum] *codd.* possunt *R* posuit *E*

4 esse] *codd.* omne *R*
5 quia] *TE* quod *PN* quod hoc *R* qui hoc *H*
6 canescere] *codd.* currere *P*
7 de] *codd.* om. *N*

6

1 quod opponitur] *ERCH* opponitur *P* oppositum *TN*
2 necessario] *codd.* necessarium *N*
3 operationibus] *codd.* comparationibus *N*
4 voluntariis] *TE* voluntatis *cett.*
5 determinatum est] *TE* determinatur *PNR* se determinat *H*
6 quandoque] *codd.* quam *N*
7 que] *codd.* quod *N*
8 ut] *N* om. *cett.*
9 paucioribus vel raro] *codd.* pauperibus vel rato *(!) sic semper R*
10 malum] *codd.* malo *N*
11 vero] *codd.* nature *N*

7

1 divisiones] *codd.* omnes *add. P*
2 dissiones] *codd.* dictionis *(!)NR*
3 quod ... secundum] *codd.* om. *N*
4 expediens] *codd.* aut sanum *add. P*

8

1 questionem] *codd.* hominem *(!)N*
2 speciei] *codd.* species *N*
3 necessitatem ... ergo] *codd.* om. *N* necessitatem habent] *TE*
necessitatis habent esse *P*
4 compositio propositionis] *codd.* propositio *T*
5 debet] *codd.* dicitur *Hᶜ* om. *H*
6 posterius] *codd.* prius *N*
7 ita] *codd.* prima *N*
8 et primo] *codd.* om. *T*
9 debet] *codd.* dicitur *N*
10 et] *codd.* vel *T*

9

1 actum] *TPCH* actualium *N* accidentium *PᶜR* accidentalium *E*
2 actus] *codd.* actuum *E*
3 a necessitate] *codd.* antecedente *C*
4 a necessitate] *codd.* antecedente *C* accidente *R*
5 motoris] *codd.* moventis et motoris *C*
6 tamen] *codd.* et tamen *N*
7 ita] *codd.* prima *N*
8 necessitatem] *codd.* necessitates *E*
9 dispositionem] *TPCH* dispositiones *NER*
10 hoc nomen] *codd.Pᶜ* om. *P*

11 debet] *codd.* dicitur *N*
12 et] *codd.* ut *E*
13 subiectam vel predicatam] *codd.* subiectivam vel predicativam *E*

10

1 verum] *codd.* rerum *(!)E*
2 predicabitur *(!)E*
3 dicentia] *codd.* significantia *H*
4 necessarium] *codd.* necessario *H* necesse *N*
5 unde facit] *codd.* ut faciat *E*

11

1 partes] *codd.* om. *T* orationis sive *add. E*
2 propositionem modalem *N* propositiones modales *cett.*

12

1 et dispositiones] *codd.* dispositiones autem *C*
2 que sunt] *codd.* om. *C*
3 denominant] *TPH^c* determinant *ERH*
4 propositionem] *codd.H^c* compositionem *CH*
5 autem] *codd.* vero *P*
6 gratia] *codd.* cum dicitur *add. N*
7 eius] *codd.* determinatio eius *P*
8 et] *codd.T^c* om. *T*
9 denominat propositionem] *TP^cE* determinat propositionem *P*
determinat compositionem vel denominat propositionem *H* om. *N*
10 denominat] *TPNH* determinat vel denominat *R* denotat vel
denominat *E*
11 denominat] *codd.* determinat *R*
12 modalis] *codd.* modis *(!)N*

13

1 eis] *codd.* ea *TP*
2 quando] *T* quod *R* quia *cett.*
3 enim] *codd.* autem *N*
4 modalis ... propositio] *codd.* om. *E*
5 dicitur] *codd.* sequitur *N* sequitur vel dicitur *R*
6 necessarium] *codd.* necesse *P*
7 dicitur] *codd.* sequitur *PNR*
8 similiter] *codd.* ita *P*
9 et sic] *codd.* et *P* sicut *E*

14

1 disponunt tamen] *P* determinant *ER* denominant *cett.*
2 et dicunt] *codd.* eum dicant *P*
3 comparationem] *TE* compositionem *cett.*
4 effective] *codd.* affirmative *E*

5 quando]*Pc* qui *P* quia *cett.*
6 vel causaliter]*codd. P^c* om. *P*

15

1 erunt]*codd.* non sunt *C*

16

1 eadem]*codd.* una *P*
2 propter potentiam]*codd.* per potentiam vel positionem *E.*
3 sedere]*coni.* esse antichristus *codd.*
4 ad legendum ... potentia]*H^c* om. *H cett.*
5 per]*coni.* ad *H^c*
6 ad currendum]*codd.* currendi *P*
7 per]*codd.* ad *NE*
8 et ... sedere]*codd.* om. *N*
9 per ipsum]*codd.* per *T* ad *E*
10 necessario]*codd. T^c* om. *T*
11 possibilitatem]*codd.* potestatem *N*
12 et]*N* om. *cett.*
13 dictiones]*T^cNRCH^c* om. *TEH*
14 propter]*codd.* per *H^c* om. *EH*
15 perpetuitatem]*codd.* possibilitatem *E*
16 perpetuis]*codd.* parte eius (!)*E* divinisque subiectis *add. P*

17

1 et]*codd.* quia *N*
2 nullus]*codd.* ergo nullus *N*
3 ut]*EH* om. *cett.*
4 universalis]*codd. T^c* om. *T*
5 illis]*codd.* aliis *N*
6 enim]*codd.* autem *P*

18

1 similiter]*codd.* simpliciter *H*
2 convertuntur]*codd.* sicut ille de inesse *add. H^m*
3 equum]*codd.* vel *add. codd.*
4 necessarie]*codd.* negative *E*
5 in eo quod]*codd.* ex eo quod *T* in esse (!)*E*
6 non ex]*codd.* ex *NE*
7 insunt]*codd.* non sunt *N*

19

1 propositiones de]*T* om. *cett.*
2 nato]*codd.* raro unito (!)*E*
3 ut]*codd.* om. *E*
4 sed differenter]*codd. P^c* om. *P* sed differunt *N*
5 contingenti]*codd. H^c* om. *TEH*
6 secundum ... equivalet]*suppl.*

7 ei] *TPN*   oportet *(!)E*   cum eo *cett.*
8 contingit] *codd.*   est *P*   licet *N*
9 sequitur] *codd.H^c*   om. *EH*

20

1 hiis] *codd.*   autem *add. N*
2 hec] *codd.*   propositio *add. N*
3 modo] *codd.*   om. *N*
4 ergo ... vera] *codd.P^c*   om. *P*
5 necessario] *codd.*   de necessitate *C*
6 contra ... animal] *codd.*   om. *C*
7 sed] *codd.*   om. *P*
8 non] *codd.*   sed non *C*
9 prima] *codd.*   omnis homo etc. *add. C*   omnis homo necessario est animal *add. H^c*
10 prima] *codd.*   hec est *N*

21

1 terminis] *codd.*   sumptis *add. H^c*
2 qui] *codd.*   quia *H*
3 habent] *codd.*   non [*? pro* cum]   habeant *H*
4 a natura] *coni.*   natura *E*   naturam [*? pro* <secundum> naturam] *TR* semper *C*   necessarium *T^cPNH*   necessarium sive a natura *H^c*
5 dicuntur qui] *codd.*   quia *H*
6 non] *codd.*   sunt *add. PC*

22

1 est] *T*   erit *cett.*
2 etiam] *codd.*   om. *P*

23

1 autem] *codd.*   om. *P*
2 compositionem] *codd.*   eam *P*
3 ampliat] *codd.*   eam *add. P*   ipsam *add. N*
4 poneretur] *codd.*   ponitur *P*   ponetur *N*
5 prima] *codd.*   est *P*
6 predicatum] *codd.*   non est vera *add. P^m*
7 prima] *codd.*   ista *N*
8 humana ... anima] *codd.*   om. *E*
9 sortes] *codd.*   si sortes *P*
10 necessario] *codd.T^c*   om. *T*
11 similiter ... simpliciter] *codd.P^c*   om. *P*
12 quando] *codd.*   quandoque *E*   necessario *T*
13 necessario] *codd.*   quando *T*
14 necessario] *codd.T^c*   om. *TE*
15 ibi] *codd.*   fallacia secundum *E*

24

1 necessario] *codd.* om. *N*
2 necessario] *codd. P^c* om. *PE*
3 necessario] *codd.* om. *N*
4 ibi assignatur] *coni.* ibi significatur *P* significatur ibi *N* hic denotatur *H^c* denotatur *cett.*
5 impossibilis] *codd.* ergo prima *add. P*

25

1 eoquod] *codd.* quia *P*
2 sic hoc] *N* sic *P* hoc *cett.*
3 semper] *codd.* simpliciter *P* om. *N*
4 et] *codd.* om. *P*
5 necessitate] *codd.* et semper *add. N*
6 inherere] *codd.* adherere *E*
7 et] *codd.* om. *T*
8 similiter] *codd.* scilicet et de necessitate *add. H^m*
9 semper ... ponitur] *codd.* om. *E* semper] *codd.* simpliciter *P*
10 sortes] *T* om. *cett.*
11 ponuntur] *codd.* poni *N*
12 in eodem subiecto] *T* in eodem *P* circa idem sive in eodem *H^c* om. *cett.*
13 necessario] *codd.* de necessitate *P*
14 mortale] *codd.* immortale *P*
15 differentia] *codd.* dictio *P*
16 sortes ... sorte] *codd.* om. *N*
17 sic] *P* om. *cett.*
18 sicut] *codd.* ut *N*
19 prius scilicet] *codd.* om. *N*
20 simul] *coni.* cur (!)*E* om. *cett.*

26

1 predictum] *TE* predicta propositio *NR* predicta propositio que est *PH*
2 falsum et impossibile] *TE* falsa et impossibilis *cett.*
3 contradictionis] *codd.* conditionalis *E*
4 claudit] *codd.* cludit (!)*P*
5 compositionem ... autem] *codd. T^c* om. *T*
6 hec dictio] *codd.* om. *T*
7 necessario] *codd.* *H^c* om. *TH*
8 determinet] *codd. T^c* om. *T*

27

1 autem] *codd.* om. *N*
2 hic] *codd.* hec *N*
3 necessario] *codd.* om. *N*
4 mortalis sortes] *codd.* om. *N*
5 sortes] *PN* om. *cett.*

6 si] *codd. T^c* om. *T*
7 sortes] *N* om. *cett.*

28

1 iuste] *codd.* iuxte *(!)T* et tantum *add. H*
2 iniuxta *(!)T*
3 iuxta *sic saepius T*
4 iusta et] *codd.* iniusta *P*
5 necessario] *T^cN* om. *T cett.*
6 propositio] *codd.* cras *add. H^c*
7 est] *codd. H* erit *EH^c*
8 scilicet] *codd.* om. *N*
9 nunc] *T* non *E* om. *cett.*

29

1 duplex] *codd.* est *add. P*
2 ita] *codd.* sic *N*
3 compositio non determinatur] *codd.* compositionem determinant *E*

30

1 vel econverso] *codd.* et econverso *T^c* om. *T*
2 super] *codd.* supra *P*
3 consequens] *codd.* consequentis *P* communitas *(!)E*
4 disiunctiva] *codd.* disiuncta *E*
5 contrariorum] *codd.* contrarie *N*
6 duplex] *codd.* dividenda *E*
7 disiunctarum] *TPNR* disiunctorum *E* disiunctivarum *H*
8 necessario] *codd. P^c* om. *P*
9 est ... falsam] *codd.* vel non sedere est falsum vel verum *E*
10 contingentiam ... dicat] *codd.* om. *N*
11 est] *codd.* contingit esse *P*
12 si ... currere] *codd. P^c* om. *P*
13 quod] *codd. T^c* om. *T*
14 hoc] *codd.* b *P*
15 est sensus] *codd.* significat est sensus *(!)N*
16 esse a] *codd.* Sequitur de hac coni.unctione an *add. T* de hac
dictione an *add. N*

TRACTATUS OCTAVUS

DE CONIUNCTIONIBUS

1

1 plura] *codd.* tria *P*
2 et quedam] *N* quedam *H^c om. H cett.*
3 obmissis | *codd.* obmissit *(!)H*
4 et dubitativis] *codd. T^c om. T*

2

1 nomen ... per] *codd. om. H*
2 interrogationem factam] *codd. om. P*
3 tertia questio est] *codd. P* tertio queritur *P^c*
4 coni.unctionibus] *codd. om. C*
5 quarta questio est] *codd.* quarto queritur *P*
6 inter] *codd.* in *P*
7 que habeat] *PRC* que habet *T* quelibet *(!)E* que hanc *(!)N*
8 quinta questio est] *codd.* quinto queritur *P*
9 quia importat] *codd.* qui important *P*
10 et] *TRCH* vel *E* in *N om. P*
11 et] *codd. om. N*
12 istos] *codd. P^c om. P*

3

1 quia] *codd.* quod *PE*
2 omnis] *T^c* si *H om. cett.*
3 sed ... accidente] *codd. om. P*
4 dubitata] *TN* dubia *T^cR* dubitive *(!)E* dubitativa *H*
5 et hec] *T^cN* hec *TE* que *H*
6 sed] *TERH* si *N* item *P*
7 per] *codd.* pro *N*
8 fiet ... adverbia] *codd. om. E* fiet] *T^c* tunc fiet *TPNR* aut fiet *H*
9 quotennis] *codd. om. P*
10 omnis ... ergo] *codd. T^c om. TN*
11 dictio] *codd. om. N*

4

1 significata] *codd.* significativa *H*
2 et] *codd. om. N*
3 quantus quotus quotennis] *codd.* quanta quotiens *(!)E*
4 et ... substantie] *codd. T^c om. T*
5 quid] *codd.* qui *H*
6 quid | *codd.* qui *H*

7 vel legit]*codd. om. P*
8 dubitata]*codd.* dubitativa *E*
9 que]*codd.P^c om. P*
10 cum legit quare legit]*N* cur legit quare legit *T* cum legisti quare legit *(!)P* sortes legit quare legit *H* quid legit quare agit *E*
11 vel]*codd. om. P*
12 cucurrit]*codd.* currit *R*
13 quando]*N om. cett*
14 fecit hoc]*TNH* fecit *R* fuit *PE*
15 sic de omnibus]*P^cE om. cett.*
16 queritur]*codd.* queratur *R*
17 quandoque]*codd.* quando *H*
18 et ... compositione]*codd.P^c* querimus *H^c om. PH*

5

1 dubitatarum]*TP^cNC* dubitabilium *PH om. E*
2 sunt]*codd.P^c om. PC*
3 dubitabilum]*codd.* dubitalium *(!)N* dubitatorum *P^c*
4 argumentum]*codd.* autem *add. N*
5 dubitatio]*codd.* duobus *(!)R*
6 adherentiam]*codd.* adherentia *R*
7 ipsius]*codd.* eius *CH* ipsi *N*
8 subiecto]*N* substantia *cett.*
9 *bis* aliquando]*codd.* quandoque *P*
10 quedam]*codd. om. P*
11 interrogativa]*codd.P^c om. P*
12 ita]*codd.* ideo *E* patet quod *add. CH*
13 dividit]*codd.* dividebat *H^c om. H*
14 interrogationem accidentis]*codd.* interrogationem *N* interrogativum accidentie *R*

6

1 secundum]*codd. T^c om. T*
2 probo]*TE* probatio *cett.*
3 hec est dictio]*E* est dictio *TCH* dictio est *N* hec dictio an est *P*
4 dictio]*codd. om. P*
5 importat interrogationem]*codd.* importata significatione interrogatione *(!)E*
6 quia]*codd.* ut *P*
7 inter ea de]*codd.* inter eadem *E* interea de *R*
8 electionem]*codd.* dubitationem *E*
9 conceptam]*PE* conceptum *cett.*
10 vel ut]*TE* aut ut *PH* sicut *N* vel ad *R*
11 affectum]*codd.* affectum assecutum *E* exercitam vel effectam quod idem est *P*
12 non]*codd.* significat *add. P* significat eam *add. N* ut significat *add. R*
13 conceptam]*P* affectum *E* conceptum *cett.*
14 omnis]*P om. cett.*

15 anime] *TPER* aut *N om. CH*
16 conceptus] *codd.* conceptio *E* conceptum *P*
17 *bis* vel] *codd.* per *add. PE*
18 ut conceptam]*P* ut conceptui *R* non conceptum *E* ut conceptum
cett.
19 affectus] *codd.* affectionis *P*
20 attectus] *codd.* effectus *N*
21 per modum] *TPNR om. cett.*

7

1 interrogandi] *codd.* sumpta *add. H*
2 quia] *TPNR om. cett.*
3 quicumque] *codd.* quicquid *(!)N*
4 ideo] *codd.* unde *C*
5 certificationis] *TERH* certitudinis *PNC*
6 disiungendo] *codd.* vel discernendo *add. R*
7 hoc] *codd.* quod *add. TPERH*
8 alterius] *codd.* ipsorum *E*
9 disiunctorum] *codd.* disiunctarum *R*
10 dictio] *codd.* coni.unctio *CH*
11 est] *codd.* hec *CH*
12 quod ... interrogativa] *codd. om. P*
13 importet] *codd.* interrogationem cum *add. H^c* interrogatio *add. R*
14 disiunctorum] *codd.* disiunctionum *R*

8

1 coniunctiones interrogativas] *codd.* dictiones interrogativas scilicet
coni.unctiones *E*
2 iste] *codd.* substantie *(!)N*
3 suppositi] *codd.* subiecti *R*
4 et differunt] *codd.* differunt autem *P*
5 disiunctiva]*PE* disiuncta *N* coni.unctiva *(!)T* copulativa *RH*
6 sed] *codd.* quando semel ponitur *add. H^m*
7 disiunctivam] *codd.* disiunctivarum *P*
8 quandoque] *codd.* quando *P* quoniam *N*
9 propter hoc quod] *codd.* et propter hoc *N*
10 currentem]*PNR* currere *cett.*
11 aliquando] *codd.T^c om. T*
12 bene] *codd.* non *E*

9

1 habeat] *codd.* habeant *E* hanc *N*
2 dictio] *codd.* coni.unctio *PR*
3 dicta] *codd.* duo *H* dicta inventa *N*
4 contradictorie ... dicta] *codd.T^c om. T*
5 opposita] *codd. om. N*
6 probo] *TE* probatio *cett.*
7 querit aliquis] *coni.* queritur *codd.*

8 in communi] *codd.* inquam *E*
9 aliquid] *codd.* aliquod *EH om. N*
10 aliquid] *codd. om. EH*
11 nisi] *codd. om. P*
12 partes] *codd.* partem *N*
13 disiunctio] *codd.* disiunctionis *N*
14 aliquid] *codd.* aliquod *R om. P*
15 coni.unctionem] *codd.* disiunctionem *N* dictionem *P*
16 partes] *codd.* disiunctionis *add. P*

10

1 unde] *codd.* quia *N*
2 deficit] *codd.P^c* desinit *P*
3 contradictionis] *codd.* dictionis *N*
4 alterum] *codd.* alteram partem *N*

11

1 circa]*R* contra *cett.*
2 ista scilicet] *codd.* etsi *P*
3 sortem currere et platonem disputare]*PH* sortem currere platonem
disputare *N* sortem currere plato est *(!)* disputare *R* platonem disputare sortem currere *T*
4 quod queritur]*N* que *E* queritur *cett.*
5 per] *codd.T^c om. T*
6 interrogationem] *TPNE* interrogationum *cett.*
7 solvitur per]*coni.* et solum *TNER* solum *cett.*
8 questio terminatur] *codd.T^c om. T*
9 quia] *codd.* que *PR*
10 ergo ... inventa] *codd.T^c om. T*
11 dicta] *codd.T* ea *T^c*

12

1 interrogatio una et] *TE om. cett.*
2 queritur] *codd.* dicitur *PE*
3 et]*PNR om. cett.*
4 est]*PEH* et *N om. TR*
5 queritur] *codd.* dicitur *E*
6 alter istorum]*N* alterum istorum *P* alterum *cett.*
7 una] *codd.T^c om. T*
8 uterque]*TNER* utrumque *cett.*
9 sit]*TPNR* scit *E* fiat *(?pro* sciat*) H^c om. H*
10 et quod] *codd.* illud quod est ut *N*
11 altero] *codd.* utro *N*

13

1 obicitur] *codd.* obicit *N*
2 disiungere] *codd.* et *add. T*
3 erit instrumentum]*N* est instrumentum *R* erit *H* est *T^cPR om. T*

4 disiungendi] *codd.* distinguendi *H* ergo hec dictio an non exercet istos tres actus *add. P^m*

5 consequentium] *TPCH* sequentium *cett.*

6 sicut] *codd.* ut *N*

7 hoc] *codd.* est *add. TPEH*

8 etiam est] *TNER* est *P* etiam *H*

9 repercutiendo] *PNR* recipiendo *T* recuperandi *E* prout repercutit *H*

10 vocalem arteriam] *codd.* vocales arterias *P*

11 hoc] *codd.* est *add. TPR*

12 repercussivus] *codd.* repercutivus *E* repersivus *(!)P*

13 aliud] *codd.* illud *H*

14 coni.unctionum] *codd.* orationum *P*

15 interrogamus ... ipsam] *codd. om. N*

16 sub] *codd.* secundum *N*

17 differt] *codd.* differunt *P*

18 sit] *codd.* sint *P*

19 per] *codd. T^c om. T*

20 predictos] *codd.* dictos *P*

14

1 posterius] *codd.* est *add. P*

2 petit] *codd.* potest *E*

3 quod oportet] *codd. om. E*

4 sciat ... respondens] *codd. om. C*

5 quod] *codd.* et *N*

6 respondens] *codd.* autem *add. P*

7 certus] *codd.* actus *(!)R*

8 debet] *codd.* dicitur *N*

9 interrogans] *codd.* opponens *T*

10 in ... specialiter et] *codd. om. E*

11 quod] *codd.* ut *P*

12 specialiter et] *T^c PNRC om. TEH*

15

1 yspania] *TNH* spania *R* yspinania *(!)E* polonia *P*

2 tamen] *codd.* cum *E*

3 scio] *codd.* scis *N*

4 neque scio] *codd.* nec scio *N* nescio *H*

5 non] *codd.* solutio *E*

6 hoc] *codd. om. ER*

7 oporteret] *codd.* teneret *NR* oporteret vel teneret *E*

8 quia] *codd.* quod *N*

9 petit] *codd.* poterit *N*

10 interrogat] *codd.* vel non *add. E*

11 disiunctorum] *codd.* disiunctivarum *ER*

12 disiunctorum] *codd.* disiunctivarum *ER*

13 huiusmodi] *codd.* noc huiusmodi *(!)N* hanc *R*

16

1 sophismate] *codd.* om. *N*
2 homo] *codd.* om. *N*
3 sit] *codd.* scit *(!) sic saepius ER*
4 ab] *codd.* a sorte vel ab *H*
5 plato sit sortes] *codd.P^c* sortes sit plato *P*
6 singulis] *codd.* aliis *PNR*
7 illo] *codd.* omni homini *P*
8 an] *TECH* vel *PN* secundum *R*
9 a sorte] *codd.* ab illo *R*

17

1 propositione] *codd.* probatione *N*
2 quoniam] *codd.* quia *TR*
3 est] *codd. T^c* om. *T*
4 sit sortes an] *codd.H^c* om. *NH*
5 omnis homo] *codd.* om. *H*
6 probatione] *codd.* propositione *P*
7 illas] *codd.* omnes illas *P*
8 deberet] *N* debet *cett.*
9 similiter] *codd.* omnes illas *P*
10 relinquuntur] *codd.* relinquentur *P*
11 deberet] *N* debet *cett.*
12 particulares] *coni.* partes] *codd.*
13 secunda] *codd.T^c* sub secunda *T*
14 distributione] *codd.* distributio est *E*
15 integra ... distributionis] *codd.T^c* om. *T*
16 particulares] partes *codd.*
17 permaneat] *TN* permaneret *cett.*
18 sorte] *codd.* et hec est falsa *add. T^mPRH* et hoc est falsum *add. N*
19 alio ... aliis] *codd.* om. *E*
20 etiam] *codd.* enim *R*
21 particulares] partes *codd.*
22 singulares ... singularibus] *codd.* significationes ... significationibus *R* omnibus *H*
23 sortes ... scias an] *T* om. *cett.*
24 tu ... et] *codd.* om. *T*
25 accepit] *H^c* accipiebat *T* accipit *T^c cett.*
26 consequens] *codd.* accidens *R*

18

1 mentiatur] *codd.* vi(n)ciatur *semper perperam E*
2 uter] *ER* utrum *TN* quis *T^c cett.*
3 negativa] *codd.* negatio *N*
4 de mentiente] *codd.* defficiente *(!)E*
5 esse] *codd.* falsam esse *N*
6 quia licet] *codd.* quod licet *P* quelibet *(!)N*
7 est] *codd.* om. *N*

8 est]*N om. cett.*
9 hoc]*codd. om. N*
10 dicitur]*codd.* esse *add. N*
11 ut]*codd.* unde *P*
12 scis]*codd.* scit *NR*
13 contingere]*codd.* contingenti *R*
14 scilicet]*codd.* si *N*
15 non]*codd.* an *T*
16 est]*codd.* esse *NR om. E*
17 semel]*codd.* solum *N*
18 disiunctive]*codd.* disiuncte *N* disiunctione *R*

19

1 sortem ... falsum]*codd. om. N*
2 sicut]*codd.* ut *N* unde *R*
3 non certa]*TPN* non *ER* incerta *H*
4 negativa]*codd.* necessaria *R*
5 illum esse sortem]*codd.* illum sortem esse *E* sortem esse illum *T*
6 mentientem]*codd.* vinciente me *(!)E*
7 non]*codd. om. T*
8 illum esse sortem]*TNER* sortem esse illum *cett.*
9 casu]*codd.* de *E*
10 alio]*codd.* alia *ER*
11 nescis]*TPNH* tu nescis *H^c* nescit *ER*
12 contingere]*codd.* vel accidere *add. P*
13 quisquis]*coni.* quicquid *E* qui *cett.*
14 illum esse sortem]*codd.* sortem esse illum *E*
15 prima]*codd.* ita *N*
16 ex qua]*codd.* et quam *(!)E*

20

1 hic]*codd.* hoc *H* quia hec est dubia ut dicebatur unde falsam est quod sit scita et in probatione est sophisma accidentis ut hic *add. R*
2 quod]*codd.* an *E*
3 enuntiabile]*codd.* annuntiabile *(!)E* esse *add. R*
4 quod falsum est]*codd. om. TP*
5 quia ... hominem]*codd.T^c om. T*
6 licet]*codd.* quamvis *TP*
7 uni]*codd.* una *NR* eorum *add. TH*
8 subicitur]*codd.* subicietur *N* subiciebatur *R*
9 reliquo]*codd.* alia vel reliqua *R*
10 unde est unum]*TE* unde unum est *PNR* unum enim est *H*
11 alterum ... eo]*codd. om. N*
12 eo]*codd.* quia sicut dictum est enuntiabile semper est de re subiecti termini sive de eo quod subicitur *add. P* et sicut dictum est enuntiabile ... subicitur dictionem *(!) add. N* Sequitur de dictione vel *add. T*

21

1 Habito] *codd.* Dicto *P*
2 disiunctiva] *codd.* om. *P*
3 queritur] *codd.* dicendum est *P*
4 dictio] *codd.* coni.unctio *C*
5 autem] *codd.* om. *NR*
6 significatum] *codd.* significant *N*
7 sit] *codd.* est *P*
8 disiunctio] *codd.* dictio *E*
9 terminum] *codd.* tertium *E*
10 disiunctum] *codd.* disiunctionum disiunctivum *(!)N* disiunctivum *R*
11 predicabilem] *TP* predicabile *NERH* predicabile esse *H*

22

1 queritur quia] *codd.* sic proceditur quia queritur *P*
2 et] *EH* aut *TPNR*
3 est] *codd.Pᶜ* om. *P*
4 et] *PEH* aut *TNR*
5 consecutiva] *codd.* disiunctiva *E*
6 dicit] *codd.* quia dicit *P* coni.unctio est ut dicit alexander in doctrinali aliorum autem vel ordinem idem *add. Pᵐ*
7 ea] *codd.* inter *add. Hᶜ*
8 permittit] *codd.* possunt *NE*
9 coni.unctio] *codd.* conclusio *N*
10 que] *codd.* quod *NR*
11 dicens] *codd.* dicendo *N*
12 significant] *codd.* om. *N*
13 hec] *codd.* om. *T*

23

1 rerum] *codd.* tunc *R*
2 disiunctio] *codd.* deiunctio vel disiunctio *E*
3 ubicumque] *E* ubi *cett.*
4 unde] *codd.* ut *P*
5 currit ... plato] *codd.* om. *N*
6 ipsa] *codd.* om. *T* in ea *E*
7 simul esse] *TᶜPN* om. *TERCH*
8 contra] *codd.* circa *P*
9 non] *codd.* om. *E*
10 quod] *codd.* quia *N*

24

1 queritur quia quod] *codd.* querit quis quid *N* queritur quid *H*
2 ente] *codd.* essente *(!)E*
3 significatum ... ens] *codd.* significat ens non *E*
4 in non] *codd.* non in *R*

25

1 obicitur quia cum] *coni.* obicitur cum *TRH* obicitur quod *N* queritur quod *P*

2 sint] *codd.* sunt *P*

3 in] *P om.. cett*

4 sed|*ER* quia *T* et *catt.*

5 aut] *NE* vel *T^cPRH^c om. TH*

6 predicamento] *codd.* predicato *N*

7 aut] *codd.* vel *P*

8 secundum] *T^c om. T cett.*

9 et] *codd.* aut *T*

10 alicuius] *codd. P^c om. P*

11 significatum] *codd.* respectus (!)*P*

26

1 sunt relationes] *codd.* habeant relationem *E*

2 et] *codd. om. N*

27

1 que est] *codd.* quoniam *R*

2 significatorum] *codd.* significativorum *N*

3 comparationes] *codd.* comparate *E* ipsorum *add. R*

4 entes] *codd.* ens *E*

5 genere] *codd.* relationis *add. H^c*

6 vicinus] *codd.* manus *E*

7 equiparantia] *TNH* equipater (!)*E* per equiparantiam *P* equivoca *R*

8 est] *codd.* sunt *P*

28

1 quia] *codd.* quod *NER*

2 coni.unctiones] *codd.* dictiones *P*

3 coni.unctio] *codd.* dictio *P*

4 aut] *codd. om. T*

5 an] *codd.* aut *T*

6 per quod] *codd.* quo *E*

7 transeat] *coni.* possit transvie *E* transit *cett.*

8 actum ... alium] *codd. om. E*

9 et ... putasne sortes currat] *codd. om. P*

10 scis] *T* scit *cett.*

11 utrum] *codd.* an *NR*

12 possit transire] *codd.* transeat *P*

13 actum] *codd. om. N*

14 enim] *codd.* omnino *E*

15 scis] *codd.* sic *E*

16 et ... currit] *codd. om. N*

17 bene] *codd.* tamen *T*

29

1 cognoscitivam] *codd.* connotivam *(!)R*
2 non motam] *codd.* et non motivam *T*
3 prout] *codd.P^c* ut *P*
4 cognoscitiva] *codd.* cogitativam *(!)R*
5 coni.unctio] *codd.* dictio *P*
6 motivas] *codd.* motans motui *(!)N*
7 motivas] *codd.* motans *N* motivum *R*
8 hiis] *TP* aliis *cett.*
9 ille] *codd.* illa *TE*
10 encleticum] *TE* encleticus *P* encletica *NH* elenticum *(!)R*
11 inclinativum] *ER* inclinativus *P* inclinativa *cett.*
12 hiis] *codd.* aliis *T^c* om. *T*

30

1 ve] *codd.* ne *R* om. *T*
2 putasne] *T* putatne *PR* putasve *NH*
3 amavitque] *codd.* vocantique *E* quia *add. N*
4 dicuntur] *T* ponuntur *cett.* semper *add. P*

31

1 disiunctus] *codd.* disiunctivus *sic semper NR*
2 vel differentia] *codd.* om. *NR*
3 vel diffinitio] *T^cP* vel differentia *NER* om. *TH*
4 omnia] *codd.* omnino *E* om. *N*
5 entia] *codd.* predicabilia *add. P^c*
6 vero] *codd.* non *ER*

32

1 predicationis] *codd.* platonis *(!)E*
2 diffinitio] *codd.H^c* differenti *E* om. *H*
3 sed] *codd.* predicatur *add. P*
4 indifferenter] *codd.P^c* differentes *P*
5 natura] *codd.* non *P*
6 indeterminate] *TPNE* indifferenter *C* determinate *H* indentitate *(!)R*
7 alicuius] *codd.* cuiusdam *E*
8 est] *codd.* etiam *N*

33

1 aliquod] *TNER* unum *CH* om. *P*
2 predicabilibus] *codd.* universalibus vel predicabilibus *E*
3 quia] *codd.* quod *N*
4 et] *codd.* om. *P*
5 et consimilia] *codd.* om. *R*
6 universaliter consignificant] *E* quoniam universaliter significant *TNR* significant quoniam universaliter *P* [cf. Arist. *De interpr.*, 17b12] quantum *(!)* universaliter significant *H*

7 sed] *codd.P^c* ergo *P*
8 vero patet] *TN* autem patet *P* non potest *R* patet *H*

34

1 disiuncto] *codd.* disiunctivo *sic saepius N* distributivo *sic persaepe R*
2 disiunctionis] *codd.* *P* distributionis *P^c*
3 distributionem] *codd.* distinctionem *(!) sic semper R*
4 quia] *codd.* et *NR*
5 potest] *codd.* possunt *EH*
6 vel] *codd.* omnis *add. P*
7 vel] *codd.* omnis *add. TE*
8 hic] *T* *om. cett.*
9 parte] *codd.* sui *add. P*
10 supra se] *codd.* *om. P* scilicet *add. NRH^c*
11 prout convenit] *P* pro naturam (!) communi *T* pro natura communi *T^c cett.*
12 quia] *codd.* et *TE*
13 sive] *codd.* vel *T*
14 quem] *codd.* quam *N* quod *R*

35

1 disiungi] *codd.* distingui *TR*
2 alio a vero] *N* alio vero *TP* a vero *R* alio *H* alio modo *E*
3 quia] *codd.T^c* *om. T*
4 vel] *codd.* et *P*
5 quicquid] *codd.* quod *add. E*

36

1 propositio] *codd.* probatio *N*
2 aliis] *codd.* singulis *E*
3 est vera] *codd.* *om. T*
4 est vera] *codd.* *om. T*

37

1 sumptam] *codd.* *om. NR*
2 non] *codd.T^c* *om. TE*
3 disiunctus] *codd.* omnis *add. P*
4 sic] *PNR* *om. cett*
5 earum] *codd.* eius *P*
6 contradictorie] *codd.* contradictiones *EH*
7 insimul] *codd.* etiam simul *T*
8 disiunctus] *codd.* omnis *add. P*
9 contradictoria] *codd.* *om. N*
10 aliquando ... disiunctionis] *codd.* *om. N*
11 singularibus] *TPR* aliquibus partibus *(!)EH*
12 alterius partis] *codd.T^c* partes *T* *om. E*
13 si stent] sistent *E* si sunt *R* si sint *cett.*

14 et cum istis sint] *TH*   cum istis sint *P* et cum istis sicut *NR* etc. iste sint *E*
15 affirmativa quam negativa] *codd.*   negativa quam affirmativa *P*
16 una] *codd.*   utraque *P*
17 propositio] *codd.*   *om. N*
18 affirmativa ... omni] *PNR*   *om. cett.*
19 oratione] *codd.*   propositione *P*
20 ibi] *codd.*   in predicta propositione *P*
21 quia] *codd.*   et *P*
22 tunc ... falsa] *codd.*   propositio disiunctiva et est falsa *P*
23 et ... disiunctiva] *codd.*   *om. P*   et falsa *P*
24 primo eorum] *TE*   prima earum *cett.*
25 secundo vera] *TE*   vera autem secunda *P*   secunda vera *cett.*
Sequitur de coni.unctione et *add. T*

38

1 coni.unctionibus] *codd.*   dictionibus *PE*
2 sit .. eius] *codd.*   *om. N*
3 fiat] *codd.*   sit sive fiat *E*   sit *R*   habet fieri *H*
4 quinto] *codd.*   autem *add. N*
5 illa diversa] *codd.*   *om. N*
6 queritur] *TEH*   *om. PNR*

39

1 quia] *codd.*   et dicunt quidam quod *P*ᶜ   et quod *P*
2 idem] *codd.*   dicit priscianus quod *add. P*ᶜ
3 orationis ... partes] *codd.*   *om. P*
4 attribuo] *codd.*   attribuit *P*
5 est quod] *codd.*   quia *P*
6 habet] *codd.*   debet *P*
7 sua] *codd.*   uno *(!)N*
8 vero] *codd.*   *om. P*
9 finis] *codd.*   predicti *add. PNR*
10 est] *codd.*   cum dico quod est pars orationis reperta ad copulandum alias *add. P*
11 quem] *codd.*   hoc *P*
12 fuit] *TE*   est *cett.*
13 qui] *codd.*   quia *P*
14 huius] *codd.P*ᶜ   *om. P*
15 coni.unctionis] *codd.*   dictionis *PNR*
16 copulatio] *TP*   copulare *NRH*
17 concedimus] *codd.*   est concedendum *E*   aliud *(!)R*

40

1 querit] *T*   queris *NR*   obicit *P*   queritur *cett.*
2 comparationem] *codd.*   compositionem *H*
3 que est] *codd.*   queritur *(!)N*
4 secundum] *PR*   *om. cett.*

5 simultatem] *codd.* similitatem *sic saepius* C similationem *(!)*R
6 hec ... et] *T^cNRC* hec T hec dictio et P coni.unctio et E *om.* H
7 eorum] *codd.* aliorum P
8 istos] *codd.* istas P istis R
9 coni.unctio] *codd.* dictio P
10 simul] *codd.* simultatem P
11 homines] *codd.* duo homines P
12 ade] *codd.* noe T
13 noe] *codd.* ade T
14 non] *codd.* *om.* N
15 bene] *codd.* unde P
16 dicitur] *codd.* sequitur NR
17 cucurrit] *codd. H^c* currit EH
18 et ... coni.unctio et] *codd. P^c* *om.* P
19 cursus ... sunt] *codd.* eri odie cras non est E
20 hesternus] *codd.* externus *(!)*TN
21 dicit] *codd.* debet H
22 coni.unctio] *codd.* dictio P
23 simultatem] *codd.* similitudinem E similationem *(!)*R
24 pari quantum est] *codd.* predicamento quantum *(!)*R
25 vel] *codd.* secundum N
26 sedet et] *codd.* videt vel E

41

1 quia] T quod *cett.*
2 omne] *codd.* esse T
3 prime] *codd.* quatuor autem predicata de quibus agitur in topicis sunt hec scilicet diffinitio proprium genus accidens anexa *(!)* autem eorum sunt alia predicata reducibilia ad hec ut idem genere reducitur ad genus comparatio [P82rb] vero accidentis ut melior fortior iustior et sic de aliis reducuntur ad predicatum de accidente idem autem simpliciter et diversum reducuntur ad predicatum de diffinitione *add* P
4 quod] *codd.* quia PN
5 unum genere ... diffinitione] T^c unum genere neque unum specie neque unum nomine vel diffinitione T unum specie neque unum genere neque est unum numero vel diffinitione P unum genere neque unum numero neque unum specie vel differentia N unum genere aut unum specie neque unum nomine vel diffinitione E unum genere neque unum numero neque unum in specie vel distinctione *(!)*R unum genere neque unum specie neque unum nomine vel diffinitione H
6 supponantur] *codd.* supponitur P

42

1 est] *codd.* *om.* NR
2 continuatione] *codd.* continuale *(!)*R
3 insertu] TNE in situ P insitione *(!)*P^c in situ *(!)* vel insertione H insertione C
4 ramo] *codd.* trunco P

5 per insertionem] *TE* per insestionem *(!)NH* per incisionem *R* perfectum *(!)P*
6 contiguatione] *codd.* contiguitate *P* continuatione *ER*
7 quando] *codd.* cuius *R*
8 nichil ... medium] *codd.* non est medium inter ea *P*
9 collatione] *E* collectione *P* collatione idest colligatione *NR* colla *(!)* idest collatione *TH*
10 non] *codd.* in *N*
11 copulatus] *codd.* copulativus *NE*
12 aggregatione] *codd.* cumgregatione *(!)E*

43

1 in contrarium] *codd. T^c om. T*
2 unum] *codd.* unum genere *P^c om. P*
3 illas] *codd.* alias *N*
4 sumuntur] *codd.* finiuntur *P*
5 predicata] *codd.* predicamenta *sic semper NER*
6 accidentis] *codd.* ad accidentia *H*
7 sic de aliis] *codd.* similia *P* que *add. R*
8 de] *codd.* dicitur de *R*

44

1 de se] *codd.* divise *R*
2 de pari] *codd.P* disparatorum *P^c*
3 substantias uni accidenti] *codd.* substantias uni actui *P* sillabus *(!)* in actum *E*
4 duo accidentia] *codd.* duos actus *PE*
5 sunt albi] *TPER* legunt *NH*
6 homo] *NERH* sortes *P* vel *T*
7 disputat] *codd.* et sic de aliis *add. P*

45

1 iam] *codd.* om. *P*
2 substantivo] *NR* suo substantivo *T* suo subiecto *E* cum subiecto *P*
3 hec] *codd.* huius *(!)N*
4 coni.unctio] *codd.* dictio *E*
5 ex predictis] *codd.* om. *P*
6 exigit] *codd.* significat *P*
7 de pari] *codd.* *P* disparate *P^c*
8 etiam] *TNE* om. *cett.*
9 accidentium] *codd.* actuum *P*
10 de ... habentia] *codd.P* habenda disparate *P^c*
11 vel] *codd.* om. *P*
12 et in] *codd.* et ab *P^c* vel ab *P*
13 accidentibus] *codd.* accidentium *P*

46

1 currunt] *codd.* currit *TH*

2 omne] *codd.* esse et *N*
3 dicitur] *codd.* dicetur *his in P*
4 aliis] *codd.* ceteris *P*
5 deus est iustus] *codd.* et deus est iustus *P om. T*
6 de deo autem] *codd. E^c* de eo autem *E* de subiecto et patre *N*
7 divinam essentiam] *codd.* differentiam essentialem *H*
8 sunt] *codd.* erunt *P*
9 indefinite] *codd.* infinite *R* indeterminate *H*
10 ergo] *codd.* et *EH*
11 sciendum autem] *codd.* sciendum tamen *P* contingit tamen *H*
12 supposita] *codd.* cum unitate significationis *add. NR*
13 de pari] *codd. P* disparate *P^c*

47

1 quia] *codd.* quod *ER*
2 ergo ... extremorum] *codd. T^c om. T*
3 debet] *codd.* dicitur *NR*
4 hec] *codd. om. P*
5 respicit] *codd.* recipit *P*
6 quando] *codd.* bene *N*
7 quia] *TNE om. cett.*
8 propter] *codd.* et propter *R*
9 est] *codd. om. P*
10 propter quam] *codd.* quia *E*
11 quando] *codd.* cum *P* quod *R*

48

1 locus] *codd.* et est locus *PNR*

49

1 sillogismus] *codd. P^c* similis *P*
2 sed] *codd.* est *add. PE*
3 hec] *codd. om. P*
4 scilicet] *codd.* hec *add. P*
5 istum] *codd.* hunc *sic saepius P*
6 aliud] *codd.* animal *R* illud *N*
7 aliud] *codd. T^c om. T*
8 animal] *codd.* animalis *N* aliud *R*
9 autem] *codd.* enim *E* iterum *NR*
10 sortes] *TEH^c om. PH*
11 in] *codd.* sub *P*
12 animal] *codd. om. P*
13 et ut] *TNH* ut *R* ut autem *P*
14 sit ... animal] *codd. om. N*
15 quod faciat] *codd.* faciens *E* cum faciat *P*
16 illa duo animalia] *codd.* animalia *P* illa duo altera *H*
17 animalia] *codd.* altera *H*

50

1 omne]*codd.* esse *N*
2 componibile]*codd.* compassibile *(!) sic semper E*
3 ergo ... falsa]*codd.* suppositionem *add. P*
4 ipsa]*PH* prima *R* tota *T*
5 unam]*codd.* *om. EN*
6 stant]*codd.* sunt *P*
7 quod est]*codd. Tᶜ* *om. T*
8 accidens]*codd.* sequitur de hac dictione nisi *add. T*

51

1 dictio]*codd. Pᶜ* *om. P*
2 que]*codd.* quoniam *R*

52

1 quod]*codd.* quando *R*
2 instantia]*codd.* *om. R*
3 enim fit]*P* enim est *Tᶜ* *om. T*
4 aliquando]*codd.* enim *add. T* autem *add. H*
5 contra totum]*codd. Tᶜ* *om. TNR*
6 ut ... totum]*codd.* *om. P*
7 extrahendo]*codd.* vel extramittendo *add. TPH* removendo *add. N*
vel extratumendo *(!) add. R*
8 extrahendo]*codd.* vel removendo *add. N* vel extramittendo vel
removendo *add. R* vel extramittendo *add. cett.*
9 Item ... tenetur exceptive]*codd. Tᶜ* *om. T*
10 iste]*codd. H* sit *add. Hᶜ*
11 duplex ... consequentia]*codd. Tᶜ* *om. T*
12 quia quedam]*codd.* quedam enim *P*
13 simplex]*codd.* simpliciter *N* cuius termini sunt simplices *add. Pᵐ*
14 mecum]*N* ad me *cett.*
15 inferre]*codd.* instare *N*
16 vel ... consequens]*codd. Pᶜ* *om. P*
17 non]*codd.* *om. P*
18 venies]*codd.* veniens *N*
19 neque]*codd.* non *PR*
20 currit]*codd.* *om. P*
21 tenetur]*codd.* ibi *add. TP*

53

1 semper]*codd.* simpliciter *P*
2 dictio]*codd.* coniunctio *P*
3 naturam exceptionis]*codd.* veram exceptionem *P*
4 hec dictio]*T* *om. cett.*
5 naturam exceptionis]*codd. Tᶜ* exceptionis *T* veram exceptionem vel
naturam exceptionis *P*
6 aliquam]*codd.* aliam *P*
7 hec dictio]*P* *om. cett.*

8 dictio] *codd.* *om. P*
9 sed] *codd.* et *P*

54

1 prius] *codd.* *om. NR*
2 obicit] *codd.* *om. N*
3 ei] *codd.* *om. P*
4 semper] *codd.* *om. P*
5 compositionem] *codd.* comparationem *NE*
6 trahitur] *TE* communiter *R* contrahitur *cett.*
7 homo] *codd.* currit *add. P*
8 non] *codd.* T^cH^c *om. TH*
9 non] *codd.* si *N*
10 instantie] *T* instantive *E* instantivam *cett.*
11 compositionem] *codd.* comparationem *E*
12 trahitur] *codd.* P^c *om. P*
13 naturam] *P* instantiam *cett.*
14 illarum] *codd.* aliarum partium vel *E*
15 per] *codd.* T^c *om. T*
16 habitudinem] *codd.* vel comparationem *add. N* vel compositionem *add. R*
17 totum] *codd.* vel comparationem *add. TPH* vel per comparationem *add. E*
18 scilicet naturam] *codd.* *om. T* secundum naturam *N* naturam *R*
19 ratione] *codd.* in ratione *P* ex parte vel ratione *E*
20 consecutivam] *PN* adversativum *R* adversativam *cett.*
21 consecutiva] *PN* adversativa *cett.*

55

1 predictis] *codd.* quod *add. P*
2 dictio] *codd.* coniunctio *PE*
3 tunc] *codd.* ergo *E* *om. H*
4 cum hoc] *codd.* P^c est homo (!) *P*
5 hoc] *P* *om. cett.*

56

1 differunt] *codd.* differt *NE*
2 quia] *codd.* quod *NH*
3 excludendo] *codd.* removendo *NR*
4 sortes] *codd.* currit *add. NR*
5 extrahendo] *TNER* excludendo *cett.*
6 toto] *codd.* parte *T*
7 parte] *codd.* toto *T*

57

1 quia] *codd.* quod *RH*
2 et in contradictionibus] *codd.* et contradicentibus *H* *om. N*
3 ita] *codd.* prima *N*

4 principium] *codd.* primum principium *N*
5 compositionem] *codd.* exceptionem *N* coniunctionem *R*
6 ex ea] *codd.* eius *P*
7 sic etiam] *coni.* sic *H* etiam *P* tunc *TNRE*
8 qualiter] *codd.* quaque *P*
9 alio] *codd.* autem *add. PN* vero *add. H*
10 non] *codd. P^c* om. *P*
11 ita] *T* similiter *H* om. *cett.*
12 per impositionem] *TE* ex impositione *NR* de sua impositione *H* om. *P*
13 negationem] *E* negatione *R* negationes *cett.*
14 dictiones] *codd.* om. *P*
15 dictio] *P* om. *cett.*
16 negationem] *codd.* negatione *R*
17 cointelligendi] *TR* intelligendi *cett.*
18 quod] *codd.* quia *N*

58

1 potius fiat] *T* possit fieri *P* potius fit *cett.*
2 non] *codd.* om. *P*
3 instantivum] *codd.* intellectuum *add. R*
4 exclusivis] *H* exceptivis *cett.*
5 exceptivis] *H* consecutivis *R* exclusivis *cett.*
6 differenter] *codd.* differat *E*
7 quod] *TP* quia *NR* et *EH*
8 et] *T^cNR* om. *TEH*
9 ordinationem] *R* ordinem *cett.*
10 ad hanc dictionem] *codd.* ad hanc coni.unctionem *P^c* om. *P*
11 unde ... adversatio] *codd.* om. *H*
12 propter *P* per *cett.*
13 preiacenti] *P^cN* preessendi *(!)P* precedenti *cett.*

59

1 hec] *codd.* om. *P*
2 non et si] *codd.* si et non *P*
3 continuativa] *codd.* consecutiva *P*
4 nisi] *codd.* non *NR* ·
5 si ... currit] *codd.* non currit si non movetur *R*
6 transmutat] *codd.* transmittat *R* transmittit *E*
7 quia] *codd.* quam *P*

60

1 si autem queratur] *T* sed queritur *R* si queratur *cett.*
2 tribus] *codd.* hiis *P*
3 dictionum] *T^cNRH* om. *TPE*
4 dicendum] *codd.* et dicendum *T*
5 instantivis] *codd.* instantie *P*
6 quia ... dictionibus] *codd.* om. *H* quia] *codd.* et *PE*

7 hic] *codd.* ibi *N*

8 maxima] *codd.* maxime *E* minime *P*

9 exceptum] *codd.* exceptiva *RH*

10 bene] *NR* om. *cett.*

11 currat] *RH* currit *cett.*

12 et] *codd.* ex hoc add. *P*

13 homo] *E* omnis homo *N* aliquis homo *cett.*

14 non currat] *NR* non currit *TPH* currat *E*

15 non] *codd.* om. *E*

16 homo non currit] *codd.* om. *R* homo] *TPNE* aliquis homo] *TᶜPᶜ*

17 currit] *TEH* om. *PNR*

18 dictionibus contradicentibus] *Pᶜ* dictionibus *P* contradicentibus] *codd.*

61

1 quaslibet personas] *codd.* personas quascumque *T* personas *H*

2 quelibet] *PNR* qualibet *E* quecumque *TH*

3 quoslibet] *codd.* quoscumque *TH*

4 coni.unctio] *TER* dictio *P* om. *cett.*

5 tantum] *codd.* om. *EH*

6 subiunctivum] *codd.* subiunctivi *N*

7 negatio] *codd.* negatio absoluta *N*

8 hac] *codd.* om. *P*

9 in intellectu uno] *NH* intellectui uno *R* in intellectu *cett.*

10 et consecutione] *codd. Tᶜ* om. *T*

11 unitur in] unitur *PE* uniuntur in *cett.*

12 ideo] *codd.* om. *N*

13 ideo ... verbum] *codd.* om. *P*

14 debet determinare] *codd.* determinabit *NER*

15 respectiva] *codd.* absoluta *R*

16 determinabit] *PNR* determinare *T* om. *H*

17 respectivam sive] *T* om. *cett.*

18 dictio] *codd.* coni.unctio *EH*

19 subiunctivi] *codd.* coni.unctivi *TP*

62

1 verum] *codd. Pᶜ* om. *PE*

2 pro vero] *TNE* in vero *P* prout quod est *R* om. *H*

63

1 tunc] *PE* tamen *TN* om. *cett.*

2 improbationis] *codd. N* probationis *Nᶜ*

3 prius] *codd.* primum *NR*

4 videndum] *codd.* modum *R*

5 improbationi] *codd. N* probationi *Nᶜ* probari *R*

6 sensus prime] *codd.* est sensus *P*

7 in hoc] *Tᶜ* om. *E* in *cett.*

8 tempus] *codd.* aliud tempus *R*

9 iterum] *codd.* om. *T*

64

1 distinctione] *codd.* dictione *N*
2 prime] *RH* *om. cett.*
3 respondeo] *TE* respondendo *N* respondendum est *cett.*
4 improbationi] *codd.* per improbationem *E*
5 dicendo quod] *codd.* dicendo quia *N* dicendo *E*
6 ergo ... instanti] *codd.* *om. N*
7 non] *codd.* *om. EH*
8 sub] *codd.* in *NR*
9 distributione] *codd.* distinctione *R* disiunctione *E*
10 distributionis] *codd.* distinctionis *sic saepius E*
11 dico] *codd.* est *NR*
12 erat] *codd.* est *T*
13 improbationis] *codd.N* probationis *Nᶜ*
14 nisi] *codd.* sit verum *add. TPERH*
15 si non est] *codd.* nisi sit *T*
16 aliud] *codd.* argumentum *add. TPN*
17 animal] *codd.* alter *P*
18 homo] *codd.* animal *T*
19 ergo animal] *TNRH* alter *P* *om. E*
20 non] *codd.Pᶜ* *om. P*
21 si ... verum] *codd.Tᶜ* *om. T*
22 ergo ... instanti] *codd.Tᶜ* *om. T*
23 antecendens] *codd.Tᶜ* accidens *T* consequens *P*
24 sic] *codd.* similiter *T* *del. Tᶜ*
25 tamen] *codd.* *om. P*
26 quod] *codd.* quia *P*
27 ibi] *codd.* *om. TP*
28 ex negativo] *coni.* negatione *R* ex negatione *cett.*
29 negativo consequente] *coni.* negatione consequenti *TEH* ex
negatione consequente *PN* negatione *R*
30 si] *codd.* *om. R*
31 ergo est animal] *codd.Tᶜ* *om. T*
32 aut] *codd.* et *P*
33 ibi aliqua apparentia] *coni.* ibi aliqua *T* ibi apparentia *PNER* *om. H*
34 ibi] *TERH* secundum *P*

65

1 aliquis] *codd.* quidam *NR*

66

1 hoc modo] *codd.* hec *T*
2 sed] *codd.Tᶜ* *om. T*
3 in hoc sensu] *codd.* secundum hunc sensum *T*
4 quia] *Tᶜ* cum *H* *om. cett.*
5 utraque] *codd.* enim *add. PNR* ens (!) *add. E*
6 est] *codd.* sit *H*

7 non] *codd.* quod *N*
8 sed] *codd.* et *NR*

67

1 possibile] *codd. R^c* impossibile *R*
2 et ... impossibile] *codd.* om. *R*
3 possibile] *codd.* impossibile *T*
4 non mori] *T^cR* iam mori *NE* mori non *PH* mori *T*
5 vel] *codd.* et *N*
6 omnes] *TPEH* homines *NR*
7 semper] *codd.* sic antecedens est possibile et *H*
8 que] *codd.* erat add. *NR*

68

1 hec reduplicatio] *codd.* habere reduplicationem *(!)E*
2 intentiones] *codd.* rationes *E* interrogationes *(!)N*
3 ipsius] *codd.* eius *P*
4 extremitatem] *codd.* vel ad medium add. *E*
5 minorem] *codd.* extremitatem add. *T^c*
6 vel ad medium] *codd. T^c* om. *TE*

69

1 subiectis] *codd. P^c* primis *P* substantiis *E*
2 similitudinis] *codd.* similitudinum *P* similitudinem *E*
3 causam] *codd.* om. *P*
4 aliquando] *codd.* enim add. *T* autem add. *H*
5 corporis organici] *codd.* organica *N*
6 autem] *codd.* enim *E*
7 omnium eorum] *coni.* eorum *E* omnium *cett.*
8 et] *coni.* ut] *codd.*
9 imponit] *RH* imponat *N* importat *P* ponit *TE*
10 operationibus] *codd.* operibus *R*
11 earum] *codd.* eorum *PE*

70

1 differunt ... conveniunt] *codd.* om. *N*
2 aliqua] *codd.* om. *R*
3 contra] *codd.* om. *R*

71

1 interemptionem] *codd.* intentionem *R*
2 falsa] *codd.* falsum *P*
3 ad] *E* in *cett.*
4 unde] *codd.* ut *P*
5 homines] *codd.* et add. *P*
6 sive omnia] *TNR* sunt entia *PH*
7 sunt] *codd. T^c* om. *T* et add. *P*
8 eo quod sunt] *codd.* uno *P*

72

1 quis] *codd.* aliquis *N*
2 quia convenientia est] *TE* quod convenientia est *NR* quia conveniunt et *P* *om. H*
3 et] *codd.* etiam *P*
4 aliquam] *PNR* *om. cett.*
5 est] *codd.* quod *add. TEH*
6 conditio] *TᶜNR* contradictio *TPEH*
7 sortes] *codd.* est *add. TPNH* dicit *add. E*
8 est] *codd.* *om. TN*

73

1 alicuius] *codd.* intentione ea *add. P*
2 equivoco] *codd. Tᶜ* univoco *TP*
3 in aliquo] *TPNR* *om. cett.*
4 oppositum] *TPE* oppositorum *cett.*
5 eius] *TP* *om. cett.*

74

1 sint] *codd.* sunt *PE*
2 univocentur] *NER* univocantur *cett.*
3 aliquo] *codd.* *om. P* univoco *add. H*
4 univocari] *codd.* equivocari *P* uniri *N*
5 univocari] *codd.* uniri *N*
6 probatio] *TNER* equivocum *(!)P*
7 quod ... patet] *codd.* quod patet per rationem *E*
8 univocari] *codd.* uniri *N* equivoca univocari *H*
9 univocari ... sed] *codd.* uniri ... sed *N* *om. P*
10 quid] *codd.* et simpliciter sed secundum quid equivocari *add. P* et simpliciter equivocari *add N* et simpliciter univocari *add. R*
11 quia] *codd.* quod *N* omnia *R*
12 univocantur] *codd.* *om. N*
13 participant ... et] *codd.* equivoca nomen unum habent *E*

75

1 dicam] *TNCH* dicitur *P* dicantur *R* indicta *(!)E*
2 debet poni] *codd.* deponet *(!)R*
3 vel habeat] *PH* vel habet *TE* ut habet *NR*
4 animal] *codd.* anima *E*
5 pulmonem ... habet] *codd.* *om. H*
6 animal] *codd.* anima *E*

76

1 nota] *codd.* sic proceditur et nota *P* sic nota *N*
2 extremitatem] *T* *om. cett.*
3 exemplum aristotilis] *codd.* exemplum quod aristotiles ponit *E*
4 bonum] *codd.* bona *sic semper H*
5 iustitie] *E* cuiuslibet iustitie *cett.*

6 sic] *codd.* om. *N*
7 dicens] *codd.* dominus *(!)N*
8 predicari] *codd.* predicare *T* predicatur *R*
9 non intelligibile] *TᶜPNE* intelligibile *T* est intelligibile *R* intellige
H
10 ipsius] *Pᶜ* om. *P cett.*
11 comprehendere *E* apprehendere *cett.*
12 natura] *codd.* om. *T*
13 predicatum] *codd.* om. *N*
14 predicantur] *codd.* ponuntur *P*
15 ars] *coni.* ar [=aristoteles] *codd.*
16 substantiam] *codd.* subiectum *N*
17 eadem autem] *codd.* eadem est *N* eademque *E*
18 quia] *codd.* quod *N*
19 esset] *codd.* essent *N*

77

1 dicens] *codd.* dicentes *R*
2 ut] *codd.* om. *N*
3 predicentur] *TH* ponuntur *P* predicantur *cett.*
4 subiciantur] *TN* subiciuntur *cett.*
5 ordinationem] *T* ordinem *cett.*
6 predicamentalem] *codd.* predicabilium *E*
7 quia] *codd.* quod *R* qui *T*
8 linea] *codd.* prima linea *R*
9 predicamentali] *codd.* predicabili *E*
10 sic ... individua] *codd.* om. *P*
11 ad] *codd.* om. *R*
12 hoc] *codd.* in hoc *R* om. *N*
13 tunc] *codd.* om. *P*

78

1 in specie] *codd.* om. *P*
2 sunt species coni.unctionum] *codd.* sicut species numerorum *P*
3 inter] *codd.* in *P*
4 dictio] *TP* coni.unctio *cett.*
5 secundum priscianum] *codd.* a prisciano *P*
6 sub] *codd.* super *N*
7 sive sub] *TN* vel sub *R* vel *P* seu *H*
8 obmittamus] *codd.* obmittimus *P*
9 coni.unctionem] *codd.* dictionem *P*
10 secundo ... consequentiam] *codd.* om. *P* et dato ... consequentiam *Pᶜ*
11 queritur] *codd.* aliquam *H*
12 an consequentiam communiter] *codd.* communiter se habentem *H*
13 omnes] *codd.* alias *add. H*
14 sit] *codd.* est *T*
15 cum] *codd.* in *T*
16 dictio] *TPR* coni.unctio *cett.*
17 subiunctivi] *codd.* coni.unctivi *R*

79

1 obicitur] *codd.* autem queritur *N*
2 et] *codd.* et ille *H* om. *P*
3 coni.unctiones] *codd.* ille coni.unctiones *H*
4 consequentiam] *codd.* consequentias *T* essentiam *N*
5 aliquarum] *codd.* aliquas *T*
6 demonstrant] *TN* demonstrat *H* denominant *R* significant vel demonstrant *P*
7 consequentiam] *codd.* essentiam *N*
8 est] *codd.P^c* om. *P*
9 potest] *codd.* possit *P*
10 sed ... animali] *codd.* om. *P*
11 hominem] *codd.* et si homo non potest esse sine animali *add. P*
12 dictio] *codd.* om. *P*
13 sunt que] *codd.* quia *T*
14 supradictum] *codd.* supradicta *R*
15 de istis] *codd.* om. *T*
16 illativa] *codd.* dictio illativa *T*
17 lectionem] *T* lectiones *cett.*
18 consecutionem] *TPN* consequentiam *cett.*

80

1 est] *codd.* hec dictio quia *add. N*
2 obicit] *codd. T^c* om. *T*
3 ponitur] *codd.* recipiuntur vel ponuntur *N*
4 vera hec] *codd.* vere *N*
5 lectionem] *TN* lectiones *cett.*
6 simplex] *codd.* simpliciter PN
7 est consequentia] *codd.* vero convenientia *E*
8 ibo tecum] *codd.* dabo tibi equum *H*
9 sequitur ... ad] *T* oportet quod unum sequatur ad *cett.*

81

1 consecutio et antecessio] *codd.* antecessio et consecutio *H* antecedens et consequens *T*
2 ita] *codd.* ideo *P*
3 significat] *codd.* om. *N*
4 hoc] *codd.* om. *T*

82

1 vero] *N* om. *cett.*
2 consecutio] *codd.* consequens *R*
3 antecedente] *codd.* antecessione *H*
4 obicit] *PNE* obicitur *cett.*
5 conclusionem] *codd. T^c* consecutionem *TP*
6 ut ... quem] *codd. T^c* om. *T*
7 est sive] *codd.* sive est *N* sive sunt *R*
8 a termino] *codd.* ad terminum *T*

9 essentialius] *codd.* essentialis *N*
10 conclusionem] *codd.* consecutionem *P*
11 infert] *codd.* insunt *E*
12 propter] *codd.* per *N*
13 conclusio] *codd.* coni.unctio *sic semper E*
14 ut] *TN* non *E om. cett.*
15 et] *TEH* sive *PR* vel *N*
16 perfectivum] *codd.* perfectum *T*
17 hec] *codd.* om. *P*
18 habet] *codd.* tenet *H*
19 consecutionem] *codd.* conclusionem *R*
20 ad] *codd.* om. *N*

83

1 et ... cognitionem] *codd.* om. *N*
2 cognitionem] *codd.* conclusionem *R* connitionem *(!)P*
3 cognitionis] *codd.* consecutionis *P* conclusionis *R*
4 ipse] *codd.* iste *P*
5 suam] *codd.* om. *N*
6 substantie] *codd.* om. *N*
7 descinditur] *P* decinditur *(!)NC^c* deciditur *TCH* deciduntur *E* dicitur *R*
8 enim] *codd.* autem *T*
9 a] *TPNR* ex *cett.*
10 ex] *codd. T^c* om. *T*
11 coni.unctio] *NE* conclusio *cett.*
12 materia] *codd.* sua *add. TERCH*
13 <ad> medium ordinatur utraque extremitas] *coni.* medium ordinem *(!)* utramque extremitatem *R* medium ordinantur *(!)* inter utramque extremitatem *NC* medium ordinatur intra *(!)* utraque *(!)* extremitatem *H* medium ordinatum inter utramque extremitatem *TPE*
14 educitur substantia] *codd.* aducitur substantie *(!)R*
15 non] *codd.* termino *E*
16 materia] *codd.* causa materialis *CH*
17 modis] *codd.* om. *ER*
18 capra] *codd.* homo *T*
19 homo] *codd.* capra *T*
20 cognitionem] *codd.* conclusionem *sic saepius R*
21 sunt] *N* causa *add. TER* causa efficiens *add. PCH*

84

1 sed ... tantum] *codd.* om. *N*
2 est tantum] *PCH* est *TE* econverso *R*
3 simplex] *codd.* simpliciter *N*
4 consecutionem] *codd.* conclusionem *R* compositionem consecutionem *N*
5 alia] *codd.* autem *add. P* vero *add. NERCH*
6 econtrario] *codd.* econverso *PR*
7 consequentiam] *codd.* convenientiam *sic saepius E*

8 huius ... simplex]*codd. om. N*
9 est]*codd. om. P*
10 sive ... consequentiam]*codd. om. R* sive consecutio]*TPNE om. cett.*
11 vero]*codd.* autem *P*
12 alias]*T om. cett.*
13 consequentiam]*codd. om. N*
14 ideo]*codd.* non *N om. E*
15 aliquando]*codd.* autem *add. P* vero *add. cett.*

85

1 quod]*codd.* quia *N*
2 ex]*codd.* a *N*
3 adverbio]*codd.P^c* verbo *P*
4 dictio]*codd. om. E*
5 composita]*TEH om. cett.*
6 trahat]*codd.* contrahit *P*
7 a]*P* ex *cett.*
8 dicimus]*T* dicendum *cett.*
9 dictio]*TNH* coni.unctio *cett.*
10 dictio]*codd.* coni.unctio *E om. H*
11 impositionis]*codd.* compositionis *N*
12 ex hoc]*TERC* ex *PN* hoc *H*
13 unde]*codd.* et *P*
14 dicimus]*T* dicendum *cett.*
15 composita]*codd.* quam *R*
16 sed]*E* quia *cett.*
17 compositiones]*codd.* significationes et compositiones *E*
18 ut quapropter]*codd.* utraque propter *(!)E*
19 ex verbis ... adverbio]*codd.* ex adverbio *N*
20 verbo ut quamvis]*codd.* nomine ut quia *E*
21 hoc etiam]*codd.* et hoc etiam *R* hec autem *P*
22 maiori]*codd.* minori *NE*
23 prepositiones]*codd.* propositiones *TR*
24 que]*codd.* quod *R*
25 causalium]*TERC* casualium *PH om. N*

86

1 significationem suam]*codd.* compositionem *P*
2 hec dictio]*TPCH om. NER*
3 quia]*TNR* quod *cett.*
4 multipliciter]*codd.* multipliciter non *N om. T*
5 componentium ... compositus]*T^c* componentium sit unus intellectus compositus *TR* componentium fit intellectus compositus *N* compositio fit unius compositi *PE* componentium sit intellectus composita *(!)H^c* sit intellectus composita *H*
6 compositum]*codd.* oppositum *N*
7 est]*codd.* ex nomine *add. P*
8 quare]*codd.P^c* quam *P*
9 est]*codd.* adverbium *add. P*

10 componentium]*TN* compositum *E* compositorum *cett.*
11 magnanimus centimanus]*codd.* magnus *(!)* cotidianus *P*
12 componentium]*codd.* compositis *P*
13 habitudinibus]*codd.* comparationibus *P* ex compositionibus *R*
14 ex comparationibus]*codd.* comparationibus *P* ex compositionibus *R*
15 duo]*codd.* *om. P*
16 dicunt]*codd.* habent *P*
17 ratione]*codd.* *om. PR*
18 causalitatis]*codd.* causalis *P*
19 adverbialis]*codd.* *om. P*
20 compositionem]*H* compositio *R* comparationem *cett.*
21 sic]*codd.* *om. NR*
22 cause]*TPC* cause vel causale *E* esse *R* *om. NH*
23 multipliciter]*codd.* materialiter *R* vel *P*
24 suam]*codd.* *om. P*
25 ideo]*codd.* tunc *E*
26 quod]*codd.* quid *N*
27 ex eo]*codd.* *om. P*

87

1 coni.unctio vero]*TNH* coni.unctio *PR* ergo non *(!)E*
2 associationem]*codd.* affectionem *P*
3 substantiarum quam accidentium]*codd.* substantialium *H*
4 significatur]*codd.* significat *P*
5 coni.unctio]*TP* dictio *cett.*
6 hoc]*codd.* *om. P*
7 quia]*codd.* quod quia *P*
8 coni.unctionis]*TRH* dictionis *cett.*
9 que est]*codd.* et *P*
10 non]*codd.* et ideo non *P*
11 immo]*T* sed est *cett.*
12 ratione]*codd.* opera *(!)N*
13 comparationis]*TE* compositionis *cett.*
14 ut]*codd.* vel *P* sive *H*
15 ipsi]*TE* isti *cett.*
16 impresentiarum]*codd.* impresentialiter *N*
17 non ex]*TE* autem non ex *PR* ex non *NH*
18 componentium]*codd.* *om. N*

88

1 quia qui]*codd.* quod *P*
2 idem est]*codd.* significat idem *E* idem significat *H^c* *om. H*
3 ostis]*TECH* hostis *P* OC idest OCTIS TIS *N* OCDYS *(!) R*
4 et os est]*TN* et oc est *R* quia os est *P* os *E* quod est *H*
5 tis]*codd.* tys *R* tix *(!)E* tis quod *H*
6 significat]*codd.* est significans *P*
7 hanc]*codd.* *om. P*

8 non ergo convertuntur]*EH* ergo non convertuntur *TP* non ergo hoc convertitur *R* ergo non convertitur *N* nec unum sequitur ad aliud *add. E*
9 ita]*codd.* prima *N*
10 supponit]*codd.* ponit *E*
11 et]*codd.* solutio *P*
12 quod]*codd. T^c om. T*
13 non convertuntur]*codd. P^c* convertuntur *P* consequuntur *H*
14 aliam]*T* alteram *cett.*
15 ut]*codd.* unde *N*
16 quod ... venias]*codd. om. H*
17 autem]*codd. om. P*
18 quod non]*codd.* quin *P*

89

1 per]*codd. om. P*
2 aliquod antecedens]*codd.* aliquid antecedens *R* aliquid *P*
3 precedat]*codd.* consequens *add. P*
4 recordatio]*codd.* relatio *P*
5 relativum]*NH* relationem *TER* recordationem *P*
6 vel]*codd.* et *H* secundum *N*
7 suppositis]*codd.* supponentis *N*
8 discretionem]*codd.* dissociationem *R* dictionem *E*
9 supposito]*codd.* suppositis *T*
10 sumitur]*codd.* est *T*
11 ipsum]*codd.* suppositum *add. P*
12 eo]*codd. om. N*
13 suppositi]*codd.* sumpti *N*
14 suppositum]*codd.* suppositionem *N*
15 autem]*codd.* est *N*
16 quia]*codd.* quod *N*
17 coni.unguntur]*codd.* adiunguntur *H*
18 non]*codd.* ut *N*
19 compositionem]*codd. P^c* dictionem *P*
20 neque]*codd.* per *add. P*
21 cum]*codd.* in *N*
22 oratione]*codd.* dictione *P* coni.unctione *E*

90

1 alia est]*codd.* aliud autem *N*
2 prout sumitur relative]*codd.* inquantum habet naturam nominis *N*
3 tyrampnum *(!)E*
4 premium accipiet]*codd.* ipsum vim *(!)* accipit *R*
5 dicebat]*codd.* significat *P*

91

1 obiciebatur]*E* obiciatur *RCH* obicitur et obiciatur *N* queritur *P* obicitur *TC*

2 solvatur] *codd.* solvitur *P*
3 coni.unctione] *codd.* dictione *P*
4 erat] *TE* erit *cett.*
5 alteram negativam] *codd.* alterius negationem *E*
6 vel ... affirmationem] *codd. T^c* om. *T*
7 ut non] *codd.* tamen *P*
8 cum] *codd. T^c* om. *T*
9 sequitur] *codd.* sequatur *P*
10 econtrario] *PRCH* econtrarione ergo (!)*N* econverso *TE*

92

1 tu] *codd.* om. *PN*
2 sis] *codd.* sit *NR*
3 ergo ... asinus] *codd. T^c* om. *T* ergo tu] *codd.* om. *N*
4 communiter] *codd.* quosdam *E*
5 dicunt enim] *codd.* om. *P*
6 negare] *codd.* negatio *P*
7 vere] *codd. T^c* om. *TH*
8 negationem huius proferre] *T^{c}N* negationem proferre *TP* negare *R* negative proferre *HC*
9 et ... asinum] *codd.* om. *P*
10 negationem] *codd.* negare idest tu non potes vere negationem *R*
11 quia] *codd.* quod *R*
12 que] *codd.* quia *P* quod *R* et *HC*

93

1 hec solutio] *codd.* adhuc illa *P*
2 potentia activa] *codd.* potestate activa *E* potentia *H*
3 negativum] *TE* negativa *cett.* ub ab anima *add. R^m*
4 potentia] *codd.* potestas *E*
5 vero] *codd.* autem *P*
6 in quod] *N* ad quod *H* in quo *cett.*
7 actio illius] *NE* actus *TPR* actus illius potentie *H*
8 ipsius] *TE* om. *N* illius *cett.*
9 easdem] *TPE* easdem et *NRC* illas eadem et *H*
10 obiectum] *codd.* subiectum *T*
11 cuiuscumque obiecti] *TP* cuiuslibet obiecti *E* cuius obiecti *NH* cui obiecto *R*
12 activa] *T* om. *cett.*
13 negativum] *codd.* negativa *P*
14 qui] *codd.* quem *N*
15 potentia] *codd.* que est negativum *add. TE* quod est negativum *add. NR* que est negantis *H*
16 quia ... subiecto] *codd. T^c* om. *T*
17 erit] *codd.* est *P*
18 univocum] *T* non equivocum *PER^c* non est equivocum *H* equivocum *NR*
19 videre] *codd.* currere *R*
20 est equivocum] *T* equivocatur *cett.*

21 visionem] *T* *om. cett.*
22 negare] *T* negandum *PERH* negationem *N*
23 quodlibet predicatum] *codd.* cuiuslibet predicati *N*
24 hanc] *codd.* scilicet *add. N*
25 negabatur] *PERC* negatur *NH* removetur *T*
26 prius] *EH* *om. cett.*
27 in ... asinus] *codd. T^c* *om. T*
28 removebatur] *coni.* removeatur *RC* removetur *cett.*
29 predicatum] *codd.* *om. N*
30 ergo non] *T^c* *om. N* non *cett.*
31 ergo ... nichil dicunt] *codd.* *om. T*
32 dicunt] *codd.* est dictu *R*
33 in casibus] *codd. T^c* in talibus *R* *om. T*
34 ergo ... preparativo] *codd.* *om. PC* et sic de aliis *add. omnes codices,* quae quidem verba *del. T^c*
35 et econverso] *codd. T* *del. T^c*
36 de ... preparativo] *T* *om. cett.* et sic de aliis et econverso si sanare dicitur multipliciter *add. TC*
37 sanativum] *codd.* et *add. PNR*
38 dicetur] sanativum dicetur *P* sanare dicetur *N* sanare dicitur *ER* dicitur *TH*
39 de eisdem] *codd.* eisdem *R* de eis *T*
40 casualium] *coni.* casuum *PEC* casum *cett.*
41 non] *codd.* *om. P*
42 sed] *codd.* sed si *N*
43 negativum] *NE* negatio *T* negatum *cett.*
44 dicitur] *codd.* dicatur *N*
45 ergo] *codd.* *om. NR*
46 a casibus] *codd. T^c* *om. T*
47 ad idem] *codd.* *om. P*
48 oratio] *codd.* ratio *P*
49 secundo sensu] *TE* sensu secundo *P* eodem sensu *cett.*
50 sic] *codd.* *om. N*
51 non] *codd. T^c* *om. T*

94

1 dicimus] *codd.* dicendum *H*
2 constructiones] *T^cNER* diversas constructiones *T* coni.unctionem *PR*
3 construitur] *codd.* constituitur *R*
4 in] *codd.* *om. P*
5 in] *codd.* *om. P*
6 quod] *codd.* quia *N* hoc quod *E*
7 sive te neges esse] *T* si te neges *P* si neges te esse *N* sive neges te esse *cett.*
8 brutum] *codd.* hoc autem *E*
9 hoc] *codd.* non *add. T^c*
10 diversa ratione] *T* diversitate *cett.*

95

1 illud] *codd.* aliud *N*
2 quin et quod non] *T* quod non et quia *cett.*
3 non] *codd.* om. *P*
4 sicut] *T* ut *cett.*
5 consecutionem] *codd.* consequentiam *T* secundam *add. Tᵐ*
6 sed ego] *codd.* si *N*
7 conclusionem secundam] *codd.* orationem *P* esse falsam *add. N*
8 esse] *codd.* et esse *N*
9 predictam] *codd.* et *add. PR* primam et *add. N*
10 consecutionem] *coni.* consequentiam *codd.*
11 quod non] *codd.* quin *P*
12 tu ... negare] *T* om. *cett.*
13 ergo ... asinus] *codd.* om. *TH*
14 falso] *codd.* hoc falso *P*
15 bene] *codd. Tᶜ* om. *T*
16 sicut] *codd.* quo *P*
17 fiat] *codd.* fuit *P*
18 constructio] *PNH* conclusio *TR* coni.unctio *E*
19 ille] *codd.* om. *T*
20 conclusiones] *codd.* orationes *P*
21 et] *codd.* sed *T*
22 non] *PE* om. *cett.*
23 non] *PEH* om. *cett.*
24 sis] *codd.* sit *T*
25 einsdem] *codd. Tᶜ* om. *T*
26 negare] *codd.* negative *R*
27 respectu] *T* sensu *cett.*
28 deberet] *PR* deberes *N* debet *cett.*
29 infert sic] *codd.* inferret sic *R* est inferre *H*
30 non] *codd.* om. *N*

96

1 probo] *TPNE* probatio *RCH*
2 tu] *codd.* non tu *E*
3 esse] *codd. Tᶜ* non esse *T*
4 si] *codd.* om. *N*
5 vere negare] *codd.* enuntiare *N*
6 potes] *NRᶜ* non potes *R cett.*
7 non] *codd.* om. *PR*
8 non] *codd. Rᶜ* om. *TR*
9 prima] *codd.* om. *N*

97

1 illatione] *codd.* illa ratione *R*
2 vere] *codd. Tᶜ* om. *T*
3 affirmare] *TPH* negare *NERC*
4 et ... tamen] *codd.* om. *R*

5 negare] *codd.* affirmare *N*
6 enuntiare] *codd.* om. *N*
7 hoc] *ER* hec *PN* om. *cett.*
8 affirmare] *codd.* affirmativa *P*
9 affirmare] *codd.* enuntiare *R*
10 esse] *codd.* non esse *P*
11 illud] *TP* ipsum *cett.*
12 deberet] *TER* deberes *N* debet *cett.*
13 negare] *codd.* om. *N*
14 esse] *codd. T^c* non esse *T*
15 enuntiare] *codd.* esse natura *(!)R*
16 contrahatur] *TPNE* contrahebatur *R* contrahitur *H* contra habeat *(!)C*
17 visu] *codd.* visum *P*
18 vero] *codd.* autem *P*
19 gustu idem est] *codd.* ergo tu non idem es *(!)P*
20 actus] *codd.* auditus *N*
21 vero] *codd.* scilicet *add. P*
21 actus] *codd. P^c* obiectus *P*
22 ut ... dupliciter] *codd.* om. *R*
23 dupliciter] *TH* om. *PN*
24 affirmative] *TNR* affirmationem *cett.*
25 negative] *coni.* negationem *codd.*
26 item ... obiecti] *codd. T^c* om. *T* item] *codd.* vel *P*
27 facta] *T^cPNR* om. *T* secunda *cett.*

98

1 nullo] *codd.* illo *E*
2 ipsum] *codd.* ipsius *H*
3 necessarium] *codd.* asinum necessarium *(!)E*
4 nullo] *codd.* illo *E*
5 necessarium] *codd.* esse necessarium *P*
6 quocumque] *codd.* quolibet *TP*
7 et] *T* quia *P* om. *cett.*
8 quocumque] *codd.* quolibet *T*
9 et] *T* om. *cett.*

99

1 nullo] *codd.* illo *E*
2 si non sit] *TH* ut si non est *E* si non est *cett.*
3 ad ... generis] *codd.* negatio speciei non sequitur ad negationem generis *P* speciei *add. E*
4 ipsum ... esse] *codd.* om. *N*
5 propositio] *codd.* probatio *N*
6 primo] *codd.* primum *P* prius *R*
7 scilicet hec] *codd.* om. *T*
8 negando] *codd.* cum negatione *R*
9 visibile] *codd.* universale *R*

TRACTATUS NONUS

DE 'QUANTO', 'QUAM' ET 'QUICQUID'

1

1 que incidunt] *T^cPERC* que incurrunt *N* *om. TH*
2 ergo] *codd.* autem *P*
3 quanto] *codd.* quantum *P*
4 cui] *codd.* sibi *N*
5 cum notatione] *coni.* cum consignificatione *H* cognitione *TE* cogitatione *R* cognitionem *N* connitionem (!)*P* agritione (!)*C*
6 istarum rerum] *codd.* ista Rerum *R*
7 relative] *codd.* respective *R*
8 tanto] *codd.* quanto *T*
9 profeci] *NH* profecisti *T^cPR* fecisti *T* perfecisti *E*
10 eadem] *codd.* hac *P*
11 quanto] *codd.* quantum *P*
12 proficiam] *codd.* perficiam *E*
13 nullo] *codd.* nullum *T*
14 trium] *codd.* *om. T*
15 calor] *codd.* color *sic semper PE*
16 aliquando] *codd.* quando *E* *om. T*
17 calor] *TNH* color *PER*
18 calefaciendi] *codd.* calidi *T*
19 intensius calefacit] *codd.* intensio calefaciendi *R* intensius calefaciendo *E*
20 citius] *codd.* fortius *E*
21 infunditur et] *codd.* *om. N*
22 premium] *codd. T^c* primum *N* *om. T*
23 labor] *codd. T^c* *om. T*
24 tolleratur (!)] *codd.* tolatur *R* relascatur *T*

2

1 quanto magis ... *etc*] *capp.* 2–3 *et* 4–5 *inverso ordine in H*
2 addiscis] *codd. H^c* addicis *PH* addiscit *N*
3 *bis* augmentatur] *codd.* amittitur (!) *E*
4 iterum] *codd.* locus *P*

3

1 quia] *codd.* et *P* et Improbatio bene tenet quia *H*
2 quod] *codd. T^c* quam *N* *om. T*
3 sit] *TH* est *cett.*
4 possit] *codd.* esse *add. PR*
5 sicut] *codd.* scilicet sicut *P*

6 submersionis] *coll. Aristot.* subversionis *E* eversionis *cett.*
7 sed] *codd.* quia *P*
8 remota] *codd. H^c* proxima *P* *om. H*
9 submersionis] emersionis *TE* eversionis *cett.*
10 eius] *codd.* navis *P*
11 quod] *codd.* que *PN*
12 maius ... quantitatibus] *codd.* *om. E*
13 quantitatibus] *codd.* qualitatibus *H*
14 magis] *TPER* maius *cett.*
15 a qualitatibus] *TPN* a qualibus *E* aqua *(!)R* quantitatibus *H*
16 dictionis] *codd.* *om. T*
17 mutando] *codd.* in mutando (*?pro* immutando) *T* multipliciter *(!)R*
18 quantitates] *codd.* qualitatis *T*
19 qualitatis] *codd.* quantitatis *T*
20 quantum] *codd.* vel quod *add. N* vel *add. R* quot *add. E*

4

1 sed ... videtur] *codd.* *om. N* sed] *codd.* et *TH*
2 contra] *codd.* quanto aliquid maius est etc. *add. P*
3 assignatur] *T* significatur esse *NRH^c* significatur est *(!)H*
4 quod] *codd.* que *P*
5 oratio] *codd.* *om. N*

5

1 esse] *codd.* omne *E*
2 maius] *codd.* *om. T*
3 videri] *codd. T^c* videre *T*
4 visus] *codd.* visio *P* *om. H*
5 coloratum] *codd.* toto *(!)R*
6 lucidum] *codd.* actus lucidus *H^c* lucidus *H*
7 aer] *codd.* vel aer *N*
8 vel] *TP* et mediante *cett.*
9 minima] *codd.* nimia *P* in minia *(!)R*
10 oculum] *codd.* ocultum *(!)R*
11 aliquando] *T* aut *cett.*
12 congregata] *T* agregata *cett.*
13 maius] *codd.* magius *(!)N*
14 debitam] *codd.* debitum *PE*
15 ponatur] *codd.* oppositum [*?an pro* opponatur] *E*

6

1 autem] *codd.* etiam *R* *om. P*
2 distinctione] *EH* diffinitione *PNRC*
3 secunda] *codd.* secundo *P*
4 importet] *P* importat *cett.*
5 tertia] *codd.* tertio *P* dictam *(!)R*
6 nomen] *codd.* unum *R* naturam *E*
7 quarta] *codd.* quarto *P* quarta questio *E*

8 fortior] *codd.* sor *(!)N*
9 quinta vero] *codd.* quinto *P* quinto vero *R*
9 quando] *PRC* quam *E* quoniam *H* cum *N*
10 comparativo] *PNC* comparatio *E* comparatione *R* nominativo *H*
11 sexta questio] *codd.* sexta qutem *P*
12 aliquando ... aliquando] *codd.* *om. P*
13 aliquando] *codd.* autem *add. NE*
14 quam] *codd.* quanam *N* aliquando cum ablativo *add. P*

7

1 fecit] *codd.* facit *E*
2 preclara] *codd.* prelata *R*
3 deus israel] *RCH* israel deus *PE* israel deus rex *N*
4 que] *codd.* quia *N*
5 quando] *PNE* que *RCH*
6 aliquid] *codd.* alium *R*
7 dives] *codd.* duos *(!)E*
8 positis] *codd.* potius *E*
9 esse] *codd.* *om. P*
10 relinquendo] *codd.* removendo *R*
11 similiter] *codd.* sumitur *R* *om. H*
12 hic hec] *coni.* hic *E* hec *cett.*

8

1 respectus] *codd.* terminus *R*
2 comparatum] *codd.* comparationem *PN*
3 cui] *codd.* ubi *E*
4 illud] *codd.* idem *R*
5 fortior] *codd.* sor *(!)R*
6 et ... comparatur] *codd.* *om. NE*
7 respectum] *codd.* *om. R*
8 comparatum] *PR* quod comparatur *cett.*
9 unde] *codd.* ut *R*
10 habet] *PNER* dicit *H*
11 respectum] *codd.* tantum *R*
12 ipsius] *codd.* tempus ipsi *(!)E*
13 excessus] *codd.* processus *N*
14 ablativo] *codd.* P^c accusativo *P*
15 sic] *NE* ita *H* nunc *R* *om. P*
16 sicut] *codd.* *om. NE*
17 et] *codd.* ad *P*
18 maioritatis] *codd.* maioris *PN*
19 quam] *codd.* quod *N*
20 respectum] *codd.* vorum *R*
21 excedens] *coni.* excedentes *P* excessum *cett.*
22 maioritatis] *codd.* maioris *PN*
23 comparativum] *codd.* comparationem *N*
24 sine mensura] *codd.* sive mensuram *NE*
25 excedens comparatum] *coni.* excessum comparativi *codd.*

26 illud]*PER* etiam *NH*
27 a comparato]*coni.* a comparativo *PH* comparativo *N* comparatio *ER*

9

1 nominativo quod]*PNR* nostro *(!)E* termino *C* et *H*
2 comparativum]*PNRC* comparationem sive ad comparativum *H* comparationem *E*
3 alicuius]*codd.* alterius *H*

10

1 respectum]*codd.* respectu *E*
2 potest]*codd.* potuit *N*
3 terminare]*codd.* determinare *P*
4 rationem]*codd.* nomen *E*
5 ut]*codd.* nisi *E*

11

1 ab]*ERCH* in *PN*
2 sive]*PNR* simul *E* vel *CH*
3 comparatur]*codd.* componitur *E*
4 alium]*codd.* illum *N*
5 idest quam plato]*codd.* *om. H*

12

1 exceditur]*codd.* excedatur *P*
2 ordinatur]*codd.* comparatur *N*
3 ipso]*codd.* uno *N*
4 comparativum]*codd.* comparatum *NH*
5 comparato]*N* comparatio *E* comparativo *PRCH*
6 re]*codd.* ratione *E*
7 stat]*codd.* fuit *P*
8 ut ... eius]*coni.* in ratione eius aut *R* in ratione eius ut *cett.*
9 quo]*codd.* qua *P*
10 aliquid]*codd.* quis *E*
11 termini a quo]*codd.* ut aqua *(!)N*
12 quando]*codd.* *om. R*
13 inquantum est excessa]*codd.* *om. P*
14 etiam]*codd.* ita *P*
15 alium]*codd.* istum *P*
16 alium]*codd.* istum *P*
17 advenit supra]*codd.* significat *(!)R*
18 primam]*codd.* *om. N*
19 semper]*CH* *om. PNR*
20 stat]*codd.* constat *P*
21 et ... quam]*codd.* *om. R*
22 sic]*codd.* *om. N*
23 propter quid]*codd.* *om. N*

24 comparativus] *codd.* *om. P*
25 comparativus] *RCH^c* compositum *(!)PNH*
26 quando|*P* quod *cett.*
27 uno ... cum] *codd.* *om. P*

13

1 ergo ... scis|*codd.* *om. N*
2 prima falsa] *codd.* hec est falsa impossibile est scire plura quam scis *N*

14

1 potentia est] *codd.P^c* *om. P*
2 quia] *codd.* *om. N*
3 alicuius] *codd.* et respectu actus essentialis ut respectu forme completive *add. P*
4 dicit]*P* ponit *cett.*
5 quia|*codd.* vel *P*
6 essentialis] *codd.* accidentalis *R*
7 ut ... ut] *codd.* et *P*
8 egredientis] *codd.* egretudinis *P*
9 rem suam]*H* relationem *PRC* relationem suam *N*
10 accusativi] *codd.* *om. H*
11 sic] *codd.* *om. P*
12 prima] *codd.* *om. H*
13 potest ponere]*N* potes ponere *R* non potest ponere *P* ponit *H*
14 vera] *codd.* falsa *P*
15 scies plura]*P* scis plura *NE* plura scis *H* suos *(!)* plura *R*
16 scis] *codd.* scies *R* *om. N*

15

1 asinum|*codd.* animal asinum *P*
2 et est]*PR* et *R om. H*

16

1 relativum]*PNH* verbum alius *(!)R*
2 aliud]*PH* scilicet aliud *N* *om. R*
3 rem aliquam aliam]*N* rem aliquam *PR* aliam rem *H*
4 nominativi] *codd.* nomen *R*
5 idest] *codd.* et *P*

17

1 ideo]*H* *om. PNR*
2 determinari] *codd.* determinandi *R*
3 quoad]*PNR* in *H*
4 consecutionem]*N* coniunctionem *PR* distributionem in se *H*
5 disiunctione]*P* distinctione *NR* consecutione *H*
6 de ipsa in]*N* in ipsa in *P* de ipsa *R* in *H*

18

1 primum]*codd.* sic proceditur et *add. P*
2 quilibet]*NH* quodlibet *R* quicquid *P*
3 per]*codd.* et *P*
4 quicquid]*codd.* quicumque *P*
5 est]*codd.* sua *add. P*
6 sive]*PNR* si *H*
7 illud]*codd.* currit movetur *add. H*
8 consecutio]*coni.* consequentia *PNRC* disiunctio *H*
9 disiunctio]*PRC* distributio *N* et consecutio sive consequentia *H*

19

1 circa secundum]*codd.* secundo *N*
2 intelligantur]*codd.* significantur *P*
3 significatione ... quicquid]*codd.* hac dictione quicquid sive in eius significatione *H*
4 consecutione]*codd.* dictione *P*
5 semper]*H* simpliciter *PRC* *om. N*

20

1 quia]*NR* quod *PH*
2 et]*RCH* vel *P* *om. N*
3 illud]*N* id *PRC* *om. H*
4 geminationem]*codd.* generationem *R*
5 quid]*codd.* *om. P*
6 quod]*codd.* *om. N*
7 interrogativum]*codd.* nomini legativum *(!)R*
8 etiam]*codd.* cum est *P*
9 oporteret]*N* oportet *cett.*
10 intelligatur]*NH* *om. cett.*

21

1 scivit]*codd.* scit *P*
2 scit]*codd.* sed scivit te esse nasciturum ergo scit te [*N 83va*] nasciturum ergo tu es nasciturus *add. N* sed scivit te esse nasciturum ergo scit te esse nasciturum ergo tu es nasciturus *add. R*
3 contra ... nasciturus]*codd.* *om. N* contra ... scit]*codd.* *om. R*
4 scivit]*codd.* nascivit *(!)R*
5 esse]*P* fore *H* *om. R*
6 scit ... ergo]*codd.* *om. H*
7 te]*codd.* deus *add. P*
8 nasciturum ... nasciturus]*codd.* *om. R*

22

1 semper]*codd.* simpliciter *P*
2 transmutationem]*codd.* mensurationem *P*
3 immobilem]*PH* immutabilem *NRC*
4 ergo ... immobilem]*codd.* *om. P*

5 immobilem]*H* impermutabilem *RC* permutabilem *N*
6 suum]*codd.* sui *N*
7 ipsa]*codd.* ipso *P*
8 sciendum quod]*P* est quia *R* quod *N* *om. H*
9 scientia rerum]*codd.* *om. H*
10 mutationem]*PN* permutationem *R*

23

1 secundum]*codd.* per *P*
2 commutatione]*PH* mutatione *R* commune *(!)N*
3 assumendo]*codd.* assumpto *R*
4 quicquid]*codd.* quid *N*
5 et etiam est ibi]*coni.* et est ibi *P* et etiam ibi *NR* etiam est ibi *H*
6 accidentis]*codd.* antecedentis *R*
7 quid]*R* quicquid *PNH*
8 motivam]*codd.* *om. N*
9 quid]*PR* quicquid *NH*
10 scilicet]*codd.* *om. N*
11 circumscripto]*codd.* scripto *R*
12 in re]*PNR* a parte rei *H*
13 quod]*codd.* *om. R*
14 predicamentalium]*R* medicabilium *cett.*
15 sunt]*T* *om. cett.*
16 Si]*T* si *PNH* *om. R*
17 sic fit]*TP* sic est *N* fit *H*
18 isti idem modi]*PN* illi modi *TR* idem modi *H*
19 sive]*codd.* *om. T*
20 vero]*codd.* *om. P*

TRACTATUS DECIMUS

DE RESPONSIONIBUS

1

1 sequitur] *codd.* ad *add. C*
2 interrogante] *codd.* interrogatione *C*
3 ut a] *codd.* tamquam a *H* ut *N*
4 interrogatio] *codd.* responsio *P*
5 per interrogantem] *T* per interrogationem *PR* per responsionem *NC* precedit responsionem et *H^c* responsionem *H*
6 suam] *codd.* om. *T*
7 interrogans] *codd.* interrogationis *R*
8 est] *codd.* om. *T*
9 est] *codd.* om. *N*
10 formare] *codd.* scire *P*
11 interrogationes] *codd.* argumentationes *H*
12 secundum] *T* per *cett.*
13 ut ad respondentem] *codd.* om. *P*
14 improbabilia] *codd.* probabilia *PR*
15 facere] *codd.* tenere *P*

2

1 solutionis] *TPN* solutionum *RC* responsionis *H*
2 solutionum] *codd.* solutionem *N* solutio *R*
3 alia] *TPCH* om. *cett.*
4 vero] *codd.* om. *P*
5 apparens] *N* sed apparens *cett.*
6 ad interrogantem] *P* ad interrogationem *TNRH* ab interrogatione *C*
7 ut] *codd.* unde *R*
8 interrogans] *P* opponens *cett.*
9 ad tempus] *codd.* a tempore *P*
10 ut quando] *codd.* unde *R*
11 ipsum propositum] *codd.* propositum huius *R^c* propositum *R*
12 eget] *codd.* indiget *P*
13 pessima] *codd.* passiva *N*
14 solutionum] *NH* om. *TPR*
15 apparentium] *codd.* apparens *P*

3

1 solutio ad orationem] *T* ad orationem solutio *H* solatio ad dictionem *N* ad orationem *R* ad rationem *P*
2 etiam] *T* om. *cett.*
3 quid] *codd.* om. *T* accidat falsum sive propter quid *add. H*

4 quia alia] *TNR* alia *P* una quidem *H*
5 vero] *codd.* om. *P*
6 divisionem] *codd.* diffinitionem *C*
7 unde ... extra dictionem] *codd.* om. *R*
8 que] *codd.* quod *N*
9 falsis] *codd.* sillogismis *P*
10 solutio] *codd.* vero *add.* TP autem *add.* C
11 divisionem] *codd.* dictionem *N*
12 debetur orationi] *codd.* om. *P*
13 peccanti] *codd.* procedenti *P*

4

1 orationem] *codd.* dictionem *P*
2 quoniam si est] *codd.* quia falsa *H*
3 sic] *codd.* si *R*
4 probabitur] *TNC* probatur *PRH*
5 fallaciam] *codd.* falsa *H*
6 aut] *coni.* vel *Hᶜ* et *H* cett.
7 et] *codd.* om. *P*

5

1 terminatis] *TRC* determinatis *PNH*
2 que] *codd.* qui *R*
3 dicuntur] *codd.* dividuntur *R*
4 secundo] *codd.* et sexto *add.* PNRCH
5 etiam] *codd.* om. *PN*
6 secunde] *codd.* om. *N*

6

1 propriam] *codd.* primam *N*
2 conversam ... proprie conclusionis] *codd.* particularem proprie
conclusionis et concludant conversam sue conclusionis *T*
3 est] *codd.* om. *T*
4 infert] *codd.* insunt *R*
5 sic] *codd.* om. *N*
6 nullum] *codd.Hᶜ* nullam *H* sillogismum *R*
7 sue ... particularem] *codd.* om. *N*
8 proprie] *codd.* om. *T*

7

1 positis] *codd.* posito *P*
2 negativi] *codd.* negative *P*
3 affirmativi] *codd.* affirmative *P*
4 universalem] *codd.* utilem *N*
5 suam] *codd.* per suam *N*
6 unde nota] *TPN* et nota *H* unde *R*
7 concludit] *codd.* concludunt *N*
8 nisi] *codd.* om. *P*

9 eadem ratione] *TR* et eadem ratione *H*
10 quintum a primo] *codd.* primum a quinto *T*
11 primo] *codd.* libro *H*
12 ubi] *codd.* ut *R*
13 principio secundi] *TN* primo secundi (!)*PR* libro *H*
14 universales ... plures] *codd.* *om. T*
15 omnes] *codd.* *om. N*
16 plura] *codd.* *om. R*
17 idest] *codd.* et *P*
18 eos] *codd.* *om. P*
19 propriam] *codd.* conclusionem *add. PNRC*
20 septimus] *codd.* sex modos scilicet *N*
21 particularis ... convertitur] *codd.* particulares negativi non convertuntur *N*

8

1 Visa] *codd.* sillogismus ostenditur duobus modis visa *N*
2 divisione] *codd.* dictio *E*
3 conclusionis] *codd.* coniunctionis *sic semper E*
4 quantitatem et qualitatem] *T* qualitatem et quantitatem *cett.*
5 lectione] *NRCH* locatione *TPE* et *add. C*
6 non] *codd.* ut *T*
7 quia] *codd.* *om. T*
8 a] *codd.* ex *T*
9 fuit] *codd.* sunt *P*
10 eorundem] *PERC* earundem *TNH*
11 ducendo] *codd.* deducendo *P* inducendo *E*
12 sive ... impossibile] *codd.* *om. C*

9

1 etiam] *codd.* autem *N*
2 termini] *codd.* terminus *E* vere *P*
3 alio sillogismo] *TER* ex alio sillogismo *P* ab aliquo sillogismo *N* a sillogismo *CH*
4 vero] *TER* *om. cett.*
5 accipiatur] *TPR* accipitur *CH* accipiat *NE*
6 interimit] *codd.* inferunt *E*
7 autem] *codd.* *om. N*
8 ex hoc ergo] *TNER* hoc ergo *CH* et ex hoc enim *P*
9 potes] *codd.* poteris *H*
10 accipiatur] *TPER* accipiat *NCH*
11 et hec conclusio] *codd.* ergo hec conclusio *R* et hoc modo *E*
12 sillogismo] *ERCH* ex sillogismo *T* de sillogismo *P* a sillogismo *N*
13 alio] *codd.H^c* alius *N* *om. H*
14 sed sillogizando] *codd.* si sillogizatur *P*
15 propositione] *T* propositione falsa *cett.*
16 si] *codd.* et *P* ut *R*
17 ducat ... inconveniens] *codd.R* *quae quidem verba del. T^c*
18 quod sit cognitum] *codd.* et sic coniunctum *T*

19 unde suum] *codd.* unde sive *P* unde tunc suum *H*
20 interimat] *TR* interimit *cett.*
21 propositionem] *T* propositionem falsam *cett.*
22 ut] *codd.* unde *H*
23 tu] *codd. om. P*
24 et ex hoc] *PNE* ex hoc *TCH* et hoc *R*
25 concludat] *NR* concludas *P* concludes *T* concludatur *E* concluditur *CH*
26 impossibile] *codd.* possibile *R*
27 nutriuntur] *codd.* convertuntur (!)*P*
28 illationem esse necessariam] *codd.* illatum esse necessarium *P*
29 vero] *codd.* autem *PN*
30 ad] *codd. om. P*
31 propositi] *codd.* propositionis *R om. E*

10

1 ergo] *codd.* autem *P*
2 quoad suam illationem] *codd.* per suam illationem *T* per figuram suam sive quoad suam illationem et *P*
3 in ... promptus] *NER* in ... peritus *T* voluerit in huiusmodi promptus (!)*P* voluerit in istis esse promptus *C* vult in istis esse promptus *H*
4 exercitari] *codd.* exerceri *P*

INDICES

INDEX LOCORUM

INDEX RERUM NOTABILIUM

addiscere
V 73; IX 2-3

adherentia
VIII 5

adiectio
sillabice adiectiones que ponunt quandam discretionem circa pronomina: VIII 89

adiectivum (sc. nomen)
adiectivum generale—speciale: III 74

admirari
adverbium admirandi: IX 7

adverbialis
intellectus adverbialis: VIII 86

adverbium
adverbium est ut *verbo adiectum*: IV 36; adverbium similitudinis—
comparandi—admirandi—indignandi: IX 7

adversari
VIII 58

adversatio
in hac dictione 'nisi' intelligitur negatio et adversatio: VIII 58

advertere
VI 30

affectus
affectus anime: I 22; VIII 6; affectus (*opp.* conceptus): II 2; per modum
affectus: VIII 6; affectus vel appetitus: VIII 29; affectus sive exercitio: II 2;
affectus sive exercitium: IV 2; affectus et inclinatio et indicatio causaliter ordinantur: I 22

affirmatio
affirmatio ut 'homo': III 53; affirmatio = *oratio affirmativa*: affirmatio
prius est negatione sicut habitus privatione: 0.5; affirmatio dat ei (=
negationi) esse: 0.5; affirmatio ponit suum obiectum et conservat: II 23;
due comparationes sunt in affirmatione: II 24; quotienscumque affirmationes sibi invicem convertuntur necesse est earum negationes sibi
invicem converti: III 53; vide etiam s.v. *contradictio*

agens
substantia sumitur ut agens in nominativo: IX 11; actus semper est ab
aliquo agente sive ab aliquo quod habet modum agentis: IX 11; a parte
agentis—a parte obiecti: VIII 97

aggregatio
unum aggregatione: VIII 42

albatio
VI 15

albedo
subiectum albedinis: III 48; substantia habens albedinem: III 48

albus
'albus' non dicit qualitatem essentialem: I 12; 'album' sumitur dupliciter: III 48

aliqualis
VII 27

aliquid
'aliquid' est extra naturalem suppositionem entis: III 30

alius
'aliud' indefinite sumptum: III 76; hoc relativum diversitatis 'aliud': IX 16

alterativus
motus alterativus: VI 9

ampliare
natura ampliandi: VII 15-16

an
de hac coniunctione 'an': VIII 2-20; quid significet hec dictio 'an': VIII 6-7; 'an' significat disiunctionem cum electione: VIII 6; qualiter differat ab aliis interrogativis: VIII 8; inter que habeat disiungi: VIII 9-12; de quadam regula:VIII 9

anima
anima est perfectio corporis organici potentia vitam habentis: VIII 69; anima forma est instrumentalis corporis: VIII 69; quanto corpus citius fit organicum, tanto citius recipit animam: IX 1; forma completiva que est anima: III 15; anima intellectiva, sensitiva, vegetativa: V 7; quelibet anima humana est ens necessario: VII 23; affectus anime: I 22; VIII 6; operationes anime: I 21; anima apprehendit significata partium orationis: VIII 27; anima inclinat se ad enuntiandum: I 20; anima potest inclinari ad res: I11; anima non potest componere nisi mediante actu: I 11; 18; anima intellectiva infusione fit: IX 1

annexus
quatuor predicata in *Topicis* et annexa eorum: VIII 43

ante
a parte ante: VI 11

antecedere
omne inferens inquantum est inferens antecedit: VIII 81; antecedens semper supponit naturam sui consequentis: VIII 88; antecedens cedit in determinationem consequentis: V 35;—antecedens (*gramm.*) cuius fit recordatio per relativum: VIII 89

antecessio
V 3-8; VIII 81-2

Antichristus
exempli causa: I 29-30; VII 22-3

antiquus
solebant dicere antiqui: III 68; dictum antiquum: I 6

apparentia
nulla est apparentia: VIII 64, neque est aliqua apparentia: VIII 97

appetitus
appetitus sensibilis: VIII 29

appositio
opp. compositio: II 3

appositum
opp. suppositum: I 17

apprehendere
apprehendere rerum similitudines: I 22-3

apprehensio
I 22

arbor
arbor Porphirii: III 33

argumentum
def.: V 41; argumentum est ratio inferendi secundum aliquam vel aliquas habitudines: V 41

arismetica
VII 4

ars
ut dicit ars: VIII 76

arteria
arteria vocalis: VIII 13

articulus
articulus dicit relationem ad ipsum suppositum: VIII 89; omnis articulus significat relationem: VIII 88; relatio importata per articulum: VIII 89-90; nulla coniunctio habet naturam articuli: VIII 88; articulus vult adiungi suppositis ponendo quandam discretionem: VIII 89; articulus preponitur suppositis: VIII 89; in lingua materna habemus articulos: VIII 89; articulus subiunctivus: VIII 88

ascensus
in numeris est duplex ascensus: III 69

assignare
III 47; V 12; 27; VII 24; IX 4

associatio
coniunctio dicit associationem: VIII 87; privatio associationis: III 6-7; associatio aliquorum de pari: VIII 44

astrum
   astra esse paria: VIII 15

attractivus
   pulmo est attractivus aeris: VIII 13

auditus
   sentire auditu idem est quod audire: VIII 97

augmentabilis
   augmentabile inquantum augmentabile: VI 15

augmentare
   augmentatur scientia: IX 2

augmentum
   augmentum motus est ad maiorem quantitatem: VI 4

aut
   de hac dictione 'aut': VIII 28-30

Bibere
   iste non comedit quin bibat: VIII 79

bonus
   'bonum' plura significat secundum prius et posterius: VII 7; cuiuslibet boni est disciplina in eo quod bonum: VIII 76; bonum est confidere in Domino quam confidere in homine: IX 7

Calefacere
   VI 15; IX 1; calefieri: VI 15

calor
   calor intensior intensius calefacit: IX 1; calor cordis: VIII 13

cartillago
   cartillagines: VIII 42

casualis
   casuale (= 'inflected noun'): III 70-1; habitudo casualis ad actum: IV 2; IV 40; VIII 8; (= 'paronym'): si unum casualium non dicitur multipliciter, neque reliquum: VIII 93

casus
   Aristotiles docet repperire multiplicitatem in casibus: VIII 93

categoreuma
   def.: 0.2

causa
   'causa' dicitur dupliciter: causa essendi, causa consequendi: V 4; diversa genera causarum: VIII 69; causa efficiens, materialis, formalis, finalis: IX 1; causa initialis: I 22; nullum oppositum est causa alterius: VIII 73; causa sui ipsius: VIII 77; Causa Prima: VI 13; 17; 19-21; VII 2; IX 22; modus reduplicationis diversificatus secundum diversitatem causarum: VIII 68

conceptus

conceptus (*opp.* affectus): II 2; per modum conceptus: II 1; VIII 6

concipio

electio ut concepta: VIII 6; exceptio ut concepta: IV 2; exclusio ut concepta: III 3; negatio ut concepta: II 1

conclusio

conclusio est argumento vel argumentis approbata propositio: V 41; premisse sunt causa conclusionis: V 4; premisse quoad cognitionem suam sunt causa efficiens cognitionis ipsius conclusionis: VIII 83; substantia (*opp.* materia) conclusionis: VIII 83; de divisione sillogismorum a parte conclusionis: X 5-7

concretio

secundum abstractionem—secundum concretionem: III 33sqq.

conditionalis

ex nulla conditionali licet inferre antecedens vel consequens VIII 64; utrum conditionalis sit sillogizabilis: V 33; ad quid feratur negatio in conditionali: V 35-6

coniunctio

coniunctio = compositio: descinditur maior extremitas a premissis et etiam minor ut ex eis fiat coniunctio tamquam ex materia: VIII 83;— coniunctio dicit associationem: VIII 87; de coniunctionibus: VIII 1-99; genera coniunctionum sunt plura: VIII 1; de numero coniunctionum: VIII 1; 78; coniunctio nata est coniungere ceteras partes orationis: VIII 61; nulla coniunctio significat relationem: VIII 88; omnis res cuiuslibet coniunctionis est comparatio: VIII 85; omnis coniunctio significat vim vel ordinem: V 4; VIII 79; nulla coniunctio habet naturam articuli: VIII 88; coniunctio causalis—rationalis (collectiva): V 3-4; VIII 78; 85; coniunctiones collective sive rationales sunt que per illationem colligunt supradictum: VIII 79; de coniunctione copulativa: VIII 38-50; de coniunctione disiunctiva: *def.* VIII 22; coniunctio dubitativa: VIII 1; coniunctio electiva: IX 7; coniunctiones encletice: VIII 30; coniunctio interrogativa: VIII 1; de coniunctione reduplicativa: VIII 68-77; de hac coniunctione 'an': VII 2-20; de hac coniunctione 'quin': VIII 78-99

coniunctivus

pars coniunctiva aliarum partium: V 4

consecutio

de consecutione: V 3-10; VIII 79-99; quot sunt species consecutionis: V 9-11; VIII 79-99; de regulis consecutionis: V 14-5; 34; consecutio illationis: VIII 80; consecutio alia simplex, alia composita sive plures: VIII 84; consecutio simplex sive consequentia simplex: VIII 84; consecutio in ipso sive ccontrario: VIII 84; consecutio ut nunc: VIII 84; consecutio cum disiunctione: IX 17-8; vide etiam s.vv. *antecessio, consecutivus, consequentia*

consecutivus

dictio consecutiva (vel illativa) vide s.v. *dictio*; natura consecutiva: VIII 54; hec dictio 'nisi' aliquando tenetur consecutive: VIII 54

consentire
anima consentit: I 21

consequens
'consequens' tribus modis dicitur: V 37; 'consequens' duo dicit, sc. consequens inquantum consequens et id quod est consequens: V 36; consequens comprehendit sub se quodlibet antecedens: III 30; *consequens* = fallacia secundum consequens: II 32 et passim;—ex consequenti (*opp.* primo): II 27

consequentia
consequentia est duplex, simplex et ut nunc: VIII 52; 80; consequentia simplex (*opp.* composita): V 11; VIII 84; consequentia naturalis: V 32; consequentia econtrario: II 10; utrum 'quin' significet consequentiam: VIII 79-83; consequentiam convertere: III 28

consequi
causa consequendi: V 4; vide etiam s.v. *consequens*

conservativus
'sanativum' dicitur de conservativo: VIII 93

consignificare
hoc verbum 'est' consignificat compositionem: 0.6

consignificatio
(*opp.* principalis significatio): VI 7

consignificativus
dicitur 'sincategoreuma' ... quasi 'consignificativum': 0.2

contiguare
VIII 42

contiguatio
unum contiguatione: VIII 42

contingens
quid sit 'necessarium' et 'contingens': VII 2; quot modis dicantur: VII 3-7; 'contingens' non potest diffiniri: VII 2; 'contingens' dicitur duobus modis: contingens quod opponitur necessario, et istud diffinitur sic: contingens est quod potest esse et non esse: VII 5; 'contingens quod opponitur necessario' dicitur tribus modis: VII 6; contingens ad utrumlibet, contingens natum (contingens ut in pluribus vel frequenter), contingens in paucioribus vel raro: VII 6; 19; contingens infinitum (= ad utrumlibet): VII 19; qualiter convertantur propositiones de contingenti: VII 7-9; de 'contingenter': VII 1-30; 'contingenter' et 'possibiliter' equipollent: VII 15; utrum 'necessario' et 'contingenter' naturam habeant ampliandi: VII 15-6; de quibusdam regulis harum dictionum 'necessario' et 'contingenter': VII 30

contingere
de hoc verbo 'contingit': VII 30

continuare
VI 16

continuatio
unum continuatione: VI 16

contractus
'compositio' contracta: I 30; specialiter sumptus et contractus: I 23

contradico
dictiones contradicentes: VIII 57-60

contradictio
dupliciter fit contradictio; sc. ex primo et ex consequenti: II 27; utrum negatio orationis faciat contradictionem: II 21ff.; posita contradictione necesse est ex ea sequi tam affirmationem quam negationem: III 50; contradictio totum est ad utramque sui partem: V 40; nichil est commune ad partes contradictionis nisi disiunctio: VIII 9

contrarietas
omnis contrarietas nata est fieri circa aliquod idem subiectum· V 20

convenientia
convenientia est secundum quod multa; VIII 72

conversivus
de sillogismo conversivo: X 8-10

convertibilis
de regula convertibilium: III 11; 17; non oportet si in uno convertibilium intelligatur relatio, quod in altero intelligatur: IX 20

copulare
terminus copulat pro: VI 34-5; actus copulandi: VIII 39-40

copulatio
VIII 40

copulativus
de coniunctione copulativa: VIII 38-50; omnis copulativa coniunctio nisi sit encletica, equaliter se habet ad utrumque extremorum: VIII 47

cor
calor cordis: VIII 13

Coriscus
cognosco Coriscum: IV 19

corruptibilis
(*opp.* generabilis): VI 12

cotidie
de hoc adverbio 'cotidie': VIII 87

cursor
'cursor' non denominative dicitur: II 4

curvus
   'curvum' dicitur de linea: 0.4; vide etiam s.v. *linea*

Dealbare
   potentia ad dealbandum: VI 15

deus
   'divinitus', idest 'a Deo': IV 37

demonstratio (*gramm.*):
   virtute demonstrationis: V 28

denigratio
   VI 4

denominare
   denominare propositionem: VII 12ff.

descindere
   descinditur maior extremitas a premissis et etiam minor: VIII 83

desinere
   de hac dictione 'desinit': VI 1-36; 'desinit' est minus commune quam 'est': VI 34

desitio
   VI 6; 24; 35; esse sine desitione: VI 31

determinatio
   determinatio materialis: VII 30

dictio
   nulla dictio significat actum quem exercet: III 2; dictio categoreumatica: 0.1; de dictione sincategoreumatica: 0.1-0.3 et passim; dictiones sincategoreumatice significant res aliquas: 0.1; in dictionibus sincategorematicis per se intelliguntur 'est' et 'non': 0.3; dictio in communi, dictio specialis: III 4; dupliciter est una dictio principium alterius, per impositionem vel per compositionem: VIII 57; de dictione composita: VIII 85-7; dictio composita multipliciter trahit significationem suam a suis componentibus: VIII 86; omnis dictio composita trahit significationem a suis componentibus: VIII 85;—de dictionibus consecutivis: V 1-56; VIII 79-99; dictio consecutiva vel illativa: VIII 80; de dictionibus exceptivis: IV 1-41; quid significet dictio exceptiva: IV 2-3; quam habitudinem denotet dictio exceptiva: IV 708; de dictionibus exclusivis: III 1-76; quare dicatur dictio exclusiva: III 2-5; quid significet dictio exclusiva: III 6; dictio exclusiva significat idem quod hec oratio 'non cum alio': III 30 (cf. 0.5); dictio exclusiva significat privationem associationis totius ad partem: III 6; dictio illativa (= consecutiva): VIII 80; dictiones illative magis se habent ad consecutionem quam ad antecessionem: VIII 82; de dictionibus instantivis: VIII 56-60; dictio interrogativa encletica : VIII 30

dies
   def. V 20-1; causa diei quoad esse: V4; 'nox' et 'dies' dupliciter sumuntur: V 20

divisio

potentia divisionis: VI 10; aptitudo infinite divisionis: VI 10; divisio excedens—divisio excessa: VII; solutio per divisionem *def.* X3

dubitare

qui dubitat de uno oppositorum, dubitat de reliquo: VIII 10; qui dubitat nescit eligere: VIII 6

dubitatio

multorum non est dubitatio una sed plures: VIII 11; 'dubitatio una' est dupliciter: VIII 12; dubitatio contraria est electioni: VIII 6

dum

gerundivum in '-do' resolvitur per 'dum': VI 30

Effectivus

VIII 93

effectus

0.4

ego

ego credo: VIII 85; 95

egomet

exempli gratia: VIII 29

electio

electio ut concepta (*opp.* electio ut affectus): VIII 6; disiunctio cum electione: VIII 6-7

electivus

coniunctio electiva: IX 7

elementatus

corpus elementatum: V 7; elementata: V 31

elongabilis

visibile est elongabile: IX 5

enclesis

'enclesis' est 'inclinatio': VIII 29

encleticus

'encleticum' idest 'inclinativum' VIII 29; dictio interrogativa encletica: VIII 30

ens

de ente et non-ente: II 5-12; 'ens' proprie significat rem unam secundum diversos modos: I 5; 'ens' (dictio equivoca) plura significat secundum prius et posterius: VII 7; ens simpliciter—ens quodammodo: I 27-33; VIII 24; ens simpliciter—ens diminutum: II 15;18; nichil est commune enti et non-enti nisi ens quodammodo: I 27; quicquid est ens simpliciter, aut est substantia aut quantitas, et sic de aliis: VIII 24; aliqua sive omnia, in eo quod *sunt,* participant naturam entis et reducuntur ad

naturam entis: VIII 71; tam substantie quam accidentia quam omne id quod significatur sive sit ens sive non-ens: VIII 87; naturaliter supponuntur per terminum tam entia quam non-entia: III 27; 30; respectus quidam repertus tam in ente quam in non-ente: VIII 24; differentie que adiciuntur enti: II 11; compositio entium—compositio non-entium: I 28; 'unum' convertitur cum 'ente': III 11-3; alii termini qui convertuntur cum 'ente': III 24; veritas entium est ens simpliciter: I 33; utrum dictio exclusiva addita 'enti' possit excludere aliquid. III 24-30; primum predicabile ut ens: II 12; vide etiam s.v. *esse*

entitas
entitatem habere: I 33

enuntiare
'vere enuntiare' commune est ad 'vere affirmare' et ad 'vere negare': VIII 96

enuntiatio
VIII 75

equalitas
comparatio secundum equalitatem est duplex: VIII 27

equiparantia
relatio secundum equiparantiam: VIII 25

equivocatio
I 5-6

equivocus
omnis dictio significans diversa est equivoca: I 4; omne nomen est equivocum, hoc est inconveniens: I 4; equivocus—univocus: VIII 73-4; dictio equivoca plura significat secundum prius et posterius: VII 7

equus
equus ex equo generatur VI 12; 'equum videt omnis homo': III 63

ergo
'ergo': VIII 79

error
impius error: VI 12

esse
unumquodque intelligitur per illud quod dat ei esse: I 25; iste actus 'esse' comprehendit sub se omnem alium actum: III 30; non potest fieri exclusio ab hoc actu 'esse': III 30; esse actuale ipsius forme est esse in materia: I 8; 'esse' et 'esse verum' convertuntur V 47; in eo quod aliqua sunt, sunt multa: VIII 70-1; aliqua, sive omnia, in eo quod *sunt*, participant naturam entis: VIII 71; quicquid *est*, aut est substantia aut accidens: VIII 3;—de hoc verbo 'est': 0.4-0.6; 'est' natura prius est aliis verbis: 0.6; in dictionibus sincategoreumaticis intelliguntur 'est' et 'non': 0.3; hoc verbum 'est' consignificat compositionem: 0.6; I, 25; 'est' quod stat in ratione compositionis: VII 29; hoc verbum 'est' restringit ad ea que sunt: VI 34; 'desinit' est minus commune quam 'est': VI 34; vide etiam s.v. *ens*

57;—*exclusiva* = *propositio exclusiva:* omnis exclusiva vera relinquit suam preiacentem veram: III 10; 20; 36; 58

exercere
nulla dictio significat actum quem exercet: III 2; VIII 39; exercere suppositionem: III 2; cursus ut exercitus in corpore: II 2; exceptio ut exercita: IV 2; 4; exclusio ut exercita: III 3; 6; negatio ut exercita: II 1; 5

exercitare
X 10

exercitio
affectus sive exercitio: II 2

exercitium
affectus sive exercitium: IV 2

expediens
dictio equivoca ut 'expediens': VII 7

exponens
(propositio) exponens: III 67

expositivus
propositio expositiva: III 53-4

extendere
extendendo 'accidens': VIII 5; extenso nomine: V 17; 26

extensio
extensio temporis—extensio motus: V 26

extremitas
descinditur maior extremitas a premissis et etiam maior: VIII 83

extremum
videtur quod extrema ponantur secundum exigentiam compositionis: I 29; 32

Falsitas
vide s.v. *veritas*

falsus
ex falso bene sequitur falsum: VIII 95; contra totam falsam (sc. propositionem) non est dare instantiam: IV 9; 33; vide etiam s.v. *verum*

farina
V 9

femininus
genus femininum: VI 7

fenestra
IV 40

figura
figura sillogismi: X 8; ex affirmativis in secunda figura nichil sequitur:

VII 19;—ubicumque figura dictionis, ibi semper est sophisma accidentis: IX 23

finis
in ratione obiecti—in ratione finis: VIII 94

forma
esse ipsius forme est esse in materia: I 8; forma minus communis
restringit ad pauciora quam forma magis communis: VI 34; 'forma
minus communis' est duplex: VI 36; forma instrumentalis: VIII 69; vide
etiam s.v. *essentia*

frequens
ut in pluribus vel frequenter; VII 6

fumus
V 9

futurus
futurum (*sc.* tempus) terminatum ad presens: VI 6

Geminare
VIII 46-7

generabilis
opp. corruptibilis: VI 12

generalis
generalis— specialis: vide s.vv. *adiectivum, exclusio, nomen*—generale:
aliquod generale: III 21;28; generalissimum, vide s.v. *genus*

generare
homo ex homine generatur et equus ex equo, leo ex leone, planta ex
planta: VI 12

generatio
generatio hominum, plantarum et aliorum generabilium: VI 12

generativus
motus generativus: VI 17

genus
'genus' dicitur dupliciter: VI 7; genus non potest predicari denominative de specie: V 21; in genere esse: VIII 25-7; (genus) generalissimum:
III 24; posito generalissimo necesse est ponere substantiam: III 32;
generalissima alia a substantia duas habent comparationes: III 33

geometria
VII 4

gerundium
gerundium in '-do' resolvitur per 'dum' vel per 'si' vel per 'quia': VI 30

gradus
gradus comparativus: IX 8-16

gustare
sentire gustu idem est quod gustare: VIII 97

gustus
sentire gustu idem est quod gustare: VIII 97

Habitudo
habitudines rerum causantur a rebus: VII 8; habitudines, accidentia, substantie: VIII 45; *logice*: habitudo localis; V 15; 41; 56; argumentum est ratio inferendi secundum aliquam vel aliquas habitudines: V 41

hemisperium
V 20

heresis
VI 18

homo
homo est res habens humanitatem: I 3; homo ex homine generatur: VI 12; non est sumere primum hominem: VI 12; 'homo' in predicato dicit essentiam, in subiecto dicit substantiam: VIII 76; 'humanitas' est nomen aliud et diversum ab hoc nomine 'homo': I 3

hostis (= ostis)
'qui' apud nos idem est quod 'ostis' apud grecos: VIII 88

humanitas
'humanitas' est nomen aliud et diversum ab hoc nomine 'homo': I 3; homo est res habens humanitatem: I 3

Igitur
'igitur': VIII 79

illatio
in omni illatione consecutio et antecessio intelliguntur: VIII 81-2; illatio respicit conclusionem ut terminum ad quem: VIII 82

illativus
dictio consecutiva vel illativa: VIII 80; vide etiam s.v. *dictio*

imaginabilis
opinabile vel ymaginabile: II 12

impar
0.4

imperare
I 22

imperatio
I 22

implicatio
VI 24

imponere
I 22

impositio
opp. compositio: VIII 57; *opp.* transsumptio: I 5

impossibilis
'impossibile' tria dat intelligere: V 42; 'non-possibile' et 'impossibile' equipollent: VI 18; de sillogismo ad impossibile: X 8-10; utrum ex impossibili sequatur quidlibet: V 39-46; 56; utrum impossibile antecedat ad quidlibet: V 39-46

impossibilitas
necessitas et impossibilitas sunt circa compositionem: V 43; ipsa compositio circa quam est impossibilitas, nichil est: V 43

impresentiarum
'impresentiarum': VIII 87

'in eo quod'
VIII 73; vide etiam s.v. *reduplicatio*

incedere
'iste incedit superbus': III 71

inceptio
VI 6; 35

incipere
de 'incipit': VI 1-36

incisivus
securis dicitur incisiva: III 5

inclinare
secundum quod homo inclinatur ad individua in quibus est, sic nominat substantiam: VIII 77

inclinatio
inclinatio qualitatis ad substantiam: I 8sqq.: I 15; inclinatio actus ad substantiam: I 15; tres inclinationes: I 15ff.; inclinatio naturalis: I 8; inclinatio perfectivi ad perfectibile: I 15; affectus et inclinatio et indicatio causaliter ordinantur: I 22; utrum inclinatio natura precedat compositionem: I 18; inclinatio = enclesis: VIII 29

inclinativus
'encleticum' est 'inclinativum': VIII 29

includere
III 68

indesinens
indesinens vel sine desitione: VI 31

indicare
I 22

indicatio
affectus et inclinatio et indicatio causaliter ordinantur: I 22

indicativus
modus indicativus: I 16

individuum
individuum vagum: VIII 77

indivisibilis
nunc est indivisibile in tempore: VI 16

inferre
inferens causat ex se illatum: VIII 82; omne inferens inquantum est inferens antecedit: VIII 81; habitudo inferendi: V 13; omne illatum inquantum est illatum sequitur: VIII 81; vide etiam s.vv. *illatio, illativus*

infinitas
VI 10; ratione infinitatis (*gramm.*): VIII 87

infinitatio (gramm.)
VIII 86

infinitus
'infinitum' proprie dicitur tripliciter: VI 10; nomen infinitum: II 9-15; VIII 86; contingens infinitum: VII 19; vacuum et infinitum et alia non-entia: III 30

infusio
anima intellectiva infusione fit: IX 1

initialis
causa efficiens remota vel initialis: I 22

insertio
unum per insertionem: VIII 42

insertus
unum insertu: VIII 42

instantia
instantia est propositio propositioni contraria: IV 3; instantia aliquando fit in toto contra partem, aliquando in parte contra totum: VIII 52; contra totam falsam non est dare instantiam: IV 9; 33; instantiam ferre: IV 3; VIII 52 et passim

instantivus
de dictionibus instantivis: VIII 56; natura instantiva: VIII 54; hec dictio 'non' intelligitur in qualibet dictione instantiva: VIII 57

instrumentum
nullum instrumentum significat actum suum: VIII 39; cf. III 5

integralis
totum integrale habet in se suas partes integrales: V 56

integrare
V 56

intellectus
intellectus non potest comprehendere idem in essentia esse diversum in essentia: VIII 76; intellectus speculativus: VIII 29;—intellectus adverbialis: VIII 86; unus intellectus ordinativus vel coniunctivus plurium dictionum vel orationum: VIII 86; habere de intellectu suo: VIII 57; de intellectu sive de significatione: IX 18

intelligere
unum intelligitur in altero dupliciter: III 35; unumquodque intelligitur per illud quod dat ei esse: I 25; hec dictio 'non' intelligitur in qualibet dictione instantiva: VIII 57

intelligibilis
est non intelligibile: VIII 76

intentio
intentiones communes logicales: VII 4; res que sunt intentiones: VII 4; habere diversas intentiones: VIII 68

intensus
calor intensior intensius calefacit: IX 1

interemptio
passim: solutio per interemptionem *def.*: X 3

interrogare
quicumque interrogat petit certificari: VIII 7; 15; interrogatio per interrogantem cognoscitur: X 1; bene interrogans quinque debet scire: X 1; solutio ad interrogantem: X 2

interrogatio
VIII 86; de diversis interrogationibus: VIII 2-20; 'interrogatio una' est dupliciter: VIII 12; interrogatio est petitio responsionis: X 1; interrogatio per interrogantem cognoscitur: X 1; de interrogatione et responsione: X 1

interrogativus
interrogativa rerum dubitatarum sunt tribus modis: VIII 5; dictio interrogativa encletica: VIII 30

itaque
'itaque': VIII 79

Latinus
latina (*sc.* lingua): VIII 89;

latio
latio solis: V 20

lectio
lectionem audire: VIII 79-80; profeci hodie in hac lectione: IX 1; in precedenti lectione: X 8

materialis
  determinatio materialis: VII 30

medicina
  sanitas finis est medicine: VIII 69

medicinalis
  'medicinale' plura significat secundum prius et posterius: VII 7

medius
  medium est tota virtus premissarum: VIII 83

mensura
  de numero et mensura: V 26; mensura excessus: IX 8

mensurativus
  quantitas est ens mensurativum substantie: II 11

minor
  'maius' et 'minus' dicuntur relationes causatas a quantitatibus: IX 3; in minus: III 41; cf. *in plus;* minor extremitas, vide s.v. *extremitas*

mobilis
  mobile inquantum est mobile existit in potentia: VI 15; mobile et solum mobile est in potentia passiva ad motum: VI 15; primum mobile: V 21; VI 12; vide etiam s.v. *motus;—logice.* distributio mobilis: IV 25; propositio exceptiva est mobilis: IV 29

modalis
  modi facientes propositionem modalem: VII 11 sqq.; in *Modalibus:* VII 11

modus
  modi sunt inclinationes animi varios affectus demonstrantes: I 23; modus in verbo: I 21; modus significandi: I 1; compositio modorum significandi I 1-2; 13; modus cointelligendi: VIII 57; modus agentis est in nominativo: IX 11; modus temporis: VI 7; modus subiunctivus: VIII 61; 91; necessitas modi: VII 3; modus sillogismi: X 8

mortalis
  hec differentia 'mortale' duplicem habet comparationem: VII 25

mos
  res moris: V 49-50

motus
  def. V 19; VI 3; 15; motus est subiectum temporis: V 23; de spatio, motu et tempore: V 24; prius et posterius debentur motui: V 22; extensio motus: V 26; motus primi mobilis sive celi est infinitus: VI 12; motus primi mobilis mensurat motum solis: V 21; tempus est mensura primi motus: VI 7; omnes motus inferiores incipiunt et desinunt: VI 9; motus inferior—motus superior: VI 9; 15; motus circularis: VI 17; motus alterativus: VI 9; motus generativus: VI 17

multitudo
  duplex est multitudo: IV 14

multus

in eo quod aliqua *sunt,* sunt multi: VIII 70-1; convenientia est secundum quod multa: VIII 72

Natura

res nature: V 49-50; accidentia nature: II 26; principia nature: VI 13; 15; principium quod est supra naturam, est Causa Prima: VI 13; secundum viam nature: VI 17; natura consecutiva VIII 54; natura instantiva: VIII 54; natura ampliandi: VII 15-6

naturalis

agens naturale: VI 20; naturalis essentia: III 29, scientia naturalis: VI 18; suppositio naturalis: III 29-30

nauta

nauta causa est efficiens salutis navis et submersionis eius: IX 3

ne

de hac dictione '-ne': VIII 1; 4; 8

necessarius

de 'necessario': VII 1-30; necessarium est ens non potens aliter se habere: VII 2; 'necessarium' duobus modis dicitur: VII 3; negare necessarium: VIII 92 sqq.; 'necessario' potest determinare compositionem vel predicatum: VII 23-9; utrum 'necessario' et 'contingenter' naturam habeant ampliandi: VII 15-6; qualiter convertantur propositiones de necessario: VII 17-9; de quibusdam regalis harum dictionum 'necessario' et 'contingenter': VII 30

necessitas

'necessitas' duobus modis dicitur; necessitas modi, necessitas rerum: VII 3; necessitas est duplex, alia substantiarum, alia actuum: VII 9; necessitas et impossibilitas sunt circa compositionem: V 43; necessitas disiunctionis vel partium disiunctarum: VII 30; duplex est signum necessitatis: VII 9; necessitatem imponere: VIII 69

negare

negare est actus egrediens ab hac potentia activa que est negativum: VIII 93; 'negare' non est equivocum ad negare quodlibet predicatum: VIII 93; signum vel instrumentum negandi: II 1

negatio

de negatione: II 1-35; 'negatio' dicitur equivoce: II 1; negatio est actus destruens suum obiectum: II 23; negatio apta nata est destruere quicquid repperit: II 23; negatio ut est signum vel instrumentum negandi dicitur tripliciter: II 1; negatio non habet esse nisi per affirmationem: 0.5; negatio quodammodo est affirmatio: II 26; secundum diversitatem compositionum diversificatur negatio: II 1; cuilibet compositioni opponitur sua negatio: II 12; negatio que est in verbo infinito, relinquit compositionem affirmatam: II 17;—negatio (*opp.* privatio): II 10; negatio termini—negatio orationis: II 3; negatio termini subdividitur: II 5; de negatione nominis infiniti: II 9-15; de negatione infinitante verbum: II

17-20; negatio preposita sive postposita termino singulari idem significat: II 28; de negatione orationis: II 21-7; de negatione duplici: negatio in genere—negatio simpliciter: V 16-8; 26; 28-9; due comparationes sunt in negatione: II 24; in dictionibus exclusivis intelligitur negatio: VIII 57; dictiones exceptive habent negationem de intellectu suo: VIII 57; ad quid feratur negatio in conditionali: V 35-6; negatio absoluta—negatio respectiva: VIII 61; in hac dictione 'nisi' intelligitur negatio et adversatio: VIII 58

negativus

'negativum' non dicitur multipliciter; VIII 93; = 'negative': propositio negativa *passim*; = 'effective of denying' (cf. *alterativus, generativus, significativus* etc.): potentia activa que est negativum: VIII 93; negativum semper est negativum alicuius et ab aliquo: VIII 93

neuter

genus neutrum: VI 7

nichil

facere ex nichilo: VI 13

nisi

de hac dictionibus 'nisi' et 'preterquam': IV 1; 41; de hac coniunctione 'nisi': VIII 51-67; utrum 'nisi' possit teneri exceptive: VIII 52-4; 'nisi' aliquando tenetur exceptive, aliquando consecutive: VIII 54; hec dictio 'nisi' habet in se naturam instantivam et naturam consecutivam: VIII 54; hec dictio 'nisi' composita est ex 'si' et 'non': VIII 54; utrum 'nisi' et 'si non' equipolleant ad invicem: VIII 55; in hac dictione 'nisi' intelligitur negatio et adversatio: VIII 58; negatio que est in hac dictione 'nisi', non est negatio absoluta sed respectiva: VIII 61; quare hec dictio 'nisi' vult semper adiungi verbo subiunctivi modi: VIII 61; utrum 'nisi' equipolleat 'quod non' sive convertatur cum eis: VIII 88-90

nomen

omne nomen significat substantiam cum qualitate: I 3-4; 6; 8; 12; cf. VIII 87; in nomine est compositio qualitatis cum substantia: I 1; cf. I 2; qualitas nominis est ratio sive principium intelligendi ipsum nomen et suam substantiam: I 6; in nomine est compositio unitorum: I 18; 'humanitas' est nomen aliud et diversum ab hoc nomine 'homo': I 3; (hoc nomen) 'homo' in predicato dicit essentiam, in subiecto dicit substantiam: VIII 76; (hoc nomen) 'album' sumitur dupliciter: III 48; transposita nomina idem significant: II 28; nomen dupliciter potest infinitari: II 13; utrum nomen infinitum predicetur de quolibet quod est et quod non est: II 9 sqq.

nominare

'pater' nominat ipsam relationem que est paternitas: III 48; nominare essentiam— nominare substantiam: VIII 77

nominativus

nominativus dicit modum agentis: IX 11

non

de 'non': 0.1 0.6; hec particula 'non': II 1; hec dictio 'non' intelligitur in qualibet dictione instantiva: VIII 57; hoc adverbium 'non' semper fert instantiam ei cui adiungitur: VIII 54; in dictionibus sincategoreumaticis intelligitur 'est' et 'non': 0.3

notatio

cum notatione 'istarum rerum': IX 1

nox

'nox' et 'dies' dupliciter sumuntur: V 20

numeralis

de toto numerali: IV 21-4

numerus

'numerus' duobus modis sumitur: III 63; de numero et mensura: V 26; numerus nichil aliud est nisi aggregatio unitatum: III 12; numerus sicut quodlibet aliud totum: III 63; omnis numerus est par vel impar: 0.4; VII 4; 30; principium numeri (sc. unum): III 12; in numeris est duplex ascensus: III 69; ratio numeri diminuitur per sibi adiunctum: V 22; utrum dictio exclusiva addita maiori numero excludat minorem: III 62-3; numerum facere cum Sorte: VIII 49; numerum facere in esse: V 51

nunc

nunc est indivisibile in tempore et continuat duas partes temporis: VI 16; terminus ut nunc: *def.* VII 21

Obiectio

resistere obiectionibus: VI 11

obiectum

obiectum in quod transit actio: VIII 93; in ratione obiecti—in ratione finis: VIII 94; a parte obiecti—a parte agentis: VIII 97

obiectus

terre obiectus: 0.4

obliquus

(casus) obliqui dicunt modum patientis: IX 11; in obliquo—in rectitudine: III 67; oblique significare: IV 36

oblongus

figura oblonga: I 5

omnipotens

VIII 86

omnis

'omnis' non significat universale sed quoniam universaliter: II 16

opinabilis

opinabile vel ymaginabile: II 12

perfectivus
inclinatio perfectivi sive perfectionis ad perfectibile: I 15; vide etiam s.v. *inclinatio*

permanens
vide s.v. *res*

perpetuitas
VII 16

pius
pius et fortis fuit Eneas: V 4

planta
planta ex planta generatur: VI 12

pluralis
omne plurale geminat singulare in terminis communibus: VIII 46

plus
in plus (*opp.* in minus): III 52; VIII 99; in pluribus: passim; ut in pluribus vel frequenter: VII 6; consecutio plures: VIII 84

pluvia
IV 40

positio
positio impossibilis: III 58

possibilis
'non-possibile' et 'impossibile' equipollent: VI 18; 'contingenter' et 'possibiliter' equipollent: VII 15

post
a parte post: VI 11

potentia
omnis potentia perficitur per suum actum: VII 5; utrum potentia incipiat vel desinat: VI 18; duplex est potentia, activa et passiva: VI 19; 'potentia passiva' sumitur dupliciter: VI 22; potentia activa duplicem habet comparationem: VIII 93; potentia divisionis: VI 10

potentialis
potentiale vel opinabile vel ymaginabile: II 12

predicabilis
primum predicabile ut ens: II 13 sqq.; predicabilis de pluribus: VIII 31-4

predicamentalis
linea predicamentalis: III 33; ordinatio predicamentalis: VIII 77; res predicamentales: IX 23

predicatio
predicatio est multis modis: V 21; communitas predicationis est duobus modis: VIII 32

predicatum
predicatum—id quod est predicatum: 0.2; dispositio predicati inquantum predicati: 0.2; VII 12; quatuor predicata in *Topicis*: VIII 43; predicatum determinatum—predicatum indeterminatum: I 14

preiacens
def. III 10; omnis exclusiva vera relinquit suam preiacentem veram: III 10; 20; IV 32; cuiuslibet exceptive vere sua preiacens est falsa: IV 32; dictio exceptiva adversatur preiacenti: VIII 58

premissa
premisse quoad cognitionem suam sunt causa efficiens cognitionis ipsius conclusionis: VIII 83; descinditur maior extremitas ex premissis et etiam minor: VIII 83; medium est tota virtus premissarum: VIII 83

preparativus
'sanativum' dicitur de preparativo: VIII 93

prepositio
prepositiones dicunt comparationem substantie oblique significate ad actum vel respectu actus: IV 36; nulla prepositio significat affectum sive exercitium sed tantum significat habitudinem casualis ad actum: IV 2

preter
hec dictio 'preter' non significat exceptionem: IV 2; 'preter' semper tenetur exceptive: IV 6; 'preter' non est adverbium sed prepositio: IV 36

preteritus
preteritum (sc. tempus) determinatum ad presens: VI 6

preterquam
IV 1; 41

pridie
VIII 87

prior
de prioribus prior est speculatio: 0.3; per prius (*opp.* ex consequenti): VIII 82; de 'prius': V 9-11; de 'prius' et 'posterius': V 22-3; significare secundum prius et posterius: VII 7

privare
privare a privatione non est privare: III 73; IV 17

privatio
privare a privatione non est privare: III 73; IV 17

processus
processus a primo ad ultimum: V 15

proportionalis
vel vere vel proportionaliter: I 11

propositio
propositio universalis est duplex, quia quedam est completa, alia incompleta: IV 26; propositio modalis—propositio de inesse: VII 3; qua

ratione dicatur propositio modalis: VII 11 sqq.; propositio necessaria—propositio contingens: VII 3 sqq.; qualiter convertantur propositiones de necessario et contingenti: VII 17-9; vide etiam s.vv. *exceptivus, exclusivus, preiacens*

pugillator
'pugillator' non dicitur denominative: II 4

pulmo
VIII 13; 75; pulmo est attractivus aeris: VIII 13; pulmo est expulsivus et repercussivus aeris: VIII 13

punctum
0.4; I 2

punctus
punctus est indivisibile in linea: VI 16; punctus continuat duas partes linee: VI 16; punctus acus: V 24

Qualificativus
ens qualificativum substantie: II 11

qualitas
qualitas est ens qualificativum substantie: II 11; qualitas accidentalis (*opp.* essentialis): I 12; qualitas substantialis: I 15; qualitas accidentalis non potest predicari de substantia: II 4; qualitas secundum se (*opp.* qualitas inclinata): I 8; qualitas nominis, vide s.v. *nomen*; qualitas ut unita substantie (*opp.* ut distans): I 10

quam
de hac dictione 'quam': IX 6-16; de multiplicitate eius: IX 7; qualiter importet comparationem: IX 8; hoc adverbium 'quam' habet rationem termini: IX 9; hoc adverbium 'quam' est ratio per quam nominativus terminat respectum comparativi: IX 10; propter quid sequatur nominativus: IX 11

quamobrem
'quamobrem': VIII 87

quando
de 'quid' et 'quando': IX 23

quantitas
quantitas est ens mensurativum substantie: II 11

quanto
de hac dictione 'quando': IX 1-5; de multiplicitate eius: IX 1; hec dictio 'quanto' aliquando dicit causam efficientem, aliquando causam materialem, aliquando causam formalem, aliquando causam finalem: IX 1

quare
'quare': VIII 86

quarta
quarta (*sc.* pars) una: V 21

que
> coniunctio encletica '-que': VIII 30

qui
> VIII 90; 'qui' apud nos idem est quod 'ostis' apud Grecos: VIII 88; huic nomini 'quod' aliquando accidit relatio, aliquando interrogatio, aliquando infinitatio: VIII 86; hoc nomen 'quod' significat substantiam infinitam cum articulo subiunctivo: VIII 88

quia
> gerundium in '-do' resolvitur per 'quia': VI 30

quicquid
> quid significet hec dictio 'quicquid': IX 18; quicquid componitur per geminationem 'quid': IX 20; hec dictio 'quicquid' uno modo importat distributionem: IX 17; quoad hoc quod hec dictio 'quicquid' importat consecutionem cum disiunctione debet determinari de ipsa in *Sincategoreumatibus*; IX 17; quatuor sunt de intellectu huius dictionis 'quicquid' sive de sua significatione: IX 18; utrum sit dictio equivoca: IX 19; utrum importet relationem: IX 20; hec distributio 'quicquid' dicit *quid*: IX 23

quid
> de 'quid' et 'quando': IX 23; dicere *quid*: IX 23; terminus dicens *quid*: III 24; VI 32-3; VIII 77

quilibet
> 'quilibet': IX 18

quin
> de hac coniunctione 'quin': VIII 78-99; utrum significet consequentiam: VIII 79-83; hec dictio 'quin' dicit consecutionem illationis: VIII 80; per prius significat antecessionem quam consecutionem: VIII 82; utrum significet consequentiam communiter dictam: VIII 84; hec dictio 'quin' est composita ex hac dictione 'quod' et hoc adverbio 'non': VIII 85; hec dictio 'quin' est dictio simplex sicut ego credo: VIII 85; 'quin' dicit consequentiam inter negationes: VIII 88; 'quin' et 'quod non' convertuntur in ratione finis: VIII 95; quare 'quin' semper coniungatur verbo subiunctivi modi: VIII 91

quisque
> 'quisque': VIII 86

quotennis
> 'quotennis': VIII 3-4

Racemus
> si vinum est, racemi fuerunt: V 11

ratio
> ratio numeri: V 22; rationes horum verborum 'incipit' et 'desinit': VI 4; quorum rationes non sunt differentes, ipsa non sunt differentia: VI 2; est alterius rationis: I 8; in ratione compositionis: I 8; in ratione finis: VIII 95; habere rationem termini: IX 9; stare in ratione: VII 29; IX 12; res

nature, moris, rationis: V 49-50; secundum rationem—secundum rem:
I 8; secundum substantiam—secundum rationem: VIII 13; ratione substantie—ratione essentie: VIII 76; ratio sive principium intelligendi: I 5;
12

rationalis
coniunctio rationalis: VIII 78

recordatio
recordatio fit per relativum: VIII 89-90

rectitudo
in obliquo—in rectitudine: III 67

rectus
rectum: 0.4; vide etiam s.v. *linea*

reduplicatio
de hac reduplicatione 'in eo quod': VIII 68-76; modus reduplicationis
diversificatur secundum diversitatem causarum: VIII 68; hec reduplicatio 'in eo quod' habet diversas intentiones secundum diversitatem
causarum: VIII 68; cf. VIII 73; utrum reduplicatio debeat poni ad subiectum vel ad predicatum: VIII 75; reduplicatio in sillogismo debet poni
ad maiorem extremitatem: VIII 76

relatio (*gramm.*)
VIII 86; 88; relatio significata per articulum alia est et diversa a relatione
significata per nomina vel per pronomina relativa: VIII 89; utrum
'quicquid' importet relationem: IX 20

relativum
hoc relativum diversitatis 'aliud': IX 16

repercussivus
repercussivus aeris: VIII 13

representare
significare et representare: I 24

res
'res' dupliciter dicitur: 0.2; res predicamentales: IX 23; res permanentes—res successive: VI 1-6; 35; de differentia successivorum et
permanentium: VI 2-6; habitudines rerum causantur a rebus: VII 8; tota
res infra suos terminos continetur: VI 6; a quibus dependet cognitio rei
priora sunt re: VI 1; res dependet ab Ipsa (= Causa Prima) tamquam a
sua causa: IX 22; via in rem: V 50; necessitas rerum est duobus modis:
VII 4; ab eo quod res est vel non est oratio vera vel falsa dicitur: 0.1; res
est causa veritatis orationis: V 47; res (*opp.* signum rei): V 50; res huius
verbi 'scire': V 56; res huius dictionis 'vel': VIII 25-7; res que sunt
intentiones: VII 4; secundum rem—secundum rationem: I 8

respectivus
(*opp.* absolutus): VIII 25

respectus
 comparatio sive respectus est duplex: VIII 26

respiratio
 VIII 13

respondens
 respondens magis certus debet esse de questione quam interrogans: VIII 14

responsio
 de responsionibus: X 1-10; interrogatio est petitio responsionis: X 1; 'responsio una' est dupliciter: VIII 12

revolutio
 revolutio celi: VI 12

Sanare
 'sanare' dicitur multipliciter: VIII 93

sanativus
 'sanativus' dicitur multipliciter: VIII 93; 'sanativum' plura significat secundum prius et posterius: VII 7

sanitas
 sanitas finis est medicine: VIII 69

sapere
 hoc sapit disiunctiva coniunctio: VIII 22

scientia
 principium principiorum in scientiis: II 21; augmentatur scientia: VI 29; IX 2; scientia reflectitur: VI 29; scientia Cause Prime semper est eadem: IX 22; scientia immobilis: IX; scientia naturalis: VI 18; scientia specialis: VII 4

sciphus
 sciphus plenus aqua: V 24

scire
 nichil scitur nisi verum: V 55; contingit scire universale ignorando particulare: VIII 15; res huius verbi 'scire': V 56; scire magis et minus: IX 2-3

securis
 securis dicitur incisiva: III 5

sentire
 sentire visu, gustu, auditu: VIII 97

sequi
 omne illatum inquantum est illatum sequitur: VIII 81; 'unum sequitur ad alterum' est multiplex: V 7; vide etiam s.v. *consecutio*

si

de hac dictione 'si': V 1-56; quid significet hec dictio 'si': V 2-8; gerundium in '-do' resolvitur per 'si': VI 30

significare

omne id quod significatur sive sit ens sive non-ens: VIII 87; dupliciter contingit significari diversa: II 4; significare plura per modum unius: IX 19; significare plura secundum prius et posterius: VII 7; significare transsumptive: I 5; nulla dictio significat actum quem exercet: III 2; 'homo' significat hominem et exercet suppositionem: III 2; significatus (*opp.* exercitus): III 7; IV 4; vide etiam s.vv. *conceptus, exercere, modus*

significatio

significatio principalis: VI 7; vide etiam s.v. *consignificatio;* significatio generalis, specialis: II 22

signum

signa sunt dispositiones subiecti inquantum subiectum est: II 16; signa non possunt infinitari: II 16; signum rei: V 50; signum universale disponit subiectum in respectu ad predicatum: II 28; duo signa universalia in eadem locutione: II 32; duplex signum necessitatis: VII 9

sillogismus

de divisione sillogismorum a parte conclusionis: X 5-7; principia sillogismorum sunt modus et figura: X 8; de ostensione sillogismorum: X 8-10; omnis sillogismus ostenditur duobus modis, quia ostenditur convertendo et etiam ducendo ad impossibile: X 8; sillogismis conversivus—sillogismus ad impossibile: X 8; de sillogismis universalibus et particularibus: X 5-7; sillogismus disparatus: VIII 83

sillogizabilis

propositio sillogizabilis: IV 1; 27-9; V 33

similis

non est simile de nomine et participio ad verbum: I 18

simultas

comparatio que est secundum simultatem: VIII 40

sincategoreuma

def. 0.2; ista verba ponuntur sincategoreumata: VI 36; in *Sincategoreumatibus*: IX 17

sincategoreumaticus

dictio sincategoreumatica: 0.1; 0.3

sol

sol lucens super terram: V 7; 9; VIII 69; motus solis: V 21

solus

'solus' est 'non cum alio': 0.5; III 74; VIII 57; qualiter 'tantum' et 'solus' differant: III 70-1; vide etiam s.v. *dictio exclusiva*

solutio

de modis solutionis: X 2-4; solutionum alia est recta, alia vero apparens: X 2; recta solutio *def.* X 3; species recte solutionis sunt due, quia alia per interemptionem, alia vero per divisionem: X 3; solutio ad orationem: X 3; solutio ad hominem: X 2; solutio ad interrogantem: X 2; solutio ad tempus: X 2

sonorus

III 24

spatium

de spatio: V 24

specialis

vide s.v. *generalis*

stare

stat in ratione: VII 29; IX 12

studiosus

'studiosus' non dicitur denominative: II 4

subdisiunctivus

'vel' subdisiunctive tenetur: VIII 32

subiectum

subiectum—id quod est subiectum: 0.2; dispositio subiecti inquantum subiectum (est): II 16; VII 12 sqq.; subiectum et propria passio dupliciter comparantur: 0.4; extenso nomine 'subiecti': V 17; 26; subiectum determinatum—indeterminatum: I 14; in quo sit tempus ut in subiecto: V 19-20

subiunctivus

vide s.vv. *modus, verbum*

submersio

submersio navis: IX 3

substantia

substantia dicitur quatuor modis: V 2; quicquid est, aut est substantia aut accidens; VIII 3; posito generalissimo necesse est ponere substantiam: III 32; dispositio substantie: III 71; VII 9; substantia sumitur ut agens in nominativo, in obliquis autem sumitur ut patiens: IX 11; per modum substantiae, per modum accidentis: III 16; VIII 4; quoad substantiam— quoad cognitionem: VIII 83; secundum substantiam—secundum rationem: VIII 13; ratione substantie, *opp.* ratione essentie: VIII 76-7; substantia exterior: I 24; II 5-6; substantia interior (intra): II 5-7; substantia interius intellecta: II 7

successivus

vide s.v. *res*

superbus

iste incedit superbus: III 71

supponere

quotienscumque tot excipiuntur quot supponuntur, locutio est impropria et falsa; IV 9; cf. IV 15; indefinite supponere: III 76; naturaliter supponere: III 27

suppositio

exercere suppositionem: III 2; quam suppositioncm habeant termini cum 'incipit' et 'desinit': VI 32-6; suppositio naturalis: III 29-30; suppositio simplex—personalis: IV 11; VI 24; suppositio ampliata—restricta: VI 24—suppositio (= hypothesis): per suppositionem—simpliciter: VIII 12

suppositum (*gramm.*):

suppositum—appositum: I 17; a parte suppositi. VIII 8

suppositum (*log.*):

diversitas suppositorum cum unitate significationis: VIII 46; ratione suppositi—ratione forme: III 14

Tantum

'tantum' est 'non cum alio': 0.5; VIII 57; qualiter 'tantum' et 'solus' differant: III 70-1; vide etiam s.v. *dictio exclusiva*

tempus

'tempus' potest sumi secundum duas comparationes: VI 17; de tempore: V 12-25; VI 7; *def.* V 22; tempus mensurat motum primi mobilis: V 21; in quo sit tempus ut in subiecto: V 19-20; utrum tempus incipiat vel desinat: VI 16-7; tempus est unum continuatione: VIII 42; extensio temporis: V 26; solutio ad tempus: X 2

terminus

terminus ad quem—terminus a quo : VI 4-5; VIII 82; terminus initialis—terminus finalis: VI 6; 35; tota res infra suos terminos continetur: VI 6; hoc adverbium 'quam' habet rationem termini: IX 9; ratione terminorum quos dicunt (sc. verba): VI 35

terminus (*log.*)

nullus terminus potest infinitari nisi subicibile vel predicabile: II 16; naturaliter supponuntur per terminum tam entia quam non-entia: III 27; termini substantiales dicentes *quid*: III 24; VI 32-3; VIII 77; terminus accidentalis: III 24; 41; VI 32-3; termini accidentales significantes res permanentes: VI 35; quod terminus dicens *quid* ... predice(n)tur ratione essentie et subicia(n)tur ratione substantie: VIII 77; terminus communis: omne plurale geminat singulare in terminis communibus: VIII 46; termini communes predicantur ratione essentie et subiciuntur ratione substantie VIII 76; terminus simpliciter *def.* VII 21; terminus ut nunc *def.* VII 21; sub terminis simpliciter non sunt sumendi termini ut nunc: VII 21; 'esse extra terminum' multiplex est: III 29; quam suppositionem habeant termini cum 'incipit' et 'desinit': VI 32-6; terminus disiunctus: utrum disiunctio faciat terminum disiunctum predicabilem de pluribus: VIII 31-4; in omni termino disiuncto duo sunt: VIII 34; vide etiam s.v. *disiunctio*;—termini sillogismi: X 9

tis
'tis' est nomen infinitum: VIII 88

totalitas
totalitas sive aggregatio: III 65

totus
'totum' duobus modis sumitur: III 63; De speciebus 'totius': IV 16-24

transire
actus non transit supra alium actum: VIII 8; 28; obiectum in quod transit actio: VIII 93; transire supra accusativum: IV 31

transitio
recipere transitionem: VIII 8

transsumptio
opp. impositio: I 5

transsumptivus
significare transsumptive: I 5

triangularis
figura triangularis: I 5

triangulus
def. 0.4; VIII 4; 75

tu
hoc pronomen 'tu': V 32

tunica
VII 18

turba
nichil est dictu 'turba preter Sortem currit': IV 13

tutemet
VIII 89

Ubique
'esse ubique' ponit tot contradictiones quot sunt loca particularia circum-scriptiva: V 32

unitas
unitas essentialis—unitas accidentalis: III 12; unitas entis: VIII 71

universalis
contingit scire universale ignorando particulare: VIII 15; signum universale, vide s.v. *signum*

univocari
quecumque participant nomen et rationem alicuius, univocantur in eo: VIII 73-4; univocari in equivoco non est univocari simpliciter sed potius equivocari: VIII 74

unus

'unus' addit discretionem numeri: III 16; 'unum' dicitur multipliciter; VIII 42; 'unum' est equivocum: III 12; 'unum' convertitur cum 'ente': III 11-3; unumquodque simulac est, unum est: III 11; ubi unum propter alterum, tantum unum est: I 6; unumquodque ideo est quia unum numero est: III 11; Aristotiles dicit si duo sunt unum esse: III 62; unum aggregatione, unum collatione, unum contiguatione, unum continuatione, unum insertu (unum per insertionem): VIII 42

utrum

de hac dictione 'utrum': VIII 1; 4; 8

Vacuus

vacuum et infinitum et alia non-entia: III 30

vagus

individuum vagum: VIII 77

ve

de hac dictione '-ve': VIII 28-30

vel

de hac dictione 'vel': VIII 21-37; quid significet hec dictio 'vel': VIII 22-3; utrum suum significatum sit ens simpliciter: VIII 24; utrum res huius dictionis 'vel' sit in genere vel non: VIII 25-7; hec dictio 'vel' non dicit rem absolutam sed respectivam: VIII 25; qualiter differat ab aliis coniunctionibus disiunctivis: VIII 28-30; 'vel' subdisiunctive tenetur: VIII 32

verbum

verbum est nota eorum que de altero predicantur: I 11; in verbo est compositio actus cum substantia: I 1; compositio actus ut distantis sicut in verbo: I 10; in verbo est compositio distantium: I 18; compositio verbi est subiectum veritatis et falsitatis: I 16; hoc verbum 'est' consignificat compositionem, et etiam alia verba: 0.6; modus in verbo: I 21; modus accidit verbo: I 24; inclinatio verbi: I 15; 25; compositio generalis (*opp.* specialis) in verbo: I 23; verbum absolutum—verbum respectivum: VIII 61; verbum subiunctivi modi: VIII 61; 91; verbum personale: IV 39-40; dupliciter removetur verbum personale ab aliquo casuali: IV 40; de negatione infinitante verbum: II 17-20; utrum verbum infinitum predicetur de omni eo quod est et quod non est: II 17 sqq.; verbum infinitum sive privativum: II 3

verificare

verificare per dictionem exceptivam: IV 33

veritas

res est causa veritatis orationis: V 47; subiectum veritatis est compositio: I 32; veritas et falsitas in oratione: 0.1; I 16; secundum veritatem: I 27

verus

ab eo quod res est vel non est oratio vera vel falsa dicitur: 0.1; 'esse' et 'esse verum' convertuntur: V 47; nichil scitur nisi verum: V 55; vel vere vel proportionaliter: II 11

via
   via in rem: V 50

videre
   actus qui est videre non est equivocum ad visionem albedinis et ad
   visionem nigredinis: VIII 93; sentire visu idem est quod videre: VIII 97;
   quinque insimul congregata sunt causa efficiens eius quod est videre et
   videri: IX 5; unumquodque visorum habet spatium quo facto non
   amplius videbitur: IX 5

virtus
   virtus in eo quod imponit necessitatem operationibus: VIII 69; virtus
   cognitiva: IX 22; virtus visiva: IX 5

vis
   vim vel ordinem demonstrare: V 4; VIII 79

visibilis
   visibile supra se recipit visionem: I 18; visibile inquantum visibile: VI 15

visio
   non sunt due visiones sed una: I 6; visibile supra se recipit visionem: I
   18

visivus
   virtus visiva: IX 5

visus
   'album' per 'disgregativus visus' adveniens 'colorato': VI 36; sentire visu
   idem est quod videre: VIII 97; liber *De visu:* IX 5

Ymaginabilis
   opinabile vel ymaginabile: II 12

INDEX SOPHISMATUM

corpus
Omne corpus preter inanimatum est animatum: IV 12

Decem
vide s.v. *preter*

desinere
Sortes desinit esse albissimus hominum: VI 23-4
Sortes desinit esse non desinendo esse: VI 30-1
Sortes desinit scire quicquid ipse scit: VI 25-7
Sortes desinit scire se nichil desinere scire: VI 28-9
Sortes desinit videre omnem hominem: VI 27

Deus
Quicquid Deus scivit, scit: IX 21-3

differre
Aliqua in eo quod conveniunt, differunt: VIII 70-2
A solo Sorte differt quicquid non est Sortes vel pars Sortis: III 60-1
Tu scis an omnis homo sit Sortes an differat ab illo: VIII 16-7

domus
tota domus preter parietem est alba: IV 18

duo
Solis tribus sola duo sunt pauciora: III 66-7

Enuntiabile
Omne enuntiabile differt ab aliquo et suum oppositum est componibile illi: VIII 50
Omne enuntiabile preter verum est falsum: IV 12
Solus Sortes scit aliquod enuntiabile quod non omnis alius a Platone ignorat: III 75-6

equivocus
Equivoca in eo quod equivoca sunt univoca: VIII 73-4

esse
Anima Antichristi necessario erit: VII 22-3
Quicquid est vel non est est: VIII 35
Si nichil est, aliquid est: V 47-51
Sortes desinit esse non desinendo esse: VI 30-1
Tantum unum est: III 11-7

et
Omne non-animal quod et Sortes sunt duo, non est Sortes: VIII 48-9

excipere
Omnis homo preter Sortem excipitur: IV 16-7

excludere
Solus Sortes excluditur: III 72-3

Falsum

Omne enuntiabile preter verum est falsum: IV 12
Tantum verum opponitur falso: III 43-4

Homo

Omnis homo necessario est animal: VII 20-1
Nullo homine currente tu es asinus: II 29-30
Nullus homo legit Parisius nisi ipse sit asinus: VIII 65-6
Nullus homo moritur nisi unus solus homo moriatur: VIII 67

Immortalis

Si Sortes necessario est mortalis, Sortes necessario est immortalis: VII
24-7

impossibile

Impossibile est aliud quam asinum genuisse te: IX 15-6
Impossibile est te scire plura quam scis IX 13-4

inanimatus

Omne corpus preter inanimatum est animatum: IV 12

in eo quod

Aliqua in eo quod conveniunt, differunt: VIII 70-2
Equivoca in eo quod equivoca sunt univoca: VIII 73-4

irrationale

Omne animal preter hominem est irrationale: IV 10-1

Lapis

Si tu scis te esse lapidem, tu non scis te esse lapidem: V 55-6

legere

Nullus homo legit Parisius nisi ipse sit asinus: VIII 65-6

locare

vide s.v. *archa*

loqui

Sortes dicit verum, si solus Plato loquitur: V 52-4

Magis

Quanto magis addiscis, tanto minus scis: IX 2-3

maius

Quanto aliquid maius est, tanto minus videtur: IX 4-5

mentiri

Tu scis an de mentiente sit falsum Sortem esse illum: VIII 18-20

minus

Quanto aliquid maius est, tanto minus videtur: IX 4-5
Quanto magis addiscis, tanto minus scis: IX 2-3

mori

    Nullus homo moritur nisi unus solus homo moriatur: VIII 67

mortalis

    Si Sortes necessario est mortalis, Sortes necessario est immortalis: VII
       24-7

Necessario

    Anima Antichristi necessario erit: VII 22-3
    Omnis anima necessario est iusta: VII 28-9
    Omnis homo necessario est animal: VII 20-1
    Si Sortes necessario est mortalis, Sortes necessario est immortalis: VII
       24-7

necessarium

    In nullo tempore aliquid est verum quin ipsum sit necessarium: VIII
       98-9

negare

    Tu non potes vere negare te non esse asinum: VIII 92-7

nichil

    Nichil est verum nisi in hoc instanti: VIII 62-4
    Nichil nichil est: II 31-5
    Si nichil est, aliquid est: V 47-51

nisi

    Nichil est verum nisi in hoc instanti: VIII 62-4
    Nullus homo legit Parisius nisi ipse sit asinus: VIII 65-6
    Nullus homo moritur nisi unus solus homo moritur: VIII 67

nullus, nulla

    In nullo tempore aliquid est verum quin ipsum sit necessarium: VIII
       98-9
    Nullus homo legit Parisius nisi ipse sit asinus: VIII 65-6
    Nullus homo moritur nisi unus solus homo moriatur: VIII 67
    Si nulla propositio est vera, aliqua propositio est vera: V 27-9

Omnis

    vide s.v. *preter*

Pater

    Si tantum pater est, non tantum pater est: III 47-50

pes

    vide s.v. *archa*

plura

    Impossibile est te scire plura quam scis: IX 13-4

possibile

    Possibile est Sortem videre tantum omnem hominem non videntem se:
       III 51-7

preter

Decem preter quinque sunt quinque: IV 21-4
Omne coloratum preter unum currit: IV 34
Omne corpus preter inanimatum est animatum: IV 12
Omnis quantitas preter continuam est discreta: IV 12
Quelibet viginti preter decem sunt decem: IV 33-4
Sortes his vidit omnem hominem preter Platonem: IV 30-1
Tota domus preter parietem est alba: IV 18
Totus Sortes preter pedem potest contineri (locari) ab (in) archa: IV 18

propositio

Si nulla propositio est vera, aliqua propositio est vera: V 27-9
Omnis propositio vel eius contradictoria est vera: VIII 36-7

Quam

Impossibile est aliud quam asinum genuisse te: IX 15-6
Impossibile est te scire plura quam scis: IX 13-4

quantitas

Omnis quantitas preter continuam est discreta: IV 12

quanto

Quanto aliquid maius est, tanto minus videtur: IX 4-5
Quanto magis addiscis, tanto minus scis: IX 2-3

quicquid

A solo Sorte differt quicquid non est Sortes vel pars Sortes: III 60-1
Quicquid Deus scivit, scit: IX 21-3
Quicquid est vel non est, est: VIII 35
Sortes desinit scire quicquid ipse scit: VI 25-7

quin

In nullo tempore aliquid est verum quin ipsum sit necessarium: VIII 98-9

quinque

vide s.v. *preter*

Scire

Impossibile est te scire plura quam scis: IX 13-4
Quanto magis addiscis, tanto minus scis: IX 2-3
Quicquid Deus scivit, scit: IX 21-3
Si tu scis te esse lapidem, tu non scis te esse lapidem: V 55-6
Solus Sortes scit aliquid enuntiabile quod non omnis alius a Platone ignorat: III 75-6
Sortes desinit scire se nichil desinere scire: VI 28-9
Sortes desinit scire quicquid ipse scit: VI 25-7
Tu scis an omnis homo sit Sortes an differat ab illo: VIII 16-7
Tu scis an de mentiente sit falsum Sortem esse illum: VIII 18-20

solus

A solo Sorte differt quicquid non est Sortes vel pars Sortis: III 60-1
Nullus homo moritur nisi unus solus homo moriatur: VIII 67
Solis tribus sola duo sunt pauciora: III 66-7
Solus Sortes excluditur: III 72-3
Solus Sortes scit aliquod enuntiabile quod non omnis alius a Platone
     ignorat: III 75-6
Sortes dicit verum si solus Plato loquitur: V 52-4

Sortes

vide s.vv. *an, animal, bis, desinere, differre, enuntiabile, excipere, excludere,
     solus, totus, verum, videre*

Tantum

Possibile est Sortem videre tantum omnem hominem non videntem se:
     III 51-7
Si tantum pater est, non tantum pater est: III 47-50
Tantum unum est: III 11-7
Tantum verum opponitur falso: III 43-4

tempus

In nullo tempore aliquid est verum quin ipsum sit necessarium: VIII
     98-9
Si nullum tempus est, aliquod tempus est: V 12

totus, tota

Tota domus preter parietem est alba: IV 18
Totus Sortes preter pedem potest contineri ab archa: IV 18

tria

Solis tribus sola duo sunt pauciora: III 66-7

Ubique

Si tu es ubique, tu non es ubique: V 30-2

univocus

vide s.v. *equivocus*

unum

Tantum unum est: III 11-7

Vel

A solo Sorte differt quicquid non est Sortes vel pars Sortis: III 60-1
Omnis propositio vel eius contradictoria est vera: VIII 36-7
Quicquid est vel non est, est: VIII 35

verum, vera, vere

In nullo tempore aliquid est verum quin ipsum sit necessarium: VIII
     98-9
Nichil est verum nisi in hoc instanti: VIII 62-4
Omne enuntiabile preter verum est falsum: IV 12

Omnis propositio vel eius contradictoria est vera: VIII 36-7
Sortes dicit verum, si solus Plato loquitur: V 52
Tantum verum opponitur falso: III 43-4
Tu non potes vere negare te non esse asinum: VIII 92-7

videre
   Possibile est Sortem videre tantum omnem hominem non videntem se:
      III 51 7
   Quanto aliquid maius est, tanto minus videtur: IX 4-5
   Sortes bis vidit omnem hominem preter Platonem: IV 30-1
   Sortes desinit videre omnem hominem: VI 27

viginti
   vide s.v. *preter*

STUDIEN UND TEXTE
ZUR GEISTESGESCHICHTE
DES MITTELALTERS

HERAUSGEGEBEN VON

DR. ALBERT ZIMMERMAN

24. MURALT, A. DE. *L'enjeu de la philosophie médiévale*. Études thomistes, scotistes, occamiennes et grégoriennes. 1991. ISBN 90 04 09254 4
25. LIVESEY, S.J. *Theology and science in the fourteenth century*. Three questions on the unity and subalternation of the sciences from John of Reading's Commentary on the *Sentences*. Introduction and critical edition. 1989. ISBN 90 04 09023 1
26. ELDERS, L.J. *The philosophical theology of St. Thomas Aquinas*. 1990. ISBN 90 04 09156 4
27. WISSINK, J.B. (ed.). *The eternity of the world in the thought of Thomas Aquinas and his contemporaries*. 1990. ISBN 90 04 09183 1
28. SCHNEIDER, N. *Die Kosmologie des Franciscus de Marchia*. Texte, Quellen und Untersuchungen zur Naturphilosophie des 14. Jahrhunderts. 1991. ISBN 90 04 09280 3
29. LANGHOLM, O. *Economics in the Medieval Schools*. Wealth, Exchange, Value, Money and Usury according to the Paris Theological Tradition 1200-1350. 1992. ISBN 90 04 09422 9
30. RIJK, L.M. DE. *Peter of Spain (Petrus Hispanus Portugalensis): Syncategoreumata*. First Critical Edition with an Introduction and Indexes. With an English Translation by JOKE SPRUYT. 1992. ISBN 90 04 09434 2
31. RESNICK, I.M. *Divine Power and Possibility in St. Peter Damian's* De Divina Omnipotentia. 1992. ISBN 90 04 09572 1
32. O'ROURKE, F. *Pseudo-Dionysius and the Metaphysics of Aquinas*. 1992. ISBN 90 04 09466 0
33. HALL, D.C. *The Trinity*. An Analysis of St. Thomas Aquinas' *Expositio* of the *De Trinitate* of Boethius. 1992. ISBN 90 04 09631 0